# Action Stations Revisited

**Other books by Michael JF Bowyer include:**

*Action Stations Revisited – The Complete History of Britain's Military*
*Airfields: No.1 Eastern England*
*Mosquito* (with C. Martin Sharp)
*2 Group – A Complete History 1936-1945*
*Air Raid!*
*Interceptor Fighters*
*Action Stations No. 6 – Military Airfields of the Cotswolds*
*and Central Midlands*
*Force for Freedom – The USAF in the UK Since 1948*
*The Battle of Britain – Fifty Years On*
*Aircraft for the Few – The RAF Fighters and Bombers in 1940*
*The Spitfire Fifty Years On*
*Aircraft for the Many – A Detailed Survey*
*of the RAF's Aircraft in June 1944*
*Aircraft for the Royal Air Force*

# Action Stations Revisited

The complete history of Britain's military airfields:
No. 2 Central England and the London Area

Michael JF Bowyer

Crécy Publishing Limited

Published in 2004 by Crécy Publishing Limited
All rights reserved

© Michael J. F. Bowyer 2004

Michael J. F. Bowyer has asserted his right to be identified as the author of
this work in accordance with Section 77 of the Copyright, Designs and
Patents Act 1988


A CIP record for this book is available from the British Library


ISBN 0 947554 94 7

Front cover photo captions:
Top: The airship R101 in its hanger at Cardington (M J Bowyer collection)
Middle: A Harrier outside the Gaydon hanger at Wittering in September 1990.
Bottom: A Balliol T.2 of No 7 FTS in July 1953.

Printed and bound in the UK by Biddles




**Crécy Publishing Limited**
1a Ringway Trading Estate, Shadowmoss Road, Manchester M22 5LH
**www.crecy.co.uk**

# CONTENTS

# Introduction and Acknowledgements

Completely re-written, much expanded and updated, the entirely new Action Stations Revisited will cover the whole of the UK in fewer volumes than the original Action Stations series (Patrick Stephens Limited), hence the extensive region covered herein. Binding and marketing costs are thereby reduced, although by being far more extensive each volume inevitably has a higher price tag.

Many of the illustrations included are new, and others have rarely appeared. They are drawn mainly from my own collection supplemented by others from good companions including the much-missed Peter Corbell and John Rawlings, with both of whom I spent so many memorable, happy hours. The late Bruce Robertson, one-time star of benchmarking Harleyford Books and later Editor of the official *Recognition Journal* and *Air Clues,* also willingly contributed. For almost six decades, Bruce, who passed away early in 2004, usually had a skilled input in books. For one last time he has helped with the mix, as he did many times previously. To George Pennick I also extend my thanks for photographs, as well as to Squadron Leader Geoffrey Phillips MBE and John Strangward, both of whom helped with the text and contributed illustrations.

For the splendid aerial view of Gatwick I am indebted to the British Airports Authority. Some other photographs are from long defunct companies proud to publicise their achievements and in a manner seemingly no longer prevalent. Thanks are due to Gordon Bruce for the kind help given with the entry relating to South Marston.

Helpful, too, has been Vic Attwood who, making me envious, spoke of how he lived close to pre-war Heston prior to a life in the airline industry. David Benfield has, from his collection, contributed some very rare items. I never thought, when in 1944 it overcame Alan Wright and me with delight, that I would see a photograph of Wittering's 'white Hampden'! David's contribution includes photographs from Jan Bos, the J Cheney Collection, M L Gibson, Brian Martin, former controller at Broadwell, R Walters and R H White.

Origins of photographs are often difficult to trace, for companies and officials, as well as private folk, readily share their treasures. Thus, some coming from company, Imperial War Museum and Crown Copyright sources were taken privately and later donated. Watch out, incidentally, for a vast deluge of photographs soon to emerge from Crown sources and snatched from destruction recently at the very last moment.

This is, of course, not primarily a picture book. As for the information within the volume, it has been gathered from very many sources. Much originates from my own recording begun in the mid-1930s, and which has continued without interruption. Since the late 1950s I have been able to supplement it with much from official sources as and when releases have been made. When transferred to the Public Record Office, relevant files and bound volumes were placed in Classes with AIR 27 containing squadron ORBs, AIR 28 and 29, carrying unit and station records. When consulting them, their appendices should never be overlooked. The National Archives website contains ever more material relating to files available for viewing, and some for on-line purchase.

While the official records embrace a vast amount of material, it is well worth searching local history collections and County Record Offices in order to obtain a more detailed and often more personal aspect on chosen topics. The Cambridgeshire Collection held in the Central Library is one of the finest of its type. Cambridgeshire, Essex and Suffolk County Record Offices all hold much worth researching. Never overlook newspapers, maps, news releases and of course the ever-increasing supply of books slender or bold. CDs have yet to play a major part in historical research, but will surely do so, and in the near future.

An ever-increasing surfeit of material on offer – good, bad, indifferent and atrocious, particularly on the 'www' – while being interesting to research, can never replace personal field study, the sensation of visiting the place where 'it' happened. Remember, though, when looking at defunct airfields, that they will probably be in private hands, and permission needs to be sought if one wishes to view them. Best of all, there can never be a substitute for being in the right place at the right time. In those respects I have to admit that I have indeed been so very fortunate.

Michael JF Bowyer
Cambridge, June 2003

# Glossary and Abbreviations

| | |
|---|---|
| AA | Anti-aircraft |
| AAC(U) | Anti-Aircraft Co-operation (Unit) |
| A&GS | Armament & Gunnery School |
| AAP | Aircraft Acceptance Park |
| AAR | Air-to-air refuelling |
| AASF | Advanced Air Striking Force |
| AB | Air Base |
| ABG | Air Base Group |
| ABS | Air Base Squadron |
| ACHU | Aircrew Holding Unit |
| AHU | Aircrew Holding Unit |
| AD | Air Depot/Air Division (USAAF) |
| ADGB | Air Defence of Great Britain (previously Fighter Command) |
| AEAF | Allied Expeditionary Air Force |
| AEF | Air Experience Flight |
| AFB | Air Force Base |
| AFCS | Air Force Communications Squadron |
| AFDE/U | Air Fighting Development Establishment/Unit |
| AFS | Advanced Flying School |
| AI | Airborne Interception (radar) |
| AID | Air Inspection Directorate |
| ALG | Advanced Landing Ground |
| ANS | Air Navigation School |
| AOC(-in-C) | Air Officer Commanding (-in-Chief) |
| AONS | Air Observer and Navigator School |
| AOP | Air Observation Post |
| APC/S | Armament Practice Camp/Station |
| APU | Aircraft Preparation Unit |
| ARC | Aircrew Re-selection Centre |
| ARF | Aircraft Repair Flight |
| ARS | Air Refuelling Squadron (US) |
| ASC | Air Support Command |
| asl | Above sea level |
| ASP | Aircraft Servicing Platform |
| ASR | Air-Sea Rescue |
| AST | Air Service Training |
| ASU | Aircraft Storage Unit |
| ASV | Air-to-Surface Vessel (radar) |
| ATA | Air Transport Auxiliary |
| ATC | Air Training Corps |

| ATS | Advanced Training Squadron |
|---|---|
| ATTDU | Air Transport Tactical Development Unit |
| BADU | Blind/Beam Approach Development Unit |
| B&GF | Bombing & Gunnery Flight |
| BAS | Blind Approach School |
| BAT/F/DU | Blind Approach Training/Flight/Development Unit |
| BCDU | Bomber Command Development Unit |
| BDTF | Bomber Defence Training Flight |
| BDU | Bombing/Bomber Development Unit |
| BG | Bomb Group (USAAF) |
| BLEU | Blind Landing Experimental Unit |
| *Bullseye* | Training exercise with AA guns and searchlights |
| BW (M) | Bombardment Wing (Medium) (USAF) |
| CAACU | Civilian Anti-Aircraft Co-operation Unit |
| CAG | Civil Air Guard |
| *Carpetbagger* | USAAF operation to assist Resistance forces |
| CBW | Combat Wing (USAAF) |
| CCF | Combined Cadet Force |
| CCRC | Combat Crew Replacement Center (USAAF) |
| CDC | Coastal Defence Co-operation |
| CF/S | Communications Flight/Squadron |
| CFE | Central Fighter Establishment |
| CFI | Chief Flying Instructor |
| CFS | Central Flying School |
| *Circus* | Bomber operation escorted by fighters to entice enemy response |
| CLE | Central Landing Establishment |
| CRO | Civilian Repair Organisation |
| CRU | Civilian Repair Unit |
| CU | Conversion Unit |
| D/F | Direction Finding |
| DFW | Day Fighter Wing |
| DME | Distance Measuring Equipment |
| DOB | Dispersed Operating Base |
| Drem lighting | System of outer markers and approach lights installed at many airfields from 1942 |
| DUC | Distinguished Unit Citation |
| DZ | Drop zone |
| EAF | Enemy Aircraft Flight |
| E&RFTS | Elementary & Reserve Flying Training School |
| EATS | Empire Air Training School |
| ECDU | Electronic Counter Measures Development Unit |
| ECFS | Empire Central Flying School |
| ECM | Electronic Counter Measures |

| | |
|---|---|
| EFTS | Elementary Flying Training School |
| ELG | Emergency Landing Ground |
| EM | Enlisted Men (USAAF) |
| ERDE | Explosives Research and Development Establishment |
| *Eric* | Night operational training mission by an OTU involving its aircraft in a 'spoof' operation |
| ETPS | Empire Test Pilots' School |
| EWS | Electrical & Wireless School |
| Exercise *Spartan* | Exercise to establish methods of making the entire complement of an airfield mobile while held intact |
| FG | Fighter Group (USAAF) |
| FIS | Flying Instructors' School |
| FLS | Fighter Leaders' School |
| FPP | Ferry Pilots Pool |
| FRS | Flying Refresher School |
| FSP | Forward Staging Post |
| FTC | Flying Training Command |
| FTCIS | Flying Training Command Instructors' School |
| FTF | Ferry Training Flight |
| FTS | Flying Training School |
| FTU | Ferry Training Unit |
| FU | Ferry Unit |
| GCA | Ground Controlled Approach |
| GCI | Ground Controlled Interception |
| *Gee* | Medium-range radio aid to navigation equipment employing ground transmitters and airborne receiver |
| GIS | Glider Instructors' School |
| GLCM | Ground Launched Cruise Missile |
| *Goodwood* | Night bombing operation including OTUs in Main Force raid |
| GP (bomb) | General Purpose high-explosive bomb |
| GR | General Reconnaissance |
| *Grand National* | Main Force operation including OTU participation, summer 1942 |
| GRU | Gunnery Research Unit |
| GS | Gliding School |
| GSU | Group Support Unit |
| GTS | Glider Training School/Squadron |
| HCU | Heavy Conversion Unit |
| HE (bomb) | High explosive bomb |
| HGCU | Heavy Glider Conversion Unit |
| HGMU | Heavy Glider Maintenance Unit |
| HGU | Heavy Glider Unit |
| *H2X* | American blind bombing aid |
| IE | Immediate Equipment |

| | |
|---|---|
| IR | Immediate Reserve |
| IRBM | Intermediate Range Ballistic Missile |
| ITS | Initial Training School |
| ITW | Initial Training Wing |
| K/TAS | Knots/True Air Speed |
| LAA | Light Anti-Aircraft (gun) |
| LAC | Leading Aircraftsman |
| Lorenz system | Method of homing using radio bearings |
| LRDF | Long Range Development Flight |
| LRFU | Long Range Ferry Unit |
| LZ | Landing zone |
| *Mandrel* | Equipment for confusing enemy ground radar |
| MAP | Ministry of Aircraft Production |
| MCS | Metropolitan Communication Squadron |
| MCU | Metropolitan Communication Unit |
| *Moonshine* | Early operational equipment preceding *Mandrel* |
| MoS | Ministry of Supply |
| MRESF | Merlin Engine Servicing Flight |
| MU | Maintenance Unit |
| NAE | National Aircraft Establishment |
| NAFDU | Naval Air Fighting Development Unit |
| *Nickel* | Leaflet-dropping flight |
| *Noball* | Operation against V-1 launch sites |
| NOTAM | Notice to Airmen |
| O&ASC | Officers' and Aircrew Selection Centre |
| OADF | Overseas Air Delivery Flight |
| OADU | Overseas Air Delivery Unit |
| OAPU | Overseas Aircraft Preparation Unit |
| *Oboe* | Navigation radio equipment/system |
| OCU | Operational Conversion Unit |
| OFU | Overseas Ferry Unit |
| Operation *Exodus* | Return of POWs from Germany to UK |
| Operation *Starkey* | Feint operation to confuse enemy into believing an invasion of the Pas de Calais was taking place, September 1943 |
| Operation *Torch* | 1942 invasion of NW Africa |
| Operation *Varsity* | Airborne operation to assist crossing of the Rhine, March 1945 |
| ORTU | Operational & Refresher Training Unit |
| ORP | Operational Readiness Platform |
| OTU | Operational Training Unit |
| (P)AFU | (Pilots) Advanced Flying Unit |
| PDC | Personnel Despatch Centre |
| PDU | Photographic Development Unit |

| | |
|---|---|
| PERME | Propellants, Explosives and Rocket Motor Establishment |
| PFF | Pathfinder Force |
| POL | Petrol, oil and lubricants |
| *Popular* | Army Co-operation Command fighter/strike/reconnaissance sortie |
| POW | Prisoner of War |
| PPR | Prior Permission Required |
| PR(U) | Photographic Reconnaissance (Unit) |
| PSP runway | Pierced Steel Planking metal sectional runway |
| PTS | Parachute Training School |
| PTU | Parachute Test Unit |
| Pundit light/letters | Airfield identity letters displayed at night and in poor weather |
| Q-site | Site flashing lights to protect an airfield and deceive enemy bomber crews |
| *Ramrod* | Day bomber raid against a target, fighter supported |
| R&SU | Repair & Salvage Unit |
| (R)AS | (Reserve) Aeroplane Squadron |
| RAT | Radio Aids Training (Flight) |
| RATO | Rocket Assisted Take Off |
| RAuxAF | Royal Auxiliary Air Force |
| RC | Reserve Command |
| RCAF | Royal Canadian Air Force |
| RCM Squadron/ Flight | Radio Counter Measures Squadron/Flight |
| RFS | Reserve Flying School |
| *Rhubarb* | Low-level fighter strike operation often relying upon low cloud |
| RLG | Relief Landing Ground |
| RNAED | Royal Navy Air Experimental Department |
| RNAS | Royal Naval Air Service |
| RNVR | Royal Naval Volunteer Reserve |
| *Rodeo* | Authorised name for a fighter 'sweep' |
| RPE | Rocket Propulsion Establishment |
| RS | Radio School |
| RTC | Recruit Training Centre |
| SAC | Strategic Air Command (USAF) |
| SAM | Surface to Air Missile |
| SBC | Small Bomb Container |
| SCCU | Support Command Checking Unit |
| SD | Special Duties |
| SDU | Signals Development Unit |
| *Serrate* sortie | Fighter sortie to help protect RAF night bombers from German night fighters |
| SFC | School of Flying Control |
| SFTS | Service Flying Training School |
| SFU | Signals Flying Unit |

| | |
|---|---|
| SHAEF | Supreme Headquarters, Allied Expeditionary Force |
| SHQ | Station Headquarters |
| SIS | Screened Instructors' School |
| SLG | Satellite Landing Ground |
| SOE | Special Operations Executive |
| SOEd | School of Education |
| SofTT | School of Technical Training |
| SOP | School of Photography |
| SRW | Strategic Reconnaissance Wing (USAF) |
| SSF | Special Survey Flight |
| SST | Supersonic transport |
| SU | Support/Servicing Unit |
| SWO | Station Warrant Officer (responsible for discipline) |
| 2TAF | 2nd Tactical Air Force (RAF) |
| TAMU | Transport Aircraft Modification Unit |
| TAW | Tactical Airlift Wing (USAAF/USAF) |
| TCC | Troop Carrier Command |
| TCDU | Transport Command Development Unit |
| TCG | Troop Carrier Group (USAAF) |
| (T)CU | (Transport) Conversion Unit |
| TCW | Troop Carrier Wing (USAAF/USAF) |
| TDS | Training Depot Station |
| TDY | Temporary Duty (overseas) (USAF) |
| TFW | Tactical Fighter Wing (USAF) |
| TRS | Tactical Reconnaissance Squadron (USAF) |
| TS | Training Squadron |
| TSCU | Transport Support Conversion Unit |
| TT | Target Towing |
| TTEE | Tri-National Tornado Training Establishment |
| UAS | University Air Squadron |
| UKADR | United Kingdom Air Defence Region |
| USAAC | United States Army Air Corps |
| USAAF | United States Army Air Force (designated thus from 20 June 1941, although the term Army Air Corps remained in common use long after that date) |
| USAF | Post-war formation from the USAAF, the United States Air Force |
| USAFE | USAF Europe |
| US TCC | United States Troop Carrier Command |
| WIDU | Wireless Intelligence Development Unit |
| *Window* | Metallic paper strips dropped by bombers to disrupt enemy radar system, also called 'chaff' |
| W/T | Wireless Telephony |

# Something to Remember

Volume 2 of *Action Stations Revisited* catalogues the histories of Second World War and post-war military airfields within a broad crescent curving from Lincolnshire to the Isle of Sheppey. With Greater London predominant, it embraces southern Essex, encircles western East Anglia and includes the East Midlands. Airfields reviewed in Volume 1 had mainly bomber connections, whereas those in Volume 2 have more diverse histories.

The landscape of the two regions could hardly differ more, Volume 2 reviewing many airfields occupying plateau sites produced by unimaginable upheavals that built the European Alps and sent 'ripples' across what is now southern and south-east England. Some airfields occupying areas 500 feet or more above sea level, have excellent approaches and clear weather.

In the north the Lincolnshire Wolds, and the rolling hills further south, provide attractive landscape settings. Good use has been made of ample flat areas in Oxfordshire and around London before Wealden influences come into play. By the Thames, chosen flat land was usually high to avoid mist brought by a river that has played a considerable part in aerial warfare.

The main criterion for inclusion is that an airfield has military connections, thus ruling out private landing strips. Heathrow has a place because of the intention to have it always ready for operational use, particularly during The Cold War. What are not included are 1914-18 landing grounds in the London area and beyond, other than those developed after the war. The 'Main features' appended to many entries appertain to December 1944, affording opportunities for comparison. 'Accommodation' relates to that available on-site only, excluding off-site billets often used by single and married personnel even in wartime. Where recent features are mentioned, some include the current official metric measurements. Many civilian airfields with strong military connections lack details of features mainly because their buildings were highly individualistic. Airfields were called aerodromes (or camps) until in 1942 the USAAF brought along the term 'field'.

Within the selected region the aerodromes fall into four categories. Most important were the RAF fighter stations, with the aircraft industry sites next. Playing a major part in the war were training stations set inland and away from operational areas, which provided initial training for pilots, and trained bomber crews, glider and transport crews. A fourth grouping includes airfields past and present used for transportation of people and freight in war and peace. Some of the aerodromes included are among the world's oldest.

During compilation of this volume it became exceedingly clear to me how the air defence of London from August 1914 came to eclipse so much and continued doing so until the rapid wind-down of ground and air defences in the second half of the 1950s. Protection of the seat of government, Britain's commercial heart, extensive industrial undertakings and a seventh of the nation's population obviously demanded priority. In 1945-46 consideration was given to their total peacetime dispersal to distant parts of Britain when the effects of atomic war were fully realised.

Before 1957 the siting of the fighter stations was largely unchanged, as this text confirms. In the 1920s and '30s they featured in the Steel-Bartholomew air defence plan agreed in February 1923 and activated in the mid-1920s. Uneasy relations, due to disagreement over German reparations, made France the only feasible foe. Fortuitously, the Plan's orientation had taken that into reckoning, the stations being well placed to encounter the German air forces well ahead of the Capital when they attacked the UK from French and Belgian airfields. Unfortunately, the same ones were too far inland to make easy offensive operations over France, for which specialist airfields like Hawkinge, Manston and Tangmere came into their own.

Under the 1922-23 Plan Central London was closely defended by anti-aircraft guns set in the Inner Artillery Zone. A belt containing eight fighter sectors (lettered A/Duxford to H in the west) faced south, south-east and east, and lay ahead of the IAZ. The fighter ring was completely surrounded by another containing Observer Corps posts. Vital Points – initially Dover, Harwich and Portsmouth – were gun-defended, and each had its own fighter station – Hawkinge, Martlesham Heath and Tangmere. Very-fast-climb interceptors would be stationed at each of those, aircraft like the Hawker Fury and its replacement, an F.10/35 design, or the equally specialised Spitfire – hence the small initial contract for the latter. To view the Hurricane and Spitfire as likes is a major misconception.

In the 1935 Reorientation Scheme the fighter belt swung directly from London to Portsmouth and extended northerly to Teesside. Southend/Rochford, Eastchurch/Gravesend and Hornchurch were allocated to defend the Thames gateway to London and dockland. Eventually the fighter station chain extended north to Wick and west to the South West and South Wales. In the 1920s and 1930s the fighter stations, each initially intended to hold one squadron and doubled in establishment very soon, also protected bomber and overseas reinforcement stations in the southern Midlands.

London's East End contained many miles of quays and warehouses lining the sides of the Thames. Specific docks were reached through lock gates, ensuring that cargo associated with large ships could be handled at any time. They plied particularly to and from the Empire and Dominions bringing essential food and reinforcements, making the docks supremely important targets. When the Luftwaffe, on 7 September 1940, switched to bombing 'London', setting the docks on fire was the prime objective and it brought about incidents as horrendous as any experienced elsewhere. At the mouth of the Thames lay oil refineries and Tilbury Docks for deep-water shipping protected, in wartime, by fighters based at Rochford/Southend Airport, Gravesend and Hornchurch.

Very noticeable was the early decline in value of the fighter stations surrounding London. By early 1941, with the Battle of Britain won, the seven principal stations were virtually put out of business. They were too far inland to deal with sudden fighter-bomber attacks on the South Coast, and too far from France to allow single-engined short-range day-fighters with a duration of about 75 minutes to carry out effective daylight operations over France. Instead, they became dormitory stations for squadrons rotating through them as in 1940, making daily use of forward airfields for refuelling, arming and operating before returning to home stations late in the day. Even additional, external tanks did little to alter the situation.

In late 1943 many fighter squadrons began gathering in organisations known as 'Airfields' in which, working as a team, they became mobile organisations able to move as one from site to site, an idea that they carried out once a toehold in France had been obtained. The famous fighter stations around London, all but redundant, were put to varied uses, some non-combatant. Their 1944 fate was further sealed when the best-known on the southern side of London found themselves in 'flying bomb ally', those early-type cruise missiles flying overhead or having to pass through the balloon barrage close by.

When reflecting upon their famous names and all that has come to be associated with them, it becomes clear just how much their squadrons contributed not just to the winning of the great battle but indeed how far they had gone to winning the war. The German Luftwaffe was prevented by them and their associated anti-aircraft gunners not only from putting them completely out of use but also from all but 'sinking' and destroying the infrastructure of Britain, its industry, aircraft production and acquisition of vital supplies through its ports. Without saving the home base the war would have been lost, with or without the tardy help of the USA.

Within the area covered in Volume 2 is the large-scale presence of Britain's aircraft industry, without which no success in the Battle of Britain could have been achieved. It called for a more specialised workforce than many industries, and recruiting one suitably skilled was easier in Greater London than in some other regions. Around London were eleven aircraft manufacturers, most of them defence contractors. The most important expansion-period fighter, the Hawker Hurricane, was built at Kingston-upon-Thames and assembled and tested at Brooklands/Weybridge where Vickers-Armstrong built the Wellington. A prime bomber-builder, Handley Page was based at Cricklewood and expanded to Radlett near St Albans. Close by was Stag Lane, and Hatfield, which became the main home of de Havilland from the mid-1930s, and Percival at Luton. Down the Thames, Short Brothers built seaplanes at Rochester on the Medway shore, and in 1936, at Rochester Airport works, set about producing the Stirling, the first RAF four-engined monoplane bomber. Fairey naval aircraft were built at Hayes, while General Aircraft at Feltham concentrated on military glider design, leaving Heston Aircraft to tackle experimental projects. Philips & Powis, better known as Miles Aircraft of Reading, designed some of the most avant-garde projects, some similar in layout to those of the 2000s. Miles nearly built Britain's first supersonic research aircraft. Most of these companies had large factories but no adjacent aerodromes, or if they did the sites were often too small. That meant component conveyance for assembly and flight test elsewhere. However, it did favour dispersed production of very small units brought together for final assembly.

Supplying aircraft to the Services by 1940 was a major task. It led to the Air Transport Auxiliary, a specially recruited force of experienced civilian pilots, men and women, who worked from aerodromes, some near London, to ferry many types of aircraft.

It remains incredible that the Germans made no concentrated attempt to wipe out the aircraft factories, when their mid-war output was beginning to seriously damage enemy war production. Additional to building new aircraft, many contractors in the area under review participated in the Civilian Repair Organisation (CRO), started in late 1939 whereby each participant concentrated upon repair and overhaul of certain aircraft types. The scheme grew to large proportions, and without it the Services would for sure have been crippled.

The third group of stations within the crescent carried out training ranging from recruit entry through trades and basic flying to operational training and development of sophisticated training methods. Its expansion started in 1935 when No 1 Elementary & Reserve Flying Training School opened at Hatfield to begin training a pool of volunteer reservists who came to form the backbone of the RAF during the war.

Another large-scale scheme initiated in 1941 was for the training of Army glider pilots, who needed to be able to fly a large and heavy glider on tow, in formation, at night, then land it before reverting to being a soldier – quite demanding, to say the least. Large numbers of such pilots were needed. Once trained, they had to repeatedly practise their skills by night and day.

Somewhat allied to those courageous souls was the transport force. At the outbreak of war the RAF's only transport and government air communications station was Hendon, long the home of No 24 Squadron. It was soon supplemented in wartime with many small Communications Flights formed to assist Groups and Commands. Not until the formation of 38 Group on 13 October 1943 and 46 Group on 1 January 1944 was there a major British tactical transport force. Even then some squadrons formed at ancestral Hendon using Dakotas there, prior to finding operational airfields able to accommodate them and large numbers of gliders needing specially enlarged, paved areas. Many gliders involved originated from within 'the crescent' and also participated from within it to play a part in the Normandy landings and Arnhem assault. Included were US IXth AF TCC Groups, which dropped large numbers of paratroops or towed gliders taken out of Cottesmore and stations in Lincolnshire.

In the war's aftermath Oxfordshire and Gloucestershire in particular accommodated British airborne forces squadrons at Brize Norton, Fairford and Upper Heyford. The discarding of gliders in favour of paratroops and short-field-performing transports saw the strength of airborne forces numerically much reduced. Their vacant bases were developed by the British and American governments into heavy bomber bases for the USAF Strategic Air Command, which, being well inland – like Cottesmore, Gaydon and Wittering – depended for protection upon forward-located RAF fighter forces and ground-to-air missiles. When the USAF left Brize Norton and Fairford, both reverted to being transport bases.

The immediate aftermath of war saw fighter stations at Odiham, Biggin Hill, West Malling, North Weald, Wattisham, Duxford and Wittering become defenders of London. They were all within a new layout, the Defended Area roughly east of the Pennines. To the west lay the Shadow Area. Into the former came London's RAuxAF squadrons, leaving most in the west, Midlands and Scotland, thus within the Shadow Area. Gun defences remained for ten years after the war.

Emphasis shifted as the ability of early warning radar probed further out to sea, allowing fast interceptors to respond rapidly to incoming bombers possibly carrying nuclear stores. By the 1970s Wattisham's supersonic fighters had the performance and weapons to engage a raider almost anywhere within the UKADR. It was now the only remaining fighter station in southern England. The others had become great names to remember. Meanwhile the capability of the few remaining fighters was in the 1980s extended when VC-10 AARs began operating out of Brize Norton.

Post-war years witnessed a steady decline in the number of airfields in the region under review. About half of those described in this volume were in use at the end of 1947, some sixty-seven by the mid-1950s and fifty-three a decade later. Currently some forty-four remain in use, although not all serve for flying. Rapid development of ballistic missiles ended the lives of many fighter and bomber airfields, their numbers further falling as defensive missiles improved.

Disbandment of the very loyal Royal Auxiliary Air Force squadrons on 10 March 1957, greeted by many as a savage blow, was a pointer to times ahead. Their Meteors and Vampires needed replacement by more advanced costly aircraft, for which extensive new crew training, maintenance and operational facilities would have been necessary. Funding requirements would have been far too high, especially in a period of rapid change. Accordingly, plans for the squadrons to re-arm with Hunters and Swifts were cancelled.

Rapidly increasing sophistication during the 1950s and 1960s, the cost of R&D and of each item forced companies to amalgamate, eventually to close, bringing widespread change in the use of sites around London. The abrupt ending of the Cold War further reduced defence expenditure, a wide assortment of military organisations contracted, and the number of aircraft further declined.

There will never again be a belt of military airfields defending London, for alternative use as offensive jump-off sites and for the training of huge numbers of fliers. There are, however, concerns and questions to pose, for 2003 witnessed disturbing developments with a bearing on aviation in the area.

In the preface to *Action Stations Revisited 1* I pointed out how history almost repeats itself, and how easy it is for 'firm' international agreements to be 'torn apart'. The European Union, little more than an undemocratic club formed by politicians for politicians holding scant regard for the views of the millions of 'ordinary' people within member countries, should be a barrier to war. Instead it could well generate terrible internal upheavals in member countries, wrecking the many good things achieved in attempts to avoid another widespread European war, something that it would be very unwise to completely dismiss.

My 2000 crystal ball was clearly working well when I also wrote that, 'The prime role of the RAF remains the safeguarding of the nation and its best interests by keeping the peace and helping in Peace Accord operations ... to support worthwhile stances taken by the United Nations.' The '9/11' terror attack upon the New York towers was an act of heinous barbarity for which the perpetrators were, at least, wiped out. Everything that could and can still be done to remove their surviving, evil companions should be given top priority. To have instead misused Britain's superb, courageous Armed Forces in an irrelevant pre-emptive strike against an impoverished and terribly tortured Third World sovereign state, with which our nation has no quarrel, drags us all down to a deplorable level. To have carried it out in the face of massive public opposition was a contemptuous act. It seems almost inconceivable that the country that fought alone so nobly for freedom, and so spectacularly from a number of the aerodromes mentioned in this book, has a Government that would act in a manner so morally wrong. Such acts may well bring about awful responses from unreasonable elements, with which no air force can effectively deal.

The military airfields described in this volume were built to defend freedom, and not as bases from which to attempt to impose our preferred life-style upon others not wishing for such an export and particularly from a country functioning internally none too well.

When heading for a holiday via Heathrow the most danger comes not from a foreign power but from the street criminal, a crazy drugged driver, the spy camera and some strange Government fellow already 45 minutes late and desperately trying to avoid the truth and something that isn't there.

# The Airfields

The accompanying map shows the approximate positions of airfields described in this volume. Under the two main development and expansion plans of the 1920s and 1930s airfields were often positioned where access to the railway was easy. Indeed, some stations – like Bicester – had their own railway line linking with the main line nearby. They were often sited reasonably near to small towns, which provided recreational facilities at a time when aircraft noise and circuit flying had little environmental effect. The 1930s expansion period saw airfields built about fifteen miles apart within suitable areas. Additional buildings, provision of satellites and other types of landing grounds increased that proximity to as little as five miles in some instances. Particularly dense was the zone around Oxford, where pilots undergoing basic and operational training were, at one time, flying within the Central Gliding Area. In wartime, that region – still a very busy one – often saw more than 2,000 movements in 24 hours.

The listed 'main features' of the airfields are applicable to December 1944 unless otherwise stated. Runway lengths and orientations are given as prescribed, although lengths were not so very precise. The longest runway is listed first, followed by the orientation of usually two wartime subsidiary runways. While often retaining all three, post-war military airfields generally were modified to have one south-west/north-east runway, the other two serving as parking areas or reserves, which, in the late 1980s, saw increasing use.

Accommodation figures give an indication of what was available, and also indicate the relative size overall and sometimes indicate the importance of the station. Off-camp billeting is not included. In the case of civilian airfields with strong military associations the complexity and one-off nature of the buildings makes it almost impossible to list/describe them. OS map references relate to the 1:50,000 series.

Plans and details of certain airfields have been chosen to illustrate a range of features. Although similar, no two airfields could in any way be identical, although they do possess similar items. The airfields depicted on the map, and whose history subsequently appears, are as follows:

1.    Abingdon, Oxfordshire
2.    Akeman Street, Oxfordshire
3.    Ansty, Warwickshire
4.    Barford St John, Oxfordshire
5.    Bedford (Thurleigh), Bedfordshire
6.    Benson, Berkshire
7.    Bibury, Gloucestershire
8.    Bicester, Oxfordshire
9.    Biggin Hill, Kent
10.   Bitteswell, Leicestershire
11.   Booker (Wycombe Air Park),
      Buckinghamshire
12.   Bottesford, Leicestershire
13.   Bovingdon, Hertfordshire
14.   Brize Norton, Oxfordshire
15.   Broadwell, Oxfordshire
16.   Brooklands (Weybridge), Surrey
17.   Broxbourne, Hertfordshire
18.   Bruntingthorpe, Leicestershire
19.   Cardington, Bedfordshire
20.   Chalgrove, Oxfordshire
21.   Cheddington, Buckinghamshire
22.   Chelveston, Northamptonshire
23.   Chipping Norton, Oxfordshire
24.   Chipping Ongar
25.   Chipping Warden, Northamptonshire
26.   Church Lawford, Warwickshire
27.   Collyweston, Northamptonshire
28.   Cottesmore, Leicestershire (Rutland)
29.   Cowley, Oxfordshire
30.   Cranfield, Bedfordshire
31.   Croughton, Northamptonshire
32.   Croydon (Waddon), Surrey
33.   Culham, Oxfordshire
34.   Deenethorpe, Northamptonshire
35.   Denham, Buckinghamshire
36.   Denton, Northamptonshire
37.   Desford (Leicester), Leicestershire
38.   Detling, Kent
39.   Down Ampney, Gloucestershire

40.   Desborough, Northamptonshire
41.   Eastchurch, Isle of Sheppey, Kent
42.   Edgehill, Warwickshire
43.   Enstone, Oxfordshire
44.   Fairford, Gloucestershire
45.   Fairlop (Hainault Farm), Essex
46.   Fairoaks, Surrey
47.   Feltham (Hanworth Park), Middlesex
48.   Finmere, Oxfordshire
49.   Gatwick, Surrey
50.   Gaydon, Warwickshire
51.   Grafton Underwood, Northamptonshire
52.   Gravesend (Chalk), Kent
53.   Grove, Oxfordshire
54.   Halton, Buckinghamshire
55.   Hampstead Norris, Berkshire
56.   Harrington, Northamptonshire
57.   Harwell, Berkshire
58.   Hatfield, Hertfordshire
59.   Heathrow, London
60.   Hendon, Middlesex
61.   Henley-on-Thames (Crazies Farm),
      Berkshire
62.   Henlow, Bedfordshire
63.   Heston, Middlesex
64.   Hinton-in-the-Hedges, Northamptonshire
65.   Honeybourne, Hereford and Worcester
66.   Hornchurch (Sutton's Farm), Essex
67.   Horne, Surrey
68.   Hounslow, Middlesex
69.   Hunsdon, Hertfordshire
70.   Husbands Bosworth, Leicestershire
71.   Kelmscot, Oxfordshire
72.   Kingston Bagpuize, Oxfordshire
73.   Kenley, Surrey
74.   Kiddington (Marworth)
75.   Kidlington (Glympton), Oxfordshire
76.   Kimbolton, Cambridgeshire
77.   King's Cliffe, Northamptonshire

78. Area of Landing Grounds at Bray, Winkfield and Waltham St Lawrence
79. Langley, Buckinghamshire
80. Leavesden, Hertfordshire
81. Leicester East, Leicestershire
82. Little Horwood, Buckinghamshire
83. Little Rissington, Gloucestershire
84. Little Staughton, Bedfordshire
85. Loughborough, Leicestershire
86. Luton, Bedfordshire
87. Market Harborough, Leicestershire
88. Melton Mowbray, Leicestershire
89. Molesworth, Cambridgeshire
90. Moreton-in-Marsh, Gloucestershire
91. Mount Farm, Oxfordshire
92. Northleach, Gloucestershire
93. North Luffenham, Leicestershire (Rutland)
94. North Weald, Essex
95. Northolt, Middlesex
96. Nuthampstead, Hertfordshire
97. Oakley, Buckinghamshire
98. Old Warden, Bedfordshire
99. Panshanger (Holywell Hyde), Hertfordshire
100. Penshurst, Kent
101. Podington, Bedfordshire
102. Polebrook, Northamptonshire
103. Radlett, Hertfordshire
104. Rearsby, Leicestershire
105. Redhill, Surrey
106. Rochester, Kent
107. Saltby, Leicestershire
108. Sawbridgeworth, Hertfordshire
109. Shellingford, Berkshire
110. Sibson, Cambridgeshire
111. Silverstone, Northamptonshire
112. Smith's Lawn, Berkshire
113. Southam, Warwickshire
114. Southend (Rochford), Essex
115. South Marston, Wiltshire
116. Southrop, Gloucestershire
117. Spanhoe (Harringworth, Wakerley), Northamptonshire
118. Stanton Harcourt, Oxfordshire
119. Stapleford Tawney, Essex
120. Stratford (Atherstone), Warwickshire
121. Sywell, Northamptonshire
122. Tempsford, Bedfordshire
123. Thame (Haddenham), Buckinghamshire
124. Thurleigh, Bedfordshire
125. Turweston, Northamptonshire
126. Twinwood Farm, Bedfordshire
127. Upper Heyford, Oxfordshire
128. Warwick, Warwickshire
129. Watchfield, Berkshire
130. Wellesbourne Mountford, Warwickshire
131. Westcott, Buckinghamshire
132. West Malling (Kings Hill), Kent
133. Weston-on-the-Green, Oxfordshire
134. White Waltham (Maidenhead), Berkshire
135. Windrush, Gloucestershire
136. Wing, Buckinghamshire
137. Wisley, Surrey
138. Witney, Oxfordshire
139. Wittering, Cambridgeshire
140. Woburn, Bedfordshire
141. Woodley (Reading), Berkshire

# The Main Airfields of Central England
# and the London Area

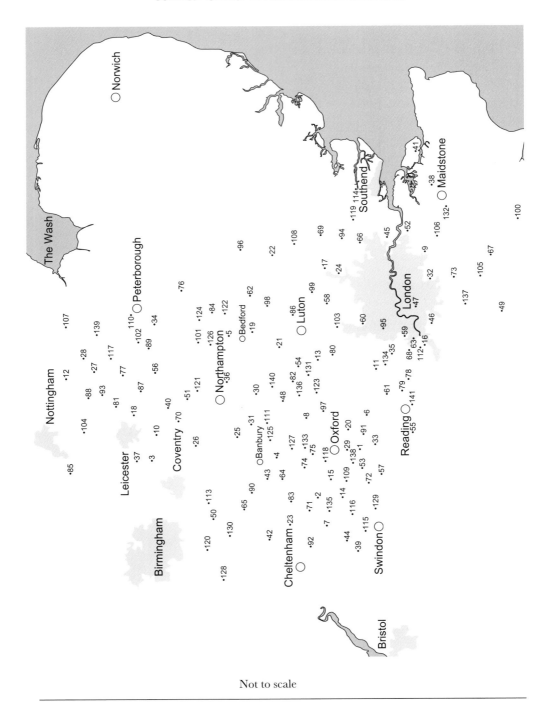

Not to scale

*Abingdon's impressive headquarters building of 1932 design.*

## ABINGDON, Oxfordshire

*51°41N/01°18W 260ft asl; SU480990. 5 miles SW of Oxford, 1 mile NW of Abingdon town*

"Approaching the guardroom check your buttons, straighten your puttees, then bravely pass – hoping the SWO isn't about. Turn sharp right and feast your eyes upon a truly magnificent headquarters castle, an outpost of Empire dominating the scene while reminding of your true place in the world." That was Abingdon, to its finality.

Conceived in the 1920s for a feasible war with France, and constructed using red bricks and slates, Abingdon looked – indeed smelled – like a typical RAF station of early 1930s vintage. Roaming around the 'tech site' and dreaming of the call of a Panther Gordon in full cry, one could easily be convinced that the Charleston must still be de rigeur in a Mess little altered throughout its career.

Abingdon's biggest change came around the time of Battle of Britain Day 1967 when, in appalling weather, the big Beverley sisters publicly waggled their tails for the very last time. Encased in thick mist, the remainder of those huge creatures soared aloft, spewing clouds of water droplets from their vast outspread wings before floating into dense fog. Soon, in formation, they ran in from the west and, in a manner more suited to a fighter, each peeled off, puffing ample exhaust smoke, which heralded a place in the stream landing. Memorable for sure, but then Abingdon holds many memories, for it was an action station for more than sixty years.

Approved on 20 July 1925, its plan called for a mere five buildings, four of them Type A Sheds, Aircraft, of which three remained to the end. Barracks blocks in the Army style of the time were soon added and regularly improved. A 1925-type white-painted water tower lasted into the 1990s, supplemented with a brick-encased 1930s chimney. Available facilities were expanded to support two single-engined, short-range day-bomber squadrons, and in wartime a Special Reserve squadron. After relatively few alterations and additions, construction started in 1929 on open flat land, an area of loam resting upon a firm shale or clay base. Clear approaches had led to the choice of site.

RAF Abingdon opened under Wessex Bombing Area control on 1 September 1932, and received its first operational aircraft on 8 October 1932. These were Fairey Gordon single-engined two-bay biplane light bombers of 40 Squadron, which arrived directly from summer armament training at Catfoss, having vacated Upper Heyford on 31 July 1932.

Permanent buildings began to be occupied on 10 October 1932, and the customary Station Flight had won an Atlas, Avro 504N and DH Moth by the end of the month. Oxford University Air Squadron arrived from Upper Heyford on 3 November and remained until 3 September 1939, by which time its Avro 504N and Atlas trainers had been replaced by Avro Tutors and a few Hawker Harts.

Central Area took control in November 1933, and on 1 June 1934 XV Squadron formed here and received Hawker Harts. Abingdon's squadrons took part in the 1935 Jubilee Review, the following October seeing 40 Squadron re-arming with Hart (Special) day bombers.

January 1936 brought clear signs of RAF expansion when construction of additional buildings began and existing squadrons in profusion sired new ones. 'C' Flight, 40 Squadron, was re-named 104 Squadron, and during the following month part of XV Squadron became the nucleus of 98 Squadron and received Hawker Hinds, more of which arrived in March 1936 for 40 Squadron.

A mere 2,000 people attended Abingdon's 1936 Empire Air Day, viewing among others a Heyford, Overstrand, Bulldog, Moth and a stripped Tutor, keeping company with two Hinds. For this treat – including a flying display – entry cost a mere shilling (5p in modern coinage, maybe around £2.50 at today's prices).

On 1 May 1936 Head Quarters No 1 Group had formed here out of HQ Central Area, and on 14 July the station became part of the emerging Bomber Command. Later it held HQ Advanced Air Striking Force, the Command's field force. So crowded was Abingdon that in August 1936 both 98 and 104 Squadrons departed. Further expansion came on 18 January 1937 when XV Squadron gave birth to a new Hind Squadron, No 52. Then on 1 May 1937 No 40 sired 62 Squadron. To afford space, 52 Squadron had moved to Upwood in late February. Interest in re-armament increasing, the 1937 Empire Air Day attracted 6,000 visitors, who were able to view what at the time seemed a most modern, very impressive and recently erected 12-Bay Type 'C' Aircraft Shed.

Cranfield received 62 Squadron on 12 July 1937, at which time Avro Tutors of Cambridge UAS were at Abingdon for summer camp. In a holding operation Hawker Nimrods and Ospreys of the FAA's 802 Squadron began detachment here in November 1937, staying until January 1938, when they boarded HMS *Glorious*; No 40 Squadron shed yet another, which, on 3 March 1938, became 185 Squadron. It flew Hinds, like 106 Squadron, formed out of XV Squadron on 1 June 1938.

More dramatic was the arrival on 13 June 1938 of the station's first Fairey Battle, and XV Squadron re-armed with Battle IIs (ie. examples powered with Merlin II engines) in June-July of that year. Another seven arrived for 40 Squadron on 7 July 1938, with examples for 106 Squadron following. The latter squadron and No 185 departed for Thornaby in August and September, while XV and 40 Squadrons, operational by late September 1938, formed 71 Wing. Although equipped by September 1938, 103 Squadron was not operationally ready.

With little warning both XV and 40 came to readiness on 10 September 1938 as the Munich Crisis deepened, war preparations – short of mobilisation – went ahead, and Station Commanders were called to HQ 1 Group for operations briefing. While they were meeting, the Prime Minister announced that war had been averted, bringing relief, realisation that precious time had been won, and deep foreboding at what lay ahead. No 103 Squadron – slowly equipped with Battles between late July and mid-September 1938 – became fully operational before leaving in April 1939.

Through spring and summer 1939, Abingdon's light bombers trained for their part in Field Force France. On 24 August, with the international situation fast deteriorating, No 1 (Bomber) Group became the Advanced Air Sinking Force, and on 1 September 1939, when Poland was invaded, ordered the Battle squadrons to prepare for movement to France. By nightfall, large civilian aircraft had arrived at Abingdon and during the night were painted in camouflage colours. Next morning they conveyed essential ground personnel to France. Mid-morning saw the departure of Abingdon's two Battle squadrons, No XV to Conde-Vraux and No 40 to Bethenville. They now formed 71 Wing AASF.

Abingdon had certainly been very much an action station and now entered a new phase by accommodating HQ No 6 (Training) Group, which, since 1 January 1939, had controlled all bomber training. Two Battle training squadrons, 52 and 63, began moving to Abingdon on 2 September to form 1 Group Pool, their role being the supply of replacement crews to AASF squadrons. Similarly, Whitley Is of 166 Squadrons, and Mk IIs of 97 Squadron, moved to Benson on 14 and 15 September 1939, there to form No 4 Group Pool. The heavy aircraft quickly degenerated Benson's grass and made it unsuitable for Whitleys. A direct swap with 1 Group Pool took place between 16 and 18 September, and into Abingdon came the type of aircraft that would

*A Barrack Block at Abingdon, of typical 1922 design.*

*Hawker Hinds of 98 Squadron,*
*Abingdon.*

dominate the wartime sky in this region. Here their task was to train and supply crews to operational 4 Group Whitley squadrons. Whitley IIIs replaced 166 Squadron's Mk Is in January 1940. Providing target facilities for air-gunners, Battles of No 6 Group Target Towing Flight were here between December 1939 and March 1940.

On 23 March 1940 two 4 Group Whitleys, landing back from night flights over the Ruhr, brought Abingdon its first involvement with operations. More noticeable was the dramatic change on 2 April when both Whitley squadrons dissolved into a new unit, changing the station's authorised title to 'No 10 Operational Training Unit Abingdon'. Whitleys of 97 and 166 Squadrons were placed in 'A' Flight while Ansons of 97 Squadron and some Whitleys of 166 Squadron formed 'B' Flight. In May 1940 a few Whitley IVs arrived.

The widespread French collapse forced survivors of the AASF, which had displayed such enormous courage in helping its ally, to vacate their forward bases. Many Battles staged through their one-time HQ airfield, no fewer than seventy-three passing through Abingdon on 15 June and six more the next day.

By mid-July 10 OTU's nominal establishment stood at forty IE plus fourteen IR Whitleys [ie. forty Immediate Equipment aircraft plus fourteen aircraft on site in reserve to replace any aircraft taken out of line] and eighteen Ansons, the former in 'A', 'C' and 'D' Flights, and the latter now in 'B' Flight. Due to aircraft shortage, and because experienced personnel manned the OTUs, those organisations commenced night leaflet-dropping over France, No 10 OTU first doing so on 21 July 1940. More such sorties were flown in August, by both Whitley IIIs and Vs. Soon after, Tiger-engined Whitley Mks II and III were largely replaced by Merlin-engined Mk Vs.

Abingdon's designated satellite, Stanton Harcourt, came into use for night-flying on 3 September 1940, and remained under Abingdon's control until 15 January 1946. 'C' Flight, 10 OTU, dispersed there from 10 September 1940 and remained until February 1941, when shortage of Whitleys forced its disbandment. 'A' Flight, which converted crews on to type, replaced it.

The need for blind approach training brought about the formation of No 1 BAT Flight at Abingdon on 12 January 1941, using Whitley IIIs and Vs and Ansons. Oxfords replaced Whitleys when No 1501 BAT Flight was established in December 1941. The Flight moved to Stanton Harcourt on 18 April 1943 and disbanded on 31 December 1943; the Oxfords remained at Abingdon within 91 Group Communications Flight.

Although the station was well inland, it did not escape enemy attention. Intruders were active at dusk in the Oxford area on 12 March 1941: while Whitleys were night-flying, a raider dropped sixteen bombs, putting Abingdon out of use. Damage was caused to a Whitley, and other bombs fell around the bomb dump. The Germans came again around 2145 on 21 March 1941, dropping twenty-six bombs across 6 Group's HQ area. Seven offices were wrecked and ceilings and windows of another ten were damaged in one of the few successful attacks on any HQ organisation in Britain during the war.

Orders given in May 1941 demanded that OTU output should be forty crews a month by more fully using satellite facilities. As a result 10 OTU made use of Mount Farm between 23 July 1941 and 12 February 1942. Availability of 10 OTU for leaflet drops was signalled in June 1941, a few sorties being despatched from Abingdon in July. OTU strength stood at around four dozen Whitleys and eighteen Ansons. In August 1941 Lysander target tugs were added, further aircraft of that type here at the end of the year being flown by a 7 AACU detachment.

Gradual replacement of front-line Whitleys released examples for alternative employment. Since late summer 1940 Whitley Vs had proven useful for ocean patrol, although the aircraft's attack profile was poor. To help to counter the U-boats a special Whitley Flight of 10 OTU formed in April 1942 and was positioned at St Eval, Cornwall. Modifications to 33 aircraft enabled them to carry depth-charges and ASV radar. Operational flying was judged good for morale for, apart from eleven *Nickel* sorties to November 1941 and eight in December, such flights were rare. Bombing sorties totalling only four had, on 30 November 1941, been despatched to Orleans/Bricy and Tours airfields.

Simultaneously to employing Whitleys for maritime purposes, 10 OTU was to participate in the 'Thousand Plan' bomber raids. That depended upon both crew and aircraft availability, and creaming off some for Biscay Patrols did not help. The detached flight therefore delayed its operational deployment, allowing twenty-one Whitleys to take off for Cologne on 30 May 1942. All returned, although one crash-landed at Manston. For the ensuing Essen raid, twenty-two Whitleys set out from Abingdon. The twenty-strong contingent operating in the June 1,000-bomber Bremen raid was less fortunate, three aircraft being lost, with one crew snatched from the sea. From 11 May 1942 until 14 April 1947 91 (Bomber) Group HQ occupied the ex-6 Group HQ building, the latest occupant controlling much of the bomber OTU establishment.

The St Eval detachment began operational flying on 4 August 1942, with twenty-six aircraft available. Each crew flew six operational patrols of nine to ten hours' duration, and for each patrol the crew was credited with a third of a bomber sortie. Four depth-charges were carried and, to make each sortie really valuable, two $9^{1}/_{2}$lb practice bombs were aimed at a rock off the Cornish coast. A long-range tank in the aircraft's belly extended its range. Crews were ordered to ditch if they met one of the Ju 88s now patrolling Biscay. Little wonder that a popular song became, with the addition of unsavoury phrases, 'I'm dreaming of a white Whitley...'. Operations ceased on 19 July 1943. By the time the detachment returned to Abingdon on 23 July 1943 it had flown 1,862 sea patrols, 6,864 flying hours, had made ninety-one U-boat sightings and fifty-five attacks, had damaged U-214, U-523 and U-591, and had sunk U-564. It had been a costly venture, however, for thirty-three Whitleys were lost.

Participation in Main Force attacks on Germany within the summer 1942 *Grand National* series included raids on Bremen, Dusseldorf and Essen, before operational training was fully resumed, interspersed with a few leaflet-dropping sorties in February and April 1943. The strength of 10 OTU in February 1943 was fifty-five Whitley Vs, eleven Ansons, three Lysanders and a Defiant. Earlier needs to night fly from the satellite to avoid bombing of the parent station being no longer necessary, the OTU was re-organised, 'A' and 'B' Flights being at Stanton Harcourt, and 'C', 'D' and 'G' at Abingdon. In April 1943 Martinets replaced the Lysander target tugs. *Bullseyes* were being flown, as well as ASR sorties. No 91 Group Air Gunners Instructors' School opened, giving a seven-day course and employing two Whitleys and two Martinets. Some of the fifty-four Whitleys at 10 OTU in August 1943 were Mk VIIs brought from St Eval. *Nickelling* was carried out in September 1943, a dozen such sorties being flown in November and sixteen in December without loss.

Into 1944 Whitleys, forever displaying their memorable nose-down attitude, droned around Abingdon, and managed twelve sorties to France in January 1944, during which they dropped 2,266,000 leaflets. Sergeant Averill was twenty-five miles into France when an engine failed. All removable equipment was jettisoned before the Whitley landed safely at Tangmere. During February 1944 10 OTU flew thirteen more sorties, dropping 1,656,144 leaflets, the most by one unit that month. A disturbing feature, however, was the loss of Whitley LA787, sent to St Quentin on 28 February 1944. As a result, Whitleys subsequently operated west of the north/south line passing through Paris, leaving only OTU Wellingtons to venture eastwards. In March 1944 another dozen *Nickel* sorties were flown.

Until 20 March 1944 Abingdon's Whitleys operated from its grass runways. Flying then switched to Stanton Harcourt, while two runways were laid at the main base and 10 OTU began to bid farewell to its faithful old Whitleys. Unit establishment was also cut, to three-quarters OTU norm. June saw four Hurricanes replace the Martinets, and in July 1944 10 OTU commenced re-equipping with Wellington Xs. Not until October 1944 did the last Whitley leave 10 OTU, and daylight flying training resumed at Abingdon on 16 November 1944.

In June 1944 there was briefly a different Whitley activity here, for 1341 Special Duties Flight was formed on 1 June. Within days at Stanton Harcourt it took on charge several Whitley Vs fitted out at Marshalls of Cambridge for an early warning role. They, and others at Finmere, were in effect the first AEW patrol aircraft, and were intended for night patrolling off France and, in Finmere's case, North Africa. No 1341 SD Flight was briefly again at Abingdon during August 1944.

*Andover C1 XS640 of 46 Squadron kneeling before an Abingdon 'A' Type hangar.*

March 1945 found 10 OTU's strength at fifty Wellington Xs, five Hurricanes and two Master IIs. Still a part of 91 Group, the OTU did not disband until 10 September 1946. Abingdon's long-time bomber role then ended, for on 24 October 1946 Transport Command took control, 525 Squadron and its Dakotas moving in five days later. On 1 December it was renumbered 238 Squadron, and on the 16th was joined by Dakotas of 46 Squadron.

Oxford University Air Squadron had re-opened on 8 October 1940 for Short Course undergraduates, functioning in wartime from its town HQ and using a Tiger Moth and an Abingdon-based Oxford. For full re-establishment it had to wait until 20 December 1946. OUAS flew Tiger Moths from Abingdon until 14 April 1949.

Major change came at the start of December 1947 when the short-range tactical transports were replaced with Avro York strategic passenger-cum-freight strategic transports of 51, 59 and 242 Squadrons, which operated scheduled services on long-range trunk routes. On 1 December 1947, and eight months after disbanding at Shallufa, 40 Squadron re-formed at Abingdon, its ancestral home, and equipped with Yorks, two dozen of which were now based here. During the Berlin Airlift they played a major part, a 59 Squadron aircraft being the first York to land at Templehof, on 10 July 1948. York operations were soon out of German airfields, reducing expense while increasing delivery and turn-around rates.

On 27 June 1949, with the Airlift ended, Abingdon passed from 47 Group to 38 Group, then, on 1 November 1949, HQ No 46 Group was re-born and functioned here until 31 March 1950. The York squadrons – apart from 242, which re-armed with Hastings – left for Bassingbourn. No 1 Parachute School, formed on 10 June 1950, arrived from Upper Heyford complete with its famous parachutists' tower and captive balloon. Renamed No 1 Parachute Training School on 1 November 1953, it stayed until 31 December 1975, when the School moved to Brize Norton.

November 1950 saw the arrival of 30 Squadron's Valettas, which stayed until May 1952. They were supplemented by the arrival from Chivenor on 19 March 1951 of No 1 Overseas Ferry Unit, whose Harvards, Oxfords and Mosquitoes trained overseas ferry crews. Responsible for delivering aircraft to overseas bases, No 1 OFU became best known for operation *Beecher's Brook,* the transatlantic delivery of Canadair F-86E Sabre jets to the RAF. The Ferry Training Unit re-formed here on 5 August 1952 moved out to Benson on 9 April 1953. Having split into three elements in 1952, the OFU was completely re-organised on 1 February 1953 when No 1 Long Range Ferry Unit (LRFU) became 147 Squadron and No 3 LRFU became 167 Squadron. Both moved to Benson on 16 April 1953.

Transport Command Training and Development Flight formed at Abingdon on 14 October 1951 and remained until 1 June 1956, when it moved to Benson. Another specialised unit was Transport Command Air Support Flight, re-formed as No 1312 Flight on 14 September 1954, which flew Hastings and Valettas. It was disbanded on 1 April 1957.

Meanwhile, in May 1953, Abingdon had resumed an operational tactical role with the arrival from Dishforth and Topcliffe of 24 and 47 Squadrons flying Hastings. No 53 Squadron, which replaced 24 on 1 January 1957, was soon ferrying troops to Kenya for anti-Mau-Mau operations.

March 1956 brought – literally – gigantic change with the arrival of the first 162-foot-span Blackburn Beverleys for 47 Squadron. Able to transport bulky loads, they could also operate from small, rough airstrips. In February 1957 53 Squadron received its first Beverley. With at one period more than 2,000 aircraft movements monthly, Abingdon was then one of the busiest airfields in Britain.

The lengthy 'F' Hangar, built to accommodate the Beverleys, passed from the contractors to the RAF on 30 April 1959, by which time the Beverleys were very actively supporting British

*Beverley XB285 'C' of 47 Squadron at Abingdon in the autumn of 1963. The doors have been removed for load drop practice.*

forces overseas. To ease operational deployment, on 28 June 1963 53 Squadron merged with 47 Squadron, crews thereafter drawing aircraft from a central pool. By 1969 'F' Hangar had been modified to permit Short Belfasts to come here for overhaul.

Until 31 October 1967 Beverleys of 47/53 Squadron operated worldwide, while the Transport Command Air Movements Development Unit, formed here in November 1959, carried out research into movement of heavy freight, and studied large-scale air movements. On 31 May 1965 it became the Air Transport Development Unit, which functioned until January 1968, latterly controlled by No 38 Group.

In summer 1966 Abingdon saw the opening of the Andover Training Flight, followed on 1 December 1966 by the formation here of No 46, the first Andover Squadron. This was based at Abingdon until August 1970 when, together with the Andover Training Flight, it left for Thorney Island. No 52 Squadron, a second using Andovers, assembled here in late 1966 prior to establishment at Seletar on 1 December 1966.

Mutely celebrated was 1 April 1968, the RAF's 50th birthday, amid ill-feeling towards a government reckoned largely unsympathetic to Service needs and certainly largely ignorant of history and tradition. One intrepid soul flew a Hunter low by the Houses of Parliament, cocking a snook at some of its incumbents who later had the cheek to rate *him* mentally unwell! Others conserved their energy for HM Queen Elizabeth II's visit to the RAF on 14 June 1968. The venue for the event, marked by a large exhibition of historic aircraft, many destined for the Hendon museum, was Abingdon, where the Queen lunched appropriately in an Officers' Mess, dating from Imperial days. During the afternoon a large-scale little-heralded fly-past was the main event in the flying display.

On 1 September 1972 the Air Support Command Examining Unit became 46 Group Air Transport Examining Unit Strike Command. The Joint Air Transport Establishment, formed here in 1971, moved from Abingdon to Brize Norton on 31 December 1975, followed by 1 PTS, and on 1 January 1976 the station was switched from 38 Group to RAF Support Command. The unique 600-foot-long, 140-foot-wide,

*Jaguar XX832 of 226 OCU undergoing third-line servicing in 'F' Hangar, Abingdon, August 1983.*

*On 14 June 1968 Abingdon hosted the RAF's 50th Anniversary event. (Bruce Robertson collection)*

50-foot-high 'F' Hangar became the centre for Third Line Jaguar Servicing and for repairs carried out by the Aircraft Production Squadron. Leconfield's 60 MU, and 71 MU Bicester, had in May 1976 amalgamated to form the Engineering Wing here, the first of many Jaguars to be worked upon arriving on 3 June 1976. Hawks and Hunters soon also came for major overhaul. Additionally, Nos 1 and 2 Aircraft Maintenance Squadrons, as well as the Rapier and Salvage Squadron, were Abingdon-based, the former to maintain fixed-wing aircraft in Britain and overseas.

From 10 August 1973 Bulldogs of the University of London Air Squadron resided here alongside Chipmunks of No 6 Air Experience Flight, and on 26 September 1975 Oxford UAS, flying Bulldogs and nudged out of Bicester, joined them. They were dwarfed by ex-British Airways VC-10s stored in giant black plastic 'bags' until called in for conversion into tanker aircraft by BAC at Filton.

Jaguar servicing declined as Tornadoes replaced them in Germany, Hunters were ever fewer, and Hawk servicing was switched to St Athan, leaving Abingdon as an expensive item. On 31 July 1992 both UASs departed for Benson, and Abingdon's days as an active RAF station were over, closure following at the end of the year. The Army took control, making it once more a 'camp' whose adjacent large field remains suitable for various activities – including aerial ones. Indeed, mid-May 2004 saw a weekend of vintage aircraft flying at Abingdon, proving that all is not lost.

**Main features:**
*Runways:* 190° 6,000ft concrete, lengthened post-war to 6,532ft, asphalt surfaced. 027° 4,200ft, lengthened post-war to 4,800ft with asphalt surface. Later had Rotary Hydraulic Arrester Gear installed on runway, by then re-listed as 18/36. *Hangars:* four Type A, one Type C. Type F, 600ft long, accepted on 30 April 1959 for Beverleys. *Hardstandings:* six spectacle, twenty-four frying-pan; in late 1950s fourteen large pans were laid. *Accommodation:* RAF officers 186, SNCOs 327, ORs 1,237; WAAF officers 17, SNCOs 25, ORs 4.

## AKEMAN STREET, Oxfordshire

*51°49N/01°31W 400ft asl; SP33S140. 3 miles NNW of Witney*

Akeman Street's title is a reminder that 2,000 years ago a Roman road passed across the site of this rudimentary wartime airfield. Selected in late 1939 for development as 2 SFTS Brize Norton's RLG, it opened for trade on 10 July 1940.

Following the bombing of Brize Norton, Oxfords of Advanced Training Squadron, 2 SFTS, immediately dispersed here and, two days after the raid, were active. By March 1941 the Oxfords were also using Southrop.

Oxford V3685, night-flying near Akeman Street at 0330 on 28 July 1941 and north-east of the airfield, was shot down, probably by Lt Bisang flying a Ju 88C intruder of I/NJG2.

Flying by 2 SFTS Oxfords continued until 14 March 1942, when 2 SFTS was re-designated 2 (P)AFU. The syllabus then changed to provide flying experience in a tougher weather environment than many pilots had met during training at schools overseas. The Oxfords remained the same.

On 14 July 1942 2 (P)AFU closed, by which time the former very modest RLG had the appearance of a slightly developed satellite airfield. Living quarters, mess buildings, shelters and a small operations block, mostly to 1941 designs, had been added by Messrs Laing aided by Messrs Thorn. Ten Over Type 65-foot Blister hangars (pattern 12512/41) had been erected, and the large metal Bellman hangar (pattern 5498/36) was thus of a style older than most. Three short grass runways closely sited on the field overlapped for much of their area.

After 2 (P)AFU's closure, Akeman Street came under the control of 6 (P)AFU, Little Rissington, which began using it in July 1942 and continued doing so until October 1945, although flying ceased on 15 August 1945. The site, briefly a Sub-Site of 3 MU, was administered by Flying Training Command until its closure on 1 February 1947. Crop sprayers made limited use of the site in the 1970s.

**Main features:**
*Grass landing ground:* Landing areas N-S 3,300ft, NE/SW 2,850ft, SE/NW 2,400ft. *Hangars:* one Bellman, ten 65-foot Blister, all buildings temporary. *Accommodation:* RAF officers 1, SNCOs 3, ORs 15, no WAAFs.

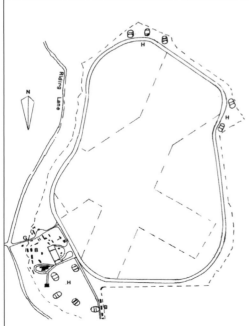

**Akeman Street**
Akeman Street was basically a large grass area encircled by a concrete track. Three portions of the grass were mown to serve as runways. Blister hangars were positioned by the concrete taxiway, to the north and north-east. The main, small camp was to be found in the south-west corner where a Bellman hanger was the most prominent item. This supplemented another five blister hangers. Other buildings were used for basic necessities and were served by the entry road. Surrounding all was a barbed wire fence. Not all RLGs were so protected; indeed in the early days of the war many had no protection and were manned by very small groups of RAF personnel.

## ANSTY, Warwickshire

*52°26N/01°24W 110ft asl; SP405830. 2 miles NE of Coventry*

For recruiting purposes the densely populated East Midlands were high on the official list, with Birmingham, Coventry and Leicester reckoned to be prime spots. The belief was that while these were not long-established as military areas, there would be ample volunteer spirit, hence the presence of several training centres in the region.

Typical was Ansty near Coventry, a relatively small grass airfield run by Air Service Training (AST) and used in the 1930s by light club and privately owned aircraft. It was here that No 9 E&RFTS opened on 6 January 1936 to train RAF Volunteer Reserve pilots. It was equipped with a wider assortment of aircraft types than many such schools, and used mainly Tiger Moths, civilian Avro Cadets and Magisters for basic training. Ansons, Audaxes, Demons, Harts, Hinds and even a Saro Cloud amphibian were available for more advanced training. Under the control of 26 Group, it passed to 50 Group in February 1939, and on 3 September became 9 EFTS, carrying on only in the basic role using Tiger Moths.

In 1938 No 4 Civil Air Navigation School was formed out of No 9 E&RFTS – hence the presence of that Cloud. Also operated by Air Service Training, its main equipment comprised a fleet of Ansons.

On 1 November 1939 No 4 CANS became No 4 Air Observer & Navigation School (AO&NS), which continued to operate a dozen Ansons. The unsuitable mix of EFTS and AO&NS aircraft ended when on 20 July 1940 the latter moved to Watchfield. Intensity of flying was such that in 1940 No 9 EFTS began using a RLG at Southam, which was supplemented through 1942-43 by Brinklow. No 9 EFTS was one of the first to close, doing so on 31 March 1944. Thereafter Ansty remained in the hands of AST, and after the war saw some use for civilian light aircraft.

On 21 March 1951 No 2 Basic FTS, run by AST and equipped with Chipmunks, opened within 63 Group, the Korean War demonstrating a need for RAF pilots. On 31 March 1953 the School closed. Ansty, with little future, was sold and became an industrial site.

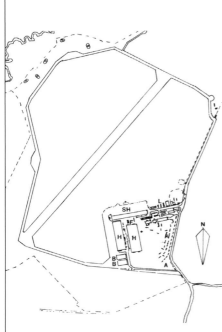

**Ansty**

Main features:

Ansty was a pre-war civilian aerodrome used first for RAFVR service, next as an EFTS, and eventually by AST when part of CRO and for repairing an assortment of aircraft types, for which a single runway was useful. The large east-west School Hangar (SH) accommodated the assorted trainers of the E&RFTS and eventually Anson navigation trainers. The two large hangars (H) similarly served for 4 CANS until they departed on 20 July 1940. Soon they were in use by AST as workshops for repair, re-doping, etc, of varied aircraft, and were supplemented by two MAP-supplied Bellman Hangars. To help accommodate the many Tiger Moths used in wartime, five Blister Hangars were earlier erected in the north-west corner and remained after 9 EFTS closed on 31 March 1944.

To the left of the Main Gate upon entry beyond the security point was the AONS ground training school building and nearby the Main Mess (M), HQ Block and a lecture block and Link Trainer section. To the south of this area was Station Sick Quarters (F) and a set of gas decontamination buildings, the years immediately prior to the war seeing very extensive anti-gas buildings erected. For the wartime trainees not billeted out, a line of barrack huts hugged the eastern perimeter.

## BARFORD ST JOHN, Oxfordshire

*52°08N/01°21W 395ft asl; SP440340. 4¹/₂ miles SSE of Banbury*

For many years, and visible for many miles, Barford's aerial farm, containing an array of tall radio masts, rose from a well-protected enclave near the centre of what was once an important airfield. A board near the entrance informed the passer-by that Barford was the home of a 'Transmitter Annexe', and in Anglo-American hands. While there was no instruction not to tune in for entertainment, one may assume that such activity, particularly during the Cold War, would have been frowned upon. Late in the 1990s the aerials on the farm were skilfully harvested. Barford's more distant past was equally fascinating and shrouded in privacy.

Activity began in earnest during mid-1941 when a small grass Relief Landing Ground for No 15 SFTS Kidlington opened and its Oxfords began circuit flying on 30 June 1941. Although undertaken well inland, such activity at night – and from hand-lit flare-paths – attracted Ju 88C intruders; late on 24 August 1941 one dropped six light bombs on the landing ground, fortunately with insignificant effect.

With the ever-increasing need for more fully-equipped airfields, Barford St John was chosen in late 1941 for upgrading to Built Satellite standard for OTU use. Additional land was acquired, and triple runways suitable for Wellingtons were laid. T2 hangars and temporary brick buildings were added. Bomber Command took control from Kidlington on 10 April 1942. Upon re-opening on 15 December 1942, it became the satellite of No 16 OTU Upper Heyford which flew Wellington IIIs.

A diversion from general activity came in March 1943 when Mustang Is of 4 and 169 Squadrons used Barford during exercise *Spartan*. Fast as they were, they would have been outpaced had they stayed a little longer, and by exotic newcomers.

Positioning Britain's early jet aircraft for test-flying brought a number of problems. Gloster Aircraft had previously relied upon Brockworth airfield for test flying, but it was too small for novel, experimental jets requiring ample take-off space and excellent landing approaches. The company was offered a wide range of sites with ample ground runs, although some featured unsuitable approaches, frequently poor weather conditions or lacked the security needed for such secret aircraft. Eventually Cranwell, then Newmarket Heath, answering needs in all categories, were chosen, but they were too distant from the Gloster works. Accordingly, a further site was requested and Barford St John was selected as a temporary base, Gloster being afforded the miserly use of half a hangar from May 1943 for flight test and development of the Gloster F.9/40, the basis of the Meteor, and for W4041/G, the Gloster E.28/39 'pioneer', Britain's first jet aircraft, and now testing a more powerful engine, the W.2/500. Between 12 and 29 June 1943 it managed twenty-three flights from Barford, then high-speed-section wings were fitted and tested before W4041/G left for Farnborough later that year.

Early on Sunday 28 May 1943 F.9/40 DG206/G, the very important Meteor Mk II fighter prototype fitted with powerful Halford turbines, made what was rated an ambitious cross-country flight from Newmarket to Barford. Already the Mk II was favoured to become a front-line fighter. It was joined on 12 June by DG205/G, another F.9/40 fitted with standard W.2B engines. Both were very active during the summer, and in August 1943 were joined by DG204/G, the much modified and ill-fated F.9/40 fitted with underslung, very advanced axial flow Metrovick F/2 engines. High thrust at idling, which would have made slow-speed flying hazardous, meant that DG204 never flew from Barford. Instead, it was earmarked for flight trials once Gloster had use of Moreton Valence near Gloucester, whence the jets eventually moved. In retrospect it does seem bizarre that revolutionary jet flying from Barford – possible only in good, calm weather – had to take second place to the training programme undertaken by 16 OTU's Wellington IIIs and later its Mk Xs. Gunnery Flight of 16 OTU was also situated here, a customary feature at satellites.

Sufficient aircrew reserves ended 16 OTU's Wellington flying on 12 December 1944 and brought major change. On 30/31 December 1944 No 1655 Mosquito Training Unit, flying mainly Mk XX and XXV Canadian-built Mosquito bombers, moved in to Upper Heyford, its conversion trainer Mosquito T IIIs and Oxfords being placed at Barford. On 1 January 1945 the unit was renamed 16 OTU and began preparing Mosquito crews for No 8 Pathfinder Group. That commitment continued until summer 1945 when flying was rapidly reduced. Mosquito B XVIs replaced the older Mosquitoes in mid-summer 1945. Positioning of traffic lights to control traffic passing the end of the main runway at Barford received much publicity in July, but within a few weeks Barford was lying rejected. The move of 16 OTU to Cottesmore in March 1946 sealed its military flying days. As to its decades as a communications centre, one must still muse upon what news items passed through its wires.

**Main features:**
*Runways:* 281° 6,000ft, 170° 4,200ft, 261° 4,200ft, concrete. *Hangars:* one T2, one B1. *Hardstandings:* 27 frying-pan. *Accommodation:* RAF officers 80, SNCOs 233, ORs 592; WAAF officers 4, SNCOs 30, ORs 108.

## BEDFORD (THURLEIGH), Bedfordshire

*52°14N/00°25W 293 ft asl; TL05602. N of Thurleigh village in open country*

When the Allies entered Germany in 1945 they discovered amazing R&D and projects being pursued by German industry, particularly within the fields of high-speed aircraft design and propulsion. Heavily camouflaged by trees growing above its buildings, the Hermann Goering Air Force Research Establishment at Volkenrode, near Brunswick, covering two and a half square miles, was found well supplied with superb wind tunnels for research into supersonic flight, armament development zones and propellant and propulsion laboratories. Visits to aircraft manufacturers revealed astonishing projects and designs planned or under way, many featuring new wing forms. By comparison, British and American research facilities were clearly inadequate, and much thinking was seemingly antique. The only way to keep Britain at the forefront of aircraft design and development would be to have a specially built research centre, a National Aeronautical Establishment (NAE), pursuing developments along German lines. To help equip it, many items large and small were snatched, particularly from Volkenrode, and were transported to Britain in RAE Hudsons, Dakotas and a three-engined Junkers Ju 352 fitted with a novel rear fuselage loading ramp that led to a capacious fuselage of square section.

Farnborough, so long the centre of R&D in Britain, could not be sufficiently expanded and enhanced to NAE standard, so a new centre was decided upon. Alternative sites for the NAE were considered in 1944, choice eventually falling on a sparsely populated plateau 285 feet above sea level north-east of Bedford.

There was now a certainty that the way ahead rested with aircraft capable of supersonic speed in level flight, which would require very long runways. Aerodynamic features involved in supersonic designs were reckoned likely to be difficult to develop and to compromise slow-flying qualities

*HS P1127 Kestrel XP980 during arrester net trials at Bedford.*

*The second prototype Harrier T2 XW175 roars off Bedford's ski-jump. (Bruce Robertson collection)*

needed during take-off and landing. Swept wings (forward or backward), compound sweep such as crescent wings and delta wings, were all expected to produce considerable handling problems. To obtain a suitably long runway, amalgamation of the existing Thurleigh airfield with nearby Twinwood, and if necessary adding Little Staughton, was suggested. Eventually a completely new airfield of more modest proportions, but still measuring roughly three miles by two and a half miles, was constructed, the largest built since the war in central England. Although cleverly planned, it was never to achieve the fame and glamour of Farnborough, whose history stretched back to the Army's use of man-lifting kites.

Utilitarian in appearance and possessing an extensive, flat, open, very bleak landing ground, the NAE around 1955 (about the time the airfield was becoming active) was somewhat unimaginatively renamed Royal Aircraft (later Aerospace) Establishment Bedford, giving the impression that this was merely a sub-station of Farnborough. Separate from the airfield was the extensive Twinwood Tunnel Site containing the Administrative Centre.

Site clearance had started in summer 1946. The airfield needed hangars suitable for large aircraft, structures and high-speed laboratories, an aerodynamics laboratory, high-altitude research plant and metallurgy laboratory. Workshops able to undertake extensive modification tasks, carry out repairs and make trial installations were also essential.

From the prestigious control tower, opened in 1957, watch could easily be kept on aircraft when afar, for the approaches were very clear. The main runway, repeatedly used for development of advanced approach and landing aids, needed to be long and wide enough to aid pilots landing aircraft difficult to handle, should they develop problems or encounter bad weather.

For all these facilities a power supply with a peak loading capacity of around 200,000hp was decided upon. Electrical power for the tunnel site was supplied by Little Barford power station. Water supplies of up to 400,000 gallons daily could be obtained from a pumping station on the River Ouse at Sharnbrook. Later, as much as 750,000 gallons would be supplied.

What had made the scheme so startling when announced in 1945 was the idea of amalgamating those three airfields, and laying the five-mile-long concrete runway linking Thurleigh with Little Staughton. A giant taxi track was to connect the runway with the Twinwood complex upon which vast hangar maintenance facilities were to be erected. This massive undertaking, intended to support the ill-starred Bristol Brabazon airliner, never materialised, but the road still dips at the spot where a wide bridge would have crossed, allowing large aircraft to pass between the two sites.

The intention was to open the Establishment in 1948, as a centre concentrating upon supersonic flight, and it was hoped to have it fully active by 1952. Instead, construction of the airfield was not started until 1951. On 12 June 1946 a contract had been agreed for construction of a vital two-mile concrete road linking the Tunnel Site with the A6 road north of Bedford. Two miles of ten-inch pipes were to be laid to convey water to the tunnel site. In August 1946 a cost of £20 million was suggested for the whole project, a large figure at that time.

First completed at Twinwood was the three feet by three feet Transonic Wind Tunnel, the main drive for which came from Volkenrode. Trials ranging from 0.9 to 2.0 Mach, the equivalent of 1,500mph at sea level, could be run with air pressure ranging over 0.1 to 2.0 atmospheres absolute. Drive equipment could reach 16,000bhp. That, the Vertical Spinning Tunnel and the High Speed Laboratory, were complete by 1952, when the first wind tunnel came into use. The spin tunnel, 80 feet high, had a diameter of 46 feet, free-fall models being tested in it.

In 1953 the thirteen feet by nine feet Low Speed Tunnel was completed, followed by the eight feet by eight feet Supersonic Tunnel made ready by 1956. The three feet by four feet High Supersonic Speed Tunnel, useful for guided weapons research, was opened in 1961, but by the late 1970s was being less used, and closed for economy reasons.

The eight feet by eight feet tunnel, the largest in its Mach number range in Western Europe, was also the largest pressure vessel. Some 90,000bhp was required to drive the main compressor and auxiliaries when running at maximum. Little wonder, then, that the power unit resembled more the engine room of a giant ship than an item of airfield equipment. In the case of the three feet by three feet high Supersonic Tunnel, designed for Mach numbers between 2.5 and 5.0, the main drive was achieved from two identical compressor sets working in parallel. A total of 300,000bhp could be generated on site.

Much of the wind tunnel testing of Concorde was undertaken in Bedford's tunnels, and also considerable work on STOL and VTOL development, including wing forms for later versions of the Harrier and AV-8.

Bedford's main 10,500-foot-long 300-foot-wide 09/27 concrete runway was built by John Laing and AMWD. Its size was reduced from the original five miles to one and a half miles, then increased to two miles. Three smaller subsidiary runways incorporated parts of wartime Thurleigh, runway 06/24 being used for carrier arrester trials and a parallel runway having a raised deck and ski-jump. Both of these runways were on the north side, in the naval trials area. The main runway's high ground position and alignment were coupled with an unobstructed horizon view extending for more than five miles, making it ideal for radar development. In 1956 the Blind Landing Experimental Unit arrived from Martlesham and, at the end of the 1970s, the Flying Wing of the Royal Signals and Radar Establishment, Malvern, moved to Bedford, bringing a variety of aircraft including Canberras, unusual looking Meteors and two Viscounts.

Within the Flight Area, on the south-west side of the airfield, were the hangars, workshops, offices, stores, laboratories, etc. The largest hangar was an all-aluminium structure with a clear span of 200 feet, a clear height of 50 feet and an overall length of 245 feet. Essential radiant heating of this and other hangars reduced the considerable heat loss when the large doors were opened. The floor surface temperature was set at 75°F. Hot-water radiant panels were sited along the hangar walls, and heated pipes were embedded beneath their tracks to nullify the effects of the doors being opened.

On the north side of the airfield was the Naval Air Section, where major items researched included the mirror landing sight, angled deck, nylon net barriers for carriers, the rolling platform for ship-based helicopters and, most famously, the ski-jump for Harriers.

Although organisation of the Establishment changed several times, the most important section remained the Aero Flight Research Department, half of which also functioned at Farnborough, and which researched aerodynamic innovations, low-speed flying during landing and take-off, and control at transonic and supersonic speeds. One of the department's striking-looking aircraft, in raspberry ripple finish, was a Gnat employed for gust research and liberally decorated with pressure measurement equipment. General development work was undertaken with helicopters, including operation in difficult weather conditions and instrument trials. A BAe 125 fitted with a laser allowed radar ranging in cloud conditions.

Vertical take-off and vectored thrust were explored using the Rolls Royce Thrust Measuring Rig XJ314 (or 'Flying Bedstead') in 1956-57, later the Short SC 1 then the Harrier family. Another major component was the Operational Systems Division, whose work included navigational systems, and the BAC 1-11 200 XX105/*G-ASJD*, which at one time was used for voice-controlled flight.

When Main Stores at the Tunnel Site was being built, a smallpox isolation hospital had first to be burned down to eradicate any remaining spores and contamination. As a hut near the airfield was being demolished in 1974 it was found to have served as a dormitory for the Americans; eight wall panels bearing artwork were carefully removed and flown to the USA for display in the Wright Patterson AFB museum at Dayton, Ohio.

Although never part of RAE Bedford, in the town of that name is the Transonic Wind Tunnel of the Aircraft Research Association. ARAL, formed in January 1952, resulted from the co-operative efforts of a number of firms that in 1951 had decided to construct a tunnel to supplement the work of the government establishment nearby. Their nine feet by eight feet tunnel came into use in the mid-1950s, building having started in October 1953.

In 1993, with major cutbacks in funding for aeronautical R&D following the end of the Cold War, RAE Bedford was a tragic casualty. Recent years had seen it being used by BA for crew training, but it was impossibly sited to have much civilian attraction, although notions were floated for its use as a freight base, possibly for the delivery of cold-store items such as fruit and flowers. Instead, it has gone the way of other superb airfields like Alconbury and Bentwaters; it just deteriorates, although the Tunnel Site for a while continued to function.

**Main feature:**
*Runway:* 09/27 10,500ft, concrete. Hangars and other buildings were one-off designs.

---

## BENSON, Berkshire

*51°37N/01°05W 200ft asl; SU631915. 13 miles SE of Oxford close to the A423(T)*

> "Watch out for the MiG coming in fast and low from the right. That's why we're using trees and terrain for cover." The Chinook banked away as steeply and as fast as it could, but it wasn't for real.

The life-like action took place in one of the simulators in Benson's helicopter air warfare block – civilian-operated, sort of. At the start of the 21st century Benson was primarily the home of the RAF's Puma force, whose crews had recently been doing so much to help the people of Mozambique during the terrible flooding of their homeland. Others retained unenviable tasks in Northern Ireland, while local Tutors gave Oxford University Air Squadron students and Air Cadets a chance to sample both flying and Service life. During 2001 Merlin helicopters trickled into No 28, a Squadron as new to Benson as to the home-based RAF. Those hectic days when Benson was the home of photographic reconnaissance seem as distant as the dinosaurs, although there are still personnel on the station who speak with pride of its links with that most magical aeroplane of all time – the de Havilland Mosquito. Between 1941 and 1953 Benson was its second home, from where the Mossie made its operational debut and regularly roamed the most distant corners of Europe. From here the Mossies flew to secure those famous amazing photographs of Peenemunde's V-1s and 2s, and even reached the Balkans during unarmed sorties requiring colossal courage. Just as remarkable were the lone pilots flying Benson's Spitfires, who commonly snapped Berlin and also took the shots that proved that the Mohne Dam had been breached. Most important of all, it was Benson's crews who had the responsibility of finding just how effective the colossal wartime investment in Bomber Command was proving to be.

What the MoD knows as Benson's 'Estate Development' has not changed very much since construction started in 1937. Nestling below the 450-foot-high Chiltern Hills to the south and thus well out of sight, Benson is also partially set among trees and still reached by road after negotiating winding country lanes. The public approach road is set almost level with the tops of four C Type hangars, no longer smothered with white paint, for the Queen's Flight has left its ancestral home. Benson is now very much the base of Army-supporting fighting forces, where the unique new, expensive and privately funded (PFI) red-brick helicopter warfare training and development centre dominates.

RAF occupation of Benson, in layout and style a typical 1937 expansion station, started early in

*Mosquito PR1 W4051 LY-J of No 1 PRU.*

1939. During the first days of April, 103 and 150 Squadrons of No 1 Group earmarked for Field Force France brought along their Fairey Battles. Clear was the preparation for war, as at similar stations, and on 2 September 1939 the squadrons flew away to France.

As planned pre-war, Whitleys at once began arriving to form No 4 Group Pool. Benson's grass surface had yet to become sufficiently firm and the heavies of the 166 Squadron advanced guard quickly damaged the turf. Plans were quickly changed so that 9 September 1939 saw the Whitleys being exchanged for Battles of 52 and 63 Squadrons and a few Ansons from Abingdon, where the Whitley Pool was re-established.

At Benson the newcomers joined the elite, for the station was home to the Airspeed Envoy *G-AEXX* of The King's Flight, for which Hendon was no longer deemed safe (the Flight Commander had, incidentally, wanted a move to Smith's Lawn, Windsor Great Park). Lacking range and defensive armament, the special Envoy had, in summer 1939, been supplemented with an internally modified Lockheed Hudson, N7263. Retained was its bulbous dorsal turret, and extra fuel tanks extended the aircraft's range to 3,000 miles. Only one passenger could now be carried. Normal bomber camouflage was retained and no special identity markings supplemented the roundels and serial number. King's Flight officers wanted, instead, to use two DH Albatross airliners, *G-AEVV* and *G-AEVW*, but the suggestion was turned down. March 1940 brought a Percival Q.6 from Northolt for the King, who shared it with the AOC-in-C Bomber Command. A second Hudson, N7364, held for a month early in 1940, served as an unmodified reserve.

To hasten crew output the Battle squadrons amalgamated on 14 September 1939, becoming No 1 Group Pool, which, together with its other half at Cranfield, provided crews for AASF squadrons in France. Unit strength increased when 207 Squadron, Cranfield, joined them in April 1940, the enlarged formation becoming No 12 Operational Training Unit Benson early in that month. Their Armament Training Flight was permanently detached to distant Penrhos, where live weapons practice was undertaken. Many Benson-trained Battle crews perished in France in May 1940.

In June the station's ground defences were rapidly strengthened against land attack, pillboxes being constructed around the perimeter. At 2355 on 29 June 1940 the enemy first visited the station to deliver from high level eighteen HEs in the vicinity of the fully lit landing ground. That led to Mount Farm, Benson's intended SLG, being brought into use sooner than intended.

*Spitfire PR IV in April 1943. Used at Benson, it was subsequently with 543 Squadron, then 8 OTU.*

July saw hectic activity as the OTU struggled to provide Battle crews to replace those lost in France. Some pilots found themselves diverted to fighter squadrons where their Merlin engine training was most useful. A memorable event of the period led to special awards to soldiers helping to defend the station. Sergeant D Jobson and Private E D Gurnham, RASC, each received a George Medal on 14 July for courageously rescuing a pilot from a crashed burning Battle.

On 13 August Polish airmen began arriving to train for the new Polish-manned Battle squadrons forming in a resurrected 1 Group. As they were being welcomed the enemy also paid his compliments, a Ju 88 diving out of low cloud to deliver three HEs and a smelly oil bomb. One HE hit unoccupied air raid shelter No 12, from which debris was hurled upon the roof of the Airmen's Mess, and between 'C' and 'D' Hangars, where an Anson was damaged. The other two exploded on waste ground and the oil bomb failed to ignite.

Construction of a perimeter track commenced in August as training of Czechs alongside Poles began. Bomber Command was eager to rid itself of the short-range Fairey Battles once current anti-invasion operations ended, and for which crews also trained at Benson. In October future re-arming of No 1 Group with Wellingtons was confirmed amid uncertainty of Benson's suitability for them. Cranfield and Twinwood were favoured as alternative sites for 12 OTU, but Mount Farm SLG's upgrade had resulted in it having metalled runways suitable for Wellington day and night flying. Any move was abandoned, leaving Benson for aircraft major maintenance and daylight flying. With effect from 1 December 1940 OTU strength was set at the equivalent of a half heavy bomber OTU, and remaining Battles were posted away.

Further reduction in 12 OTU's establishment made space for No 1 Photographic Reconnaissance Unit, which arrived from Heston on 27 December 1940, heralding Benson's long and famed association with photo-reconnaissance. Its arrival brought strange, unusually coloured camera-equipped Spitfires for highly secret work, still viewed to be of a somewhat experimental nature. A few Blenheim IVs and Hudsons accompanied them, and operations were resumed almost immediately.

Meanwhile, Wellingtons were arriving for 12 OTU, which began the first new equipment training course on 4 January 1941 – six complete crews would be trained each fortnight. Airfield extension had already been decided upon before the afternoon of 30 January, when nineteen HE bombs and incendiaries fell within the station's boundary without causing damage. In another attack on 27 February 1941 an enemy aircraft strafed and bombed the aerodrome, destroying a Wellington.

By March 1941 12 OTU's average intake had fallen to only four crews a fortnight because it was also converting 1 Group Battle squadron crews to Wellingtons. Bad winter weather and the thaw had played havoc with the landing ground, bringing the loss of three Wellingtons in a month, one overrunning its chocks and smashing into No 1 Hangar.

As winter passed, Spitfire PR operations increased, but not without loss, for on 10 April 1941 a Spitfire was shot down on a sortie to Brest. Another managed to secure PRU's first photographs of

*Valetta C1 VW855 of No 30 Squadron, Benson. It provided backing for aircraft ferrying overseas.*
*(John Rawlings)*

Copenhagen, and Flt Lt A L Taylor photographed Le Bourget before strafing the airfield. Four days later, Sergeant W Morgan managed quite an incredible feat when, in a Spitfire, he photographed Genoa and Spetzia before landing at Hawkinge in Kent after an amazing seven-hour ten-minute flight, at the end of which he had only two gallons of petrol left; he had established a record for such operations. On the previous day Pilot Officer S H Dowse had been less fortunate when four Bf 109s intercepted his Spitfire over Bergen. After escaping, he courageously turned into Germany, came out over Wilhelmshaven and force-landed, short of fuel, near Ipswich at the end of an action-packed five-hour flight. April's successful sorties totalled fifty-five, and a further seventy-nine were flown in May. Wellingtons of 12 OTU also operated in June 1941, flying a few *Nickels*.

On 17 June No 1 PRU established another record: in the course of thirteen successful sorties, thirty-seven films were run from which 6,800 prints were made between 1230 and 2210 hours. Marylands were, at this time, coming to Benson to be fitted with cameras, prior to operating in the Mediterranean Theatre.

Following a decision to place Benson in 18 Group Coastal Command, Chipping Warden was chosen as a new home for 12 OTU, whence the advance party moved on 10 July 1941, thus depriving themselves of witnessing that magic, exhilarating moment when, on 13 July, No 1 PRU received the RAF's first Mosquito. Benson's strength was further expanded when five Bomber Command Spitfires and a Blenheim IV of 3 PRU arrived from Oakington for absorption by 1 PRU. Mount Farm was passed at this time to 15 OTU. By early September 1941 12 OTU had completely moved into Chipping Warden and Benson was now fully in Coastal Command. Photographs were despatched daily to the interpretation unit at nearby Medmenham for analysis.

It was to Sqn Ldr R H Clerke that the honour fell on 17 September 1941 of being the first pilot to take a Mosquito (W4055) on an operational sortie, during which he passed over Bordeaux, La Pallice and Brest. Flt Lt Taylor took the aircraft on its second operation, three days later, to the Heligoland-Sylt area. The Mosquito was already ranging widely.

Fast times and long duration were common to Benson's complement, nearly always flying without defensive armament. Two long Mosquito flights, on 12 and 28 February 1942, were to Danzig and Gdynia in Poland respectively. By March Mosquitoes were largely handling the Scandinavian commitment from Wick, watching for German capital ship movements and leaving Spitfires to survey other areas. There were, however, notable exceptions such as a brave low-level run by Victor Ricketts and Boris Lukhmanoff to photograph the bombed Renault works at Billancourt. Augsburg, too, was photographed in April 1942, after the Lancaster low-level daylight raid on the MAN works. Damage assessment flights over Germany were mainly flown by Spitfire IVs, many of which differed individually by way of technical and equipment features.

In September 1940 a de-luxe DH Flamingo, R2766, had arrived for The King's Flight. Alongside its RAF roundels it carried the civil registration *G-AGCC*, allowing it to readily cross neutral territory in an emergency. Gp Capt Fielden had pressed for a communications aircraft and, rather curiously, was offered the captured Me 108 *G-AFRN*, held at Farnborough. Displeasure greeted this, so instead an Avro Tutor biplane, K6120, which had joined 63 Squadron at Benson in November 1939 and had passed to 12 OTU, was now put at the Flight's disposal. The Flamingo raised a number of problems, for it was an unarmed, unfamiliar shape, needing a fighter escort, and for that reason was disposed of to 24 Squadron. Questions then arose about the continued existence

*National Emergency Standby Puma HC 1 ZA935 of 33 Squadron in Benson's 'C' Type Hangar, May 2000.*

*A May 2000 view of Grob G.115E Tutor G-BYUP, operated by VT Aerospace Ltd at Benson and used by Oxford UAS. The plastic strips hanging in the doorway reduce heat loss via the large hangar mouth.*

of the Flight, and also its low utilisation. Some things never change! Eventually it was decided that The King's Flight would disband, and that the King would fly mainly in aircraft provided by a VIP detachment of 24 Squadron based at Northolt. Accordingly, disbandment took place at Benson on 14 February 1942. The Hudson, N7263, which had been used as the Royal aircraft early in the war, joined 161 Squadron at Tempsford, the Percival Q.6 leaving for Halton in May 1942.

Another squadron that used Benson in the winter of 1941-2 was No 140. Formed to provide photographic coverage of enemy movements during an invasion of Britain, and as 1416 Flight based at Hendon, it gradually became a strategic reconnaissance unit for GHQ Home Command, controlled by Army Co-operation rather than Coastal Command. It moved to Benson early in September 1941 flying a mixture of Spitfires, and held several Blenheim IVs for night duty. Operations over coastal France commenced on 1 October 1941, and in November night operations by the Blenheims started, photographs being taken using flash bombs. Another task was photographic support of the Army within Britain, particularly of its use of camouflage. Early in 1942 the squadron began to photograph Channel shipping, until 4 May, when the entire establishment and role changed. Next day No 140 moved to Mount Farm to concentrate on Army strategic reconnaissance needs by making flights leading to the Dieppe landing. The move had another purpose, for, as 140 Squadron left Benson, the building of concrete runways began.

Clear summer weather allowed a great increase in successful photographic reconnaissance operations. No 1 PRU expanded fast, frequently detaching aircraft to other bases at home and abroad. For administrative purposes the PR force was re-organised into squadrons, the Unit dispersing on 18 October 1942, its dozen Mosquitoes being placed in 540 Squadron, while 14 Spitfire PR IVs became 541 Squadron. An assortment of nineteen Spitfires became 542 Squadron, and another fifteen equipped 543 Squadron, leaving a mixture of Marylands, Ansons, Spitfires and Wellington IVs to call themselves 544 Squadron.

Benson was certainly an action station, despatching sorties over the whole of Europe and inspecting and recording the effects of the Battle of the Ruhr. At 0725 on 17 May 1943 Fg Off F G Fray set off in Spitfire IV EN343 of 542 Squadron to photograph the results of the attacks on the Mohne and Sorpe Dams. Next day Fg Off D G Scott and EN411 observed and photographed the extent of the Ruhr flooding, and on the following day Benson Spitfires flew another three sorties, to the Sorpe Dam. During their ever-deeper penetrations into Germany, Mosquitoes of 540 Squadron returned with photographs of Peenemünde, confirming its purpose and, for the British, the development of the V-weapons. Experimental night photography using Mosquito IVs of 544 Squadron began in February 1943. Two-stage supercharged Merlin engines led to refinements of both Spitfires and Mosquitoes. The Spitfire PR Mk XI came into use at Benson in May 1943, joining a handful of re-engined Mosquito Mk IVs, redesignated as PR VIIIs, introduced in February 1943. In June 540 Squadron began operating PR IXs.

During October 1943 543 Squadron left Benson, leaving behind Spitfires of 541 and 542 Squadrons and Mosquitoes of 544 and 540 Squadrons until March 1945. Before 543 Squadron vacated Benson its 'B' Flight was hived off to form the nucleus of 309 Ferry Training Unit, also known as 309 Ferry Training and Aircraft Despatch Unit, which held a few Master IIs and Spitfire IVs for the training of pilots prior to their ferrying of reconnaissance Spitfires overseas.

Frequent attempts were made from Benson to photograph the German capital at the start of

1944 and throughout the Battle of Berlin. Then the station began its vital part in the run-up to the invasion of France, with 544 Squadron photographing much of northern France. From mid-1944 both Benson Mosquito squadrons employed pressure-cabin Mk XVIs. The Spitfire squadrons used a few Mustang IIIs, and received the first of the Griffon-engined PR Mk XIX Spitfires. In midsummer 1944 the nominal strength of Benson's four operational squadrons was eighty aircraft. A few were detached to Dyce in August, and also to the USSR, to observe the movements of the battleship *Tirpitz* for potential Bomber Command attack.

At the end of hostilities Benson had a few very-long-range Mosquito PR 34s, which were despatched on their first operational sortie (by 544 Squadron) to Norway on 7 May 1945. Unlike most operational stations, Benson had an exceptionally busy post-war period ahead, for damage-assessment flights over Europe were needed aplenty so that rehabilitation and rebuilding could commence after the tremendous destruction wrought in the closing months of the war. Photographic survey sorties were flown over Britain, Malta and various other overseas territories. Benson became the centre to which such agencies as the Ministry of Agriculture and Town and County Planning could turn for help, and such was the quantity of material required that Benson's equipment, such as continuous processing machines coupled to fast drying techniques, were as useful now as in the closing stages of the war. Advances in survey photography had been quite amazing, while processing had changed from laborious hand or tank development to machines churning out thousands of prints in a day. The value of photography for mapping purposes, particularly of uncharted areas, became an adjunct to the activities at Benson, as a result of which a handful of Lancasters were acquired and, on 1 October 1946, gathered to form 82 Squadron. They were soon overseas photographing vast tracts of Africa. No 542 Squadron disbanded on 27 August 1945, and 544 Squadron on 13 October 1945. On 30 September 1946 540 and 541 Squadrons were also disbanded. From them arose 58 Squadron, manned and equipped by the old hands and armed with Mosquito PR 34s and Ansons modified for survey work. A new 541 Squadron was formed in November 1947, and another, 540 Squadron, the following month. The former operated Spitfire PR XIXs in a tactical role, while the latter, equipped with Mosquito PR 34s, was for strategic reconnaissance. For night photographic duty, 58 Squadron received a few specialised Mosquito PR 35s.

It was not only the needs of civilians that required attention in peacetime. Attitudes in eastern Europe caused all sorts of devices and methods to be used, under the label of 'reconnaissance'. Specialised training being essential, 8 OTU was retained and spasmodically flew from Mount Farm, Chalgrove and Benson. It became 237 OCU on 31 July 1947, and did not leave the area until the start of December 1951, by then equipped not with Harvards and Spitfire XIXs but with Meteor 7s and 9s and Mosquito PR 34s.

Jet aircraft, due to their short duration, came late to the reconnaissance scene in Britain, the first intended for the role – the Meteor V – proving very troublesome. Meteor PR 10s were little more than short-duration tactical aircraft, and it was not until the first Canberra PR 3s reached 540 Squadron at Benson, at the end of 1952, that the PR force moved into the new age. Meteor PR 10s had joined 541 Squadron just before it left for Germany in mid-June 1951.

At the end of October 1952 82 Squadron's Lancasters returned to Benson, among them the famous Lancaster PA474, still active within the Battle of Britain Memorial Flight. The squadron's stay was brief for, in March 1953, together with the other PR units and squadrons at Benson, it moved to Wyton. A great partnership, Benson and PR, had ended.

Benson's transfer to RAF Transport Command came in March 1953, when the station became an aircraft despatch centre. No 30 Squadron, using Valettas, was briefly here before moving to Dishforth. Two squadrons with similar roles, 147 and 167, arrived at Benson in April 1953 and later amalgamated to become the Ferry Squadron.

An unexpected event was the re-forming of 21 Squadron here on 1 May 1959, for a duty reminiscent of the RAF's pre-war colonial policing. It trained with four Twin Pioneers before leaving in mid-September 1959.

There were even more unlikely occupants in the mid-1950s. Culham being unsuitable for jet fighters, 1832 Squadron, RNVR, set up shop at Benson in July 1955 to fly Attackers shared with 1836 Squadron. In October 1956 Sea Hawk Is started to replace the Attackers, but the Navy's stay was brief, for on 10 March 1957, in keeping with the disbandment of RAuxAF fighter squadrons, the RNVR squadrons were also paid off.

Transport Command had important plans for Benson. The new medium-range, unconventional-looking, tail-loaded AWA Argosy twin-boom freighter intended to be able to reach Cyprus non-stop when fully loaded, would be based here; the first for RAF service arrived on 18 November 1961. It joined a training unit that became 242 Operational Conversion Unit before moving to Thorney Island in April 1963.

No 114 Squadron re-formed at Benson on 1 October 1961 to operate the Argosy, equipping commencing in February 1962, at the same time as 105 Squadron received Argosys. It flew them from here for four months before moving overseas. No 267 Squadron began to equip in November 1962, operating from Benson until the Argosy's withdrawal and its disbandment on 30 June 1970. Another recipient had been 215 Squadron, which worked up on Argosys at Benson between May and August 1963. Unable to match the RAF's range requirements, the Argosy had a short career.

With the disbandment of 114 Squadron on 31 October 1971, Benson's troop and freight transport role ended – but not that of passenger-carrying. Royal wartime flying had been the task of 24 Squadron and later of Hendon's Metropolitan Communications Squadron. The King thought highly of its Dakotas and, in a world where flying was ever increasing, The King's Flight had re-formed at Benson on 1 May 1946, Air Commodore Fielden resuming his Captaincy. Originally The King's Flight was to operate a VVIP York and three Vikings, two with VVIP fit and the other with the normal passenger layout. Instead, only four cheaper Vikings were allotted, the additional one serving as an engineering support aircraft. To speed delivery, BEA surrendered two early Vikings, allowing one, as VL245 – the normal passenger aircraft – to be collected from Wisley for the Flight on 11 August 1946. It joined Dominie RL951, already in use and whose career ended abruptly in a crash at Mount Farm in November 1946.

All four Vikings were at Benson by January 1947 and a month later flew to Brooklyn Air Base, near Cape Town, from where they were used during the South African Royal Tour. Later in 1947 they were active during the wedding of Princess Elizabeth and Prince Philip, and subsequently carried the Royal Family many times.

Prince Philip commenced flying lessons in 1952. Using Chipmunk WP861, he made his first solo flight on 20 December 1952. Subsequently he flew another Benson-based Chipmunk, WP912, then made use of Devon VP961, stationed at White Waltham, from which airfield he had undertaken most of his flying training.

For Queen's Flight purposes the Devon, though a reliable and pleasant aircraft for pilot and passengers, was too small, so one of its larger derivatives, a Heron, was ordered for Prince Philip. Vikings remained very active, but the little-used workshop aircraft was disposed of in November 1953 when the future of the Flight – renamed The Queen's Flight on 16 November 1953 – was under review. A plan emerged by which the Heron would reach the Flight early in 1954, and the Vikings be replaced by three Viscounts. With the Flight temporarily at Northolt while its Benson hangar was being renovated, discussions concerning new equipment went ahead bringing sufficient confidence for Vickers to earmark Viscount airframes in production for completion to VIP standard. A firm commitment was awaited for 18 months before official sanction was given for the Flight's new establishment to comprise one Viscount 700D, one VVIP Viking, a Heron and two Whirlwind helicopters.

The problem ever facing the Flight was how to maintain value to set against the cost of capital equipment and maintenance over a long period. For Her Majesty to have made use of one of the finest airliners of its time would certainly have given that a prestigious boost, for which reason the purchase would have been sensible. The decision not to go ahead with the Viscount scheme, irrespective of the economics involved, cannot be considered as wise.

September 1954 brought to the Flight and Benson their first helicopter, a small Westland Dragonfly, HC4-XF261, from CFS South Cerney; although intended for temporary service, it actually resided at Benson for four years. Sanction for The Queen's Flight to operate two VVIP helicopters was given in July 1954, and the first Royal helicopter journey came on 6 September 1954 when Prince Philip flew in the Dragonfly from Buckingham Palace to Shinfield. Although many members of the Royal Family used XF261, it mostly carried Prince Philip, who, in 1955, qualified as a helicopter pilot. His Heron C3, XH375, joined the Flight on 18 May 1955. Upon its highly burnished finish it wore an Edinburgh Green cheat line in keeping with its pilot's title. Both Devon and Heron were positioned at White Waltham until July 1955, when they moved to Benson.

Summer 1955 saw Prince Philip making use of a naval Whirlwind 22, the Dragonfly being switched to route and landing area survey. Satisfied as to the value of helicopters, the Air Council agreed to Whirlwinds being added to the Flight's establishment the following spring. Various delays arose, and not until July 1958 was a contract for two VVIP Whirlwind 8s placed, for 1959 delivery. Meanwhile a Whirlwind 4 replaced the small Dragonfly. Trouble with the Alvis Leonides Major engine, which powered the Whirlwind, delayed the Mk 8's Benson debut until October 1959. Not until 23 September 1960 did the new Whirlwind make its first Royal passenger flight, from Kensington Palace to Papworth.

Replacements for the Vikings were ordered in April 1956 in the form of two Heron C4s. Two years later they came into use, Prince Philip's Heron – together with Vikings VL233 and VL246 – having long borne their Royal role. Not until 22 April 1958 did the last Viking flight take place, with the two new Herons arriving within a few days.

Subsequently the Royal Herons – bright red overall from 1960 – were used in many distant parts of the world. Their payload/range characteristics were limited, and for the Royal Tour of India and the Himalayas two Dakotas (KN452, previously used by the AOC Malta, and KN645, once the transport of Field Marshal Montgomery) were acquired. Nevertheless, a fourth Heron joined the Flight in June 1961 and was used during Princess Alexandra's tour of the Far East, despite dissatisfaction with the aircraft's overall performance.

In March 1964 the first of two turbo-engined Whirlwind 12s to replace the Mk 8s came into use at Benson as agreement was reached to replace the Herons with Andovers. The first two of those came into the Flight in July-August 1964.

Prince Philip flew to the North Sea rig, *Sea Quest*, in a 72 Squadron Wessex during June 1967 as consideration was being given to the Flight having such aircraft. HM Queen Elizabeth the Queen Mother came to be quoted as saying that 'the chopper' had changed her life as much as it did Anne Boleyn's, but whether the use of helicopters would continue came into doubt on 7 December 1967 when Whirlwind XL487 crashed as a result of a rotor shaft fracture. Air Commodore J H L Blount, Captain of The Queen's Flight, was among those killed, and all Whirlwinds were promptly grounded pending a court of enquiry. Not until the end of March 1968 did The Queen's Flight resume helicopter flying.

The last Royal Heron, XM296, left on 25 June 1968 after ten years' service and an accumulation of 4,310 flying hours.

Several Wessex helicopters were used before mid-1969. The VVIP Wessex HCC4's first task was to carry the Prince of Wales to his Investiture at Caernarfon. Later that year a Basset was placed at Benson for the Prince's use and also for general communications flying. It remained at Benson until 16 September 1971, when it was despatched to 32 Squadron, Northolt.

In 1972 HQ 38 Group arrived, together with No 38 Group Tactical Communications Wing. They stayed until 1976, the former then leaving for Upavon, the latter going to Brize Norton. In 1977 Support Command Signals HQ and the Radio Introduction Unit arrived from Medmenham, joining 115 Squadron, which had arrived from Cottesmore and was now flying Andovers. Also with them was the Andover Training Flight and the Andover Servicing Flight. The Support Command Checking Unit was also here. The Andovers departed for Brize Norton in January 1983 and the SCCU disbanded early in 1987.

At the start of the 1980s The Queen's Flight, Benson, consisted of three Andover Mk CC2s – XS789, XS790 and XS793 – together with two Wessex HCC4s – XV732 and XV733. On 23 April 1986 the first of two BAe 146 CC Mk 2s, able to carry twice the Andover's load at almost double its

*An Aw Argosy XR443 by one of Benson's hangars.*

speed, was handed to the Royal Flight, the second in June, and a third in December 1990. Two of the Andovers were then passed to 32 Squadron, Northolt, when the 146s arrived.

A highlight for the station had been provided on 12 June 1989 when the Queen's Colour was awarded here to the Royal Auxiliary Air Force.

On 1 November 1992 The Queen's Flight joined the new 38 Group, and on 1 April 1995 merged with Northolt-based No 32 Squadron to become No 32 (The Royal) Squadron.

The Queen's Flight helicopters were not the only Wessex helicopters using Benson, for in March 1992 No 60 Squadron was re-established with Wessex HC2s at Benson on their return from Northern Ireland.

Modern warfare makes much use of helicopters, and Benson plays a major part in British involvement. Within the Joint Helicopter Command, formed in October 1999 to jointly train RAF, Army and Navy crews in multi-skills, by day and night, it has become main base for Puma and Merlin.

Benson's 1998 population of 1,600 personnel (200 of them civilians) rose by 2003 to 1,700, whose dependants numbered 2,700. Aircraft movements (all types) total around 51,000 a year – and in an area of exceptionally busy sky. The annual cost of running Benson is in the region of £43m. Impressive figures indeed.

No 33 Squadron and its Pumas arrived from Odiham in July 1997, the Puma OCF following in 1998. Pumas soon played a prominent part in operation *Barwood*, which provided relief for those stricken by terrible flooding in Mozambique. Ordered to move from Benson on a Tuesday evening, personnel were expecting to join exercise *Joint Winter* in Norway, to where Pumas have long been committed. Instead, they left Brize Norton on Thursday 2 March and arrived at SAAF base Hoedspruit the next day. Four dismantled Pumas were flown out in an Antonov, and two were re-assembled ready for the 50-minute flight to Maputo, Mozambique, by the morning of 5 March. Operating from Palmeira, they first rescued people stranded on small islands, then undertook supply flights carrying food and medical supplies – demanding tasks in heat and high humidity. They rescued 725 people, transported 43,350kg of freight, flew 363.5 hours in two weeks, and used 185,010kg of fuel.

Indicative of more typical operational commitments, May 2000 found the squadron holding ten Pumas at high readiness for Joint Reaction Force use. Four Pumas were committed to Rapid Reaction Force Nato and two – together with seventy-five personnel – were at Pristina, Kosovo, participating in operation *Agricola*. One Puma was on standby for any important National Task, the latter role involving Pumas in assisting alleviation of distress during UK flooding and within operation *Peninsula*, the appalling foot and mouth episode. No 33 Squadron, with a nominal strength of fifteen Pumas, has kept a small detachment with the 'peace keeping' force in Kosovo and maintains a few Pumas at Aldergrove, Northern Ireland.

In March 2003 Benson's Pumas were part of the Joint Helicopter Force, which, at the start of operation *Telic*, supported the assault on Iraq's Al Faw Peninsula by 40 and 42 Commando. Flying at around 50 feet in atrocious conditions caused by a sandstorm, they flew by night and day moving troops and supplies. Two were assigned to a Tactical Medical Wing, which involved collecting more than forty serious front-line casualties needing urgent attention. Benson's Pumas were subsequently busily engaged in supporting British land forces in the Basrah area. On 12 December 2003 six of Benson's Pumas were placed in a newly reformed No 1563 Flight, for which Benson provides aircraft, engine and electrical servicing and support through the supply and mobility squadrons.

*No 28 Squadron operates Merlin helicopters (like S-ZJ134) from Benson.*

Recent activity at Benson relates in particular to the Merlin helicopter. On 17 July 2001 No 28 Squadron re-formed to operate a fleet of eighteen Merlin HC3 medium support helicopters, each able to carry between twenty-four and thirty troops, a 4-ton load and fly for more than three hours when cruising at 150K IAS. Benson received its first Merlin on 6 November 2000, the type entering service in January 2001. Pilot training on the Merlin OCF started in January 2002. Final delivery came in November 2002, operational capability beginning in 2003. The 'Required Operating Fleet' figure (modern name for 'establishment', and now without reserves) calls for as many as twenty-two Merlins at Benson.

An important new feature at Benson is the CAE-devised Medium Support Helicopter Training Facility (MSHTF). Opened in 2000, it includes six of the latest simulators (three for Chinook, two for Merlin and one for Puma, which might still have a useful career ahead). A computerised battle scenario theatre allows most realistic helicopter combat scenarios to be explored. The first Private Finance Initiative tactics installation, it is run by Canadian CAE, which leases it to the MoD.

Other developments related to the increased importance of helicopters include a refurbished 'D' Hangar, a new MRESF and Blade Bay, a special Merlin spares store – there is no Merlin MU backing – and a new MT complex. Benson is also home to the Rotary Wing Operational Evaluation and Training Unit.

Also Benson-based is No 606 Chiltern Squadron, RAuxAF, formed on 1 October 1996 as a Helicopter Support Squadron. Manned by civilians with special skills, who undertake twenty-seven days training a year to work alongside Regulars in war, its role is to generally assist under the terms of the Reserve Forces Act 1996.

A Mobile Catering Supply Unit arrived in November 1992 to train personnel who man three portable Air Combat Support Units, each able to cater in the field for 500 personnel. Also here is the Mobile Meteorological Unit, and No 612 (Volunteer) Gliding School comes under the station's control, the latter flying from Abingdon. With the closure of Abingdon, the ULAS, Oxford UAS and 6 AEF in July 1992 found a home at Benson. They fly Tutor T1s, which provide 6,000 flights annually for 6,000 Air Cadets.

As one enters RAF Benson, which nestles in fine surroundings beneath the adjacent Chilterns, there is a reminder of times long gone in the form of a replica of 'EN343', the Spitfire PR XI used to secure in the early morning after the raid the famous photograph of the broken Mohne Dam. A plaque unveiled on 17 November 1989 recalls the sortie, flown by Fg Off Fray, and serves as a very good reminder of just what went on in times past at Benson.

Benson's possible future raises concern, for to adapt defence spending in order to maintain Eurofighter contracts and thus probably for the wrong reasons, and also to produce two aircraft carriers for questionable purposes, rumours suggest that Benson and its Pumas might be sacrificed. Whatever the outcome, Benson and its aged Pumas have served far better than most politicians.

**Main features:**
*Runways:* 06 5,700ft, 190 4,260ft, concrete and tar with woodchip surface; post-war development included runway 01/19 5,981ft of asphalt and concrete. *Hangars:* Four Type C, three Over Blister, four Extra Over Blister. *Hardstandings:* Ten 120ft diameter concrete. *Accommodation:* RAF officers 182, SNCOs 113, ORs 2,903. Two large Married Quarters areas to SE flank the domestic site.

The 490ft Chiltern Hills lie a mile to the south. Benson, in an area of much air activity, handles many light aircraft and military helicopters. It lies beneath the Oxford AIAA with high traffic density airways and the approaches to London.

## BIBURY, Gloucestershire

*51°46N/01°50W 521ft asl; SU123975. 6¹/₂ miles NE of Cirencester, 2 miles N of Bibury village*

Bibury-on-the-Plateau might have been an apt name for this one-time landing ground bisected by a road leading to idyllic Bibury village. It is hard to accept that once close by was an active night-fighter station, and even more difficult, when admiring delectable Arlington Row, to picture a summer's day when, near noon, three rare, lumbering Bombay transports, protected by six Spitfires of 92 Squadron, helped bring along their squadron from Pembrey. Being 19 August 1940, such a trio would have been tempting to a marauder – hence the escort, which was coming to Bibury for night stand, and at a landing ground that had already shown itself suitable for night fighters.

Situated on an extension of Ablington Down, it was very remote even if it was close to one of England's most picturesque vistas. Yet within two hours of the Spitfires' arrival Ju 88As of III/KG 51 crept in to operate singly over Gloucestershire. One crew, by intent or maybe chance, called on Bibury, making a fast run to bomb and strafe the airfield. One Spitfire was destroyed, another seriously damaged, three hit by stray bullets and an airman killed.

Such impudent intrusion on a showery summer afternoon engendered rapid reaction. Two pilots jumped into their Spitfires for a fast and long chase, then a short and sharp combat followed, as a result of which the bomber and crew perished in the Solent. Flying Spitfire R6703 was Flt Lt T S Wade, the well-known late-1940s test pilot of Hawker Aircraft, who had to force-land and was lucky to be clear before his fighter exploded.

As well as night fighters, Bibury witnessed early jet activity, so with envy you may ascend to Ablington Down to view the airfield site. It's still easy to spot, for it retains the appearance of a one-time flying field. By the Northleach road long remained two Blister hangars, a picket hut, and fractured remains of other buildings with concrete roads as further recognition points.

Bibury Farm, as the camp was first known, was selected as a grass relief landing ground in April 1939 to permit increased flying by 3 SFTS South Cerney. When the first aircraft touched down seems not to have been recorded, at least officially, but the site was certainly in use as an RLG for Oxfords by April 1940. When invasion involving troop transports seemed possible, No 23 Group Training Command, controlling the landing ground, ordered it to be blocked with old motor bodies, which littered it for weeks. The road to the site was closed to all but official traffic and local residents, with the LDV enjoying great, delectable power.

With the initial scare passed, night-flying training commenced on 6 July 1940, so that 3 SFTS's more permanent and expensive home could remain cloaked in darkness. Presumably the residents of the homes around were none too well aware of that aspect! Night-flying took place over many months, with day training a daily item helping to relieve congestion at South Cerney.

A complete change overtook the camp when, on 7 August 1940, 'A' Flight of 87 Squadron, Exeter, arrived together with its Hurricane 1s. Their role was night-fighting, so the claim of a quick kill of a He 111 by Plt Off Comilly on the night after arrival must have raised morale. The detachment stationed here to help defend Birmingham stayed briefly, and in mid-August was withdrawn and replaced by part of 92 Squadron, also administered by 10 Group. Spitfires flew a few night sorties from Bibury, pilots including Flt Lt C B Kingcombe. On 8 September 1940 92 Squadron left Pembrey for Biggin Hill, and the detachment joined the parent. Next it was the turn of 'B' Flight, 87 Squadron, which, on 3 September, heralded detachment rotation from that squadron, which continued until mid-December 1940.

The night following 'B' Flight's arrival proved ideal for night-flying. Visibility was excellent, the moon bright and Fg Off Beaumont aboard Hurricane V7285 damaged a Ju 88 near Bristol. The next night he and Pilot Officer Jay each fired at a Ju 88, but without success. After a week their Flight was recalled, but it was back again for night patrols on 10 September, and thereafter the two Flights of the squadron rotated, each having a week at Bibury. Action was limited, and keeping a Flight out of battle was hardly morale-boosting. So, on the afternoon of 30 September, 'B' Flight and Flt Lt I R Gleed went to Exeter. From there they hurried to Portland where Pilot Officer Maclure and Sergeant H Walton ran into a group of bombers escorted by fighters. Maclure claimed a Bf 110 and damaged a Ju 88, but Walton was shot down and slightly injured. Pilot Officer Cook also claimed a He 111 and damaged a Bf 109. Meanwhile, Gleed, flying above cloud, suddenly found himself confronting about sixty He 111s, so chose a rear bomber, which he shot out of the formation then watched it go vertically through the thick clouds. By then the whole of the German force had turned upon him, so he had little choice but to race for safety.

Weekly rotation of 87 Squadron to Bibury continued, and on 24 October 'B' Flight's arrival was marred by an accident when Pilot Officer Cook and Pilot Officer Jay collided during formation flying. Jay baled out but was unable to open his parachute.

The only other night engagement took place on 24 November 1940 when Fg Off Rayner, seeing a He 111 lit by searchlights, fired a six-second burst. On 18 December 1940 87 Squadron finally vacated Bibury, leaving it to the Oxfords of 3 SFTS, which by mid-January 1941 had seriously damaged its surface. There were many soft patches, and ruts caused by pilots pivoting their aircraft on one wheel, thus reducing Bibury's usefulness. The AOC of 23 Group visited on 10 February 1941 and, seeing the poor accommodation and sanitation arrangements, ordered an improvement, and also decided that the landing ground must be extended.

South Cerney's Oxfords used Bibury until snowy conditions closed it from January until 1 March 1942, when Oxford flying was resumed, by which time the SFTS had become 3 (Pilots) AFU. On 15 April 1943 1539 BAT Flight formed at South Cerney, moving to Bibury on 13 July 1943, where it remained until 15 November 1944. Blind approach training was administered in buildings close to the road, near the main technical site and WAAF communal site.

Improvements to the airfield in 1942-43 resulted in two Sommerfeld Tracking runways, but buildings remained of 1941-42 style, including five Over Type Blisters – three near the road, by which the fourteen-bay metal 'T1' was erected between two Blisters. Accommodation in temporary brick Laing huts was provided in four dispersed sites, three to the west of the road passing through the camp, and one on the far eastern side. An instruction site was fitted alongside the limited technical facilities.

When 1539 Flight vacated the airfield, 3 (P)AFU was also in the process of leaving, and by the end of November 1944 flying had ceased. On 1 December 1944 the station was taken over by 40 Group, Maintenance Command, and 7 MU, which used it as a domestic equipment storage sub-site at least until late 1945. Disposal is believed to have taken place in early 1950.

**Main features:**
*Runways:* No 1 04/022° 3,180ft, No 2 09/270° 3,540ft, both Sommerfeld Tracking, no permanent lighting. *Hangars:* four Over Double 65ft Blister and a single 65ft Over Blister (all 12532/41), and one metal T1 (0659/42). *Hardstandings:* Nil. *Accommodation:* RAF officers 79, SNCOs 154, ORs 310; WAAF officers 4, SNCOs 3, ORs 93.

## BICESTER, Oxfordshire

*51°55N/01°08W 270ft asl; SP595245. 1¹/₂ miles NE of Bicester town, by the A421*

In 1916, on Callers Field near Bicester town, British and Canadian engineers – assisted by Chinese and Portuguese workers and press-ganged German POWs – started building an RFC Training Depot Station for Southern Army Command. Americans – here near the start and almost at Bicester's demise – generated the only electric power station in the district in late 1917, when the camp opened.

In January 1918 118 Squadron RFC began mobilising here to operate HP 0/400 bombers, but the plan lapsed. Instead, No 44 Training Depot Station opened at the start of October 1918, and 118 Squadron left the next month. In August 1919 44 TDS was renamed 44 Training School within No 2 Group. No 2 Squadron, here from mid-February 1919, moved to Weston-on-the Green and was immediately replaced, on 19 September 1919, by 5 Squadron and its Bristol Fighters brought from France. No 44 TS closed in December 1919, No 2 Squadron disbanded on 20 January 1920, and Bicester passed to care and maintenance in March.

*Overstrand K4561 of 101 Squadron stands between Bicester's 'A' and 'C' Type hangars.*

Positioning bomber squadrons in central England under the 1924 plan led to Bicester's extensive reconstruction, which started during 1925. Technical site buildings were arranged within a pentagonal area, one Aircraft Shed Type 'A' (pattern 1154/27) being on the south-west side, another on the south-east, with plans allowing for another four. Main Stores (978/25), close to the MT Section and aero engine test rig (702/26), had a rail link to the main line. A circular, elevated 30,000-gallon water tank (1178/25) supplemented the camp's 100,000 gallon reservoir. Bicester's ultimate and very smart guard house (925/25) retained much of the original building. A 192-seat Airmen's Dining Room, modified in 1925 and 1933, stemmed from a 1923 design. Earlier Airmen's Barrack Blocks Type E, based on 1922-23 designs, each accommodated three NCOs and eighty men. Behind the 1924-25 SHQ was the camera obscura, while on the airfield a fifty-foot-diameter concrete compass swinging platform was laid.

Revised RAF Bicester opened in January 1928. Hawker Horsleys of 100 Squadron, which arrived on the 10th of the month from Spitalgate, stayed until November 1930, when they left for Donibristle, being replaced by 33 Squadron's Hawker Harts on 4 November 1930. Equipped at Eastchurch in February 1930, 33 was the first squadron to operate the fast Hart day bomber, and resided at Bicester until November 1934. Replacing it came 101 Squadron on 4 December 1934, the only squadron to fly Boulton & Paul Sidestrands. Between October 1935 and late July 1936 Overstrands – the RAF's first bombers with power-operated gun turrets – trickled in replacing the Harts, the first (K4547) arriving on 14 October 1935. On 25 November 1935 No 48 (GR) Squadron re-formed, then moved to Manston in mid-December to be equipped.

During the 1930s RAF Expansion period Bicester had a further facelift. Two 'C' Type Aircraft Sheds (1581/35 and 2392/37) supplemented the older pair, and Barrack Blocks Extended Type E (2489/37), accommodating an NCO and ninety-six ORs. By the start of 1939 nine Barrack Blocks had been added, as well as nine Married Quarters units for airmen, and six for officers together with the long-surviving Watch Office and Tower (1959/34). East of the playing-fields was built the splendid Officers' Mess.

Bicester came under Western Area control on 1 April 1936, became part of 3 Group on 30 April 1935, and was transferred to 1 Group on 17 August 1936.

No 144 Squadron was formed from 'C' Flight, 101 Squadron, on 11 January 1937, and moved to Hemswell on 8 February 1937, allowing 'A' Flight 101 Squadron to become 90 Squadron on 15 March 1937. Initially equipped with Hawker Hinds, 90 Squadron began re-arming with Blenheim Is in May 1937. Overstrands equipped 101 until August 1938, re-equipment with Blenheims having begun in June 1938.

Soon after the last Overstrands left the station the Munich Crisis pushed the Blenheim squadrons into advanced readiness. On 9 May 1939 both squadrons moved to West Raynham and into 2 Group, making way for Fairey Battles of 12 and 142 Squadrons, which, as part of the AASF now concentrated in Oxfordshire, moved to French bases on 2 September 1939.

On 12 September 1939 Blenheims returned, this time in the hands of 104 and 108 Squadrons, which used Ansons for navigator training. Two days later they merged to form No 2 Group Pool, which trained crews for its squadrons, a task similarly undertaken hereabouts in different guises almost to the end of the war. Controlled initially by 6 Group, the pilots and observers were from flying training schools and observer schools, whereas many air-gunners came

*Harts (including K2438 and K2461) of No 33 Squadron, Bicester.*

from 2 Group squadron groundcrews. Although specialised aircrew, the latter for a while retained airman rank and, even more miserly, their miserable rates of pay. British governments are rarely generous to those in greatest need! Training a Blenheim crew at this time took six months.

Bicester's personnel received a morale-booster early in the war. Vehicles from Handley Page's Cricklewood works delivered a large bomber secretly erected in the hangar by Launton Road. It was L7244, the Halifax prototype, which on 25 October 1939 made its first flight from Bicester and soon left for Boscombe Down.

On 8 April 1940 2 Group Pool became No 13 OTU Bicester. Crew training rapidly increased to replace 2 Group's crippling losses of the French campaign, and HM King George VI visited the station on 19 July 1940 to help boost morale. Many he met that day soon died in the terrible punishment incurred by 2 Group over the next fourteen months. During the period January 1940 to November 1941 No 15 MU made limited use of Bicester for aircraft storage.

On 22 July 1940 control of 13 OTU passed to 7 Group, and RLG Weston-on-the-Green came into use for night-flying while Grendon Underwood dummy airfield was ready to attract enemy bombs. During November Hinton-in-the-Hedges came into supplementary use for night-flying. That month saw Lewis gunners at a Bicester ground defence post claim hits on passing Ju 88 L1 + LS, which crashed at Blewbury, Berkshire.

During its first year 13 OTU trained 217 pilots, 240 observers and 273 air-gunners, and flying hours totalling 26,670. Blenheim crews were needed for home and overseas squadrons, and 2 Group's merciless anti-shipping campaign, which took a terrible toll. After that campaign ceased in autumn 1941, Blenheim crews were trained at 13 OTU mainly to meet Middle East needs. The OTU's second year produced 32,718 flying hours and 297 complete crews, 121 of them going overseas. The closest Bicester's bombers came to participating in offensive action was flying air/sea rescue searches after the '1,000 bomber' raids. From July 1942 part of the OTU output went to conversion for heavy bombers.

Finmere, first used from 31 July 1942 to 28 November 1942, replaced Hinton-in-the-Hedges as a satellite station. Turweston was also used, from 1 October 1942 to 28 November 1942 and, like Finmere, again in mid-1943. Both were Built Satellites having metalled runways, something Bicester never possessed. No 13 OTU had been passed to 7 Group on 15 July 1940, the Group being renumbered 92 on 11 May 1942. Bicester was home to 7 Group Communication Flight and 92 Group Communications Flight until 14 September 1942. The Blind Approach Calibration Flight under 26 (Signals) Group control moved in on 3 July 1942 and became No 1551 BAC Flight on 20 November 1942. It used Ansons, Master IIs and Oxfords before disbanding on 15 April 1943, being absorbed by the Signals Development Unit, Hinton-in-the-Hedges.

During Operation *Torch*, Blenheim Vs (often called Bisleys) at last went into action, their crews being drawn from 13 OTU. Replacement Mk Vs became urgently needed in Africa, and since they could only be flown there, No 307 Ferry Training Unit was formed at Bicester to perform the role. From 24 December 1942 thirty ferry crews were trained using seven Blenheim Vs.

On the afternoon of 5 April 1943 five Blenheims of 13 OTU flew a North Sea ASR sweep, the last such operation. At the time there were only twelve crews per course, and training was about to switch to producing crews for Bostons and Mitchells, which flew from the satellites because they needed hard runways.

On 1 June 1943 13 OTU left Bomber Command and joined 70 Group, Fighter Command, in preparation for training 2TAF crews. For the present Blenheims – mainly dual-control Mk Vcs – remained on strength for twin-conversion flying, and a few Spitfires were available for fighter affiliation training.

No 9 Group had control from 1 November 1943, then specialised formations of 84 and 85 Groups' TAF arrived to train for their supporting roles. The administration became known as the Forward Equipment Unit and served both Groups. No 420 Repair & Salvage Unit formed here on 1 February to support 84 Group, and as 84 Group Support Unit moved south later that month.

All thirteen OTU Blenheim flying ceased on 25 February 1944, the last short-nosed Blenheim I leaving Bicester three days later.

Bicester's backing of 2TAF became increasingly more important. No 12 Group took over 13 OTU, and as soon as 38 Group vacated runway-equipped Harwell in mid-October 1944, it moved there. Subsequently Bicester served almost exclusively as a 'non-flying' station. The Forward Equipment Unit of 85 Group became 246 MU on 1 January 1945 and transferred to 40 Group, Maintenance Command. As a transit centre for despatch of equipment to 2TAF on the Continent, it was also an assembly point for its vehicles and in particular those equipped with radio. Bicester also served as a Command Centre for aero engines and vehicle spares. BAFO was supplied until September 1945, then the station became a motor transport depot between late 1946 and 1 April 1949. Headquarters 40 Group, which arrived from Andover during February 1947, stayed until closure on 28 July 1961. A return to flying came during a brief stay by the Beam Approach Calibration Flight in July 1947.

No 246 MU disbanded on 1 April 1949, parachute-packing and servicing taking their place. Part of No 3 MU arrived from Akeman Street Sub-Sites and functioned between May 1947 and 20 May 1958. Between 3 September 1951 and 30 January 1954 the Civilian Supplies Technical Officers' School functioned here. No 71 MU opened as a 43 Group lodger unit on 15 December 1953, to repair, salvage and transport Service aircraft involved in flying accidents occurring south of a line drawn roughly between Aberdovey and the Wash. Assistance was also rendered to incidents involving civilian aircraft. Within 71 MU were a Bomb Disposal Flight and the Historic Aircraft Exhibition Flight, responsible for the restoration of the RAF Museum's famous Lancaster.

Chipmunks of Oxford University Air Squadron moved into Bicester in 1959 and remained until September 1975. As part of the Strategic Reserve, No 5 Light Anti-Aircraft Wing formed here in 1967 and included No 2 Light Anti-Aircraft Squadron, which had been in Malaysia defending RAF bases during the Indonesia confrontation. The Wing disbanded in 1970, by which time the RAF Gliding and Soaring Association had established itself, and although it has continued use of the landing ground, Bicester closed as an active RAF station on 31 March 1976, and was placed under Abingdon control for care and maintenance. Transfer to the Army Department followed on 20 May 1976. Unexpected further RAF presence resumed when use of the barracks recommenced on 22 November 1978. Then the station (parts of which were steadily disposed of) served as a storage site for USAF Upper Heyford. An adventure school also functioned here.

Sale of buildings – including Married Quarters – to civilian agencies has taken place over a very long period, and some retained buildings now within the enclave span an eighty-year period, making the station of considerable architectural interest. Developers with an eye to money-making have seen the flying ground as ripe for picking, while others have viewed it as suitable to accommodate a major new road. Thus its future looks insecure. An asylum seekers' residence lies beyond the airfield site. In view of its long military career, it certainly is surprising that Bicester never despatched even one offensive sortie.

**Main features:**
*Grass runs:* NW/SE 3,200ft, SW/NE 3,300ft. *Hangars:* two Type A, two Type B. *Hardstandings:* forty-one on tarmac apron, thirteen in flying safety zone. *Accommodation:* RAF officers 172, SNCOs 428, ORs 1,211; WAAF officers 13, SNCOs 11, ORs 576.

## BIGGIN HILL, Kent

*51°19W/00°02E 600ft asl; TQ415605. 5¹/₂ miles SSE of Bromley*

Bastion of freedom (Churchillian style), Battle of Britain, 'The Few' with their Hurricanes and their Spitfires – they and Biggin Hill will all for ever be one.

Built on a plateau topping the North Downs, Biggin Hill for most its military life was devoted to air defence. That began with the opening of the station's HQ on 14 February 1917, and the arrival of the Wireless Testing Park, which on 14 December 1917 became the Wireless Experimental Establishment specialising in W/T communications. Called the W/T Establishment from 2 April 1918, it existed to meet air defence needs.

By then the station was within the Inner Patrol Zone London Air Defence Area and attracted 141 Squadron's Brisfits, which joined in on 8 February 1918, and were supplemented by those operated by 140 Squadron between 1 May and 4 July 1918, when the squadron disbanded through lack of trade. However, on 19/20 May 1918 141 shared with 143 Squadron a Gotha, which fell near Harrietsham, Kent. On 1 March 1919 it moved to Ireland. No 37 Squadron, flying Snipes, replaced 141 on 17 March, and on 1 July 1919 became 39 Squadron at half squadron strength until leaving in 1922.

The Instrument Design Establishment, born here on 1 November 1919, evolved from the W/T Establishment and probably left for Farnborough in mid-1922. A special Navigation Flight had

*Vickers FB 26 Vampire 1
B1484 was evaluated at
Biggin Hill by No 141
Squadron early in 1918.
(Bruce Robertson)*

arrived in March 1920, and a Signals Co-operation Flight formed here in April 1921. Both vacated the station in 1922.

Unit moves resulted from implementation of the Steel-Bartholomew Plan, placing Biggin Hill in the Fighting Area to the south-east of London. The changed role from 'radio in warfare' development to fighter defence was in evidence on 7 May 1923 when 56 Squadron and its Snipes came from Hawkinge. Those were replaced in autumn 1924 with Grebe IIs. A touch of the experimental nevertheless remained, for on 1 July 1923 the Night Flying Flight (NFF) was formed, equipped with three Vimys and an F2b. Its role was to assist in the development of sound locators for early warning of approaching raiders, diverse aircraft later being employed.

No 56 Squadron departed for North Weald on 12 October 1927, making way for extensive building and upgrading of Biggin Hill. Hitherto the buildings had been on the site's southern side, but now a completely new technical site was constructed on the northern side involving General Service Sheds, workshops, stores, messing, barrack blocks, administration offices, etc. The existing ex-RFC Officers' Mess by the Bromley-Westerham road, opposite the main camp, was retained.

Two fighter squadrons occupied the 'new' station in September 1932, leaving Kenley to have a facelift. No 32 flew Bulldogs, and 23, using Bulldogs, switched entirely to Demons by Spring 1933.

Still based on the south side, the NFF became the Anti-Aircraft Co-operation Flight on 22 October 1931, supplying Horsley and Wallace target-towers to train London's AA gunners. On 14 April 1936 the Flight rose to Unit status, and was then renamed No 1 AACU on 10 February 1937. On 11 April 1938 its HQ moved to Farnborough. Subsequently two of its Flights used Biggin Hill, 'E' from October 1938 to January 1939 and 'H' from April 1939 to 29 September 1939, by which time Battle target-towers were in use.

No 23 Squadron's move to Northolt on 21 December 1936 allowed 'B' Flight, 32 Squadron, flying Gauntlets since July 1936, to be detached and become 79 Squadron on 22 March 1937. The Munich Crisis saw 601 (County of London) Auxiliary Squadron flying Demons to use its war station from 29 September to 2 October 1938, then the all-biplane force changed dramatically when No 32 re-armed with Hurricanes in October and No 79 during December 1938. Station strength was enhanced when 3 Squadron's Hurricanes joined them on 2 May 1939. By then Biggin Hill, like all the fighter stations, had taken on a grim and all-camouflaged, very toned-down and business-like appearance. Ominous signs were the plentiful slit trenches and stacks of sand-bags.

On 2 September 1939, as peacetime ebbed away, 3 Squadron moved to Croydon, Biggin's satellite,

*Black-and-yellow-striped
Westland Wallace K4344 of No
1 AACU at Biggin Hill.*

*Siskin IIIa J8967 of 32
Squadron, Biggin Hill.*

making way for Blenheim I(f)s of 601 Squadron. Sector defence and Channel shipping protection patrols were undertaken, often from more forward stations. Two Hurricanes (L1716 and L1718) of 79 Squadron were the first to destroy an enemy aircraft off Britain's southern shores, a Dornier Do 17P shot down on 20 November 1939. On 12 November 79 had departed for its forward base, Manston, and on 3 January 1940 32 Squadron went to Gravesend. That allowed the laying of a tarmac runway measuring 4,800 feet by 150 feet. Two more, each of 2,370 feet by 150 feet, were added later.

The May 1940 German Blitzkrieg resulted in 610 Squadron's Spitfires being at Biggin Hill from 10 to 26 May. No 242 Squadron from France joined them between 21 May and 18 June, together with 213 Squadron from 9 to 18 June. By then Biggin Hill's two permanent squadrons were back, 32 on 4 June and 79 next day. Although the latter had passed through the trauma of French decay, it moved to Hawkinge and into the front line on 2 July. No 610 Squadron replaced it and, with 32, fought from Biggin Hill through much of the Battle of Britain. On 28 August 79 Squadron relieved 32, and on 14 September 72's Spitfires relieved 610 Squadron. No 79 was replaced by Spitfires of 92 Squadron on 8 September, allowing 72 Squadron to retire on 13 October, by which time the Battle had abated and the Biggin Legend had been born. Its exhausted pilots had fought with enormous courage against the odds, and helped to win freedom for the world – including the United States – in the most important battle of all time. In so doing Biggin Hill encountered terrible torture, a lasting reminder of the ferocity of the fight.

During July the station's fighters had frequently moved forward, particularly to Hawkinge, to engage raiders. Not until 18 August was Biggin Hill heavily bombed for the first time. Around 1330 nine Do 17Zs of 9/KG 76 raced in very low, hurling mixed loads on to the main site. Responding, 32 and 111 Squadrons destroyed two attackers, two others crashed in the English Channel, and another three force-landed in France. Later than intended, three waves of Ju 88s from II/KG 76, operating at between 12,000 and 18,000 feet, soon unloaded more than 150 HEs, mainly cratering the landing ground, while anti-personnel bombs were aimed at the defending AA gun sites. Fighters destroyed two Ju 88s, one falling to 92 Squadron's famed Flt Lt Stanford Tuck.

Late afternoon of 30 August saw Ju 88s, flying at about 1,000 feet, deliver the next sharp attack, dropping sixteen 500kg HEs on the technical site and destroying communications, water and power links. The attack killed thirty-nine and wounded twenty-six personnel. No 79 Squadron claimed two of the raiders.

*Hurricane 1s of No 79
Squadron, Biggin Hill, in
1939.*

*High-level bombing of a much-
camouflaged Biggin Hill on 18 August
1940, bombs bursting centrally on the
buildings.*

Next day brought two major onslaughts.
Around midday two Staffln of He 111s, carpet-
bombing from 12,000 feet, destroyed two GS
Sheds, hit messes and quarters and smashed and
fired the Sector ops room, which was soon
replaced by a primitive ops room in a Pantiles
butcher's shop. One Heinkel was shot down. At
around 1730, low-flying Ju 88s with Bf 110s of
Erpro 210 delivered another attack, no warning
of which was given to station personnel. Although
brief, the attack was highly damaging, with thirty
HE bombs bursting mainly on the technical site,
destroying workshops, stores, barracks and
WAAF quarters, and finishing off a hangar.

Three notable raids developed at 1330 the next day, 1 September, when the station was
attacked from high level. However, the most memorable assault came at around 1800, when Do 17s
made another of their low-level attacks, this time scoring the famous hit on the station operations
room. For continuing to work the defence lines, three WAAF teleprinter operators received the
Military Medal for bravery.

Biggin Hill, now able to operate only one squadron, accommodated the Spitfires of No 610.
Few buildings remained habitable, and undamaged equipment was salvaged while basic utility
services and communications remained out of action. A permanent site for the operations room was
later established in requisitioned Victorian 'Towerfield' by Keston crossroads, some two miles from
the airfield. However, the Luftwaffe had still not finished punishing the station, although most
bombs fell wide and along the Westerham Road during the next main attack. Group Captain Grice,
the Station Commander, ordered on his own initiative that the badly damaged hangars be
demolished to discourage further attacks.

With night-bombing increasing, 141 Squadron returned for five days – 13 to 18 September –
flying Defiants in the Sector and acquiring operational experience.

*No 92 Squadron spent almost a year at Biggin Hill and used Spitfire Mk Vb R6923 in early 1941.*

On 15 September, now Battle of Britain Day, Spitfires of 72 and 92 Squadrons fought from the station. Over the ensuing weeks they and 74 Squadron tackled Bf 109 and Ju 88 day attacks until those faded. No 421 (Reconnaissance) Flight arrived from Gravesend on 6 November and left on 15 November.

Early 1941 saw the Spitfire squadrons switching to offensive activity, including bomber escort. In January 92 Squadron became the first to equip with Spitfire Mk Vs, making its first kill using X4272 on 3 February.

For a share in night defence, 264 Squadron, Biggin-Hill based, operated Defiants between 11 January and 13 April 1941. Throughout that year the station's fighters operated over France as well as flying defensive sorties.

In 1942 133 'Eagle' Squadron was twice based at the station, additional American visitors in August being Nos 2 US and 307 US Pursuit Squadrons flying Spitfire Vbs, and at Biggin Hill for a month's operational learning. During operation *Jubilee* the Biggin Hill Wing claimed fifteen enemy for a loss of six pilots. That same month Spitfire F IXs were seen at Biggin Hill for the first time. By July 1942 the station had claimed 900 enemy aircraft destroyed, the claim in good faith reaching 1,000 on 15 May 1943. Post-war verification was impossible, but there can be no doubt that the Sector score was extremely high.

With German fighter-bombers attacking South Coast towns, Typhoon-equipped 609 Squadron moved in on 18 September 1942 to respond, attack and carry out low-level strikes on Continental targets. On 20 January 1943 Fw 190s, roaring in very low, circled the aerodrome and strafed and bombed it as they headed home. That usual tactic gave the resident defenders time to scramble, and in the ensuing fight six German aircraft were shot down for no loss to the RAF. On 9 February 1943 defences were strengthened, Typhoons of 1 Squadron being brought in from Acklington; after a five-week stay they moved to Lympne.

July 1943 saw the arrival of 485 (New Zealand) Squadron, which opened a Commonwealth phase. On 19 September 1943 St George's Chapel of Remembrance was dedicated, Group Captain 'Sailor' Malan unveiling the altar during the service.

On 13 October HQ No 126 Airfield arrived, and with it three Canadian Squadrons, Nos 401, 411 and 412, replacing 485 Squadron. The Airfield remained until 15 April, when the organisation left for Tangmere. During its stay three Repair & Salvage Units formed before being integrated into the pre-*Overlord* organisation: 403 (October-December 1943), 405 (15 November 1943 to 26 January 1944) and 410 (26 January to 18 February 1944). The Canadians departed in April, 401 to Fairwood Common on 7 April, and 411 and 412 moving with the Airfield to Tangmere on 15 April.

One week after D-Day the first V-1 cruise missiles made their debut over England. Biggin Hill's position on the line of fire to London soon also placed it within the defensive balloon barrage belt, and at the end of June the station was taken over by Balloon Command. Six V-1s crashed inside the airfield boundary.

Balloon Command moved out in September 1944, Station Headquarters returned from Redhill, and squadrons moved in, joining 141 Wing ADGB here between 18 October and 1 November 1944. The Spitfires carried out fighter escort to RAF Lancaster and Halifax bombers carrying out daylight raids on Germany. Nos 154 and 322 Squadrons, which took over from 91 and 345, remained for the rest of the year. No 322 moved to Holland on 3 January 1945, leaving only 154 to soldier on until 1 March 1945.

The fighters had in 1945 been joined by aircraft of Transport Command using Biggin Hill as a terminal for services to various parts of Europe. First to fly from Biggin Hill was a detached flight of 168 Squadron RCAF, operating seven Dakotas.

In June 1945 Biggin Hill was transferred from No 11 Group Fighter Command to No 46 Group Transport Command, and No 168 Squadron RCAF and 314 Squadron USAAF made use of the station. In December 1945 168 Squadron returned to Canada, and was replaced by Dakotas of another Canadian squadron, 436. Flights were being undertaken to Schiphol (Amsterdam), Evere (Brussels), Munster and the home base, Down Ampney. No 436 Canadian Squadron returned to Canada in June 1946.

Fighter squadrons based at Biggin Hill during the period January 1941 to 1945.

| Squadron No | Aircraft | Dates in situ | From/to |
|---|---|---|---|
| 92 | Spitfire I | 8.9.40-9.1.41 | Biggin Hill/Gravesend |
| 264 | Defiant I | 11.1.41-13.4.41 | Gravesend/West Malling |
| 74 | Spitfire IIa | 15.10.40-20.2.41 | Coltishall/Manston |
| 72 | Spitfire Vb | 26.7.41-20.10.41 | Coltishall/Gravesend |
| 92 | Spitfire Vb | 20.2.41-24.9.41 | Gravesend/Gravesend |
| 609 | Spitfire Vb | 24.2.41-27.7.41 | Warmwell/Gravesend |
| 609 | Spitfire Vb | 24.9.41-21.11.41 | Gravesend/Digby |
| 401 | Spitfire Vb | 20.10.41-18.3.42 | Digby/Gravesend |
| 124 | Spitfire Vb | 8.11.41-3.5.42 | Castletown/Gravesend |
| 72 | Spitfire Vb | 22.3.42-22.6.42 | Gravesend/Martlesham Heath |
| 72 | Spitfire Vb | 29.6.42-30.6.42 | Martlesham Heath/Lympne |
| 133 | Spitfire Vb | 3.5.42-11.7.42 | Kirton-in-Lindsey/Gravesend |
| 19 | Spitfire Vb | 1.7.42-7.7.42 | Perranporth/Perranporth |
| 72 | Spitfire Vb | 7.7.42-2.8.42 | Gravesend/Duxford |
| 340 | Spitfire Vb/ IXb (10.42) | 28.7.42-20.2.43 | Westhampnett/Turnhouse |
| 602 | Spitfire Vb | 16.8.42-20.8.42 | Peterhead/Peterhead |
| 133 | Spitfire Vb | 30.8.42-23.9.42 | Kirton-in-Lindsey/Great Sampford |
| 401 | Spitfire Vb | 8.42-8.42 | Martlesham Heath/Lympne |
| 2 USA | Spitfire Vb | 8.42 | |
| 3 USA | Spitfire Vb | 8.42 | |
| 611 | Spitfire IXb | 23.9.42-1.7.43 | Redhill/Matlask |
| 1 | Typhoon | 9.2.43-15.3.43 | Acklington/Martlesham Heath |
| 341 | Spitfire IXb | 21.3.43-15.10.43 | Turnhouse/Perranporth |
| 41 | Spitfire XII | 21.5.43-21.5.43 | Hawkinge/Friston |
| 485 | Spitfire IX | 7.43-10.43 | Merston/Hornchurch |
| 401 | Spitfire IX | 10.43-4.44 | Staplehurst/Fairwood Common |
| 411 | Spitfire IX | 13.10.43-17.4.44 | Staplehurst/Tangmere |
| 412 | Spitfire IX | 13.10.43-15.4.44 | Staplehurst/Tangmere |
| 91 | Spitfire IXb | 7.10.44-29.10.44 | Deanland/Manston |
| 345 | Spitfire IX | 18.10.44-1.11.44 | Deanland/Wevelghem |
| 322 | Spitfire XVIe | 1.11.44-3.1.45 | Fairwood/Woensdrecht |
| 340 | Spitfire IXb | 2.11.44-17.12.44 | Wevelghem/Drem |
| 154 | Spitfire IX | 16.11.44-1.3.45 | Re-formed/Hunsdon |

Biggin Hill's post-war phase started when, on 10 May 1946, two Auxiliary Air Force squadrons, Nos 600 (City of London) and 615 (County of Surrey), re-formed, and in August 1946 the station joined Reserve Command. In October 1946 London UAS re-opened and moved to Fairoaks on 15 December 1947. Biggin Hill returned to Fighter Command in November 1949 and, as part of the Regular Air Force, both RAuxAF squadrons re-armed with Meteors in 1950, being joined on 29 March 1951 by a regular Meteor 8 squadron, No 41 from Church Fenton. The latter converted to Hunters, and in 1957 the main runway was improved for safer operation of the faster jets. Drastic reductions in fighter strength resulted in both RAuxAF squadrons disbanding on 10 March 1957. With the station lacking strategic value, 41 Squadron disbanded on 31 January 1958.

No 61 Group Communication Flight Kenley found a new home here on 1 March 1958, before disbanding on 15 January 1959. July 1957 had seen the formation of the Historic Aircraft Flight, and on 21 February 1958 it became The Battle of Britain Flight, which left for North Weald on 28 February 1958. On 8 September 1958 No 1 Air Experience Flight formed, equipped with ten Chipmunks, which each weekend gave about 140 ATC cadets living in the South East a chance to fly. On 7 February 1959 No 1 Air Experience Flight moved to White Waltham. Also flying here since 1949 was No 162 Gliding School, and when it disbanded on 31 August 1959 RAF flying ended.

North Camp now accommodated the Ground Officers' Selection Centre, opened in April 1959. The Aircrew Selection Centre moved in on 9 April 1962, the two at once amalgamating as the Officers' and Aircrew Selection Centre.

*Meteor F8 WH253 R of No 600 Squadron. (John Rawlings)*

South Camp was leased to Surrey Aviation for private flying, and with Croydon's closure other operators chose Biggin Hill as their base, giving it a new lease of life. The airfield was subsequently bought by the London Borough of Bromley.

In late 1979 the Government confirmed its earlier decision to close the RAF camp at Biggin Hill and demolish the remaining buildings except for the Officers' Mess, which became the RAF Chaplains' School and the chapel. When, on 9 September 1992, the O&ASC left for Cranwell, RAF tenancy was virtually at an end, and probably the most famous RAF station was left to business and private fliers. Among the variety here in 2003 were the Alouette Flying Club, Biggin Hill Helicopters, Biggin Hill School of Flying, Civilair, Classair, EFG Flying School, Surrey & Kent Flying Club, and TropAir Services. There is increasing business flying, including the coming and going of sophisticated jet transports.

**Main features:**
*Runways:* 215° 4,800ft x 150ft, 235° 2,850ft x 150ft, 295° 2,850ft x 150ft, concrete and asphalt. *Hangars:* two Bessoneau, twelve Blister, one Type F. *Hardstandings:* nineteen single-engine, twelve protected pens, single-engine. *Accommodation:* RAF officers 162, SNCOs 154, ORs 2,077; WAAF officers 14, SNCOs 8, ORs 729.

*Special note:* Gravesend served as Biggin Hill's main satellite, Croydon also being used early in the war. In late 1944 a number of other stations had become Affiliated: Forward Airfields Detling, Gatwick, Hawkinge, Kenley and West Malling (night-fighter). Other Affiliated stations were Friston, Gravesend. Lympne, Penshurst and Redhill.

*Post-war:* main runway 03/21 was lengthened to 6,017ft for jets, and 11/29 reduced to 2,677ft. Current are 03/21 1,808m x 46m, 11/29 816m x 24m, with light aircraft parking on northern area. Heavier aircraft and biz-jets on the southern apron are returning the South Camp to its former prominence.

---

## BITTESWELL, Leicestershire

*52°27N/01°14W 420ft asl;SP510847. 2 miles W of Lutterworth on the A427 and the junction of the A5*

In 1940 construction of Bitteswell commenced, the airfield coming into use in July 1941 as 18 OTU Bramcote's satellite, a role in which it served until February 1943. The OTU's Wellingtons – mainly Mk 1cs and Mk IIIs – and also its Ansons, had been a daily sight, many flown by Poles training for 1 Group squadrons. Initially administered by 6 Group, which became 91 Group on 11 May 1942, it functioned under 93 Group from 1 September 1942.

No 18 OTU was reduced by half in strength, and on 1 June 1943 Bitteswell became 29 OTU, Bruntingthorpe's satellite. Wellingtons – Mks III and X – used the airfield until October 1944.

---

On 22 November 1944 the station returned to Bramcote, now home to 105 OTU, a Transport Command unit flying Dakota IIIs and IVs until OTU closure on 17 July 1945. On 10 August 1945 No 1381 (Transport) Conversion Unit opened at Bramcote from the remains of 105 OTU, limited Dakota flying being undertaken from Bitteswell until November 1945.

Bitteswell was transferred to care and maintenance under Bramcote, where No 266 MU had been formed as an equipment disposal depot unit. Between January 1946 and January 1947 Bitteswell functioned as its sub-site. The Transport Command Aircrew Examining Unit, based at Bramcote between December 1945 and August 1946, also made use of Bitteswell, but the airfield had long been extremely busy with very different civilian activity.

Late in 1943 Armstrong-Whitworth Aircraft started using Bitteswell for final assembly and flight test of Baginton-built Lancasters, and when the RAF departed in July 1946 Armstrong-Whitworth and Armstrong-Siddeley, the aero-engine manufacturer, took over the site. Plentiful flight testing of

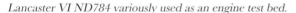

*Lancaster VI ND784 variously used as an engine test bed.*

Armstrong-Siddeley turboprop engines and AWA-built aircraft followed. A Dakota tested the Mamba, and a Lincoln the Python, and it was here that the tailless AW 52G glider and the two twin-jet, all-wing AW 52 high-speed mail carriers undertook flight trials.

By the 1950s Bitteswell was being used as a development and flight test centre for the Meteor night-fighter range, Hunters Mks 2 and 5, Seahawks, the Argosy twin-boom transport, and Javelin all-weather fighters. It remained in use after Armstrong-Whitworth lost its individual identity within the Hawker Siddeley Group and Armstrong-Siddeley ceased involvement with jet engines.

As part of British Aerospace, Bitteswell later served as a repair and modification centre handling Shackletons and upgrading Vulcan 1s.

**Main features:**
*Runways:* 042° 6,000ft x 50ft, 108° and 358° 4,200ft x 50ft, concrete and wood-chips in wartime. *Hangars:* one T2 and one B1. *Hardstandings:* sixteen spectacle type, eleven dispersal pans. *Accommodation:* RAF officers 90, SNCOs 353, ORs 732; WAAF officers 3, SNCOs 16, ORs 84.

*The Armstrong-Whitworth AW 52G flying-wing glider test-flown from Bitteswell.*

**BOOKER** (Wycombe Air Park), Buckinghamshire

*51°36N/00°48W, 515ft asl; SU828910. 3 miles SW of High Wycombe by the B482*

Booker, conceived as Marlow Airport, became instead the home of civilian-operated No 50 E&RFTS, which received its first aircraft in late May 1939. After initial training on Tiger Moths, pilots flew a handful of Audax and Hind biplanes. The School (controlled by No 50 Group) closed when war commenced, Booker then being requisitioned by the Air Ministry.

A more ambitious technical site was established in 1940 on the eastern side of the landing area, hutted domestic accommodation for staff and EFTS pupils being added close by. On 1 June 1941 Booker become busy when Airwork Ltd, operating under 50 Group overall, opened No 21 Elementary Flying Training School, which used Magisters for a while and Tiger Moths continuously until disbandment on 28 February 1950. RLGs at Bray and Denham helped to reduce pressure of wartime activity at Booker. From November 1947 No 21 EFTS undertook glider pilot training until disbandment. These were not the first glider fliers, for in August 1943 No 126 Gliding School opened to give ATC cadets a taste of piloting. Not until 1 September 1955 did it close, by which time it had witnessed many changes.

*Tiger Moths of No 21 EFTS Booker, including T-5426 FIWD, T-7365 FIWE and DE-663 FIWE. (George Burn)*

On 20 December 1950 a new training unit opened to provide pilots needed for the 1950s limited re-armament scheme. No 1 Basic Flying Training School was run by Airwork Ltd and 65 Group – later 62 Group – and operated de Havilland Chipmunks. This 'emergency' school closed on 21 July 1953 after sharing Booker with the Joint Services Staff College Flight, formed here on 15 January 1947 flying Austers, Proctors and a Dominie until unit closure in November 1952. Also in residence from 6 October 1950 until 12 January 1956 were the Chipmunks of the University of London Air Squadron. Nearby HQ Bomber Command had since October 1946 based its Communication Flight here. On 1 February 1956 it was raised to squadron status and stayed to the end of March 1963, variously flying Ansons, Chipmunks, Devons, Proctors, Tiger Moths and, later, a Pembroke. Its small Meteor and Canberra jet contingent used Benson.

Military activity was replaced when Wycombe Air Park was established, the single paved runway proving useful. A busy civilian airfield, it is used by many private and group-operated aircraft as well as flying clubs, with Wycombe Air Centre and British Airways Flying Club, Helicopter Services and a gliding club contributing to the active circuit. Engineering company Personal Plane Services often works on the exotic aged aircraft of Florida-based collector Kermit Weeks. Bianchi Aviation Film Services operates the Blue Max Museum of items and aircraft used in its aviation film work, and the 1975 film *Aces High,* about First World War fighter pilots, was largely filmed here. The company also operates the sole remaining airworthy Spitfire Mk 1a, AR213 alias *G-AIST*. All four Bellman hangars remain as a reminder of Service days.

**Main features:**
*Runways:* wartime all grass: NE/SW 1,133yd, N/S 970yd, E/W 920yd, NW/SE 900yd. *Hangars:* four Bellman each 175ft long x 90ft wide, two with maximum 25ft entry height and two with 71ft entry height; also four EO Blister hangars. *Hardstandings:* five. *Accommodation:* (hutted) for RAF personnel only: 56 officers, 88 NCOs, 507 ORs.

*Mosquito Squadron,* loosely based upon the legendary Amiens prison raid (see Hunsdon). As a tailpiece some aircraft stars of the film *Battle of Britain* were publicly displayed here at the end of filming.

Although in 1962 the Americans departed, flying continued over the next few years, before 1968 brought the announcement by the Ministry of Defence that Bovingdon was to close. That should have provoked no surprise, for the hangars had recently been renovated! The Southern Command Communications Squadron moved to Northolt on 1 January 1969, and Ministry of Defence property was steadily disposed of by 1976, leaving only some Married Quarters to eventually be put up for sale.

Through war and peace Bovingdon had been a popular posting, for it existed in a beautiful setting with easy access to the capital. Little remains of Bovingdon today, Amey Roadstone Corporation having worked with too much efficiency.

**Main features:**
*Runways:* 220° 4,800ft x 150ft, 270° 4,200ft x 150ft, 350° 3,900ft x 150ft, concrete with asphalt surface. *Hangars:* four T2. *Hardstandings:* 36 loop type, 1950s dispersal areas on NE, E and SW perimeter areas with two ASPs and a warm-up pad added. *Accommodation:* USAAF Officers 635, enlisted men 2,214.

## BRIZE NORTON, Oxfordshire

*51°45N/01°34W 270ft asl; SP295060. 6 miles SW of Witney*

Brize Norton, the largest operational station in the RAF and active every hour of every day in the year, has a population of 3,800 Service personnel and 600 civilians. Run on an annual cash budget of about £105 million, it is also one of the last bastions of our great past, for here strategic need merges with the tactical, long-range tanker transport. Its four squadrons fly some 21,000 hours annually, transfer 15,000 tonnes of fuel during AAR operations, handle 150,000 passengers, and lift 8,000 tons of freight. Of 6,600 yearly aircraft movements through the station, 2,500 are civilian. To 'Brize' the casualties from recent conflicts have returned to be treated, remembered, honoured. Through its superb, sadly ageing VC-10s, Brize provides an almost final link with so many world-beaters from what could be, and should still be, the world's top aviation industry. It remains the place from where important people fly, or obtain their aeroplanes – and they can fly Royal Air Force in the knowledge that its 'airline' has an unbeaten safety record. Nice, too, when one sees – maybe touches – a comforting roundel instead of some nasty, cheap, garish civilian 'dot com' contraption!

Brize Norton sprawls before the Chilterns for miles across smooth Oxfordshire, its bold buildings prominent even from the A40. Outstanding, too, are the white TriStar tanker/transports of 216 Squadron, the heaviest aircraft any RAF squadron has operated in some numbers.

Naming this station posed a problem, however, for it lies mainly within Carterton, a name too reminiscent of Cardington to be suitable. So instead Brize Norton took its title from a nearby village when construction started in 1935. Exceptional was the completion of five 'C' Type hangars, planned for many stations but rarely built. Even more astonishing, there were 44 assorted hangars here in December 1944 – two 'C' Type had been destroyed in 1940.

No 2 FTS moved in to an incomplete Brize Norton on 13 August 1937, bringing Hawker Hart variants received in April 1935. Audaxes were introduced in May 1936, Hawker Furies helping until the first monoplane arrived, an Airspeed Oxford that joined the FTS on 22 February 1938; thereafter they trickled in, allowing more realistic pilot training. A divorced, motley group of buildings was also erected, including Type D and E hangars and six 'Lamella' grass mounds in the

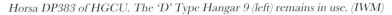

*Horsa DP383 of HGCU. The 'D' Type Hangar 9 (left) remains in use. (IWM)*

south-east corner, to store 6 MU's treasures. A 41 Group ASU, it opened on 10 October 1938, attracting its first two lodgers, Saro Cloud amphibians, on 30 January 1939.

More audible was the change overtaking 2 SFTS in March 1939, for ten Harvard Is arrived. Another thirteen came in June, bringing a din sure to annoy any populace. Close by, 6 MU quickly hid another thirteen, and by the start of the war more Oxfords were with the SFTS.

When war commenced Blenheims of 101 Squadron quickly 'scattered' both here and at Weston-on-the-Green, Brize Norton's satellite. No 6 MU was soon supplying Gladiators to Finland and Blenheims to Yugoslavia, while training at 2 SFTS increased its pace.

The fall of France, demanding more fighter protection for the south and west of Britain, led to Middle Wallop becoming a fighter station and forcing out 15 SFTS. Half of its Oxford/Harvard strength began lodging at Brize Norton on 11 June, awaiting space at Kidlington. HQ 15 SFTS followed, then acquired residence in Oldner House, Chipping Norton, which it reached on 10 July. Brize Norton was accommodating many personnel and aircraft, for the MU had a large holding too.

Enemy knowledge of this possibly provoked the catastrophic attack on a cloudy 16 August. In the late afternoon, groups of raiders penetrated deeply into Britain between Harwich and the Isle of Wight. Several reached Oxfordshire, bombing Stanton Harcourt and Harwell at 1745, where no warnings were sounded. Almost simultaneously two Ju 88s delivered a devastating half-minute onslaught upon Brize Norton, where some thirty small HE bombs and a few incendiaries were dropped, hitting Nos 1 and 3 C Type hangars, and damaging a barrack block and the Institute. A civilian was killed and three injured, together with thirteen RAF men. Fuelled trainer aircraft sheltering for the night packed those hangars, and forty-six were destroyed, mainly by fire, others suffering blast damage. Fires raged into the night in this most devastating bombing of home-based aircraft during the entire war. Luckily, many serviceable aircraft were dispersed, at Akeman Street and Southrop. No 15 SFTS hurriedly left, on 19 August, and although Brize Norton was attacked three more times it suffered little further damage.

Throughout 1940 and 1941, 2 SFTS trained RAF pilots while 6 MU handled a multiplicity of aircraft types, particularly Blenheims, Hampdens, Hurricanes, Spitfires and Fairey Battles. No longer fighting machines, the Battles languished long at Brize Norton.

In November 1941 the first EATS pilots arrived for acclimatisation flying, and 25 BAT Flight formed. Renamed 1525 BAT Flight on 18 February 1942, it stayed until 13 July 1942. No 2 SFTS also changed, on 14 March 1942, becoming No 2 (P)AFU. Numerically superfluous, some such units soon closed, including No 2 on 14 July 1942.

Next day Brize Norton entered the transport field, which has subsequently dominated its history. Arriving from Shrewton came the recently formed Heavy Glider Conversion Unit (HGCU), changing the base into the school where Army glider pilots would learn to handle the hefty Horsa, backbone of the airborne forces. No 6 MU erected and despatched many Horsas during the next three years. HGCU trainees came from GTSs, the course strength being sixty-two pupils. Aircraft establishment was set at fifty-six Horsas and thirty-four Whitley V glider tugs. Glider handling was no simple matter; it took time to marshal the glider, attach the tow rope and position the tug, flying accidents were frequent, and night training difficult. On 21 October 1942 a Glider Instructors' School formed, staying until February 1944 when it moved to North Luffenham.

Storing many aircraft, 6 MU acquired the use of 34 SLG Woburn in November 1941, relinquished for No 28 SLG Barton Abbey on 8 February 1943. Woburn then passed to 8 MU, Little Rissington. No 22 SLG Barnsley Park was also used.

Unwieldy Whitley/Horsa combinations with their wide turning circle were difficult to integrate in the Central Gliding Area with small tugs and Hotspurs on their daily rounds. Cross-country routes were

*The interior of the recently completed Junior Ranks Cotswold Restaurant.*

therefore awarded to the HGCU, whose
Whitleys and Horsas paraded alone
widely and well-spaced. Between 10
February and 20 April 1943 they flew
from Grove while Brize Norton's
runways were resurfaced. After the
HGCU had trained sufficient Horsa
pilots for the Sicilian landing, it switched
to the main task – training for the
Normandy invasion. When that was
completed, HGCU strength fell to forty
Whitley Vs and thirty-six Horsas. It
moved to North Luffenham in March
1944, then Brize Norton became a 38
Group operational station. A new SHQ
opened on 13 March 1944, and within
hours Albemarles of 296 and 297

*The well-appointed Barrack Block, 2002-style.*

Squadrons arrived. They collected their Horsas from bomber bases, then on 20 March 1944
operational training commenced in earnest, dropping paratroops and releasing gliders accurately.

On 5/6 June 1944 eighteen Albemarles drawn from both squadrons carried the 5th Parachute
Brigade to LZ 'N', by the River Orne in Normandy, where a landing ground was fast prepared for
seventeen Horsas towed out of Brize Norton. Another two, brought by 297 Squadron, landed by the
Merville coastal gun battery.

The early evening of 6 June saw forty Horsas towed across the Channel from Brize Norton,
carrying part of the 6th Airborne Division in operation *Mallard*. Albemarle squadrons subsequently
flew supply-dropping sorties over France, while maintaining their glider-towing skill. Because of
their limited range and the possibility of engine overheating during long tows, Brize Norton's
Albemarles flew to Manston on 15 September 1944. Twice they operated, towing gliders to Arnhem
during operation *Market*, before returning to Brize Norton. Both squadrons were soon converting
to Stirling IVs and, on 29-30 September, left for Earl's Colne, taking with them ninety-four Horsas.

Arnhem's high casualty rate brought a need to train more glider pilots for another Rhine crossing
attempt, so the HGCU's Whitleys and Horsas returned from North Luffenham on 15 October 1944.
One unit could not train sufficient glider pilots so additional units formed, Brize Norton's school
becoming No 21 HGCU. American Waco Hadrians were added to the strength in November. An
Instructors' School, which arrived in October, remained until December 1945.

Increased local activity caused 6 MU to repossess Woburn SLG for storing surplus Stirlings.
No 21 HGCU's Whitleys began to be replaced with Albemarles in January 1945, and by February
there were enough glider pilots for another Rhine crossing operation. Training nevertheless
continued, against possible Far East needs.

As soon as hostilities ceased in Europe,
the few aircraft enthusiasts of those days
began to experience unforgettable
moments. Over the following weeks some
200 captured enemy aircraft were flown to
Britain for examination. Most went to RAE
Farnborough, some to ATTDU Gosport or
Ford, with 6 MU support. Many flew in
from Schleswigland, and shuttled between
RAE and 6 MU, Brize Norton, occasionally
venturing further afield.

Brize Norton's first captive was,
satisfyingly, a Ju 88, which landed there on
10 May 1945. An Arado Ar234B-2 140008
came from Farnborough on 30 June, and a
Heinkel He 162 touched down on 2
August. Many exciting shapes followed,

*VC-10C Mk 1 XV105 of 10 Squadron with AAR
pods and grey finish, seen during checks in the
MPBW Lacon 7203/64N hangar lately modified to
house a C-17.*

among them Focke-Wulf Ta 152H 150168, which flew in from RAE on 18 August and stayed until 22 October. Heinkel He 219A-7 Air Min 20 came on 21 August, another following ten days later. An Me 410 and 6158, one of the two Dormer 217Ms selected for examination, were among others brought here. Oh, to have been by the road passing the runway end on those days! 'Why didn't someone save them?' you may well ask. Conservation was unknown, and anything Nazi unpopular. Most weathered away or met harsh dismemberment.

Halifaxes replaced Albemarle tugs before 21 HGCU left for Elsham Wolds in late December 1945. Then Brize Norton re-joined Transport Command – apart from 6 MU. The School of Flight Efficiency and Transport Command Development Unit arrived from Harwell, leaving Hampstead Norris and Finmere under Brize Norton's control.

TCDU explored airborne delivery of mixed loads using Dakotas, Halifaxes, Hamilcars, Horsas, Liberators, Stirlings, Yorks and a few Hoverfly helicopters. Glider towing trials involved the Hastings and Valetta. In May 1946 the Army Airborne Trials and Development Unit arrived. Activity here attracted American interest and a Fairchild C-82 Packet towed a Horsa, a most unusual combination. Does anyone have a photograph?

On 5 September 1946 Halifax A IXs of 297 Squadron arrived and stayed until August 1947. September 1946 also saw a Douglas C-54 fly here automatically from America. Meanwhile 6 MU was disposing of very many aircraft, particularly Spitfires. In January 1948 the MU received its first Meteors.

TCDU left for Abingdon on 30 June 1949 and on 4 July Brize Norton came under 21 Group Training Command. Buzzing Harvards of Examining Wing, CFS, were joined in mid-August by Mosquito T.3s and 6s of 204 AFS. Emphasis had most definitely returned to training, with Fairford as the RLG. CFS remained until 16 May 1950, Mosquitoes leaving for Swinderby early in June. By then the station was administered by 23 Group, but not for long. Just before the trainers left, news broke of alien times ahead. Bomber Command seized Brize Norton on 1 June 1950 on behalf of the United States Strategic Air Command.

Soviet intransigence over Berlin led to US B-29 Groups moving into temporary bases in Britain; these were within the eastern fighter belt, whereas the Americans wanted bases to its rear. Chosen sites – for use by the RAF after the USAF moved out – were finally agreed in May 1950 as Fairford, Greenham Common, Upper Heyford and Brize Norton. Each needed a runway of 9,000 feet, broad perimeter tracks, strong dispersals, alert and warm-up pads, and very secure weapons dumps.

*VC-10 XV102 of 10 Squadron and Belfast XR370 of 53 Squadron outside Brize Norton's Lacon hangar.*

*Tristar C2 ZE702 of 216 Squadron departing Brize Norton 12 June 1997. The 'C' Type hangar, high-intensity apron lights and Gateway House terminal are visible.*

On 7 June 1950 the first Americans arrived from Marham, and on 16 June the 7503rd Base Complement Squadron (USAFE) was activated and became an Air Base Group on 7 July. The official hand-over to the USAF took place on 16 April 1951, the 7503rd becoming an Air Support Wing on 25 May 1951. The 7523rd Air Base Squadron was here from 10 March to 27 May 1952. On 27 June 1952 came the first most spectacular deployment, twenty-one assorted B-36Ds and B-36Fs from Carwell's 11th Bomb Wing (H), to spend fifteen days at Brize Norton. The 7503rd Strategic Wing ran the base aided, since January 1951, by the 3920th Air Base Group (SAC), which took over on 1 December 1952. Regular SAC rotational TDYs then commenced, December's arrival being B-29s belonging to the 301st BW (M). B-50As of 65 Squadron, 43rd BW (M), replacing them, were here from March to May 1953. Preparations then started to support B-47Bs, two squadrons of MacDill's 305th BW being in residence from 4 September to December 1953.

From Limestone AFB, Maine, next came a squadron of B-47Bs of the 22nd BW (M) on TDY from December to February 1954. May 1954 brought the 320th BW, which stayed until August 1954 and was replaced immediately by B-47Es of the 43rd BW, deployed until November.

In December 1954 the base's first tanker squadron, the 321st Air Refuelling Squadron, using KC-97Gs, arrived; it was replaced in March 1955 by more KC-97Gs, this time of the 310th ARS. From June to September 1955 more from the 40th ARS were here, then the base saw its runway under repair.

It re-opened in July 1956, limited use being made by B-47Es of the 307th BW. Fewer aircraft were now usually on base, only one squadron residing from each of these Wings – No 384 (January-April 1957), 380 (April-July 1957), 68th (October 1957-January 1958), and 100th (January-April 1958). During that period of reduced numbers the first Boeing B-52B to land in Britain, 3395 *City of Turlock* of the 93rd BW (H), touched down on 16 January 1957 after a flight from Castle AFB, California.

KC-97 deployments in late 1957 and thereafter were 90 ARS (October 1957-8 January 1958) and 376 ARS (8 January 1958 to 1959). During 1958 B-47Es of the 2nd BW were also here.

On 27 March 1958 came the debut of another type when two KC-135A tankers, the first to come to Britain, landed at Brize Norton. Of the 99th ARS, Westover AFB, Maine, they made record Atlantic crossings. Amazing, isn't it, that KC-135s have been around so long?

April 1958 saw six B-52Ds of the 92nd BW (H) participating in the annual Anglo-American bombing competition from a relatively empty Brize Norton, as the 100th had left early in that month. Under 'Reflex Alert', now under way, as few as nine B-47s would be at 'Brize' for a three-week stay. For company they had, for varying periods, detachments of the 55th, 98th and 301st SRWs flying reconnaissance variants of the RB-47 for spying missions directed at Eastern Europe and the USSR. When the 308th BW (M) was in Britain late 1959 it deployed eleven B-47s at Brize Norton, together with KC-97Gs.

Assorted detachments continued into early 1960, and from 28 February involved basing KC-135s here for thirty-day periods. Much excitement was generated when, in January 1964, a 43rd BW Convair B-58 Hustler, the world's first supersonic bomber, touched down from Carswell AFB, Texas. Never more than a handful ever visited the UK, but B-47s continued to come although there was a gradual swing towards ICBMs for SAC, and American-based B-52s.

On April 1 1965, when 'Reflex' ended, Brize Norton returned to the RAF, but not before it had attracted exotic Americans including U-2s, Gary Powers and ERB-47s. When B-47E 53-1884, of the 380th BW (M), departed on 3 April 1965, the American era ended.

Britain's transport forces were expanding, with large aircraft requiring a suitable base, extensively equipped and strategically well situated. Brize Norton was an obvious choice. Cargo and passenger terminals were added, as well as custom-built maintenance facilities. A hangar large enough to hold half a dozen aircraft of the Belfast/VC-10 size was built as the cantilever MPBW Lacon 7203/64N, an amazing 1,039ft 6in in length and 193ft 6in wide. The slanting roof rises from 52ft 5½in to 88ft 2in at the top of the ridge. Within the structure are eleven bays alternately of 91 feet or 80ft 6in width. Completed in June 1967, this became the largest cantilever structure in western Europe, and cost nearly £2m.

In waiting were Belfasts of 53 Squadron and VC-10s of 10 Squadron, both squadrons operating from Lyneham and Fairford until they moved in during mid-1967. On 1 August 1967 Transport Command was re-arranged as Air Support Command. VC-10s of 10 Squadron worked the Hong Kong service supporting Britain's worldwide commitments, while transportation of heavy items was left to 53 Squadron's Belfasts. Both Britannia squadrons, Nos 99 and 511, arrived from Lyneham to make way for the Hercules fleet. 'Brits', excellent performers, had a good field performance overseas. Brize Norton hit the summer headlines in 1974 when its force rapidly lifted more than 7,500 Service and civilian personnel when trouble flared in Cyprus.

When requirements for large military passenger transports declined, Britannias and Belfasts were phased out. The run-down of the former began in April 1975, and of the latter in June 1976, but removal of the Belfast came as the RAF Hercules force needed spar replacements, and only the Belfast could convey such to Britain. Vital components continued arriving, in XR366, into autumn 1976 – 53 Squadron disbanded on 14 September 1976. Brize Norton then appeared almost empty.

Cottesmore, once in line for TSR-2, had now been earmarked for the Tri-National Tornado Training Unit, so its Argosy E1s of 115 Squadron were, in February 1976, moved to Benson. February 1978 saw the last Argosy replaced by the Andover E1. Meanwhile, crew training for the mixture of transport types at Brize Norton had continued to be given by 240 OCU using borrowed aircraft.

No 1 PTS arrived from Abingdon in 1976, attracting Hercules from Lyneham for paratroop drops at South Cerney and Weston-on-the-Green; the 'Falcons' parachute team, which provides summer delights, is part of 1 PTS. No 38 Group Tactical Communications Wing was also based here, and the Joint Air Transport Establishment, the modern equivalent of TCDU. Brize Norton was also used for Concorde pilot training and, following the Paris accident, some development work.

Since 7 July 1966, when at Wisley Lord Portal handed to the RAF the first of its fourteen VC-10 hybrids with Super VC-10 wings and tail, more powerful engines and a forward freight door, the elegant VC-10 C Mk 1s of No 10 Squadron have been a beautiful sight in Oxfordshire's sky. Normally each could carry 139 passengers, or eight cargo pallets, or thirty-five stretcher alternatives, but often, and somewhat incongruously, the VC-10s have conveyed bombs and ammunition to war zones.

Flying personnel and freight to Ascension during the Falklands campaign, they also participated in 'casevac' duties. The value of AAR, so strongly evident during that action, resulted in 10 Squadron's aircraft having from 1989 a Mk 32 in-flight refuelling pod beneath each wing, making the eleven VC-10 C1Ks (also known as C 1 Combi) very useful dual-role aircraft. In 1997 VC-10 XV108 was permanently and luxuriously modified, at considerable expense, to serve as a transport for the incoming Prime Minister. No VC-10 has ever had a permanent Royal layout.

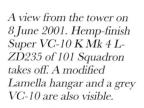

*A view from the tower on 8 June 2001. Hemp-finish Super VC-10 K Mk 4 L-ZD235 of 101 Squadron takes off. A modified Lamella hangar and a grey VC-10 are also visible.*

Sadly, the beautiful VC-10s are showing their age, as a brief glimpse of the cockpit confirms. Major servicing at Brize Norton takes fifty-one days and costs between £3 and £4 million. Second-line servicing, involving random rectification, is also undertaken in the huge hangar. Each VC-10 has a yearly major check, and every fourth year undergoes a ninety-five-day 'major' at St Athan. How long the VC-10 will continue to serve is impossible to say with certainty, but final withdrawal by 2010 seems feasible.

The VC-10s, whose prescribed availability is 75%, are likely to retain their role until the introduction of the future strategic tanker aircraft (FSTA), a £7.8 billion long-term project very likely to be civilian owned, which raises fundamental operational issues, including the question of who will man the aircraft, and when and where they will be based.

The success of the Falklands air bridge's AAR Hercules led to the RAF acquisition of nine TriStar strategic transport/AAR aircraft modified for the RAF by Marshall Aerospace at Cambridge. They comprised three C Mk 2/2A pure transports, two K Mk 1 tankers and four KC Mk 1 dual-role examples, the latter voted best. Plans for a three-refuelling-point version involving wing pods were foolishly dropped, leaving one centre-line AAR system with obvious inefficiencies.

In June 1983 two ex-British Airways TriStars commenced trooping flights from Brize Norton, giving a chance to explore the use of a wide-bodied transport, the largest transport aircraft ever in RAF squadron service. In October 1983 crew training began, aided by BA, and on 1 November 216 Squadron re-formed. The first RAF TriStar joined the squadron at Brize Norton on 25 March 1986, and soon they were operating twice weekly the continuing service via Ascension to Mount Pleasant in the Falklands. No 216 Air Transport/AAR Squadron, relying on sixteen crews, half of them trained for both roles, has been very active ever since. Its dual role was put to good use in the Balkan and Iraq campaigns, and during the last years of the Cold War, when TriStars supported Tornado F3 activity in the UKADR.

The third Brize Norton-based aircraft type is 101 Squadron's VC-10 pure tanker. Participants in recent major conflicts, they gave support to RAF and US Navy AAR probe-fitted aircraft. No 101 Squadron theoretically flies nine VC-10 K Mk3s and K Mk4s, and is the RAF's main AAR refuelling force. It now shares the station's north-side facilities, which support all VC-10 activity.

On 30 March 1999 four 101 Squadron aircraft began their part in operation *Engadine*. During 7hr 10min round trips from Bruggen, three VC-10s and six Tornado GR1s flew via southern France to carry out operations against Serbia. Transferring 250 tonnes of fuel meant that the VC-10s needed to refuel from a TriStar while the Tornadoes carried out their bombing attacks. Under operation *Allied Fair* in May-June 1999 five 101 Squadron aircraft flew sixty missions from Bruggen and eighty-three from Ancona. In all, 2,500 tonnes of fuel were transferred during about 600 linkages, and at an average altitude of about 20,000 feet.

Taken from storage at Abingdon, those VC-10s were converted for the RAF at Filton. The first of five VC-10 K2 three-point hose/drogue refuelling aircraft, ZA141 made its maiden flight on 22 June 1982. Four Super VC-10s were modified into K3s, which 101 Squadron currently operates, each able to carry a 70-tonne fuel load, and five into K4s, with an 80-tonne load. These, the only three-point refuellers in the RAF, each have two wing-mounted Mk 32 pods with 50 feet of hose and a Mk 17 fuselage drum holding 80 feet of hose. AWACS and Nimrods use centre-line refuelling, but not usually the fighters. Normal transfer rate is 40 tonnes of fuel per hour, training towlines being trailed over nine regions off the UK east coast. When VC-10s escort RAF fighters across the Atlantic for training in North America about a dozen top-ups are needed in order to reach Nellis AFB, Nevada. No 101 Squadron's aircrew number some sixty, the ground support teams totalling around 150. No 101 Squadron has had a K3 detached to 1312 Flight, supporting four Tornadoes on twenty-four-hour stand-by in the Falklands.

In 2000 99 Squadron re-formed to operate four C-17 Globemaster III strategic heavy lift transports on seven-year lease from the USA at a cost of £500 million. The first reached Brize Norton on 23 May 2001, and two were used in the desert exercise *Saif Sareea* the following autumn. Their heavy load-carrying ability has since been put to good use during the Afghan and Iraq operations. Utilisation is about 3,000 FH per year.

Prior to the 2003 Iraq campaign Brize Norton maintained Standing Detachments near Iraq over a number of years. Operation *Resinate North* saw VC-10s based at Incirlik, Turkey, while *Resinate South* involved VC-10s at Bahrain. Operation *Deliberate Forge* involved 216 Squadron TriStars at Ancona.

Additionally, Brize Norton is the base for the Joint Air Transport Evaluation Unit, Tactical Communications Wing, 2624 (County of Oxford) Regiment Field Squadron RAuxAF, RAF Air Movements School, and 4624 Movements Squadron RAuxAF. Within the Aircrew Ground Training School are two VC-10 simulators, a TriStar simulator and both civilian and military instructors. Around 2,500 trainees (from basic to special forces) pass through No 1 (The) Parachute Training School in a year, making some 50,000 descents.

Whatever the future holds for the station, its present-day occupants have some excellent accommodation in new twenty-room barrack blocks alongside well-lit streets. New garages are available and the Junior Ranks Cotswolds Restaurant, a fine bungalow-type building, is excellent on every count. To old-timers the smart oval tables and comfortable chrome frame chairs would probably cause a culture shock, likewise the wide choice of fine food and a variety of non-alcoholic cold drinks and hot drinks – and ultimately the bill, which allows personnel living off camp (of which there are many) to have meals during duty. Yes, Service life has changed – a lot!

### Main features:

*Runways:* 224° 6,000ft x 150ft, 266° 6,000ft x 150ft, concrete with wood chips. *Hangars:* four C Type, two D Type, two E Type, six 'Lamella', two Bellman Standard, one Bellman Oversize, five T2, two standard Blister, five Over Blister, fifteen Robin 'blister'. *Hardstandings:* nil. *Accommodation:* RAF officers 170, SNCOs 319, ORs 1,493; WAAF officers 8, SNCOs 9, ORs 331.

Present-day Brize Norton has a 10,007-foot asphalt 08/26 runway, has seven distinct taxiways and retains some of the main, permanent hangars. A prominent feature is the large passenger terminal building.

## BROADWELL, Oxfordshire

*51°45N/01°38W, 340ft asl; SP250065. 3 miles S of Burford*

From the A361 Burford-Lechlade road just beyond the Cotswolds Wild Life Park, which aircraft from Brize Norton make every attempt to avoid overflying (by NOTAM), turn on to a road that crosses an open area. A few huts, the Watch Office and a distant Braithwaite water tower are the remains of RAF Broadwell.

Opened on 15 November 1943 by a 70 Group working party, Transport Command took control on 24 January 1944. No 46 Group was rapidly expanding, although its Dakota strength remained small in number. An advance party of Group personnel arrived from Down Ampney on 2 February 1944 and, four days later, were joined by representatives of 512 and 575 Squadrons from Hendon, whose Dakota IIIs (and main parties) arrived on 14 February 1944, some Dakotas bringing Horsa gliders.

Like other 46 Group stations, Broadwell's role was three-fold: delivery of airborne forces and their equipment; transportation of mixed supplies to the Continent; and retrieval of wounded troops. To organise the ambulance service, elements of Nos 91, 92 and 93 Forward Staging Posts arrived at the station on 29 February 1944, by which time 220 commissioned and 1,400 non-commissioned men were stationed there. No 94 FSP stayed until June 1944, whereas the other two left soon after arrival.

On 4 April 1944 Broadwell's Dakotas participated in Exercise *Dreme*, their first taste of a major, intensive practice troop landing. Paratroops of the 1st Air Landing Brigade were carried in thirty Dakotas supplied by the two squadrons. A major 'navex' followed, involving thirty-five aircraft, and glider tow practices were undertaken. On 21 April came exercise *Mush* in which, at dawn, 248 men parachuted from nineteen Dakotas. Rapidly returning to base, eighteen glider attachments were made and all the combinations departed within an hour. Night leaflet dropping over France was also undertaken, four crews of each Broadwell squadron participating on 2 April 1944.

In a pathetic gesture the Luftwaffe deposited three unexploded HEs on the southern extremity of the airfield on 23 April. Had the enemy dropped incendiary loads upon the many wooden Horsa gliders now here… Luckily, the potential of such a blow was clearly not appreciated. On 24 and 25 April both Dakota squadrons showered information leaflets on to St Lo and Vire in the course of twenty-one effective night sorties.

May brought a rapid increase in exercises, *Exeter* being watched by Their Majesties King George VI and Queen Elizabeth, who saw the dropping of paratroops at Netheravon where

*Rebecca/Eureka* radio beacons had been set up at the dropping zone to lead in thirty Dakotas from Broadwell to drop 300 troops of the 6th Airborne Division.

Surplus Horsa gliders were towed away at the end of May to Ramsbury by USAAF C-47s, by which time tension was rising quickly. The invasion of the Continent was clearly imminent, especially so when orders were given to seal the station and impound all mail from 1400hrs on 2 June. By then, Broadwell was hosting more than 1,000 troops for the assault on Normandy.

Upon receipt of the executive order on 5 June, a final briefing for those taking part was arranged for 2000hrs. Fifty-nine Dakota crews attended, including six spare crews. Present at the briefing for operation *Tonga* was the AOC, 46 Group, who stressed the vital importance of the venture before the crews and troops boarded their aircraft.

Leading Broadwell's contingent was Wing Commander Coventry of 512 Squadron, who at 2314 was first away. His thirty-two Dakotas were airborne in 15 minutes. Then came Wing Commander Jefferson and 575 Squadron. By 2336 the whole force was on its way. Their paradrop went well – 952 troops parachuted on to the two dropping zones – and all aircraft returned home safely.

At 1400 on 6 June crews of both Broadwell squadrons were again briefed – eighteen from 512 and nineteen from 575 – for operation *Mallard*. This time they were to tow loaded Horsa gliders to Normandy in daylight, protected by a massive fighter screen. One aircraft encountered trouble before take-off, which meant quickly attaching its glider to a spare Dakota. All returned except for one, which ditched in the Channel. Additional Dakotas took part after dark in *Robroy*, a special operation involving supply dropping.

Commencement of Broadwell's third operational phase on 17 June set the tone for the rest of the war. At 0600 fifteen Dakotas of 575 Squadron took off for Holmsley South, taking aboard 191 RAF personnel and their kit. One Dakota became unserviceable, leaving the others to make history by touching down at B5 landing strip (Camilly), the first Dakota squadron to land in France in force after D-Day.

Such activity was chancy and two damaged Dakotas had to be left there while the others hurried to B2 (Bazenville) to retrieve 254 casualties who were back in England before mid-afternoon. This was the first huge input to the Air Ambulance Pool. No 6 Casualty Evacuation Unit began working up here in May to cope with such activity, which continued until unit closure on 24 August 1944.

Apart from retrieving the wounded, Dakotas of both squadrons aided other squadron moves to and within the European mainland, then returned with casualties, often from Coulombes (B6). Such activity, supported by Nos 104 and 105 Staging Posts, here from 16 August until September, continued at fever pitch throughout summer and into autumn, Dakotas returning with both stretcher-cases and walking wounded, before mid-September brought the tragedy of Arnhem.

Broadwell's contribution on 17 September comprised twenty-two aircraft of 512 Squadron and twenty-four of 575 Squadron, with one from 437 Squadron, each Dakota towing a Horsa glider. Low cloud base during take-off led to five glider pilots casting off before the Suffolk coast was reached. The pilot of another glider was killed by machine-gun fire near Oustahouet. Finally, forty-one gliders (carrying 544 troops of the 1st Border Regiment No 1 Airborne Division, together with twenty-two jeeps, thirteen trailers, thirty motor-cycles, seventeen ordinary cycles, thirty-four hand-carts and seven anti-tank guns) were launched on to a landing zone west of Arnhem. All Broadwell's Dakotas returned safely.

Re-supply on 18 September involved twenty-four Broadwell Dakotas. One crew, captained by Fg Off Henry, flew in error on to a southerly route towards the LZ, Henry being killed when AA guns opened up south of Turnhout. His navigator was wounded and the aircraft's rudder badly damaged before the second pilot took over. The initial intention was to turn back and release the glider over British lines. Instead, its pilots at once cast off, giving Warrant Officer Smith and the Dakota an easier chance of reaching home. He landed safely at Martlesham. A Dakota of 575 Squadron was involved in an alarming incident over the DZ when the tow rope from an aircraft overhead wound itself around the wing of Flying Officer McTeare's machine, making it very difficult to fly, before he landed at Framlingham. One Dakota of 512 Squadron did not return.

On 19 September thirty Dakotas operated, both Broadwell squadrons losing an aircraft. Next day thirty-one crews were involved, and 512 Squadron lost another Dakota. With the situation at Arnhem desperate, it was decided to place one Dakota squadron much nearer to the dropping zones. On 23 September the crews of sixteen Dakotas of 512 Squadron found themselves taking personnel of 575 Squadron to B56 Brussels/Evere, with that squadron's eighteen Dakotas tagging along. Late in the afternoon 575 Squadron set out to drop food and ammunition west of Graves.

About 75% of the supplies appeared to reach Allied troops, so a second operation was ordered. Eventually four aircraft took off next day and faced plentiful flak. On 25 September seven crews operated to a dropping zone west of Arnhem where nearly 800 men were desperate for supplies. This time the formation flew to Antwerp to meet its fighter escort before unloading seventy-nine panniers of rations, twenty-eight of medical supplies and three bundles of bedding. There was again much machine-gun fire, which damaged four Dakotas. All returned except KG 449, which was hit in the port elevator and rudder, but flew on quite well. Some 10 miles north-west of Eindhoven the aircraft ran into intense flak which, put the port engine out of use. Nevertheless it flew on while gradually losing height, and force-landed near Pael, the crew having a lucky escape.

Arnhem passed, the round was again transportation of various loads to the Continent and a return with casualties. For operation *Varsity* Broadwell's Dakotas advanced to Gosfield. After the drop they landed at B56, returning to Broadwell on 25 March. No reduction in the number of sorties flown followed the end of hostilities in Europe, for troops still needed supplies and there was repatriation flying to be done. By this time there were many Horsa gliders in storage at Broadwell.

The immediate post-war phase ended for 512 and 575 Squadrons when they moved to Melbourne and Holme-upon-Spalding Moor, on 6 August 1945. Replacing them came 10 and 76 Squadrons, here to equip with Dakotas prior to Far East service. On 29 August 1945 77 and 78 Squadrons began arriving for similar conversion. Soon the move of 78 Squadron was halted, and it was instead to go to the Middle East.

Conversion of the squadrons was rapid, 10 and 76 setting off for St Mawgan and Portreath on 28 August. Training was intense at Broadwell, with the two squadrons completing 720 glider tows and dropping 2,050 containers. No 77 Squadron left for India in October 1945.

On 5 October 1945 Dakotas of 271 Squadron moved in from Odiham, continuing scheduled services within Transport Command's extensive continental network. To ease administration Broadwell was switched from 46 to 47 Group on 9 October 1945 and, by December, 271 Squadron was flying along the busy trunk route to India. A 271 Squadron Dakota normally took four days to reach India.

Broadwell was returned to 46 Group early in April 1946. Throughout that year 271 Squadron concentrated on passenger and freight services mainly to Europe, particularly to areas where British Forces were stationed.

Closure of Broadwell was discussed towards the end of 1946, as was a new positioning of 271 Squadron. At the end of October 1946 Bicester was announced as the chosen location, but Broadwell had more to offer by way of accommodation – and it had concrete runways. The move was therefore cancelled.

On 1 December 1946 271 Squadron was renumbered 77 Squadron and continued the pattern of passenger and freight services to, among others, Warsaw, Rome, Prague and particularly Buckeburg. Broadwell's end was, however, not far off, and on 17 December 1946 most of 77 Squadron left for Manston. On the final day of 1946 station strength was reduced and preparations for closure began. With the rear part of 77 Squadron gone by 9 January 1947, closure began, with 31 March 1947 marking the last day of RAF tenure of the station.

**Main features:**
*Runways:* 190° 6,000ft x 150ft, 070° 4,200ft x 150ft, 310° 4,200ft x 150ft, all concrete with wood chip surface. *Hangars:* two T2. *Hardstandings:* forty-eight and two loading aprons. *Accommodation:* RAF Officers 275, SNCOs 361, ORs 1,405; WAAF Officers 13, SNCOs 20, ORs 220

## BROOKLANDS (WEYBRIDGE), Surrey

*51°21N/00°28W 75ft asl; TQ066625. SW of Weybridge just north of the A245 at By fleet*

> "Brooklands? An airfield? A famous concrete oval motor racing track, yes – but an aerodrome? Maybe aeroplanes visited on race days, surely that's all."

No, that is not all, for from Brooklands great events took place. Hawker's prototype Hurricane flew from here, where Vickers built many aeroplanes – Wellingtons, Viscounts, VC-10s and lots more – and in an unusually shaped wooden building, famed Barnes Wallis developed brilliant ideas.

True, there was a famous racetrack here before any aeroplane. Built in 1906/7 on land owned by the Honourable Hugh Locke King, 1,500 workers constructed the circuit in less than a year.

Measuring 4,730 yards long and 100 feet wide, it was officially opened on 22 July 1907 by S F Edge, then a leading motorist. Brooklands might well be looked upon as 'a mechanical sports arena', and early aviation pioneers evidently thought along such lines. In 1907 Moore-Brabazon tried, unsuccessfully, to fly his home-built craft from here.

The first person to make a flight from Brooklands was A V Roe who in 1908 made what is regarded as the first successful aeroplane flight in Britain. His activities were not universally popular with the motor-racers, especially after he crashed his first triplane in the middle of the track. In 1909, after being very strongly encouraged to continue his activities elsewhere, he disposed of his small aeroplane shed for £15. His experiments were continued on Lea Marshes, Essex, before he moved to Manchester, where his flying proved so successful that the Brooklanders in 1910 invited him to return. Very soon he was flying from his original haunt and was soon joined by other famous pioneers. Short Brothers were soon there too, building aeroplanes, and in 1910 Martin and Handasyde set about constructing a very successful Martinsyde monoplane, bringing excitement and glamour to Brooklands. The *Daily Mail* round-Britain Air Race started from here on 22 July 1911. Then in 1912 Vickers opened a flying school, making Brooklands racetrack a focal point for aviation before the outbreak of the First World War. Among pupils trained at the school, and destined for fame, were Sir Sefton Brancker, Marshal of the Royal Air Force, Viscount Trenchard and Air Chief Marshal Lord Dowding.

The aerodrome, sited in the centre of the Brooklands motor track, was not without obstructions, for there were high-tension cables on three sides, two tall chimneys to the east and a wooded hillside 2 miles distant. Byfleet sat to the south-west and Weybridge to the north, with the racing circuit passing close to Weybridge railway station.

The First World War saw Brooklands become a training station for ab initio pilots, instruction being given using Maurice Farman Shorthorns and Avro 504s. Military association began in earnest with the arrival of No 1 Squadron from Farnborough in August 1914 for a stay almost to the end of the year.

On 1 January 1915 No 8 Squadron re-formed at Brooklands as a general duties squadron equipped with BE 2cs. A fortnight later 10 Squadron came from Farnborough, both squadrons leaving during April to make way for IX Squadron, which re-formed on 1 April commanded by Major H C T Dowding, the 1940 AOC-in-C of Fighter Command. No IX Squadron, equipped with Avro 504s, moved to Dover on 28 July 1915. Established earlier in that year, the Wireless Testing Park left in August for Joyce Green.

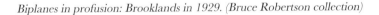

*Biplanes in profusion: Brooklands in 1929. (Bruce Robertson collection)*

*A 'popular' dare, as a Sopwith*
*1¹/₂ Strutter flies under*
*Brooklands Bridge.*
*(Bruce Robertson collection)*

By 1915 Sopwith was building aeroplanes at Brooklands, while Harry Hawker, his test pilot, perfected the art of flying a Pup under the Byfleet bridge. Vickers, too, opened an aircraft factory, on the site of the Itala motor works, where it built the Vickers Gunbus, the company's first successful military aeroplane. Vickers went on to turn out more than 1,650 of its famous SE 5 single-seat fighters in 1917-18. More than 4,600 aircraft were produced at Brooklands aircraft factories during the 1914-18 war, for which reason Brooklands became No 10 Aircraft Acceptance Park, taking SE 5s from Bleriot, Martinsyde and Vickers, as well as Snipes from Sopwith. Storage was in one hangar measuring 190 feet by 70 feet, and seven of 170 feet by 80 feet. On 31 January 1917 No 2 RS, at Brooklands since early times, moved to Northolt.

Despite its unusual siting, the aerodrome continued to be used after the war, although post-war cutbacks and recession reduced activity. Many well-known wartime manufacturers closed before new names replaced them. Hawker, which took over the Sopwith concern at Kingston-upon-Thames, built a huge new hangar at Brooklands for final assembly of its products that were flight-tested here. Vickers Ltd embarked upon the design and construction at Brooklands of a line of large civilian aircraft. In 1919 the first transatlantic crossing was made by a Vickers Vimy, which covered the 1,890 miles from Newfoundland to Ireland in 15 hours 57 minutes at an average speed of 120mph. A trickle of orders kept Vickers in business, the firm expanding its Weybridge works by adding a hangar similar to Hawker's. The mid-1920s saw the Vimy develop into the Virginia bomber range, mixed in with Victoria then Valentia transports supplied to the RAF for overseas use.

The late 1920s saw an outburst of light aeroplane flying in which Brooklands played a leading part, the Henderson School of Flying initiating activity in 1927. Club owner Colonel G L P Henderson designed and built several aircraft, including the Gadfly, which in May 1929 broke the world's height record for light aircraft. Duncan Davis, Chief Flying Instructor, took over the Henderson School in 1928 and renamed it the Brooklands School of Flying. With financial assistance he was able to purchase three Avro 548s, and the school proved very successful, particularly when it sent two red Avros to an area between Canvey and The Wash. Using several landing sites, they carried necessary ladders and tents strapped to the aircraft! By April 1929 the School held eight aeroplanes, and in 1929 more than forty pupils gained their 'A' licences. That same year 'Mutt' Summers became Chief Test Pilot to Vickers and George Bulman took on the same role for Hawker Aircraft.

Spring 1930 saw the opening of the Brooklands Aero Club, with a sole DH Gipsy Moth. Flying lessons cost £2 per hour, and by mid-1931 advanced and blind flying were on offer as well as aeronautical engineering courses. The latter led to the opening in October 1931 of the College of Aeronautical Engineering, which formed its own aero club in 1932. The Brooklands School of Flying expanded into new premises embracing a control tower and quite elaborate club facilities in 1932. Much remaining from that period is safeguarded by a preservation order.

*Hawker Hurricane 1 L1580 during its final*
*acceptance process in 1938.*

The Vickers factory was rebuilt in 1932, by which time tenders were being invited for advanced bomber aircraft, in particular the B.9/32 that was eventually produced as the Wellington. Meanwhile the motor-racing circuit remained in the forefront of its sport, club flying flourished, and private owners were basing their aircraft at Brooklands. By 1934 the Club held five Gipsy Moths, on which Duncan Davis was still instructing. The new Hawker sheds were being used for assembly, then testing of the Hart family and fast Furies by Lucas, Bulman and Hindmarsh.

October 1935 brought a very special event, the arrival of the prototype Hawker Hurricane K5083 by road from the Kingston works. Amid mounting excitement. on 6 November George Bulman first flew the small silver monoplane. Another highlight came on 15 June 1936 when the prototype Vickers B.9/32 K4049, piloted by 'Mutt' Summers, also made its first flight from Brooklands. Its production derivative, the Wellington, whose geodetic construction mirrored that of the R-100 airship, became the dominant wartime sight at Brooklands, generally known by then as Weybridge, where the Vickers main factory stood. Production there totalled 2,514 Wellingtons, with many others passing through the repair area of the works.

In 1936 the Vickers Wellesley entered production here. A large single-engined aeroplane whose high-aspect-ratio narrow chord wings conferred upon it exceptional range, its bomb load was conveyed in under-wing stores containers in modernistic style.

Private flying continued, but in the run-up to war Brooklands had become a major aircraft production centre. The first production Wellington left the works in 1938, while at Hawker erection and delivery of Hurricanes rapidly increased. These two activities were stepped up when the war came, replacing private flying.

It was inevitable that the enemy would attack such an important aircraft industrial complex, yet the Germans, expecting quick victory, seemed not to appreciate how important it was. Not until 4 September 1940 did they send some twenty-five Bf 110s to deal a heavy blow to Brooklands. Certainly the damage inflicted on Vickers was serious, eighty-three of the work-force being killed and more than 400 injured. Considerable damage was caused to the aircraft repair hangar, machine shop and electrical wiring department. More important, Hawker's erecting shops luckily escaped major damage, and Hurricanes continued to flow forth to shoot down Bf 110s. Apart from small-scale incursions, the enemy ignored Brooklands.

Hawker moved out of Brooklands to concentrate production at Kingston-upon-Thames and its Langley complex, using the large airfield for trials and production test flying. That left Brooklands Weybridge to Vickers Armstrong, which, as well as producing Wellingtons, tested, developed and then produced Warwicks as bombers, ASR, and general reconnaissance aircraft to the end of the war. By 1944 Vickers was using Wisley for development of new types and for general experimental work. In 1945 the company produced a twin-engined airliner, the VC-1 Viking. The first post-war British airliner to fly, it had Wellington ancestry and in its early form retained geodetic wing and tail construction.

In January 1948 the whole of Brooklands – including the remaining motor-racing circuit – was bought by Vickers Armstrong for £330,000, following which a concrete runway was laid and factory premises were extended and improved. The company's main interests now were invested in a four-turbo-prop airliner, the VC-2 Viscount, and a four-jet bomber, the B.3/48 Valiant. The turbo-prop Viscount constructed at Weybridge was soon widely acclaimed as a major advance in airliner development. The first production Viscount, *G-ALWE*, flew from Weybridge on 20 August 1952. Valiants were also Weybridge-built, the first production example flying in December 1953.

*The first production Wellington 1, L4212, at Brooklands (Weybridge) in the autumn of 1938.*

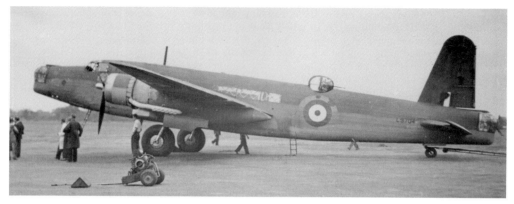

*The Warwick 1 prototype L9704 at Weybridge after installation of Pratt & Whitney Twin Wasp engines in 1940. (Vickers)*

July 1957 brought the unveiling by Lord Brabazon of a Brooklands Memorial comprising a bronze plaque with a relief map carrying an illustration of the circuit and a brief history of the site.

On 20 January 1959 the prototype Vanguard airliner, *G-AOYW*, lifted off for the first time from Brooklands. Orders for this 'big brother' Viscount ended at forty-three, its effectiveness being dented as turbojet engines became sufficiently economic for use in airliners.

Much effort was also devoted to the Vickers 1000, a large elegant jet-propelled transport government backing for which was withdrawn after much design work had been completed. Vickers proceeded with the VC-10 variant, the last aircraft entirely designed and constructed by Vickers, the prototype of which first flew at Brooklands on 29 June 1962. Production examples were constructed at Weybridge, then flown to Wisley for acceptance flight tests.

Vickers Weybridge became part of the British Aircraft Corporation in 1960, at which time the TSR2 high-performance aircraft was being designed in conjunction with English Electric at Warton. The prototype, built at Weybridge, was transported from Brooklands to Boscombe Down, where it first flew on 27 September 1964. The acrimonious saga surrounding the TSR-2 undoubtedly severely damaged the British aircraft industry and its international standing.

Meanwhile, the VC-10 in BOAC service became the most publicly preferred jet transport. The longer Super VC-10 was flown for the first time at Weybridge on 7 May 1965. Fifty-four VC-10s and Super VC-10s were built, the last one taking off from Brooklands in February 1970. The event heralded the closure of the runway and the end of Brooklands as a fixed-wing airfield. Helicopters occasionally called.

Closure came in 1987, after which industrial units were built on the site with roads crossing the closed runway.

An excellent overall view of the history of Brooklands can be had by visiting the on-site Brooklands Museum (Tel 01932 857381).

*A Brooklands-built Valiant XD870 after conversion into an air-to air refueller.*

## BROXBOURNE, Hertfordshire

*51°44/00°01E 85ft asl; TL378065. 1¹/₂miles E of Broxbourne, near Nazeing*

"What happened to Broxbourne, its Tigers, Hornet Moths and Proctors?" you may well ask.

The answer is that, if they didn't catch fire, they fled – in this case to Stapleford Tawney – leaving their home to be assaulted by ugly gravel-gouging contraptions disgorging hideous mounds of stones and ruining the view.

Little Broxbourne was born in those heady early 1930s days when club flying emerged. An area of flat agricultural land east of Broxbourne village and close to the Essex border was one site acquired, and on 13 November 1930 it became licensed to the then new Herts & Essex Club. Typical were the founders, the Frogley brothers, with roots in motor-racing, or more precisely the speedway arena, and who between them owned DH 60 Moth *G-EBVK*.

A clubhouse – essential item – and an aircraft shed were soon in situ, and on 14 June 1931 popular comedy actor Will Hay, together with Jim and Amy Mollison, undertook the aerodrome's official opening ceremony during a flying display with all the normal ingredients of carefree times.

Broxbourne rapidly became such a popular flying venue that the landing ground had to be increased in area. More accommodation was made available for men, women and their machines as well as the additional flying organisations that were attracted, among them the London Transport Flying Club. Flying lessons were available, although the loss of W R Bannister, CFI, who died when a Rapide came down in the English Channel in 1935, was a bitter blow. By 1937 Broxbourne was a thriving private flying aerodrome, and the following year an outpost of the Civil Air Guard was established here. The landing ground was too small for an RAFVR school to open, but Herts & Essex expertise was drawn upon by the award of a contract to run the E&RFTS at Waltham, Grimsby. In late 1938 more than 200 CAG members were being trained at Broxbourne by the Club, which operated twenty-four aircraft, had thirteen instructors, and employed fifty ground staff.

As at all such places, civil flying ceased on the day war broke out. Some time followed before aircraft suitable for military light communications duties were impressed, leaving others to degenerate. In 1942 a new aircraft shed and other facilities were added, in which a variety of RAF light communications aircraft were overhauled, repaired and re-painted. Most were Proctors, but late wartime saw Canadian-built Harvards come for modification to suit the RAF and RN standards.

The Herts & Essex Club (1946) was quick off the mark when private flying resumed on 1 January 1946. Moths, Proctors, M.38s and Austers all became a common sight, until their presence was incenerated on 22/23 June 1947 by a major fire that destroyed two hangars, two Proctors and seven Tiger Moths, another five of which were damaged. Although it was a bitter blow, the Frogley brothers fought back and Autocrats, Tiger Moths, a Hornet Moth, Proctors, Rapides and Miles were soon active again. The Aero Club amalgamated with Herts & Essex Aviation Ltd in 1948. In 1953, with airfield extension impracticable, the site was sold and the Club moved to Stapleford. If you wish to find where the aerodrome once existed, look for much disturbed gravel, then weep if such things disturb you.

**Main features:**
*Landing area:* N/S 1,350ft, NE/SW 1,890ft, E/W 1,500ft, SE/NW 1,680ft. *Hangars:* fourteen small lock-up aircraft sheds (ten 26ft wide, four 30ft wide). *Accommodation:* Club house with restaurant and sleeping accommodation.

## BRUNTINGTHORPE, Leicestershire

*52°29N/01°17W 450ft asl; SP599665. 10 miles S of Leicester*

A typical temporary, three-runway wartime bomber station, Bruntingthorpe opened in November 1942, and to the end of the war was a Bomber Command OTU. From its debut until 30 May 1943, it was a second satellite of No 29 OTU North Luffenham. Wellington IIIs flew from here, continuing to do so after 24 May 1943 when the station became the home of No 29 OTU during runway construction at North Luffenham. The move also brought Bitteswell into being as a satellite of Bruntingthorpe, an arrangement lasting until November 1944 when OTU strength was reduced by 25%. Wellington Xs largely replaced Mk IIIs in 1943. The OTU depended upon Ansons for navigation training, and progressively employed Lysanders, Defiants then Martinets for gunnery practice. Fighter affiliation was, from 5 June 1943, provided by No 1683 Bomber (Defence) Training Flight, unusually equipped with six Curtiss Tomahawks based here until transfer to Market Harborough at the start of February 1944. No 29 OTU was disbanded on 27 May 1945.

Bruntingthorpe's survival partially stemmed from its association with Bitteswell, where industrial activity resulted in the latter airfield becoming a major test site for jet aircraft. Bruntingthorpe possessed good approaches and, between December 1944 and 1947, Power Jets and others made use of it for test flying. It was also kept alive by the January 1946 arrival from Loughborough of the ATC's No 42 Gliding School, which stayed until transfer to Bramcote in January 1947. Thereafter the airfield existed through care and maintenance.

Its suitability for expansion had long been realised, the main runway having feasible extension to 12,000 feet. When the USAF asked for bomber bases in the Midlands behind the fighter protection belt, Bruntingthorpe rose high on the list. On 13 November 1952 it was allocated to the Americans; however, contractors were already upgrading the four bases earmarked for the USAF, so plans for Bruntingthorpe's development were halted and in 1953 the site returned to British care and maintenance. As a result of further policy change, Bruntingthorpe was re-allocated to the USAF on 13 February 1957. Two days later SAC's 3912th ABS (upgraded to Combat Support Group on 1 January 1959) moved in, with runway extension to 10,500 feet coming under way to allow fully laden B-47 bombers to operate.

January 1959 saw B-47Es of the 100th Bomb Wing arrive from Portsmouth AFB, New Hampshire, as part of 'Reflex Action', then at its peak. Under that scheme small numbers of Stratojets were rotated among home and overseas US bases. At Bruntingthorpe such activity ceased as early as April 1959.

In September 1959 the 3912th was replaced by USAFE's 7542nd ABS as part of *Red Richard*. Bruntingthorpe now became a satellite of the 10th TRW Alconbury, whose 19th Tactical Reconnaissance Squadron using RB-66Bs arrived and remained until September 1962, when it left for Toul AB, France. The 7542nd was rapidly inactivated and Bruntingthorpe returned to UK control on 28 September 1962.

Despite its excellent runway and proximity to the M1 and M6 motorways, Bruntingthorpe held no further military use. Instead, the main camp site, hangars and other areas were acquired by Talbot, the motor manufacturer.

Aeronautically all has most certainly not been lost, for here one now finds the British Aviation Heritage Collection, a fine gathering of twenty-six aeroplanes. Included is the last 'airworthy' Vulcan XH558, hoping to fly again helped by the Heritage Lottery Fund and public support, a Boeing 747 to serve as a conference centre, and a most impressive Super Guppy. Nearby sits the last Comet 4C to fly, XS235. The Walton family owns the site and hopes to expand its collection. The Buccaneer Preservation Society and the Lightning Preservation Group are other residents – and you can have a splendid time among the Hunters, Harriers, Gnats and Jet Provosts on any Sunday for a mere £4!

**Main features:**
*Runways:* 245° 6,000ft x 150ft (later lengthened to 10,500ft), 132° 4,200ft x 150ft,.185° 4,200ft x 150ft, concrete with wood chips. *Hangars:* four T2, one B1. *Hardstandings:* thirty frying-pan type. *Accommodation:* RAF officers 214, SNCOs 656, ORs 894; WAAF 10 officers, 10 SNCOs, 420 ORs.

## CARDINGTON, Bedfordshire

52°06N/00°25W 55ft asl; TL008470. 3 miles SE of Bedford by the A600

Once seen never forgotten, 'tis said. I can vouch for it in the case of that giant among flying machines, the R-101 airship. As its nose slipped from view when low over our roof the tail had still to appear. As young as I was, the R-101 presented to me an image remaining as clear now as upon that magic day. The thump of its engines, the curiously whirring propellers, that huge 'G' on the fin and the absolutely colossal bulk of this flying ship were to influence the rest of my life.

Deciding to visit close relatives in Goldington, Bedford, Dad guided our ageing Jowett via Cardington on the morning of the airship's notorious departure for India. We passed close by as the huge silver cigar was being manhandled by 700 or so helpers, completely dwarfed by this colossal flying Queen Mary. My cousins had set up a telescope, which they held so that little me could periodically peer at his pin-up on that fateful Saturday, 4 October 1930.

Cardington's watchers were not unduly large in number, although many were aware of the imminent departure. Maybe the drizzle was discouraging, while a delayed departure caused some to drift away before the R-101 slipped its mooring and sailed at around 1900. It carried fifty-four people on its gruesome voyage, amidst concern about its readiness to undertake such a journey. Put simply, the lift/weight ratio of the airship was worrying, and there were various concerns about its envelope, possible leakages and the ship's frame.

R-101 had been launched on 12 October 1929. Two days later it made a 5hr 38min flight giving Londoners a view of the wonder of the age. On 18 October Midlanders glimpsed it, and in the course of a 7hr 15min flight on 1 November R-101 paraded before HM King George V in residence at

*The R-101 airship at Cardington's mooring mast.*

Sandringham. Another flight came on 2 November, and on the 3rd the Isle of Wight was visited. Two local flights followed on 8 and 14 November, before a tour of Britain on 17/18 November 1929 became its longest, having a duration of 30hr 41min. Each flight terminated at the southern end of Cardington where the ship was attracted and anchored to the 200-foot mooring mast with the aid of a huge electromagnet. On 30 November it was manoeuvred into Cardington's No 1 Shed for six months of weight reducing modifications, which did little to improve handling.

In June 1930 a contingent of airmen from Cardington and Henlow – supplemented by Bedford's unemployed – tugged the airship from its cocoon. Inherent buoyancy made the task of 'carrying' it relatively easy – the difficulty was to ensure that it was correctly guided. Therefore the task needed to take place in calm weather, at dawn or dusk. Similar conditions placed constraints on all ground manoeuvring and sailing.

Flight trials were resumed on 26 June, with its readiness questionable. The next day's 12-hour flight coincided with a practice for the 1930 RAF Display at Hendon where, on the morrow, R-101 was displayed to boost political egos. Then it re-entered No 1 Shed for more weight reduction treatment and attention to a various snags.

Drastic was the programme now undertaken, for the hull was sliced vertically to permit insertion of a new central section containing additional gas bags to improve the lift/weight ratio and increase R-101's length to 777 feet. Its diameter was 132 feet, and its volume now 5,500,000cu ft. Lavish passenger accommodation – including a lounge, dining-room, sleeping accommodation and a promenade deck – was a feature of the R-101, heavy wooden features contrasting oddly with very expensive (in 1930) lightweight Bakelite cups and plates, some of which have been preserved to prove their existence.

Major concern was directed at the porous nature of gas bags, and evidence that some easily chafed against the metal frame. In the vast airship shed, assembly of the metal airship structure had taken place with the aid of steel cables hanging from the roof, which contained three catwalks.

On 1 October 1930 the 'slave labour' force again tugged out the 'Socialist airship', thus named to distinguish it from its happier, capitalist rival, the R-100, in which the brilliance of Barnes Wallis was evident. Considerable concern arose during a long overnight flight on 1/2 October, for the R-101 still handled poorly. Without doubt it was inferior to the Graf Zeppelin, which had visited Cardington in April 1930, and very poor when compared with the R-100, which had recently come to Cardington following a triumphant voyage to Canada.

Competitive pressure was placed upon the staff and fliers of the Royal Airship Works to get the R-101 into service, while cautionary voices were being raised publicly and privately. Brushing that aside, the fifty-four people, including Lord Thomson, the Secretary of State of Air, and Sir Sefton Brancker, the Director of Civil Aviation, were aboard the R-101 when, with little ceremony, it slipped from its mooring mast in the early evening of 4 October 1930, circled Bedford, then set off at 1,500 feet towards the South East and France. Capable of up to 80mph, adverse winds reduced

*Low Zone Mk XI barrage balloon and winch in 1938 during acceptance flying.*

its ground speed to 25mph, its five 580hp Beardmore diesel engines pulsating deeply. Weather forecasts did not indicate favourable conditions, which were soon worse than expected, including strong gusts among generally bumpy, thundery conditions and rainstorms. Handling the tail-heavy R-101 was far from easy in good weather, let alone in bad conditions and with a full load.

The likelihood seems to have been that in rough weather the fabric and a gas bag tore, releasing hydrogen. Height was lost over France, a crew member later recalling that the R-101 was at the height of Beauvais Cathedral when it sailed passed about a kilometre to the north. Shortly afterwards, at 0200, the watch, maintained in nautical style, was changed, and at a very critical moment. A few minutes later the R-101 was probably caught in a strong gust. There was a tremendous explosion as the airship bounced 60 feet high on striking a hillside near Allonne. Only six of the fifty-four occupants survived the conflagration.

Not a lot materially remains of that event. On a heat-seared silver watch the hands remain set at 0203, and through an unusual twist of fate the RAF Ensign aboard the airship survived. Little charred, it was found fluttering at the extreme stern of the wreck, and now it hangs proudly in a small exhibition of memorabilia in Cardington Parish Church, well worth visiting. Among the many dead were Lord Thomson, Sir Sefton Brancker and Major Scott. They are commemorated on road nameboards at Cardington.

The disaster near Beauvais spelled the end for large British airships. In July 1932 the Directorate of Airship Development was quietly transferred from the Air Ministry to Cardington, which two months later was placed on care and maintenance, although the Royal Airship Works remained, in title, until 1938. The R-100 programme cost £471,000 – a vast sum at the time – and ended when the ship was stripped of its fabric, broken up and sold for a mere £450. Cardington's mooring mast, as much a landmark as the airship sheds and built in 1926 for £150,000, was broken up in 1943 and melted down. At that time the 50-foot radio mast remained on the tower at the rear of the headquarters building of the RAW, a memorial to ghastly messages flashed one October night. That, too, has long gone, but until the airship sheds still dominating their region are no more it will remain difficult to pass without thinking of a giant that filled the sky.

If you like sensations from the past, don't ever miss an opportunity to set foot inside one of Cardington's hangars, the largest of their type in the world. The bigger of the two – they differ in detail – is the northernmost one, the No 1 Shed built for the Admiralty and used by Short Brothers during the First World War for airship building. On 16 November 1930 close on 7,000 voices were raised in this sepulchral structure in a memorial service for the disaster victims. A report of the day recalled how 'the great roof echoed and re-echoed to the music of the hymns', and that 'the final chords resounded in the girders and had to be allowed to fade gradually before the service could continue. Voices were amplified and echoed from the great emptiness at either end of the shed' from the huge crowd that occupied only half of the floor of the vast hangar.

The mammoth steel-framed 1916-17 shed has a cross-section in the form of a three-pin arch supported on A-frames. Between the pins it is 180 feet wide, at its base 272 feet. Originally the height to the pins was 63ft 3in, the minimum clearance at the roof centre 110 feet, and the overall hangar length 700 feet. The capacity of the hangar above the floor was 17,100,000cu ft, staggering even then. Over the steel framing was fitted ungalvanised corrugated sheeting. Annex coverings

*Cardington's gigantic twins.*

were finished with 'Hybrid' covered with cement mortar. Three rows of windows extended the entire length of the building, which was finished in dark grey, a colour repeatedly applied until the 1970s when it was overtaken by light green. Painting the sheds, let alone maintaining them, will always be a mighty task. To improve ground handling of the airships, giant screens 70 feet high and 700 feet long were erected to deflect the wind, and remained until the mid-1920s, giving added evidence of the enormity of airship operation.

To be commercially viable, airships needed to be large. Although the spaciousness and luxury of ocean liners could be variously challenged, the problem of very limited payload remained. Large airships needed huge sheds, one coming into use at Howden where Vickers built its R-100. Before the Government R-101 could be constructed at RAW Cardington, the First World War hangar needed enlarging. Four additional bays were fitted, adding 112 feet to the overall length. Raising the centre of the roof by 35 feet and the doors by 46 feet was far more difficult. Already those structures were very high, and the construction of a new roof by the Cleveland Bridge & Engineering Company Ltd of Darlington was no mean achievement. Liverpool Street Station would now have fitted into it, as well as a building as tall as Nelson's Column. The modified No 1 Shed enclosed 26,600,000cu ft and covered 4³/₄ acres. Its internal height remains 156ft 8 in with a height to the crown pin of 174ft 6in, and to the top ridge of 179ft 6in. Modification, commenced in October 1924, was completed in March 1926, the hangar by then being 812 feet long.

Cardington's other hangar came from Pulham, Norfolk, where it was dismantled in 1928 for re-erection as Cardington's southern or No 2 Shed. Visiting Cardington one surely cannot but be overawed by the size of these sheds, and no less by the truly gigantic doors at their western ends, their opposite ends being sealed. Each half door weighs an amazing 470 tons. Massive steel girders anchor each door to two large horizontal beams that rest upon four-wheel bogies, themselves of no mean proportions. Each wheel supports a 33-ton load in calm conditions, and twice that when the wind blows strongly. Electric power closes the doors, an operation taking 15 minutes. Nevertheless, on one occasion a 70mph gust lifted a bogey from the 3ft 6in gauge track, which gives an idea of the vulnerability of these huge structures.

Viewing of No 1 Shed reveals seemingly unending bays, cross-braced by thick cables. Ascending any of the stairways leading to the roof catwalks (upon which the workforce spent much time when the giant airships were constructed) is not for the faint-hearted.

The 200-foot-high steel-framed mooring mast comprised eight columns rising from an octagonal base 70 feet across. A 40-foot-diameter passenger boarding platform, some 170 feet above the ground, was reached by a lift. The base of the mooring turret was of a 25-foot diameter, and the tower could withstand a pulling force equivalent to 30 tons. In two huts at the tower's base, both long existent, were three steam winches used to pump water at a rate of 5,000 gallons an hour and gas through a 12-inch pipe into the airship for purposes of maintaining its centre of gravity under varying conditions. When the water was jettisoned it was a case of run fast – or be drowned!

Without entering Cardington it is possible to view the now much-run-down intended palatial passenger terminal-cum-hotel, which later became Station Headquarters. Supported by Grecian-style columns, the facade carries the inscription MCMXVII, a reminder that Cardington has long been an action station. The magnificent entrance hall with its high ceiling, ravaged by time until the 1980s, contained treasures from the station's historic past. Some walls were tiled, and the entire building once had the air of an Edwardian stately home. For many years it contained the ship's wheel from the R-100.

The terminal faced Shortstown. Short Brothers had long been involved in airship building at Cardington, having tendered to an Admiralty requirement for two rigid airships, Nos R-31 and R-32. The firm, lent £110,000 to purchase land and erect a 700-foot-long hangar and sundry buildings, acquired suitable land at Cardington in 1915. It was chosen because of the ample space for development, the close proximity of the river Ouse, useful for industrial purposes and sewerage disposal, good road and rail links, and the closeness of Bedford. By 1917 800 people were working here, 300 of them women, and most of whom came from Bedford. Shorts built a housing estate opposite the intended passenger terminal and named it Shortstown, by which title the crescent of houses is still known.

R-31, launched at Cardington in August 1918, suffered a structural failure during its delivery flight to East Fortune. Its sister ship, R-32, entered service in September 1919 for training and experimental purposes. R-37, 675 feet long and 78ft 8in in diameter, and based upon Zeppelin L 48, was partly built at Walney Island, Barrow, then moved to Cardington in 1917. Some £300,000 was spent before building halted in February 1921. A second, larger airship, R-38 – metal, and rigid too – was ordered from Shorts in September 1918; the Admiralty was proposing to take over Cardington, leaving Shorts to run the station and build new airships there, but the company wanted better terms, and the R-38 order was cancelled. The Admiralty informed the company that Cardington was to be immediately nationalised and, by April 1919, Shorts was vacating the factory.

The Royal Airship Works thus came into being, and work on the R-38 was resumed, being completed in 1921. An impressive airship, it had a 3,000-mile action radius and a 211-hour cruise potential. Initial plans called for an airship of 750 feet long and with a 3,000,000cu ft capacity, but since that would not have fitted into any existing shed a revised scheme called for an airship 695 feet long and 85$\frac{1}{2}$ feet in diameter, having 2,724,000cu ft capacity and 65 hours duration when cruising at 65mph. R-38 encountered numerous problems during flight trials and broke in two on 24 August 1921. As a result Cardington was on care and maintenance between 1921 and 1924.

Between 1923 and 1925 plans for the future of large rigid airships were further discussed, and the R-33 was reconditioned here before being test flown from Pulham. As a result of these trials the go-ahead was given for the R-100 and R-101. After its successful flight to Canada, the R-100 landed at Cardington, never to fly again.

Following the R-101 disaster, recrimination was bitter and prolonged, even extending to present times. Without airships what use was Cardington? In 1933 No 2 Aircraft Storage Unit was established here, and supplied aircraft to the RAF until 1938.

A new stage in Cardington's history was then highly visible. The military use of balloons was long established, and the mid-1930s idea was to fly enough to form a barrage forcing enemy bombers to fly high and thereby ruin their aiming; destruction of enemy aircraft colliding with a balloon cable would be a by-product. No detailed official appraisal seems to have been produced summarising the effectiveness of the barrage, although recent suggestions for barrages have been considered. An official report listed a likely total of fifty-three cable collisions by hostile aircraft over the United Kingdom between 3 September 1939 and 31 March 1941, resulting in twenty-four enemy aircraft crashing. Against this is a certain figure of ninety-one friendly aircraft hitting cables, causing thirty-eight to crash. The first enemy aircraft to be brought down was a He 111, which collided with a cable at Billingham on 20 June 1940, and the only ones to be brought down for certain in the Midlands were a Ju 88 near Coventry on 16 September 1940 and two He 111s, which collided with the Birmingham barrage on 31 March 1941 and 10 April 1941. An enemy aircraft that hit the Birmingham barrage on 31 July 1942 proceeded on its way.

*The intended passenger hotel and terminal for airship services. Plans to open it as a hotel have faded. The circular window framing resembled a ship's wheel.*

Many balloons were needed for a barrage, their testing, construction and storage being undertaken at Cardington. Just as important here was the production of vast quantities of hydrogen, something well provided for by the Cardington plant. SHQ Cardington formed on 15 December 1936, by which time the RAW had become the Balloon Development Establishment. On 9 January 1937 No 1 Balloon Training Unit formed to train personnel to control the barrage balloons and handle ground equipment. The ASU left in 1938 and the Research and Development Establishment joined the Balloon Development Unit.

Already Cardington was echoing to another facet that would etch itself into the memories of thousands, the sound of the tramp of boots, for in September 1937 No 2 RAF Depot moved in from Henlow. Its purpose was to provide basic indoctrination and training for RAF recruits who, instead of 'square bashing', could experience an alarmingly loud indoor variant in those huge hangars. Another intention was for No 2 Group Pool to form here, an idea abandoned on 1 January 1939. Control of the station instead passed from Training Command to Balloon Command, and over the next decade many balloons were test floated over the landing ground daily. No 2 RAF Depot remained under Training Command, and when war commenced the station became the main RAF recruit centre.

By October 1939 plans were complete for the release of swarms of Cardington-developed 10-foot-diameter 'M' balloons over Germany from bases in France. From the balloons would fall propaganda leaflets. More sinister were trials with balloons whose cables carried grenades, useful against enemy aircraft. Linkages, cables and ground equipment were all progressively modified to produce an active barrage. These activities were pursued by the Balloon Development Establishment here between November 1939 and August 1945.

Ever greater numbers of recruits joining the RAF at Cardington needed more medical personnel to ensure that they were fit for service, and more balloon handling squadrons also formed here. In July 1940 camouflage painting of the sheds was completed. No 26 Maintenance Unit formed out of No 26 EU on 10 February 1938 to service the balloons and their gas and equipment needs, and functioned until 15 April 1947. Cardington remained the base of No 2 Recruit Centre, and with it the Aircrew Medical Board, Central Trade Board and later a Selection Board. By the time No 1 Balloon Training Unit closed in 1943 more than 10,000 RAF and WAAF handlers had been trained, in addition to 12,000 balloon operators and drivers. Squadrons continued to form until August 1944, the final introductions being established to help counter flying bombs. Most of the training units moved out, then the station passed to Maintenance Command and 28 Group. That tramp of boots, though, continued to echo around the camp – No 2 RC was too firmly entrenched for it to march easily away.

From the Balloon Training Unit the Balloon Development Unit re-formed on 1 August 1945 under 12 Group Fighter Command. November 1945 brought the amalgamation of the Balloon Development Unit and the Training Aids Development Unit, resulting in a Research and Development Unit.

By May 1945 No 102 Personnel Despatch Centre had formed here, to demobilise wartime personnel. Call-up, induction and initial training of recruits would be events ever remembered by more than 250,000 people who joined the Service here where basic drill and discipline were generously meted out to more than 100,000 men and NCOs between 1936 and 1953.

On 15 April 1948 the RDU became the Balloon Unit, which moved to Hullavington on 31 October 1966. The Balloon Development Establishment (BDE) became the Research and Development Establishment in 1945,

*Advanced Technologies AT-10 G-AOTG at mooring on 24 March 2003.*

under the control of the Ministry of Supply, and later the Ministry of Technology. It became RAE (Cardington) under the control of MoD (PE) as an outstation of RAE Farnborough, and was concerned mainly with weather research. Hydrogen for its balloons was still provided by the Gas Factory established in early airship days to produce hydrogen by the 'steam-over-iron' process. Wartime needs for barrage balloons brought fast expansion, then, in 1948, the unit was named 279 MU, its task being to produce compressed gasses for the entire RAF. A similar unit at RAF Wellingborough joined 279 MU in 1955, the combination becoming 217 MU.

Since 1947 the Department of the Environment has had units here, the Driving Examiners' Establishment looking after the Department's needs for driving test examiners, and housed in excellent quarters far removed from the rows of wooden huts familiar to thousands of servicemen. No 2 Hangar has served as a Mechanical and Electrical Test Laboratory, carrying out trials connected with heating, vibration, ventilation and intruder alarm systems, while the Fire Research Unit tests such items as fire-resistant materials, and studies fire-fighting with the aid of full-sized structures built in the hangar. The Civil Engineering Laboratory, a branch of the Directorate of Civil Engineering Development, tests materials.

Balloons at Cardington in the 1980s were still of the Kite Balloon Mk XI and smaller Mk XV types used by RAE. The former was a version of the Low Zone Mk XI used in wartime barrages. The Meteorological Research Unit researched into the earth's boundary layer and recorded vertical profiles of temperature and fog.

BDE conducted research into the development of fabric adhesives, and was responsible for the development of inflatables such as the ML inflatable wing aircraft.

Apart from a small air rally, conventional flying has not taken place from Cardington for a very long period. Recent years have, however, witnessed periodic returns of airships to Cardington where a new breed developed. Hitherto, most commonly seen have been Goodyear ships like the Europa, 192 feet long, 45.92 feet in diameter, and 202,700cu ft capacity, a shadow of former giants, but a useful platform for advertising and filming.

Aerospace Development's AD500, built here and similar in size and layout, first flew in 1979 and was intended for use in under-developed countries. It suffered a common fate when, like Lord Ventry's small airship Bournemouth, it was damaged beyond repair in gusty conditions.

On 28 September 1981 the first flight of Airship Industries Skyship SKS 500, *G-BIHN*, took place. High hopes rested upon this 164.04-foot-long airship with its maximum diameter of 45.93 feet and a volume of 181,200cu ft. A 2-ton payload was coupled with a 600-mile range and a cruising speed of about 52 knots on a 120hp power rating. Helium-filled – which makes modern airships much safer – it had an unusual VTOL capability offered by employing two swivelling, ducted fans. Polyester-coated polyurethane formed the envelope and the crew and passengers occupied a one-piece plastic gondola.

In 1996 Airship Technologies arrived, a US company whose products are found around the world, having been in the airship business since 1972. It opened its No 2 Hangar Cardington base in June 2000 as the Advanced Technologies Group, and has diversified into diesel engines and UAVs. Its AT-10 airship first flew on 28 March 2002, and by spring 2003 was entering phase II of its trials, having flown for more than eighty hours. A special feature is the use of two vectored-thrust 100hp diesel engines, which promotes short take-off and landing. Moored alone, the AT-10 looks quite large. See it close to one of the hangars and its makes them look like the giants they are.

**Main features:**

For much of its existence Cardington has featured two enormous hangars visible for many miles, and workshop buildings for the Royal Airship Works, some of which remain near SHQ. The grass aerodrome remains but the mooring tower has long gone. In 1938 many wooden accommodation huts were erected on the northern part of the site for use by RAF recruits, who entered the Service here in vast numbers. Circular gas tanks have long been an obvious feature.

## CHALGROVE, Oxfordshire

*51°40N/01°04W, 230ft asl; SU635980. 10 miles SE of Oxford by the B480*

Nature greeted the arrival at Chalgrove of its occupying power with torrential rain, the Americans having come from Culham railway station. Welcoming them to Oxfordshire was

*Meteor III EE416, which was used for early ejector seat trials. (Martin Baker)*

the task of Chalgrove's Adjutant. On 23 November 1943 this muddy, desolate quagmire joined the RAF, the experience of HQ 70 Group's opening party being similar to others repeated at a number of new sites during that winter. By mid-January 1944 about 1,000 9th AF Americans had arrived to brighten the camp, but for the hapless RAF party there would soon be a miserable repeat performance at Kingston Bagpuize.

Chalgrove's first operational unit, the 30th PR Squadron USAAF, reached the airfield on 4 February 1944 when forty-five officers and 297 men moved in. As the Americans were sorting themselves out, two intrepid Englishmen, Fleet Air Arm pilot Sub Lieutenant Fellows and a Mr P Goodsir from Thame, enquired as to whether they might borrow the airfield to test model gliders built by International Model Aircraft, part of toy-maker Lines Brothers, widely known to pre-war aviation enthusiasts as the folk who produced the gorgeous 'Frog Penguins'. In a world of wood, they introduced superb replicas in plastic kit form of the aircraft of the day. Goodsir, the gliders' designer, needed runways for the testing of what were no model kits. Thame, where they worked, had no runways, so the resident RAF officer, Squadron Leader Monckton agreed and on 10 February 1944 two gliders arrived by road. Chalgrove was starting its career as a base for test flying – one glider was quickly erected and next morning a Defiant and a Martinet arrived to undertake towing. 'Little America' watched as in an international setting an unusual display commenced. After a lot of checking the combination was pronounced ready. Towing off a manned glider was never easy, and this was pilotless. Satisfied with his preliminary checks, Flt Sgt R Hitchin chanced his luck and the combination safely ascended. Getting back would not be easy, but a landing with the target glider in tow was also successfully accomplished. A second glider, having double the wing span of the first, was tested just as successfully. International Models were subsequently told to produce these gliders, which saw wartime and post-war service as towed targets and were tested from here beyond the end of hostilities.

Chalgrove's first operational aircraft had also arrived, an F-5 photo-reconnaissance variant of the twin-boom P-38 Lightning. On 15 February 1944 the band of the US 9th AF played as the British national anthem sounded and the RAF ensign was lowered. In its place was raised, doubtless to the suppressed satisfaction of the 'Brits', a much-torn Stars and Stripes, which fluttered to the strains of 'The Star Spangled Banner'. Chalgrove was now USAAF Station No 465. The 'Yanks' had come and the RAF opening party was free to leave.

Operational training was quickly initiated and directed to a singular purpose. Chalgrove would be the base from which photographic and visual reconnaissance of German forces in France would take place prior to and immediately following the Normandy landings. Information would be gathered to allow

*Meteor WL419,*
*photographed in 1990,*
*remains in use for ejector*
*seat trials.*

tactical attacks by 9th AF squadrons operating from East Anglia and southern England. On 21 February HQ 10th Photographic Group took control, and on 23 March the 31st Photographic Reconnaissance Squadron was established within the 10th. Six days later the 34th Squadron joined the Group, which was raised to full strength by the arrival on 27 April of the 33rd Squadron.

A variety of PR tasks were soon being undertaken, in particular low-level operations. Photographs were thus secured of enemy airfields and especially coastal defences and ports prior to the Normandy landings. Damage assessment material was gathered following 9th AF attacks on airfields, marshalling yards, bridges and tactical targets, allowing Marauder crews to view the effectiveness of their operations. The 10th's low-level 232-sortie photo survey of the enemy coast from Blankenburg to Dunkirk – a strongly defended zone – and from Le Touquet to St Vaast-la-Houge, undertaken between 6 and 20 May 1944, won a Distinguished Unit Citation. On 6 June the 10th Photo Group held fifty-four F-5s, thirty-eight fully serviceable, with some F-3s, F-6s and light liaison aircraft sharing the base.

Once the Allies were ashore in France, the 10th concentrated upon photographing enemy troop concentrations, bridges, artillery posts, road and rail junctions, airfields and targets about which it was necessary to be well informed. Such intelligence gathering was essential for neutralising resistance during the break-out from the Normandy beach-head towards St Lo.

On 27 June 1944 the 15th Tactical Reconnaissance Squadron transferred from the 67th Tactical Reconnaissance Group to the 10th, bringing P-51s and F-6s to Chalgrove. They were replacing the 30th PR Squadron, which, on 9 June 1944, had at Middle Wallop joined the 67th Tactical Reconnaissance Group. As soon as the advance was well under way, the 10th packed its bags and in mid-August moved quickly to an airfield near Rennes. Chalgrove's main operational span was ended. It had nevertheless played a vital part in the invasion of France, and now came under the control of the US IXth Troop Carrier Command.

Contraction of USAAF PR units in March 1945 resulted in the 7th Photographic Group (Reconnaissance) moving in from Mount Farm. On 26 March P-51s and F-5s of the 22nd PR Squadron arrived, followed by the 14th Squadron on 2 April and the 13th on 8 April, then the 27th, which returned from France on 22 April as the European war entered its final phase.

New tasks commenced after the ceasefire as a Europe ravaged by bombing and ground fighting was photographed to allow overall viewing of the plight of its people. That work was undertaken from here until mid-October 1945 when the 7th Group split. The 13th Squadron moved to Grove on 13 October while the 14th and 22nd Squadrons left for Villacoublay. The 27th Squadron vacated Chalgrove for Germany on 14 October 1945, but not until December did Group HQ vacate the airfield.

Between 6 August and November 1945 Chalgrove used Mosquito PR VXIs of the 653rd Bomb Squadron, removed from the 25th Bomb Group in August 1944 to provide weather reconnaissance data for the 9th AF. On 21 November 1945 the 7th Reconnaissance Group was de-activated at Chalgrove, its squadrons being posted overseas.

With the USAAF gone, the station came under Benson's control, and very soon a new phase in its history unfolded. Martin Baker Ltd of Denham was concentrating upon the development of ejector seats and, in need of a base from which to fly the aircraft used in seat trials, obtained an agreement allowing the use of part of Chalgrove. Testing involved ejections from Meteors, one of which, on 24 July 1946, when flying over the airfield at 320 knots at 8,600 feet, was used by company employee Mr Bernard Lynch, who volunteered to make the first live ejection from a Martin Baker ejector seat, and the first in the UK. He also ejected from Meteor III EE416 on 19 August 1947 using the first production seat. Success resulted in orders for its installation in RAF and RN fighter aircraft.

On 8 July 1946 remnants of 8 OTU, which trained pilots and observers for the RAF's photo-reconnaissance squadrons, arrived at Chalgrove to share it with the civilians. When 8 OTU left in October 1946, post-war reductions had brought the strength down to three Spitfire XIs and two Mosquito PR 34s. Subsequently Benson-based PR aircraft made use of the station for continuation training.

Chalgrove is still Martin Baker's test airfield, and perhaps even more astonishing is still the home of two modified Meteors, WA638 and WL419, which continue to play an almost unsung yet vitally important part in ejector seat development. The Company's Dove and, until 1981, Dakota kept them company. The modified Meteors permit test ejections to a speed of 450 knots. A well-maintained runway and perimeter track, a T2 hangar and a few buildings remain, and if your luck is in you can still see and hear the unmistakable sight and sound of a Gloster Meteor helping to develop the means whereby already over a thousand lives have been saved.

**Main features:**
*Runways:* 140° 6,000ft x 150ft, 250° 4,200ft x 150ft, 190° 4,200ft x 150ft, tarmac on concrete. *Hangars:* two T2. *Hardstandings:* fifty loop type. *Accommodation:* USAAF officers 364, EM 2,193.

## CHEDDINGTON, Buckinghamshire

*51°50N/00°40W 94 ft asl; SP905160. 7 miles ENE of Aylesbury*

On 15 March 1942 Cheddington opened as the satellite of No 26 OTU Wing. The first four aircraft – Ansons – moved in on 22 March 1942, and began training flights on 26 March. Two new Flights of the OTU, 'B' and 'C', formed here on 31 March 1942, and Wellington Ics then began arriving, both types using the station until 3 September 1942. Transfer to the 8th USAAF came on 7 September, when Cheddington was placed under the administration of Bovingdon, Little Horwood replacing Cheddington as 26 OTU's satellite. Four days after the Americans took control the 44th Bomb Group arrived and stayed into October. Return to the RAF and 92 Group took place on 31 December, Wellingtons of 26 OTU briefly using the station during February 1943. Hotspur gliders and Master II tugs of 2 GTS spent seven weeks here before work started in March 1943 to improve Cheddington. Flying was still possible – indeed, on 13 April 1943 eleven Wellingtons were detached from Little Horwood for a five-day stay, and sundry other aircraft called, among them three B-17s on 27 April. Next day Sqn Ldr H C Todd took command of the station, whence personnel from Bovingdon were transferred. During May 1943 No 4263 Anti-Aircraft Flight briefly resided here, and on 15 May more Bovingdon B-17s called.

On 17 July 1943 No 1139 MP Company arrived. The Americans seemed ever a part of Cheddington, as on 25 July when B-24 240801 made an emergency landing. Next day Wellington X3399 of 26 OTU with starboard engine trouble landed, its pilot mistaking the airfield for Wing. The 'Wimpey' overshot and belly flopped near the D/F station.

Conversion of the airfield into USAAF Station 113 took place on 16 August 1943, and the 2nd Combat Crew Replacement Centre, providing crews for the 2nd Air Division, was established here, a role performed until the summer of 1944. Earlier that year additional crew training units had arrived and in February 1944 Cheddington came under the control of the US 8th USAAF Composite Command.

A change to specialised night operations followed the arrival, on 19 June, of the 858th Bomb Squadron (H), flying B-24s brought from North Pickenham. It at once commenced operations, continuing to do so until 4 August 1944. Next day the squadron joined the 492nd Bomb Group, and on 10 August moved to Harrington where the 406th Bomb Squadron (H) came, followed by its sister squadron, No 36. Both under the 8th USAAF Composite Command, were switched to the 8th USAAF Fighter Command on 1 October 1944, then to the 1st Air Division on 1 January 1945, flying night special duty and leaflet dropping sorties. The 36th returned to Harrington on 28 February 1945, followed by the 406th on 16 March.

Variety was certainly prevalent here, for next in were P-47C/DSs of the 551st and 552nd Squadrons, and the 495th Training Group, which came from Atcham and stayed only until June 1945. No 91 Group Bomber Command repossessed the station and returned it to 26 OTU on 12 July

1945. Four days later No 1 Overseas Packing Unit opened, together with the Road Vehicle Disposal Unit, which handled vehicles for public auction. From 1 February 1946 a variety of equipment arrived from the Vehicle Disposal Unit, Hinton-in-the-Hedges, but all vehicle work ceased on 20 February 1946. The packing unit moved to RAF Drayton, vacating the station by 20 March 1946, by which time the seventy-five RAF and sixty-five WAAF personnel domiciled here worked either at the Meteorological Signals Centre, Dunstable, or the Medical Training Establishment and Depot, Halton. Cheddington passed to Technical Training Command control at the end of April 1946, ending its RAF days in February 1948. Between that date and 1978 part of the site was used by the War Department for special purposes.

**Main features:**
*Runways:* 200° 4,200ft x 150ft, 140° 4,200ft x 150ft, 260° 1,800ft x 150ft, concrete with wood chips. *Hangars:* four T2. *Hardstandings:* thirty-seven loop type. *Accommodation:* USAAF officers 558, EM 1,993.

---

## CHELVESTON, Northamptonshire

*51°8N/00°32W 292ft asl; TLO15685. 4 miles NE of Rushden*

Construction of an RAF bomber station at Chelveston started in 1940, hence the inclusion of a J Type hangar, supplemented by two T2s. On 15 August 1941 Fg Off J B Townsend and ten men of No 2 Group took the station into RAF hands. After being passed to 8 Group, which handled administration of new bomber stations, it functioned under Polebrook control until 2 September 1941, when it separated and became self-accounting with its own Station HQ. Extension of the main runway to 2,000 yards was completed in late March 1942, the other two remaining at 1,400 yards. Installation of *Drem* lighting was still under way when in December 1941 the Central Gunnery School arrived here as a lodger unit until Sutton Bridge was ready. Chelveston's future was obvious after Air Vice-Marshal Alan Lees brought General Eaker USAAF to view the station.

Before any Americans moved in, the new runway saw use for glider trials by the Airborne Forces Experimental Establishment. Their advance party arrived on 5 May 1942, initially to explore the Stirling's suitability as a Horsa tug. A variety of glider trials followed, and not without incident. A Hotspur broke up in the air, the crew being lucky to escape, and on 19 July 1942 the half-scale Hamilcar, on tow behind a Stirling, made an emergency landing at Thurleigh.

Other landings pointed more to Chelveston's future. On 10 June the 12th Troop Carrier Squadron USAAF arrived, and next day the 10th and 11th Squadrons, all part of the 60th Troop Carrier Group. Between 20 and 28 July forty-eight C-47 Skytrains – Dakotas to the British – arrived here and the Americans took on the responsibility of running the station, even to the extent of feeding to the RAF personnel a diet that astonished them.

Tenure of the tan-coloured transports was brief. On 7 August 1942 the 60th TCG, moving to Aldermaston, made way for B-17Fs, the latest Flying Fortresses, which began arriving on 9 August, nineteen of them crewed by the 352nd and 419th Squadrons, 301st Bomb Group, US 8th USAAF. Seven more, of the 353rd Squadron, touched down on 16 August. That was the day when testing started of the amazing-looking Twin Hotspur glider, whose two fuselages were to carry twice the normal load. Another eight B-17Fs flew in on the 26th, the 352nd and 419th Squadrons soon being fully equipped. During August glider testing centring upon the giant Hamilcar tank carrier was switched to Newmarket Heath. Some 352nd Squadron B-17s temporarily lodged at Podington to allow battle training to start, then on 2 September the Group's assets assembled at Chelveston.

The 301st Group commenced operations on 5 September 1942, five crews of the 352nd and seven of the 419th Bomb Squadrons setting off for the engine sheds at Rouen. One crew of each squadron aborted, leaving the rest to attack, after which bomb plots showed poor aiming. Next day thirteen B-17s made a diversionary raid on St Omer/Longunesse; one crew mistook Fort Rouge as the target, while another bombed rail yards at Abbeville. When fourteen crews of the two squadrons were sent to attack Schiedam Docks at Rotterdam on 7 September, the Group's first kill, a Fw 190, was confirmed. All four squadrons operated together for the first time on 26 September, but poor weather bought confusion and recall. On 14 September 1942 the 301st was switched to the XIIth AF, although it remained operating with the 8th.

On 2 October 1942 the Potez Meaulte factory was attacked by eighteen of the twenty-five crews of

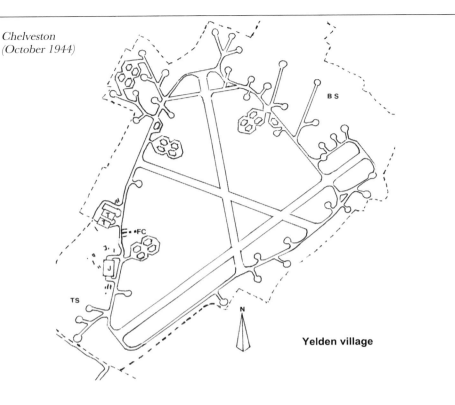

*Chelveston*
*(October 1944)*

**Yelden village**

## CHELVESTON

Depicted is the basic layout at Chelveston in October 1944. It was planned in late 1939 as a bomber station, having a single metal Aircraft Shed Type 'J' (12705/40) of Errol construction (J) instead of the two featured by its immediate predecessors. Their more elaborate buildings were also largely superseded by a range of fast-to-construct Temporary Brick buildings supplemented by an assortment of other temporary buildings, later examples being partly pre-fabricated. Of the 186 listed items as being on the No 1 Site (Airfield), fifty-two were Temporary Brick buildings, many of them latrines and ablutions to 1940 designs. Station HQ (14850/40) was of similar construction, like the 15596/40 Operations Block, SHQ (14850/40), Main Stores (14981/40), and Main Workshops (14982/40), all situated within the Technical Site (TS) area. The MT Section buildings were of brick, and 5,000 gallons of petrol were stored underground. Also on the Technical Site were metal Nissen huts, one, 24 feet long, serving as the Briefing Room. Another three were used as Air Ministry Works Standard Stores.

In 1941 flying control towers were becoming standard features, their design reflecting local layout and topography. Chelveston's Type 518/40 (FC) was brick-built. Funnel approaches led to the beacon projected beam approach system.

Two metal Aircraft Sheds Type T2 (3654/42) supplemented the 'J' Type. Aviation spirit, initially held in two 70,000-gallon underground tanks (11574/40) fed by an underground pipeline, was later supplemented with two additional tanks, one added in 1944.

On No 1 Site, Airmen's Quarters were in Laing huts. Small buildings from a wide assortment of manufacturers and in varying styles were also to be found. Within such diversity were Romney huts, timber buildings and others of plasterboard, corrugated iron, asbestos and of SECO design.

Triple runways were imposed during 1941 and available by opening time. Details of the saga leading to runway introduction in Bomber Command may be found in *Action Stations Revisited No 1*. Bomb Stores (BS) was situated in an area known as Top Gorse.

the 301st who were engaged by a strong group of Fw 190s, three of which they claimed to destroy without loss. Then came participation on 9 October in the largest USAAF raid so far, against the Fives-Lille steel and engineering works, to which the Group contributed twenty-three aircraft drawn from all four squadrons. Of these, eighteen attacked. An RAF ASR launch rescued the crew of one that force-landed about a mile off the North Foreland, the first such successful rescue involving a B-17 crew. Another force-landed in East Anglia and two were damaged in exchange for the possible destruction of ten German fighters. The Lille raid of 8 November 1942 proved to be the last before the 301st moved to North Africa. Before departure, on 13 November, the Squadron was honoured with a visit by HM King George VI, making his first visit to the 8th AF, arriving with Generals Spaatz and Longfellow.

The next red letter day was 6 December 1942, when the 305th Bomb Group began to move in from Grafton Underwood, whose runways needed attention. Leading the Group was the soon to be famous Colonel Curtis LeMay, whose command extended to 18 May 1943. Immediately after arrival the Group prepared to operate its four Squadrons, the 364th, 365th, 366th and 422nd. They were briefed for Lille, but bad weather caused postponement. When the attack was launched the sixteen aircraft altered course too soon to bomb, and Fw 190s brought down a B-17. Next they were pitted unsuccessfully against Romilly-sur-Seine, an operation repeated on 20 December when twenty-two B-17s of the four squadrons operated.

Tactics employed in daylight bombing needed to be well thought out, a task particularly pursued by LeMay. Not all of this tough man's ideas met with approval. In December a large-scale trial used Horsham St Faith as primary target and Cambridge as secondary, and fighters explored escort tactics with the bombers. Ideas formulated were tested on 30 December when twenty-four B-17s of the 305th took part in an attack on Lorient's Keroman shipyards. Only thirteen bombed and claimed six enemy fighters, which were engaged after the bombers had faced ferocious AA fire during their tightly packed run-in. Enemy fighters forced a B-17 into the sea, and damaged two, one limping into St Eval and showing what could happen to anyone who broke formation. Some P-38s placed at Chelveston in January 1943 assisted in the exploration of fighter tactics.

On 3 January 1943 the target for twenty-two crews was the torpedo station at St Nazaire, part of the attack of eighty-five B-17s led by the 305th to try out a staggered formation. Heavy flak damaged half the entire force. Formation was held on the run-in, the 305th claiming three enemy fighters. Lille was raided on 13 January and Brest on the 23rd, then the Group took the great plunge, the first raid on Germany. With the weather fine on the 27th, the raid, led by Thurleigh's 306th Bomb Group, was ordered, and eighteen B-17s from Chelveston participated in this first American B-17 attack on Germany. Cloud prevented bombing of the primary aiming point, so the formation bombed its secondary in the naval dockyard at Wilhelmshaven. There was also cloud there, and bombing spread beyond the target. The 422nd lost B-17F 124623, last seen in the target area, and the only B-17 missing on this historic occasion.

The next milestone was the Emden raid of 4 February 1943 in which seventeen crews of the 305th took part. The weather was poor, pin-points impossible to find, and the raid cost two 305th crews. Bad weather also resulted in recall as the bombers headed for a Hamm attack on 14 February. Vegesack was bombed by seventeen crews on 18 March 1943, and very accurate results were obtained by the 305th when Lorient was bombed on 16 April. The 305th's hardest fight so far came the following day when twenty-eight B-17s left Chelveston for the Focke-Wulf factory at Bremen, and opposition was plentiful. This came at the end of the first phase of B-17 operations, for Chelveston was handed over by the RAF to American control in April, coming under the command of Brigadier General Anderson.

By the end of May 1943 the 305th had a champion twenty-mission B-17F in hand, *Wham Bam,* and the 305th had won a Distinguished Unit Citation for its courage during the Paris raid of 4 April. During the second half of 1943 the Group was to penetrate deeply into enemy territory, attack a nitrate works in Norway, industrial targets in Berlin, the Merseburg oil refinery, and shipping at Gdynia. An interesting and initial departure from such operations came when the 422nd Squadron switched to night-bombing operations between 8 September and 4 October 1943 during the *Starkey* invasion feint period. Ten days later the 305th suffered decimation, losing thirteen aircraft during the infamous Schwemfurt raid of 14 October. Assembly in cloudy conditions over Britain had placed the Group in the wrong position within the 1st AD, laying it wide open to savage fighter attack. Between 7 October 1943 and 24 June 1944 the 422nd Squadron carried out night leaflet dropping over Germany.

Evidence of the horrific experiences faced by crews during operations was abundantly clear on 20 February 1944. First in the 305th to be awarded the Medal of Honor was 1st Lieutenant W R Lawley. A head-on fighter attack set fire to one of his B-17's engines, and Lawley was seriously wounded, together with seven more of the crew. Bombs remained aboard the aircraft, the co-pilot was dead, and the crew too badly injured to bale out. As Lawley nursed the aircraft homewards enemy fighters set another engine on fire. Then the crew managed to jettison the bomb load, but Lawley soon collapsed, having lost much blood. Mason, another crew member, took control until Lawley revived just in time to land the Fortress at Redhill.

On 11 April 1944 it was 1st Lieutenant E S Michael who showed courage in a situation similar to that encountered by Lawley. His B-17, *Bertie Lee,* hit during a head-on attack, spun down followed by fighters. Both pilots and others were wounded, and part of the burning incendiary load could not be jettisoned. The crew baled out apart from the pilots and the wounded bomb-aimer. Then the bombs were crew jettisoned and cloud cover was found. Very weak, Michael nevertheless revived sufficiently to land the battered aircraft and was awarded the Medal of Honor.

During the run-up to D-Day, the 305th attacked airfields, V-sites and, following the invasion, tactical targets. They supported the St Lo break-out and the airborne landings at Arnhem. The 422nd Squadron, using *H2X,* adopted a pathfinder role during day-bombing operations between 22 March and 23 May 1944. Since October 1943 the 305th had operated as a three-squadron Group, but in June 1944 the 422nd resumed a mainstream bomber role and recommenced bombing on 6 July 1944 by raiding V-1 launch sites. When operations ended on 25 April 1945 337 raids had been despatched. Instead of returning to the USA in late July 1945 the 305th assumed garrison duties in Belgium, leaving Chelveston to be taken over by the RAF in October 1945, when it became a satellite for 25 MU before being switched to care and maintenance. In 1951 a small area served the 300-man RAF radio equipment unit.

During 1952 the rebuilt main runway was extended to 9,000 feet for B-45s, an overrun taking it to almost 11,000 feet. On 1 December 1952 the USAF took control after the arrival of the 7523rd Air Base Squadron (ABS). The 7523rd Supply Squadron formed on 1 January 1954 and disbanded on 1 September 1954. On 1 November 1955 the base was transferred from the Third AF to the Seventh Air Division, SAC, and the 3914th Air Base Group, SAC, ran what was now a SAC Stand-by Base.

From late 1958 to mid-1959 RB-47s of the 301st SRW Reflex Force rotated through Chelveston, the 3914th functioning from 1 January 1959 as a Combat Support Group. That was inactivated in September 1959 when the base was returned to the Third AF and administered by the 7541st ABS.

On 25 August 1959 the 10th Tactical Reconnaissance Wing arrived as a result of *Red Richard,* bringing RB-66Cs (and initially some WB-66Ds) of the 42nd Tactical Reconnaissance Squadron (red trim), whose aircraft carried electronic jammers. From the 47th BW thirteen B-66Bs, carrying *Brown Cradle* ECM in their bomb bays, were received, this stand-off jammer being used to protect fighters. In their tail cones the 66s carried Type 113 ECM jammers and chaff dispensers. The 42nd remained until March 1962, when it moved to Toul AB, France. The 7541st ABS disbanded in August 1962 when Chelveston was reduced to DOB status before return to the UK on 19 June 1964. On 1 January 1967 it returned to the AFE for use as a storage annexe under the 7518th Supply Squadron (redesignated CSS on 15 April 1967). Chelveston was retained for use as a family housing annexe for Alconbury personnel, and since 1959 the Americans have had a small enclave wherein a microwave relay station exists administered by AFCS. The RAF maintains a presence, but the long runway has been attacked by demolition workers. A hangar remains.

**Main features:**
*Runways:* 060° 6,000ft x 150ft, 180° 4,167ft x 150ft, 120° 3,600ft x 150ft, concrete and tarmac. *Hangars:* one J Type (all other buildings temporary), two T2. *Hardstandings:* fifty loop type. *Accommodation:* USAAF officers 421, EM 2,473.

## CHIPPING NORTON, Oxfordshire

*51°55N/01°31W 690ft asl; SP325255. 2 miles SSE of Chipping Norton by the B4026*

Chipping Norton's name derives from the medieval word Chepynge, meaning a long narrow market place central to this hamlet. Of the enhanced RLG, little remains.

Chipping Norton became active on 10 July 1940 when Headquarters 15 SFTS arrived, accompanied by Oxfords of the Advanced Training Squadron (ATS). Both needed a home because 10 Group had nudged them out of Middle Wallop.

Three grass runways were marked out in July 1940, the overshoot featuring a disturbing drop away to the south-west. Two Bellman hangars and a few wooden huts formed the technical section, personnel living in a line of bell tents in a corner. Stores and messing arrangements were by the B4026 road, and mains water was drawn from a temporary link with Chipping Norton's supply. All electricity was generated at the camp.

July 1940 saw 15 SFTS begin to re-equip with Harvard 1s, twenty of which arrived here by the end of the month, joining twenty-seven Oxfords on site and the remains of R6266, which had crashed into stationary Oxford N4580, causing both to burn. Three days later Oxford P1890 collided with N6326 over Charlbury with literally shattering results. HQ 15 SFTS now occupied Oldner, Chipping Norton, about a mile north of the aerodrome.

On 2 August 1940 the school was informed that it was to be consolidated at Kidlington, with the ATS remaining at Chipping Norton. A return of 31 August 1940 showed forty-one Harvards and fifteen Oxfords based here, the former being desperately used for training fighter pilots. Headquarters moved to Kidlington on 1 October 1940, and on 13 October Chipping Norton came into use as Kidlington's RLG. The enemy called on 29/30 October, incendiaries falling nearby. High-explosive bombs fell a mile to the east on 5/6 November.

The end of 1940 saw Kidlington's RLG provision reconsidered, and in February 1941 this RLG was completely released from 15 SFTS use. Since 16 November 1940 it had served 6 SFTS Little Rissington, whose Oxfords used the RLG particularly for night-flying. The Luftwaffe welcomed 6 SFTS by placing several HEs on the landing ground on 18/19 November 1940.

Extended facilities constructed in 1941-42 included a Watch Office (pattern 13726/41) and an instruction site to the rear of the technical area. Four Over Type 69-foot Blister hangars and a single 65-foot Over Type now supplemented the Bellman hangars, and two Sommerfeld runways were laid on QDMs 11/29 and 04/22. Unusually, the perimeter track only partially circled the field. Sub Site 1 held the engine repair facilities, general maintenance, servicing and stores buildings, while on Site 2 were found the ground staff room and flight offices. Dormitory huts (2965/42) and ablutions were found at Site 5.

On 1 April 1942 6 SFTS was renamed No 6 (Pilots) Advanced Flying Unit, which made use of Chipping Norton (upgraded to satellite status by 1944) until mid-July 1945. From mid-November 1942 until 22 May 1945 No 1517 BATF (affiliated to No 6 (P)AFU) operated out of Chipping Norton. During October 1945 No 265 MU, Kidlington, placed some of its equipment at Chipping Norton, the site being disposed of in the early 1950s.

**Main features:**
*Landing ground runs:* 117° 3,030ft, 064° 2,280ft, farm buildings prominent on centre south side. *Hangars:* two Bellman on north side, ten 65ft Blisters. *Accommodation:* RAF 110 officers, 208 SNCOs, 886 ORs; WAAF 4 officers, 3 SNCOs, 180 ORs.

## CHIPPING ONGAR, Essex

*51°43W/00°17E 65ft asl; TO585055. 2 miles NE of Chipping Ongar*

Typically a mid-war temporary operational airfield, Chipping Ongar was built with one purpose in mind, to house a tactical bomber Group of the USAAF, which materialised as the 387th BG flying B-26B/Cs. The Group came to Britain aboard the *Queen Mary,* and began to move into the new airfield on 21 June 1943. Assigned to the 3rd BW, 8th ASC, the Group had trained for low-level attack, but for the B-26 that had proven disastrous. A new training scheme was introduced whereby the B-26 Marauders would operate in formations basically of eighteen, and at a medium level, carrying our carpet bombing of mainly tactical targets. The 387th flew its first mission on 15 August 1943, but further plans took it into the 9th AF on 16 October 1943, by which time it had operated twenty-nine times. Its last 8th AF raid was mounted on 9 October, the main targets being airfields.

The second operational phase, again involving tactical bombing formation attacks, extended to 18 July 1944, then the Group advanced first to Stoney Cross and, in August 1944, to France. In the winter of 1943-44 it carried out attacks on V-1 sites, and during the so-called 'Big Week' of 20-25 February 1944 bombed the airfields at Leeuwarden and Venlo. In the weeks just before D-Day it concentrated upon bridges and coastal batteries, and on 6 June carried out attacks on German coastal defences in Normandy. In the following weeks the targets were railways, bridges, defiles, POL depots and road junctions. By moving south the Group was better placed to support the break-out from St Lo.

Chipping Ongar had played its part and after the Marauders left was used as a support airfield for the forces in France. During October 1944 it did have an interesting occupant, part of No 1426 Enemy Aircraft Flight from Wittering, which visited USAAF fighter bases nearby. Closure came in 1945 and the site was sold in 1947.

**Main features:**
*Runways:* 030° 6,000ft x 150ft, 090° 4,200ft x 150ft, 150° 4,200ft x 150ft, concrete with wood chip surface. *Hangars:* one T2. *Hardstandings:* fifty loop type. *Accommodation:* USAAF officers 443, EM 2,327.

---

## CHIPPING WARDEN, Northamptonshire

*52°08N/01°16W, 457ft asl; SP495495. 6 miles NE of Banbury*

"There's plenty at Chipping Warden – it's on care and maintenance."

That 'plenty' meant asset-stripping to improve comfort in huts at Wellesbourne. A working party set forth to snatch good linoleum from buildings at Chipping Warden, leaving bare concrete floors. By such methods in the late 1940s was the route to bare site disposal followed.

Constructed to 1940 plans, Chipping Warden, with one Type J hangar (5836/39), typified ideas at the time of its birth. Three T2s (8254/40) and later a fourth were added, together with additional maintenance facilities, to temporary brick buildings. As usual two standard 72,000-gallon aviation fuel tanks and a 500-gallon oil tank were underground. The high-level water tower (14285/40) held 60,000 gallons.

The station completion date repeatedly slipped. It was incomplete when 12 OTU advance party arrived from Benson on 10 July 1941, followed on 23 July by the Mount Farm echelon. Night-flying commenced on 24 July 1941.

Chipping Warden opened for general flying on 1 August 1941 under 6 Group control. A Flight of 12 OTU became operational on 15 August 1941, and the fully assembled OTU Wellingtons and Ansons on 1 September. Turweston and Edgehill were available for additional flying training.

The early hours of 12 October 1941 brought the station its first German visitor, intruding upon Wellingtons' night-flying. Eight small HEs and a container of incendiaries slightly damaged two Wellingtons.

In mid-November 1941 the station prepared for aircraft diverted during night-bombing operations. Up to twenty crews could be accommodated. On 16 December a Lysander, nucleus for a drogue TT flight, joined two Wellington Ics modified to tow sleeve targets, all three temporarily placed in No 5 Navigation Flight. January 1942 saw 1517 BAT Flight's eight Oxfords join 12 OTU's 40 plus 14 Wellingtons, 14 plus 4 Ansons and target-towing aircraft. Single-pilot manning for Wellingtons came in March, crew composition changing to pilot-observer/bomb-aimer and wireless-operator/air-gunner.

For the 30/31 May 1,000 Plan Cologne raid, twenty-two Wellingtons set off from Chipping Warden, all returning safely. Next they took part in the Essen raid of 1 June, and on 25/26 June, of twenty Wellingtons despatched to attack Bremen, four did not return. L8800, flown by Sergeant Bagley, ditched 25 miles east of Cromer due to a damaged fuel pipe; two and a half hours later a minesweeper rescued the crew. Pilot Officer Cowsill's DV952 was attacked near Wilhelmshaven by a Ju 88; the Wellington's tail-gunner opened fire and the attacker spun away, glowing red, and was claimed as a probable victory. Flt Lt Kerwan evaded another Ju 88 45 miles north-west of Bremen.

On 13 June 1942 Chipping Warden acquired Gaydon as its satellite, retained until that station's transfer to 22 OTU Wellesbourne on 1 September 1942. By then 12 OTU had re-armed with Wellington IIIs, the first arriving in July. The Anson flight disbanded in August and a separate Gunnery and TT Flight formed.

On 31 July 1942 12 OTU took part in a *Grand National*, one of a series in which OTUs supplemented the main force as in the 1,000 Plan raids. The thirteen Wellingtons, including Mk IIIs, set off for Dusseldorf carrying mixed incendiary and 500lb HE loads. About 40 miles east of Nordland the tail-gunner of N2856 'T-Tommy' spotted a Ju 88, which closed, guns blazing. The Wellington's tail-gunner accurately poured his shots into a soon burning foe. On 16 September 1942 nine Wellingtons, two of which did not return, set out for Essen. From one, badly shot about, the rear-gunner baled out before the blazing bomber crash-landed. 'A' Flight 12 OTU moved to Turweston on 23 November 1942, instructors training Wellington crews while 12 OTU's dedicated satellite remained under construction.

On 24 November 1942 a flash bomb ignited in the chute of Wellington BK261 and exploded, killing the entire crew; the wreckage fell near Shotteswell, Oxfordshire. Another horrendous accident unfolded at midday on 1 December 1942. Sergeant McMurchy's BK250 was taking off when a crosswind gust forced it off the runway. Out of control, it headed towards the fire tender bay. McMurchy steered it clear and away from a group of civilians, but it smashed into the control tower, hit a civilian car then hurled itself on to a hangar, which erupted in flames. Ambulancemen and the medical officer were quickly on the spot and found the crew badly burned, two civilians dead and frantic efforts being made to extricate the control tower staff from burning offices. Casualties totalled twenty-four, including two severely burned crew members. The geodetic construction conferred great strength, and the Wellington's fabric covering burned fiercely, always making crew extrication difficult.

Leaflet drops over Roubaix on 28 November 1942 by four Wellingtons marked a return to operational flying. Another quartet visited Orleans on 22/23 December 1942, 12 OTU thereafter periodically participating in leaflet dropping on French towns. Plans made for further acceptance of 'cuckoos' (aircraft diverting from home bases) were first enacted on 4 February 1943 when a 4 Group Wellington landed from Lorient and two Halifaxes from Turin. Such activity thereafter increased. Edgehill, the station's new satellite, was taken over from 21 OTU on 12 April 1943. Next day two of the Unit's newly acquired three Martinets were lost, HP372 crashing near Bicester and HP373 overturning during a forced landing.

Both Flights of 12 OTU then at Turweston moved into Edgehill on 27 April, establishing Unit disposition for the rest of the war. Wellington conversion flying took place at Edgehill, leaving operational flying training to be given by two Flights at the parent station. Leaflet dropping (*Nickelling*) over France, *Bullseyes* and ASR searches followed.

When four Wellingtons left to *Nickel* in the Rennes area on 13/14 July 1943, Wg Cdr Bray crossed into France some way off track. He altered course for the Mortain-Domfront area, 50 miles north-east of Rennes, and at about 0120hrs at 16,500 feet, heavy predicted flak burst immediately below his aircraft, damaging the port mainplane and engine. Bray turned for home, re-crossing the French coast at his point of entry. Heavy flak making the Wellington impossible to handle, there was no choice but to ditch. The crew, including Bray with a broken nose and Fg Off Parkinson with broken ribs, managed to scramble into their dinghy in which they were afloat for three hours before rescue came.

More *Nickels* followed, and during August 1943 the first Wellington X arrived. Wellington IIIs were used as bombers when 12 OTU raided the Fôret de Hesdin and Fôret de Raismes in the Pas de Calais during the run-up to operation *Starkey*. Such raids took place over five nights.

Another memorable incident involved Stirling R9249 of 1657 CU, ordered to land at Chipping Warden because of bad weather during the night of 22/23 October 1943. In heavy continuous rain the crew mistook the perimeter track for a runway, and during landing approach the bomber clipped a tree, then rooftops in Aston le Walls before crashing and burning. Four of the crew were killed.

The final active months of 1943 saw leaflets dropped upon Chartres, Versailles, Melun, Montagris, Cambrai, St Quentin and other areas. There were *Bullseyes* too, during one of which, on 22 December 1943, 12 OTU's contingent became enmeshed with German bombers over the London area.

Further *Nickels*, each time by four aircraft, took place over northern France on 14/15 January 1944, 8/9 February and 2/3 March, at which time Chipping Warden was frequently receiving 'cuckoos'. On 24 March the OTU first dropped *Window* during a special exercise. Even more eventful was the seven-crew operation on 24/25 April 1944 during which the gunner in LP456 opened fire on an unidentified aircraft with unobserved results. That night Wellington III BK542 was missing in uncertain circumstances after being last seen losing height over the North Sea. *Bullseyes*, *Erics* and *Nickels* continued, leaflet drops taking place around Cherbourg on 15/16 May, following the loss of Wellington LP155 on 4 May when there was enemy activity off Portsmouth. *Nickels* became fewer as the available area became limited, although on 13/14 August four sorties took the Wellingtons to Chalons, La Roche, Charlette and Monteuil/Bellay.

By the start of 1945 there were fewer personnel on courses, making it increasingly difficult to meet commitments. Training flights over France were more safely undertaken, and there were still diversions, as on 8/9 April 1945 when fifteen Lancasters of 415 Squadron and two others landed from Hamburg and Lutzkendorf. Brief, totally unexpected 'excitement' came early on 4 March 1945 when an enemy aircraft (possibly an Me 410) came in low and fast aiming three short bursts of cannon fire at the airfield. The Pundit light was on, but there was neither damage nor casualties. No 12 OTU was by now flying only Wellington Xs, Oxfords, Hurricane IIs and Master IIs, the two latter types for gunnery training.

On 1 June 1945 the last cross-country detail was flown by Flying Officer Begg and crew in Wellington X LN158. Over the next few days Master IIs and Hurricanes – based at Edgehill until vacated on 7 June 1945 – were disposed of. By the end of the month all that was left of 12 OTU's bomber force were two Wellingtons, NC971 awaiting disposal and LP648 awaiting repair. The OTU closed on 14 June 1945.

Chipping Warden then left Bomber Command and joined 25 Group Flying Training Command, and was cared for by a party from Harwell until August 1945, when an assortment of Wellingtons and Ansons of 10 ANS arrived for a stay until Swanton Morley was, in November 1945, ready for it. No 1517 BAT Flight, lodging here since 1942, and whose eight Oxfords were used mainly by 6 SFTS/6 (P)AFU, disbanded on 17 December 1945.

On 31 January 1946 the station passed to 41 Group and became No 114 Sub Storage Unit of 6 MU Brize Norton, used to hold Horsa gliders prior to their sale as surplus material. RAF Chipping Warden closed in December 1946. During the mini-re-armament phase of the early 1950s, 8 FTS Wellesbourne Mountford used Chipping Warden between September 1952 and September 1953 as an RLG for its Oxfords. The site was mainly disposed of in the late 1950s.

**Main features:**
*Runways:* 253° 4,800ft x 150ft, 011° 4,200ft x 150ft, 133° 3,300ft x 150ft, concrete. *Hangars:* one J Type, four T2. *Hardstandings:* thirty frying-pan type. *Accommodation:* RAF officers 171, SNCOs 610, ORs 1,704; WAAF officers 12, SNCOs 15, ORs 417.

## CHURCH LAWFORD, Warwickshire

*52°21N/01°20N, 366ft asl; SP455355. 3¹/₂ miles WSW of Rugby*

Church Lawford was an unusual training station. Three hard-surfaced runways, a legacy from its intended bomber role, brought about post-war retention for flying purposes even though most buildings were of a 1940 brick-built style. A Type J hangar (10680/39) kept company with six Bellman hangars, and across an intervening road lay the domestic area. The short north-east/south-west runway was used for radio approach training, and aircraft clustered around the airfield perimeter. Four Over Type Blister hangars and six Extra Over Type were added in time for the opening by a party from Cranwell on 12 May 1941.

Since its formation on 17 August 1919 the Central Flying School has been the RAF's authority on flying, and has trained flying instructors. A minimum course of two and a half months, including seventy-eight flying hours, was maintained until the late 1930s. RAF expansion made great demands upon the CFS, additional to which was far greater emphasis on night-flying together with fast, new aircraft to master. On 9 March 1940 the decision was taken to form an additional school, at Cranwell, for flying instructors under Wg Cdr Darvell. When it opened as No 2 Central Flying School on 19 September 1940, equipment consisted of Avro Tutors from 24 MU and Airspeed Oxfords, which accompanied the School when, on 30 May 1941, it was ordered to leave for Church Lawford. No 1 CFS Upavon would concentrate upon training instructors for single-engined aircraft, although from each course of forty-five a third would learn to instruct on twin-engined aircraft. No 2 CFS would train instructors solely for multi-engined aircraft. Three instructors for twin-engined aircraft would be trained against each single-engined aircraft instructor.

On 9 January 1941 the policy was introduced whereby all flying instructors must be trained to serve at EFTSs if necessary; special courses for OTU instructors were introduced in June 1941. Gone were notions that a pilot from an operational squadron could simply be posted to an OTU and at once become an instructor. The great importance of No 2 CFS Church Lawford is thus apparent.

The move here of No 2 CFS with its Tutors and Oxfords was completed on 17 June 1941, No 11 Course having just completed training. Almost immediately flying also commenced at Southam RLG, and Sibson was also used for circuit flying. At the end of July 1941 the School's strength stood at ten Oxford Is, forty Oxford IIs, twenty-eight Tutors and a general 'hack' GAL Monospar. An unusual event occurred on 21 August when an Oxford, after taking off from Sibson, crashed into a water tank, defying all laws by burning itself out. Two detached Flights of No 2 CFS, which had remained at Cranwell, moved in late October to Montrose and Dalcross, taking along their Tutors and Oxfords and divorcing themselves from the parent unit.

Five schools were now training instructors, and on 19 January 1942 they were renamed Flying Instructors' Schools; 'CFS' was, however, retained by Upavon, and from it the Empire Central Flying School formed. No 2 CFS became No 1 Flying Instructors' School Church Lawford responsible for training SFTS and (P)AFU instructors to give twin-engined flying tuition. Special courses were run for OTU instructors using the twenty-four Oxfords Is, thirty-six Oxford IIs and thirty Avro Tutors. RLG Warwick replaced Sibson, which was transferred to Peterborough. Oxfords of 1509 BAT Flight were at Church Lawford from 6 April 1942 until leaving for Dyce in May. By August Hockley Heath RLG was supplementing Warwick.

At the end of September 1942, with No 1 FIS's strength at twenty Oxford Is, thirty Oxford IIs and eighteen Tutors, its training commitment was completed. On 27 October 1942 it became No 18 (P)AFU, using Oxfords only and remaining in 23 Group. No 1533 BAT Flight formed the same day, operating alongside the main unit that, at the end of October 1942, held twenty-two Oxford Is and thirty-one Mk IIs with a Tutor and a couple of Ansons for communications flying. A course graduated each month and, at the end of May 1943, ninety Oxfords were in hand.

Snitterfield satellite came into use on 7 May 1943 when overall strength was 100 Oxfords. By the end of August 1943 it totalled 136 and four Ansons. The BAT Flight held another eight Oxfords. Strength at the end of March 1944 reached 123 Oxford Is, 23 Oxford Mk IIs and four Ansons, together with seven Oxford Is of 1533 BAT Flight – 159 aircraft some away at Snitterfield. Peak strength had still to be reached.

Soon after 0400hrs on 27 April an Me 410 entered the circuit. Almost immediately there was a blinding flash for the intruder had collided with Oxford LX196 whose Canadian pilot and two others aboard were killed instantly.

Nos 1514 and 1546 BAT Flights also used the station where Oxford strength on 30 June 1944 totalled 164 and, by September 1944, had reached an amazing 172. Large numbers remained in use in 1945 with 18 (P) AFU still using Snitterfield and Warwick RLG. March saw No 21 Group Communications Flight move in bringing a Dominie, Harvard and two Proctors. Soon after a much slimmed 18 (P) AFU moved to Snitterfield disbanding there on 29 May 1945. Meanwhile, No 20

*A Tiger Moth parade at Church Lawford in February 1948. (R J Burgess)*

FTS was established at Church Lawford on 3 April 1945 equipped with Harvards, and on that day No 1533 BAT Flight disbanded. No 20 FTS became No 20 SFTS on 4 September 1946.

On 23 July 1947 No 20 FTS was re-designated No 2 FTS, had Tiger Moths added and left for South Cerney late March 1948. Flying now halted at Church Lawford where No 68 MU re-formed on 1 December 1954. An airfield construction depot within 43 Group, it was replaced with an equipment depot before the station was disposed of in the late 1950s.

**Main features:**
*Runways:* 355° 4,200ft x 150ft, 270° 4,200ft x 150ft, 045° 3,600ft x 150ft, concrete with tarmac surfaces. *Hangars:* all temporary except one unusual ARS two-bay hangar measuring 300ft x 200ft converted from an Abbotsinch Shed. Six Bellman, ten 65ft Over Blister. *Hardstandings:* nil. *Accommodation:* RAF 203 officers, 145 SNCOs, 787 ORs; WAAFs 10 officers, 410 ORs.

## COLLYWESTON, Northamptonshire

*52°36N /00°30W 282ft asl; TF025032. 3 miles SW of Stamford by the A43*

> "Where's Collyweston gone?" you may well ask. Simple – it was swallowed by its
> very close neighbour, Wittering, into which it disappeared in 1946.

Originally called Easton, and a First World War site, it was prepared during the winter of 1939/40. The day before opening it was awarded the exciting title 'K3', K identifying its Sector affiliation, and 3 meaning the third airfield within the Wittering clutch.

Nightly positioning of 266 Squadron Spitfires started here on 26 May 1940, and 23 Squadron was soon undertaking night-flying training from this Unbuilt Satellite where Blenheims nightly dispersed to carry out night operations from June 1940. That month also found Hurricanes of 229 Squadron using Collyweston, where No 1 Squadron Hurricanes were also often seen. A detachment from 29 Squadron Digby commenced night stand-bys in September.

As winter deepened, night-fighter Hurricanes of 151 Squadron began making use of the airfield, working with the 29 Squadron detachment. The arrival of 25 Squadron at Wittering on 27 November 1940 brought more dispersal activity before 229 and 1 Squadrons left when they moved out of Wittering in December 1940.

June 1941 saw 266 Squadron's Spitfire IIs make the satellite their usual home, Mk Vs replaced them in August 1941. On 24 October 'K3' was redesignated 'WB3' and became a satellite of Digby. Wittering's replacement satellite was the newly opened King's Cliffe, whence 266 Squadron moved the same day.

On 6 April 1942 Master IIs of 1529 BAT Flight took up residence after leaving Wittering; the Flight disbanded on 7 December 1942. No 152 Squadron, here since September 1942, withdrew, and No 118 briefly dispersed at Collyweston in January 1943. On the 2nd 1530 BAT Flight's Oxfords arrived from Wittering, whence they returned on 19 January. Over the next two years detachments of AACU organisations flew from the satellite, 116 Squadron residing here in April 1943 and 288 Squadron in late 1944.

The main event of that period, though, was the placing here of the exotic 1426 Enemy Aircraft Flight. The passage of a He 111, Ju 88, Bf 109 and Bf 110, often grouped and escorted for safety, had become commonplace over the Eastern Counties. On 24 March 1943 the collection of ex-enemy aircraft moved in from Duxford, followed on 12 April 1943 by its ground echelon, the Flight remained at Collyweston until disbandment. Collyweston thus held some really unusual 'RAF'

*Fw 190A4/U8 PN999 of No 1426 (EA) Flight at Collyweston in November 1943. It had been captured after a forced landing at Manston on 20 May. (via Don Bradfield)*

aeroplanes. Initially there was the well-worn He 111H AW177, brought down in the Lammermuir Hills, several Ju 88s, and the Bf 110 AX772, forced down in Dorset. In June 1943 Henschel Hs 128B-1 NF756 arrived, in August 1943 Bf 109F NN644 and a week later Fw 190A-4 PN999.

'Tour 10' by the 1426 Enemy Aircraft Flight commenced on 6 November 1943 and was carried out by the He 111, Ju 88 HM509, and the new Bf 109F. On 19 November they reached Polebrook to afford the Americans a close look at these enemy aircraft. Then came a flying display that went dreadfully wrong when the He 111 and Ju 88 both commenced taking off from opposite ends of the main runway. The Heinkel's pilot fully opened up and as he turned to port AW177 went into a stall turn, killing seven of the eleven men aboard.

Another two Fw 190s arrived in December 1943, together with a Bf 109G. At the end of the month 'Tour 11' began, extending to 1 February 1944, during which period many stations in the Midlands were visited. On 23 March 1944 Collyweston's *circus* set forth again, this time touring airfields in Essex and Suffolk and taking along a new Bf 109, VX101, which had joined the Flight on 4 February 1944. Before they returned, yet another Fw 190, PE882, had arrived.

Adding variety, Auster AOPs of 658 Squadron called on 14 March 1944 as they headed south from Otterburn. Another arrival stayed longer. This was the Gunnery Research Unit, which came from Exeter on 14 April 1944 bringing a Wellington X, Defiants and – most fascinating of all – L5776, one of the last Fairey Battles surviving in Britain. Delivered to the RAF in July 1940, it joined the GRU on 10 September 1941, remaining with the Unit – apart from a two-month stay at Farnborough at the end of 1942 – until written off on 12 December 1944. GRU remained until disbanding on 12 March 1945.

Ever a very lively performer for 1426 Flight was a Ju 88R-1 that joined the EAF on 6 May 1944. After a forced landing at Dyce, it came to Collyweston for tactical evaluation, and in pseudo-German markings it resides today in Hendon's Battle of Britain Museum. Three days after the Ju 88's arrival at Collyweston, 1426 Flight took some of its aircraft to Thorney Island to give Channel gunners a chance to improve their aircraft recognition prior to D-Day. The Flight's final tour came in August 1944, when, liaising with 100 Group, it used Little Snoring. In September 1944 a Ju 88S-1 joined the Flight.

For the next four and a half months, '1426' remained variously engaged, then on 17 January 1945 the Flight was ordered to dispose of its aircraft, which were passed to CFE on 21 January. Long an Operational Satellite (night-fighter), Digby Sector, Collyweston was transferred to 21 Group, FTC, on 1 April 1945, resuming its old role as a satellite of Wittering. In an extensive rebuild later that year it was integrated into that station's landing area, in whose confines it remains.

**Main features:**
*Landing ground runs:* N-S 4,500ft, NE-SW 4,380ft, E-W, 3,000ft, SE-NW 3,780ft. *Hangars:* four Over Blister. *Hardstandings:* six. *Accommodation:* RAF officers 24, SNCOs 98, ORs 552; WAAF officers 2, SNCOs 4, ORs 60.

---

## COTTESMORE, Leicestershire (Rutland)

*52°42N/00°39W 462 ft asl; SK905155. 5¹/₂ miles NNE of Oakham*

Hot war, cold war, no war. Brits, Yanks, Germans, Italians and many others. Fine planes, Skytrains, vertijets and Victors, atomic bombs and Antonovs, hopeless power plants and propaganda leaflets. Friendly families days, tattoo days, magnificent German bands and incredibly spotless hangar floors. Cottesmore has as many associations as any celebrity – but then it is a celebrity! For some it will be the worries of the Hereford, the Victor scrambles, going up vertically, parachuting down to Ste Mere Eglise. For others there will surely always be the discovery that, when Fairford closed for two years, the International Air Tattoo (Royal) would be using Cottesmore. "Far too small," said many – until the traffic problems were fewer, the walking less and, on departure day, those in the stands had photographic opportunities to delight every enthusiast.

West of the Great North Road and Woolfox Lodge, in fields north of Cottesmore village, work began in 1935 on this Permanent RAF Station. Although incomplete, it opened on 11 March 1938 in No 2 (Bomber) Group. A two-squadron station, it received from Worthy Down No 35 Squadron, flying long-range Vickers Wellesleys, and No 207, armed with Battles. The latter departed to Cranfield in April 1939, and 35 Squadron, after re-arming with Battles, joined it during August. No

*A Fairey Battle of No 35 Squadron refuelling at Cottesmore in the summer of 1938.*

185 Squadron from Thornaby replaced them on the outbreak of war, bringing fifteen Hampdens, a single Hereford and four Anson navigational trainers. 'Hereford' would for months blight Cottesmore. Concurrent with change, Cottesmore entered No 5 (Bomber) Group.

By mid-September 1939 No 106 Squadron had arrived, also armed with Hampdens, the intention being that they should combine, making No 5 Group Pool to train Hampden crews. Instead, No 106 left in October for Finningley and operations, leaving 185 Squadron to become a supplementary training squadron at Cottesmore within No 6 (Training) Group. On 5 April 1940 No 185 merged with SHQ Cottesmore to form No 14 OTU Cottesmore, its establishment being thirty-two Hampdens, sixteen Herefords and twenty-four Ansons. A new No 185 Squadron formed, only to disband on 17 May.

On 26 June 1940 Cottesmore was attacked, causing little damage, for the aircraft were well dispersed on hard pans around the perimeter. As at other pre-war stations, families had been evacuated from married quarters, allowing occupancy by Service personnel only.

Hampdens carried out 14 OTU's first operation, a *Nickel* drop over Northern France, on 25 July 1940. By 23 December thirty-five such Hampden sorties had been flown without loss.

The tempo of crew training had been impeded by serious problems with the sleeve-valve Napier Dagger engines powering the Hereford. There being no simple cure, the Herefords were replaced with Hampdens, a process that, when completed, allowed increased crew output by 1941.

Further enemy attacks on Cottesmore came in April, May and June 1941, little damage being caused.

Hampden crew training continued into 1942, a major break from routine coming on 30/31 May when Cottesmore participated in the 1,000 Plan Cologne raid, despatching twenty-nine Hampdens, three of which failed to return. After the second 1,000-bomber raid on Essen, flown on 1/2 June, all twenty-four participants came safely home. When Cottesmore also took part in the third 1,000 Plan raid on 25/26 June 1942, then target being Bremen, one of the twenty-two Hampdens operating failed to return. Operational employment was unusual, the last in 1942 taking place on 16 September when a dozen Hampdens joined a *Grand National* on Essen. A total of 151 operational bombing sorties were flown in 1942, resulting in the loss of nine aircraft and twenty-three crew members.

On 1 August 1943 No 14 OTU moved to Market Harborough, ending Cottesmore's wartime training duty. During 1942 the OTU output had totalled 1,047 pilots, navigators, wireless-operators and air-gunners, but not without loss: throughout the OTU period sixty-three aircrew were killed.

*A Hampden of No 16 OTU, with a Hereford alongside, in 1940.*

Cottesmore was now on care and maintenance for laying of concrete runways essential for the heavier aircraft. In April and May 1943 thirty-two Horsa gliders had been delivered by Whitley and Albemarle tugs for dispersed storage; they were tended by a detachment from No 2 HGMU, Snailwell.

When Cottesmore re-opened in August 1943 its three concrete runways and widened perimeter track fed thirty-five concrete and seventeen tarmac hardstandings. On 8 September 1943 it passed to the US Troop Carrier Command (TCC) and became USAAF Station 489, the glider maintenance team being the only RAF unit remaining. On 24 September 1943 Headquarters TCC (soon renamed HQ IXthTCC) took control before moving to St Vincents, Grantham, on 1 December 1943. By then the 50th Troop Carrier Wing HQ also had come, which left for Bottesford on 18 November 1943.

The winter of 1943/44 saw continued build-up of USAAF personnel, Cottesmore being the arrival and transit base for many ground formations until 16 February 1944, when twenty-six C-47s arrived. Under Colonel Burton R Fleet, the incoming 316th TCG comprised Nos 36, 37, 44 and 45 Squadrons flying C-47 Skytrains, C-53 Skytroopers and Hadrian gliders. Next day the 52nd Troop Carrier Wing HQ arrived elements of four TCGs, the 61st, 313th, 314th and 316th passing through. By 20 February fifty aircraft were on the airfield, supported by nearly 3,700 personnel. To accommodate them tented accommodation was erected and local properties requisitioned, including Exton Hall, home of the Earl of Gainsborough.

February also saw the establishment of the Pathfinder School, IXth USAAF TCC. Equipped with seven C-47s, two carried *Gee* and the others SCR-717 radar. However, its intensive training interfered too much with the other resident formation, so on 22 March the Pathfinder School moved to North Witham.

The 316th trained intensively for the invasion of Europe, many paratrooper drops being carried out during the course of ever larger exercises flown by day, then in darkness. Visiting on 9 May 1944, Prince Bernhardt of the Netherlands saw a demonstration of the glider snatch technique.

Exercise *Eagle* held on 11/12 May saw all the Troop Carrier Groups of the 50th, 52nd and 53rd Wings participate. Heavy clouds covered most of England and, as the 52nd TCW assembled over March, Cambridgeshire, two aircraft of the 316th TCG collided, killing their pilots, Lt Col Burton R Fleet and Lt Shorber. Lt Col Harvey Berger was appointed as the new Commanding Officer.

For *Overlord* on 5/6 June 1944, seventy-two aircraft of the 316th TCG took off from the 'new' 2,000-foot runway carrying US paratroopers of the 1st and 3rd Battalions, 505th Paratroop Infantry Regiment, who were dropped at DZ 'O' and gliders released near Ste-Mere-Eglise. The 316th commenced landing at Cottesmore before 0400, initial sorties being followed later the same day by reinforcement operations.

Training and supply drops to forces in France followed. Then came a part in the 17 September 1944 operation to seize the Rhine bridges. An amazing ninety C-47/C-53 transports took off from Cottesmore between 1035 and 1050 carrying 1,362 American paratroopers of the 82nd Airborne Division, including General Jim Gavin, the 82nd Airborne Division Commander, and war correspondent Ed Morrow.

The following day eighty-two aircraft towed off Waco CG4A gliders carrying 384 American troops, twenty-eight Jeeps, five 75mm howitzers and nearly 44,000lb of supplies for the Arnhem area. By the third day the weather had closed in, and poor conditions made it impossible to fly another mission until D+6. The final support mission was flown on D+9.

After the failed operation the 316th resumed training for the next major airlift, and flew supply missions to the Continent into 1945. At 0100 on 4 March 1945 a German night intruder attacked the base, dropping seventeen anti-personnel

*A C-47 of the 36th Troop Carrier Squadron, 316th Troop Carrier Group, at Cottesmore in 1944. A Waco CG-4A pokes into the picture. (Don Bradfield)*

*No 7 FTS, re-established at Cottesmore, was partly equipped with Harvards.*

bombs and damaging two aircraft and a Waco glider. On 21 March all the transport aircraft moved to Wethersfield, Essex, in preparation for the Rhine crossing operation of 24 March 1945.

Immediately the war in Europe was over, the Americans began to depart. A final parade was held on the base attended by Lt Gen Lewis H Brereton, Commander, First Allied Airborne Army. During the parade a cheque was given to Oakham hospital, and a bronze memorial plaque was mounted near the main entrance. By 11 June the brief American presence had ended.

The station was returned to the RAF and on 17 September 1945 Lancasters of No 1668 HCU moved in from Bottesford. By the end of the month more than 2,000 Service personnel had arrived, including WAAFs. Many were awaiting demobilisation which, by January 1946, reduced the station complement by half.

Cottesmore's resumed training role ended in March 1946, when No 1668 HCU disbanded. Its output reached fifty-seven crews, who had flown 4,285 hours. No 16 OTU replaced it with fifteen Mosquito T3s and FB VIs, as well as four Oxford radio bombing trainers. Flying, curtailed by acute shortages of servicing personnel, was halted during the severe winter of 1946/47. In February no aircraft flew from the airfield, conditions being so bad that on 6 March a Lancaster from Lindholme dropped essential food and medical supplies to the beleaguered station.

By the end of March 1947 all bombing training had ceased, the role of the unit following a new course as 16 OTU became No 204 Advanced Flying School flying Mosquito Mark 3s and 6s. Overall control changed, the station transferring to No 21 Group, Flying Training Command.

On 10 March 1948 No 204 AFS moved to Driffield and was replaced on 16 April by No 7 SFTS equipped with Tiger Moths and Harvard IIbs. Control then changed again, the station becoming part of No 23 Group. Percival Prentices replaced the Tiger Moths, and by June 1950 7 SFTS was managing some 2,500 training flights a month. To ease circuit pressure Spitalgate was used as a relief landing ground for Prentices, and Woolfox Lodge for the Harvards.

In March 1953 the Harvards were replaced with Boulton Paul Balliol T2s, whose use was brief, for on 14 April 1954 No 7 SFTS was disbanded. The Women's Royal Air Force also departed as Cottesmore prepared for a very different role. In May 1954 it was transferred to No 3 Group, Bomber Command, and on 20-22 May four front-line high-level-bombing Canberra B2 squadrons, Nos XV, 44, 57 and 149, arrived from Coningsby. No 149, the first permitted to bomb from 40,000 feet, departed for Ahlhorn on 24 August, the others to Honington on 20 February 1955. Cottesmore, put on care and maintenance on 15 February 1955, was to be developed into a V-bomber base.

The following three years witnessed construction of an extensive, complex airfield whose main, rebuilt runway extended to over 9,000 feet. New taxiways and four-aircraft H-pattern hardstandings were built, allowing rapid movement to the runway. New buildings accommodated electronic, radar, radio, crew clothing, navigation and briefing sections, while secure weapons areas were also added. The domestic site was much enlarged to cope with an increase in staffing. Messing arrangements were greatly extended and also modernised before the station re-opened in March 1958 as an operational V-Force base under the command of fighter ace Group Captain 'Johnnie' Johnson. On 15 April No 10 Squadron re-formed, equipped with Handley Page Victor B1s, then on 1 September 1958 the second Victor squadron, No XV, re-formed here.

*Italian-marked Tornado I-42:MM55000 of TTTE at Cottesmore on 8 June 1996.*

Much faith and money was invested in the V-Force amid claims that Britain would have about 4 minutes' warning of an imminent air attack. To respond with an all-out nuclear response producing mutual destruction, fighter-style scrambles were practised. To achieve this, modifications were made, allowing all engines to start simultaneously so that four Victors could become airborne in less than 4 minutes. The strength of a V-Force squadron was nominally six aircraft, four of which were always at stand-by and two were undergoing base servicing. Another pair would be undergoing major updating elsewhere.

In November 1961 'C' Flight No 232 OCU moved in from Gaydon to undertake intensive flying and Service trials of the Victor B2. March 1962 saw the unit renamed Victor Training Flight, and in February 1964 it moved to Wittering. The Victor occupancy of Cottesmore was winding down, and on 1 March 1954 No 10 Squadron disbanded, followed by XV Squadron on 31 October.

On 2 November Nos IX, 12 and 35 Squadrons arrived from Coningsby, bringing Vulcan B2s to form the Cottesmore Wing of No 1 Group, which had both nuclear and conventional roles. Activities ranged through stand-bys, normal crew training and overseas flights. In 1965 the Vulcans were deployed to Gan, Butterworth and Takoradi during the confrontation with Indonesia. Policy changes and increased vulnerability of a surfaced-based deterrent force led to transfer of the nuclear response to Royal Navy submarines. That led to reduction of the V-Force, the role of which had changed to one of low attack using special weapons other than nuclear. No 12 Squadron disbanded on 31 December 1967. Extensive change overtook the entire RAF, leading, on 30 April 1968, to amalgamation of Bomber, Coastal and Fighter Commands as Strike Command; Bomber squadrons were gathered as No 1 Group.

During January 1969 Nos 9 and 35 Squadrons moved from Cottesmore to Akrotiri, Cyprus. After 1,551 consecutive days, Quick Reaction Alert ceased at Cottesmore on 31 January 1969.

Three weeks after the Vulcans left, No 90 Group took control of Cottesmore, and in April 1969 Nos 98, 115 and 360 Squadrons began moving in. They were concerned with radio and radar, operationally,

*German Luftwaffe Tornado 43+05 G-24 of the TTTE undergoing maintenance in June 1996.*

for training and calibration. No 98 Squadron flew Canberra E15s for airfield radar checking, and No 115 Squadron, flying Argosys since February 1968, was responsible for checking navigational aids and airfield runway approach systems at RAF stations worldwide. No 360 Squadron, comprising 75% Royal Air Force and 25% Royal Navy personnel, was a joint RAF/RN electronic warfare training squadron flying mainly Canberra T17s with a limited operational capability. On 19 May 1969 No 231 OCU Canberra training unit arrived from Bassingbourn to produce crews for all the squadrons. In 1971 these 90 (Signals) Group squadrons became part of No 1 Group.

The 1975 Defence Review resulted in twelve stations closing and brought more change to Cottesmore. No 360 Squadron moved to Wyton in August, and early February 1976 saw a slimmed No 231 OCU leave for Marham. No 115 Squadron, fully equipped with Argosys since August 1970, took them to Brize Norton in February 1976. Finally it was the turn of No 98, which, in the process of disbanding on 27 February 1976, passed its Canberras to No 100 Squadron. Its squadrons gone, Cottesmore was placed on a C&M between 31 March 1976 and 31 March 1978. During that period further extensive work was undertaken, ranging from detailed office changes to runway resurfacing, new hardstandings and conversion of one hangar into an aero-engine centre, as a result of which a fine floor shone in a pristine environment. Additions included refined accommodation blocks, a far cry from those wartime tents. All this was to make Cottesmore fit to become the home of the Tri-National Tornado Training Establishment (TTTE), one of the most important military bases in Western Europe, where all British, German and Italian pilots and navigators in accord with the 1979 Tri-National Memorandum of Understanding would learn to fly the Tornado, examples of which exhibited the international markings of the three nations. The importance of the task is clear from the fact that 671 operational Tornadoes and 138 trainers with operational capabilities were ordered, of which 385 were for the RAF, 324 for the German forces, (including 112 for the German Navy), and 100 for the Italian Air Force. As a consequence German and Italian aircrew and their dependants took up accommodation at the tri-national station.

On 22 October 1979 the first RAF Support Command Tornado Ground Servicing School (TGSS) course started. At peak time Cottesmore housed some fifty Tornados, the first two arriving on 1 July 1980. The three-squadron TTTE opened on 29 January 1981 in 1 Group, plans calling for a maximum output of 300 crews per year. To the end of the Cold War the international force learned to handle the Tornado GR1/IDS here. In 1998 agreement was reached for the three nations to go their separate ways, and in June 1998 RAF Tornado training was switched to No XV (Reserve) Squadron. TTTE closed on 31 March 1999.

There was now a need to find a home for RAF squadrons being withdrawn from Germany. Cottesmore's proximity to Wittering (all too close to the A1) now played a part in the scheme, for it was chosen as the base for JF2000, which, as Joint Force Harrier, was created on 1 April 2000. The three operational Harrier GR7 squadrons moved in – No IV on 13 April 1999, No 3 on 11 May 1999, both from Laarbruch, and No 1 Squadron from Wittering on 28 June 2000.

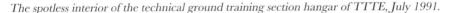

*The spotless interior of the technical ground training section hangar of TTTE, July 1991.*

*Harrier GR7 ZD410 of No 3
Squadron at Cottesmore in
July 2000.*

In July 1999 No 3 Squadron was detached to Gioia del Colle, Italy, to take part in operation *Allied Force*, which entailed operating over Kosovo and Serbia. Subsequently No 3 Squadron joined Nos 1 and IV Harrier squadrons rotated to police the Balkans within operation *Deliberate Forge*, in which they were involved until April 2001. On 1 April 2000 No 3 Squadron had joined JFH, and in May 2001 joined HMS *Illustrious* to take part in exercise *Linked Seas*. The carrier, carrying the squadron's Harriers, was soon re-tasked to support the Sierra Leone Government.

Expectation that shore-based Royal Navy fleet protector Sea Harrier FA2s of Nos 800 and 801 Squadrons would move to Cottesmore ended with a disturbing announcement on 28 February 2002 that they were to be withdrawn from service in 2004 to save money. RN personnel with Harrier experience would still move to Cottesmore, which might, in 2012 or the more distant future, become the lair of the JSF. To extend their operational usefulness, RAF Harrier squadrons have trained aboard HMS *Ark Royal*.

Cottesmore's Harriers on detachment to Kuwait during operation *Telic*, the 2003 Iraq conflict, flew almost 700 close air support/reconnaissance day and night sorties of the 2,500 flown by the RAF during the main combat phase, and went into action on 21 March, the first night of operation *Telic*. Firing the Maverick anti-armour missile for the first time, the chosen target 200 miles inside Iraq was a mobile Scud launch unit. The missile's infrared seeker passes target images to the cockpit, the pilot then directing the missile to the chosen target. The 3 Squadron force returned to Cottesmore on 18 April and IV Squadron on 8 May 2003.

Much of service activity does, of course, have a lighter side My most cherished memory of Cottesmore came on April Fool's Day 1961 when the then Prime Minister, Harold Macmillan, decided to heal the wounds inflicted upon the RAF by Duncan Sandys's missile threat to its aircrews. After delighting us with amazing antics at Cranwell, the 'press *circus*' and the PM flew to Cottesmore where the latest aircraft were on show – including a Lightning F3 carrying a real, very hush-hush Firestreak missile. I watched the PM inspect it closely, and to my amazement he removed the red cap covering its heat-seeking nose. He then beckoned to me and said, "You'll get a better picture now, if you're quick."

There must be a very special name for rare PMs who do nice things for the people – like me…

**Main features:**
*Runways:* 230° 6,000ft x 150ft, 280° 4,800ft x 150ft, 190° 4,500ft x 150ft, tarmac. *Hangars:* four C Type, one T2. *Hardstandings:* thirty-five concrete, seventeen tarmac. *Accommodation:* RAF officers 237, SCOs 240, ORs 2,236.

Re-build for V-Force resulted in Runway 05/23 9,003ft, concrete/asphalt, later with RHAG arrester gear, crossed by closed runway 280°, four sets of four-pan linked dispersals, and four paired dispersals by the widened perimeter track. Remnants of wartime dispersal and the third runway are visible to the NW of the present active area. An ASP was later added in the SE area and another large 'technical area' or apron was built before the hangars for Harrier use.

*KC-130T 164441/NY of
VMGR-452 taxies, followed
by two more C-130s,
providing an impressive
departure from RIAT in July
2000.*

## COWLEY, Oxfordshire

*51°43/01°11W 120ft asl; SP555035. 3 miles SE of Oxford, along the A4142*

Civilian Repair Units utilised sites ranging from small motor garages to huge business premises, and one of the latter was established as No 1 Civilian Repair Unit, Cowley. Seriously damaged aircraft – particularly Hurricanes and Spitfires – were conveyed to its Salvage Centre aboard 60-foot 'Queen Mary' trailers for repair, cannibalisation or often for write-off, in which case final remains were handled by No 1 Metal Produce & Recovery Depot, Cowley. Initially, personnel of No 2 Salvage Centre, opened on 11 September 1939, did the collection, but from 4 October 1940 the task was undertaken by No 50 MU aided by 67 MU, which harvested the aircraft to be worked upon in southern and south-western England. So great did the task become that, on 1 April 1941, 90 MU opened as another salvage collector, until absorption by 50 MU on 30 April 1943. Between early 1940 and 1946, No1 Metal Produce & Recovery Depot coped with metallic items beyond restoration.

*Hurricanes awaiting delivery after re-working at Cowley. (Bruce Robertson collection)*

Mainly civilian-manned, the extensive Cowley organisation was masterminded by Lord Nuffield, whose Morris Motors factory was largely converted into aircraft workshops. Flight test hangars fronted a grass landing ground that held two runways, and the spring of 1940 saw those facilities replace the use of Abingdon for flight testing.

No 1 CRU provided essential back-up during the Battle of Britain, civilian staff working around the clock to return damaged aircraft to MUs and squadrons. The close proximity of Nos 6 and 8 MU led to some unusual aircraft types being dismembered here. When hostilities ended, the site fast reverted to civilian use. Some buildings used by 1 CRU remain, while the airfield partially resides beneath the Oxford Ring Road.

Morris Motors, Cowley, produced more than 3,000 Tiger Moths. Argument has long raged over the precise number constructed, many spare parts having been built for Tigers. Certainly Cowley's wartime Tiger Moth production was considerable, many a Tiger still flying owing its survival to the Morris works.

## CRANFIELD, Bedfordshire

*52°04N/00°37W 336ft asl; SP945425. 8 miles SW of Bedford, S of A422, reached via a by-road from Astwood*

The likelihood of Cranfield becoming a University, and simultaneously a source of Japanese cars, would have been laughable in wartime. But then a wartime use for the pre-war Walls 'Stop me and buy one' ice-cream salesmen's pedal tricycle would have been rated just as unlikely. When I came upon that bizarre sight, and on Cranfield's sacred parade ground, it beggared belief. Nobody joined the RAF to pedal around a barrack square on a tricycle. In fact, they were night-fighter pilots wearing dark glasses and improving their night vision.

I have other Cranfield memories. I bagged a ride in Oxford R6350 to circle the station on a crystal clear eve in summer 1944 to gaze down upon Cranfield when it was an aircraft enthusiast's paradise. Grouped on the south side were about 100 Spitfires in varied hues and many forms, with scattered among them fifteen Typhoons and fifty Mustang IIIs, many conspicuously wearing 'invasion stripes'. In the north-east corner rested Mosquito IIs, the first of which joined resident 51 OTU in July. Close by were ten Beauforts and a fine assortment of Beaufighter Is and VIs. By now this night-fighter OTU, training crews for 100 Group, Bomber Command, was overshadowed by the other resident, No 3501 Servicing Unit, working through hosts of front-line fighters of both ADGB and 2TAF in for rapid modification and servicing.

Very cautiously nosing around, notebook in hand, I found four still-novel Tempest Vs, and by the tower (smaller than now) a Spitfire XIV, the first production example, which I examined closely. Artists' impressions of RB174: DL-T that appear from time to time do not quite equate to my afternoon's careful production of the original!

*Cranfield's one-time Officers' Mess. The games room and ante-room flank the main entrance, with accommodation at either end, and the dining room to the rear.*

Also lying around were 51 OTU Wellington XIs, still wearing Coastal colours, and fitted out as flying classrooms for converting fighter crews to handle AI Mk X centimetric radar. Some of the Beauforts retained Coastal white/grey camouflage, and several had dorsal turrets. Others wore standard grey/green night-fighter finish. Four Hurricane IIs had recently joined them, and an unusual fully marked yet unpainted Spitfire, MJ963, rested close by. Add communications and ferry aircraft such as Ansons, Arguses, Harvards, Magisters and Proctors – not to mention a Flamingo sailing serenely by – and 2 August 1944 remains memorable, like the hairy run in that Oxford between small fruit trees in an orchard. I kept my eyes closed until we were back on firm ground. No, I never mentioned it to my mother!

Cranfield had the ambience of all Permanent RAF Stations. Its Station Headquarters opened on 1 June 1937, and the aerodrome on 1 July 1937, under control of No 1 (Bomber) Group. On 6 July 108 Squadron's Hinds arrived in formation from Farnborough, more of the same (belonging to 82 Squadron) finding their way from Andover two days later. Yet more breezed in on 12 July, for 62 Squadron was vacating Abingdon. Cranfield's operational contingent, three dozen Hinds initially intended to deal with France, were now intended to give close support to the Army – until something more modern came along.

When other new stations opened, Cranfield's squadrons moved, No 108 leaving for Bassingbourn in February 1938, just as Blenheim Is were arriving for 62 Squadron. Blenheims were delivered to 82 Squadron in March 1938, then both squadrons transferred to 2 Group on 15 July 1938. September's Munich Crisis brought them to high readiness, hazardous tasks on

*The one time Airmen's Mess at Cranfield. The ground floor held a large dining area, while upstairs were the Institute ('NAAFI') and writing and games rooms. The Parade Ground has become a car park.*

offer within the Western Plan including raids on German power resources. After the situation calmed, training became very realistic. Fuel consumption trials took place and training flights were made over France to cement the entente cordiale.

Cranfield's partnership broke apart when in August 1939 62 Squadron began moving to the Far East, the sea party setting forth on 12 August for the troopship *Neuralia*, which took them to Singapore. When on 23 August two Flights each of eight Blenheims left Cranfield, they were commencing a journey that at the time was extremely demanding. Another eight crews set forth on 26 August, and some of the aircraft being ferried were destined to be hurled into an impossible attempt to stem the 1941 Japanese advance into Malaysia. After 62 Squadron had gone, No 82 Squadron moved to Watton, to be replaced, on 25 and 28 August, the advance elements of Nos 35 and 207 Squadrons, arriving from Cottesmore in Fairey Battles to train replacement pilots and observer/air-gunners for XV and 40 Squadrons, AASF, in France. Thirty men were trained over every six-week period, the squadrons amalgamating on 1 October 1939 to form 1 Group Pool, still under 6 Group control.

The intention was to re-arm Battle squadrons in France with Blenheims, some of which arrived at Cranfield in late 1939. Almost simultaneously, both Battle squadrons left, as construction of three runways had commenced. A Servicing Flight remained until 1 February 1940, when it moved to Upwood.

Dramatic change came with the arrival from Kinloss of Airspeed Oxford trainers of 14 SFTS. A first-rate station adjacent to the operational area, and one of the first with runways, was surely being wasted. Consideration was given in May 1941 to changing it into a Coastal Command OTU, but it was rated too far from that Command's activities. Instead, a night-fighter OTU would open in early August 1941 after 14 SFTS moved to Lyneham, thus making way for 51 OTU, which had partially formed at Debden. By 3 August seven Blenheims and two Oxfords had reached Cranfield. The establishment set mid-month was for thirty-nine IE plus thirteen IR Blenheim I/IVs or Havoc Is (six to come from 85 Squadron re-arming with Havoc IIs), eight dual-control Blenheims or Hudsons, and ten Oxfords for navigation training and five communications aircraft.

Had the night-fighters arrived much sooner they might have engaged the enemy when he first attacked Cranfield on 27/28 August 1940 with incendiaries and two HE bombs, which fell to north and south of the airfield. At 2107 on 24 September 1940 a parachute mine exploded in a field, damaging and shops in Cranfield High Street. On 13 October 1940 a second mine complete with parachute was discovered dangling from a tree in Hulcote Wood, 1½ miles south of the aerodrome, reckoned to have been dropped with the other example. It was safely dealt with the next day. Winter nights cloaked Ju 88Cs lurking in the area; in one skirmish an Oxford was landed by a pupil pilot after his instructor was wounded.

*A typical small gathering at a large-scale PFA Rally – Stampe SV 4 G-AZGA, Piper G-ATBX, and Auster G-APJK.*

*Supermarine Swift F7*
*XF114 in 1967, used by*
*Cranfield College of*
*Aeronautics for runway*
*aquaplaning investigation.*

No 51 OTU opened on 25 August 1941, Blenheims aplenty having moved in and the first Havocs on 18 August. Cranfield's OTU fast assumed major importance, and it acquired a satellite at Twinwood, where Blenheim V trainers for type conversion came into use in April 1942. The first Beaufighter for 51 OTU arrived on 8 August 1942. Protracted re-equipment followed, Blenheim Is remaining on strength into 1943. Beaufighter Is and a few VIFs served until 51 OTU's closure.

Snarling Sabres first shattered Cranfield's air during March 1943 when 181 and 183 Squadrons tarried briefly during exercise *Spartan*. More interesting was a brief American call between May and June 1943 when USAAF crews learned to operate AI Mk VIII-equipped American-marked Beaufighters, which equipped a few of their north-west African night protection squadrons. Rumours that Northrop P-61 Black Widows were coming generated enough local excitement to frighten them away!

Dual-control Beauforts were used for twin-conversion training, the unit's diverse equipment in July 1943 being listed as seventy-eight Beaufighter IFs (AI Mk IV), four Beaufighter VIFs, four Beaufighter IFs without AI, ten Blenheim Vs (dual-control), six Beauforts (dual-control), three Blenheim Is, one Blenheim IV, three Lysanders, five Martinets (which had arrived in May), four Magisters and a Dominie. Additional was No 2 Delivery Flight, which arrived from Colerne on 23 July 1943. Each night-fighter course numbered about thirty men. High-intensity flying reduced aircraft serviceability often to less than 50%, but never low enough to prevent, in November 1943, a few operational night sorties. During March/April 1943 seven Wellington XIs had arrived to help train 100 Group Mosquito crews.

On 13 July 1943 No 3501 Servicing Unit was set up to handle overhaul, mainly night-fighters transferred from squadrons to OTUs. By 1944 single-engined fighters were also modified and overhauled here, particularly those of 2TAF once the invasion was under way. Also included were aircraft of ADGB when the flying bomb campaign made heavy demands upon home-based day-fighters There were plenty of pilots available for flight testing because No 3501 Pilot Replacement Unit was also here until early September 1944, when No 3501 SU moved to Middle Wallop.

On 5 July 1944 Mosquito IIs for the training of No 100 Group crews began supplementing 51 OTU's Beaufighters, equipping its No 4 Squadron by September. February 1945 saw the last Beaufighters withdrawn, although many stayed here inactive. On 14 June 1945 No 51 OTU disbanded, and during the last week of June the remaining Mosquitoes, Beaufighters and Beauforts were flown away.

*Blenheim 1 L1131 'R' of 62 Squadron.*

A group of Canadian airmen waited at Cranfield for home passage within the Canadian Aircrew Holding Unit, under the command of Wg Cdr Bob Iredale of Mosquito fame. Some 120 Australians also waited here for passage home. All Cranfield's aircraft had left by the end of August, and No 16 Aircrew Holding Unit (ACHU) disbanded on 13 September 1945.

Extensive rumour was surrounding the de Havilland Vampire jet fighter. A variety of development aspects had deprived the experimental fighter of combat, and countless stories circulated concerning it. In reality the few built were mostly at Hatfield and Boscombe Down. An unlikely rumour about a Vampire at Cranfield turned out to be true, because Geoffrey de Havilland Junior force-landed one there on 15 October 1945. Next day he gave one of his unsurpassed Vampire demonstrations before leaving the area. Jet fuel was available at Cranfield because during October 1945 the Empire Test Pilots' School had partly vacated Boscombe Down for a new home here, a move completed on 16 November 1945, after which jets became a permanent feature.

The first ETPS course at Cranfield opened on 2 January 1946 when the School held four Lancasters, three Mosquito VIs, two Boston IIIs, four Meteor IIIs, three Spitfire IXs, three Tempest IIs, three Tempest Vs, two Oxfords, Harvards, a Dominie, a Swordfish and a Tiger Moth. Post-war needs for test pilots in Britain and many other parts of the world were increasingly met by ETPS graduates. However, having them closer to the latest developments in aviation and testing techniques became desirable, so ETPS moved to Farnborough in August 1947.

Military Cranfield seemed ready for closure, although by the early 1950s 23 Group Communications Flight resided here using an Anson 19, Provost and Vampire T 11.

Cranfield's civilian future was more assured, however, when in 1946 the College of Aeronautics, a government-sponsored institution still at Cranfield today, was founded. Soon it was offering advanced courses in aeronautics and engineering, mainly to post-graduates, and some of the College's original equipment came from wartime German research establishments. Low- and high-speed wind tunnels were erected in a hangar, and facilities provided for in-flight demonstrations. One-year degree courses and two-year non-degree courses were offered, studies ranging widely over project definition, structures, aircraft propulsion – for which rocket engine demonstrations were given in the one-time bomb dump – as well as in other associated aviation fields.

Following the harmful Sandys White Paper of 1957, the College decided that it must expand into other fields of advanced technology, its catchment area becoming worldwide in the process. At this time Cranfield was used by the Fairey Development Flight for guided weapons trials with a Meteor NF 11 and a Swift F 3. It was also a Swift that served for aquaplaning experiments along sections of a runway, flooded to a depth of several inches.

In the 1950s and 1960s Cranfield's collection of museum aircraft included such rarities as the Supermarine 535, Lincoln and Tempest II prototypes, as well as a TSR-2, all of which attracted much interest. For reasons of space they were dispersed elsewhere. Aeroplanes for demonstration of research techniques included two Jetstreams. However, none of the aircraft flown from here will ever be more enjoyed than Lancaster PA474, which had served with 82 Squadron and now provides a link with earlier times. Above its fuselage, a hefty aerofoil section was carried for ice accretion and boundary layer research. PA474 was a common sight over the Midlands before the RAF repossessed it; it is now part of the Battle of Britain Memorial Flight, providing a reminder of Bomber Command's wartime mainstay.

On 14 July 1954 Cranfield's runway was the scene of a terrible disaster when WB771, the prototype Victor, engaged on high-speed low flying, suffered catastrophic tail unit failure. Four of the crew were killed when it hit the runway. Ironically, it was at Cranfield that Bruntingthorpe's Vulcan XH558 gave its last public display in RAF hands.

Cranfield Institute of Technology played an important part in post-graduate training of aviation engineers and designers. Staff at the College produced their own aerobatic aircraft, the Cranfield A1, and the curious Edgeley Optica had a main home here. Cessnas and other light aircraft come and go, as at the PFA Rally, the last of which at Cranfield was held in 2002.

A three-campus University is now sited at Cranfield, Silsoe (Beds) and Shrivenham Defence Academy UK. As well as the College of Aeronautics there are also the Advanced Materials Department, Cranfield School of Management, and Motorsport Engineering. A multiplicity of activities have been pursued, among them the orderly and rapid safe exit of passengers from burning aircraft.

Although Cranfield's academic activities are much to the fore, plentiful aviation activity continues. Based here are the Bedfordshire School of Flying, College of Air Training, Cranfield Aero Club, Bonus Aviation, Cabair, Flyteam Aviation, Euroair Flying Club, Patriot Aviation and Taylor Aviation.

**Main features:**
*Runways:* 265° 6,000ft, 224° 4,800ft, 156° 3,300ft, concrete. *Hangars:* four Type C, nine E O Blister, one T3. *Hardstandings:* twenty-five circular concrete pads. *Accommodation:* RAF officers 89, SNCOs 187, ORs 1,389; WAAF officers 6, SNCOs 7, ORs 645.

For civil use from the 1950s there were two main runways, 04/22 5,928ft and 08/26 5,988ft, both asphalt. By the mid-1990s 04/22 had become the main one with 18/36 (620m x 18m) the secondary. 08/26 had become a taxiway.

## CROUGHTON, Northamptonshire

*51°59N/01°10W, 450ft asl; SP563325. By the B4031 SW of Brackley*

Brackley Landing Ground became Croughton in July 1941, the A43 affording a clear view across the plateau upon which the landing ground was sited. As early as February 1940 Brackley LG was used by three Whitleys of 78 Squadron, and on 4 June a 16 OTU Hampden crashed here, all shortly before Brackley became 16 OTU's satellite and attracted dispersed Ansons and Hampdens. The most memorable event during that unit's tenure occurred on 20 September 1941 when Ju 88Cs were intruding in the area. One, flown by Oblt Semrau, came across Hampden P5314 approaching well-lit Croughton. Flying at 500 feet, he opened fire with his cannon and shot down the Hampden before dropping eight 50kg bombs across the airfield. Another bombing attack was made in December 1941.

In July 1942 Croughton was chosen by 23 Group for glider training, being larger and preferable to Thame. Control of the station passed to 1 GTS on 19 July 1942, and on 1 August the air party of the gliding school arrived at Croughton, leaving a few personnel at Thame to form the Glider Instructors' School. No 1 GTS held eighteen Hotspurs, towing being undertaken by a fleet of fourteen Hectors, although Master IIs began replacing those shortly after the move.

*Miles Master GT 2 DL 457 of No 1 GTS Croughton in the spring of 1946.*

When sufficient glider pilots had been trained for scheduled airborne operations, No 1 GTS was absorbed into 20 (P)AFU, and on 24 March 1943 Kidlington took control of Croughton. Pilot training Oxfords soon replaced gliders at Croughton, the AFU placing its No 2 Squadron at Croughton by July 1943. Oxfords in profusion patrolled local skies, together with those of No 1538 BAT Flight, formed here on 15 April 1943. Use was also made of nearby landing grounds, including Mixbury Farm.

The intention was that Croughton would serve out its days as a pilot training station, but heavy glider pilot losses at Arnhem changed that. On 18 October 1944 No 1538 Flight disbanded and 20 (P)AFU retired to Kidlington, clearing the way for the rebirth of 1 GTS on 1 November 1944. Reinforcements for the Glider Pilot Regiment were now trained, a large number of Hotspur IIs and ample towing Master IIs being used. Glider pilot training continued in 1945 to meet possible Far East requirements.

Harvard II BD130 came to Croughton in July 1945 from ECFS for assessment of its suitability as a Hotspur tug. It was unsatisfactory, so instead a number of American-engined Master IIIs were fitted out as tugs and used into 1946.

In August 1945 1 GTS took over Gaydon, its strength was reduced, and it then came under the control of 21 HGCU based at Brize Norton. Flying continued using Croughton, where it ended on 25 May 1946. Gliders and tugs – those worth keeping – were sent to Wellesbourne, and Croughton fell quiet.

Giant USAF-owned 'golf balls' and mixed large aerials have for years dominated Croughton's skyline, making the airfield unusable. The station was allocated to the USAF on 16 October 1951 for use as a communications centre, and until disbandment on 1 July 1966 it was run by the 7562nd Air Base Squadron and since 1965 has been controlled by the Defence Communication Agency (UK) under US Air Force Communication Service control. Until its closure Croughton had strong connections with the 20th TFW Upper Heyford. A memento of that affiliation is an F-100D decorated in 20th colours, which guards the gate with an F-105, a curious, rare companion for sure.

**Main features:**
*Grass runs:* E-W 6,600ft, NE-SW 4,300ft, NW-SE 4,940ft. *Hangars:* four T2, ten 65ft Blisters. *Hardstandings:* fifteen frying-pan, six double fighter pens. *Accommodation:* RAF officers 133, SNCOs 300, ORs 640; WAAF officers 3, SNCOs 6, ORs 182.

## CROYDON (WADDON), Surrey

*51°21N/00°07W 215ft asl; TQ306635. 2¹/₂ miles SW of Croydon*

According to the Met Office, the air temperature was 22°F. I didn't doubt it when on 3 January 1946 I made a lone pilgrimage to Britain's most famous airport, its importance already being usurped by a soulless muddy upstart named Heathrow. Getting to Croydon wasn't easy, for it involved a penny-ha'penny tube ride from Liverpool Street, a 2s 8d return train trip and a tupenny ticket on a 194 bus to Purley Way. How things really have changed! Nothing, though, can erase the magic of 'Croydon', a word that stirs the heart, for from there flew the braves like Amy Johnson and Jean Batten, who undertook epic, lonely long flights, and from there also flew those gorgeous, huge, Warren-girdered '42s gathered so proudly and displaying the gold, blue and black proclamation with such pride: 'Imperial Airways London'. Dear Croydon, indeed the real dear old London, for you are so much missed too – both loved ones all gone, all gone…well almost.

On that bitterly cold Thursday there were a few shadows of past magic, like DH 86B *G-ACVY* slipping in from Speke, ABA Sweden's DC-3 SE-BAC, Rapides *G-AGUF* and *G-AGUR* of Railway Air Services, and Olley's *G-AGSI*. Sabena DC-3 OO-CBB landed at 1233 from Brussels, quickly followed by the Railway Air Services Avro XIX *G-AGVA*. Sundry 110 Wing RAF Dakotas, and an Expeditor, sat watching by the hangars, together with Dakotas *G-AGHK* from Cairo and *G-AGHE/HP*. Three BOAC Lancastrians, *G-AGMK/ML/MM*, sheltered a BOAC Mosquito and Lockheed 14 *G-AGAV*. As I left, an anonymous RAF Ju 52 3m/z whirred in. Civilian flying had barely started, but when it did Croydon, packed with Rapides, Consuls, Avro XIXs, and years later that mass of Tiger Moths awaiting disposal, was a joy to experience.

Like many aerodromes around London, Croydon came from a 1915 need to protect the capital from zeppelin bombers. They were quite a serious threat and caused considerable casualties and damage. Within London's protecting ring of night landing grounds was an area flanking Plough Lane at New Barn Farm, Beddington, approved for use on 13 December 1915. Doubling as a training aerodrome featuring Bessoneau hangars and tented accommodation, and called Beddington Aerodrome (sometimes Wallington), two BE 2cs moved there during January 1916. Six mechanics followed, together with Royal Engineers with a searchlight. April 1916 saw them join the 18th Wing, the detachment being part of No 39 Home Defence Squadron. However, Beddington's use faded, for in May defence detachments were more suitably repositioned mainly east of the capital. Space at Beddington was filled during 1916 and 1917 by No 17 Reserve (Training) Squadron. Three brick 1917-style RFC hangars were erected, and hutted accommodation was supplemented by requisitioned housing to allow for more personnel including Canadians.

No 40 Training Squadron, RFC, replaced No 17 in 1917, stayed until early 1918, then moving to Tangmere. The early months of 1918 also saw No 141 Squadron, Biggin Hill, using the landing

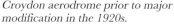

*Croydon aerodrome prior to major*              *Croydon aerodrome in 1930.*
*modification in the 1920s.*

ground, where No 29 Training Squadron had arrived. Winning his 'wings' here in 1919 was Prince Albert, later King George VI, who was joined by the Prince of Wales, later King Edward VIII.

A summer eve in 1919 saw Winston Churchill crash at Beddington just after taking off, his pride suffering most. Beddington was used by some squadrons back from France – London's proximity much popularising it.

July 1919 found the aerodrome also being used by the Air Council Inspection Squadron and No 1 Group Headquarters. In October three squadrons (Nos 32, 41 and 207), none holding aircraft, arrived to disband, although No 207 survived until 16 January 1920. The RAF quit the aerodrome the following month and civilians moved in.

At this time two landing grounds existed, Beddington and Waddon, separated by Plough Lane running from Stafford Road to Purley. National Aircraft Factory No 1, which opened in January 1918 and delivered its first DH 9 in March, was built at Waddon at the northern end of the aerodrome and was managed by Cubitt Ltd. Adjacent ground was used for test flying. At the start of 1919 NAF became No 3 Aircraft Salvage Depot, which on 15 March 1920 became the Aircraft Disposal Co Ltd, acquired by Handley Page the following month. Refurbishing and sale of wartime aircraft and equipment at once got under way, more than 10,000 aircraft being handled in the following decade.

Beddington Aerodrome and the flying field at Waddon became Croydon Aerodrome, which on 29 March 1920 became the London Terminal Aerodrome, replacing Hounslow and also becoming the Customs airport for London. Airlines soon attracted included Air Transport & Travel, Handley Page and Instone Air Lines. Later in 1920, KLM, Sneta (later Sabena) and William Beardmore started using Croydon. KLM inaugurated an Amsterdam-Croydon flight, and two main French airlines, Compagnie des Messageries Aeriennes (CMA) and Compagnie des Grands Express Aeriens (CGEA) – merged in 1923 as Air Union and the forerunner of Air France – introduced the prestigious Paris-Croydon scheduled flights with Spad S.33s and Farman Goliaths, the latter bomber development being a frequent sight at 1920s Croydon.

Airport development continued, April 1921 seeing the R-33 airship briefly moored here, but subsidies were needed because airline running costs were high. Handley Page Transport obtained

*G-AACH AWA's first Argosy,*
*a large biplane transport,*
*seen at Croydon in 1929.*

a dual subsidy from the British and Swiss Governments to allow an HP 0/10 service between Croydon and Zurich via Paris. Croydon was now calling itself 'The London Terminal – The Continental Airport'.

To ease funding and improve efficiency, the 1923 Hambling Committee for Air Transport proposed that British commercial airlines should combine to form one. That led to the inauguration of Imperial Airways on 1 April 1924, brought about by merging Instone, Daimler Airways Ltd, Handley Page Transport Ltd and the British Marine Air Navigation Co Ltd.

In 1925 there was more expansion. A Croydon-Amsterdam-Hamburg-Copenhagen-Malmo service opened, with Imperial Airways running the Croydon-Amsterdam leg from 15 May, employing de Havilland 34s, and leaving Swedish Air Lines to complete the run using Junkers-G23s. On 16 November Alan Cobham for Imperial Airways started out on a survey flight to Cape Town and back using a de Havilland 50, a journey of 8,100 miles including thirty stopping places. It took five months.

With passenger traffic fast increasing, and inadequate buildings on the airport's Wallington edge, plans were made for an impressive terminal topped by what is surely the world's best-known control tower. Included would be a private hotel, passenger handling and booking facilities, and a restaurant. Aircraft still taxied from Beddington's one-time RFC hangars (used until 1927) across Plough Lane to the landing ground; now the two were to merge. Plough Lane was sealed, and the sites fully integrated. These plans for the world's first purpose-built international airport were set in motion by Parliamentary approval of the 1925 Croydon Airport Act, work beginning on the new buildings in 1926.

That year Lufthansa started a Croydon-Amsterdam service, Sabena began a Croydon-Brussels run and, in mid-July, Imperial Airways introduced the three-engined Armstrong-Whitworth Argosy on its Croydon-Paris service. December 1926 saw a survey flight to Delhi, a 62-hour journey.

*Croydon was the home of Imperial Airways and its memorable 130-foot-wingspan, maximum-weight 28,000lb HP 42s like G-AAXC 'Heracles'. Its top speed was 120mph, minimum speed 51mph, and range 500 miles: still a gorgeous sight and sound.*

*Westland IV airliner taxiing out at Croydon*

By January 1927 a Cairo to Basra Imperial Airways service was running, fed from Croydon, and in May Imperial Airways obtained a spectacular publicity coup by opening a popular *Silver Wing* lunchtime service to Paris using 'silver' aircraft.

Arousing great interest, Charles Lindbergh, the first man to fly the Atlantic solo, flew into Croydon on 29 May 1927 in his *Spirit of St Louis*. The welcoming crowd numbered an amazing 120,000, rated enormous at the time. Landing at Paris/Le Bourget, he covered 3,610 miles in 33hr 30½min, then brought his 230hp Ryan monoplane via Brussels to Croydon. He was followed by two of his countrymen, Schlee and Brock, who on 28 August landed at Croydon during their round-the-world flight.

In January 1928 new airport buildings situated alongside Purley Way and south of the NAF factory were completed, the wartime RFC structures having been at last demolished. Official opening of Croydon Airport took place on 2 May, and was performed by Lady Hoare. The new buildings received wide acclaim, and were copied in several foreign cities, including Moscow. By 1929 Croydon was Europe's busiest airport and the most successful financially. Smaller companies had joined in to operate local flights, and even Imperial Airways, for more than three years, flew 'tea flights' over London for £2 and 2 shillings (210p then, possibly £110 today).

The 20th anniversary of the first cross-Channel flight was celebrated on 27 July 1929 when M Louis Bleriot flew from France to Dover, then visited Croydon. Three days later a three-engined ANT-9 monoplane, piloted by M Grommoff and carrying ten passengers, touched down here. Bringing 1929 to a close, Francis Chichester left Croydon for Australia in his Gipsy Moth, a name he bestowed years later on his round-the-world yacht, now at Greenwich and worth a visit.

To extract maximum value from Croydon, several small companies were encouraged to open aeronautical manufacturing businesses. In December 1928 Desoutter Aircraft was established in part of the ADC premises to build Koolhoven light transports, concentrating upon the FK 41 design. Production amounted to 28 Desoutter Mk I and 13 Mk II high-wing single-engined transports. Surrey Flying Services, here in the late 1920s and into the 1930s, manufactured aircraft components, and during October 1929 the Robinson Aircraft Co also took up residence. Re-named Redwing Aircraft in March 1931, the company built light aircraft and supplied components into the late 1940s. Another similar contractor was Captain W. A. Rollason's factory, opened in 1937, and Croydon-based (as well as also functioning elsewhere) until 1973. After the war it specialised in handling light aircraft including transports and a large number of Tiger Moths. General Aircraft Ltd, formed at Croydon on 21 March 1931 out of the Monospar Wing Co, moved to more extensive premises at Feltham in October 1934.

The 1930s saw Croydon feature in many famous record-breaking and pioneering flights by such famed aviators as Charles Kingsford Smith, Bert Hinkler and Jim Mollison, but those by Amy Johnson are probably the best known. She left Croydon on 31 May 1930 on her famous flight to Darwin, Australia, becoming the first woman to fly solo the 9,960 miles from Britain to Australia, in de Havilland DH 60 Gipsy Moth *G-AAAH*, preserved in the Kensington Science Museum. Records were at this time frequently broken, and in November 1937 A E Clouston broke the London-Cape Town record previously held by Amy Johnson.

*Hurricanes of 615 Squadron landing at Croydon in the summer of 1940. (IWM)*

On 11 May 1937, the day before the Coronation of King George VI, Hermann Goering arrived at Croydon Airport uninvited in a Junkers Ju 52 3/m. After spending the night at the German Embassy with the Ambassador, Herr von Ribbentrop, he was driven back to Croydon, uninvited and unwanted at the Coronation. Germany's Lufthansa was operating a scheduled service, often in bad weather, perfecting instrument flying and the use of the Lorenz beam system. The final pre-war Lufthansa departure was made by Ju 52 D-AXOS on 31 August 1939.

By then Croydon was hosting impressive monoplanes like the DH 91 Albatross, AW Ensign and Douglas DC-2s and DC-3s. But the end was very close now, for on 1 September 1939 Imperial Airways and others dispersed to other airfields.

Plans to use Croydon as a satellite of Kenley were enacted on 2 September when Gladiators of No 615 (County of Surrey) Auxiliary Squadron moved in, soon joined by Hurricanes of No 3 Squadron from Biggin Hill, which took over the two southern hangars. No 17 Squadron's Hurricanes were here before the day ended, and No 3 Squadron scrambled for the first time on 4 September. On 9 September No 17 Squadron moved to Debden, then on 10 October No 145 re-formed at Croydon and equipped with Blenheim I(f)s. Gladiators of No 607 (County of Durham) Squadron staged through on 14 October and next day left for Merville, France, together with 615 Squadron and some impressive, aged transport aircraft. No 3 Squadron often sent detachments to Manston, and from 17 December to 10 February 1940 had detached aircraft at Hawkinge. On 29 December 1939 No 92 Squadron, flying Bristol Blenheim I(f)s, arrived, and in March started re-equipping with Spitfire 1s, while 145 Squadron converted to Hurricanes. No 3 Squadron had returned to Kenley on 29 January 1940, No 145 Squadron moved to Filton on 7 May, and next day No 92 moved to Northolt.

A battered No 607 Squadron arrived from France on 22 May, with transport aircraft bringing in wounded to Croydon, then the squadron's personnel left for Usworth on the 21st as No 501 Squadron arrived from Jersey. No 501 left for Middle Wallop on 4 July. Meanwhile, on 4 June No 111 Squadron arrived from North Weald and was almost at once very active over France and the Channel.

On 4 July Canadians were back at Croydon, when an advance party of No 1 Royal Canadian Air Force Squadron began to arrive. At Croydon it was to receive Hurricanes shipped from Canada; two-blade-propeller types, they had three-blade propellers fitted on arrival in the UK. On 10 July 111 Squadron fought a fierce battle over the Channel, marking its first encounter during the Battle of Britain. The squadron was now moving forward daily to Hawkinge, from where it fought.

After a few tented nights, the Canadians were found quarters off camp. Some ate in Croydon tea-rooms, paid for from their own pockets; excellent teas were still available as rationing had yet to bite hard. But such activity was just the lull before the storm, and when the Luftwaffe struck Croydon it did so without warning and most ferociously.

Beautiful, that summer eve when shortly before 1900 on Thursday 15 August a group of Canadians were watching a group of twin-engined aircraft in blissful ignorance. Suddenly an airman of 111 Squadron yelled, "They're bloody Jerries!" It did not at once get through to the Canadians until the intruders dived and their bombs could be seen falling away. It was all over in a few minutes. The attack had been delivered by Erprobungsgruppe 210, a fighter-bomber unit specialising in low attacks using Bf 110s and 109s. Its Swiss-born Commander was Hauptmann Walter Rubensdorffer.

*Dakotas of No 110 Wing in early 1945.*

At 1815 some seventy or so raiders had appeared on coastal radar screens and at 1850 No 111 Squadron had scrambled nine Hurricanes from Croydon with orders to orbit base. The situation changed very fast, with the German formation at 10,000 feet splitting in two. Rubensdorffer may well have mistaken Croydon for nearby Kenley, and at 1859 he dived and released the first bomb on the aerodrome. As the raiders (possibly twenty-five in number) attacked, the Hurricanes went among them trying to disrupt the attack, causing some bombs to be dropped wide, resulting in civilian casualties in the airport's proximity.

The attackers fled individually, Rubensdorffer's Bf 110 speeding south-east and being shot down in flames near Bletchinglye Farm, Rothersfield, Sussex by Sqn Ldr Thompson; the crew were killed. No 32 Squadron was quickly on the scene, and the Bf 109s fled, for they were none too well supplied with fuel. Having to protect themselves, the Bf 110s formed one of their defensive circles, but it did not stop three in all from being destroyed, two by 32 Squadron.

In a few minutes Croydon had been considerably damaged. The armoury had taken a direct hit and the pitted landing ground resembled a lunar landscape. 'C' Hangar, used by Rollason Aircraft Services, received direct hits by incendiary bombs, and all the training aircraft stored inside were destroyed. The terminal building and control tower were damaged, and Rollason's factory and workshop were badly hit, causing many civilian casualties. 'D' Hangar received serious blast damage and was raked by cannon fire. 'A' Hangar escaped, having only a few windows broken. The Officers' Mess was reduced to a heap of rubble by extreme blast. Five airmen of 'Treble-One' Squadron and one in SHQ died in the attack, whereas sixty-two civilians were killed. Four 111 Squadron airmen, an officer of No 1 (RCAF) Squadron, two civilian telephone operators and 185 other civilians were injured, for the British NSF factory had also received a direct hit – thirty died there alone. Following the attack No 111 Squadron was diverted to Hawkinge while repairs to the airfield were carried out.

At about 1930hrs the BBC reported that Croydon had been dive-bombed – such a newsflash was previously unheard of. In lurid terms it told of the raid, clearly for propaganda purposes. That the Germans had the cheek to bomb Croydon, which most people knew, showed what terrible people they were. They would be sure to get a very bad press coverage. That Croydon was a fighter station somehow was overlooked.

*'DC-3' OO-AUY of SABENA about to touch down at Croydon in 1947.*

*Ju 52/3mg8e G-AHOF at Croydon in 1947, one of ten used by BEA for domestic services between November 1946 and August 1947. BEA*

Within two days the craters had been filled in and Croydon was again operational – then on Sunday 18 August it again came under attack, this time by high-level raiders. No 111 Squadron was scrambled to orbit Kenley at 3,000 feet. Croydon, undefended, was an easy target for the high-flying Dornier 17s, which within five minutes dropped a shoal of HE bombs, some with delayed-action fusing.

Next day 'Treble One' Squadron retired for rest and No 85 Squadron's eighteen Hurricanes came from Debden to take over, led by their CO, Sqn Ldr Peter Townsend. The Canadians had moved to Northolt on 16 August.

At 1255 on 31 August, Croydon was yet again bombed, by a dozen Bf 110s that damaged a hangar and an air raid shelter. During the resulting engagement Peter Townsend was shot down and injured. On 1 September Spitfires of 72 Squadron moved in, allowing 85 Squadron to retire to Castle Camps. Such was the horrendous toll of battle that during the squadron's stay fourteen of its pilots had been shot down, three had been killed and five wounded. No 111 Squadron returned to Croydon on the 2nd, the day that the first Hurricane IIs to enter squadron service arrived. On the 3rd there were ten here for 111 Squadron, which became the first to operate the Mk II. It had a Merlin XX that boosted the top speed to 335mph at 21,000 feet. The aircrafts' stay was brief, however, for they left for *Drem* on 8 September after having fought on the 7th during the first large-scale daylight raid on London. Their replacement on the 8th was 605 Squadron, which soon saw its first fighting in the Battle of Britain. On 14 September it was 72 Squadron's turn to move, in this case to Biggin Hill. With the accent now on Wing activity, on 15 September Nos 253, 501 and 605 Squadrons fought as the Kenley Wing. Increased Bf 109 fighter-bomber raids drew 605 Squadron up from Croydon until the tempo decreased.

The station had been twice again bombed and was attacked by lone bombers on 15, 19 and 23 October. No 605 began re-arming with Hurricane Mk IIas in November, but it was February before the change-over was completed, and on the 25th the squadron left for Martlesham in an exchange with 17 Squadron and its Hurricane IIs, which moved in on 28 February 1941. Part of the Kenley Wing, they participated, from Croydon, in offensive operations over France. No 17 returned to Martlesham Heath. on 31 March, then it was No 1 Squadron's turn. It arrived on 7 April, joined the Kenley Wing, and on 1 May moved to Redhill, remaining in the Kenley Wing. That brought to an end the use of Croydon as a fighter station.

The change was apparent when 11 Group Flight occupied the vacant tenancy on 6 June 1941. Using Blenheim IVs and Lysanders, it assisted with the training of GCI operators, and carried out more generalised AA co-operation activities. On 19 November 1941 the unit at Croydon became No 287 Squadron, and remained here until 4 July 1944.

A second change came on 12 August 1941 when No 414 (RCAF) Squadron formed as an Army co-operation squadron equipped with Lysanders and Tomahawks. During June 1942 414 Squadron re-armed with Mustang Mk Is and flew operationally for the first time on 30 June, when three Mustangs flew an anti-fighter-bomber patrol along the south coast.

On 1 July 1942 Nos 302 and 317 (Polish) Spitfire Squadrons arrived to participate in a combined operation on the French coast, which was postponed, so they soon departed. For 414 Squadron the eventual raid on Dieppe of 19 August brought it its first combat victory. During a tactical

*Croydon-based Airspeed Consul G-AIAH of Morton Air Services, the last firm to operate a scheduled service there.*

reconnaissance Fg Off H H Hills was attacked by three Fw 190s and destroyed one. From the same operation two Mustangs did not return, but their pilots were rescued. During that day pairs of Mustangs flew nine tac/recce operations. No 414 Squadron left Croydon on 2 December 1942 for Dunsfold.

On 12 December 1943 No 116 AAC Squadron arrived, but with 287 moved out on 2 July 1944, making way for Croydon to pass to Transport Command next day and at the same time for No 110 (Transport) Wing to form, its task being the handling of Dakota passenger flights to liberated Europe.

On 5 September 1944 No 147 Squadron re-formed at Croydon with Dakotas, under the control of 110 Wing. On 13 November scheduled services to Allied-occupied Europe commenced, and the same month BOAC started limited operations from Croydon. The first private civil air service to operate since the war was inaugurated by Railway Air Services, linking Croydon with Belfast, via Liverpool. A detachment of No 271 Squadron's Dakotas arrived on 2 April 1945, but after only five days moved out. By the end of hostilities other companies, including Scottish Airways, Jersey Airways and Morton Air Services, had moved into Croydon. RAF activity continued and on 23 September1945 No 110 Wing carried its 100,000th passenger. RAF operations continued until 4 February 1946, when BOAC took over the European services. No 110 Wing disbanded on 15 February 1946.

On 9 October a detachment of ten from No 435 (RCAF) Squadron, Down Ampney, joined Wing operations, the Canadians remaining until 16 March 1946. No 147 Squadron disbanded at Croydon six months later.

*A J Whitmore's Tiger Moth collection at Croydon on 27 March 1954 included K4259, ex-No 2 Grading Unit. Disposed of on 18 November 1953, it became G-ANMO.*

*A 2003 view across what was Croydon Airport landing ground looking WSW from Purley Way. (Colin Richardson)*

Although in 1946-47 Croydon was the centre for many internal scheduled flights and charters, international flights were gradually transferred to Northolt or Heathrow. The coming and going of hosts of Consuls, Rapides, Avro XIXs, Ju 52s, Dakotas and a few much larger aircraft was always a joy to behold. What brought an end to such delights was the introduction of aircraft needing longer take-off and landing runs on metalled runways. There was no possibility of Croydon expanding, and on 25 March 1946 Heathrow was designated London Airport.

In 1947 BEAC and BOAC departed for Northolt and Heathrow, leaving only small companies remaining at Croydon. A Government report of the mid-1950s sealed its fate and Croydon officially closed to flying on 30 September 1959, on which day Croydon's last scheduled service involved DH Heron *G-AOXL* of Morton Air Services. Maintenance companies moved to Gatwick and small operators and clubs to Biggin Hill.

Much of Croydon Aerodrome's landing ground has been buried beneath the houses and gardens of the Roundshaw Estate, where roads carry names to remind the populace of former great days. The terminal building and control tower are safeguarded by preservation orders. To the north some of the NAF buildings are still in use. On 28/29 August 2004 an airshow was held, a DH60 and Tiger Moth having earlier flown in.

The Croydon Airport Society, formed in 1978, runs the Visitor Centre, open between 1100 and 1600 on the first Sunday of each month. In two galleries in the terminal and control tower it contains memorabilia and displays outlining the airfield's history. Outside is a DH Heron. It seems confused, probably because the grass spreading before the terminal is merely a play park.

**Main features:**
*Grass runs:* NW-SE 3,900ft, NE-SW 3,300ft, E-W 3,600ft. *Hangars:* four EO Blisters, pre-war civil and engineering hangars also partially used. *Hardstandings:* twenty-two twin-engined type. *Accommodation:* RAF officers 83, SNCOs 140, ORs 436; WAAF officers 5, SNCOs 6, ORs 204.

## CULHAM, Oxfordshire

*51°39N/01°13W 190ft asl; SU052958. 1¹/₂ miles SE of Abingdon, by the A415*

A naval base at Oxford seemed incongruous at the time, and now it seems even more unlikely. Yet where Culham Laboratory stands, and clever folk try to harness the power of the H-bomb for peaceful purposes, there once rested HMS *Hornbill*. The twenty-one hangars of the former occupant, clustered on its north-west side, exist where the runways were completed in September 1944 and the Aircraft Receipt & Despatch Unit was commissioned on 1 November 1944. Many types of aircraft passed through Culham's RN Ferry Pool (later known as No 1 Ferry Flight) including Ansons, Fireflies, Reliants and Seafires.

Post-war Culham was a centre for naval reservists residing between London and Oxford and in the surrounding areas. No1832 Squadron was commissioned on 1 July 1947 to train them to use Seafire Mk IIIs, XVs, XVIIs and FR 46s. Harvard IIbs and Mk IIIs also served the squadron, which later re-armed with Sea Fury FB 11s. A move to Benson came on 18 July 1953 as Culham was run down. No 1840 RNVR Squadron formed from 1832 Squadron on 14 April 1951, and operated

*Seafire F 17s at Culham: SX198-101/CH nearest, alongside SP343-126/CH.*

Firefly Is, IVs and Harvards before leaving for Ford on 30 June 1951.

Two further reserve squadrons commissioned at Culham on 1 October 1952 were Nos 1832A and 1832B, which became 1836 and 1835 Squadrons respectively in April 1953, prior to moving to Southern Air Division Benson on 18 July 1953, taking along its Sea Fury FB 11s.

An interesting small unit that formed here on 1 May 1947 was 739 Squadron, known also as the Photographic Trials & Development Unit, equipped with Sea Mosquito TR 33s, Sea Hornet F 20s and PR 22s, and a Dominie. Culham's aircraft carried the tail identity letters 'CH'.

HMS *Hornbill* was paid off on 30 September 1953, subsequent to which the Admiralty used Culham as a store until the Atomic Energy Commission moved in during early 1960.

**Main features:**
*Runways:* 10/28 4,200ft x 90ft, 00/24 3,600ft x 90ft, 17/35 3,600ft x 90ft. Perimeter track 40ft wide. *Hangars:* twenty-one 87ft 6in x 60ft. *Hardstandings:* sixteen.

## DEENETHORPE, Northamptonshire

*52°30N/00°35W 330ft asl; SE965930. 6 miles NE of Corby, by the A43*

Deenethorpe came into use late in 1943. During the first few days of November 1943 the four squadrons of the 401st BG (612, 613, 614, 615) moved in with B-17s. Deenethorpe was a typical three-runway wartime temporary airfield with a couple of T2 hangars and a usual style of control tower.

Operations commenced for the 401st on 26 November 1943, and after even a few operations it was clear that it was setting very high levels of bombing accuracy, maintained to the end of hostilities. Targets varied and included factories, submarine facilities, shipyards, marshalling yards, V-weapon sites and airfields as it took its place in the 1st Air Division's campaign.

The first DUC was awarded after the 401st attacked Oschersleben airfield on 11 January 1944, a second following their bombing, in the face of fierce opposition, of Leipzig/Mockau airfield on 20 February 1944. In the D-Day run-up, the 401st played an active part supporting the landings, then the break-out from St Lo. It took part in August's reduction of the Brest garrison, bombed Peenemunde on 25 August 1944, and fought in the Arnhem misadventure, in the Battle of the Bulge and during the Rhine crossing. From October 1944 its good bombing accuracy was put to particular use, the Group specialising in attacking oil targets. Most USAAF Groups had particularly bad days – that for the 401st came on 26 May 1944 when seven B-17s were lost in action. Generally, though, the Group's losses were comparatively low. When the war ended the Group had participated in 255 operations from Deenethorpe, flown 7,430 sorties, and lost ninety-five B-17s.

Return to the USA took place between 30 May and mid-June 1945. Personnel who did not fly home returned in style on the *Queen Elizabeth*, and many must have felt satisfaction when sailing on both 'Queens', for their journey to Britain in October 1943 had been aboard the *Queen Mary*.

Barely had they left Deenethorpe when the RAF took over, placing No 11 Recruit Centre here in June 1945. Military flying days, though, were finished at Deenethorpe, for no flying unit moved in before its closure in mid-1946. Long dormant, it was almost all sold off by 1963. Part of a runway remained in use for aircraft bringing visitors to the steelworks then at Corby, and for which purposes Deenethorpe in recent years flew a windsock.

**Main features:**
*Runways:* 050° 6,000ft, 100° 4,200ft, 151° 4,200ft, concrete with wood chips. *Hangars:* two T2. *Hardstandings:* fifty loop type. *Accommodation:* USAAF officers 421, EM 2,473.

## DENHAM, Buckinghamshire

*51°35N/00°30W, 225ft asl; TQ030886. 2 miles NW of Uxbridge*

Situated between the A412 and A413 roads, this small site came into use during the latter part of the First World War when, from 8 September 1917 to 15 February 1919, it was the home of Nos 5 and 6 Schools of Military Aeronautics. They provided eight weeks of ground instruction for pilots and observers before they embarked upon flying training. Subjects taught included the fundamentals of aero-engines, rigging, armament, photography and map-reading. Pupils passed out as 2nd Lieutenants, then proceeded to a Training Depot Station. The airfield, surrounded by woodland, was abandoned after the departure of the schools.

James Martin, who came to Denham in August 1929, was keen to design and build aeroplanes. He found the facilities primitive for there was no water supply. Poor roads and a shed built of breeze-blocks and wood stood by three ramshackle ex-wartime wooden huts. Nevertheless, he teamed up with Captain Baker and they went ahead and opened the Martin Baker Company. Steadily it expanded, the factory having over 130,000 square feet of floor area.

The MB 1, the company's first aeroplane, was a very unusual tourer whose wings folded. Far more unusual was the positioning of its power plant behind the cabin, the propeller being driven by a shaft passing between pilot and passenger. The advantage was that it placed the pilot well to the front of the single-engined machine. First flown in April 1935, it had a top speed of 125mph.

The MB 2 was a simple eight-gun fighter whose fuselage was longer that its 34ft 6in wingspan. Belief was that was a 'trouser' undercarriage (one where the undercarriage oleo leg and wheel are encased in a large, wide trouser-like fairing) suited the unsophisticated aircraft. It first flew from Harwell on 3 August 1938. The company built a helicopter designed by Raoul Hafner, which was test-flown at Heston.

The company's later aircraft needed more operating space than Denham could provide and were test-flown where they could be accommodated. In the case of the MB 3 six-cannon, Sabre-powered racy-looking fighter, Captain Baker had just taken off from Wing on 12 September 1942 when he had a catastrophic engine failure that cost him his life.

Meanwhile, military interest in Denham aerodrome was re-awakened at the start of the war. Two Bellman and three Blister hangars were erected, but the runways would remain grass only, their runs extending 3,150 feet north/south, 2,580 feet north-east/south-west, 4,150 feet east/west, and 2,400 feet north-west/south-east.

From 18 November 1941 to 9 July 1945 Denham served as an RLG for the Tiger Moths of 21 EFTS Booker. For local ATC cadets No 125 GS opened in August 1943 and functioned here until 1947. A detachment of No 38 Group Flight was here for a short while in 1944.

In 1946 private flying was resumed and has continued since. Air Schools Ltd started operating from here and Elstree in 1952 and many concerns have since been based here. A major improvement was the addition of the 006/24 779-metre-long, 18-metre-wide asphalt runway. The 12/30 540-metre runway is of grass. In 2003 Bickerton's Aerodromes Ltd was Denham's operator. The Pilot Centre operates Cessna 152s and 172s, also Piper PA-28s.

Denham remains the headquarters of Martin Baker Ltd, world famous for its ejector seats, which, to the end of May 2003, had saved 6,994 lives. One in ten of the seats manufactured saves a life. Testing is carried out from Chalgrove.

**Main features:**
*Grass area:* N/S 3,150ft, NE/SW 2,580ft, E/W 4,140ft, NW/SE 2,580ft. *Hangars:* three EO Blisters, one Bessoneau 156ft x 25ft x 22ft high and one 156ft x 50ft x 12ft high. Hardstanding: one rectangular pan. *Accommodation:* for personnel, nil.

## DENTON, Northamptonshire

*52°12N/00°47W 365ft asl; SP830580. 6 miles ESE of Northampton*

Denton was once a large meadow used not for grazing of cows but for the needs of Tiger Moths. It came into use as an RLG for 6 EFTS Sywell in summer 1940, its secondary role being for night-flying, allowing permanent airfields to be unlit. During night-flying, on 17/18 July 1941, an intruder, attracted to the bright lights of Denton, dropped ten small bombs near the boundary. By then the parent unit, 6 EFTS Sywell, was increasingly training Free French airmen.

The most spectacular of the inevitable accidents occurred during night-flying on 12 December 1941. Flt Lt E M Frisby and Leading Aircraftsman D Q May, flying a night circuit, collided with a 15 OTU Wellington. Both aircraft dived in, killing the Tiger Moth's crew.

During 1941 and 1942 accommodation at Denton slowly improved, and Blister hangars were added. Some Tiger Moths used here were noteworthy by reason of age or origin. L6923, a 1937 build, was involved in an accident when taking off on 8 April 1944. On 25 July 1944 Tiger Moth BB699 (used by Brooklands Aviation pre-war as *G-ADGY*) crashed into power cables at Turvey, both occupants dying. Excitement was generated when, on the afternoon of 10 April 1944, Beaufighter NE480 crashed on the landing ground and was burned out.

When in late 1944 Sywell was badly flooded, Denton proved most useful until 9 July 1945, when flying from the RLG ceased.

**Main features:**
Grass field runs: N-S 2,700ft, NE-SW 3,000ft, E-W 2,460ft, NW-SE 2,640ft. *Hangars:* two Extra Over Blisters, eight Standard Blisters. *Accommodation:* RAF only, officers 2, SNCOs 4, ORs 120.

## DESBOROUGH, Northamptonshire

*52°28N/00°48W 460ft asl; SP815860. Approximately 6 miles NNW of Kettering*

Late 1942 saw conversion commence of an ironstone upland into RAF Desborough, a typical temporary heavy bomber airfield to accommodate 84 OTU. Unfortunately its opening on 1 September 1943 was marred by a crash on the airfield of a No 22 OTU Wellington, fortunately without serious crew injuries.

Controlled by No 92 Group Bomber Command, 84 OTU (founded on the opening day) had an establishment of forty plus ten Wellington III/Xs, five Hurricane IIs for fighter affiliation, four Martinet target towers and two Master IIs for gunnery training. By 1944 monthly hours were averaging around 2,000, and not without serious accidents. On 21 January 1944, for instance, Wellington LN238 crashed into Geddington Chase Wood four miles north of Kettering, killing three of the crew and injuring four others. Six days later there were two more fatal accidents, Wellington X3392 crashing at 2014 hours near Molesworth, followed 2½ hours later by HZ484 at Arthingworth.

Every two weeks eleven aircrew trainees for each role were posted in – pilots, navigators, wireless-operators, bomb-aimers and rear-gunners – and formed into individual crews to undertake a ten-week course embracing about eighty hours as a team.

Harrington, the OTU's satellite between 6 November 1943 and 26 March 1944, was transferred to the US VIIIth AF on 1 April 1944. Establishment of the OTU was reduced on 9 May 1944 to three-quarters of OTU level, while remaining centred on Wellington Xs. The final course, No 38, which opened on 17 April 1945, was cut short, for the OTU closed on 14 June 1945 and the Wellingtons departed.

Following runway maintenance, Dakotas of No 107 (Transport) OTU Leicester East used Desborough for practise until August, when the station was placed on care and maintenance.

On 4 October 1945 Desborough – still administered by Transport Command – passed from No 44 Group to No 4 Group. No 1381 (Transport) Conversion Unit moved in from Bramcote on 19 November 1945, bringing Dakotas that remained until 1 January 1947, when they moved to Dishforth.

Desborough reverted to care and maintenance, limited activity involving Cadet gliders of No 108 Gliding School, ATC, operating here between 1945 and 1949.

Cold War fighter pilot needs brought the opening of No 102 Refresher School North Luffenham, whose trainees – Meteors, Spitfires and Vampires – used Desborough as an RLG between May and November 1951. After again being held on care and maintenance for several years, the site was sold for civilian use, and very little now remains of its airfield days.

**Main features:**
*Runways:* 272° 6,000ft x 150ft, 321° 4,200ft x 150ft, 201° 4,200ft x 150ft, tarmac and wood surfaces on concrete. *Hangars:* four T2, one B1. *Hardstandings:* twenty-nine frying-pan type. *Accommodation:* RAF officers 159, SNCOs 394, ORs 1,004; WAAF officers 8, SNCOs 15, ORs 297.

## DESFORD (LEICESTER), Leicestershire

52°38N/ 01°17W 425ft asl; SK480020. S of Desford, between the A47 and B582 roads

A small grass airfield triangular in shape and bounded by roads, Desford opened in 1935 as a base for the Reid & Sigrist-operated No 7 Elementary & Reserve Training School, which opened on 25 November of that year and became equipped with Tiger Moths, Ansons and Hart variants. Sited south of the village after which it was named, the aerodrome was also known as Leicester, being close to the city.

In September 1939 the school became No 7 EFTS, opened under 51 Group, Training Command using Tiger Moths as its main equipment. To help increase pupil output from the School, Desford used Braunstone RLG from November 1939 to July 1945.

In mid-July 1940 Desford entered the CRO, Reid & Sigrist undertaking the repair of Harvards, Mitchells and particularly Defiants.

No 7 EFTS continued functioning after the war, becoming No 7 RFS on 9 May 1947, which, like its predecessors, was run by Reid & Sigrist. Unlike most RFSs, its equipment ranged through Tiger Moths to Prentices and Ansons. The School disbanded on 31 July 1953.

*Reid & Sigrist's post-war 'Desford', a small twin configured for prone piloting trials at RAE and visiting Old Warden on 29 July 1973.*

*Flying instructors of 7 EFTS Desford in 1941. (via Don Benfield)*

Reid & Sigrist was the manufacturer of twin-engined light aircraft, the Snargasher and the post-war Desford, which was acquired by the MoS for research into prone pilot flying.

The airfield closed soon after the RFS was disbanded, and such buildings as survive are in private, industrial use.

**Main features:**
*Landing area, grass:* NE/SW 3,600ft, E-W 2,700ft. *Hangars:* Two civilian hangars, one Bellman (MAP), thirteen Standard Blister, one Over Blister, one EO Blister. *Hardstandings:* nil. *Accommodation:* RAF only.

## DETLING, Kent

*51°18N/00°36E 600ft asl; TQ182595. 3¹/₂ miles NE of Maidstone off the A249*

In Africa, America, Australia, 'Ambling Annie' was ready to train anyone, any time, any place, anywhere. In contrast, at Detling during the toughest wartime days she displayed a very nasty, highly offensive attitude by tackling the Luftwaffe's best with astonishing success. A 'flying greenhouse' bearing a huge armed cupola resembling a parrot cage, the manoeuvrable crawler presented a surprisingly difficult target when escorting a coastal convoy. Many times the Avro Ansons of 500 Squadron saw off pirates of all sizes, sometimes causing them to involuntarily sample British seawater. No 500 Squadron managed its task skilfully and very courageously, for to face a Bf 109 in an Anson was not everyone's idea of fun. Not surprising, then, that the enemy retaliated with ferocious attacks upon Annie's Detling dwellings.

Despite a long, varied history, Detling, atop the North Downs, remains publicity shy. Opened in 1915 as a Royal Navy Air Station for the defence of Sheerness and Chatham, that commitment passed to the RFC on 3 April 1917. BE 2cs and 12as of 'A' Flight, No 50 Squadron, soon came to help tackle Gotha day raids. In summer the Squadron temporarily operated Sopwith Pups, after which it relied on BE 12as and AW FK 8s. Following No 50's departure on 8 February 1918, No 143 Squadron filled the space in March and brought along FK 8s, which in May were replaced with SE 5as. The squadron remained until disbandment on 31 October 1919, the station soon after being held on care and maintenance prior to reversion to agricultural use.

RAF expansion in the 1930s led the Air Ministry to review the Detling site, then acquire it for development. Upon re-opening during summer 1938 its nautical association was repeated when it became administered by 16 Group, Coastal Command. Then on 28 September 1938 No 500 (County of Kent) Auxiliary Squadron, flying Hawker Hinds, moved in from Manston. Its role was, on 7 November 1938, changed to general reconnaissance, re-arming with Ansons commencing during March 1939.

When the war started 500 Squadron began flying convoy protection patrols off Kent. Generally regarded as out-of-date training aircraft, the Ansons proved very useful protectors, able, because of speed disparity, to survive in battle with fast fighters. When in June 1940 three patrolling Ansons were jumped by nine Bf 109s, No 500 Squadron claimed two without loss.

Throughout the campaign to save France and retrieve the BEF, 500 Squadron was hyper-active despite obvious risks. More Ansons of No 1 Coastal Artillery Co-operation Flight joined them on 18 May, and they remained – supplemented with Blenheim IVs – till late 1940.

Retreating from France, No 4 Squadron and its Lysanders on 22 May stayed for three days before space could be found for them elsewhere. Between 26 May and 24 June Blenheim IVf maritime fighters repeatedly used Detling as they, like 500 Squadron, helped to protect the withdrawal of the BEF from France.

On 30 May 1940 an Anson returned to Detling with engine trouble. As the pilot attempted a wheels-up landing, an engine blazed furiously and soon the aircraft caught fire. With a full-bomb-load explosion likely, Corporal Daphne Pearson, a WAAF medical orderly, most courageously dragged the injured pilot clear, shielding him with her body as the wreckage exploded. Her gallantry led to the award of a Commission in June 1940, and in August to the award of the Empire Gallantry Medal, which was exchanged for the newly introduced George Cross during November 1941.

When the Battle of Britain began, 500 Squadron's Ansons, Blenheim IVs of 53 Squadron (here between 3 July and 20 November 1940) and 801 Squadron, Fleet Air Arm, flying Skuas and Rocs, were all protecting convoys and carrying out strikes. As part of the anti-invasion force, they attracted ferocious enemy attention.

Detling's first vicious raid, at 1710 hours on 13 August 1940, was carried out by some forty Ju 87 Stukas of IV/LG1. They struck as personnel were heading for evening meals, killing many in the three Mess buildings. Eight Blenheims were destroyed, eight Ansons mauled, hangars were left blazing, and the landing ground was cratered while living accommodation and administrative buildings were severely damaged. Gp Capt Edward Davis, Station Commander, was killed in the operations room, which received a direct hit. Casualties included sixty-seven killed.

Another sharp raid took place at 1730 on 30 August, more than fifty bombs falling on the landing area and putting it out of use until the next day. A small arms store was also hit, a Blenheim damaged and there were more casualties. Next day at 1006 assorted Bf 109s and Bf 110s strafed the station, setting petrol and oil stores alight and destroying the electrical power system.

On 1 September it was the turn of a few Ju 88s, escorted by Bf 109s, to bomb and machine-gun the station, causing five slight injuries. Two large bombs fell near the operations block, and a follow-up night raid started a fire in the already damaged Officers' Mess.

At 1316 on 2 September thirty high-flying Do 17Zs of 9/KG 3 carpet-bombed Detling with HE bombs. They pounded a 500 Squadron hangar and put the station out of use for four hours. So severe was the overall damage by now that repairs continued into 1941.

What had not been destroyed was the indefatigable will and great spirit of Detling's 1940 personnel. On 12 July Plt Off Pain of 500 Squadron was escorting a convoy when nine He 111s attacked it. Tackling the violators, the Anson crew shot down one of them. On 18 July Sgt Barr and crew bagged a Bf 110 before Spitfires came to help protect his charge, one of fifty-one convoys escorted in July during the course of which 201 sorties were flown in a hazardous area. In August 161 sorties were flown, the Ansons escorting fifty-seven convoys, September's comparative totals being 115 and 52. No 500 Squadron continued convoy escorts into 1941 before changing its role, for which it was re-armed with Blenheims in April. Emphasis was shifting to offensive operations now that the risk of invasion was receding, and fighters were available to protect shallow-water convoys. A few weeks later 500 Squadron received Hudsons and moved to Bircham Newton on 30 May 1941 to attack shipping. Coastal Command's No 16 Group Communication Flight took up residence at Detling during June 1941 and stayed – later as a lodger – until January 1945.

As No 500 departed, and with the airfield largely repaired, change set in. 'D' Flight 2 AACU arrived on 11 June 1941 for a long sojourn. It became 1624 AAC Flight on 14 February 1943, was upgraded to 527 Squadron on 1 December 1943, staying until mid-November 1944. During that time it flew Defiants, Gladiators, Hurricanes, Oxfords and Martinets. A No 6 AACU Detachment worked with it between mid-September and November 1943.

Between 23 January and 1 August 1942 PR Spitfires of 'K' Flight, No 1 PRU, operated from Detling, where, on 10 February 1942, No 280 Squadron assembled, equipped with Ansons. In June 1942 it began air/sea rescue operations off the south-east coast prior to departure on 31 July 1942. No 2368 Squadron RAF Regiment was also stationed here, and for two weeks in April 1942 some members mounted guard duty at Buckingham Palace.

Detling transferred to 11 Group Fighter Command in 1942 and became a forward fighter airfield affording lodger facilities for Coastal Command. Mustang Is of No 26 Squadron twice used the station, from 12 January to 27 February 1943 and from 21 June to 11 July 1943. No 318 (Polish) formed on 20 March 1943 to fly Hurricane 1s and left for overseas in August.

Preparations for D-Day brought HQ 125 Airfield to Detling on 21 September 1943 for a stay extending to 4 May 1944. As part of the Airfield, Nos 132 and 602 Squadrons were at Detling between 12 October and 18 January 1944 flying Spitfire IXs and accompanied by No 184, which arrived on 12 October 1943 flying Spitfire Vbs, re-armed with Typhoons in December and left on 6 March 1944. After APC training, Nos 132 and 602 Squadrons returned on 11 March and stayed until 18 April 1944.

On 19 May 1944 three Spitfire IX squadrons arrived, Nos 80, 229 and 274, their special task to afford rear protection over UK bases for UK-based squadrons returning from action during the early phase of the invasion. That task completed, they departed on 22 June 1944.

A new operational phase started with the arrival on 11 July 1944 of 504 Squadron, and No 118 on the next day. They were reinforced on 24 July with No 124, which, like other Spitfire IX squadrons, faced the V-1 assault and provided support for Bomber Command heavies during day raids. The latter was the prime task for their replacements, Nos 1 and 165 Squadrons, based here between 10 August and 16 December 1944. Following their departure Detling passed to care and maintenance from 1 January 1945.

The station's flying days were not over, however, for on 1 July 1949, and administered by Reserve Command, the Reserve Command Glider Instructors' School opened, becoming the Home Command Glider Instructors' School on 1 August 1950 and later leaving for Hawkinge. No 141 Gliding School was here from 1951 to disbandment on 1 September 1955, and Detling was also home of Auster VIs of No 1903 AOP Flight, which departed in January 1956. Another ATC unit using the station was No 615 (Volunteer) Gliding School, at Detling in 1955 and leaving for Kenley at the end of that year. The Kent Gliding Club then flew from the airfield until it used Challock.

Detling was eventually returned to its former landowners, and several hundred acres were subsequently purchased by Kent County Council, part of the one-time aerodrome now providing a permanent showground for the Kent County Agricultural Show. Only fragments remain of airfield days, and it is certainly hard to believe that 'Annies' of '500' once chugged around where the show still goes on, even more so that the Third Reich kept trying to spoil everything.

**Main features:**
*Grass Runways:* NE/SW 4,200ft, N/S 2,700ft, E/W 2,700ft. No permanent lighting. *Hangars:* assorted individualistic pre-war hangars replaced with one Bellman, one Bessoneau, and fourteen Blister type. Only permanent buildings left after 1940 raids were Married Quarters. *Hardstandings:* eleven Spur type, twenty-three BRC Fabric. *Accommodation:* RAF 41 officers, 79 SNCOs, 1,386 ORs; WAAF 281 ORs only.

## DOWN AMPNEY, Gloucestershire

*51°40N/01°50W 265ft asl; 7 miles NNW of Swindon*

> "And what happened to you, Edwards?" asked the King, to which the big man is reputed to have responded, "I burned my bum, Sir."

Rarely have five simple words produced such stunning effect. A ripple of laughter is said to have swept across the awards parade while His Majesty turned away laughing – very privately, of course! How sad that so few who delighted in a delectable weekly dose of *The Glums* on the radio knew just what Jimmy Edwards had endured on a dreadful Arnhem day.

He was forever uttering a sombre reminder that there are old pilots, bold pilots, but there aren't many old, bold pilots. He knew, because he was 'a pilot when Pontius was a Pilate'. What he rarely recounted were the ghastly moments aboard KG 444 when he was a very brave pilot.

The run to the DZ went well, all panniers being released, but about five minutes into the return flight two Fw 190s delivered six damaging passes on the Dakota from astern. From the astrodome, Bill Randall, the wireless-operator, shouted instructions to his captain as cannon fire riddled the fuselage and seriously wounded three dispatchers. A further pass set the Dakota's engines blazing. With no hope of getting home, Flt Lt Edwards ordered the crew to abandon, the second pilot and navigator baling out. The wireless operator could not manage it because he was wearing a bulky harness. Edwards, only partly out of the aircraft when it crashed, was thrown clear, but the ordeal was far from over. A Fw 190 then strafed the wreck and its survivors, none of whom, mercifully, was hit. The injuries Edwards sustained amounted to severe burns on both his face and left arm, and according to legend his posterior suffered when his pilot's seat caught fire.

After five minutes the survivors were cheered by English voices telling them to hide in a wood. A doctor came later and, under cover of darkness, they were taken to a farmhouse. There they discovered that two crew members, Harry Sorensen and Alan Clarke, were POWs. Next morning a car carried the party first to Grave, then to the 186th Field Hospital, where their wounds were dressed.

Horrendous injuries and ghastly misfortunes arrived at Down Ampney in vast numbers, for this was a main reception airfield for casualty evacuation flights coming from France following the D-Day landings.

As an airfield, Down Ampney's time was brief, like others in 46 Group. As an action station its days were frenetic. An advance party from Broadwell opened it on 7 February 1944, the first aircraft to land here, on 18 February, being the Proctor of Air Commodore Fiddament, AOC 46 Group. The deadline for the opening of 46 Group's three Dakota bases had been 1 February, at which time only half of Down Ampney's buildings were complete, likewise the runways and roads carved across farmland in recent weeks. Not until 24 February did Down Ampney's first squadron, No 48, arrive. Five days later, 271 Squadron's main party moved in, the squadron soon holding thirty-eight Dakotas and nineteen Horsa gliders. An establishment for a hundred of the latter caused major problems, for there were insufficient dispersals and essential hardstandings to accommodate so many. Nevertheless, by mid-March operational training had begun, and on 16 March No 91 Staging Post arrived.

Down Ampney's squadrons trained to carry out four tasks: freight delivery, casualty evacuation from French airstrips, paratroop drops, and glider towing. These later began to be featured in April's major exercises involving aircraft and gliders. On the 9th, thirty-five Dakotas were within a large formation that, with formation lights blazing, flew a spectacular night navigation tour of central England. More glider towing and careful formation flying followed, the danger clear when two Dakotas collided with grievous results. One of the largest paratroop exercises held in the early morning of 21 April involved more than 700 aircraft. A week later, and watched by the AOC 46 Group, forty Dakotas towed off their Horsas in 27 minutes, a time soon bettered. For the forthcoming invasion, crews needed to fly very accurately at night, and to face searchlights, for which reason Dakota crews participated in Bomber Command *Bullseye* exercises. They also flew *Nickels* late in April, relying upon *Gee* fixes over Normandy and adjacent areas. Just before April ended, the movement of Staging Posts to be opened in France for 'casevac' was practised on a wide scale. May saw a number of large-scale, increasingly efficient glider landing exercises and paratroop drops, which, by the end of the month, were being combined with cross-country night-flying exercises as D-Day approached.

Operation *Tonga* began with the first take-off at 2248 on the night of 5/6 June 1944. Seven Dakota/Horsa combinations and thirty-nine paratroop carriers of 48 and 271 Squadrons participated, the gliders being released on to LZ 'V'. All the aircraft were airborne by 2320, carrying the 3rd Parachute Brigade HQ under Brigadier J Hill DSO MC, and the 1st Canadian Parachute Battalion under Lt Bradbrook. With visibility good, the drops went well, all the Dakotas returning safely.

During the evening of 6 June, fifteen Dakotas of 271 Squadron and twenty-two of 48 Squadron towed thirty-seven Horsas across the Channel in operation *Mallard* to release them on LZ 'N'. A Dakota of 48 Squadron ditched in the Channel, two of the crew returning to Down Ampney within two days. On the night of 7 June, both squadrons assisted during operation *Robroy* with a supply drop.

'Casevac' Dakota operations, commenced on 18 June 1944, started after personnel of 2TAF Tangmere were carried in eleven Dakotas to airstrip B4 in Normandy. There the Dakotas were loaded with 183 casualties, which were flown to Down Ampney. Late in the evening of 21 June ninety more wounded arrived.

Down Ampney's Dakotas conveyed the personnel and stores of 122 Wing to B6, then on 25 June took 125 Wing from Ford to B11, each time returning with wounded. A daily average of a hundred injured during the previous twenty-four hours were brought home. Many, urgently needing surgery, had been given simple dressings, while around a third were walking cases, lots had head wounds and most had tissue destruction. About one-third had been blinded, and quite a high proportion received penicillin treatment. It was the most seriously wounded who were air evacuated, and many had not flown previously. The alternative three-to-four-day journey by land and sea would have meant large numbers dying.

For ground personnel at Down Ampney stretcher-bearing was exhausting physically, but of course greatly rewarding emotionally. The sick had also to be fed, tended, and lifted into ambulances. By the end of June, 869 casualties had been flown into Down Ampney, flights usually taking about 90 minutes. More than 3,000 wounded had reached the station by 20 July.

Living nearby, HM Queen Mary visited the wounded, inspecting Dakota KG 419 'AV' of 271 Squadron in the process. To have been greeted by such a majestic lady, discover her grace and experience her true caring, must have been memorable for many.

Gradually the evacuation airstrips moved a little further away, July flights being mostly out of B14. Freight to the battle zone and 'casevac' remained Down Ampney's major tasks, although supply drops were also undertaken, one of which was laid on to Chambois on 21 July. Flown by Wg Cdr Sproule, KG 421 left Down Ampney at 0530 hours and encountered very bad weather with cloud base at 300 feet. Sproule flew low, finding his DZ marked by fires. Enemy gunners also found a target, the slow Dakota, and soon damaged its wings and engines. More enemy fire pouring through the windows hit the navigator in the shoulder, cut the second pilot's face and injured the captain. First aid was given to the navigator by the wireless-operator and the course set for B14. The rudder was useless so the crew tried maintaining course using engine power while the dispatcher threw out disposable items, heavy rain keeping height and direction was difficult. Then more flak hit the batteries. Oil temperature fell, controls overheated and, although the engines at maximum revs, the ASI showed only 110mph.

The inevitable crash came after the aircraft clipped the top of a tree. Wg Cdr Sproule ordered crash stations then skilfully put down on a hilltop west of Jurques. A shelter from the rain was made although the crew knew that the aircraft was likely to explode at any moment. Two soldier dispatchers unsuccessfully went for help before the pilots set off with a compass, following tank tracks in the belief that they would at least miss mines. Three hours later, and with guidance from a farmer, they located British soldiers and late that afternoon they all reached B14.

Each day, and sometimes twice a day, the casualties continued to flow into Down Ampney. Some 20,000 had arrived by early August, and with the battle intense the station was alerted on 8 August 1944 to be ready for 1,000 casualties in one load, far beyond its ability to cope.

Broadwell and Blakehill assisted, 527 casualties eventually passing through Down Ampney in twelve hours. This meant providing 1,100 meals with all ranks distributing food and comfort as best they could. By 1800 hours the entire accommodation for wounded was full. Well into the night, loading of an ambulance train took place, and not until 0300 hours on the 9th was the backlog cleared.

Other squadrons were helping – Nos 24, 511 and 525 among them – and using B14 as their pick-up point. By early September, B50 and B56 were in use. No 120 Staging Post opened on 5 September, then came a break while the 46 Group squadrons prepared for operation *Market*.

For the initial Arnhem assault, on 17 September, forty-nine Down Ampney Dakotas each towed a Horsa, thirty-nine being released at the LZ. Next day fifty Dakota/Horsa combinations sallied forth to LZ 'S', then came the start of re-supply on 19 September by thirty-two Dakotas. Drops were made near DZ 'V' before twenty-seven Dakotas eventually returned to Down Ampney; three others were shot down. The weather was poor, and eight of the Dakotas suffered various degrees of damage. Later in the day twenty other crews delivered petrol containers to both B56 and B58 for the advancing ground forces.

During the day's supply drop one of the Dakotas was flown by Flt Lt Samuel Anthony Lord, who showed total disregard for personal safety and maximum consideration for his crew, and indeed for those fighting for survival below. At about 1,500 feet the aircraft's starboard wing was hit twice by AA fire, then an engine was set on fire about three minutes' flying time from the DZ. Lord came lower for an accurate drop, all but two of his containers being released before he joined the stream to drop the remainder. For eight minutes Lord's aircraft came under intense fire, and with no hope of a safe return he ordered his crew to bale out. The aircraft soon crashed in flames and only Flt Lt Harry King escaped. Lord, posthumously awarded the VC, was buried in Oosterbeek cemetery.

On 20 September re-supply went well for the Down Ampney squadrons, but on the 21st it was different. German fighters attacked the Dakotas, for the expected Allied fighter escort was not in place. Plt Off Cuer's aircraft was set on fire soon after its pannier drop, while Flt Lt Beddow's aircraft was damaged by fighters, the crew being lucky to survive and land at B56. Flt Lt Hollom also force-landed and KG 512 was shot down. Flt Lt Mott and crew, together with four RASC dispatchers, baled out after fighters twice attacked their Dakota. Flak cut oil and petrol lines in Sqn Ldr Duff Mitchell's machine, forcing him also to land at B56. and of course there was tragedy aboard KG 444.

With such heavy losses, the Arnhem venture could not succeed, but before it was ended Down Ampney's Dakotas went again, twenty-three of them on 23 September, before a return to 'casevac'. Casualty numbers, although falling, could still reach 250 a day. Good medical centres were being established in France, and Down Ampney's Dakotas frequently took blood supplies to them. They still assisted squadron moves and carried mixed freight. On 28 October 1944, for instance, blood supplies were taken to B57 and B58, and twenty casualties retrieved by aircraft of 271 Squadron – 109 casualties in all arrived that day – while fifty-nine aircraft flew a glider tug exercise. Next day, 271 Squadron flew a load of oranges to B78 for a hospital, and 241 casualties were brought to Down Ampney where, during 4 October, 291 casualties arrived. On 8 December the Duchess of Kent met the 20,000th wounded soldier arriving at the airfield.

Serious casualties were now being sent to Stratton St Margaret's Hospital, Wroughton. Daily arrivals were averaging 158, with 3,893 passing through that month. Bad weather prevented 'casevac' operations on nine days, a new feature of the casualties being the number resulting from road accidents in wintry conditions. December's activity showed a further decline, an average of eighty-five arriving daily, and a month's total of 2,646.

The New Year saw a general run of freight and passengers, lifts to the Continent and a gradual decline in the casualties brought in. On 24 March 1945 sixty Down Ampney Dakotas took off from Gosfield towing Horsas for a part in the Rhine crossing airborne lift. It was on this occasion that the enemy made his only attempt to interfere with the Dakotas on the ground when, just before take-off, a V-1 crashed quite close to Gosfield airfield.

For 46 Group, and indeed the whole of RAF Transport Command, the end of the war and its immediate aftermath was its busiest ever time. There was much trooping, movement of displaced persons, retrieving POWs and carriage of freight. A break-up of Down Ampney's comradeship came on 9 July when 48 Squadron was ordered to get glider snatch gear fitted to its Dakotas. The work extended into August, at the close of which 271 Squadron – which throughout its stay here had sent detachments to other transport bases – moved to Odiham. Replacing it came two Canadian Dakota transport squadrons, Nos 435 and 436, overseen by 120 Wing. The latter squadron, operational from 15 October 1945, flew scheduled services to the Continent into 1946 before the Canadians prepared for home.

Down Ampney's run-down began in April 1946. Between 0913 and 0938 on 22 April ten Dakotas took off for Leeming, the last to leave being KN256 flown by Plt Off Hadfield. In all, forty-five Dakotas had left for Canada, and on 30 June 1946 120 Wing folded. It but remained to wind down depleted Down Ampney, in many respects a typical temporary wartime airfield.

Little remains of RAF days. At the end of the runway – on private property – a memorial stone recalls the station's existence, and every September those who served here are remembered at a memorial service. Buried in the churchyard are the ashes of Wireless Operator L Gaydon, together with a sole survivor of a 271 Dakota flown by Plt Off Len Wilson and shot down at Arnhem on 21 September. Courage and terrible adversity were once here in distressing profusion. One can rest pensively on memorial seats in the churchyard and recall the words of the hymn 'For All the Saints', the usual melody for which was written by Ralph Vaughan Williams, who lived close by. As you pass through the beautifully kept lych-gate, recall the words of 'Come down, oh love divine', another most suitable hymn for awful events past, and also with local connections. You may well catch a glimpse of cows still grazing on meadows once the lair of the Dakotas, and possibly pass the site of the casualty centre, which brought desperate hope, tears and surely love divine to thousands.

**Main features:**
*Runways:* 030° 6,000ft x 150ft, 090° 4,200ft x 150ft, 150° 2,400ft x 150ft, concrete. *Hangars:* two T2. *Hardstandings:* fifty loop type. *Accommodation:* RAF officers 240, SNCOs 510, ORs 1,386; WAAF officers 12, SNCOs 20, ORs 252.

# EASTCHURCH, Isle of Sheppey, Kent

*51°23N/00°51 47ft asl; TQ985695. 4¹/₂ miles SE of Sheerness*

Should you have the misfortune to find yourself an unwilling guest of one of the two HM Prisons now near Eastchurch, try gaining a little satisfaction in the knowledge that you are, at least, on very hallowed ground. It is virtually the birthplace of British naval aviation and an ancestral home of Short Brothers. Ironically, our 1940 enemies viewed Eastchurch not as a place on incarceration, but as a bastion of freedom, a place from where their invasion of Britain might well have been halted. Consequently they attacked it, ferociously. If time drags, you might consider studying its fascinating history – and try to discover photographs of historic days long gone, for this was one of the earliest flying fields.

Eastchurch's aviation career began when, in late 1909, and only a year after the first flight was made in Britain, Mr Frank McClean purchased a large tract of land on the southerly side of nearby Stanford Hill. He leased it to the Aero Club of the United Kingdom, then using a marshy site at Leysdown; the rent he charged was a mere 'one bob per annum'. Short Brothers, also using Leysdown landing ground, joined the exodus to the new land.

Distinction of being first in at Eastchurch fell to a Short (Wright) biplane piloted by the Hon C S Rolls, which touched down on 20 November 1909. On the same day Mr McClean's similar machine (Short No 1) arrived by road, also from Leysdown. In February 1910 the Aero Club became the Royal Aero Club.

Movement to Eastchurch was all but complete by the end of April 1910, by which time, in its better premises, Short Brothers was preparing to manufacture and repair aircraft. By autumn eighteen sheds had been erected at Eastchurch, their pioneer users including Messrs Batchelor, Colmore, Grace, McClean, Moore-Brabazon and W L Travers; the Hon C S Rolls had been killed at Bournemouth in July.

On 18 December 1910, piloting a Howard Wright biplane (ENV engine), famed Mr T O M Sopwith flew from Eastchurch to Thirlemont, Belgium, a distance of $177^{1}/_2$ miles, in $3^{1}/_2$ hours, and won the Baron de Forest prize of £4,000 for the longest flight yet from England to mainland Europe.

The activity at Eastchurch aroused the interest of the Admiralty, the force responsible for delivering powerful punches beyond Britain's shores and from British-occupied territories. In February 1911 McClean offered the Admiralty the loan of two aeroplanes for the exploration of aviation and for providing flying instruction for naval officers, a generous offer readily accepted. Volunteers were invited to apply for instruction at Eastchurch, and more than 200 applied. Six were selected for the first course, which started on 2 March 1911, participants including Lts G R Samson, K Gregory, A M Longmore, and Captain E L Gerrard RNLI. Mr O B Cockburn of the Royal Aero Club voluntarily instructed them for a year, the pioneering project thus costing the Admiralty very little.

Additional to flying instruction, the officers received technical training at Shorts' works, visited French aeroplane factories and attended the 1911 Military Aeroplane Trials at Rheims.

One of the two aircraft loaned to the Admiralty was being flown by Cecil Grace when he was killed on crashing in the English Channel during December 1910. A replacement was supplied and plans to acquire more were laid. Of the first three Short Farmans, Nos 26, 28 and 34, the latter two were later purchased by the Admiralty.

A further four of McClean's aircraft were flown by naval pilots during 1911 and early 1912. Among them were a Bleriot monoplane and two Shorts, including S 27 No 39 (McClean's No 10), fitted with two 50hp Gnomes and known as 'The Triple Twin', later purchased by the Admiralty.

Late 1911 saw facilities at Eastchurch granted to the London Balloon Company, Royal Engineers, for it to sample aeroplanes. Two Short Farman Gnome-engined pushers were put at their disposal by Lt Samson, while flying instruction was given mainly by Mr L Travers and maintenance handled by Horace Short. The War Office most emphatically disapproved of

*The RFC's principal bombs displayed at Eastchurch: from left to right they are Incendiary, 20lb, 110lb, 112lb and 230lb. (Bruce Robertson collection)*

fraternisation with such contraptions, and in February 1912 ordered that 'personnel of the London Balloon Company should not be trained in aeroplane work'. Four officers had, however, already availed themselves of the offer: S P Cockerell, who had already obtained Aero Club Certificate No 132, H D Cutler (No 189), V A Barrington-Kennet (No 190), and C W Meredith (No 193). All qualified at Eastchurch on 5 March 1912.

In October 1911 Lt Samson persuaded the Admiralty to establish at Eastchurch a naval aviation school and in December agreement was reached between the Royal Aero Club, the brothers Short and Mr F K McClean for the Admiralty to rent the aerodrome for an annual fee of £150. A proviso stated that the Admiralty could, if it so desired, purchase the ground at the rate of £16 per acre as from 25 December 1918. However, the aerodrome was taken over under the Defence of the Realm Act early in the war and was indeed purchased by the Air Ministry in December 1918. The Naval Flying School opened in February 1912 and, under various guises, remained here until April 1918.

Towards the end of 1911 Shorts had constructed experimental floats at Eastchurch, and fitted them to a now amphibious pusher biplane erected at Shellness. Lt A M Longmore RN (later Air Commodore, RAF) carried out several flights to Sheerness Harbour using the machine, alighting, then taking off from the water for return to Shellness. On 12 January 1912 newspapers announced that Lt G R Samson had recently flown from Eastchurch to Sheerness, where his Short S 38 (a pusher biplane fitted with wheels and floats) had been lifted on to a platform above the bow of HMS *Africa*. He flew the aircraft off the vessel while it was at anchor, making the first such flight from a British ship. In May 1912 Samson flew the same machine off HMS *Hibernia* when it was proceeding at 10 knots, and in so doing made the first flight ever from a moving ship. The S 38 and S 41 amphibians – Eastchurch-built and arguably the first dedicated British float-fitted naval aircraft – were designed for shipboard launch, but were incapable of take-off from water.

In March 1912 Colonel J E B Seely, Under Secretary of State for War, announced in the House of Commons that thirty or forty naval officers would be required for a Naval Wing about to form. The constitution of the Royal Corps, including the Naval Wing (headquarters at Eastchurch) and a Military Wing, was promulgated by Royal Warrant of 13 May 1912.

Summer 1912 saw the beginning of Admiralty interest in wireless use in aircraft. It resulted in the appointment of Lt R Fitzmaurice RN to conduct trials at Eastchurch. November saw a M Rouzet bring from France an engine-driven wireless set, which, fitted in a Short biplane at Eastchurch, was able to transmit for up to thirty miles.

Bomb-carrying gear and weapon trajectory were also subjected to Admiralty enquiry at Eastchurch. Spring 1913 witnessed experiments connected with the destruction of enemy airships. Use of a towed explosive grapnel suspended from an aeroplane and intended to contact the side of an airship was abandoned in favour of dropping a sensitive fused bomb or the firing of Hale grenades at the target, preliminary trials taking place in October 1913. Early 1914 brought experimentation with machine-guns fitted in aircraft, testing taking place at the Isle of Grain, while at Eastchurch development of airborne wireless equipment continued.

On 23 June 1914 the Naval Wing became the Royal Naval Air Service, the Naval School being jointly administered by the Air Department of the Admiralty and Sheerness Central Air Office.

*It can snow heavily on Sheppey as K2957, a Bulldog IIa of No 1 AAS, is discovering.*

July's highlight was the Royal Review of the Fleet at Spithead by HM King George V, participating naval aircraft being concentrated at Eastchurch. On 21 July sixteen seaplanes flew over the Fleet, saluting the monarch aboard the Royal Yacht. Two Flights, each of three aeroplanes in vee formation and led by Commander Samson, followed them.

On 31 July 1914 very new faces arrived when two Flights of No 4 Squadron, RFC, commanded by Major G H Raleigh, arrived to temporarily assist the RNAS in patrolling the coast during mobilisation.

War broke out on 4 August and next day Mr (later Lieutenant-Colonel Sir) F K McClean, responsible for training the first naval pilots, joined the RNAS as a Flight Lieutenant, making his private house at Eastchurch Aerodrome available for officers' quarters. The station became the main base for RNAS units. Both RFC Flights left for Amiens and the BEF on 13 August.

From Eastchurch aerial coastal patrols were often flown, as well as by detached Flights operating from East Coast sites. Another force, comprising three BE biplanes, two Sopwith biplanes, two Bleriot monoplanes, a Henri Farman biplane, one Bristol biplane and a converted Short seaplane, was sent to Ostend racecourse, from where for three days they carried out reconnaissance flights in the Bruges-Ghent-Ypres area before returning to Eastchurch on 30 August, only to be immediately directed to Dunkirk where they remained until February 1915 for operations against zeppelins.

On 17 October 1914 No 2 (RNAS) Squadron formed here and mainly used 80hp Gnome-engined Bristols for development work at Eastchurch.

Its place was taken by No 4 Wing, which, as No 4 (RNAS) Squadron, had formed at Dover in April 1915 and left for Petit Synthe, Dunkirk, in April 1916. Wireless experimental work continued until May 1916, when it was moved to Cranwell.

On 16 April 1915 eight aircraft from Eastchurch were involved in intercepting the first German army raider to operate against the UK, an Albatross BII, which, just before noon, crossed the English coast at Kingstown and dropped HE bombs at Sittingbourne and Swile. In response, fourteen British aircraft unsuccessfully tried to catch the intruder. The second attempt came on 23 May when two RNAS Sopwith Tabloids from Eastchurch and two aircraft from Westgate attempted unsuccessfully to deal with an Albatross floatplane attacking ships near the Goodwins.

Two BE 2cs tried to intercept the L 10 that dropped ten bombs across Eastchurch on 9 August 1915, the crew believing that they were over London. A few windows were broken at Eastchurch.

Twice in 1916 aircraft from Eastchurch attempted interceptions, first on March 5/6 when a BE 2c tried to engage the L 13, and on 23/24 September when three BE 2cs were involved in indecisive engagements.

A further detachment to France began on 29 March 1916. Four Nieuport Scouts were sent to Abeele, headquarters of No 6 Squadron, RFC, to co-operate for eighteen days with the RFC, under military command.

At the end of March 1916 the decision to enlarge Eastchurch was taken, a station head-quarters forming under Wg Cdr J L Forbes. While more sheds were erected on the eastern side of the site, the School ceased to operate, re-opening on 1 May. In September 1916 Wg Cdr A M Longmore became the Station Commander, and remained in command until February 1917.

In a new departure, a gunnery school opened in 1916, and in August the Design Flight arrived from the Isle of Grain. Early 1917 brought the opening here of a Marine Observers' School, all greatly extending the importance of Eastchurch.

Ten Gothas attacked Kent coast targets on 22 August 1917, and three Sopwith Camels from Eastchurch took off – for the last time – to face the enemy's arrival, together with many other RFC and RNAS defenders. Bombs fell at Margate and Dover, three raiders being brought down.

April 1918 saw the gunnery school divide, the ground section staying and the Aerial Fighting and Gunnery School using Leysdown. Closure came at the end of 1918.

Formation of the Royal Air Force on 1 April 1918, which all but ended the Navy's tenure, led to the formation of No 58 Wing at Eastchurch, based here until disbandment on 21 December 1918. On the RAF's founding day, the Naval Flying School became No 204 Training Depot Station, acquired its assorted aircraft, and functioned until March 1919. Short Brothers' consolidation of business at Rochester during Autumn 1917 freed considerable facilities, which the Government purchased, allowing for the 1918 opening of the School of Technical Training (Boys), based here until the end of 1919

In July 1918 No 1 Observers' School, flying DH 9s among other types, arose from the existing fleet observers' unit. Renamed No 2 Marine Observers' School on 28 December 1918, it disbanded in June 1919.

A special event that originated at Eastchurch on 18 April 1919 was an attempt at a transatlantic crossing using the two-seater Short Shamrock. Carrying petrol for forty hours' flying, Major J C P Wood and Captain C C Wylie intended to fly to Curragh. Unfortunately an errant fuel feed system caused the Rolls-Royce Eagle VIII engine to cut out after only $3^{1}/_{2}$ hours, forcing the aircraft into the sea about twelve miles from Holyhead. The occupants were rescued and the aircraft towed ashore.

On 18 February 1920 the School of Technical Training (Men) formed, becoming No 3 Boys' Training Centre on 16 March, and moving to Manston in May 1920. Emphasis was then being placed upon attracting youth to apprenticeships within the RAF.

Care and maintenance now overtook Eastchurch, which served as a useful centre for official handling of the May 1921 Kent coal-mining dispute. Rejuvenated, the station was re-activated on 1 April 1922 within 1 Group as the RAF's all-ranks main Armament & Gunnery School derived from the School of Air Gunnery and Bombing. On 1 November 1924 the Air Ministry Meteorological Flight formed within the A&GS, its Sopwith Snipes remaining until January 1925, when the unit moved to Duxford. Also attached to the A&GS, from 1 December 1924, was the Coastal Defence Co-operation Flight, employing DH 9As and Fairey IIIDs and IIIFs. On 1 April 1926 the A&GS passed to No 3 Group, then to 23 Group on 12 April 1926.

No 207 (Bomber) Squadron arrived from San Stephano, Turkey, on 3 October 1923, joined in May 1924 by No 100 (Bomber) Squadron from Spitalgate, which stayed until July. A third front-line squadron, No 33, flying Hawker Horsleys, arrived in September shortly after reforming at Netheravon. In November 1929 No 207 Squadron left for Bircham Newton, while No 33 Squadron moved to Bicester.

On 1 January 1932 the Armament & Gunnery School became the Air Armament School, its Bulldogs, Gordons, Harts, Wallaces and Wapitis seeing varying use. The CDC Flight left for Gosport on 23 May 1933. The AAS was re-named again on 1 November 1937, becoming No 1 Air Armament School controlled by the Armament Group, which had formed on 1 February 1934 to administer all air armament training. Further re-organisation in RAF Training Command saw it become No 25 (Armament Training) Group, whose HQ was here from 1 December 1937 until it moved to Brize Norton in June 1939.

With the formation of SHQ Eastchurch on 15 July 1938, a new organisational structure paved the way for change. The air armament training units left for Manby on 15 August 1938 and were immediately replaced by Hinds of No 21 (Bomber) Squadron from Lympne. Ansons of No 48 (General Reconnaissance) Squadron followed on 1 September 1938, both squadrons remaining until spring. Although armament training had been reduced, 'D' Flight of No 2 AACU Gosport was on detachment here from 16 February to 4 September 1939.

December 1939 brought new faces and sounds as the first of many Polish Air Force personnel, who had courageously made long treks to join the RAF, arrived for necessary training and general acclimatisation. They were joined, during the debacle in France, by what was left of No 53 Squadron and its reconnaissance Blenheim IVs, which temporarily occupied Eastchurch between 1 and 13 June 1940.

On 6 August 1940 the station was transferred to No 16 Group, Coastal Command, and thirty-two Fairey Battles of Nos 12 and 142 Squadrons – on loan from Bomber Command – moved in on 12 August. Their orders were to prevent Boulogne's E-boats from attacking Channel shipping. Instant Luftwaffe response to their arrival came after dark, then, at around 0700 on the 13th, Do 17s of KG 2 dropped more than a hundred HEs on hangars, the Officers' Mess, airmen's quarters and the operations block. Ammunition and equipment burned furiously, sixteen personnel died and forty-eight were seriously wounded. In another attack during the afternoon of 15 August the landing ground was cratered, resulting in No 142 Squadron using Detling for operational flying.

The afternoon of 20 August brought twenty-seven Do 17s of KG 3 escorted by Bf 109s. Fierce combat overhead, resulted in two Dorniers being shot down. Eastchurch was next bombed on the 28th, two of 142 Squadron's Battles being destroyed. Still the enemy had the station in his sights for on 31 August the Dorniers returned, a night raid followed, then on 2 September the bomb dump was fired by incendiaries causing 350 HE bombs to explode and devastate a wide area. Five Battles were destroyed before a second attack came that day. Dive bombing and strafing on 5 September left a delayed-action HE by the SHQ, which had to be vacated; a temporary HQ was set up in the village. Both Battle squadrons withdrew from their hazardous location to Binbrook and Bomber Command on 7 September.

Several times the Battles had operated against Boulogne. A dozen, escorted by Blenheim fighters, sought the E-boats at dusk on 17 August, and next evening they attacked again. A few more night sorties resulted in attacks on Calais and on Le Crotoy airfield.

With the squadrons gone the battered old station very slowly recovered, and it was not until August 1941 that it came back to life when, under No 27 Group, Technical Training Command, RAF personnel came to be trained in the use of parachute and cable rocket weapons for airfield defence. Formation here of the RAF Artillery School followed in February 1942.

Midsummer 1942 saw Eastchurch become a satellite station for Gravesend. As a result Spitfire Vs of 124 Squadron were positioned here from 30 June until 5 July. Another brief front-line interlude came between 14 and 20 August 1942 when, with space at a premium due to many squadrons moving south for operation *Jubilee*, Spitfire Vs of No 65 Squadron came from Gravesend to participate in the Dieppe combined services raid from Eastchurch. On the 17th they flew a Channel sweep, and on the 19th operated four times claiming two Do 217Es without loss.

Departure of the RAF Artillery School to Filey at the start of April 1943 was followed by the arrival of HQ 123 Airfield here to participate in exercise *Spartan*. Included was No 132 Squadron, replaced by 122 Squadron on 18 May. They stayed until the exercise ended on 1 June. Between 4 and 11 May Typhoons of 184 Squadron were also here. Alongside them – from 14 April to 26 July 1943 – were Martinets of No 1493 (Target Towing) Flight.

Despite a brief operational period Eastchurch remained a training centre in No 54 Group, Flying Training Command, which had taken control of the station in April 1943. A combined Aircrew Re-selection Centre opened in June following 123 Airfield's departure, and assumed duties hitherto performed at Brighton, Blackpool and Uxbridge. That was the station's main use until ARC disbanded in mid-1946.

Lodger facilities for up to two single-engined fighter squadrons had been available since 1942, an option used twice by 2TAF in 1944. On 21 January No 174 Squadron's Typhoons noisily arrived for pre-D-Day ground attack live firing practice using the Essex marshland ranges. The course completed, they left on 4 February. No 181 arrived two days later, and its departure on 21 February was followed by Typhoons of four other squadrons, also here for APC training: No 175 (24 February to 8 March), No 184 (11 March to 3 April), No 263 (1 to 24 April) and No 245 (25 to 30 April). Eastchurch, with the marshes just across the river, had most usefully reverted to its pre-war armament training role.

A second plan started with the arrival of 247 Squadron, whose Typhoons raucously disturbed Sheppey on 12 May. They came as part of a holding operation prior to an order to cross the Channel when suitable airstrips were established in France. They lodged at Eastchurch until 22 May, when a more suitable jump-off point was chosen further south. No 183 Squadron came on 14 July for the same reason, stayed until 25th, then crossed to France; the same route was followed by No 263 Squadron, which tarried at Eastchurch from 23 July until 6 August 1944.

The end of Eastchurch was relatively abrupt. Following closure of the ARC in 1946 the station, now in 21 Group, Training Command, was reduced to care and maintenance and parented by RAF West Malling. RAF Eastchurch, declared inactive in December 1948, was transferred to the Prison Commissioners in June 1950 to become an open prison site, which role it retains.

**Main features:**
*Landing area:* SE-NW 1,600yds, N-S 1,200yds, E-W 1,200yds. *Hangars:* three Bellman. *Hardstandings:* fifty-one rectangular constructed of Sommerfeld matting. *Accommodation:* Ample pre-war school buildings and permanent technical buildings, some used for accommodation. RAF officers 118, SNCOs 81, ORs 1,809; WAAF officers 16, ORs 294.

The station was served by the Sheppey Light Railway, Southern Railway.

## EDGEHILL, Warwickshire

*52°05N/01°28W 628ft asl; SP365435. 3 miles SE of Kineton*

The 1939-45 war years were times unequalled for amateur and private spying, and no topic attracted it more than jet propulsion – unless you lived in Cambridge, where the atom was first split. There you explored (with risk) amazing rumours about a bomb that, when exploded, would set off an unstoppable chain reaction. Ah, happy days.

It was spring 1941 when our 'agents', visiting Gloucestershire to deliver Blue Circle cement, confirmed the existence of a small, fast aeroplane with an amazing feature – it was propellerless. Excitement climaxed when a driver later produced a sketch made 'near Chipping Norton'. Emphatically, he claimed that 'it had a pipe sticking out of the back'. That clinched it – rocket propulsion was involved, not a version of that strange Caproni CC2. Using his representation, we soon had models of this secret 'rocket plane' and, like 'the professionals' we, too, gave it a magic number to cloak its identity. Thus was the 'CN/1' born. Soon, another 'agent', who drove close to the wonder plane, brought news of 'a big hole' in the nose. Derrick, always in the forefront of knowing more than one should, at once lectured us on the Caproni Campini CC2 Italian gas-turbine aircraft, and bamboozled us with words like 'the Coanda effect'. It is, he declared, a gas-turbine-driven aeroplane. Obvious – once you know the truth.

*The general layout of many wartime airfields remains visible, as with Edgehill (alias Shennington) in 2003. The runway orientations remain, together with several circular dispersals. The private flying and gliding centre is at the picture's top. (Mike Rudkin)*

In my curly haired, little lad days, an RAF member of the family, seconded to read Engineering at Cambridge, used to bring a colleague along for tea. Very polite, he was for ever congratulating my mother on the quality of her scones and confirming his satisfaction by the rate at which he consumed them. When in September 1944 photographs appeared, I was amazed to discover that 'our Frank' also carried the name 'Whittle'. After seeing W4041/G at Farnborough in 1944 I was relieved that 'Frank' did not visit us in 1941, spot my reasonably accurate 1/72nd replica and ask some awkward questions!

But why such thoughts while gazing upon the chicken houses, vacant runways and strange control tower at Edgehill? Simply because this little-known airfield played a part in the development of British jet aircraft and engine development.

Edgehill was completed in October 1941 as a satellite for 21 OTU Moreton-in-Marsh. Night-flying by aging Wellington Ics started in August, 12 OTU also using the station before its official opening on 21 October 1941.

On 14 May 1941 the Gloster E28/39 Pioneer W4041 was first flown at Cranwell and, after ten hours' flying, returned by road to Gloster's for a new engine. Cranwell being a long way from Gloster's, and Brockworth being unsuitable for jets, alternatives were considered, and eventually Edgehill, with one 1,600-yard and two 1,200-yard runways, was selected. Rather like Barford St

John, it was situated on a high plateau. One mile south-west was the 745-foot Edge Hill, while half a mile south was the 750-foot Shenlow Hill. At the western end of the runway was a dramatic escarpment face that fell away to a valley below. Otherwise the airfield approaches were good, so, despite that fall-away and the high hills, it was deemed suitable for the jet. A Robin hangar was erected to secretly house it, and agreement was reached whereby the Pioneer would fly from Edgehill and the Gloster F9/40 experimental fighters from Cranwell or Newmarket during 1942.

At Edgehill W4041, now powered by a W.1A engine, first taxied on 4 February 1942, flight-testing beginning almost immediately. Now quieter and smoother in flight, all went well till 24 March 1942 when part of a turbine blade broke away in flight, forcing a rapid return to Edgehill.

The station's prime occupants, Wellington 1cs and Ansons of 21 OTU, were now also very busy. A dozen of them participated in the Cologne raid of 30/31 May 1942. As DV598 was taking off it hit a tree, and two other crews aborted, leaving nine to complete their sorties. In the Essen raid eleven crews operated, and ten took part in June's 1,000 Plan Bremen attack, from which X3179 failed to return.

Now it was time for the jet to capture the limelight – in secret of course. 'Jerry' Sayer it was who piloted W4041 when flight trials were resumed in June 1942, and not without moments of concern. Fuel starvation was encountered, and a flame-out also brought a quick return home. Throughout that hot summer the jet was frequently test-flown, and on 27 September 1942 a group of visitors arrived for a demonstration, among them Americans. Just as the Pioneer was getting airborne oil pressure fell dramatically and, conserving what he had by reducing power, Sayer was seen to sink below the edge of the escarpment. Great relief came as he was seen safely pulling away. Keeping his speed low he managed a neat forced landing. Not many days later, while testing a Typhoon off the North East coast, Sayer was killed, possibly in collision with another aircraft.

His place at Edgehill was taken by Michael Daunt, who resumed E.28/39 flying in November 1942. After four flights, W4041 was conveyed by lorry to Farnborough for engine development work. That freed the circuit for 21 OTU's Wellingtons.

W4046, the second E.28/39, arrived at Edgehill in February 1943. It was powered by a Rover-built W.2B engine, first flew during the evening of 1 March 1943 piloted by John Grierson, and was capable of reaching just over 400mph after an unstick run of 330 yards. Such success permitted it to be flown to Hatfield on 17 April 1943 for a few days of demonstration, the $19^{1}/_{2}$-minute flight being the first cross-country jet journey undertaken.

Very strict flying restrictions were applied to the early jets, which, from Edgehill, were allowed to venture up to five miles away or fly within a corridor two miles wide between Edgehill and Cheltenham, a distance of about thirty miles. The duration of early jet aircraft was also very limited. When on 3 May 1943 W4046 was taken to RAE Farnborough, Gloster's use of the Pioneer ceased, like jet flying from Edgehill.

There had shortly before been another alteration for, on 12 April 1943, Edgehill became a satellite station of No 12 OTU Chipping Warden. Two Flights of the Unit under Wing Commander C W Scott arrived from Turweston on 27 April 1943 flying Wellington IIIs, replacement by Mk Xs starting in August 1943. Edgehill also accommodated 12 OTU's gunnery flight's Martinets and Hurricanes, as well as the initial training element of the OTU, until unit closure on 7 June 1945.

Between July 1948 and December 1949 Edgehill acted as a sub-site for No 25 MU, an equipment storage unit, then was placed on care and maintenance. Flying was resumed in July 1952 when Edgehill opened as an RLG for Prentices of No 1 FTS, and continued until October 1954.

Visit the site now and few typical wartime airfield buildings used by light aircraft remain.

**Main features:**
*Runways:* 172° 4,620ft x 150ft, 239° 3,300ft x 150ft, 284° 3,300ft x 150ft, concrete and tarmac. *Hangars:* one T2, one B1. *Hardstandings:* twenty-seven heavy bomber frying-pan type. *Accommodation:* RAF officers 70, SNCOs 291, ORs 646; WAAF officers 2, SNCOs 5, ORs 108.

# ENSTONE, Oxfordshire

*51°55N/01°25W 550ft asl; SP395255. 5 miles E of Chipping Norton, by the B4030*

Enstone opened as the second satellite of 21 OTU, Moreton-in-Marsh, on 15 September 1942, but was inactive until 12 April 1943, when it replaced Edgehill. Wellington Ics were used until April 1944, although Mk IIIs were phased in late 1943, and Wellington Xs in February-March 1944. No

21 OTU's 'X' Flight (Gunnery) arrived on 17 May 1943 equipped with Martinets, and left for Moreton-in-Marsh on 24 February 1944. From Enstone 21 OTU carried out leaflet-dropping operations over France, a somewhat unusual activity from a satellite.

Interesting arrivals from Stanton Harcourt, on 26 February 1944, were five Curtiss Tomahawks of No 1682 Bomber (Defence) Training Flight, which used Enstone until disbandment in August 1944. From April 1944 the Flight was Hurricane IIc-equipped, the Tomahawks departing during May.

No 21 OTU had a post-war presence but used Honeybourne from August to October 1945 as runways were repaired. Flying, resumed in October, ceased at Enstone in November 1945. The station passed to Maintenance Command on 17 January 1946 and became a sub-site of Quedgeley, Gloucestershire. On 28 October 1946 it was transferred to Flying Training Command, a detachment of Oxfords and Harvards of 17 SFTS, Coleby Grange, arriving on 10 November. Next day they became equipment of the Refresher Flight. Giving flying practise to aircrew returning to flying, on 17 December 1946 they moved to Moreton-in-Marsh to form the basis of No 1 Refresher School. Enstone subsequently saw limited use as an RLG for Little Rissington.

Although the RAF left long ago, civilian flying continues under the Oxfordshire Sport Flying Club Ltd, which flies motor gliders and has two maintenance hangars on the north side of the site. Enstone Flying Club is also active, as is Pegasus Flight Training, which uses microlights. Available to them are the 08/26 asphalt runway, 1100 metres long and 40 metres wide, and an 800-metre by 40-metre grass strip alongside. The main runway was at one time used for surface trials. Whereas at many airfields contractors smash concrete, at Enstone they have busily made it, at an industrial area embracing the hangar and wartime buildings at the east end of the airfield. Enstone hit the headlines when the only Bristol Freighter to have ventured into Britain's skies for decades crashed here during taking-off.

**Main features:**
*Runways:* 256° 6,000ft x 150 ft, 329° 3,975ft x 150ft, 195° 3,600ft x 150ft, concrete. *Hangars:* one T2, one B1. *Hardstandings:* twenty-seven frying-pan type for heavy bombers. *Accommodation:* RAF officers 72, SNCOs 261, ORs 450; WAAF officers 2, SNCOs 4, ORs 158.

## FAIRFORD, Gloucestershire

*51°40N/ 01°46W 260ft asl; SP150990. 2 miles S of Fairford town*

After Fairford has crumbled, how will it be remembered? As the base from which B-52s carried horrendous loads halfway across England to deposit on an irritating Third World territory? For its part in the Concorde story, or the Normandy invasion? For a lucky few it must be standing by the runway wishing one dare use the camera and shoot the B-36 stream landing in February 1953. What a thought! For most, though, it will surely be hot, bright sunny days when NATO displayed its generous nature by supplying hundreds of combat aircraft to the RAF Benevolent Fund International Air Tattoos and pleasing huge crowds – before the Soviets passed away and crazy terrorists spoilt it all. Of those days, few thrills were better than sharing the taste of freedom enjoyed by a 'Russian' Bear peacefully – and noisily – sampling England.

Fairford has always had a desire to be American, for the original intent of 1943 was that a USAAF transport/air observation base should be built south of Fairford town. Instead, the airfield, at birth, was surprisingly earmarked for RAF Bomber Command and probably for an OTU. Its situation was rather too far south for that, and instead it was, on 14 January 1944, transferred to AEAF control. An opening-up party arrived four days later, and Fairford joined 38 Group, Transport Command, on 2 March 1944. Stirling IVs of 620 Squadron, which arrived from Leicester East, were joined by 190 Squadron's contingent later that month. A flock of Horsa gliders followed, then cross-country glider-towing practise mingled with demanding exercises. Both squadrons flew night sorties for SOE, generally from Tarrant Rushton. Of several accidents, that of 17 April 1944 was certainly spectacular, for Horsa LJ263 was destroyed when it crashed into Fairford's control tower, killing its pilot.

Shortly before midnight on 5 June 1944 the first of forty-five Stirlings carrying 887 paratroops of the 6th Airborne Division began to roll. Participants in operation *Tonga*, their task was to help secure the Orne Bridge and an area east of that river. Three Stirlings of 620 Squadron failed to return, and twenty-seven others were battle-damaged or unserviceable. Nevertheless, by 1800 on 6 June twenty-five Stirling IVs were ready for operation *Mallard*, the main landing that took place near Ranville and

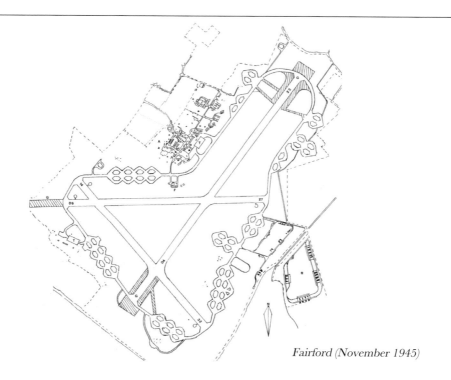

*Fairford (November 1945)*

## FAIRFORD

Fairford in the 21st century resembles a vast concrete playground. That has come about by widening and extending the main runway, turning its subsidiaries into parking areas and merging them with wartime dispersals. View the sketch map and parts will be recognised as still existent, including the public road skirting the eastern perimeter fence first erected in 1951 and repeatedly strengthened. Dispersal pans from the past remain but much enhanced, and the bomb storage area to the east is still prominent, although the proximity of Welford bomb store has nullified its use. Luria hangars long ago replaced the sole T2 on the northern side.

Depicted is No 1 Site Fairford as in November 1945, its still present wartime temporary and more permanent brick buildings mostly embracing 1942 and 1943 styles mixing with Nissen huts, one of which served as the Station Armoury. Squadron and Flight Offices were to be found in Temporary Brick buildings (1431/41), as well as Operations, both Parachute Stores and the Tow Cable Maintenance and Storage Section (9523/42). The Crew Briefing Room was accommodated in a Nissen hut (228/43) and two Main Stores were found in Romney Huts measuring 96ft by 38ft (2981/43). Like the Army Supply Accommodation, the Main Workshop was in a BCF hut. A 16-foot Nissen hut served as a Flame Float Store (2196/43). Although envisaged as a bomber base, wartime Fairford emerged as a British transport glider and tug station. Glider pilots had their own crew room and large glider assembly areas constructed from metal netting were laid at the runways ends (seen shaded), as also at, for instance, Down Ampney. Two Aircraft Sheds T2 (23) (3653/42) were available for essential indoor repairs, otherwise the tug aircraft occupied dispersals while the many gliders were strongly picketed, many without their control surfaces so susceptible to storm damage.

involved the 6th Air Landing Brigade. By 1901hrs, when the first Stirling/Horsa combination roared off from Fairford, thirty-six combinations were about to participate. Thereafter the Stirling crews generally supported the Normandy invasion and trained with airborne forces for the next major operation.

*The din, the size! An RB-36 proclaims 'I'm a big, tough, noisy American. Don't mess with me, oh, and NO photography.'*

At 1400 on 16 September 1944 the station was sealed. From Fairford's two squadrons thirty-eight Stirlings were detailed for pathfinding and glider-towing in the next day's commencement of the Arnhem operation. On 18 September another forty-three Horsas were towed towards Arnhem, thirty-seven landing on the planned LZ. Next day Fairford's re-supply force faced intense flak, operating in daylight at low level in the heavy four-engined Stirling being no sinecure. Although on one day 696 containers and 116 panniers were delivered, it cost two Stirlings of 620 Squadron and three of 190 Squadron. Disaster struck hardest on 21 September when German fighters penetrated the fighter cover and viciously attacked the Stirlings. Seven of 190 Squadron's ten Stirlings and two of 620's were shot down. Some idea of the intensity of activity at this time is given by the 613 daylight take-offs and 669 landings made by Fairford's Stirlings and station visitors during September 1944.

October 1944 brought the demanding operation *Molten*. Sixteen crews of each squadron set out, towing thirty-two Horsas across France to Rome/Ciampino. By 10 October, twenty-seven had arrived safely and departed for Pomigliano, near Naples. Problems were many, not least the strain on crews, aircraft and engines. All the Stirlings returned to Britain in November, but not to Fairford, for mid-October 1944 saw 190 and 620 Squadrons depart for Great Dunmow, Essex, together with RAF Fairford's station organisation and much equipment.

Fairford now became a satellite of Keevil, where No 22 Heavy Glider Conversion Unit formed on 20 October 1944, equipped with Albemarles. Its task was the rapid training of glider pilots to replace Arnhem losses. Flights 'C', 'D' and 'F' used Fairford, their strength amounting to twenty-nine Albemarles with twenty-three gliders – Horsas and inferior Waco CG-4A Hadrians. The presence of the latter gave pilots a chance to fly gliders likely to be used in the Far East. No 22 HGCU moved to Blakehill Farm in mid-June 1945, keeping Fairford as its satellite until 21 October 1945, when it withdrew, and Fairford was placed on care and maintenance.

In 1945/46 the station hosted BAT/RAT Flights of Oxfords, No 1555 forming on 15 September 1945 when the station was in 4 Group. No 1556 came in December, No 1529 on 27 January 1946, and No 1528 on 1 February. The latter was absorbed mid-month by No 1555 Flight. No 1529 disbanded on 16 February, No 1556 on 1 April, and No 1555 moved to Blakehill Farm on 30 April 1946.

A more important phase started in late September 1946 when Fairford regained an airborne forces role as home for 47 Squadron's Halifax A Mk VII/ IXs. A second Halifax squadron, No 113, re-formed on 1 May 1947, and was joined by Nos 297 and 295 Squadrons on 10 September 1947. Halifax strength amounted usually to almost forty examples at the Halifax's final main bastion. All the squadrons wound down in September-October 1948, after experimental glider flying had taken place. In December 1948 Fairford was once again placed on care are maintenance.

It was on the occasion of re-awakening in June 1950 that the Americans at last gained their prize, the 7507th ABS (USAFE) arriving on 7 July to claim it. The Americans wanted to enlarge, lengthen and strengthen runways, build 'special storage areas', give it a US domestic feel, and generally brighten Fairford. On 25 May 1951 the 7507th was raised to ABG status, erection of three Luria hangars began in June, then on 1 July Fairford was transferred to the Americans and their 7th Air Division, Strategic Air Command. On 10 March 1952 the 7522nd ABS formed and left to prepare Stansted for SAC spies on 10 November. The 7507th disbanded on 16 October. Also here from 1 July 1952, the 7582nd ABS moved on 1 August 1952 to Molesworth. Activated on 16 October 1952 was the 3919th ABG SAC, here until 1955. Strongly guarded compounds, high fencing and self-important perambulating perimeter guards had by now converted Fairford into a typical SAC base of the period, and it was ready for big tenants.

The biggest bombers of all, they began moving in just after shattering the dawn on 7 February 1953, seventeen whopping great B-36 bombers arriving from Carswell AFB, Fort Worth, Texas. Another, flown by Lt Col Herman Gerick, did not quite make it. Encountering trouble in the circuit, the crew of fifteen baled out leaving the B-36 to fly on for thirty miles before spiralling down out of control near Laycock, its wreckage fortunately scattering widely over the countryside. Another B-36 in the deployment had already come to grief en route for Gander, Newfoundland.

The next newcomer to Fairford, and making its UK debut, was the Boeing B-47B Stratojet, a futuristic shape and weird undercarriage layout marking it out as highly unusual. After a flight of 5hrs 21min, the first of the two B-47s touched down at Fairford from Limestone AFB on 7 April 1953 for a brief stay. They heralded the first B-47 Wing TDY deployment of 45 Stratojets of the 306th Bomb Wing, which arrived at Fairford on 2 June 1953. The three B-47B squadrons (Nos 367, 368 and 369) made their 4,500-mile homeward dash on 4 September 1953.

While in Britain they hosted another B-47, which, on 4 August, flew from Goose Bay to Fairford in 4hrs 14min. Its return was made non-stop to Tampa.

The 305th BW(M) from Limestone AFB was next in, to occupy Brize Norton and Fairford, placing one squadron at the latter base. The third B-47 TDY Fairford deployment of late 1953 was the first to bring B-47Es. Subsequent Bomb Wings deploying to the UK usually based only one squadron at Fairford, reducing vulnerability to attack. Among them was the 98th BW from Lincoln AFB, here between June and September 1954. Interesting aircraft at Fairford that year included a few RB-47Es of the 68th SRW, home base Lake Charles, Louisiana, more of which were at Fairford between May and July 1955. A few RB-36Fs of the 5th RW visited Fairford in July 1954, and at the same time three squadrons of B-47Es of the 43rd BW(M) moved here for a three-month stay. Use of Fairford, somewhat spasmodic, declined from autumn 1955, although B-47s remained a common sight, and B-36s occasionally called.

In January 1958 twenty-one-day 'Reflex' deployments started. Small numbers of B-47Es would spend three weeks at one base then move elsewhere to prevent heavy losses during a pre-emptive strike. Those deployed to the UK were drawn mainly from Nos 2, 308 and 384 Bomb Wings.

Soon after 'Reflex' ended on 26 June 1964, Fairford reverted to being an RAF station, CFS using it as an RLG. Gnat Trainers of 'C' Flight CFS moved in at the start of 1965 and stayed until September 1966. Perhaps symbolically, the RAF Aerobatic Team, the 'Red Arrows', formed on 1 March 1965, lived here until 1 August 1966. At the other extreme was No 53 Squadron, which re-formed here on 1 November 1965 to operate giant Short Belfast freighters before moving to Brize Norton in May 1967. Fairford had been increasingly used by VC-10s while Brize Norton's runway was resurfaced.

*Free fall 'iron bombs' aboard, B-52G 92579 of the 806th BW (P) taxies out at Fairford on 25 February 1991, bound for Iraq. (Robert A Edwards)*

*Eurofighter Typhoon ZJ699 makes the type's public RAF service debut at RIAT 2003.*

The tranquillity of summer 1967 soon faded, for in September Fairford re-opened as an independent station in Air Support Command for the RAF's then new C-130K Hercules. Here, on 25 February 1968, 47 Squadron re-formed to operate them, and Fairford entered 38 Group on 1 March 1968. A second squadron, No 30, equipped here with Hercules in June 1968, and both squadrons were soon trooping and generally airlifting freight.

Fairford must have been thrilled when, on 9 April 1969, it was designated the BAC Concorde Flight Test Centre, catching the public imagination. Soon the home of Concorde 002, it also became the test base for production Concordes. The last Hercules departed for Lyneham on 10 February 1971, Station HQ disbanded, and Air Support Command's tenancy was terminated on 30 April 1971. Fairford again became an RLG, also a reserve airfield and satellite of Brize Norton and, of course, a Concorde lair.

SST trials continued until the lease expired on 31 January 1977, and necessary runway and taxiway resurfacing commenced in April 1977. In September Fairford resumed a reserve airfield role before July 1978 brought an announcement, not universally applauded, that studies showed Fairford a suitable second UK base for USAF KC-135 AAR tankers. On 12 September 1978, five KC-135s slipped in for an autumn NATO exercise to prove the point. After flying up to four sorties daily, they departed on the 28th.

On 1 February 1979 the 7020th Air Base Group (USAFE) descended to make Fairford fit for six-week rotations of small numbers of KC-10s and KC-135s cared for by the 11th Strategic Group (SAC), which was also to handle brief deployments of B-52 bombers. Fairford was, on 1 June 1979, upgraded to a USAFE Primary Installation, and on 13 September 1979 the first resident KC-135 arrived. RAF Support Command had a unit on base from 3 September 1979, and an RAF liaison party formed, before the station was transferred again to the US 3rd Air Force on 20 September 1979.

Small numbers of mainly KC-135s rotated to Fairford over the next decade, the high spot coming on 14/15 April 1986 when three KC-10as of the 2nd BW together with KC-135s drawn from eight Wings were part of the in-flight refueller force that supported F-111s sent to disturb Gaddafi's Libyan power base during operation *El Dorado Canyon*.

In January 1990 tanker operations were entirely transferred to Mildenhall, and Fairford remained a USAF forward operating location put to use at the start of 1991 for operation *Desert Storm*. On 1 February 1991 the first of ten B-52G bombers, gathered into a special 806th BW (Provisional), arrived. On 9 February they flew their first long-haul sorties to the Iraqi-Kuwait border. In the course of sixty effective sorties, the last on 25 February, they released 1,158 tons of munitions. The Wing de-activated on 6 March 1991.

The following months saw small detachments of B-1s and B-52s calling, and B-1s operated from Fairford during the Kosovo campaign. To be better able to support heavy bomber and heavy transport operations, Fairford received an all-over facelift between 2000 and 2002. New dispersal pads were included, where special hangars could be erected for use by B-2s, although operation *Iraqi Freedom* saw only fourteen B-52Hs operating from Fairford to bomb targets in Iraq during March-April 2003 as the sole bomber types used. U-2s passed through, and occasionally C-17s call, large pans being built with them in mind. Fairford is surely here to stay as a forward operating location.

### Main features:
1944: *Runways:* 230° 6,000ft x 150ft, 280° 4,200ft x 150ft (additional 600ft of American Track), 330° 3,200ft x 150ft, asphalt and concrete. *Hangars:* two T2. *Hardstandings:* fifty-two spectacle type. *Accommodation:* RAF officers 172, SNCOs 648, ORs 1,562; WAAF officers 8, SNCOs 6, ORs 302. Post-war: *Runway:* 09/27 9,974ft, take-off distance available 10,023ft

## FAIRLOP (HAINAULT FARM), Essex

*51°35N/00°06E 85ft asl; TQ460905. 3 miles NE of Ilford*

'Twice Temporary' might be a suitable sub-title for Hainault Farm (maiden name) and Fairlop (grown-up title), a site that first attracted interest in 1915.

Named after nearby Hainault Farm, it appears to have been first used operationally on 13/14 October 1915, by a pair of night-operating BE 2cs (detached from No 14 RA Squadron, Gosport) trying to engage four zeppelins raiding London. No 17 RAS in January-February 1916, and No 19 RAS in March-April 1916, used Hainault as a launch site for night defence sorties until the upgrading on 15 April 1916 of No 19 RAS into No 39 (Home Defence) Squadron, one of the first specifically for home defence. With HQ at Hounslow, No 39 Squadron permanently placed its 'C' Flight here, from where it first operated its BE 2cs on 25/26 April. Based here by June 1916 were four BE 2cs, two BE 12s and two Bristol Scouts, to protect eastern London.

It was a zeppelin raid of 23/24 September 1916 that brought the first night victory to 'C' Flight, 39 Squadron, when 2nd Lt A de B Brandon, flying a BE 2c, so severely damaged L 33 that it crashed in flames at Little Wigborough. Despite the damage, its structure revealed features later incorporated in the British R-23 airship.

On 25 May 1917 twenty-one Gotha bombers set out to bomb London in daylight. Encountering cloud, they aimed their bombs instead at Folkestone. The British response to this sudden change of tactics was to form three Home Defence Day Squadrons in July 1917, one of which was No 44, which, in Eastern Wing, commenced formation at Hainault on 24 July, temporarily armed with Sopwith 1½ Strutters. In August they re-equipped with fifteen Sopwith Camels, first operating them on 12 August 1917 against Gothas raiding Southend. At one time their Commanding Officer was Major A T Harris (later Sir Arthur of Bomber Command fame).

No 39 Squadron, here until early August 1917, first employed operationally one of its new Armstrong-Whitworth FK 8s on 4 July 1917 against a day raid. Later that month it was flying Sopwith Camels for day interception duties and soon vacated the camp. Although busily involved against Gotha daylight raids on South East England between May and August 1917, the Sopwith Camels had little success. In August-September 1917 No 44 Squadron pioneered the use of the Camel as a night-fighter, but not until 28/29 January 1918 did success come, when two pilots from 44 Squadron achieved the first unqualified Camel night combat victory by bringing brought down a Gotha at Wickford.

When the need for home defence began to decline, No 207 Training Depot Station Chingford in May 1918 began using Hainault Farm as a sub-station. No 151 Squadron, formed on 12 June 1918, left for France four days later. By August Hainault had become No 54 Training Depot Station, but reduced training needs and strength reduction brought closure in February 1919. No 153 Squadron, forming as the conflict ceased, remained at Hainault Farm until disbandment on 13 June 1919. No 44 Squadron folded the following month. Closed by the end of the year, Hainault Farm reverted to agricultural use.

A search in the mid-1930s for a north London airport site again raised interest in Hainault Farm, which had been acquired for council development. Gathering war clouds soon brought abandonment of what was now being referred to as Fairlop. Being very suitably positioned for the air defence of London, the Air Ministry acquired the site from the Council, although not until 26 September 1940 did contractors commence preparing the landing ground before adding three runways and the technical and domestic sites.

Sqn Ldr H Ovendon took command when the station opened on 18 August 1941, personnel from Hornchurch carrying out organisational duties. On 1 September 1941 Gp Capt Harry Broadhurst from Hornchurch made trial landings, and on 10 September Fairlop opened for flying.

As Hornchurch's satellite it first accommodated Spitfires of No 603 Squadron, which touched down on 12 November 1941. Their tenure ended on 15 December 1941 when they left for Dyce. No 411 RCAF Squadron, 603's replacement, spent two weeks here between 13 and 22 February 1942.

Changes were a reflection of those made to the Hornchurch Wing, with Czechs of No 313 Squadron using Fairlop between 30 April and 8 June 1942, their replacement on 17 July being No 81 Squadron, resident until 1 September 1942. Using Spitfires Vs, it typically flew fighter sweeps, and helped provide cover for the 19 August Dieppe raid. Its companions were No 122 Squadron's Spitfire Vs. No 154 also operated from the station twice between 27 July and 15 August.

Next came No 64 Squadron, which at Hornchurch had just become first to operate the superb Spitfire F IX. Arriving on 8 September, it remained until 14 November 1942, during which time '64' provided cover for USAAF B-17 raids. In mid-November and early December No 122 Squadron was back flying offensive sweeps, convoy patrols and bomber escorts. On 2 January 1943 No 64 Squadron returned from Hornchurch, staying until 15 March 1943, on which day 350 (Belgian) Squadron brought along Spitfire Vs for a week's stay, and closing this phase in Fairlop's life.

Now it played an important part in exercise *Spartan*, which tested the concept of moving in full an airfield's squadrons together with maintenance and administrative personnel. Testing the plan, HQ No 121 Airfield opened on 5 April 1943, and on 31 May moved en bloc to Selsey. During that period seven squadrons staged through, Spitfire Vs of No 19 Squadron and Typhoons of 182 and 247 Squadrons arriving on the opening day, with No 19 staying until 18 April. No 182 remained until 29 April, and 247 until 28 May. Between 18 and 31 May Spitfires of 65 Squadron used Fairlop, and Typhoons of No 245 Squadron tarried briefly, from 28 May to 1 June 1943. Other callers were No 602 Squadron's Spitfires, which moved out on 1 June.

Following occupancy by Mustang Is of No 239 Squadron from 21 June to 27 June 1943, Spitfires of No 302 (Polish) Squadron arrived from Perranporth on 19 August 1943 and, two days later, No 317 (Polish) Squadron joined them. The Poles departed on 18 and 21 September respectively, making way for another complete change.

Now the squadrons specialised in ground attack, Hurricane IV fighter-bombers of No 164 moving in from Manston on 22 September 1943. Next day Typhoons of 195 Squadron joined them, and both continued attacks on ground targets in France.

Preparations for the June 1944 Normandy invasion were well under way when HQ No 136 Airfield opened at Fairlop on 22 November 1943 within No 84 Group, 2TAF. It took over Nos 164 and 195 Squadrons and the former began re-arming with Typhoons in January 1944. No 195 disbanded on 15 February 1944, and was replaced on 20 February by Typhoons of No 193 Squadron.

On 11 February 1944 No 164 Squadron moved out to Twinwood Farm and was replaced on the 20th by No 193 Squadron, which arrived from Harrowbeer and stayed until 15 March 1944. On that day No 136 Airfield HQ left for Thorney Island, then a period of calm descended.

Fairlop switched to becoming North Weald Sector's Operational Satellite, and in September 1944 became No 24 Balloon Centre, holding Nos 965, 967, 970 and 998 Balloon Squadrons until September 1945. Apart from the ATC's No 146 Gliding School activity, wind-down proceeded, closure coming on 22 August 1946.

**Main features:**
*Runways:* 245° 4,800ft x 150ft, 205° 3,300ft x 150ft, 290° 3,300ft x 150ft. *Hangars:* eight Blister type. *Hardstandings:* twelve suitable for Blenheims, two 50ft frying-pan type, twenty-four hardcore and asphalt. *Accommodation:* RAF 45 officers, 48 SNCOs, 958 ORs; WAAF 9 officers, 32 SNCOs, 112 ORs.

## FAIROAKS, Surrey

*51°20N/00°03W 80ft; TQ005623. 2 miles N of Woking, south of the A319*

Once known as Dolley's Farm, Fairoaks is a product of the 1930s need to train RAFVR pilots, for which hangars and offices were constructed in the north-western corner of the chosen area, close to the A319. Operated by Universal Flying Services, parented by General Aircraft Ltd, No 18 Elementary & Reserve Training School opened on 1 October 1937, No 26 Group taking control in February 1938 and No 50 Group a year later. The main equipment was a fleet of Tiger Moths, advanced training being provided using assorted Hart variants, a few Battles and Ansons. Private flying flourished alongside the RAFVR element.

On the outbreak of war the School became No 18 Elementary Flying Training School, absorbing No 19 E&RFTS, which had functioned at Gatwick. Concentration upon elementary flying training, still under 50 Group, resulted in aircraft other than Tiger Moths being posted out.

In 1940 nine Blister hangars were erected – on the opposite side of the road from the landing ground – to cope with intensive flying. Additional hangars were erected because of participation in the CRO, which led to Bristol twins in particular being repaired/overhauled during the war by Universal Flying Services working for General Aircraft.

*Chipmunk T 10 WB617 of 18*
*RFS, Fairoaks.*

The airfield surface remained grass, with Tiger Moths steadily increasing in numbers, remaining in use throughout the war. Relieving circuit congestion, the School made use of four RLGs, at Bray (February 1941-April 1942), Smiths Lawn (July 1941-February 1945), Waltham St Lawrence (1945-46) and Winkfield (May 1941-July 1945).

The ATC had a presence from October 1943, No 167 Gliding School using Grunau Baby and Kirby Cadet gliders until 1948 brought cessation.

On 21 April 1947 18 EFTS passed to 23 Group, Flying Training Command, before on 14 May 1947 it became No 18 Reserve Flying School administered by 65 Group Reserve Command. Tiger Moths remained, but in smaller numbers, and were replaced by Chipmunks.

On 15 December 1947 Tiger Moths of London University Air Squadron moved in from Biggin Hill, where the squadron had re-formed in October 1946. Its title reverted to that of pre-war times, University of London Air Squadron, on 1 December 1949, and before movement to Booker on 6 October 1950 the squadron had received Chipmunks.

Transferred to 61 Reserve Group on 1 February 1951, the RFS acquired several Anson T21s before disbandment on 31 July 1953. Throughout its time the School had been run by Universal Flying Services.

After the war various civilian organisations and private fliers made use of Fairoaks, which in 1967 was purchased by Mr Douglas Arnold, who had the site refurbished and named Fairoaks Airport. The Fairoaks School of Flying opened to give pilot training together with pleasure and charter flights. The main hangar was completely renovated and a ground instruction centre and aero club facilities provided. Distribution of Cessna F-172s in the UK was then undertaken. Helicopter flying instruction from Alan Mann Helicopters is available at the flourishing 'Fairoaks Flight Centre', while 'Flying Pictures' operates hot air balloons for promotional and hospitality purposes.

**Main features:**
*Grass area:* N-S 2,550ft, NE-SW 2,850ft, E-W 2,640ft, NW-SE 2,850ft. *Hangars:* Civil: one 80ft x 80ft, one 350ft x 90ft, one 110ft x 100ft, one 240ft x 114ft. Military: one civil hangar requisitioned, two Double Standard Blister, five Standard Blister, one Double EO Blister, one EO Blister. *Accommodation:* RAF SNCOs 39, ORs 136 only.

Modern Fairoaks remains well supplied with hangar space. Its 06/24 asphalt runway is 813 metres long and 27 metres wide. The airfield, operated by Fairoaks Airports Ltd, lies just within the southern boundary of the London Control Zone.

*Tiger Moth G-ANDG of*
*Universal Flying Services,*
*Fairoaks, on 17 April 1955.*
*(John Strangward)*

## FELTHAM (HANWORTH PARK), Middlesex

*51°27N/00°25W190ft asl; TQ105716. SW of London between Staines and Richmond*

There are a few British aerodromes that, almost throughout their existence, attracted the rare, exotic, fascinating and strange, never failing to provide many magic moments. Feltham, commonly called Hanworth or London Air Park, was most certainly one of them. It flourished until its one-time RLG cheekily expanded, re-named itself London Heathrow, and forced the closure of heavenly Hanworth.

Sandwiched between two main roads, Hanworth resembled a park across which fencing, then coils of barbed wire, stretched to persuade one not to enjoy an enquiring short-cut. Houses, from which some splendid views must have been enjoyed, fringed its eastern and southern borders. A small off-centre forest long hid an estate's manor-house-cum-hotel, aircraft manufacturing areas skirted the northerly fringes, and a stream meandered (almost secretly) across part of the landing ground. What more could one want?

Hanworth Park became a flying ground when, on Mr Whitehead's pleasant parkland in the First World War, 21 storage sheds and twelve hangars were erected. Feltham Aircraft Acceptance Park served for service preparation of Sopwith Pups and DH9s built in the works along its western edge. After the war financial problems closed the business and the buildings were put to other commercial usage.

*A Feltham product of the 1930s, BA Eagle G-AFAX, finely restored, passes at Duxford in 2003.*

Feltham awoke when, on Hanworth Park Estate, the Hanworth Air Park, which also called itself the London Air Park, opened on 3 August 1929. Its manor house, surrounded by tall trees, became a hotel and clubhouse and, unusually set almost in the middle of the landing ground, gave the impression of being an island floating on a sea of grass. To the north manufacturing and commercial interests were found. While the southern part provided a home for private fliers and the London Air Park Club. Hangars were erected along three edges of the northern site and one on the flying ground's southern perimeter.

On the eastern side was the hangar of the Cierva School of Flying, giving autogiro handling lessons, the Cierva Autogiro Company moving in during April 1937. The prototype of the Cierva C.30 had been assembled by NFS Ltd in 1933, and although most C.30As were Avro-built they were distributed to owners from Hanworth.

More buildings, on the aerodrome's north-west perimeter, were occupied by three firms. General Aircraft Ltd, which came to own the aerodrome, was the most important, while the others were the British Aircraft Manufacturing Co Ltd and Rollason Aircraft Services Ltd, the latter being a smallish company that in peacetime overhauled and repaired privately owned light aircraft, and in wartime was much involved with Hurricane repair and modification.

General Aircraft Ltd, founded at Croydon Aerodrome and needing more space in which to produce its twin-engined, all-metal, low-wing Monospar cabin monoplanes, arrived in October 1934 after the National Flying School went into receivership in June 1933. Monospar production totalled 59 aircraft, the best variant being the ST 25 Jubilee, an example of which, *G-AEYF*, was modified for ambulance work. Painted white and bearing bold red crosses on wings and fuselage, it had an upward-hinging door in the port side of the fuselage allowing a stretcher to be loaded. Medical equipment was carried, as well as a seat for a nurse. The British Red Cross eventually took delivery of the prototype and five more were produced. Another Monospar became the first aircraft built in Britain to be fitted with a pressure cabin, following which GAL designed a high-altitude pressure-cabin fighter. Under sub-contract in 1936-37 the firm also constructed 89 Hawker Fury Mk IIs and went on to convert Hawker Hind bombers into Hawker Hind trainers and upgrade Blackburn Sharks. In 1938 GAL took over CW Aircraft and developed its Cygnet into the nosewheel undercarriage GAL 42, of which ten airframes were built. A further development also tested here was the Owlet, an open-cockpit version first flown on 5 September 1940 and pushed with little success by a company aware of impending deliveries from the USA of nosewheel-fitted combat aircraft. Another specialised GAL pre-war design was the grotesque-looking Fleet Shadower. Devised for ultra-slow flight, it could all but hover, allowing the crew to observe enemy warships and chart their progress. It first flew, from Feltham, on 13 May 1940. Cancellation resulted from the aircraft's operational vulnerability.

The British Aircraft Manufacturing Company/Kronfeld developed and produced its Drone here in the mid-1930s. Formerly known as British Klemm Aircraft Limited and using the former Whitehead factory, it built under licence German-designed Klemm monoplanes including the Swallow, a large low-wing, two-seater wooden monoplane first flown here in November 1933. Production amounted to 28 Mk 1s and 105 Mk IIs. The British Aircraft Company also produced the Eagle low-wing wooden cabin monoplane and the wooden high-wing cabin twin-engined Double Eagle before GAL purchased the business in January 1938. Activity was certainly diverse.

At Feltham the Tipsy B light monoplane was built. Designed by E O Tips in the Belgian Division of Fairey, his layout was modified at the Hayes factory in 1937 to meet UK requirements. Of the eighteen Tipsy aircraft built in Britain, three were constructed post-war as *G-AISA/ISB/ISC*.

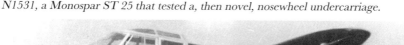

*N1531, a Monospar ST 25 that tested a, then novel, nosewheel undercarriage.*

*No, it won't bite, and it's quite tame – the GAL Shadower at Feltham. GAL*

*Behind No 239 Squadron Lysanders HB-T P1674 and HB-F in early 1941, the stands of Gatwick racecourse can be seen. (John Robertson)*

Agreement was reached, with an Air Ministry proviso that if it needed the aerodrome the airlines must vacate it within twenty-four hours. Since the airfield was not being much used, No 92 Squadron, Croydon, placed a Spitfire training element at Gatwick during February to aid their conversion from Blenheims. The detachment quickly returned to Croydon in May when the German onslaught on France and the Low Countries began.

On 6 June 1940 Airwork formally joined the CRO, and extended the range of aircraft repaired during the years ahead. On 17 July 1940 Southern Aircraft, following a similar path, concentrated on repairing impressed light transports.

By then dramatic scenes had unfolded, for the battered remnants of Nos 18 and 57 Blenheim IV Squadrons, Air Component, BEF, came to Gatwick on 26-27 May. Re-established and re-armed, they moved out on 11-12 June, and the next day were replaced by what remained of No 53 Squadron, also ex-BEF and flying Blenheim IVs. During its re-establishment, the squadron was billeted in the racecourse grandstand. It moved to Detling on 3 July, by which time survivors of an horrific event were at Gatwick.

Off St Nazaire on the afternoon of 17 June 1940 the Luftwaffe, after two attempts, sank the liner SS *Lancastria*. The third attack was horribly successful – the liner, carrying 5,000 troops, was set on fire and quickly sank. Among the few survivors were men of 98 Squadron who, with a party from 70 Wing, Air Component, arrived at Gatwick on 28 June with memories as bad as can be. No 70 Wing dissolved into SHQ Gatwick on 1 July 1940 and came under the control of No 22 (Army Co-operation) Group, then part of Fighter Command. A re-formed 98 Squadron equipped

*Wartime Gatwick, much involved with Army Co-operation, accommodated among others 239 Squadron, two of whose Lysanders are seen flying near Gatwick in January 1941. (John Robertson)*

with Battles flew to Newton on 26 July, ending a dreadful period of Gatwick's wartime existence.

Gone, at least for now, was any civilian use. Gatwick was about to become an operational military aerodrome. The terminal had many uses, additional technical and domestic features were added, local defences were strengthened, and by September 1940 light anti-aircraft guns were in position. No 26 Squadron, repeatedly attacked at West Malling, brought along its Lysanders on 3 September, confirming Gatwick's wartime Army link and staying until 14 July 1941. Between 18 September and 24 October it had as company a detachment of Defiant night-fighters of Biggin Hill's No 141 Squadron, here to improve night-flying skills.

The Lysander squadron, part of the anti-invasion force, was chosen to carry out gas spray attack – should it be demanded. Gatwick held a stock of forty-seven 250lb gas canisters.

In January 1941 Gatwick passed to No 71 Group on the formation of Army Co-operation Command. February 1941 saw a small 'C' Flight of 26 Squadron detached to Old Sarum for conversion to Curtiss Tomahawk reconnaissance fighters. Replacement was being sought for the unwieldy large Lysander, and while agile dive-bombers were required, a fighter for low-altitude reconnaissance had much to commend it. On 14 March 1941 Air Marshal Sir Arthur Barratt, AOC-in-C Army Co-operation Command, and Lt-Gen Alan Brooke, C-in-C Home Forces, visited 26 Squadron to discuss trials comparing the Lysander and the Tomahawk. The latter had a lengthy take-off run, was prone to ground loop and was powered by a troublesome Allison V-12 engine. Yet it was nimble, fast low-down and able to fight the opposition. For a while No 26 Squadron continued using both types, for only the Lysander was suitable for gas spraying.

Since late September 1940 Lysanders of 'A' Flight of No 239 Squadron had supplemented aircraft strength at Gatwick, from where they flew coastal watch dusk and dawn patrols. Joined by the remainder of the squadron on 22 January 1941, No 239 can be regarded as Gatwick's 'own' for – with brief detachments – it resided here until 21 October 1942. In June 1941 its Lysanders were replaced by Tomahawks, supplemented between January and May 1942 with Hurricane Is and IIs. It then converted fully to Mustang Is. Throughout its stay it participated in Army exercises large and small, and constantly complained about the poor standard of accommodation available on camp.

On 22 August 1941 No 71 Group disbanded, being broken into smaller Wings able to maintain closer touch with Army units. Gatwick and its squadrons, together with No 414 Squadron at Croydon, were assigned to a new No 35 Wing.

Laying of two Army Track wire-mesh runways was completed in September, allowing winter operations. Further improvement followed when, next month, No 803 Road Construction Company arrived from Iceland to improve the runways, one of which, 4,200 feet long, extended into the racecourse. By now six Blister hangars had also been erected.

Although operational sorties were later flown from Gatwick, No 26 Squadron sent a detachment to Manston in October 1941, from where, on the 16th, it flew four cross-Channel *Rhubarb* sorties. Similar operations were undertaken in two phases during November. On 22 January 1942 the squadron flew its final Tomahawk operation, from Gatwick.

Great excitement arose on 5 January 1942 when the first North American Mustang I to join any squadron was received at Gatwick by No 26, which was to review its suitability for use as a low-altitude reconnaissance fighter. So excellent was the newcomer that on 24 January the decision was taken to re-equip ten Army Co-operation squadrons with Mustangs. Thus one of Gatwick's prizes is that the P-51 Mustang made its world debut here in front-line service. No 26 returned on 23 February after two weeks' armament training at Weston Zoyland, and 'A' Flight

*Koolhoven FK-43 PH-NAU of the Luchtvaart Schule Ypenburg at the 19 June 1948 Gatwick International Air Rally, parked near the 'beehive'.*

*DC-7C EC-ATQ of Spantax at Gatwick on Saturday 14 August 1965. The background includes two Torair C-46s, IL-18 YR-IMD of Tarom, and DC-7C N90801 of Saturn Airways. (George Pennick)*

began re-arming with Mustangs. In May they were declared operational and carried out their first operational *Populars* on 14 July. Six sorties were flown, but AG415 failed to return.

With sufficient Mustang Is in hand, No 63 Squadron re-formed at Gatwick on 15 June 1942, while fourteen Tomahawks were fed into re-forming No 171 Squadron the same day. No 171 departed for Odiham on 11 July and No 63 to Catterick on 16 July.

No 35 Wing had four Mustang squadrons providing tactical reconnaissance support for operation *Jubilee* on 19 August. The resident Gatwick squadrons operated along the front from Le Havre to the Somme Estuary. By the end of the day No 26 Squadron had lost four aircraft. Two days later, Marshal of the Royal Air Force Viscount Trenchard visited the station to commiserate and also to congratulate the squadrons on their part in *Jubilee*.

No 171 Squadron returned to Gatwick on 25 August, re-equipped with Mustangs in September, and flew its first operational patrols on 3 October. From Gatwick it undertook mainly low-level interception patrols, the squadron's first mission over France coming in mid-November when two aircraft flew a French coast photo-reconnaissance mission. On 7 December the squadron left for Hartford Bridge. Two days later the 'Hurribombers' of No 175 that replaced them came to obtain close Army support experience prior to settling at Odiham in mid-January 1943.

Winter months saw squadrons similarly sending detachments to Gatwick for Army support experience. No 4 Squadron was one, No 309 (Polish) another, detached to No 35 Wing from mid-December to mid-January 1943. On 12 January No 26 Squadron departed to Detling, terminating its lengthy continuous stay. March saw the coming of No 655 (AOP) Squadron's Austers for a month's stay.

The formation in 35 Wing as part of HQ 123 Airfield on 7 April marked a new feature in Gatwick's career. Nos 26, 175 and 239 Squadrons were assigned to this unit, which was to practice moving rapidly from one site to another. It was to undergo squadron changes, Typhoons of 183 Squadron replacing No 175 on 8 April. On 21 June Nos 26 and 239 Squadrons returned for brief training before the Airfield moved to Odiham on 23 June. Accommodated under canvas, 183 Squadron had flown a few patrols, and mounted its first raid on 19 April when four of eight Typhoons operating from forward airfield Ford dive-bombed Yainville power station. The squadron left for Lasham on 3 May, the other pair also departing in May.

Upon the formation of the 2nd Tactical Air Force on 1 June 1943, No 35 Wing was placed in 84 Group, and on 28 June the Wing moved to Odiham. Formation of 2TAF resulted in the establishment of many specialist supporting units. One was 403 ARF, formed on 10 May and here until July 1943. Another was No 404 Air Stores Park, Gatwick-based between 4 June and 13 August 1943, which held spares for the ARF.

Another Airfield, No 129, formed at Gatwick on 4 July 1943, and immediately acquired Canadian Mustang squadrons, Nos 414 and 430, which carried out *Rhubarbs*, *Populars* and weather reconnaissance flights. All the Airfield and squadron personnel were accommodated under canvas.

No 414 Squadron moved to Weston Zoyland on 30 July, returned to Gatwick on 10 August, and two days later left for Ashford in Kent, followed by Airfield HQ next day. Gatwick, at last quiet, entered a period of care and maintenance. No 2875 Squadron, RAF Regiment, was posted in, together with No 2306 Squadron. The airfield was now being used as a haven for battle-damaged fighters and bombers needing to make emergency landings. It also housed No 84 Group Communication Squadron between 29 August 1943 and 1 March 1944, No 83 Group Communications Flight (a Squadron from 1 March) working alongside from 10 October 1943 to 15 April 1944.

In mid-October 1943 operational activity was resumed with Nos 19 and 65 Spitfire IX Squadrons arriving for a ten-day stay, leaving for Gravesend on 24 October. Left behind was No 430 (RCAF) Squadron, busily taking obliques of the French coast until late March 1944.

To prepare for 1944's intensive operations, Sommerfeld Track replaced the Army Track runways before 6 March 1944, when No 168 Squadron moved in, also to undertake low-level photographic missions. At the end of the month both squadrons moved to Odiham.

Bolstering the invasion build-up, No 130 Airfield, part of No 35 Wing embracing No 2 (Mustangs) and No 4 (Spitfire XI, Mosquito PR XVI) Squadrons, arrived at Gatwick on 4 April. Four days later 268 Squadron (Mustangs) joined them. All undertook tactical reconnaissance.

On D-Day, 6 June 1944, the two Mustang squadrons, Nos 2 and 268, were mainly engaged in spotting for the naval gunners bombarding coastal targets, but dense cloud prevented No 4 Squadron from photographing the battle area. In the weeks following D-Day all the squadrons busily carried out photographic/armed reconnaissance sorties. On 27 June Nos 4 and 268 Squadrons departed for Odiham, whereas No 2 waited until 30 July before moving directly to Plumetot ALG, Normandy.

No 35 Wing was replaced by three home defence Spitfire IX squadrons, Nos 80, 229 and 274, here for just over a week. The flying bomb assault had been under way for two weeks, and now to protect London a balloon barrage was flown, which put Redhill Aerodrome and ALG Horne out of use. The balloon barrage came to within 2,000 yards of Gatwick, which prevented squadrons using the airfield until the V-1 campaign subsided.

On 27 August Nos 116 and 287 AAC Squadrons brought along their Oxfords, Hurricanes, Ansons and Spitfires from North Weald. For company they had No 1 Aircraft Delivery Unit between 27 August and 17 October 1944, as well as a small outpost of No 49 Maintenance Unit. In autumn a Canadian 'casevac' unit set up base receiving wounded troops for transfer to local hospitals. No 116 moved out on 5 September, followed by No 287 and the 'casevac' unit on 20 January 1945. By then Gatwick was classed as a Forward Fighter Airfield in the Biggin Hill Sector of Fighter Command.

January 1945 saw the formation here of No 1337 Wing, SHAEF, and on 1 February the station, placed on care and maintenance and parented by Biggin Hill, became occupied by SHAEF's disarmament unit. Following the ending of hostilities in Europe, Gatwick became the satellite of

*Gatwick seen from a Boeing 767 during take-off in October 1988. Parked aircraft encircle the 'beehive'.*

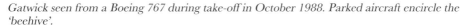

*Looking down on the South Terminal area in October 1988.*

Dunsfold. In August No 103 Air Disarmament Wing passed through on its way to the Continent, replacing SHAEF occupancy, and Nos 83 and 85 Group Communication Squadrons made use of Gatwick in the autumn. There was still a considerable amount of activity due to the proximity of London. Airwork Ltd was at this time overhauling Wellingtons, and Southern Aircraft remained within the CRO. The next few months saw the steady run-down of RAF activities. A personnel holding unit sojourned briefly, and a release centre functioned before Gatwick was derequisitioned on 31 August 1946 and taken over by the Ministry of Civil Aviation.

Had Gatwick any future? In 1943 two post-war uses were proposed. One was for a small airport serving Continental routes. The other, far more ambitious, was for a second long-haul airport for London. Heathrow had been chosen to become London's No 1 airport, so the Government considered disposing of Gatwick for housing development. Pressure not to do so was applied by interested parties, who pointed to a likely increasing need for a charter airlines airport to replace Croydon, and in November 1946 a licence permitting passenger flying from Gatwick was issued. Without metalled runways the airport was disadvantaged, and only small charter operators like Horton Airways and Ciros Aviation Ltd made use of it. Airwork Ltd still used the hangars and technical installations for the repair and servicing of, among others, Sea Hornets and Seafires. In summer 1948 an international light aircraft rally was held around 'the beehive', something much removed from current activity.

That year saw Airports Ltd still running Gatwick, but it was informed that the Government intended to de-requisition it in September because Stansted had been chosen as a second London airport. Mr M Desoutter and Peter Masefield, Chief Executive of BEA, immediately championed Gatwick, traffic figures suggesting to Peter Masefield that Heathrow would be unable to handle all BEA's London movements by the mid-1950s. He pointed out that Gatwick was nearer the Continent, and already had a good rail link with London. After much prevarication the Government agreed in 1952 that Gatwick, not Stansted, should become London's second airport. How the pendulum swings!

It took four years for work to start on a long Gatwick runway, new hangars and terminal building – all similar to those proposed in 1943. There would, however, be only one runway to restrict environmental damage on the area around the airport. In March 1956 all companies moved out, and Gatwick closed for reconstruction.

It re-opened for flying on 30 May 1958, an official re-opening being declared by HM Queen Elizabeth II on 9 June 1958. Possessing the single 7,000-foot runway and a large apron, Gatwick had a huge new terminal building connected with a new railway station.

Although BEA made use of Gatwick, charter operators predominated. Formation of British United Airways in 1960 brought a marked increase in both scheduled and charter business, at a time when inclusive tours and passenger numbers were multiplying fast. To cope, two long piers were extended from the terminal, featuring covered walkways leading from pier gates to the aircraft and mirroring the forethought of the 1930s. As the number of passengers grew, so the airport expanded to accommodate them, and the larger, heavier aircraft types entering service to carry them. The runway was lengthened first to 8,200 feet in 1964, and later to around 10,000 feet. In 1977 major modification of the terminal resulted in the inclusion of a multi-storey car-park and a direct access road to the new M25 motorway. Whereas the excellent 30-minute rail link with London had been important as envisaged, the immense increase in road traffic had to be catered for with far more parking areas.

In the 1980s the second or North large terminal came into use, by which time the names of some of Gatwick's airlines were household words – Dan Air, British Caledonian, British Midland and the ill-fated Laker. No longer were they using cast-off main-line aircraft, but were investing in new, high-performance airliners including BAC 1-11s, DC-10s and TriStars. From humble beginnings some climbed to great heights, while others dramatically fell by the wayside.

By the start of this century, twin terminal/one runway Gatwick was handling around 32 million passengers annually, about one-fifth travelling for business reasons, the remainder for leisure. About 14 million passengers are inbound. Within the terminals are 140 retail outlets and twenty-six refreshment areas, with three hotels close by. Around one-fifth of the passengers arrive by rail, London being thirty minutes away. Half arrive by car, clearly causing a major problem, with about a tenth using bus/coach travel. A forecast 45 million passenger flow by 2008 is leading to much effort being put into persuading passengers, and the 45,000-strong workforce, to make use of ever improving public road transport and the railway.

'The Gateway to Spain' might well describe Gatwick, with BA and the GB franchise alone flying to fifteen destinations. There are, however, more services to the USA from here than from any other UK airport, with flights to Florida and the Caribbean region attracting many leisure fliers. Operators to America from Gatwick are BA, Virgin Atlantic, Continental Airlines, American Airlines, Delta Airlines, Northwest, and US Airways. A dozen destinations in the UK and Eire also are served by some of Gatwick's eighty airlines, which also operate to many European destinations within a grand total of around 200. About a quarter use the North Terminal, which, like its companion, has recently been extended.

Work likely to cost £80 million started on Pier 6 in 2003. Put in position in May 2004 was a 197 metre long, glass enclosed, 2,500 ton passenger bridge set 32 metres high and linking Pier 6 with the North Terminal. It has completely changed the Gatwick skyline. Crossing a main taxiway, and

*A general view of Gatwick Airport in 2002 looking south-westwards. (BAA)*

allowing 747-400s to pass beneath, it is the first of its type in Europe. The only similar structure is at Denver International airport, USA. With the prospect of ultra-large airliners looming, these bridges may well become indispensable.

Large airports inevitably generate noise, smell, and movement on a grand scale. None of those can be hidden. They also provide employment, bring trade, attract huge sums of money – and unfortunately terrorists siring an ever-booming security, protection and intensive manual search industry, which, although essential, can so easily spoil air travel. Plans for more runways related to traffic forecasts for many decades ahead need very close scrutiny. The progress of aviation has always deviated, like its speed, from the forecasts. Thirty years in the world of aviation is a mighty long time!

**Main features:**
December 1944: *Runways:* 238° 4,200ft, 277° 3,600ft, both Army Track, NW-SE grass run, 3,000ft available. *Hangars:* one Bellman, six Blister. *Hardstandings:* twelve Blenheim type, three 50ft frying-pan, seventeen 100ft frying-pan. *Accommodation:* RAF officers 79, SNCOs 111, ORs 720; WAAF officers 6, SNCOs 4, ORs 202.

December 1994: Main Precision Instrument Runway 08R/26L for all Cat II/III operations, take-off run available 10,364ft, take-off distance available 10,863ft, landing distance available 9,075ft, concrete/asphalt. Five approach crossbars, green threshold wingbars, red end lighting, rapid exit taxiway indicator lights. ILS Cat III (Localiser and Glidepath), DME, NDB. The 08L/26R 2,850m runway is available when the main runway is temporarily non-operational, and has surveillance radar, DME and NDB. There are 109 aircraft stands. Piers are twenty-five for 747/777, fourteen medium for DC-10/767, and fifteen for smaller aircraft (757/737). Non-pier stands for twenty-five, fourteen and fifteen respectively.

## GAYDON, Warwickshire

*52°11N/01°29W 410ft asl; SP355555. 7 miles SSE of Leamington*

Gaydon's selection as the first V-bomber station was due to the existence of fighter belts to the east able to defend it. A completely new 9,000-foot-long runway was built south of wartime Gaydon, with three groups each of four dispersals leading directly to the runway for fast response. A special 'Gaydon'-type hangar, reminiscent of the Type J of the 1940s, housed Valiants, later Victors. An electronics servicing block was added, as well as secure weapons areas and a new operations block – all essential at all V-bomber bases. A much-increased population meant the addition of more messing and domestic quarters.

Gaydon first came into use in early 1942, before opening on 13 June 1942 as a satellite for Chipping Warden's 12 OTU. When that unit acquired Edgehill as a permanent satellite, on 1 September 1942 Gaydon was transferred to 22 OTU Wellesbourne Mountford, a 91 Group station whose runways were under repair.

'A' and 'B' Flights of 22 OTU moved to Gaydon, which was the base for Training Wing's Wellingtons to the end of the war. Wellington Ics were first used, Mk IIIs were introduced in October 1942, and from 1943 Mk Xs were used.

Because of those 1942 runway repairs, 22 OTU used Gaydon as the starting point for bombing sorties within the operation *Grand National* series (during which OTUs enhanced Main Force strength) during September 1942. In 1943 *Nickelling* sorties were flown from the station, and by the end of 1943 Gaydon's Wellingtons had delivered reading material to the inhabitants of Grenville, Nantes, Orleans and Rennes. Autumn 1943 saw few bombing sorties despatched preceding operation *Starkey*, gun emplacements near Boulogne being targeted. Additionally, daylight ASR flights over the North Sea took place from Gaydon, and quite a number of diversions were made here by bombers returning from operations by day and night.

Training by 22 OTU ceased at Gaydon on 1 July 1945, and control of the station, although still held by Wellesbourne, passed like that of the latter to 23 Group Flying Training Command on 24 July. That resulted in the immediate arrival of 3 GTS from Exeter, bringing Master IIs, Hotspur gliders, Tiger Moths and an Oxford. From Croughton on 28 May 1946 came the Glider Instructors' Flight, whose stay was brief for Gaydon closed to flying on 15 August 1946. From 28 August 1946 Gaydon was held on care and maintenance, but although it was not active it became 21 (P)AFU's satellite in 1947. It returned to care and maintenance in May.

*Valiants of No 138 Squadron and the OCU at Gaydon on 19 March 1956.*

Rapid rebuilding began in 1953, and on 1 March 1954 it re-opened. On 1 January 1955 138 Squadron re-formed at Gaydon as the first V-bomber squadron. Equipped with Valiants, it became operational prior to moving to Wittering on 6 July 1955. No 232 Operational Conversion Unit formed on 21 February 1955 to train Valiant crews, and Canberra T4s were used for runway approach aid training. No 543 Squadron, which re-formed at Gaydon on 1 July 1955 to fly strategic reconnaissance Valiants, left for Wyton on 18 November 1955.

*A Victor B1 of No 232 OCU at Gaydon in 1961.*

Once the Valiant force had formed, aided by 232 OCU, Gaydon began training Victor crews, the first of seven aircraft arriving for the OCU on 11 November 1957. All Victor 1 bomber crews were trained at 232 OCU alongside replacements for Valiant squadrons. On 1 April 1962 'C' Flight moved to Cottesmore and became the Victor Training Flight.

V-bomber training continued until 30 June 1965, when the Victor OCU disbanded to make way for Flying Training Command, and on 1 September 1965 No 2 ANS and its Varsities began moving in to Gaydon. The School departed for Finningley on 1 May 1970 to become part of 6 FTS. Gaydon remained under 23 Group until 10 June 1970, when it was transferred to HQ CFS. The Strike Command Special Avionics Servicing Unit of No 1 Group lodged at Gaydon until disbanded on 1 December 1971. Control of Gaydon passed to 71 MU Bicester, Maintenance Command, on 1 April 1972, and the station was once again put on care and maintenance until closure on 31 October 1974. British Leyland later acquired the site, which has since served a variety of motor manufacturers.

**Main features:**
*Runways:* 248° 5,800ft x 150ft, 178° 4,200ft x 150ft, 316° 4,200ft x 150ft, concrete with tar and sand surface. *Hangars:* one T2, one B1. *Hardstandings:* twenty-seven heavy bomber type. *Accommodation:* RAF officers 87, SNCOs 340, ORs 1,224; WAAF officers 2, SNCOs 8, ORs 185.

## GRAFTON UNDERWOOD, Northamptonshire

*52°25N/00°38W 338ft asl; SP925815. 4 miles NE of Kettering*

As Maurice Chevalier once so famously said, "Ah yes! I remember it well", for the sun was beaming and the *spartan* wartime tea was waiting when a sound like an overgrown Anson passed overhead. I raced outside, binoculars in hand, and quickly espied the long-awaited. On the pale bluish underside of the B-17E was the proclamation 'U S ARMY'. They sure had taken their time, but the Yanks were here – at last. One, anyway.

They weren't too good at security in 1942, for the first American I met, in his gas-guzzler, asked the way to Thrapston. A quick follow-up chat easily confirmed that Grafton Underwood (near Thrapston) was a lair of the early USAAF Flying Fortresses.

On 5 August 1942 cousin Roger and I set forth early on the long cycle ride from Cambridge, and by lunchtime – after a lot of pedalling – we were on the winding Slipton road off the A604, which our maps indicated (no signposts then) would lead us to Grafton Underwood. Already excitement had welled as US lorries passed perilously close and we had our first sighting of a Jeep. We were on the right track, but of B-17Es nothing was seen or heard.

Grafton we found to be a most picturesque village, but no airfield was visible. Then – curse upon curses – the road ahead was closed, an American sentry barring our way. We retreated to a by-road to rest, bite the margarine and jam sandwiches and rejuvenate hope. The only engine notes came from skylarks, plentiful that summer. On returning to the village we found a winding path skirting a high wall and blocking the view towards where we knew the aerodrome – sorry, the Field – was obviously situated.

Suddenly there was a rough cough and an engine burst into life. No mistaking it, this was a Cyclone. Roger, more American-orientated than me thanks to the Inkspots and such souls, was frantically trying to dislodge a large, loose boulder from the wall, assuming that a splendid view might appear. He pushed, and I fumbled for the binoculars.

What an incredible sight presented itself. A gigantic US 'bum' deposited itself right in Roger's cavern, completely blocking the view. I'm sure he did not mean to do that and, being an American, had he known how far we'd cycled to view an American, he would probably have taken away his posterior – had we the nerve to have requested it.

Instead we quietly crept away hopeful of another vantage point. Through a crack I spied 19038 taxiing quite close by, its deep orange-coloured 'tail number' belying the usual claims of yellow. Moments later the pilot opened up its engines and the B-17 hurried off.

We retreated to open country to plan another attack before accepting that a clear, close view of sunny, breezy Grafton was not to be ours. We had to be satisfied with a distant view of a stream take-off by six B-17Es, our binoculars informing us that 19047 was leading. Over the next hour the formation flew around low, engraving images to store for life.

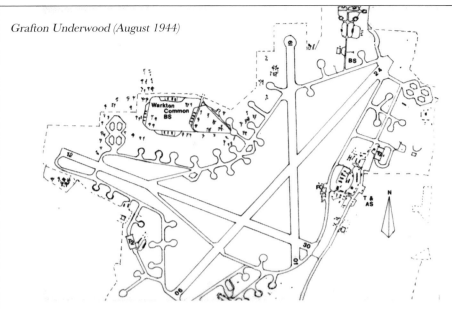

Grafton Underwood (August 1944)

## GRAFTON UNDERWOOD
This was a Built Satellite of 1941 style to serve Polebrook, and it performed in that role even after the USAAF took over both stations during May 1942. After the 97th BG moved out late 1942 it was much enhanced, developing into a more elaborate than usual version of a standard wartime temporary three-runway bomber station, and ultimately embraced more then 500 buildings spread over a wide area. In all, the station covered twelve Sites and had two sewage sites. Additional to the usual pair of 72,000-gallon aviation fuel tanks (pattern 9846/41) were added a further two, one for 48,000 gallons and the other containing 24,000 gallons. Two unglazed T2 hangars (pattern 3653/42 – marked T2) were later erected. A total of twelve Sites were constructed, No 1 Site (illustrated) being the airfield; the others were dispersed sites and mainly domestic in essence, of which No 7 was intended as the WAAF domestic site. One held an M/F D/F station. Grafton's development resulted in the closure of two local roads, one feeding into the Technical & Administration Site (marked T&AS), comprising surprisingly few buildings, with the flying control tower (FC) on its edge.

Originally, twenty-four circular 'frying-pan-type' dispersed hardstandings were laid. Early 1943 saw a dozen angular-type hardstandings added. Finally came three sets of 'spectacle-type' hardstandings, so that 50 stands were ultimately available. To reduce lengthy taxying, two unusual track spurs crossed runways 12/30 and 06/24. A circular pad at the end of runway 19 allowed aircraft to about turn. Runway headings are more precisely listed under 'Main features'.

Having two bomb storage areas (BS) – one in the north-east corner with ten buildings and the other on Warkton Common – was unusual. Silver birch trees grown in profusion on the latter provided camouflage for associated buildings including some of the five HE bomb stores, four incendiary bomb stores, component sheds, four bomb fusing buildings, a pyrotechnics store, and several aircraft hardstandings. Also unusual were two retractable Oakington Pillboxes (8992/41).

The long, hard haul home was not without incident, for while resting in a shady hedgerow (still there) near Spaldwick, we had an unexpected bonus, the appearance of a USAAF P-38 Lightning – the first we had seen – scurrying northwards, possibly to Goxhill?

There had been Americans at Grafton since May 1942. They had sailed to Britain aboard the SS Andes before stepping ashore at Liverpool docks. These were men of the 15th Bomb Squadron, soon to take the Douglas Boston into action spearheading American bombing operations. Their stay was brief, however, for they moved to Molesworth on 9 June.

*97th BG B-17E 19043 gets airborne from Grafton in August 1942. (IWM)*

Grafton had come into use in late 1941, and by the start of 1942 temporarily served as the satellite of Polebrook, where 90 Squadron used Fortress Is and now the RAF's 1653 Conversion Unit was acquiring Liberator IIs. American bombers were nothing new to this area. On 10 June twenty-nine officers and 412 enlisted men made a dusk arrival at Grafton to prepare for the first B-17Es.

Possibly the enemy knew about it, or maybe a load of incendiaries from a passing Ju 88 intended for Thrapston's ironworks went astray. Whatever the truth, they fell upon a Nissen hut, giving the Americans a most unfriendly welcome and their first taste of war. Into Grafton the ground echelon of the 342nd Bomb Squadron moved on 10 June, followed by the 414th next day. Their aircraft soon followed. Remaining squadrons of the 97th Bomb Group placed themselves at Polebrook, together with the Group's HQ, the whole coming under the control of No 1 Bombardment Wing, US VIIIth Bomber Command. July and early August 1942 saw acclimatisation flying and fighter affiliation with RAF Spitfires, then by mid-August the Group was ready to commence operations.

On 17 August 1942 the battle began. First away were Polebrook's B-17s, flying a mid-afternoon feint. Then at 1627 the first of twelve B-17Es rolled along Grafton's runway to launch the mighty offensive with which the 8th AF carved its place in history. Ironically, that first B-17 had as co-pilot Major P W Tibbets, who was to captain the B-29 from which the atomic bomb fell on Hiroshima to all but end the war. By 1635 the dozen B-17s were airborne, one from the 340th Bomb Squadron, five from the 342nd, and six of the 414th. Aboard 19023 *Yankee Doodle,* leadship of the second formation, was another who would achieve fame, General Ira Eaker.

Hordes of Spitfires gathered to protect them as they tracked towards the exit point, Beachy Head. Providing high cover were the latest Spitfires, F Mk IXs of Nos 64, 401,402 and 611 Squadrons. Rear cover was provided by Spitfire Vs of Nos 129, 131, 412 and 309 (USA) Squadrons (the latter operating from Tangmere), with 133 and 307 (USA) Squadrons, Biggin lodgers, aiding them. Many other RAF Spitfires protected the diversion.

With forty-five 600lb and nine 1,100lb HE bombs aboard, the Fortresses entered France east of St Valery, and from 23,000 feet, between 1739 and 1746, aimed at Rouen's Sotteville railway complex. At the coast one of the B-17s suffered flak damage. About fifty enemy fighters responded from Beaumont-le-Roger, 64 Squadron claiming two of them and 401 Squadron another, for the loss of two Spitfires. A Fw 190 was chased into the fire of a waist gunner, Sergeant West, in *Birmingham Blitzkrieg,* and a ball turret gunner fired at a Fw 190, both being inconclusive.

As the returning B-17s came into view at Grafton around 1900, all were seen to be safe. It was a splendid summer evening, but there would be many more when no amount of sunshine could dispel the anguish and terrible carnage found aboard many a bomber.

*Bombs away from B-17Gs of the 384th Bomb Group, Grafton Underwood. (USAF)*

*Boeing B-17E 19043 'Peggy D' of the 342nd BS, 97th BG, up from Grafton in the summer of 1942. (USAF)*

On 19 August, 'Dieppe Day', twenty-four B-17Es of the 97th – six from each of the four squadrons – attacked Abbeville/Drucat airfield in support of the landing. Next day a dozen raided Amiens marshalling yards and, on 21 August, a raid by twelve on Rotterdam displayed to the Americans the vital need for precise time-keeping: they were sixteen minutes late at the rendezvous, so the Spitfires could cover them for only half of the journey. Three bombers aborted, and the remainder were ordered to abort at the Dutch coast. Abandonment came too late, for twenty-three Fw 190s were sweeping in to attack. Two were shot down, but B-17E 19089 was soon in trouble. Five fighters set about the lagging bomber, killed the co-pilot and injured the captain. A courageous crew miraculously nursed the Fortress home.

Le Trait shipyards, Avions Potez Meaulte, Courtrai/Wevelghem airfield – all had been raided by the end of August 1942. The largest raid yet came on 7 September, twenty-nine B-17s attacking Rotterdam. Enemy fighters rose in strength, B-17 crews optimistically claiming twelve of them.

At the end of the first week of September 1942 the 342nd and 414th Squadrons moved to Polebrook, making room for B-17Fs of the 305th Bomb Group at Grafton, there by September. In late November 1942 the 305th moved to Chelveston, for Grafton was now to be much enhanced with additional dispersal areas, improved runways, and better and more accommodation.

By mid-April 1943, with the work complete, four squadrons of B-17Fs of the 96th Bomb Group arrived, but only for a brief stay. At the end of May they left for Andrews Field, Essex, their place taken by the 384th Bomb Group, which began battle on 22 June 1943. During the course of 314 operations, the 384th ('P' in a triangle) attacked targets over a very wide area ranging from Orleans/Bricy airfield, engine works at Cologne, Gelsenkirchen coking plant, a components factory at Halberstadt, a steelworks at distant Magdeburg, and the ball-bearing factory at Schweinfurt. Leipzig, Emden, Hamburg, Mannheim, Berlin – all felt the crunch of Grafton's bombs.

*The control tower at Grafton. R Walters. (via Don Bradfield)*

Two Distinguished Unit Citations were awarded to the 384th, one for the raid of 24 April 1944 when, although greatly mauled, the Group led the 41st Wing through great opposition to bomb a factory and airfield at Oberpfafenhofen.

After assisting with the softening up of French coastal targets, prior to the June 1944 invasion, the 384th helped the Americans break out from St Lo, supported the Rhine crossing assaults, and on 24 April 1945 was the last Group in the 8th AF to drop bombs in anger, making Grafton's contributions to the 8th AF campaign both first and last.

In June 1945 the 384th moved to France, the RAF repossessed the station and 236 MU arrived to dispose of many surplus motor vehicles here. Military ownership of Grafton ceased in February 1959.

Visit Grafton now and a good view across the site of the airfield can be had. On dispersals among silver birch trees the 'Forts' used to stand. Runways in part remain, as well as the perimeter track. Call at Grafton's village post office and you may find out more about the historic field. The nearby church is also worth a visit, for items recalling days long gone are much in evidence here. A memorial by the Geddington road provides a physical reminder, if one is necessary.

**Main features:**
*Runways:* 045° 6,000ft x 150ft, 293° 4,200ft x 150ft, 358° 4,200ft x 150ft, concrete with asphalt and wood chips. *Hangars:* two T2. *Hardstandings:* fifty frying-pan type. *Accommodation:* USAAF officers 421, EM 2,473.

## GRAVESEND (CHALK), Kent

*51°25N/00°23E 240ft asl; TQ665720. 2 miles SE of Gravesend*

"I don't believe it! You're kidding – this little thing couldn't make Cape Town and back in four days. The cockpit is only a couple of feet wide, and you can't even see where you're going. Who was the pilot, then, and where did he start from?"

"Pilot? He was Alex Henshaw who became the Chief Test Pilot at the wartime Castle Bromwich Spitfire factory, and his amazing journey started and ended at Gravesend."

"Gravesend? Surely not that place by the Thames? I've often been there and never seen any sign of an aerodrome."

"I most certainly do mean that Gravesend – or should it be Bravesend? Some of the most famous pioneer aviators flew from there including Amy Johnson, later Amy Mollison, Jean Batten, Kingsford Smith. During the war many celebrated fighter pilots flew from Gravesend, and with many famous fighter squadrons, for it was Biggin Hill's satellite. It's mainly covered with houses now, and only microlights manoeuvre into the area."

Unless you are an 'aviation person' you may well never have heard of Gravesend aerodrome. Visit the site and you may need a lot of convincing that the following events really did take place here, that Typhoons thundered over land where the refuse cart now clangs away.

Aviation came to the scene when Australian aviator, Captain Edgar Percival, began using a small grass area to the south of Chalk for flying. Local interest promoted its development into the 148-acre site soon called 'Gravesend Airport'. Set 240 feet above sea level between the A2 and A226 roads, it overlooked the river, sitting above the fog level. Two hangars, a control tower, clubhouse, fuel and oil stores and ancillary buildings lined its eastern side by risqué-titled Thong Lane.

Activity increased in June 1932 when the Gravesend Aviation Company was inaugurated, headed by two pilots, T A B Ternan and W A C Kingham. Herbert Gooding, a local builder, became managing director, and Mr A D Carroll the first Chief Flying Instructor. A rally at the site on 25 August 1932 attracted more than twenty light aircraft, although there were then only four permanent residents – two DH Moths, an Avro Avian and a Desoutter belonging to the Gravesend School of Flying, strictly run and offering instruction up to commercial pilot standard.

At the grand official opening on 12 October 1932 Alan Cobham's *circus*, including his strange Airspeed Ferry three-engined biplane, joined in the fun. The Airport's future suddenly brightened in November when a Fokker airliner, PH-AEZ of Royal Dutch Airlines (KLM), ferried in ten passengers. Officials aboard were much impressed with their welcome, and the airport's layout. Herbert Gooding, who had strongly invested in the airport, tried hard to promote Gravesend, which KLM again used on 24 February 1933. A snowstorm, preventing a landing at Croydon Airport (sometimes fog-bound), had ironically promoted Gravesend's value – as an emergency landing ground. This led to its being styled as 'London East – Gravesend'. KLM, Deutsche Lufthansa, Sabena and Swissair all made use of it when inclement conditions closed Croydon, but hopes that they might regularly use Gravesend failed to materialise. Instead, only the flying school became busier.

Soon to become the most extensive user of Gravesend, the RAF made the first use of the strategically well-sited aerodrome in July 1933, three Hawker Audaxes and an AW Atlas using the airport during a coastal exercise.

Later that year serious negotiations with KLM were undertaken, and a new 130ft by 125ft hangar was completed by summer 1934. However, KLM, using well-equipped Croydon with its superior passenger-handling facilities and better land links, decided to continue using that facility as its London terminal. Gravesend didn't not look as if it had any future.

There was, however, another player at the field, Edgar Percival, whose small aircraft company had established sales and servicing facilities in 1932. Percival Aircraft Ltd had designed the Gull, a three-seat low-wing monoplane test-flown from West Malling, and had built a small factory at Gravesend. Hangar space was now rented and a production run of two-dozen Gulls initiated. Some twenty-two were eventually built, including *G-ADPR*, flown to New Zealand by Jean Batten, *G-ADZO* used by Amy Johnson, and Sir Charles Kingsford-Smith's *G-ACJV*. Using these, record and pioneering flights were made to Africa, Australia and South America.

The exotic, exquisite Percival P6 Mew Gull, a sort of aerial racing-car that emerged in March 1934, was the first 200mph-plus light aircraft. A centre of gravity dangerously aft when fully loaded made it demanding to fly, and the view from its cockpit was so bad that it was often taxied by a pilot walking alongside who, with the cockpit cover raised, controlled the throttle.

Percival Aircraft's success overtook Gravesend's facilities and the company moved to Luton in October 1936. Its place was taken by Essex Aero Ltd, which concentrated on modifying and customising aircraft. Several aircraft types made their maiden flights from Gravesend at this time, among them the prototype Short Scion *G-ACJI* and, in September 1936, the sole CLW Curlew, *G-ADYU*.

That year Amy Mollison, née Johnson, set out from Gravesend in a Gull on her second flight to the Cape, breaking all records for the duration of the return flight, as well as the round trip.

The airport's financial problems were now all too obvious. Airports Limited, which owned Gatwick, stepped in and purchased Gravesend, but found it so unprofitable that it offered the airport to Gravesend Council for use as its municipal airport. No transfer fee could be agreed, then the Air Ministry stepped in, leading to the formation here, on 1 October 1937, of No 20 Elementary & Reserve Flying Training School. This trained not only RAFVR pilots, but also Royal Navy pupils in a region with traditional naval links, and used assorted Hart variants and Tiger Moths.

In February 1939 Gravesend suddenly entered international prominence when Alex Henshaw, in his Mew Gull *G-AEXF,* piloted it from its birthplace on an amazing record-breaking flight to Cape Town and back. Henshaw had won the 1938 King's Cup Air Race in the P6, covering a

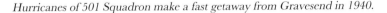

*Hurricanes of 501 Squadron make a fast getaway from Gravesend in 1940.*

*Lysander ASR III V9517 of 277 ASR Squadron, Gravesend-based in 1942.*

1,012-mile track at an amazing average speed of 236.25mph. Now, in four days, he covered the 6,377 miles to Winkfield, Cape Town, in 39hrs 23min, and took 39hrs 36min to fly back to Gravesend. He had beaten the existing world record by an amazing 66hrs 42min!

During his lone journey he took off ten times, endured that cramped cockpit, whose canopy almost touched his head, and had flown one leg taking 6³/₄hrs. Heavily fuel-laden, the small aeroplane – wingspan 24 feet, length 21ft 11in, all-up weight 2,125lb – could cruise at 240mph at 7,000 feet, and was seriously unstable, giving Alex a bumpy ride, high fatigue and maximum stress. His navigation skills were brilliant, for he traversed desert and jungle almost without guiding landmarks, flying through storms, haze, fog and darkness aided with inadequate maps and having no margins for error. He recounts his amazing epic in the book *The Flight of the Mew Gull.*

When war broke out civilian flying ceased, and the E&RFTS closed. Requisitioned by the Air Ministry, Gravesend became Biggin Hill's satellite, so it is hardly surprisingly that so many famous RAF fighter squadrons and their personalities flew from here. Sparse accommodation led to aircrew being billeted in the small control tower and at Cobham Hall, while groundcrews used the Laughing Waters roadhouse on the A2 road, or were billeted locally.

First in were Hurricanes of No 32 Squadron, which arrived on 3 January 1940 and stayed till late March. The Blitzkrieg of 10 May led to more Hurricanes, this time of 56 Squadron, which spent three days here before Spitfires of No 610 'County of Chester' Squadron arrived on 26 May, staying until 2 July when they moved to the parent station. Between 1 and 6 June they had been reinforced by 72 Squadron, brought from Acklington to help protect the BEF's withdrawal from Dunkirk. Replacing 72 came Blenheim Ifs of No 604 'County of Middlesex' Squadron to undertake day and night interception patrols between 3 and 26 July.

On 25 July 1940, with early skirmishes of the Battle of Britain being fought, Hurricanes of No 501 'County of Gloucester' Squadron arrived at Gravesend, their main Battle of Britain station. Among the pilots were pre-war original Auxiliary members, as well as the famous Sergeant Pilot J H 'Ginger' Lacey.

The squadron's first major engagement on 29 July meant tackling Ju 87s escorted by Bf 109s. No 501 claimed six of the enemy and six damaged. To allow earlier interception Hawkinge was used as a forward airfield, 501 flying there daily from soon after first light.

Within a few days the squadron – like others in No 11 Group – was being stretched to its limit.

Heavy bombing temporarily closed Hawkinge so, between 12 and 15 August, No 501 operated from Gravesend and participated in hectic battles over Kent.

Bombs fell on the aerodrome on 2 September, injuring two soldiers, a day on which 501 Squadron lost four aircraft. Three pilots were injured, and Fg Off A T Rose-Price was killed – on his first day with the squadron.

Early on 6 September approximately one hundred enemy aircraft were engaged over Ashford, the fight claiming three pilots. No 501 Squadron was at last relieved on 11 September, by Spitfires of No 66 Squadron, which remained until 30 October 1940. They too fought daily from Gravesend or the forward site, Hawkinge.

Unusual was the manner of formation here, on 8 October 1940, of No 421 (Reconnaissance) Flight. Drawing upon 66 Squadron's resources, and as a result of Winston Churchill's intervention, its task was to undertake high-level early warning patrols to spot the build-up of Luftwaffe formations, and also to observe Channel enemy shipping movements. Armed with Hurricane IIas, the small specialised Flight left, on 30 October, for West Malling.

No 141 Squadron flying night-fighter Defiants in Biggin Hill Sector began using its satellite on 3 November, continuing to do so until 29 April 1941. They were supplemented from 23 November with night-fighting No 85 Squadron under Sqn Ldr Peter Townsend, flying Hurricanes. Without AI radar, these fighters had little chance of night successes. No 85 left for Debden and re-equipment on 1 January 1941. Replacing it briefly, Defiants of No 264 resided at Gravesend between 1 and 11 January, when they moved to Biggin Hill.

From November 1940 the station was self-accounting with its own SHQ, meaning that squadrons were now posted to the station and not detached from Biggin Hill, although Gravesend remained in its Sector. Additional buildings were erected during the 1940/41 winter.

After the Defiants departed at the end of April 1941, Gravesend accommodated many Spitfire squadrons whose tasks were mainly offensive. Those operations meant that the two-cannon Mk Vbs were operating at their extreme range, making the use of forward airfields essential. No 124 Squadron was an exception, based here with high-flying Mk VIs positioned to oppose expected Ju 86R high-level bombers; they flew four top-cover operations during operation *Jubilee*. In May 1942 the squadrons hitherto flying as part of the Biggin Hill Wing began to operate as the Gravesend Wing, and Nos 124, 133, 232 and 165 were all available to cover the Dieppe landings. Since summer 1941 bomber escorts, *Rodeos*, shipping protection and defensive operations had been flown as needed.

Spitfire Squadrons using Gravesend from May 1941 to November 1942 were:

| Squadron No | Period |
| --- | --- |
| 65 | 29.7.42-14.8.42 |
|  | 20.8.42-26.9.42 |
| 71 (Eagle) | 3.5.42-30.6.42 |
| 72 | 8.7.41-26.7.41 |
|  | 20.10.41-22.2.42 |
| 74 | 1.5.41-9.7.41 |
| 92 | 24.9.41-20.10.41 |
| 111 | 3.5.42-30.6.42 |
| 124 | 3.5.42-30.6.42 |
|  | 14.8.42-20.8.42 |
| 133 (Eagle) | 31.7.42-22.8.42 |
| 165 | 14.8.42-1.11.42 |
| 232 | 31.7.42-22.8.42 |
| 350 (Belgian) | 30.6.42-7.7.42 |
| 401 (Can) | 19.3.42-3.8.42 |
| 609 | 27.7.41-24.9.41 |

A role change started on 7 December 1942 when air/sea rescue Lysanders, Spitfires and Walruses of No 277 Squadron moved in to operate around the Kentish coast. The lengthy stay of their HQ element extended to 15 April 1944.

Gravesend's increasing use led to much improvement and increased size. North-south and east-west runways were considerably lengthened, the former to 5,100 feet, the latter to 5,400 feet. Sommerfeld steel tracking was laid, and *Drem* lighting installed. Fuel storage for up to 32,000 gallons of aviation spirit, 400 gallons of oil and 1,500 gallons of MT spirit allowing Gravesend to support three squadrons and make a switch to tactical support operations.

Raucous change was only too audible on 24 March 1943 when 181 Squadron and its fighter-bomber Typhoons arrived. They were joined on 31 March by 245 Squadron. No 174 replaced 181 on 5 April, then No 247 took over from 245 on 28 May. No 247 left on 4 June and 174 on 12 June.

Then the operational organisation structure changed. Typhoons were replaced by Spitfire Vs of Nos 19 and 132 Squadrons on 20 June 1943, and on 24 June they came under the control of HQ 125 Airfield. No 19 departed on 26 June, No 132 moving out with the new HQ on 3 July.

HQ No 139 Airfield formed on 10 July and attracted Nos 2 and 4 Squadrons flying Mustang Is. They joined on 16 July and moved to Odiham, with the Airfield HQ, in the second week of August.

Typhoons returned, this time with No 193 Squadron, Gravesend-based between 17 August and 18 September 1943, No 266 Squadron joining it between 7 and 10 September.

Assisting the build-up of tactical forces, HQ 122 Airfield was here between 20 October 1943 and the end of April 1944. Initially it controlled three Spitfire IX squadrons, Nos 19 and 65 from 24 October and No 122 from 8 November. Soon after, 65 Squadron commenced re-arming with long-range escort Mustang IIIs, the first squadron to do so, and was followed by Nos 65 and 122 in February 1944. For company at Gravesend they had No 18 Armament Practice Camp, formed on 18 October 1943 from 1493 Flight and operating four Martinet target-towers. The APC departed for Eastchurch on 26 December 1943.

Tactical activity was ever increasing. HQ 122 Airfield left as No 122 Wing 2TAF, formed on 12 April, the departure of the Mustangs to Ford taking place on 15 April 1944. Throughout their stay they had taken a very active part in operations over northern Europe.

Quite dramatic change was exhibited on 12 May 1944 when No 140 Wing, part of No 2 Group and 2TAF, formed here. Its squadrons would mount an interdictor campaign by night against all German movement in Normandy, employing the Mosquito FB VIs of Nos 464 RAAF and 487 RNZAF Squadrons. On the morning of 5 June, a No 464 Squadron diarist wrote: 'A chilly morning with high wind; however, an air of expectancy pervades the squadron – something seems to indicate that we have not long to wait.' How right he was, for that night the Gravesend squadrons put up maximum effort to destroy enemy road traffic as D-Day unfolded. They found little – the enemy had not yet realised that the invasion had begun. The Wing's stay was, however, cut short when on 13 June 1944 the first V-1 flying bomb landed at Swanscombe. Gravesend was in the enemy's direct line of fire, so the Mosquitoes, with a vital role, were moved to Thorney Island on 18 June. Gravesend's great days were over and activity was much reduced. The remaining personnel helped to control aircraft through new balloon barrage belts designed to help defeat the V-1 onslaught.

Between mid-February 1945 and April 1946 No 3 MU operated a sub-site here for equipment handling, while No 212 MU handled barrack supplies and clothing through Gravesend from 1 May to 2 July 1945. Flying had not ceased, with light gliders of No 149 Gliding School flying from here until November 1945. The airfield then passed to care and maintenance.

Essex Aero, which throughout the war had maintained a small factory on the airfield making self-sealing aircraft petrol tanks, purchased two Walruses and two Sea Otters, but plans for their use came to nothing and the company went into liquidation during March 1956. The Air Ministry relinquished site control in June 1956, and within two years the large River View Park private housing estate was engulfing the one-time airfield. Two schools, playing fields and Thong Lane Sports Centre occupy much of the airfield's wartime extension area.

The great are not forgotten. A plaque in the sports centre commemorates the fourteen pilots who died when flying from Gravesend during the Battle of Britain. Hopefully, the children in those schools will become well aware of Gravesend Airport's history.

**Main features:**
*Runways:* Originally grass, but by 1944 concrete runways had been laid: N-S 4,260ft, extended to 4,550ft, ENE-WSW 4,350ft, extended to 4,440ft. *Hangars:* eight Blisters and one T1, additional to mixed civil buildings. *Hardstandings:* six for twin-engined aircraft, thirty 65ft frying-pan. *Accommodation:* RAF officers 42, SNCOs 71, ORs 1,197; WAAF officers 6, SNCOs 12, ORs 200

## GROVE, Oxfordshire

*51°36N/01°26W 275ft asl; SU395900. W of village, 1 mile N of Wantage*

Grove, a three-runway 91 Group bomber airfield, was in 1942 placed under Brize Norton's control, although Wellingtons of 15 OTU used the airfield in August 1942. Grove had been intended to replace Hampstead Norris as Harwell's satellite, but with so much glider activity close by, that scheme was abandoned. Grove was instead transferred to Flying Training Command.

Brize Norton's Whitleys and Horsas used Grove during the first four months of 1943. On 11-12 March Typhoons of 174 and 184 Squadrons lodged here, participating in exercise *Spartan*. Grove was still incomplete, awaiting decisions on possible use by the Americans. In early May 1943 Oxfords of 'K', 'L' and 'M' Flights of 15 (P)AFU used the station for circuit flying, as well as Greenham Common and Ramsbury, which were also awaiting decisions regarding possible American occupation.

When 15 (P)AFU began using Grove its runways were unfinished, and the airfield surface was marred by depressions and ditches. Such was the intensity of flying in the area that 15 (P)AFU moved to Andover in July 1943, its Oxfords vacating Grove on the 3rd.

The US 9th AF Support and Tactical Air Command then took control of the airfield. A Tactical Air Depot opened, where C-47 Dakotas, and later C-46 Commandos, were repaired and maintained. Unusually, it was supplied with six T2 hangars. Communications flights of the 9th AF, at Grove in 1944, used Proctors, Oxfords, UC-64s and UC-78s.

On 2 March 1944 the exotic Vickers-Armstrong Windsor DW506 force-landed in poor weather and was written off as a result. The large, unconventional and highly secret bomber was being flown by a pilot new to the type when a piece of metal became lodged in the constant speed unit of the starboard inner propeller which could not be feathered. In the ensuing crash the bomber broke its back.

Grove had acquired an unconventional appearance by the end of the war. Additional to assorted wartime temporary buildings were the six T2 hangars (3653/42), one set aside for the storage of aircraft parts. Two others served as assembly shops, while in two Robin hangars (2204/41) parts (including propellers) salvaged from crashed aircraft were held. The airfield's ultimate seventy-eight dispersal pads, mainly on the east side, were far in excess of the norm. On the west was the bomb store, a reminder of the original plan.

In February 1946 the RAF took back Grove, using it as an RLG. No 6 MU Brize Norton, busily disposing of many surplus aircraft, also made use of Grove, much of which was ultimately overtaken by a housing estate; there has also been a Harwell outpost here, where the industrial application of isotopes was researched.

**Main features:**

*Runways:* 220° 6,000ft x 150ft, 340° 4,200ft x 150ft, 270° 3,600ft x 150ft, concrete. *Hangars:* six T2. *Hardstandings:* twenty-four frying-pan, twenty-six spectacle type. *Accommodation:* USAAF officers 214, EM 3,188.

---

## HADDENHAM (THAME), Buckinghamshire
See **THAME**

---

## HAINAULT FARM, Essex
See **FAIRLOP**

*Sopwith Camels of No 44 (Home Defence) Squadron at Hainault Farm. (Bruce Robertson collection)*

## HALTON, Buckinghamshire

*51°46N/00°43W 360ft asl; SP875010. 4 miles SE of Aylesbury*

In 1912 three aeroplanes and an airship participating in Army manoeuvres used the grounds of Halton House, owned by Alfred Rothschild, and Halton, one of the oldest RAF stations, was in essence born. In 1914 he offered his estate to the Army for training purposes – provided they left within six months after the war ended and returned it in the condition in which they received it. In the 1914-18 war Halton served as an overspill camp for Aldershot, some 15,000 men being billeted there.

Technical training was undertaken at CFS Netheravon until the ever-increasing need for skilled technicians led to establishment of a 1,000-trainee school at Farnborough and, by 1916, another at Coley Park, Reading, for riggers and fitters. A larger training depot was established in Halton Park, Wendover. When in 1917 the Boys' Training Depot formed there, the decision was taken to create a special technical training school for both men and boys, and on 10 September 1917 the Halton RFC School of Technical Training was established. Alfred Rothschild died in January 1918 and the War Office decided to buy the estate.

At Eastchurch on 6 April 1918 a Boy Mechanics' Training School formed to supplement a Boys' Training School at Cranwell, and a Boys' Training Depot at Letchworth, formed in June 1918. The end of hostilities brought changes to technical training, and resulted in the Halton School of Technical Training (Boys) coming into being on 9 October 1919, although the title remained unused until 23 December, possibly because the Letchworth depot did not close until site disposal. Scheme revision at Halton from 1 January 1920 resulted in a further name change on 16 March 1920, to No 1 School of Technical Training (Boys) Halton.

Lord Trenchard's memorandum of November 1919 laid the foundation of the Halton apprentice scheme. He considered it impossible for RAF mechanic requirements to be met by recruiting skilled men. The RAF, he argued, must train its own mechanics, and enlisted the aid of local education organisations and others to find boys suitably educated for technical trades. Course entry could only follow examination success in grades equivalent to the School Certificate, thus ensuring a sufficiently high standard of education. Boys, he argued, should complete their apprenticeship in three instead of the five years customary at Cranwell and in civilian life. Cranwell's first entry under the new scheme started in February 1920. At Halton it became effective in January 1922, with No 1 School of Technical Training, a title retained until 1993. RAF Halton's badge incorporated the Rothschild coat of arms, the five arrows of which represented Lord Rothschild's five sons. A four-bladed-propeller backing represented the RAF Apprentices.

After passing a medical examination, boys were allotted their trade and enlisted for twelve years' service following their eighteenth birthday. Their choice from available trades resulted from examination success, while bearing in mind any trade training previously acquired. Trades on offer were fitter, carpenter and electrical and wireless trades, further broken into specialist fields of armourer, airframe, engine and wireless-operator/mechanic.

From August 1926 apprentices learning mechanical trades trained at Halton. Wireless training was undertaken at Cranwell, and some boys, upon changing stations, took with them bagpipes, which resulted in the formation of Halton's well-known pipe band. This was not the first Halton band to achieve fame, for early in 1917 a brass band formed; but it was not until 1922 that a flute, drum and trumpet band was assembled, to participate in the 1924 Olympia Royal Tournament.

*From the left, DH 9As, 504Ks and Sopwith Snipes (E7545 and E7716 nearest) at Halton for training purposes on 3 June 1923. (Bruce Robertson collection)*

Halton's training programme continued into the 1930s in relative tranquillity – apart from very audibly encouraged discipline, which, to many of today's youngsters, would doubtless seem incredibly severe. Even in the mid-1930s' expansion the problem was to find sufficient teenagers to become apprentices! Meanwhile, building proceeded apace at Halton. By the outbreak of war there were four Wings of apprentices, each holding 1,000 boys under its own Commanding Officer and occupying a separate block of the camp.

Within each Wing, apprentices were assigned to a Squadron and Flight. They spent twenty hours a week in workshops, did nine hours of 'PT' and drill, had eighteen hours of academic schooling, and were encouraged to take part in sports. In their quarters they prepared for strict inspections, ensuring that the barracks were spotlessly clean in time-honoured style. For recreation there was a cinema, clubs and ample games facilities. Competition to join was keen, and those so desiring could proceed to Cranwell for permanent commissions.

Apprentice training was reduced in wartime. On 22 March 1940 the scheme was re-organised, output changing to fitters, armourers, cooks and medical orderlies. By 1945 22,000 apprentices had passed out of Halton since 1920, and more than 4,000 had become commissioned. Former Halton apprentices, 'Trenchard's Brats', had been awarded more than 800 decorations, including a George Cross, and Sergeant Thomas Gray's bravery had been acknowledged with a Victoria Cross. More than 1,800 had been mentioned in despatches by May 1945 when No 1 STT celebrated its Silver Jubilee and Lord Trenchard inspected his brainchild. A year later, the re-adjusted intake once more included a high proportion of apprentices.

When wearing uniform they were easily identifiable. With men and boys in the same camp, a badge was deemed necessary to distinguish them apart – to identify who should not, for instance, be smoking. Originally it incorporated a bee motif superimposed upon a propeller boss, but the design adopted – in December 1918 – featured a four-bladed propeller.

*The modern equivalent, as RAF aircraft, retired from active life, find use for technical training at Halton, including Whirlwind 10s and Jet Provosts.*

As well as the aforementioned training, Halton has seen much else, including the RAF hospital, which opened in 1919 with limited medical and surgical facilities. It was superseded by a larger hospital opened in 1927 by HRH Princess Mary and named after her. Its facilities were heavily drawn upon in wartime, particularly the burns unit established in 1940, which became a leader in the field of plastic and maxillo-facial surgery. By the middle of the war Princess Mary's Hospital had more than 700 equipped beds, and in 1957 the first Artificial Kidney Unit in Britain was set up here to deal with cases of acute renal failure. Facilities existed for its rapid mobile deployment at home and overseas, for civilian as well as service personnel. Two-year nursing courses lead to Halton's students becoming State Enrolled Nurses.

Much early involvement concerned Empire outposts, and specialised RAF staff were needed to deal with tropical diseases. A small laboratory was established at Finchley, an offshoot of the RFC Officers' Hospital at Hampstead. In 1925 the tropical medicine unit moved to the new Halton hospital and was re-titled the RAF Pathological Laboratory. It functioned until 1935, when it was re-named the RAF Institute of Pathology and Tropical Medicine. The Institute has played a major part in the RAF's medical service, undertaking laboratory investigations and handling a variety of medical situations. The Department of Aviation and Forensic Pathology has been responsible for medical investigation into causes of fatal flying accident casualties throughout the Services, and has acted for the Department of Trade and Industry.

*Many non-operational stations hosted gliding schools. Shown at Halton in 1947 is Slingsby Primary Glider (Dagling Type) TS467. (Bruce Robertson collection)*

Halton's RAF Institute of Community Medicine opened as an offshoot of a long-established unit known, upon formation in 1919, as the Hospital Orderlies Training Depot. This became the Medical Training Establishment and School, later the Institute of Hygiene and Medical Training. Apart from running specialised medical courses, the school has investigated a variety of health problems arising from noise, ventilation, heating, etc. The Joint Services' School of Physiotherapy has run courses for up to twenty male and female students from the Services and civilian life each year. Dental health was the responsibility of the Institute of Dental Health and Training.

Wartime Halton's grass landing ground attracted a variety of mainly light aircraft. In November 1940 No 112 Squadron RCAF was briefly here, but more widely known was a mid-war arrival. Formed here on 15 June 1943 under Fighter Command control, No 529 Squadron (originally No 1448 (Calibration) Flight) flew Cierva C30a autogiros. Since 1940 used for radar calibration, they had become widely seen in the UK as they serviced coastal radar stations. At their Halton HQ they were supported by a few long-life DH Hornet Moths. The controlling HQ No 80 Group is thought to have had its HQ Flight here in 1942-43. On 19 August 1944 529 Squadron vacated Halton for a site near Henley-on-Thames.

Between 23 March 1940 and 1944 No 60 Group Communication Flight was based at Halton, where HQ 24 Group Flight also functioned between December 1944 and December 1945. Bomber Command Communication Flight formed at Halton on 12 May 1942 and remained until October 1946, by which time its Mentor, Q6 and early Ansons had been replaced by Proctors and later Anson variants.

Well-known by many ATC cadets was the Air Training Corps Flight formed on 1 January 1943, whose Dominies/Rapides and Oxfords provided air experience for so many prior to its closure in November 1945. Local cadets could also learn to glide with No 121 Gliding School between early 1944 and late 1945. From October 1946 to disbandment on 15 September 1947 HQ 23 Group Communication Flight was based here. On 1 September 1953 No 613 (Volunteer) Gliding School opened from 123 GS, and is still Halton-based using Vigilant and Venture 2s. In 1963 No 1 Mobile Glider Servicing Party began working out of Halton, supporting ATC needs until summer 1981, when gliders were brought here for attention. That ceased on 1 July 1988.

The landing ground offered a 'last landing' for time-expired 'old warriors' joining No 1 SofTT, where the procession of aircraft through the workshops has been voluminous. The most spectacular arrival, without doubt, was a very lightly loaded Vulcan I, which joined Jet Provosts, Gnats, Canberras, Argosys, Whirlwinds and Sea Vixens acquired as they were withdrawn from use. From October 1978 electricians trained on them following the transfer of their School from St Athan.

For No 1 SofTT the end of its long sojourn came with closure on 9 September 1993. The Apprentices moved to Cosford, leaving Halton to become the School of Recruit Training. Basic trade training is provided for chefs and Mess stewards, clerks, RAF police and equipment suppliers. Officers are also trained for administration, catering and provost duties, together with specialised tasks. Space on courses is now sold to civilians through the business development office. Also here are the RAF Institute of Health, HQ Defence Dental Agency, and No 613 (Volunteer) GS, flying Vigilant T1s. In 1997 Halton became the first RAF Station to be presented with the Queen's Colour, only the ninth awarded to the RAF.

When a group of senior German officers visited Halton shortly before the war they witnessed an amazing march-past. The column paraded around the camp so that its head joined its tail providing a never-ending body of men. Such a sight would now surely gladden the heart of many a long-retired SWO, just as the sight of a silver Siskin or Halton's collection of grounded Blenheim Is would have others jumping for joy. Alas, the world has changed so much that while we're all going to be disappointed we might be able to pay for a proper cookery course – a very stylish one in nice, historic surroundings. 'Start cooking now,' as the man might say.

**Main features:**
*Landing ground:* grass area allowing runs as follows: N-S 3,000ft, NE-SW 1,860ft, E-W 2,070ft, SE-NW 2,070ft. *Hangars:* none permanent but assorted removable types. Extensive permanent workshops and accommodation buildings for trainees and medical facilities. All vary greatly in design and age. *Hardstandings:* none. *Accommodation:* RAF officers 184, SNCOs 383, ORs 8,326; WAAF officers 134, SNCOs 71, ORs 1,770.

In 2002 Halton had two grass runways, 02/02 1,130m x 45m and 80/26 826m x 45m, and a helipad. Light aircraft, motor gliders and winch gliders use the airfield.

## HAMPSTEAD NORRIS, Berkshire

*51°29N/01°13W 376ft asl; SU530765. 9 miles NE of Newbury, via the B4009*

Hampstead Norris, opened in summer 1940 as Harwell's satellite and dispersal field, provided a base for the initial stages of OTU day and night flying. Personnel initially used tented accommodation. Hampstead's value was greater than many of its type because of its metalled runways. Laid to an unusual and imposed pattern, they made it a Built Satellite early in its life. They also made it noticeable, and had possibly caught the enemy's attention when three bombs, directed at the aerodrome on 16 September 1940, fell harmlessly. By that time Wellington Is of 15 OTU were using Hampstead Norris. On 4 April 1941 another raider followed in a landing Wellington and tried to bomb it. At this time there was increased use of satellites to clear the winter backlog of night-flying training.

Hampstead was used in particular as a starting point for ferrying Wellingtons overseas. The first three (T2825, T2840 and T2873) left on the night of 9 May 1941 and flew direct to Gibraltar, averaging 8hrs 41min journey-time for the first leg. Then, by way of Malta, they proceeded to Egypt.

Clearly knowing of this new venture, the Luftwaffe placed ten HEs and one hundred incendiaries on the airfield on 12 May 1941, damaging the tailplane and wing of a Wellington. The southern taxi track was also damaged, and a bomb hit the flare path while flying was in progress. This did not halt ferry flights, and on 15 May three Wellingtons left for Gibraltar, a long and demanding flight. On this second occasion, Sergeant McManus force-landed T2572 on a Portuguese beach, Es Edro du Muel, where the crew burned their aircraft. Bad weather raised in-transit loss rates, as on 19 June when Z8722 came down off Aguiles, Spain, and rapidly sank. X3211ditched in the river estuary at V der Castelle, Portugal, while two others survived disastrous electrical storms.

Before heavily laden bombers could use Harwell it needed hardened runways. When in July 1941 their construction began, 'D' Flight and the Middle East Despatch Flight of 15 OTU temporarily moved out to Hampstead Norris. Only two of the twenty-six Wellingtons – twenty-two of them Mk IIs – despatched from there in September 1941 were lost en route. Life at Hampstead Norris was certainly more eventful than at many satellites. Plt Off Fenton. flying Z5588 on 11 October 1941 was six miles south-east of Filey when a Ju 88C opened fire, to which his rear-gunner replied with two bursts that drove away the enemy. That month thirty-one Wellingtons departed for overseas use, and twenty-nine arrived safely, one crossing France to reach Malta. In November 1941 twenty-five made the journey to Gibraltar after their crews trained with the newly formed Ferry Crew Training Flight. Wellingtons usually came from Kemble ready for delivery flights. Between 10 May and 31 December 1941, 218 Wellingtons (162 Mk Ics and 56 Mk IIs) carrying 1,308 airmen were despatched from Hampstead, but only four flights were direct to Malta. The overall loss rate was 11.5%, three crews being interned. By the start of 1942 transit flights began at Portreath, Cornwall.

Main Force night diversions were then arriving, eleven Wellingtons of 214 Squadron landing from Brest on 11 January 1942. This brought an influx of faces – some old, some new – as well as needs for meals, aircraft refuelling, interrogation, etc, which stretched the satellite's resources.

Between 1 January and 30 June 1942 330 Wellingtons were despatched overseas from Hampstead or Harwell, superintended by 1443 Flight built from previous ferry organisations. A record number of eighty-one Wellingtons was despatched in April. By the end of 1942 a further 120 had been delivered, including Mk VIIIs and some torpedo-carriers. In January 1943 fourteen Mk VIIIs were despatched, mainly from Harwell. Overseas delivery pressure was removed from 15 OTU when, in July 1942, No 1444 FTF at Moreton-in-Marsh, and 21 OTU, began ferry flights. Hampstead remained the conversion training centre for 15 OTU, also holding its Gunnery Flight's three Lysanders. Harwell nearly lost control of the improving satellite when, in August 1942, plans were mooted for its replacement by Grove. Although 15 OTU did some flying there, substitution never took place.

In October 1942 Bomber Command reviewed Hampstead with a view to extending its runways to 7,200 feet and 4,200 feet. During that month the first Ferry Command crews trained at 1443 Flight, Harwell, before delivering nine Wellingtons from Hampstead in December. On 12 December 1942 six Oxfords of 1516 BAT Flight arrived from Middleton St George, the intention being that they would move to Harwell once 1443 FTF disbanded. Unexpectedly, delivery of Wellingtons to the Near East was extended, and the BAT Flight moved instead to Pershore on 13 April 1943. No 310 Ferry Training Unit formed on 30 April equipped with Wellington IIs and Xs and also a couple of Ansons, and disbanded on 17 December 1943.

Three Martinets replaced the gunnery Lysanders in March 1943, both 'A' and 'B' Flights continuing to use Wellington Ics until October. In September 1943 re-equipment with Wellington IIIs and Xs started, and by November 15 OTU had largely converted, but, with a limited future input, it closed on 15 March 1944.

Hampstead Norris was raised to self-accounting status within 38 Group on 1 March 1944. No 101 Course of 15 OTU, then in training, was posted to Westcott and the Wellingtons transferred to Moreton and Wellesbourne Mountford OTUs. In place of 15 OTU came the Operational & Refresher Training Unit, giving refresher courses to glider pilots originally trained to take part in the airborne assault on Sicily and now preparing for the Normandy invasion. The ORTU held thirty-three Tiger Moths, nine Whitleys and twenty Albemarles, together with Horsas. Elementary flying training took place at Shrewton. Equipment with Albemarles raised ORTU to operational status, and four of them participated in an RCM ruse during operation *Tonga*. For company, ORTU had the eight Oxfords of 1526 BAT Flight until the letter disbanded on 9 November 1944.

The ORTU was here until 27 February 1945, then moved to Matching, Essex. Hampstead reverted to being Harwell's satellite, and Mosquitoes of 13 OTU arrived on 15 March 1945, mainly from 60 OTU. They joined remnants of ORTU, and not until 8 April 1945 was the last glider towed away. About half of 13 OTU's Mosquito IIs and IIIs were based here, staying until 13 OTU left for Middleton St George in July. From 13 March to 14 July, Hampstead served again as Harwell's satellite, then it was placed on care and maintenance. Hampstead's final use was as an accommodation centre for the Glider Pilot Regiment and redundant RAF glider pilots, a role it shared with Finmere, its sister satellite.

**Main features:**
*Runways:* 230° 4,800ft x 150ft, 140° 3,300ft x 150ft, 276° 3,300ft x 150ft, tarmac with concrete extensions. *Hangars:* one T2, one B1, one Bessoneau. *Hardstandings:* twenty-eight frying-pan type. *Accommodation:* RAF officers 64, SNCOs 100, ORs 528; WAAF officers 4, ORs 156.

## HANWORTH PARK, Middlesex
### See FELTHAM

*Hawker Hart (T) K6486 of No 5 E&RFTS.*
*Blackburn B.2 G-ACRA is alongside.*
*(Don Mckay)*

## HARRINGTON, Northamptonshire

*52°23N/00°51W 520ft asl; SP765799. 5 miles SE of Market Harborough*

On 15 September 1943 No 84 OTU formed, with an establishment set at fifty-four Wellington IIIs and Xs, and flying commenced on 22 October 1943. The OTU's designated satellite, Harrington, was incomplete on 27 September 1943 when it received its first flying caller, a Wellington of 14 OTU with engine trouble.

The intention was to open Harrington on 9 November 1943, but it failed to meet necessary requirements. However, with the need for OTUs receding, Harrington was accepted lacking some usual features. Built mainly by the US 852nd Engineering Aviation Battalion, transfer to 92 Group, RAF Bomber Command, took place on 6 November 1943 and was attended by Air Chief Marshal Sir Arthur Harris. As the ceremonial band stopped playing, three of Desborough's Wellingtons flew over, saluting the work of the Americans.

Not until 26 December 1943 did a party come from Desborough to organise the arrival of 84 OTU. The airfield was still incomplete in February 1944 and now the intention was to remedy that by 16 March 1944. Before then Headquarters Bomber Command decided that the RAF had no need for the station. RAF personnel left before April, and 84 OTU's size was reduced.

Replacing the RAF, the 801st Bomb Group (Provisional), US 8th AAF, formed on 28 March 1944. It comprised two squadrons – the 36th and 406th (Bomb) – flying B-24s. The 406th had arrived at Harrington on 25 March 1944 and stayed until 10 August, when both squadrons left for Cheddington to continue *Carpetbagger* operations – upon which they had been engaged – from that new base. The 801st expanded with the arrival at Harrington of the 788th Bomb Squadron, but the squadron left for Rackheath and the 467th Bomb Group on 10 August. The 850th Bomb Squadron was here between 11 May and its departure for Eye on 12 August 1944. All supported European Resistance forces by delivering arms, equipment and men. Previously Alconbury-based, the B-24s flew their first support sorties from Tempsford on 4/5 January, 1944.

On 5 August 1944 B-24s of the 492nd Bomb Group began assembling at Harrington. This Group had incurred serious losses, so its squadron numbers were now applied to units at Harrington flying *Carpetbagger* operations. Using C-47s, landings were made in Vichy France during July and August 1944. On 16 September the Group was committed to the rapid supply of cans of oil and petrol to sustain the American advance in Europe. In December 1944 the 859th Bomb Squadron left for Italy.

Some intermittent night-bombing of airfields, oil refineries, ports and tactical targets was carried out by the other squadrons. Training had commenced in October for these raids, begun in February 1945. They continued until 18 March 1945 when the Group returned to *Carpetbagging*. Now in use were B-24s, A-26 Invaders and Mosquito XVIs, the latter used by 856 Squadron between September 1944 and March 1945 to drop leaflets and intercept ground signals transmitted by Resistance forces.

After hostilities ended the Group conveyed personnel to the Continent before returning home. The 406th Squadron, which returned to Harrington in March, left for the USA in July-August 1945.

Harrington gradually acquired Agricultural Airfield status, although parts remained Government property. In 1958 Harrington became the base for three Thor intermediate range ballistic missiles after No 218 Squadron re-formed on 1 December 1959, but brief was their stay because of surface weapon vulnerability and political antics. No 218 disbanded on 23 August 1963, Harrington then being disposed of.

**Main features:**
*Runways:* 184° 6,000ft x 150ft, 230° 4,200ft x 150ft, 298° 4,200ft x 150ft, concrete. *Hangars:* four T2. *Hardstandings:* thirty-six spectacle type. *Accommodation:* USAAF officers 229, EM 1,553.

## HARWELL, Berkshire

*51°34N/01°18W 375ft asl; SU465925. 6 miles S of Abingdon*

Atoms and Arnhem, Wellington and Nun May, energy and excitement, Fairey Battles, anemometry and Ansons – all have a niche in Harwell's history, for sited here was Britain's prime nuclear research centre. Now Harwell is the International Business Centre for Science and Technology, and some seventy organisations occupy the site, employing 4,000 people. Construction of the new Diamond UK Synchotron is the largest science project initiated in the UK for 30 years. Nearby is the Rutherford Appleton Laboratory.

*Battles of Harwell's 105 Squadron.*

Harwell's aeronautical history is worth reviewing in some detail for it provides a typical history of wartime activity in the central area. Its setting is superb, the Lambourn Hills stretching from east to west to form a southern rim. Greensand and the close proximity of Didcot's rail link with London made fruit-farming in the area viable in days now gone. Official requisition of some of the Upper Chalk level land preceded its use as a temporary night landing ground, upon which, in April 1935, a decision was made to develop it into a Permanent RAF Station for light bombers. Construction began in June 1935.

Harwell came under RAF control between 2 and 12 February 1937. Two weeks later *The Times* recorded that the 220-acre site had been purchased for £11,650. In April 1937 No 226 Squadron arrived from Upper Heyford with Hawker Audaxes, which type also equipped No 105 Squadron, re-formed here on 26 April; shortage of bombers had forced both squadrons to use Army Co-operation aircraft. In June 1937 four squadrons of Avro Ansons were detached here to participate in the Hendon Display fly-past. Harwell's third squadron, No 107, moved in from Old Sarum on 14 June, bringing Hind bombers.

On 18 August 1937 K7571, the first Fairey Battle, arrived for 105 Squadron. Fully re-armed by September, they were followed by 226 Squadron in October 1937. Portentous indeed was the November sighting of a mushroom on the landing ground, but even more interest surrounded the first flight of the Martin Baker MB 2 fighter from Harwell on 3 March 1938.

HM King George VI and the Chief of the Air Staff, Air Chief Marshal Sir Cyril Newall, visiting Harwell on 9 May 1938, were received by Air Chief Marshal Sir Edgar Ludlow Hewitt, AOC-in-C, Bomber Command, and the AOC 1 Group, which controlled the station. The Battle squadrons were training realistically and, in August, 107 Squadron received Blenheim Is in time for the Munich Crisis. All the Merlin I-engined Battle Is of 105 and 226 Squadrons were exchanged for Cottesmore's Merlin II Battle IIs of 35 and 207 non-mobilisation squadrons; these two squadrons were not earmarked for the AASF, where no Merlin I spares would be held. The switch came in October 1938, well before the airfield became a winter quagmire. Experiments were undertaken in the use of netting, as well as cinders for surface improvement, but only concrete – or better weather – could achieve that.

During May 1939 No 107 Squadron moved to Wattisham, leaving the Battle squadrons to work up for a clearly coming conflict. On 2 September 1939 the Battle squadrons formed No 72 Wing and left for France to become part of the AASF.

Their replacement was complete by 17 September 1939, and now great change overtook Harwell with the arrival of 75 and 148 Squadrons flying Wellington Is. Under 6 Group's control, Harwell became 3 Group Pool on 14 September 1939. Army-manned machine-gun posts were set up around the airfield perimeter, and a Q-site opened on 3 September. Training concentrated upon Bomber Command's intention to operate in formation and in daylight. However, by January 1940 it was a case of all change, for Bomber Command, for reasons of protection, would now operate principally at night. Excellent navigation skills were essential, and Ansons already in hand

*A general view of Harwell's domestic site looking north in 1944. The MT Section is bottom left, and Married Quarters top right. The Barrack Blocks are in the central foreground, with one H Block. The central double-fronted building is the Airmen's Mess. (UKAEA)*

were to play a vital and overlooked part in bomber crew training. Conversion of some Battle squadrons to Blenheims, while having no direct effect upon Harwell, brought in exotic movements. On 1 December 1939, with bad weather closing in, DH 86 *G-ACVY* (see Heston entry) and HP 42 *G-AAXC* were forced to land, and left for France next day.

On 30 January 1940 operational truths were forcefully related to the Wellington trainees by Wing Commander Griffiths of 99 Squadron, who had participated in the shattering operations of December 1939. Harwell now lay deep in snow, and rapid clearance from operational areas had barely been contemplated. The surest means of removal was by hand and the use of a shovel. On 14 February 1940 a Heinkel III was reported in the area, claims still neither confirmed nor discounted. About this time Ryman and Canning devised the 'Harwell boxes', three tall structures built for gunnery and navigation purposes and copied at other stations.

Wellington Ias began arriving in March 1940, some having flown operationally with 149 Squadron. On 4 April 1940 both 75 and 148 Squadrons amalgamated, SHQ closed and the whole station was rejuvenated as 15 OTU Harwell on 8 April; the title change taking account of the fact that SHQ Harwell was replaced by HQ 15 OTU. It remained within 6 Group, its establishment of Wellingtons and Ansons increasing. An arrival on 20 May was Wellington I L4265, ex-149 Squadron, which operated against Brunsbuttel's shipping on 4 September 1939. It was eventually lost without trace on 18 March 1942 while flying a training exercise.

Fighting in Norway, then France, called for the great expansion of operational training. It also brought, on 24 May 1940, the first operational diversion to Harwell, a Whitley of 77 Squadron flown by Plt Off Mahaddie, later of Pathfinder fame. Increased flying led to more accidents, in one of which Anson N5186 crashed in flames near the bomb dump, killing the pilot, Wg Cdr Hughes.

On 15 July 1940 the Unit moved from 6 Group into 7 Group. Operational flying by 15 OTU commenced on the night of 18/19 July 1940, three Wellingtons dropping leaflets over the Dunkirk-Boulogne area. On 23/24 July another trio crossed the Channel to Amiens, Cherbourg and Rouen. Dieppe, Evreux, Beauvais and Caen were visited on 27/28 July. Such activity was reckoned good for crews and recipients.

The afternoon of 14 August saw twenty Whitleys arrive from Driffield, Harwell becoming their point of departure and return for a long haul to Milan that night. They had headed home before the station came under attack for the first time, at around 1800 on 16 August. A raider swept in over Rowstock and dropped four bombs, setting fire to two 400-gallon petrol bowsers, one of which was courageously towed away. Three Wellingtons were destroyed, and two of the seven casualties were fatal, for which strafing was responsible. Station defences at the time amounted to a few twin Vickers gun emplacements and a 3-ton Bedford lorry mounting twin Vickers guns on a Scarff ring.

Soon after midnight another six bombs aimed at 15 OTU caused neither damage nor casualties. Later that day Harwell was ordered to disperse aircraft by using the satellite at Hampstead, and to place some AA defences there because large-scale night attacks were forecast for the coming moon period.

The Luftwaffe's obsession with Harwell continued, and during the afternoon of 19 August a Ju 88 bombed and strafed the station, destroying another three Wellingtons. Another raid on 26 August resulted in bombs exploding near the bomb dump, causing six RAF and ten civilian casualties. That night six of Dishforth's Whitleys operated from Harwell.

Despite enemy interference and invasion alarms – when Ansons stood ready, each carrying two 112lb bombs – 15 OTU managed 1,594 daylight and 665 night hours of flying training in August, an average fifty Wellingtons and seventeen Ansons providing higher pupil output numbers than larger units in 6 Group. Accidents nevertheless marred the programme, especially at night. Undercarriage collapse due to heavy landing was frequent. There were bent wings, too. Night-flying was from the grass runway marked by about ten or so goose-necked flares, which consisted of long spouted cans filled with paraffin, fitted with thick wicks and placed so that the wind blew the flame away from the fuel reservoir. From time to time aircraft would knock them over, bringing hazardous moments. Additional to Harwell's lights were those at the large Didcot railway installation, which distracted more than one pupil pilot.

In what later became the Plastics Technology Building was a bombing teacher and a Wellington fuselage for training purposes, which allowed crews to become familiar with the aircraft's layout. Another trainer was equipped with radio aids.

On 7 September three Wellingtons went *Nickelling* in a defiant gesture, and if there were worries about balloon cables L4322 on 18 September 1940 survived after colliding with one over Yeovil. Another six *Nickel* sorties were flown over three nights in October 1940.

Enemy presence was proven on 13 November when Ju 88, LI +LS, Werke Nr 6557 of LG1, flew across Oxfordshire and was brought down by 611 Squadron. It crashed at Blewbury and three of the captured crew were taken to Didcot, the fourth being buried at Harwell on 19 November. King Haakon of the Norwegians, visiting the station on 12 December, was treated to a fly-past by three Ansons, then one shed part of a cowling when pulling too steeply out of a dive.

Two attacks on Harwell's Q-site on 5 March 1941 put ground defences on high alert. Anson N5078 was twelve miles north of Banbury at 2045 when it became coned by searchlights that refused to extinguish even when a recognition signal was flashed. The aircraft's captain decided to fire the Very light colour of the day, but unfortunately the pistol discharged within the aircraft, setting it ablaze and forcing the crew to quickly bale out.

Early on 11 April 1941 the enemy came yet again to Harwell. After circling, a raider dived, released two bombs, repeated the action, then machine-gunned the station. A crew, walking between two hangars, thought they saw a cat run by; in fact it was a bomb bouncing along the tarmac, which came to rest in the solid fuel dump without exploding. Another went through the superstructure on the west side of what became known as Hangar 8 and came to rest unexploded under a starter trolley at the north-east corner of Hangar 9. A third bomb exploded by Hangar 2 (renamed No 8) while the fourth rested by the water tower. In 1946 a member of the Nuclear Physics Division dashed into Building 30 to announce that a bomb was lodged in No 8 Hangar's roof. However, all was well. It was only the tail unit of one of April's delivery of five years earlier.

Harwell's life changed abruptly when Group HQ despatched a signal on 30 April to the effect that 15 OTU was each month to train fifteen crews, each to ferry a Wellington to the Near East. Such ferrying had previously been undertaken by 3 Group squadrons starting out from Stradishall. The new pattern was for the aircraft involved to be collected from OADF Kemble by 15 OTU, and for departure to take place from Hampstead Norris, whence the first three left on 9/10 May 1941. On 24 May the commitment required twelve crews a fortnight from the OTU, ten for ferry duty and overseas service. *Nickelling* had continued into 1941, the twentieth operation having been mounted on 6/7 May.

In June 1941 No 15 OTU was the busiest in 6 Group. During 3,040 flying hours there had been fourteen flying accidents for an output of ninety pilots, forty observers and eighty radio-operator/air-gunners – roughly a quarter of the entire Group output.

On 18 July the decision was taken to lay two hard runways of 3,300 feet and one of 3,000 feet. As a result Harwell was declared non-operational with effect from 21 July. That halted *Nickelling* until 14 October, when six Wellingtons carried out Operation No 34 to central France, from which R1275 and R1783 failed to return.

The OTU had meanwhile placed 'A' and 'B' Flights at Mount Farm on 24 July and moved its ferrying sections to Hampstead Norris on 28 July. Flying did not entirely cease at Harwell, however, for while the flare path was lit, it was twice attacked on 20 September. During that month 15 OTU still managed to fly for 3,367 hours.

The station re-opened to flying on 23 November 1941, the McAlpine concrete runways almost complete. A Lorenz beacon lined up with the main runway helped to maintain winter flying, for which Grove was to be available if ready in time.

During February 1942 the 50th Course passed out of 15 OTU. Overseas deliveries continued, control passed from 7 to 91 Group on 11 May 1942, and twenty Wellingtons set off from Harwell on the Cologne '1,000-bomber' raid; two did not return. For the June Essen raid twenty-one took off and safely returned. Bremen was attacked by eleven of nineteen Wellingtons despatched on 25/26 June, two being lost. Harwell also participated in *Grand Nationals*, after which OTUs again concentrated upon training instead of operations. A Gunnery Flight was added to the OTU in August.

Flying accidents at rates too high still plagued all OTUs. X3209, carrying full fuel and bomb loads, was halfway along the runway when it flopped on to its belly and careered into contractor's excavations. The starboard engine burst into fierce flames while the crew remained inside the aircraft too severely shocked even to leave. Wg Cdr Dabinett, close by, raced to the aircraft, courageously clambered aboard and switched off the fuel flow. Then the fire crew tackled the blaze, knowing that there were bombs board.

Another spectacular incident involved T2557, which was returning to Harwell on 21 August 1942. Its night flight had almost ended when the Wellington suddenly rammed into an Oxford over Chipping Norton. Both showered down on to the town in a mass of flames. Four nights later a further mid-air collision occurred, over Odstone Bombing Range: DV595, night-flying from Harwell, collided with N2775, operating from Hampstead Norris and lining up for Stanton Harcourt. The pilot of N2775 regained control for a single-engine crash-landing at Stanton Harcourt, and DV595 crashed near Uffington.

During summer 1942 some overseas delivery flights started from Harwell instead of Hampstead Norris, many adventures overtaking their crews. W5565 and crew bravely carried out an eight-hour transit from Harwell to Gibraltar in daylight on 8 November 1942. They then headed along the West African coast for Bathurst, but never arrived. Plt Off A B Kidson and crew had been shot down near Dakar by Vichy French fighters.

In September 1942 twenty-five Wellingtons left Harwell for a new departure point, Portreath, but only nineteen of them reached Gibraltar, one later force-landing off Sicily. For bombing raids on Italy in late 1942 Harwell again served as an advanced operating base. On 20/21 November nine Wellingtons of 420 and five of 425 Squadrons left here for Turin. Next night they carried out mining sorties. Both squadrons again operated similarly later that month. On 7 January 1943 Lancaster W4330 of 460 Squadron became the first of its type diverted here.

No 15 OTU was now participating in *Bullseyes* and resumed *Nickelling* on 4 December 1942. Night diversions increased, as on 17/18 January when Lancasters (five of 97 Squadron, one of 50 Squadron) landed from Berlin, and overseas deliveries of Wellington continued into 1943, fourteen setting forth in January, and twenty in February. Control of the operation, initially by the Ferry Training and Despatch Flight/Unit of 6 Group, was from 21 January 1942 undertaken by 1443 Ferry Training Flight (equipped with two Ansons and two Wellingtons) and administered by 91 Group from 11 May 1942.. A new flying control building (which later held Harwell's General Administration Department) opened on 17 February 1943 as a flying and operations control centre, and watch was kept from there over the departure of forty Wellingtons overseas, as well as during two *Nickelling* operations in March. The 73rd OTU course passed out on 27 February 1943.

Increased sophistication failed to prevent accidents. Wellington Ic X3171, on a solo cross-country flight, crashed mid-afternoon on 1 March in Northumberland and the crew died. On 3 March HF906, practising overshoots from Hampstead Norris, was overcome by power-setting problems, smashing into cottages at Common Barn, near Hermitage; its crew, two civilians and livestock were killed. On 11 March came another fatal accident involving one of 15 OTU's first Wellington IIIs, while on 3 April two Wellingtons collided during circuit flying; such an event was unusual despite the intense activity. The collision risk increased during fighter affiliation when it was all too easy for a Martinet to get out of control, as happened on 11 May. Another problem with so many airfields in use was the selection of the correct runway at the right airfield. On 19 May 1943 Wellington HZ437 of 310 Ferry Training Unit, which emerged from 1443 FTF on 3 April 1943, crashed two miles from Turweston. It was approaching the wrong runway and, close to landing, the pilot realised his error, but with insufficient speed to go round again, the bomber spun in.

Mediterranean departures continued from Harwell, thirty-nine in April and thirty-three in May. Involvement with operations also continued, and late June 1943 saw 1 Group Wellingtons diverting here after carrying out mining. *Nickelling* and *Bullseyes* continued into 1944.

Overseas delivery flights ended in October 1943, the FTU disbanding on 17 December. Still mainly equipped with Wellington Ics, 15 OTU sometimes flew ASR searches. December found the Unit re-equipping with Wellington Xs, whose stay was short for, on 3 March 1944, with the need for Wellington bomber crews reduced, the OTU closed.

When Harwell re-opened on 1 April 1944, its role had dramatically changed, and it was now within 38 Group, Airborne Forces. Two Albemarle squadrons arrived, Nos 295 and 570, and with them sufficient Horsa gliders for Harwell's participation in exercise *Dreme* on 4 April. The next night ten Albemarles flew *Nickel* sorties over France, and another seven on 10 April. A night navigation training tour was laid on, and more sorties over France. Exercise *Posh*, flown on 16 April, included two Albemarles of 570 Squadron as Pathfinders, practising their part in the Normandy landings by dropping twenty troops and supplies at Winterbourne Stoke. Another three practised at Tarrant Rushton. Similar, even larger exercises followed in rapid succession.

An interesting diversion was provided on 23 May when the first flight of the very fast, extremely impressive Martin Baker MB 5 fighter took place. Invasion training was now more important, and by the end of May all was ready for Harwell's vital contribution to the Normandy invasion. One hour before midnight on 5 June 1944, three Albemarles from each squadron took off to spearhead *Tonga*. Each dropped ten men to set up *Rebecca* radio beacons to guide in the Main Force. Another twelve Albemarles brought part of the main paratroop force, and a further twenty-eight towed Horsas, one carrying General Gale and Divisional HQ.

Crews then rested before operation *Mallard* during the early evening of 6 June, the large-scale towing of loaded Horsas to Normandy, in which thirty-eight Harwell combinations took part. SOE supply drops and further training followed. Albemarles were only stop-gap glider tugs, being used until sufficient four-engined aircraft were available. Harwell's first Stirling IV arrived on 14 June, and a count of the aircraft available here on 11 July shows what now seems an amazing sixty-four Albemarles, nineteen Stirlings and eighty Horsas. Night SOE drop operations using Stirlings began on 27 July and continued spasmodically until early September 1944 and the next airborne assault. Before then the enemy briefly counter-attacked, using a V-1 flying bomb, which crashed on to Harwell on 30 August, destroying three grounded aircraft.

Already the airborne forces were preparing for their next major venture, and it materialised on 17 September. Shortly after 1100 Stirling IVs of 295 and 570 Squadrons began to set forth to lead operation *Market*, the attempt to secure a bridge at Arnhem. By mid-afternoon all of Harwell's contingent was safely home, and groundcrews were already preparing gliders for Phase II on the morrow. Mist delayed the event, but eventually thirteen Stirlings towed off Horsas, and another thirty-two Stirlings carried containers for ground forces. Re-supply became a vital, daily task, flak taking a steady toll of the transports, which, unable to vary their routing,. needed plentiful fighter protection. On 20 September that failed to appear, but Harwell's squadrons suffered less than others. Final drops were made on 23 September, and AA guns brought down four of 570 Squadron's contingent, while two others force-landed. Harwell's Stirlings were still having their wounds dressed when they moved to Rivenhall, Essex.

A further twist in Harwell's history unfolded on 12 October 1944 when it again hosted an OTU, No 13 under 12 Group, ADGB, and a training centre for 2 Group TAF. Fighter-bomber Mosquito crews were expected to train here, but when 60 OTU merged with 13 OTU on 1 March 1945 it was all change. Mosquito training was split between Finmere and Hampstead Norris, Mosquitoes arriving at both satellites on 15 March. At long last 13 OTU entered 2 Group, an event that should have happened years before. Harwell briefly housed 13 OTU's Mitchells and Bostons, training using the latter ceasing on 19 March. That left Harwell holding sixty Mitchells, seven Spitfires and an Anson. Mitchell training ended on 28 May 1945, and 13 OTU contracted prior to moving in late July 1945 to Middleton St George.

On 22 July Harwell and its satellites returned to 38 Group, and the satellites went to care and maintenance. A party from the School of Air Transport arrived at Harwell on 27 July, only to return to Netheravon, for Harwell was unready. On 21 August the School of Flight Efficiency, Transport Command, arrived, followed by the Transport Command Development Unit from Netheravon on 1 September. The delay was due to necessary last-minute runway intersection repairs.

Barely had all settled when the Ministry of Supply began to take over Harwell for atomic research. RAF units then began leaving for Brize Norton on 14 December 1945, finally vacating the station on 31 December 1945.

A British atomic bomb had been suggested in March 1940. By the end of 1942, with more resources and greater safety available in America, development was switched there. By autumn 1944 Britain clearly needed its own nuclear experimental establishment – but where should it be? Airfields offered ample space and facilities, roads, water and power facilities, and hangars suitable for adaptation to hold nuclear plant. Close proximity to a major university and the Clarendon or Cavendish Laboratories, at Oxford or Cambridge, was necessary.

The Air Ministry listed seventeen airfields that they were prepared to release. Most had limited facilities, preference among scientists being for a site near Cambridge. The Air Ministry was not keen, for East Anglia lay within the new Defended Area. Eventually Duxford and Debden were offered, but since radioactive waste was then to be buried on site, a low water table was essential, as well as an ample water supply. Debden, with a high water table, was rejected, and Duxford because of its poor water supply. Benson was then reviewed before Harwell was deemed the most suitable. Service personnel, unhappy at losing their fine estate, were given Brize Norton to console them. Sir John Cockcroft and his team privately confirmed their choice in Harwell's nearby 'Horse and Jockey'.

The Air Ministry produced reasons why it should not release the station. Its runways were suitable for Bristol Brabazon flying, they claimed, and the Thames Conservancy was concerned about effluent discharge. The scientists had their way, however, taking control on 1 January 1946. Their studies would range over particle physics, large reactors, nuclear fuels and the production of radio isotopes for medical and industrial purposes. By the mid-1950s, of Harwell's ninety-four buildings, only thirty-four had known RAF days. The C Type hangars were serving purposes as far from the original intention as could be imagined, for one housed a large reactor. By 1957 the Atomic Energy Research Establishment was so vast that parts were hived off: the National Institute for Research into Nuclear Sciences used the original Harwell buildings, and the Rutherford Laboratory – under the control of the Science Research Council – was on a site adjacent. At Winfrith a new 1959 development was to explore power reactor development, and fusion research would be undertaken at Culham Laboratory. At Grove airfield, research would take place into industrial applications of isotopes, the task returning to Harwell in the 1970s. A later off-shoot from AERE was the Medical Research Council unit, researching into protecting human tissues from radiation.

Flying did not cease in December 1945. In an alarming episode years later a USAF pilot flying a Lockheed T-33 jet trainer encountered a problem and in making an emergency landing mistook Harwell's closed runway for an active one. Although RATO bottles were strapped in place, and an intrepid soul tried to take off, it proved impossible.

**Main features:**
*Runways:* 295° 6,000ft x 150ft, 258° 4,200ft x 150ft, 151° 3,900ft x 150ft, concrete. *Hangars:* four C Type. *Hardstandings:* forty-five frying-pan type, ten tarmac pads. *Accommodation:* RAF officers 284, SNCOs 464, ORs 1,606; WAAF officers 8, SNCOs 5, ORs 307.

## HATFIELD, Hertfordshire

*51°45N/00°15W, 250ft asl; TL206090. W of the A1 at Hatfield*

In his worst dream Sir Geoffrey de Havilland could surely never have imagined that beloved Hatfield, home of such a precious company, would be turned by Americans into an imaginary battlefield to save Private Ryan. That was quite bizarre. What should have been saved was Hatfield. In great times, now faded beyond belief, it was from the plain of Hatfield that the Mosquito, the world's finest combat aircraft of all time, set forth to the fight, that a multitude of lovely Moths took flight on summer eves, that Britain's first supersonic jet and the world's first jet airliner to enter commercial service were brought to life among some very special, exceptionally able people and all to the sound of "Ah, de Havilland!"

Captain de Havilland learned to fly at Brooklands in 1913, and with intuitive talent hatched his earliest designs in North West London. Very successful in the 1914-18 war, and needing more space and a suitable base, on 18 November 1921 his company purchased 76½ acres of land for £21,000, upon which the Stag Lane works had been built. There it was that in 1928 the much desired 100hp-plus engine to replace the Blackburn Cirrus in light aircraft, the de Havilland Gipsy, came alive, to be fitted into a DH 60. An important part had been played by a very able freelancing engineer, Major Halford.

Almost a decade later, and requiring yet more space for larger aircraft and, hopefully, increased production, de Havilland management purchased around 400 acres of farmland near Hatfield. The latter never replaced Stag Lane, a 14-acre factory being retained into the 1960s. The 1930s move to Hatfield came gradually. Occupying the northern part of the site, the landing ground was separated from the remainder by a stream, and weight restrictions were imposed on aircraft and vehicles crossing the 'bridge'. A hangar, flying school clubhouse and petrol installation were positioned in the south-east corner. Just after Christmas 1933 construction of the large new factory on the eastern side began. An impressive art nouveau office block confronted the A1, for all to see.

The unusual de Havilland Flying School had opened at Stag Lane on 1 May 1923, using DH 9s to provide refresher courses for RAF officers. Moved to Hatfield in May 1930, it then used DH Moths. In an early 'PFI', the flying instructors were civilians.

Pacemaker airliners like the DH 84 Dragon, DH 86 Express and the DH 88 Comet Racer were all Stag Lane-built. Hatfield output was the four-engined DH 91 Albatross and the metal twenty-passenger twin-engined DH 95 Flamingo airliner, first flown from snowy Hatfield on 28 December 1938. Only sixteen of these were built before the war started.

*The prototype Mosquito W4050 under camouflage wrapping at Hatfield in November 1940. DH*

Very successful in the 1930s was the Dragon Six, better known as the DH 89 Dragon Rapide, a Hatfield production. Cruising for four hours at 135mph, it could carry five to eight passengers. In place of the DH 84's rectangular planform wings, the 89 had an elegant tapered form, a well-tailored trouser undercarriage, and metal propellers. First flown in April 1934, 210 Rapides were built pre-war, 200 post-war, and 275 as Dominies by Brush Coachworks at Loughborough in wartime.

The most significant event at Hatfield in the mid-1930s was the interest in radical advances in aviation, particularly in the USA. Monoplanes were replacing biplanes, undercarriages retracted, flaps assisted take-off and landing, skinning was stressed, and propellers were blessed with variable pitch. Most, put together, did much to make the twin-engined two-seat DH 88 Comet racer a winner.

Over lunch, Charles C. Walker, DH Chief Engineer, recalled for me how during breakfast at Hatfield one April 1934 morn, a small management team decided to accept the challenge to build a sleek racer for the coming October McRobertson Air Race from Mildenhall to Melbourne, Australia. Putting the latest ideas together, they sketched a suitable layout on the back of a cigarette packet and the famous Comet (No 1) was conceived, and sired the company's future.

De Havilland, recognising the excellence of the American Hamilton variable-pitch metal propellers, acquired rights to produce them in the UK, and de Havilland Propellers was born. By the outbreak of war 10,000 propellers had been built at Stag Lane and Lostock works. The introduction of propellers able to cope with rapidly increasing engine power demanded continuous development, undertaken at a new facility on the western side of Hatfield aerodrome. De Havilland-made variable-pitch propellers first flew on 17 March 1936, fitted to a Whitley at Baginton.

A major item from DH Propellers was the constant speed unit (CSU), examples of which, between June and 16 August 1940, were fitted to 1,051 RAF fighters, conferring on them a much faster climb rate and a higher ceiling. DH CSUs made a considerable contribution to the winning of the Battle of Britain.

At Hatfield ideas behind the DH 88 were applied to an all-wood four-engined fast mail and passenger plane suitable for a non-stop London 'to Berlin' service. As the DH 91 Albatross, it first flew from Hatfield on 20 May 1937, the seven built serving with Imperial Airways on routes from Croydon to Brussels, Paris and Zurich.

*In February 1944 Hatfield is packed with Mosquito PR16s and mainly FB VIs.*

Hitherto de Havilland had concentrated on civilian aircraft, but when Airspeed entered the de Havilland camp, Hatfield set about producing Oxfords. With war increasingly likely, that made sense. Production lines were already in place for Tiger Moths and radio-controlled Queen Bee anti-aircraft target aircraft, 210 of which were completed here pre-war and 110 in wartime. Also produced just before the war were ninety Moth Minor monoplanes intended for Civil Air Guard use. With conflict looming, de Havilland, wedded to aeroplanes for peace, wanted to build something special for the war, a bomber Comet-cum-Albatross. Made of smooth, strong wood – in ample supply – it would be unarmed because defensive armament added unproductive load. It would be 'a bomber with fighter speed'.

High-speed bombers had been officially considered for some time, but the Air Ministry and the RAF took a lot of convincing on the wisdom of relying upon speed rather than protective weapons for defence. Not until late 1939 were de Havilland's ideas accepted, but applied to a fast unarmed reconnaissance machine, the PR Mosquito.

*Typhoon MN655 and Spitfire 14 RB144 (with contra-prop) at de Havilland Propellers on 21 November 1944.*

While the Battle of Britain raged, the prototype Mosquito was secretly assembled at Salisbury Hall, once the haunt of saucy Nell Gwynne and later the Churchills. At Hatfield Hurricanes arrived for repair, the first coming on 23 May, and leaving after repair a mere six days later. Hereward de Havilland was then flight testing a Tiger Moth carrying eight 20lb bombs on a light series carrier, and in the factory 1,500 sets of the gear were built for EFTSs to use for dive-bombing German invaders.

That summer saw bombs falling around Hatfield, but not until 1130 on 3 October 1940 was a determined attack made by a lone, very low-flying Ju 88, which strafed the site and positioned four 250kg HEs on Hatfield's grass. They skipped into the sheet metal shop, killing twenty-one and wounding seventy of the workforce. Nine months of work and 80% of all Mosquito material vanished in a flash. Elsewhere Oxfords were blazing and other buildings were broken. The raider from Laon, hit by ground fire, crashed at Hertfordbury.

Hatfield had suffered a setback, but the Mosquito was safe at Salisbury Hall. It came from there by road to Hatfield, where it first flew on 25 November 1940. Its performance was as outstanding as forecast, and at Boscombe Down in February 1941 it easily outpaced a Spitfire. The company team celebrated their success and a highly satisfied Geoffrey de Havilland Jnr, having exceeded safe consumption limits, began to shed his entire body cover. Excitedly enjoying the resultant freedom, he encouraged his companions to enjoy themselves. Such was the resultant furore that the landlady of the hotel said that she neither knew nor cared who they were and why they were acting so disgracefully. Ordered out, never to return, they followed the line of another well-known person – they took to the straw in a barn.

Although the first Mosquito photo-reconnaissance aircraft entered service in July 1941, failure to appreciate its amazing performance delayed the bomber variation from operating before 31 May 1942. A night-fighter version was already doing so well that, without building space at Hatfield, the Second Aircraft Group opened at Leavesden to build the fighters. Hatfield then concentrated on bomber and PR Mosquito production throughout the war, together with development that made this the most ubiquitous warplane of all time.

In a moment of inspiration the de Havilland team realised that the aircraft's bomb bay could accommodate a 4,000lb 'cookie' bomb. Using the Mossie's speed, two deliveries to Berlin in one night using one aircraft could be made, and there would be just long enough to do a newspaper crossword puzzle on the way home – each time. Fitment of two-stage Merlin engines and a 2 psi pressure cabin further improved performance. Wartime Mosquito production at Hatfield totalled twenty-one in 1941, 389 in 1942, 806 in 1943, 1,203 in 1944, and 635 in 1945. At the 1946 SBAC Radlett Exhibition, the prototype, W4050, now back at Salisbury Hall de Havilland Museum, had lying before it a kitchen sink, about the only thing it did not carry.

*VW120 'DH 108 Mk II', the third prototype 'Swallow', at Hatfield in August 1947. (DH)*

In 1941 the DH Engine Company was set up to handle development and production of the Gipsy (10,212 were Stag Lane-built in wartime), and considered the possibility of building a gas turbine. The company again contacted Frank Halford for help and developed a centrifugal flow design for which it built the E.6/41 flying test bed. On 13 April 1942, 248 days after the go-ahead, the engine that became the Goblin was bench-run. It was soon delivering 2,000lb st (static thrust) amid hopes that it would reach 3,000lb. Other jet engines were producing only around 1,100lb st, so a pair of Goblins were wedded to an F.9/40 Meteor prototype. Its performance was so stunning that 450 production Meteor IIs were ordered, only to be cancelled when hopes were pinned to even better things. Instead, the Goblin-powered test bed first flew on 20 September 1943, the combination entering production in 1945 as the Vampire fighter. A more powerful Goblin became the Ghost.

The build-up to war and the war years had found Hatfield ever more busy. On 4 August 1935 the reserve school became No 1 E&RFTS, equipped with Tiger Moths and Hart variants, and No 1 Elementary Flying Training School on the outbreak of war. To reduce congestion at Hatfield, on 7 September 1942 it moved to Panshanger.

Another feature of life at Hatfield was the constant departure of new aircraft and the input of others for repair. As well as the EFTS there was the Air Transport Auxiliary Women's Section, which opened in January 1940 and became 'D' Section, 3 FPP, in June 1940, later uprated to 5 FPP in November 1940. Amy Johnson was one of the ferry pilots, the Hatfield group being among the first people to learn of her death on Sunday 5 January 1941. Amy had set off from Squires Gate, Blackpool, to deliver Airspeed Oxford V3540 to Kidlington, a routine flight of about an hour's duration. Nearly three hours after she was overdue, the Oxford was reported down in the Thames Estuary, just off the Kent coast, in freezing water and nearly 100 miles off course. Much speculation remains as to how such a famous flier came to grief, for the Oxford had enough fuel for $4^{1}/_{2}$ hours flying. No 5 FPP moved to Luton on 1 April 1942, operating from there until disbandment on 18 May 1943.

On 8 June 1940 Hatfield had became an operational RAF station into which Lysanders of No 2 Squadron moved from Bekesbourne within the overall anti-invasion strategic plan. They were joined on 18 September 1940 by No 239 Squadron, re-formed here from elements of 16 and 225 Squadrons; all flew Lysanders. No 2 Squadron left for Sawbridgeworth on 24 October 1940, and 239 Squadron moved out on 22 January 1941. On 17 February Lysanders of 116 Squadron came for a short stay lasting until 24 April 1941.

Immediately after the war DH flew its 1943-designed eight-passenger monoplane Rapide successor. As the DH 104 twin-engined Dove, it first flew five weeks after the end of hostilities. It had high passenger appeal, but its Gipsy Queen engines did not do it justice. The larger, four-engined Heron derivative was used by The Queen's Flight.

In 1947 Hatfield's concrete 6,000-foot runway, construction of which had been held back so as not to interrupt wartime activity, came into use. Since 1943 the Hatfield team had been planning a jet-propelled airliner, tailless for some time then conventional in design yet revolutionary. As the DH 106 Comet *G-ALVG*, it first flew discreetly on the evening of 27 July 1949. The thirty-six-passenger 105,000lb production version operated at around 500mph eight miles up on stages of about 1,500 miles, shrinking travel time around the world and changing human communication for all time. There was nothing comparable, no competitor and none yet emerging, and it was entirely British. On 2 May 1952 the Comet flew the first fare-paying jet passenger service. However, in September, at the SBAC Show, there came a major setback that tarnished the company's image.

Flown from Hatfield by John Derry, the prototype DH 110 all-weather fighter was performing before Farnborough's Saturday crowd. Following a sonic boom, produced in a dive, it banked to cross Farnborough and suddenly began breaking apart. The cockpit crashed by the runway, the two engines rammed into the crowd, and the main section fluttered vertically from the fracture zone. The reasons for the disaster were found to be complex, and probably followed wing-tip failure and aileron flutter. Whatever the cause, the company suffered a massive blow and the loss of a popular pilot and a worthy companion.

The Comet's supremacy made the two 1954 Comet disasters all the worse. The Comet entered service with a fully approved Air Registration Board C of A allowing passenger operations. There can be little doubt that the catastrophes resulted from metal fatigue, probably induced by thinner skinning than was desirable. Much was also attributable to a harsh learning curve. Once the necessary remedies had been made, Comets operated as efficiently as any other jets of their era.

As jet propulsion overtook ever more of the aircraft market, propeller needs for large and fast aircraft declined. In 1951 the propeller firm, changing course, signed a contract to develop guided weapons, and in April 1952 secured a contract to develop Blue Jay, the infra-red heat-seeking missile called Firestreak in RAF service. In 1957 Lostock works was ready to begin production.

Large de Havilland post-war civilian aircraft were Hatfield-built. Their very successful DH 125 business jet was mainly a DH Chester production, while at Hatfield the DH 121 Trident jet airliner

*Percival Vega Gull G-AFEA at the 1951 National Air Races held at a rainy Hatfield.*

took precedence. Meanwhile, the military team that had projected a rocket fighter, next turned their attention to the TSR.2 specification. However, neither DH scheme was proceeded with, leaving the DH 121 as the main Hatfield line. BEA was the prime customer for the new twin-engined airliner, with a third engine to boost its pull-away. BEA wanted something smaller, only to change its mind too late for de Havilland when calling for increased passenger capacity. When in Japan the 121 Trident competed with the Boeing 727 for a new customer, the latter won because the Trident was rated too small. The contract loss was a major blow, and the small Trident 1 entered BEA service in 1963.

On 17 December 1959 de Havilland had merged with Hawker-Siddeley, whose domineering attitude even led to the 'HS 60G Gipsy Moth'. Not surprisingly, 'HS' lacked popularity at Hatfield. Bristol Siddeley Engines acquired the DH Engine Co in November 1961.

The propeller company was now very much involved with missile guidance and propulsion and designed Britain's only IRBM, Blue Streak, for which Duxford was in view as an operational base. The prototypes were built at Hatfield, the engines being tested at Spadaeum. Being a vulnerable surface-based weapon, the giant rocket was soon cancelled.

In June 1970 the People's Republic of China took delivery of four ex-Pakistan International Airlines Tridents, and the following year the Hatfield sales team were invited to China and secured an order for six Trident 2Es, worth £20 million. A year later another six were ordered.

*Foreign sales of Tridents were disappointing: 4R-ACN of Air Ceylon rests by the 1950s-built main flight test hangar in July 1969.*

Further change came in 1977, when Hawker Siddeley Aviation, Hawker Siddeley Dynamics, the British Aircraft Corporation and Scottish Aviation merged to become British Aerospace. The corporation was divided into two groups, Aircraft and Dynamics, and Hatfield became the headquarters of the Hatfield-Chester Division of the Aircraft Group.

Over the years the Hatfield site had expanded, and now occupied nearly 1,600 acres. It comprised the factory, whose buildings covered nearly 1,500,000sq ft, and a large new hangar. The 6,000-foot paved runway was supplemented with taxiways, an engine-running bay and three wind tunnels. About 600 acres of land were still farmed. With more than a hundred departments at British Aerospace Hatfield, the workforce numbered over 4,000. Hatfield Division, British Aerospace Dynamics, became well-known for its work on 'Sky Flash', and with 2,500 employees the Division had extensive research, design and test facilities.

A reminder from far-off days was a wooden hut, the original design office of the de Havilland Aircraft Company, at Stag Lane, which stood near the works entrance and served to house the the de Havilland Museum.

The final production at Hatfield was the BAe 146 feederliner unveiled on 20 May 1981. Hatfield design staff had long worked on what now would be called a regional airliner. Via the DH 126 and larger twin 136, the 146 emerged powered by four Avco Lycoming ALF 502R-3 turbofans.

The first production aircraft, 001, was *G-SSSH*, providing a reminder that this was a low-noise-level aeroplane. BAe 146s were at first assembled at Hatfield, to which four other British Aerospace facilities supplied parts: the centre fuselage was built at Bristol, the rear fuselage at Manchester, the fin at Brough, and the engine pylons at Prestwick. Hatfield built the front fuselage and flight deck.

The BAe 146 was not an unqualified success, partly because it employed four engines instead of two, and there were ample competitors sharing the sales market. BAe 146 work moved to Manchester, and with no other designs in vogue and ample capacity in a soon shrinking defence market, BAe closed Hatfield in April 1994. The factory closure was a bitter blow; many among the workforce had been born and had always lived in the community where Hatfield *was* de Havilland. Many had given their entire lives and total loyalty to DH, and recalled tremendously exhilarating moments and terrible tragedies. Perhaps loyalty never edges into the lives of young folk used to job changes, but for the older folk the hurt long remains, like the memories.

**Main features:**
*Grass runs:* N/S 3,750ft, NE/SW 6,000ft, E/W 3,000ft, SE/NW 3,150ft, no RAF buildings.
*Hardstandings:* none. *Accommodation:* RAF officers 85, SNCOs 22, ORs 88.

---

## HEATHROW, London

*51°28N/00°27W 80ft asl; TQ075755. 11 miles W of London, access from the A4 and M4 and Staines by-pass*

Rain fell until lunchtime. By 1400 only a few puddles remained beneath a cloudy sky and already the aeroplane that would change the world was on the apron. The date was 2 May 1952. At about 1420 airmail bags were unloaded from an incongruously ancient vehicle and placed in the belly of their conveyor. A few people were watching, many with famous faces, when, with great excitement, came the specially decorated coach bringing 36 trendsetters. Conversation with the small contingent was exchanged, causing Customs men to be visibly shocked at the sight of ordinary mortals let loose on the apron beyond 'immigration' and probably engaging in smuggling. At 1440 the lucky three dozen began boarding, led by a gentleman carrying a raincoat (just in case). We stood well back for engine start, for still there was a feeling that one might easily be sucked in, or blown away, by four jet engines.

*Fairey Battle prototype K4303 in 1936 over Fairey's Great West Aerodrome, which was later engulfed by Heathrow.*

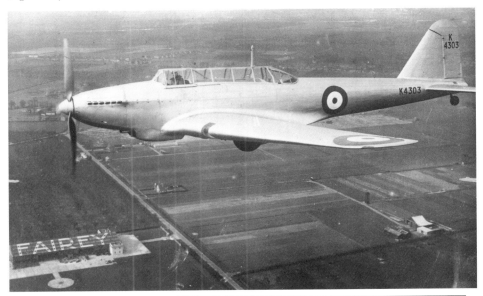

*Bristol Britannias at the 1950s BOAC maintenance base.*

At a few minutes before 1500 Comet *G-ALYP* edged timidly forward then slowly swung on to the westbound peritrack and left, passing the original tower. At 1501 the engines snarled and we watched in awe the first fare-paying passenger jet take-off the world had experienced. History was being made at Heathrow: a British aeroplane with British engines flown by a British crew from a British airport was leading one of the greatest changes the world has known. Nearby someone mentioned 'B for British'. That was a phrase I was to hear many times years later when Martin Sharp of de Havilland and I produced the authorised Mosquito history. By the time I was back in Cambridge, 'LYP had called at Rome and was heading for Athens. It seemed incredible that anyone – with sufficient funding – could now move at such speed.

London Heathrow I'd observed from its opening in January 1946, when mud encircled the concrete area called 'North' where large camouflage tents and war-surplus trailers accommodated the basic things airports need – forms to fill, scales, tea bars, wicker chairs in tatty lounges, toilets, nasty Customs men, strange sleek immigration chaps and many appended souls maintaining a living of a sort. Passengers, all correctly attired, carried raincoats, wore hats, stood in smart shoes and were clearly well-heeled.

A second pointer to the future had arrived at around 1925 four days before that Comet departure: the first Pan-American Douglas Super DC-6B (N6519C) to visit London. *Clipper Liberty Bell* looked so very long and could carry up to 86 people, a lot at that time.

While I was gazing at it over the barrier at the main entrance, a tall, distinguished figure came alongside. Looking intently over the apron, he turned and said, "That's what I call an air bus. One day high-density-load aircraft like that will carry lots of passengers who will simply arrive, buy a ticket and board it – just like getting on a bus, an air bus. It will carry lots of people, all wanting to travel with little fuss."

Already I had recognised my companion as Sir Peter Masefield, one-time editor of *The Aeroplane Spotter,* who later became head of British European Airways. For sure he was right: in America people would use aeroplanes as if they were long-distance buses and with little fuss, until selfish, jealous, extremely evil men spoiled the dream.

*Production Fairey Albacore X9151, a common sight at the Great West Aerodrome.*

*On leaving the apron, BOAC Constellation G-AHEJ passes the single-storey north-side buildings in May 1953.*

Heathrow now dominates Hounslow Heath, where highwayman Dick Turpin aboard Black Bess hijacked the Bath flyer. Long before, a Celtic temple was on the site, and at nearby Perry Oak probably the last wild wolf in England was caught. During the First World War an important night defence landing ground was established at Hounslow, from where, on 25 August 1919, a London-Paris air service was inaugurated and early mail deliveries took place.

In December 1928 Fairey Aviation purchased for £15,000 a 150-acre area of land serving as a market garden near Harmondsworth, just north-east of Stanwell, Middlesex. After draining, levelling and grass sowing, it opened in June 1930 as Fairey Aviation's flight centre, replacing Northolt. Variously known as Harmondsworth and, more usually, the Great West Aerodrome, it remained Fairey's until 1943, when the Government compulsorily purchased it. The Royal Aeronautical Society held garden parties there, where more than 1,500 Fairey aircraft were test flown and the Airspeed Horsa glider made its first flight, towed behind a Whitley V. To the coming London Airport was bequeathed Fairey's huge hangar, at one time the world's largest.

In mid-1943, when the Brabazon Committee formulated post-war civil airliners, it was clear that London would need a new airport suitable for large high-performance aircraft needing long runs and plentiful facilities – not to mention good land links. A developed Gatwick was a serious possibility, whereas sites to the east were ruled out because of frequent inclement weather and the risk of many bird strikes over the Thames Estuary and Essex Marshes. No sites suitably near for development existed to the north of London, but to the west was an area long favoured for flying. With good approaches and easy-draining gravel sub-soil, in 1943 Hounslow Heath was chosen for a very large-scale development. The Great West Aerodrome was included.

There seems little doubt that from the start the new airfield was envisaged as a future civil airport for London, although the scheme called for a 'Transport RAF Terminal Station'. Military use meant that a public enquiry could be avoided, likewise criticism claiming a diversion from the war effort. Acquiring land by using the 1939 Defence of the Realm Act meant that there could be no Right of Appeal. Oft-repeated claims that a B-29 bomber base had been envisaged are a misreading of the truth and are mentioned later.

Construction commenced in June 1944 of an airfield having three runways, 280° of 9,000 feet by 300 feet, and 156 and 232 each being 6,000 feet long and 300 feet wide. A single paved parking area would cover 75,000 square feet, sufficient to hold 30 large transport aircraft. Accommodation

*BOAC Canadair DC-4M Argonaut G-ALHY departs in June 1952.*

*BOAC Lancastrian G-AGLW in 1946 soon after bleak Heathrow opened. The dark green tents by the Great West Road contained 'check-in' and pre-flight 'lounges'.*

would be for 51 RAF officers, 28 SNCOs, 80 ORs, 5 WAAF officers, 5 SNCOs and 150 ORs. The war conveniently ended before the airfield could be put to military use, while still allowing it to go ahead with its conventional layout. A specially established committee considered a requirement that aircraft must be able to land or take off in a 4mph crosswind, their decision resulting in the runway pattern commonly called 'the Star of David'.

Far from complete, the airfield passed to the Ministry of Civil Aviation on 1 January 1946, and on 31 May 1946 was officially opened for operations. Prominent by then were BOAC and the new British South American Airways led by dynamic Don 'Pathfinder' Bennett, one of whose Lancastrians had set out from Heathrow on 1 January 1946 to make the first official (route-proving) flight. BSAA Lancasters and Lancastrians as well as Yorks were early users of the mud-engulfed airfield. By the end of 1946 57,109 passengers had made use of Heathrow.

By 1947 three runways were open for flying and a further three had been earmarked for aircraft dispersal and emergencies. A collection of prefabricated huts serving as offices and a passenger terminal edging the North Apron had replaced the scruffy tents. Passengers still walked or were bussed to aircraft, which, on departure, merely turned off the apron and followed the perimeter track to the active runway.

By now development of the airport was planned to take place in four phases. For some years the North Terminal area alongside the Bath Road would remain and be variously improved. Second, all runways and parking aprons were to be active by 1950. Third, very extensive maintenance areas would be built mainly in the south-east corner. Finally, a large permanent and main central passenger terminal complex would be constructed and reached through a large tunnel passing under the main north No 1 Runway. At this time a central terminal involving a concept somewhat similar to that which produced pre-war Gatwick seemed a good idea. To Heathrow, however, there was to be no vital, major rail link. Decades later, with an enormous input of vehicular traffic, the tunnel became a bottleneck, making Heathrow's layout no longer looking so clever. Easy it is to criticise, much harder to be far-seeing. For a while passenger numbers and available finance were less than expected, so construction of the central terminal area did not commence until November 1951, and the North Terminal – planned to close sooner – remained in use until 1954. Interestingly

*Trans World 'Connie' N6018C being hand-loaded on North Apron in June 1952.*

in view of recent suggestions, an area north of the Bath Road had been acquired for additional runways, but it was sold because the conclusion was that they would not be needed. Instead, the airport would cover an area of about $4^{1}/_{2}$ square miles.

In the south-east was constructed the imposing 240-acre No 1 Aircraft Maintenance Area. The BOAC/BEA extensive maintenance building consisted of two pairs of roofed pens, each spanning 336 feet and sufficiently high to give tail clearance for the largest foreseeable aircraft. Two huge reinforced-concrete cantilever arches fronted the pens. The vast structure was designed to accommodate huge aircraft like the ill-starred Bristol Brabazon. Fairey's hangar was retained and for many years put to good use within the maintenance area.

No 2 Maintenance Area, covering 70 acres, was for the use of foreign airlines, which continue to use it. No 3 Maintenance Area was a 91-acre site in the south-south-west of the airport, in which was built the fuel farm. Parts of this zone were available for parking, cargo operations and visiting aircraft, but the main idea was to hold this section for expansion or development as needed.

As soon as Runway 5 parallel to No 1 (the main runway) was functioning, the latter closed and work began on digging a deep and wide trench linking the northern area to the central terminals. Boring a tunnel was not possible due to the gravel sub-soil, so a concrete shell measuring 2,000 feet by 86 feet was built in the giant gulley. There were four traffic lanes with special lighting to make entry into and departure from bright light safer. Eventually there were in effect not one but three self-contained terminals. Tunnel opening came in November 1953, in time for the London to New Zealand Air Race.

Central area design was by Mr Fred Gibberd, who envisaged two terminals and an aircraft traffic control building overlooking the airport as well as the 158-acre central area. First to open, in 1955, was Terminal 2, Queen's Building, to handle European services. Terminal 1, mainly for domestic services, opened considerably later, and between them the two had stands for 34 aircraft. Terminal 3 was added to cope with long-haul operations. All three terminals remain in use, performing the same roles, although much additional building, refurbishing, structural change and adaptations have been made to cope with the vast amount of traffic at this busiest of all airports. Vehicle controls and car parking have become rigidly controlled and a bus station has been incorporated. All has been compounded by increased threats from terrorists, although such activity is far from new.

By March 1953 airport construction had cost £15m, the overall cost being estimated as £32m, but those figures were to be massively exceeded. They took no account of the colossal rise in passenger numbers, operators, baggage handling and a host of spin-off ancillary services.

The initial general layout remained until the mid-1980s. Vastly increasing traffic density and the high passenger numbers generated by wide-bodied aircraft now led to the building, on the south-side reserved space, of Terminal 4, mainly for the use of British Airways long-haul services. Siting Terminal 4 on its own surrounded by aircraft stands means at least a 10- to 20-minute underground transfer, which is far from ideal. Extension of the Piccadilly Underground line to both central and southern terminals was a great advance, further improved with a fast non-stop City Rail Link.

By the 1980s passengers were rarely bussed across the apron to their aircraft. Instead they walked directly from gated piers, often boarding and leaving an aircraft without even seeing it. That might aid security and help those nervous of flying, but few things could be more annoying to aircraft enthusiasts!

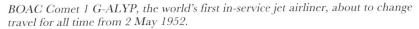

*BOAC Comet 1 G-ALYP, the world's first in-service jet airliner, about to change travel for all time from 2 May 1952.*

*How could anything as splendid as Swissair fail? A DC-3, like these on North Apron, arrived daily at 4pm – exactly. Ideal for watch-setting, they were.*

*DC-6B N6519C 'Clipper Liberty Bell', the first high-density aircraft, seen here on 29 April 1952 – Heathrow's first 'air bus'.*

*From 1946 to 1953 Avro Yorks of BOAC, like G-AGNP and 'NS, were common sights.*

*Most post-war air transport trends have been evident at Heathrow. SABENA passengers here leave Convair Cv 240 OO-SCP on foot for the Queen's Building.*

*Avro Tudor 5 G-AKBZ of BSAA on the southern-side maintenance area at Heathrow in 1948.*

*BEA's Viscounts were the world's first regular in-service turboprop airliners.*

*Conveyance to and from aircraft like DC-3 EI-ACD was soon in specially designed buses.*

One of the most noticeable changes in all terminals has been an amazing increase in the number and type of retail outlets offering a wide range of goods and services, duty-free or otherwise. Food and drink provision, too, has multiplied. In 2003 approval was at last given for Terminal 5, also on the south side, a £2.6bn venture possibly to open by 2007. Technological advances could well make extra runways unnecessary. As for noise intrusion, I spent several weeks in college under Heathrow approach and discovered it to be far quieter than I expected. The slow passage of piston-engined large aircraft making low-angle approaches to London Airport and generating considerable noise was something I lived with for more than two years during the 1950s. I found that far more noticeable than the sounds of the 1960s and '70s.

An interesting aspect of Heathrow's history is that it is one of the few major airports to have seen the entire development pattern of air transport since 1946. When it opened low passenger numbers carried by ex-military aircraft and civilian derivatives like the Lancastrian, Halton and York provided much of the traffic. Their US equivalents were C-47s and Dakotas, DC-4s and the first L-749 short and elegant 'Connies', while from Italy came the unusual SM 95 and from Paris the SO 161 Languedocs. Britain then fielded its half-way civilian designs based upon military aircraft, the HP Hermes and unhappy Avro Tudor. Long before its time came the two-deck Boeing Stratocruiser, a sort of small Airbus A380, while from Canada came the Merlin-engined Canadair DC-4M – the BOAC Argonaut Class – one of which *(G-ALHU)* conveyed home our Queen from Kenya soon after her father's sudden death in February 1952.

The next period marked the introduction of the short-haul piston liners, BEA Elizabethans and Convairliners, then very dramatically the superb and almost vibrationless Vickers Viscount, which in 1953 largely replaced BEA's Dakotas and Vikings that had begun switching their activity here from Northolt in May 1950.

Application of the turboprop to a long-haul aircraft brought along that fine whispering giant, the Bristol Britannia. But it came in on borrowed time, because the Comet was already in service. Although the jet's progress was soon marred by tragedy, that could not halt the move towards jet-powered long-haul aircraft. Meanwhile came the first conventional aircraft with fuselages lengthened to allow them to carry more passengers and sufficient fuel for non-stop Atlantic flights. More impressive still, the L-1049 long 'Connie' could fly over the North Pole non-stop to Tokyo, an amazing advance. Then, with military support, came the next great clan, the Boeing 707 family, which, in the tail of the Comet, ushered in widely the gas turbine transport.

*An architect's model of the Central Terminal area.*

*Heathrow Central Terminal area under construction.*

*The North Terminal at Heathrow in 1952.*

*Boarding and disembarkation from the early 1980s was via a 'pier', as first tried from pre-war Gatwick's 'beehive'.*

The four basic trends in commercial aviation have been clearly evident at Heathrow. Aircraft have been seen to fly faster and higher, affording increased passenger comfort, and further, with often less comfort, and with a steadily increasing passenger capacity that promotes more problems in passenger and baggage handling. The first reached its peak when Concorde was introduced, halving the time needed for trans-Atlantic non-stop flights. Its withdrawal in October 2003 may become to be seen as a confirmation of the greater need to carry more passengers economically. The introduction of the Boeing 747 showed such a trend, although it brought great surges in passenger and baggage arrival. Feeding 400 or so passengers during long-haul journeys has meant meal production on a massive scale.

Heathrow terminals by the 1990s were largely shared by twin-engined aircraft powered by exceptionally good engines and suitable for very more economic long-haul flights. Included are the Airbus 300 and 310, as well as Boeing 767s and 777s. The short-haul market relies upon Boeing 737s, 757s, Airbus A320s, SAABs and Embraers.

One of the greatest changes seen at Heathrow has been sociological. Whereas from 1946 to the early 1950s high fares restricted flying to the well-to-do, desire to travel far for business or pleasure has changed the clientele. To cope with that, along came the ever smaller seat pitch, clearly defining classes by fare structure – pay extra for more space and better food – as was the case on ocean liners until the 1960s, when they became single-class. That trend is now happening on aircraft. There has also been a change in the status of travellers whereby a celebrity of any sort has become more feted. In yesteryear only the really great achievers in science, industry, the arts, politics, sometimes games and Head of State visitors achieved a hard-won press welcome. Heathrow has become a microcosm of sociology and life-styles as much as of aviation.

You might, incidentally, wonder why Heathrow appears among the military airfields in *Action Stations Revisited*. The answer is that London Heathrow has long featured in military planning, receives military transports and would have even had a Vulcan call had not catastrophe overtaken it at the last moment. More specifically, in 1951, under a war reinforcement plan, agreement was reached for USAF Boeing RB-29/RB-50/RB-47 strategic reconnaissance aircraft to operate from the airport in wartime. It is probably that fact which prompts the erroneous idea that Heathrow was built as a base for B-29s. When that agreement lapsed, Heathrow became the War Station for Javelin all-weather fighters squadrons stationed at Waterbeach, Cambridgeshire.

Heathrow is in size and use a quite breathtaking place, one of the greatest airports in the world and always busy. With a current workforce of around 60,000, superlatives abound.

**Main features**:
*Runways:* Heathrow has two parallel main concrete/asphalt runways to either side of the central terminals. Runways are 27L 12,000ft x 147ft and 27R 12,800ft x 147ft, both supported with ILS/DME. Short asphalt runway 23 is 6,434ft long and 147ft wide and is an upgrade of an original runway. Upon the airport's three-runway wartime layout was superimposed a mirror image, giving the 'star of David' plan, Nos 1 and 5 roughly directed east-west becoming the main runways. Shorter Nos 4 (eastern) and 6 were shorter and SE/NW orientated, while Nos 2 (eastern) and 7 were aligned SW/NE. A maze of taxiways linked them to the central area. *Buildings:* These remain essentially as described in the text, with the central area holding the three main terminals.

## HENDON, Middlesex

*51°36N/00°14 170ft asl; TQ215905. Colindale Avenue, now occupied by RAF Museum*

Cream teas in elite enclosures, Gladiators tied together with tape, Heyfords skittle-bombing, the 'set piece', pupil and instructor and, of course, The New Types Park – all that and much more was 'Hendon'. Like 'Farnborough', one magic word in the 1920s and '30s meant a day when so few brought so much delight to so many.

Hendon meant so much, for it was active in the early days of flying. Indeed, its share began when Everett and Edgcumbe's unhappy 1909 aeroplane was housed in a shed on a field at the end of Colindale Avenue, the road that now leads to the RAF Museum.

In February 1910 Claude Grahame-White, who kept his Bleriot in that shed, took out an option to buy adjacent land, which became the London Aerodrome where eight hangars were erected. Three were used by the Aeronautical Syndicate, the rest by Grahame-White.

During April Louis Paulhan, a Frenchman, erected his Farman, and on 29 April 1910 set off to attempt the first flight from London to Manchester to be completed in under 24 hours. Claude Grahame-White had already tried and failed, but the Frenchman had stolen a march on him by starting out while he was having a late-afternoon snooze. Awoken with the news that Paulhan was already on his way to Manchester, Grahame-White was soon airborne. Overtaking Paulhan meant that he must undertake his first night flight, but the Frenchman reached Manchester before Grahame-Wight.

By 1 October 1910, when the London Aerodrome officially opened, the small landing ground had been expanded to cover 250 acres. The eight sheds were housing a variety of aircraft including Horatio Barber's Valkyrie canard monoplanes and the Bleriot School of Flying.

In summer 1911 Grahame-White began to hold weekly flying meetings, which between 1912 and 1914 did much to popularise aviation. His flying school offered a complete course for 50 guineas on monoplanes or biplanes. For 75 guineas one could learn to fly them both. Socially appealing race meetings took place at weekends, activity being boosted when the Blackburn Flying School moved in from Filey, Yorkshire.

A military flying display at Hendon on 12 May 1911, devised by the Parliamentary Aerial Defence Committee, was laid on to arouse Government awareness of the potential of the aeroplane. Between 9 and 18 September 1911 Hendon witnessed the first airmail service in Britain, during which Gustav Hamel carried over 100,000 special letters and cards between Hendon and Windsor in part to celebrate the coronation of King George V.

On 20 September 1912 the first round-London 80-mile air race, watched by an estimated half a million people, was flown from Hendon, where more than 45,000 spectators paid to see the 'show'. Next month Handley-Page aircraft started regular flying from here, following the company's move to Cricklewood. In May 1913 Grahame-White became the agent for UK manufacture of Morane Saulnier aircraft in Britain.

*A Hawker Hart of No 24 Squadron, Hendon.*

*'Where's the Kodachrome, then? Surely you didn't leave it at home?' Show-stopper Siskin IIIas of 43 Squadron pass over the Hendon Display crowd, sunshades up and not one camera around – except, evidently, for brave Auntie Annie's!*

The first acrobatic and parachuting displays in Britain took place at Hendon, where, in November 1913, inverted flying and loops were first demonstrated by British fliers G L Temple and B C Hucks respectively. Not to be outdone, Grahame-White established a passenger-carrying record using his Charabanc biplane, when, on 2 October 1913, it flew for nearly 20 minutes carrying nine people.

Unusual night-flying displays took place in June 1913 using aircraft outlined with electric bulbs. Grahame-White incorporated more sinister, meaningful demonstrations, including the 'bombing' of a set piece – mock ship or fort – in the centre of the airfield.

A very wide assortment of aircraft flew from Hendon before the war, and the range of flying schools included the Hall School of Flying (1913-15), Bleriot, the Beatty School of Flying and the Ruffy-Baumann School of Flying, between them offering instruction on a wide assortment of aircraft types.

*Everyone at the Display headed first for the New Types Park, where the Vickers PVO-9 prototype looks down on two Anson-like forms and the distant Bombay prototype.*

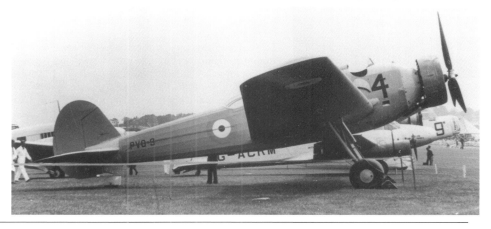

*Bristol Bulldog IIs of No 3 Squadron at the 1930 Hendon Display.*

When war was declared on 4 August 1914, Hendon aerodrome and the Grahame-White aircraft business were requisitioned under the Defence of the Realm Act, the aerodrome for use by the RNAS. Grahame-White, showing his strong patriotism, flew a night sortie on 5/6 August while the enemy stayed at home. Hyde Park or Hendon were earmarked as landing grounds for defensive fighters. Hendon was chosen and became a Royal Naval Air Service Station, where, on 7 August 1914, a Caudron arrived to became London's both first and only defensive fighter. In October a captive balloon used for zeppelin spotting began to be flown, then in December four fighters were kept on the aerodrome.

The first night scramble came on 31 May 1915, when a Gunbus sent to engage a Zeppelin crashed in Hertfordshire, killing the crew. Relatively few such sorties were flown before January 1916, when the RFC began working at Hendon alongside the RNAS in fighter defence of the capital. Detached Flights of Nos 17 and 19 (Reserve) Squadrons operated using BE 2cs.

Hendon's assortment of civilian flying schools started training pilots for the services at the start of the war. On 22 September 1916 the RFC took over the civilian schools functioning here, which, to the end of the war and controlled by the 18th Wing, were known as the Civilian Flying School of Instruction. Until that takeover, civilians – including women – had learned to fly alongside military personnel. Grahame-White's school, the largest, trained nearly 500 military pilots in wartime. Among them were famous fighter 'aces' Mannock, Ball and Warneford, each destined to be awarded a Victoria Cross.

By the close of 1914 there were, near Hendon, three aircraft factories manufacturing military aircraft. Handley Page had in September 1912 became established at Cricklewood and began flying its aeroplanes from Hendon the following month. The Aircraft Manufacturing Company (AIRCO), formed in 1911 to build Henri and Maurice Farman aeroplanes, now had factories beside Edgware Road, and Grahame-White on Hendon Aerodrome. All provided aircraft for acceptance at Hendon.

During the night of 9 December 1915, prior to its first flight, the prototype 0/100, wings folded, was towed along Colindale Avenue to Hendon aerodrome. To aid its passage Frederick Handley Page and companions sawed off obstructing tree branches, to the chagrin of their owners. Test-flying began on 17 December. Subsequent Handley Page bombers were test-flown from Cricklewood aerodrome and flown to Hendon for acceptance.

Throughout the war Hendon maintained close links with local contractors whose output amounted to about 8,000 aircraft. Besides the company's works on Aerodrome Road, Grahame-White had in 1916 erected a new factory where were built Avro 504s, BE 2s, DH 6s and Henri Farman FH 20s under licence.

In February 1917 the RNAS installation passed to the War Office, which opened No 2 Aircraft Acceptance Park here and for which fourteen-aircraft sheds were erected and some of Grahame-White's buildings acquired. No 2 AAP received DH 4s and DH 9As from AIRCO, Waring & Gillow and Berwick built DH 9 Camels from Hooper and Nieuport aircraft and Handley Page bombers. In June and July 1917 2 AAP also operated a Flight of DH 4s and DH 5s, which participated in attempts to intercept Gotha attacks.

At its Edgware Road works AIRCO, whose Chief Designer since 1914 was Geoffrey de Havilland, produced DH 1s, 2s, 4s, 5s, 6s, 9s, 9As, BE 2Cs, Avro 504s and Farman Longhorns, many of which were flown at and delivered via Hendon, where in June 1916 the DH 4 was first flown and, in February 1918, the DH 9A. Formed in June 1917 the British Aerial Transport Co (BAT), which built aircraft at Willesden, test-flew them from Hendon.

Diversity was certainly the watchword here, for in 1917 an experiment involved an Avro 504, flown by Flight Commander R E Penny RNAS, being launched from a compressed air catapult, the prototype of those used on ships.

Hendon remained a seat of much and complex activity. In February 1919, the year when 2 AAP closed, No 86 (Communications) Wing was formed, controlling Nos 1 and 2 (Communications) Squadrons, which carried out ferry duties between Hendon and Paris during the Versailles conference. Handley Page 0/400s carried passengers and DH 4s the mail before the squadron moved to Kenley in April 1919. By then the 0/400 bombers at Hendon were being dispersed, leaving the aerodrome in mid-1919, for the AAP had become No 1 Aircraft Salvage Depot, whose task was to gather on a very extensive scale aircraft and equipment for sale by the Croydon Aircraft Disposal Co.

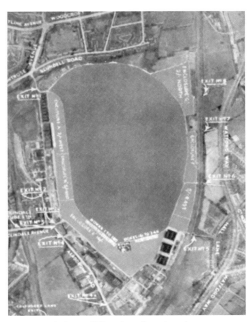

*An aerial view of Hendon showing the spectator enclosures indicated for the 1937 RAF Display.*

Although the station remained under military ownership, civilian organisations were moving in or, in some cases, departing. Claude Grahame-White, plagued by financial problems and realising that his aeroplane production was no longer needed, turned to making car bodies and furniture. By January 1919 more than 100 of his two-seater 'Buckboard' cars were leaving Hendon each week. He kept some Avro 504s and DH 6s for joy-riding purposes, but stopped flying in 1920, leaving the airfield to become a race venue. In 1919 BAT briefly operated air services to Birmingham and Amsterdam, but only until early 1920. AIRCO-owned Aircraft Transport & Travel used Hendon as a maintenance and air taxi base, operations ceasing in December 1920. SE 5As converted by the Savage Skywriting Co used Hendon as their base between 1921 and 1925.

By then the airfield's future looked assured, for in 1920 it was used for the RAF Tournament, inaugurating a spectacular, fashionable event subsequently called 'the Pageant', and later the Royal Air Force Display, staged annually until 1937, by which time the international situation demanded maximum effort be devoted to operational training. It was reckoned that more than 4,000,000 visitors in all flocked to the events, which became the highlight of the British aviation calendar. Not only was it always a superb publicity spectacle, but the displays were excellent channels for RAF recruiting purposes.

*Beech JRB-6 39795 of the US Navy, 21 July 1951.*

*Bombs burst on Hendon's east end,*
*25 October 1940.*

When the airfield was sold to the Air Ministry in 1926, resident were the London Flying Club and the Skywriting Corporation. De Havilland had left the area for Stag Lane in 1920, and Handley Page was ensconced at Cricklewood. Only the Skywriters stayed alongside the RAF, until 1932.

RAF activity much increased in 1927. On 15 January DH 9As and Avro 504s of No 601 (County of London) Squadron arrived from Northolt, followed on the 18th by DH 9As of No 600 (City of London) Squadron, both of the Auxiliary Air Force. On 16 April 1928 the Home Communications Flight joined them, setting in train Hendon's associations with similar organisations.

Wapitis replaced the Auxiliary DH 9As in autumn 1929, Hawker Harts taking the Wapitis' place in 601 Squadron during early 1933, and two years later in 600 Squadron. They in turn were replaced by Demons in 600 Squadron in spring 1937, and in 601 Squadron during August 1937, by which time there had been other significant events, the most important of which was the arrival of No 24 (Communications) Squadron from Northolt on 9 July 1933, which next day absorbed the Home Communications Flight. Under a variety of guises, '24' remained here until 25 February 1946, when it moved to Bassingbourn, leaving behind elements that remained to the end of flying at Hendon. Many Government Ministers, senior civil servants and high-rank officers experienced the value of aviation through 24 Squadron's de Havilland DH 86 Express, Rapide and Flamingo airliners when these transported them around the UK and Europe. In 1940 it was 24 Squadron's Flamingo that took Winston Churchill from Hendon to France on the most critical days of the war.

Another newcomer was The King's Flight, formed here on 20 July 1935 and holding the blue, red and silver VIP Royal aircraft, the best known being the Airspeed Envoy *G-AEXX*. The Flight moved to Benson on 15 September 1939.

Two other auxiliary squadrons with Hendon connections were No 604 (County of Middlesex), formed here on 17 March 1930, and No 611 (West Lancashire), formed at Hendon on 10 February 1936. The latter then took its Hawker Harts to Speke on 6 May 1936. Nos 600, 601 and 604, initially bomber squadrons, changed to a fighter role in 1934, whereas No 611 was a fighter unit from the outset. During the September 1938 Munich crisis No 600 deployed to war station Kenley, No 601 to Biggin Hill and No 604 to North Weald. In November No 601 had a brief flirtation with Gauntlets, but in January 1939 600 and 601 converted to Blenheim 1(f) interim/strike fighters. No 601 moved to Biggin Hill on 2 September, and No 600 to Hornchurch on 2 October. No 604, initially equipped with DH 9As, had used Wapitis between June 1930 and June 1935, Harts from September 1934, and received Demons in June 1935. It had also been flying Blenheim 1(f)s since January 1939, and returned to North Weald on 2 September 1939. These moves left no operational aircraft at Hendon, which became home to unusual aircraft and non-flying organisations, more of which set up offices and depots in nearby areas in wartime. No 50 Group Communications Flight, for instance, had functioned at Hendon from formation on 1 February 1939 until 2 September 1939.

*Dakota III 'NQ-I' FD903 of 24 Squadron, Hendon-based in the summer of 1943.*

An anomaly was the formation here on 17 May 1940 of 257 Squadron, which received Spitfires – possibly in error – and which quickly re-armed with Hurricanes, becoming operational on 1 July and moving to Northolt on 4 July 1940. Between 5 and 26 September 1940 No 504 Squadron's Hurricanes operated from here.

Hendon was bombed several times, and Colindale Underground station, via which many visit the RAF Museum today, was completely destroyed. On 7 October 1940 an oil bomb burned out No 24 Squadron's hangar, and on 11 November HE bombs fell across the East Camp, landing ground and on West Camp.

No 1 Camouflage Unit arrived on 8 November 1940 and worked alongside 24 Squadron until 1 June 1942, when it moved to Stapleford Tawney. On 10 March 1941 No 1416 Flight formed, equipped with PR Spitfires and Blenheims partly for internal survey operations, and left for Benson in September 1941. Lysanders of No 116 Squadron arrived on 20-24 April 1941, their role being to allow AA gunners to calibrate their predictors and carry out general practice activities. Before the squadron moved to Heston on 20 April 1942 it acquired Hurricanes to give AA gunners aim practice against dive bombers and low-attack fighters. A swarm of Tiger Moths joined them at Hendon, also to assist AA gun calibration. In August 1941 No 151 Wing personnel staged through en route for the USSR.

*Devon VP955 of No 31 Squadron in Grahame-White's Hendon hangar.*

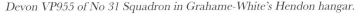

On 15 October 1942 'A' Flight of 24 Squadron was re-named No 510 Squadron, and disbanded on 8 April 1944 to become the Metropolitan Communication Squadron, whose role was UK internal communications flying for Government and service purposes.

With 46 Group airfields in short supply, No 512 Squadron formed instead at 44 Group's Hendon HQ base on 18 June 1943 to await equipping with Dakotas. No 575 followed a similar path, being formed on 1 February 1944. As soon as equipped they departed for Broadwell.

On 30 June 1944 a flying-bomb hit a wing of Colindale Hospital and four airmen were killed. On 3 August another exploded in front of a brick barrack block, damaging five huts in the south-east corner of the airfield, killing nine airmen and injuring 25.

Hendon ceased to be administered by 44 Group on 7 July 1944, command passing to No 116 Wing, which had formed on 1 January 1944 and arrived from Hendon Hall to occupy No 2 Mess, Hendon. Transport Command Communication Flight formed here on 8 April 1944 as a third Flight of MCS, stayed until May 1946, then left for Upavon. This was a period of local change, for on 12 June an Allied Flight had formed within 24 Squadron, which, within MCS, provided communications flying for the Belgian and Dutch in the UK. On 7 July No 1316 (Dutch Communication) Flight formed from Allied Flight and used a Beechcraft D-17, Lockheed 12a and Koolhoven FK 43. It also had Dominies, and by the end of hostilities was operating six Dakotas. The Flight disbanded on 4 April 1946. Its noisy Beech 'Staggerwing' was not the only one here, for at the start of the war the US Embassy was using a Hendon-based example; later in the war it added at least one Beech 18, and later still had assorted 'C-47s', more of which, in USAAF hands, briefly stayed in late summer 1944 before leaving for Bovingdon.

By autumn 1945 24 Squadron and the MCS were dominant. Here since 1942, the Air Ambulance Unit and its training section, which carried out much specialised air ambulance work, had departed. In February it was time for '24' to end its long tenancy, its departure, to operate aircraft needing longer runways, also making way for a return of the auxiliaries.

On 10 May 1946 both Nos 601 and 604 Squadrons reformed as medium-altitude fighter squadrons and received Spitfire LF 16es. Their residence ended on 28-29 March 1949 when they moved to North Weald to re-arm with jet fighters. During their stay the Fighter Command Communications Squadron was detached here from April 1946 to July 1947 while runway improvement took place at Northolt. On 23 April 1949 the RAF Antarctic Flight formed, received an Auster 6 and a T7, and was based here until disbandment in January 1951. ATC cadets were trained at No 143 GS between 1950 and August 1953, while No 1958 Reserve AOP Flight, formed on 1 July 1949 as part of 661 Squadron, flew its Auster AOP 4s, 5s and 6s from here until disbandment on 10 March 1957. Only the Metropolitan Communications Squadron remained faithful, but Hendon, in a congested and residential area, was too small for modern aircraft, so in November 1957 the Metropolitan Communications Squadron left for Northolt. Hendon closed to flying on 2 November 1957, although gliders of No 617 (Volunteer) GS, which formed here in

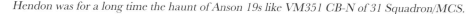

*Hendon was for a long time the haunt of Anson 19s like VM351 CB-N of 31 Squadron/MCS.*

*Now suspended in Auckland Airport, NZ, the Percival Vega Gull G-ADPR used by Jean Batten for pioneering flights was part of the 1951 Daily Express Hendon static aircraft display.*

January 1958, functioned until 31 March 1968. The RAF Main Gate continued to fly the ensign, and facilities remained allowing personnel proceeding overseas from the London area via Brize Norton to assemble in a transit centre until RAF Hendon closed on 1 April 1987.

Somewhat surprisingly, Hendon came fully awake for just one more day. On 19 June 1988 a huge Blackburn Beverley XH124 flew in and won a place for itself in the main car park. Alas, its tenure was relatively brief, for it was – perhaps surprisingly – scrapped in January 1990.

The Royal Air Force Museum, established in 1963, was opened by HM the Queen on 15 November 1974. On a 10-acre site, the main aircraft hall recalls the history of the service, and displays in pristine condition more than 40 aircraft from the Museum's collection of over 150. The large Battle of Britain and Bomber Command Museums on the same site hold superbly maintained items. Departments handling books, company drawings, extensive data records and photographs can be visited by prior arrangement. If you have never visited the RAF Museum, then it is time you did so!

Where aviation is concerned it is good policy not to assume that anything has completely faded. A forlorn-looking Grahame-White factory and hangar faced the main RAF Museum, and their cries for a saviour were at long last heard; the National Lottery rewarded them and in 1997 it was announced that the factory and part of the hangar would be taken into care on the RAF Museum site. As a result a precious part of our aviation heritage has been saved.

**Main features:**
*Runways:* 339 3,975ft, 014 3,060ft, 290 3,000ft, tarmac surface. *Hangars:* Two Belfast Roof General Service Sheds, one built of steel trusses and brick, one large shed converted into three hangars, three Bellman. Factory building opened for Grahame-White Co and adjacent hangar. Numerous 1920s permanent buildings, and some non-permanent. *Accommodation:* RAF officers 80, SNCOs 246, ORs 911; WAAF officers 15, SNCOs 10, ORs 399.

## HENLEY-ON-THAMES (CRAZIES FARM), Berkshire

*51°31N/00°51W 180ft asl; SU795824. 6 miles NNE of Reading*

Henley-on-Thames opened in the early part of July 1940 as a grass-surface RLG for No 13 EFTS White Waltham, whose Tiger Moths used it until December 1940. Then it became the RLG for Woodley, and between 3 February 1941 and 21 September 1942 Magisters of No 8 EFTS used it. When in 1944 Tiger Moths of No 10 Flying Instructors' School were very active, they, too, used Henley.

Radical change came in mid-August 1944 when No 529 Squadron arrived from Halton. Formed on 15 June 1943 from No 1448 Flight (Radar Calibration Duties), the unit had been operating Cierva C 30s for coastal radar station calibration Their autogiros (commonly called 'spider planes') always aroused interest as they whirred overhead in wartime and made sinister overnight stops at unlikely places. The unit also operated Oxfords, Hornet Moths, and in May 1945 received a Hoverfly 1 to become the RAF's first helicopter-equipped squadron. It disbanded at Henley on 20 October 1945, after which the RLG (still Woodley-controlled) was closed.

**Main features:**
*Landing area:* Grass, longest run SSW/NNE 2,100-2,400ft. *Hangars:* three standard Robin, two Standard Double Blister and two Standard Blister. *Accommodation:* none, but messing and ablutions provided and tents for up to 70 ORs.

## HENLOW, Bedfordshire

*52°01N/00°18W 150ft asl; TL165365. 5¹/₂ miles N of Hitchin; the A600 and A6001 roads pass through the camp site*

At Henlow one can still be convinced that the 1930s, even 1920s, are still around, for some original buildings survive, although the wizardry within must amaze them. Yet Henlow exudes no indications of its great part in past victories. From its 13 MU, hordes of Hurricanes headed for Malta, Africa, the Far East and the USSR, together with technicians to care for them. Travelling on HMS *Furious*, they faced the fury of the sea as well as the foe. Some were aboard HMS *Ark Royal* when she was torpedoed off Gibraltar.

On flat ground near industrial Luton, and with good communications, Henlow was chosen in 1917 as the site for an aircraft repair depot. Construction began in April 1918, and Service personnel started arriving from Farnborough on 10 May to establish No 5 Eastern Area Aircraft Depot. Three months later they were overhauling Bristol Fighters and de Havilland aircraft. In October 1918 around a hundred Americans arrived, only to leave soon after the Armistice. By that time 300 women were fabric-working or doing clerical work, but soon after the Armistice repair work stopped. Much of Henlow's equipment was scrapped, stored aircraft selling at 'ten bob' for a small one, 'a mere quid' for a big bomber. Just imagine their worth now! Some went to Australia, but most were scrapped.

Henlow hit the headlines when, on 1 April 1919, airmen about to be demobbed mutinied because the Government wanted to extract all it could from them by forcing them to work excessive hours. Long jail sentences were given to some of the fifty-six tried by Courts Martial. Modern old folk had better watch out!

Site retention was certain in February 1920 when an additional 161 acres were purchased from a farmer for use as a flight-test airfield, and on 16 March 1920 Henlow became the Inland Area Aircraft Depot. By 1922 its monthly handling amounted to about fifteen engines and ten aircraft. Shed 186 was designated for aircraft repair, overhaul or modification, engines were dealt with in Shed 187, and metalwork in No 188. Assembly and flight-test checks were undertaken in 189.

A wide array of aircraft passed through the workshops including Fairey Fawns, Flycatchers, '504s, Grebes, Snipes, IIIFs and Vimys. From a public address system intended for the colonies and being tested on a modified Handley Page Hinaidi, Shakespearean words once penetrated the clouds above Henlow, mesmerising its neighbourhood. There is a legend claiming that a camp building intended for a Hendon 'pickle factory' was erected at Henlow in error. Within it, large Handley Pages were instead repaired.

From Farnborough, the Officers' Engineering School arrived in April 1924. Three months later the first course commenced within the Engineering Instruction Section, which, variously re-named, functioned almost to the 1970s. It represented an extension of Lord Trenchard's plan by which, after five years of flying, an officer pursued a ground trade for two years.

Early 1920s home air defence plans required new fighter squadrons for which suitable stations were few. Despite its poor strategic position, Henlow became a temporary choice. Nos 23 and 43 Squadrons re-formed on 1 July 1925 and used Snipes. In April 1926 No 23 became the first Gloster Gamecock squadron, and left for Kenley in February 1927. No 43 re-equipped with Gamecocks in spring 1926, and left for Tangmere the following December.

Henlow, under 21 Group, was renamed the Home Aircraft Depot on 4 April 1926. In September 1925 the Parachute Test Section formed, and in October 1926 was joined by Northolt's Parachute Training Section. This combination became the Parachute Test Unit and initially employed Vimys. To test a parachute an airman hung on to the bomber's interplane struts, faced

*Henlow under construction on 29 August 1918. (Bruce Robertson collection)*

*Radio-controlled DH Queen Bee K4229 '10', test-flown pre-war at HAD Henlow.*

the direction of flight, streamed out his parachute, then allowed himself to be pulled away. It was reasonably safe, and at this time free fall was reckoned far more hazardous.

In the 1930s, Thursday brought a half-day holiday for Cambridge schoolboys like me, providing very useful spotting opportunities at a time when activity was ever-increasing. One windy afternoon a PTU Virginia 'raced' across at a snail's pace. As I watched, the big, clumsy and drifting biplane turned into a strong wind, then, to my fascination, momentarily hung motionless before being very slowly blown backwards for some moments before it found enough strength to overcome the gale and head for Henlow at such a slow speed that it took more than fifteen minutes to pass from sight.

LAC Dobbs of the PTU was one involved in parachute testing. Participating in one test, involving the use of a balloon, he was suddenly lifted over low obstacles near Henlow and carried into an 11,000-volt electricity system. Although not so devastating for them, airmen from Henlow helped on 1 October 1930 to pull the R-101 airship from its Cardington hangar for its fatal flight.

The opposite of such disasters was to involve a young Flying Officer, Frank Whittle, who joined the engineering course in August 1932. He completed it in less time than usual, and while here he continued his theoretical work on gas turbines. In mid-1934 Whittle entered Cambridge University to spend two years reading engineering.

By August 1935 the RAF Expansion Scheme was making such demands upon ground technician provision that the Home Aircraft Depot became an airframe riggers' school. No 1 Wing trained machine-tool operators and Fitter 1, and Nos 2 and 3 Wings flight riggers and flight mechanics. New accommodation was erected in the north-west corner of the station and other huts between the road through the camp and Henlow village.

Training of MT drivers and operatives began in January 1937, and cookery courses were soon running. An offshoot of the RAF Depot, Uxbridge, was established in July 1937 to provide initial RAF training for more than 1,000 men. There were now so many troops at Henlow that the basic trainees had to live in tents. Two months later ITU moved to Cardington, where wooden huts had been erected for the 'rookies'.

*The Sheds remain, but 1944 Canadian-built Mosquito B25 KB669 has long gone. (De Havilland)*

By 1938 Henlow's pupil population had reached 5,000 men. Repair activity had ceased, but war plans called for its resumption in the event of hostilities. The PTU remained, and since December 1936 the engineering school had been known as the RAF School of Aeronautical Engineering. Additional were the three Training Wings and the MT Training School.

In September 1938 two-thirds of the Training Wing moved to St Athan, and No 2 Mobilisation Pool formed to prepare for an increased repair role. The Home Aircraft Depot became 13 MU in October 1938, and in April 1939 No 1 Wing moved to Halton, only small training units remaining at Henlow. Shortage of space for new squadrons caused No 80 to arrive from Kenley on 15 March 1937 with Gauntlet IIs, receiving Gladiator Is before moving to Debden on 9 June 1937. An unusual arrival in October 1936 was the Pilotless Aircraft Section from Farnborough, its de Havilland Queen Bees being handled, from January 1937, by the Base Training Unit operating from Hangar 186A. This Unit was responsible for test-flying the radio-controlled Queen Bees preparatory to their despatch to AA gunnery training formations. The PAS moved to Hawkinge on 22 February 1940.

No 13 MU was undertaking aircraft modification, manufacture of replacement parts and handling armament tasks when war began. Suggestions for a No 6 Group Pool here did not materialise, but No 21 Aircraft Depot did form and quickly moved near Nantes in France on 26 September 1939. When the British were forced out of France, 21 AD withdrew through St Nazaire. In June 1940 some 3,000 of its officers and men re-assembled at Henlow, many to work incredibly long hours modifying and repairing Hurricanes, about a dozen of which were returned to squadrons each week during the Battle of Britain. Another intensive task was unpacking, assembling and testing Canadian-built Hurricanes, which arrived crated.

More than 6,000 personnel were now at Henlow serving in 13 MU, No 13 School of Technical Training, the School of Aeronautical Engineering, the test-flying section and manning the station; No 13 School of Technical Training alone had on roll more than 2,000. Soon it was renamed 14 SofTT because having two No 13s on the station brought problems.

Enemy action against Henlow was limited, but on 26 September 1940 a bomb fell between two hangars Two houses in Station Road, Lower Stondon, were demolished and three servicemen killed. In another raid a bomb passed across the roof of Hangar 530 and rammed itself into soft ground.

In 1941 13 MU prepared for operation *Quick Force.* Parties of fitters, numbering between fifty and a hundred, served on aircraft carriers, in particular HMS *Furious.* Their task was to prepare, dismantle and pack Hurricanes for shipment to Malta. About thirty men sailed with the Hurricanes and prepared them when the time came for them to be flown off the aircraft carrier's deck when it was about 300 miles west of Malta. The last of these deliveries was aboard *Ark Royal* when she was torpedoed by U-81 on 14 November 1941. Seven RAF survivors reached Henlow on 22 November.

Parachute trials having long taken place at Henlow, instructors were sought from here when an airborne troop force was formed. For parachute testing the ancient Virginias were not replaced until 1941, when Whitleys arrived. Later development work involved using Dakotas and a Halifax for parachuted test drops of items for Resistance forces.

No 13 MU maintained and modified many aircraft, in particular Hurricanes, Mosquitoes and Typhoons. Between June 1940 and October 1943, 1,004 Canadian Hurricanes were erected and tested at Henlow. Many Bristol radial engines were also handled, and modifications to Halifaxes made, among them the fitting by working parties of rectangular fins and rudders and, to some aircraft, turretless 'Z' Type noses. During March 1943 a Whitley IV was modified to enable it to snatch personnel from the ground by means of a long line, in preparation for fitment of a similar device to Dakotas. Another 13 MU idea was a mobile link trainer for Continental squadrons. Henlow used three sub-sites, one from 1939 sited in the north-west of the camp. A second was close to Meppershall water works, and a third near Clifton village.

During a visit I paid to Henlow on 19 April 1944 a mixture of Mosquitoes could be seen spread around the field. It was to 13 MU that Canadian-built Mosquito B20 and 25 bombers were flown to be fitted out to the required operational standards. Also visible were a number of Lockheed Hudsons, among them a grey/green specially equipped example of 161 Squadron from nearby Tempsford. A 'half yellow' Blackburn Shark – dusty, complete, wings folded – was in a hangar close to a couple of Hawker Fury biplanes, an 'all-silver' Hind, a Gladiator and a Fulmar. Several Mosquitoes were flying on air tests and Typhoons were being prepared for 2TAF use.

As the war drew to a close Henlow twice came under enemy fire – by chance. At 1900 on 10 December 1944 a V-1 landed near the camp, damaging windows and ceilings and causing two slight civilian casualties. The final attack came at 1420 on 10 January 1945 when a V-2, making the furthest penetration into the UK by a long-range rocket, came down in a field near Henlow, causing no damage.

After the war Henlow's status as a technical training centre increased. The need for suitable accommodation for 1948 Olympic Games contestants led to them using the Signals Development Unit site at West Drayton. That caused the unit to move to Henlow on 19 October 1947, being renamed the Radio Engineering Unit on 1 January 1950. During other changes at Henlow, the School of Aeronautical Engineering became the Technical College on 15 August 1947, and concentrated on running courses for senior engineering officers. Then 13 MU was run down, as was No 3 Ferry Pool, another 24 Group unit based here.

Association with RAF Debden commenced on 20 October 1949 when its Empire Radio School became Signals Division, RAF Technical College, and which moved to Henlow on 8 April 1960. The Technical College Armament Division at Manby, once the Empire Armament School, moved to Lindholme in 1949, and in February 1951 to Henlow, where it became the Engineering and Armament Division, Technical College. Next month saw it again re-named, this time as 'Henlow Division'. No 1 Recruit Centre functioned here for a year, then returned to improved quarters at Cardington. It had held 1,000 men, and by the time it left had become No 1 Recruit Training Squadron. No 14 SofTT amalgamated with 10 SofTT Kirkham on 6 June 1952, and the space vacated was taken over by the Technical College, barracks being converted for technical training use. The Sergeants' Mess became students' quarters, while huts remaining from 1918 now provided modernised accommodation. From April 1951 the school offered courses in guided weapons technology.

Henlow's importance was such that it was raised to Group status, and from June 1953 was commanded by an Air Commodore. When the Debden Division arrived in 1960, Technical College embraced HQ and five Wings – Basic Studies, Technical Engineering, Electrical Weapons Systems, Engineering and Cadet Wing. This arrangement was short-lived, however, for on 31 December 1965 Technical College was amalgamated with the RAF College Cranwell.

Thenceforth Henlow diversified, undertaking RAF Museum storage and restoration tasks, had a part in the *Battle of Britain* film and in *Those Magnificent Men in their Flying Machines*. RAF bandsmen brought joyful notes to the camp, and the English Electric P.1 WG760 began guarding the buildings used by the Officer Cadet Training Unit, which arrived from Feltwell in 1966. By 1970, of only four original wooden huts remaining, three served for messing and social purposes. A much reduced Parachute Test Unit provided another link with the past. Officer cadet training ceased here on 24 April 1980, and a depleted station passed, on 21 March 1980, to the Radio Engineering Unit which, on 1 January 1975, had celebrated its 25th year at the camp, which it then shared with the Land Registry.

Henlow, caught up in a hi-tech world, nevertheless retains a recognisable image of a pre-war 'camp', which for thousands was 'where you learnt yer trade', did your 'square bashing', and worked staggering hours preparing aircraft vital for Britain's survival and that of a grudgingly grateful Malta. The western area is a smart RAF enclave, while the eastern section of the technical site thrives as a civilian transport depot, with many of the hangars being used in a pristine state. Close to the camp through road, the one-time SHQ remains in fine health, guarded by a Hunter that is overlooked by flourishing houses on the domestic site opposite. The four-grass-strip landing ground is used for Air Cadet flying, civilian flying events and free-fall parachuting.

**Main features:**
*Runways:* 210° 4,650ft x 150ft, 330° 3,900ft x 150ft, 280° 3,450ft x 150ft, Sommerfeld Tracking with grass overrun areas. *Hangars:* six Bellman, six General Service Sheds, nine Blisters, one Type D2 permanent. *Hardstandings:* thirteen Chevron (metal, temporary). *Accommodation:* Permanent: RAF officers 270, SNCOs 277, ORs 2,202; WAAF officers 18, SNCOs 28, ORs 849. Temporary: RAF officers 12, SNCOs 283, ORs 5,115; WAAF ORs 108.

---

# HESTON, Middlesex

*51°29N/00°23W 100ft asl; TQ118781. 1¼ miles SSW of Southall*

Back from his autumn break in Bavaria, and looking satisfied, 'the umbrella man' proclaimed 'peace in our time' while flourishing a piece of paper that he and the German Chancellor, Herr Hitler, had autographed. With it, wily old Chamberlain had saved face and time. Meanwhile Hitler, in a sense, had signed away his fate. Well, that is probably not everybody's judgement of events! Although his end was far from nigh, Chamberlain probably by chance had bought just enough time (at others' expense) to produce enough Hurricanes and Spitfires with which in 1940 to save the world from Nazi tyranny.

*An aerial view of Heston in the 1930s.*

That famous event took place upon the area now occupied by the BA Sports Club. Heston Service Station occupies another portion of Heston Air Park, and a sea of houses flows over other parts of the one-time place of fascination called Heston, conceived by Sir Nigel Norman and Alan Muntz. Private pilots as well as members of the Auxiliary Air Force, they had travelled around Europe. As a result they purchased land near the village of Cranford upon which, by the end of 1928, construction of an aerodrome had begun. As Heston Air Park, it was officially opened on 6 July 1929, and control was vested in Airwork Ltd, also formed by Norman and Muntz.

Heston's design was unusual. From the air its buildings in plan could be seen to be laid out to resemble an aeroplane, with hangars serving as shops in which aircraft for sale were displayed. A main complex contained the control tower, offices, Heston Aero Club house, a restaurant and, at the eastern end, a small hotel. The western part was occupied by the Airwork Flying School.

Heston was the first aerodrome in Britain to have a large concrete apron. The concrete floor of its hangar measuring 100 feet by 80 feet can still be found at what was the first private aerodrome to feature a Customs section, established in 1931. Floodlighting made night-flying feasible, and from 1936 it was backed by a Lorenz blind landing system. Progressive indeed was this state-of-the-art international airport.

*Customs and flying control at Heston 1933. (via Vic Atwood)*

*Also test-flown at Heston was the Fane G-AGDJ flying observation post.*

Its popularity fast grew, the Household Brigade Flying Club moving in from Brooklands not long after Heston opened. In 1931 it was both the starting and finishing point for the King's Cup Air Race, and by 1934 was a base for commercial airlines. First came Spartan Air Lines, those following including United Airways, Jersey Airways and Commercial Air Hire Ltd.

A handful of small aircraft manufacturers also used Heston as a manufacturing base in the 1930s and 1940s. The Comper Aircraft Company, which arrived from Hooton Park in 1933, was taken over to become the Heston Aircraft Company Ltd., and opened for business on 18 August 1934. Its products included six attractive Heston Phoenix high-wing, retractable-undercarriage light transports, the first of which flew on 18 August 1935. Far more spectacular was *G-AFOK*, the 2,000hp Napier Sabre-engined high-speed Type 5 Racer. During its first flight on 12 June 1940 it encountered an engine problem that led to a rapid heavy landing and a broken back.

Novelty, like the stream of light aircraft types first flown here, seemed ever-present. In September 1935 the Hafner AR III Gyroplane, an autogiro with features akin to a helicopter, made its first flight here. The Luton Minor also first flew from here, in March 1937, and the Taylor Watkinson Ding-Bat in 1938, after Heston had its share of Flying Fleas, with *G-ADMH* flying from the site in 1935. Chrislea Aircraft, born in October 1936, is probably best remembered for its novel Ace high-wing nosewheel cabin monoplane, which appeared in autumn 1946. A decade earlier it had devised its two-seat Airguard light monoplane. Chrislea functioned here until April 1947, when it had to move to Exeter. Also at Heston was the Carden-Baynes Aircraft Ltd, which, born in April 1936, built a novel light aircraft whose mainplane could swing through 90 degrees to ease hangar storage. In wartime imaginative ideas certainly did not desert Heston. Fane Aircraft opened for business in August 1939, and designed a two-seat, short-take-off pusher monoplane, the Fane Flying Observation Post, first flown in March 1941, by which time Taylorcraft had snatched the lead. After the war Heston Aircraft produced its light liaison twin-boom design, which was similarly outclassed.

The most important pre-war development here was surely the formation of British Airways Ltd on 1 January 1936, brought about by merging Spartan and United Airways. Heston was its London terminus until the summer, when it moved to newly opened Gatwick. Waterlogging of the latter in February 1937 brought British Airways back to Heston, where it remained until the outbreak of war.

Expansion continued. A main hangar was completed in 1935, and a new Customs and Immigration centre opened in 1938. Government interest was such that the Air Ministry backed Heston and purchased adjacent land to allow extension. What irony that a less developed aerodrome nearby ultimately became London's No 1 Airport. Storm clouds threatening Europe ended the plans.

Heston's place as a famed airport was assured when on 30 September 1938 Mr Neville Chamberlain, the Prime Minister, back from Munich, stepped from a Lockheed 12 on to that famous apron to wave his wretched – or worthwhile – piece of paper. He was, unfortunately, wrong about peace in our time. A year later, with war declared, Heston was taken over for use as Northolt's satellite, and in another year was being bombed.

Fame again shone through when on 24 September 1939 the Heston Flight formed, headed by the able Sidney Cotton. Before the war using a Lockheed 12 to visit Germany (like Chamberlain), and also

*British Airways Lockheed 12a G-AEPN at Heston in 1938. (Bruce Robertson collection)*

To five countries and three of the most important capitals in Europe British Airways fly daily. Entrusted with the carriage of His Majesty's mails to Scandinavia by day and night, British Airways have gained a notable reputation for speed, comfort and operational efficiency. We would welcome the responsibility of flying you to Paris in 90 minutes, or to Amsterdam, Hamburg, Copenhagen, Malmö and Stockholm in a few hours of comfort.

**BRITISH AIRWAYS LTD**

## *BRITISH AIRWAYS*

TERMINAL HOUSE, VICTORIA, LONDON, S.W.I.    Phone: SLOANE 6091

as a civilian, he illegally photographed assorted foreign objects, realising the importance of photo-intelligence in any future conflict. Although not the originator, he was a pioneer of the modern style of such activity. Indeed, on 22 March 1939 a decision had been made to form a PDU – when practicable. Cotton told Air Marshal Tedder just after the start of the war that he felt certain that photographic intelligence would have a vital role, and requested the use of two Spitfires. Instead, two Blenheim IVs, standard reconnaissance aircraft, were delivered for his use from Heston, to where unit personnel had been told to report on 3 October 1939. Their base was in the hangar of the Airwork Flying Club, the Officers' Mess being in the Post Hotel. Fighter Command was in charge.

Blenheims were 100mph too slow and flew too low for what Cotton had in mind, so he arranged a meeting with Air Chief Marshal Lord Dowding at HQ Fighter Command, Bentley Priory, Stanmore. As a result two Spitfires slipped into Heston next day. Cotton's team fast removed guns and equipment, reducing the all-up weight so much that the Spitfires' speed rose from 360 to almost 400mph and their feasible flight track to more than 1,000 miles. Approval – without Air Ministry authorisation – was far from universal. As a suitable cover-up title Heston Flight became No 2 Camouflage Unit on 1 November 1939 with a detachment, the Special Survey Flight, operating Lockheed 12a *G-AFTL* (impressed on 15 December), a Hudson, Blenheim and Spitfires.

On 5 November a detachment of SSF took to France one Spitfire, one Hudson and the Lockheed 12a. The first trial flight on 18 November flown between base and Nancy proved fruitless due to cloud, but on 21 November very good results were obtained flying Trier-Saarlouis-Bitburg. The detachment returned to Heston on 11 January 1940.

Cloud over the German coast hampered reconnaissance, making it 10 February before photographs were obtained of Emden and the Schillig Roads. Clouds still abounded, and it was clear that fuel states would always need to be watched.

Meanwhile, 19 January had seen No 2 CU renamed the Photographic Development Unit, which promptly despatched to France two Flights holding a few Spitfires, and which operated between 10 February and 18 June 1940 as No 212 Squadron, while the home-based element operated between January and July 1940 via Horsham St Faith or Stradishall. During operational sorties from French bases fine pictures were obtained from more than 30,000 feet allowing Cotton to press for more aircraft and a team of professionals to extract the maximum information from the many photographs. During three months, RAF Blenheims had photographed 2,500 square miles of enemy territory with losses, while Heston's Spitfire detachment photographed 5,000 square miles of enemy territory during a mere three sorties. On 18 January 1940 the first operational flight from Heston – thwarted by cloud – was attempted using Stradishall as a refuelling stop, and as a result priority was given in January 1940 for the modification of more Spitfires. The first arrived at Heston on 7 February. More pilots were also posted in, but resistance to the activity remained.

To emphasise the potential, at 1100 on 10 February Flt Lt 'Shorty' Longbottom took off from Heston, encountered some cloud but still managed to photograph Emden and the Schillig Roads from nearly 30,000 feet. At 1520 he landed after photographing the battleship *Tirpitz*, his chief quarry. Even such worthy pictures failed to impress some.

On 18 June the PDU became the Photographic Reconnaissance Unit and was transferred to 16 Group, Coastal Command. Expansion came on 1 July when 'A' Flight was formed at Wick and 'B' Flight at St Eval. 'C' and 'D' Flights remained at Heston, each holding four Spitfires and a Hudson. 'E' Flight, added at Heston on 25 July, carried out development work using a Wellington for night activity and a PR Spitfire.

During May sorties at up to 33,000 feet were flown over Borkum, Nordeney and Texel, mainly to investigate naval activity. Flt Lt Wilson in P9308 very successfully reconnoitred Cuxhaven-Hamburg-Bremen on 18 May, three days after a Spitfire had force-landed short of fuel. emphasising

*DH 86A G-ACVY, with Heston's memorable gasometer in the distance.*

*Just completed a Heston-built Fairey Firefly FR4 TW693. (Fairey)*

the need to watch consumption rates. In June Blenheims and Hudsons penetrated well into France while Spitfires continued the naval watch. During July 57 out of 78 sorties from Heston were effective, producing 5,325 useful exposures, and in August 93 of 112 sorties to the Dutch coast were productive. Action was now concentrated upon observing German preparations for their invasion of Britain, as was explained when the King visited on 22 July.

It was on 19 September 1940 that disaster struck mightily. At 2248 a parachute mine exploded on the tarmac in front of the main hangar, the roof of which crashed down, damaging or destroying seventeen aircraft. Five precious PR Spitfires were damaged, as well as Cotton's famous Lockheed 12 and the Percival Q6 used by the Inspector General. Blast damaged the Operations Room, and a small hangar also suffered roof damage.

Operations were not halted, 100 of 129 sorties flown in September being effective. Included were eight on 7 September over Channel ports, and another eight on the 8th, both days being at the height of invasion alert. The daily average was five sorties.

On 16 November the Unit became No 1 PRU, and more bombing of Heston came in mid-November, 28 HEs hitting the site. By then the value of PR was only too obvious, and to provide more space and better facilities – as well as more protection – No 1 PRU was transferred to Benson in 16 Group on 27 December 1940.

Heston returned to Fighter Command and joined No 81 Group (Training). No 53 OTU was formed here on 18 February 1941 using Masters and Spitfires for pilot conversion. On 1 July the OTU moved to Llandow, leaving behind 'A' and 'C' Flights; on 9 June 1941 these had become the nucleus of No 61 OTU, which left for Rednal on 15 April 1942.

No 1422 Flight was formed at Heston on 12 May 1941 to investigate possible operational use of the Helmore Turbinlite, trial installations of which Heston Aircraft had undertaken resulting in Boston IIIs and Havocs IIs having searchlights installed in their noses. Wellingtons and Ansons served as target aircraft during trials. Relying upon giant batteries, they projected an intense narrow beam, which, it was hoped, would illuminate German raiders. Hurricanes flying at the Havocs' wing-tips could then attack the enemy. Improvements in AI radar soon nullified the need for Turbinlite aircraft. Development was then directed towards the Helmore rocket weapon carried under the wings of Hurricanes and tested operationally before the unit moved to RAE Farnborough in March 1944.

From October 1940 Heston Aircraft, part of the CRO, made use of various premises in the area. It built and, in the spring of 1941, flew the half-scale model of Boulton Paul's twin Vulture cannon turret fighter design. Repair work involved more than 600 Spitfires, and modification of Seafires and other types of naval aircraft was undertaken. The company fitted nitrous oxide engine power boost to Mosquito NF 19 night-fighters used against V-1s in 1944. This wide range of activity certainly made Heston a place of interest.

In April 1942 the station was returned to 11 Group to become a forward operational fighter station linked with Northolt. For two years a succession of squadrons – many Polish-manned and mostly flying Spitfires – participated in main-stream operations from Heston. The squadrons based here were:

| Squadron No | Period | Type |
|---|---|---|
| 316 (Polish) | 22.4.42-30.7.42 | Spitfire V |
| 302 (Polish) | 7.5.42-21.9.42, 29.9.42-2.2.43 | Spitfire V |
| 308 (Polish) | 30.7.42-1.9.42, 21.9.42-29.10.42 | Spitfire V |
| 303 (Polish) | 5.2.43-5.3.43, 12.3.43-26.3.43, 8.4.43-1.6.43 | Spitfire V |
| 350 (Belgian) | 1.3.43-5.3.43 | Spitfire V |
| 302 (Polish) | 1.6.43-20.6.43 | Spitfire V |
| 317 (Polish) | 1.6.43-21.6.43 | Spitfire V |
| 306 (Polish) | 21.9.43-19.12.43, 1.1.44-15.3.44, 20.3.44-1.4.44 | Spitfire V |
| 308 (Polish) | 21.9.43-29.10.43 | Spitfire V |
| 315 (Polish) | 13.11.43-24.3.44, 28.3.44-1.4.44 | Spitfire V |
| 129 | 16.3.44-30.3.44 | Spitfire IX |

Between 20 April 1942 and 12 December 1943 Oxfords and Tiger Moths of No 116 AAC Squadron operated out of Heston, where, between 29 October 1942 and 31 May 1943, No 515 Squadron's Defiant IIs flew carrying *Moonshine* radar-jamming equipment, from which *Mandrel* was developed.

In May 1943 the USAAF 27th Air Transport Group arrived, and by spring 1944 a variety of communications aircraft – C-64s, C-78s and L-4s – were calling. The Americans departed in October 1944. Like many stations, Heston had experienced the invasion build-up. No 405 R&SU, 83 Group, formed on 4 July 1943 to support Nos 126 and 127 Airfields, moved out on 14 August 1943. Working alongside was No 4 Aircraft Delivery Flight, Heston-based from 24 July to 21 September 1943, whose purpose was to keep 13 and 14 Groups supplied with fighters. HQ No 133 Airfield (ex-No 1 Polish Wing) formed on 1 November 1943 in No 18 Wing to control Nos 306 and 315 Squadrons, and moved to Coolham on 1 April 1944. On 2 February 1944, Heston-based, it had been designated to act as a Forward Airfield, Tangmere Sector, No 11 Fighter Group, because Northolt's fighters were mainly moved further south. It returned to Northolt Sector in June 1944.

The AEAF Communication Flight, formed on 13 December 1943, used Ansons, Oxfords, Proctors, Austers and other types. Raised to squadron status in June 1944, on 15 October 1944 it became SHAEF (RAF) Communication Squadron, and moved to Gatwick five days later. No 85 Group Communication Squadron was also here, between 3 June 1944 and October 1944.

Major change started in April 1945 preparation for Heston's transfer to Fairey Aviation, forced out of its Great West/Harmondsworth or Heathrow Aerodrome home because it was scheduled for

*The third prototype Fairey Spearfish TD 1, RA 363, at Heston in April 1947. (Fairey)*

development as London's premier airport. Three 'T2' Type hangars, added where the bombed hangar once stood, were for Fairey's use. On 13 January 1945 Heston was transferred to the Director General of Civil Aviation for operation on behalf of the Ministry of Aircraft Production, and Fairey moved in. Components for its aircraft were manufactured at Hayes works and transferred to White Waltham for assembly. Completed aircraft were flown to Heston for painting and fitting-out, then returned to White Waltham for acceptance testing.

Summer 1945 saw the arrival of No 701 Royal Navy Communication Squadron and its Harvards, Seafires and sundry other types for a stay extending to the end of December 1946, by which time the fate of the airfield had been decided.

Opening of Heathrow ended Heston's days, its demise being announced on 13 April 1946 by Lord Winston, Minister of Civil Aviation. Before Fairey moved out at the start of 1948 they had, on 7 December 1947, first flown the Gyrodyne *G-AIKF* and commenced air-to-air missile design and development.

To the very end Heston was home for the unusual. To a Proctor IV fuselage, Youngman full-span double slotted flaps were fitted, the aircraft, constructed by Alan Muntz as VT789/*G-AMBL*, being first flown on 5 February 1948. The last fliers from Heston were almost certainly gliders of No 144 GS opened there in May 1945 and closed in March 1948.

Part of the airfield was returned to agricultural use. The control tower and adjoining buildings survived until demolition in 1978, while the 'T2s' and sundry buildings on the eastern side became warehouses. The M4 motorway bisects magic Heston, much of which has become covered by housing, commercial and leisure premises.

Throughout is fascinating life Heston seemed forever beckoning anyone and anything that could excite aviation-minded folk. In October 1945 a privileged few came to enjoy a memorable display of Britain's latest naval aircraft. Geoffrey de Havilland Jnr delighted them by closely circling fast the famous nearby gasometer in a whistling Sea Vampire. For me one of the most unusual joys late in 1946 was a Northrop P-61 Black Widow, too near Heston's fence to photograph. Just what was that doing at Heston?

**Main features**:
Grass *Runways:* E-W 4,975ft, NW/SE 4,551ft. *RAF Hangars:* Six T2, six Blister. *Hardstandings:* Six twin-engine type, one frying-pan 100ft diameter, 33 Sommerfeld 60ft squares. *Accommodation:* RAF officers 69, ORs 340; WAAF officers 8, ORs 181. Many more billeted off site.

---

# HINTON-IN-THE-HEDGES, Northamptonshire

*52°01N/01°12W 505ft as; SP545370. 2¹/₂ miles W of Brackley*

Living up to its name, taken from Sir William and Lady Hinton who lived hereabouts in manorial style during the 1300s, Hinton was ideally placed for some very special activities. What the ancient incumbents would have made of the goings-on defies imagination! The airfield is best reached along a narrow road leading off the A422 about four miles west of Brackley. Sharp left and right turns lead into a lane wending its way to Walltree Farm, once part of the airfield. Hinton's remoteness must have played a part in its history.

The hangars have gone, but the control tower shell remains, as well as parts of the peritrack and runways. Opened in November 1940, 13 OTU's Bicester-based aircraft were the first to use it as their RLG. Between March and May 1941 the airfield was unsuitable for flying, but it resumed on 5 May 1941 when 'D' Flight 13 OTU placed its Anson navigational trainers here. Blenheims from Bicester also flew circuits and, in October 1941, 'A' Flight brought along Blenheim IVs.

In July 1942 Hinton switched to becoming 16 OTU Upper Heyford's satellite when Croughton was transferred to Flying Training Command. Hinton's alliance with 16 OTU's Wellington Ics was somewhat brief for, in April 1943, its 'A' Flight left Hinton for Barford St John. Then came a fascinating period.

July 1942 had also seen the formation at Upper Heyford of 1473 Flight, which used Finmere for assorted radio trials. No 1478 Flight, an offshoot, formed at Hinton on 15 April 1943 as part of 26 Group's Signals Development Unit. The Flight's highly specialised role involved flying five Whitley flying radio stations over a battle area while assault troops went into action, like a J-Stars or Sentinel of today. Equipped with point-to-point VHF R/T, M/F D/F and R/T, radio contact with forward troops was possible and details of the battle situation could be relayed to rear areas. All was exceptionally advanced in concept.

The prototype battlefield control radio station Whitley V, BD286, was with 1473 Flight Finmere when 1478 Flight formed, whereas operational aircraft came to Hinton where a Marshall of Cambridge working party fitted the radio installations. The first two aircraft modified, Z6977and Z9165 – the latter a veteran from 51 Squadron – were set aside for training; Z6977, with aged Merlin engines, was soon unusable.

The Whitley, excellent for the intended purpose and being able to operate from quite small airfields even at maximum weight, which carried radio gear such as Types 9, 11 and 14 Radio Stations. Eventually only the Type 9 was fitted because the weight of petrol-driven generators was high. Apart from numerous radio aerials, the Whitleys externally resembled normal examples.

On 18 April 1943 BD286 arrived at Hinton, and was soon joined by BD203, LA854, LA887 and LA889. Long-range tanks were installed in their bomb bays and, early in June 1943, the four operational examples left for Portreath. They vacated Cornwall on 12 June for North Africa, but LA889 encountered trouble over the Bay of Biscay, as a result of which some radio gear was discarded. After refuelling at Marrakech it left to help control a ground situation from off Algiers, a task also undertaken by others that reached the operational area via Casablanca and Oran. By patrolling off-shore, early warning of marauding German bombers could be given; Whitleys are not generally associated with the Mediterranean war, making this a rare event. The Flight consolidated itself at Maison Blanche before disbanding on 30 June 1943.

A taste for the unusual remained Hinton's hallmark to the end of its active military days, with the Signals Development Unit on the station using mainly Ansons and Beaufighters. The Unit, which formed from BADU in 92 Group, took over No 1478 Flight and three BADU Flights, retaining 'A' Flight's Masters, Oxfords and Ansons at Hinton to help develop beam and ground controlled approach (GCA) systems. 'B' Flight's Ansons undertook calibration duties from Bicester. On 16 April 1943 the SDU joined 26 Group. At the end of August 1943 all three Flights assembled at Hinton, and on 24 September 'A' Flight moved to St Eval for further GCA development. On 29 July 1944 SDU disbanded, its personnel moving to SFU Honiley, leaving Hinton under care and maintenance. From November 1946 to November 1947 a sub-site of 246 MU, Bicester, it undertook MT servicing.

Private flying continues from Hinton-in-the-Hedges, where the operator is Mr R B Harrison. Daily activities include Hinton Skydiving, gliding and flight training. A 700m x 18m section of asphalt runway 06/24 remains in use.

**Main features:**
*Runways:* 244° 5,700ft x 150ft, 280° 3,300ft x 150ft, 326° 3,300ft x 150ft., concrete and tarmac. *Hangars:* one T2, one B1, one Blister. *Accommodation:* RAF officers 56, SNCOs 95, ORs 594; WAAF officers 2, SNCOs 8, ORs 200.

## HONEYBOURNE, Hereford and Worcester

*52°04N/01°50W 178ft asl; SP025300. 4³⁄₄ miles E of Evesham*

Follow the A46 Stratford road from Broadway and at Weston Subedge turn sharp left for Honeybourne. Turn left at the first crossroads and the remains of Honeybourne airfield are to the right.

Honeybourne, a typical 1940-41-style parent station, featured mainly temporary brick buildings supplementing a metal Type J hangar, the presence of which shows the station's 1939 planning origin. Little remains of the typical triple runway layout and the thirty circular dispersal pads, laid mainly on the west and north-west airfield perimeters. Backing the Type J hangar were four T2s (12705/40 pattern). A few wartime Laing huts (14887/40) for thirty-two men and an NCO survive. Identical buildings served as Officers' Quarters, each containing only six officers and 'two servants'. Maybe officers physically required more space than slimmer other ranks! In like buildings resided up to twenty-seven air women and a lady NCO – strange, because one would have expected WAAFs to be of more slender form than airmen, generally!

The main gate, its position still recognisable, was on the eastern side. Two standard aviation fuel dumps each contained 72,000 gallons, and there were three EWS tanks, each of 20,000-gallon capacity. In front of the hangars were four ground defence features known as 'Oakington Pillboxes'.

As early as 3 December 1940 Honeybourne was earmarked for a 6 Group OTU with nearby Long Marston as its satellite. October 1941's RAF arrival was therefore unexpected, for the opening party was of 44 Group, which undertook aircraft ferry duties. During November 1941 Kemble's Service Ferry Squadron became the Ferry Training Unit, which moved to Honeybourne in mid-November. On 18 November training began of crews to ferry Hudsons and Beauforts. For company the FTU had 1425 Flight, formed at Prestwick on 30 October 1941, to run a passenger and freight ferry service to the Middle East, with a trans-Africa route preceding return from West Africa. No 1425 Flight moved to Honeybourne on 16 November 1941, established at three rare Liberator Is. The trio of crews trained to fly them were commanded by Sqn Ldr N M Boffee DFC. Since all the occupants were of Ferry Command, they were lodgers at Honeybourne, and remained until the intended OTU formed. Flying training using Liberators commenced on 25 November 1941, crews for 1425 Flight being aided by experienced members of 120 Squadron, several of whose aircraft at Prestwick, awaiting conversion into maritime Liberators, would now serve as transports.

On 1 January 1942 AM913, Honeybourne's first Liberator I, arrived. Five days later came AM922, not fully equipped as a transport. The intention was to start operations on 15 December 1941, but now there was more delay because snow fell throughout January, allowing flying on only fourteen and a half days that month. February proved little better.

Liberator services operated out of Hurn, to where AM913 was despatched on 9 January 1942. It set off the following evening with a modest load of one passenger and 2,500lb of freight. Return to Hurn came on 28 January 1942. AM919 had arrived at Honeybourne on 24 January 1942, but flew no operational sorties while based there. AM922 flew the second service, leaving Hurn on 10 February. Before the Liberators went to Hurn each flew a height/range fuel consumption trial to ensure sufficient endurance.

During March, while the Liberators undertook lengthy journeys, the FTU trained crews to ferry aircraft overseas. On 10 March 1942 the unit began moving to Lyneham, finally vacating Honeybourne on 28 March. No 1425 Flight moved to Lyneham in early April 1942 when that station also took on Hurn's role.

As the FTU moved out, 24 OTU came alive. Officially formed on 15 March 1942, it equipped not with the expected Wellingtons but with Whitley Vs, the first five of which arrived together. By the end of April the unit, with only ten Whitley Vs and two Ansons, was unable to participate in the Cologne 1,000-bomber raid. Strength increased in May-June, sufficient Whitley Vs being available for sixteen to participate in the Bremen 'Thousand Plan' raid. It was a costly venture, for three Whitleys were lost, including BD379, which came down in the Netherlands. Mainly fire bombs had been carried, 50,494lb of small incendiaries, 288 30lb incendiaries and twenty-two HE bombs. On 31 July 1942 24 OTU's Whitleys took part in the *Grand National* attack on Dusseldorf and lost two of their number.

Output from 24 OTU, nominal holding fifty-four Whitleys and five Ansons, was fourteen crews per fortnight. On 21 June 1942 Battle L5416 was assigned for target-towing, two Lysanders joining it in August. The Battle departed in October, Lysander strength being maintained until May 1943.

On 14 October 1942 three C-47s flying from Burtonwood to Keevil brought excitement when they landed due to bad weather. A more pernicious fate overtook Whitley EB389 on the night of 9/10 December 1942, when it exploded in flight and fell in pieces near Shipston-on-Stour.

*Wellington X
TY-C of No 24
OTU, 1944.*

Spasmodically during 1943 Whitleys dropped leaflets over France. Five such sorties were flown in January before bad weather halted such activities. Returns to HQ 91 Group in March showed the average unit strength as fifty-five Whitleys, eleven Ansons, a Defiant and two Lysanders. The target-towers were replaced on 28 April 1943 by three Martinets. Doubtless the latter were as disappointed as we are not to have been at Honeybourne on 11 March 1943 when a rare Brewster Bermuda FF557 put down for refreshment on its way to trials at Boscombe Down.

Five *Nickels* were flown in May, then, on 2 June 1943, the inevitable happened. High ground to the east of Honeybourne is very apparent, and hillside crashes were inevitable. Such a fate befell Z6639 in cloud and rain at night and the crew perished.

Six *Nickels* were flown in June and seven in July, for the loss of one aircraft. By August 24 OTU was using a few Whitley VIIs surplus to Coastal Command's needs. Establishment was still set at forty IE plus fourteen IR Whitleys. To enjoy the sight of them – and doubtless write down their serials and maybe peep in to see if there were fat WAAFs in each barrack block – the AOC winged in on 21 August 1943 in another Monarch, W6464, once *G-AFJZ* and now of 91 Group CF. Ten days later a visitor arrived in more alarming circumstances. On approach, Wellesbourne Wellington XN-I-HE356 hit electric cables near Honeybourne church and burst into flames. The crew miraculously escaped, only one having serious injuries.

By September 1943 Whitleys were participating in *Bullseye* exercises. BD368 failed to return from *Nickelling* on 3 September 1943, 91 Group's only operational loss that month. In October twelve leaflet-dropping sorties were despatched and ten in November. Of 91 Group's December effort of seventy-eight *Nickels*, twenty-one were flown by 24 OTU, which still had some Whitley VIIs. In January 1944 the OTU flew sixteen of the Group's eighty-five *Nickel* sorties and dropped 756,880 leaflets out of the Group total of 9,871,258. A *Bullseye* with Green Park in London as target, flown on 21 January 1944, turned out to be quite hazardous. It was to end with a demonstration drop of target indicators at Otmoor. Six OTUs took part, and 24 OTU was flying at 13,500 feet when the Luftwaffe opened operation *Capricorn*, the surprise mini-Blitz on London. Great confusion ensued, especially when the raiders dropped lots of *Duppel*, strips to distort British radar activity, ground and airborne.

Adding incentive to *Nickelling*, OTUs were authorised in March 1944 to carry bombs. Both 10 and 24 OTU were each to make a dozen Whitleys available, half carrying SBCs and the remainder each carrying four 500lb GP HEs in addition to leaflets. In March 1944 24 OTU flew twenty *Nickel* sorties, and on 24/25 March took part in a *Bullseye* routed over France, a diversion for an attack on Berlin.

On 8/9 February 1944 Whitleys dropped *Nickels* over Versailles and Paris, one crew having a lucky escape when their aircraft was badly damaged by enemy fire. With wings, rear turret and fuselage shot about, the aircraft was guided safely to Exeter. Poor weather cut *Nickel* sorties to eleven in April, additional to *Bullseyes* and two diversion sweeps flown over the North Sea.

Front-line bomber squadrons had bidden farewell to the Whitley in 1942, and now its time was ending in the OTU. With ample Wellingtons available, the switch started in April, establishment changing to fifty-four Wellington III/Xs with effect from 20 April 1944. By June strength equated establishment, and four Hurricane IVs replaced the Martinets of 'C' Flight, although it was August before the latter left. The last Whitley vacated 24 OTU in July, leaving Ansons to soldier on to the end of the year.

Disbandment of the OTU came on 24 July 1945, and Wellingtons of 21 OTU, nudged out of Enstone due to runway work, replaced it at Honeybourne from 11 August to 6 October 1945. Then the station passed to 8 MU control as 107 Sub Storage Unit. With so many Wellingtons to tend, 8 MU placed many here. In January 1946 fifty Hamilcar gliders – some powered Mk Xs – joined them, awaiting the inevitable. Honeybourne is now largely agricultural land.

**Main features:**
*Runways:* 233° 1,400ft x 150ft, 292° 3,900ft x 150ft, 171° 3,300ft x 150ft, concrete. *Hangars:* one Type J, four T2. *Hardstandings:* thirty frying-pan type. *Accommodation:* RAF officers 298, SNCOs 389, ORs 1,216; WAAF officers 10, SNCOs 9, ORs 363.

## HOLYWELL HYDE (PANSHANGER), Hertfordshire
See **PANSHANGER**

## HORNCHURCH (SUTTON'S FARM), Essex

*51°32N/00°12E 36ft asl; TQ530845. 2 miles SE of Romford*

Thoughts of Hornchurch surely head towards that horrendous, well-recorded moment when bombs burst among its Spitfires racing in desperation across the green field to help save their homeland. Overlooked, perhaps, is the fact that on the first night of the war Hornchurch Spitfires were the first ever to be scrambled. When victory looked quite possible, on to that same Hornchurch big lawn came the first superlative Spitfire IXs to enter the front line, not long after famous 'Paddy' Finucane, Hornchurch Wing Leader, failed to return. If one had to name *the* Spitfire operational station, then it might well be Hornchurch, for it fielded them and some of their most famous pilots almost throughout the war, only to eventually crumble into little more than oblivion and rich memory. Its fame is, of course, not only built upon Spitfires, for it was when flying from here in 1916 that Lt Leefe-Robinson was first to destroy a German airship over Britain. Hornchurch is, indeed, hallowed territory.

The land around Mr Tom Crawford's Sutton's Farm being judged suitable for London air defence landing ground LG No 11, a requisition order was issued in 1915 and the selected site, 900 feet across, was acquired. The distinctive title Sutton's Farm was adopted and, with two small canvas hangars in situ, a BE 2c flown by 2/Lt H MacD O'Malley, No 13 Squadron Royal Flying Corps, became the first aircraft to land here, on 3 October 1915. On 13/14 October the first night operational sortie was flown by a BE 2c flown by 2/Lt John C Slessor, who had taken off to challenge one of five German airships wishing to damage London. For many months a pair of BE 2cs, some from 17 (RA) Squadron, were held on 'the Farm' at night readiness.

By 1916 Sutton's Farm was part of the 18th Wing controlling London's air defences, and on 15 April 1916 No 19 (RA) Squadron became 39 (Home Defence) Squadron, whose 'B' Flight, based here, held eight aircraft including BE 2cs, BE 12s and a Bristol Scout. The Flight was active almost immediately, Capt A T Harris (future C-in-C Bomber Command) engaging without success the LZ 97 on 25/26 April. At the grass field, wooden hangars, workshops and personnel accommodation were in place.

Although many night patrols were flown, not until 2/3 September 1916 was a kill made, Lt W Leefe-Robinson being first to achieve it. He was about to land at Sutton's Farm when he noticed a red glow to the north-west. Investigating, he soon came across a Schutte-Lanz SL 11 bombing a London suburb. On his third attempt, and using the latest ammunition, he set fire to the airship, which at 0225 fell at Cuffley, Hertfordshire. For courageous attacks he was awarded a Victoria Cross. More success came on 23/24 September when 2/Lt Frederick Sowrey shot down the L 32 near Billericay, and 2/Lt Brandon destroyed the L 33.

Gotha day raids in summer 1917 had marked effects upon Sutton's Farm. BE 12s and AW FK 8s were in June 1917 introduced into 'B' Flight 39 Squadron. Fighters possessing more agility were needed, like the Sopwith Pups of 66 Squadron, which passed through between 8 and 10 July on the way to France. To strengthen home defence the Pups of No 46 Squadron flew in from France on 10 July to operate from Sutton's Farm until 30 August. Impressive and highly trained, No 46 fielded outstanding pilots including Major Philip Babington and J T B McCudden. 'B' Flight No 39 Squadron, still operating BE 2c/es as well BE 12s and a few SE 5s, left in late July to consolidate at North Weald, making way for Pups of 61 Squadron. SE 5as replaced them, and later Camels. On 20 September 1917 78 Squadron bolstered the day-fighting force, its FE 2ds and Sopwith 1¹/₂

*Gladiators of 65 Squadron up from Hornchurch.*

*Gladiator pilots of 54 Squadron practice 'Scramble!'*

Strutters being replaced by Camels in December 1917. Both new squadrons operated frequently in the defence of London until 19/20 May 1918 when SE 5as of 61 Squadron and 78 Squadron's Camels flew the last operational patrols from Sutton's Farm during a night that saw thirty Gothas setting out to bomb London, whose protection was always the reason for the station's existence.

No 189 (Night Training) Squadron, here since 1 April 1918, disbanded on 1 March 1919. No 78 Squadron, re-equipping with Sopwith Snipes as the war ended, disbanded on 31 December 1919, No 61 Squadron on 13 June 1919.

Sutton's Farm then closed, its buildings demolished and the territory returned to its former state. By 1921 the aerodrome – apart from a few scattered sheds – was farmland.

The Steel-Bartholomew 1922 defence policy review identified needs for a fighter station near Romford within the capital's protective ring, and Sutton's Farm, as before, was ideally placed. November 1922 saw its suitability reviewed as a permanent aerodrome. Mr Crawford, having only recently recovered his land, and being unsupportive, caused a further search to be initiated. With no feasible alternative, New College, Oxford, from whom the land was rented, agreed to sell 120 acres on the understanding that Mr Crawford be allowed to keep farmland and his home north of the landing ground. The Air Ministry agreed and ordered construction of a Permanent RAF Station to commence.

Technical and domestic areas were earmarked for the site's north-western corner, the landing ground spreading over former building positions. Two metal A Type Sheds were erected in an arc, having central space for a third, which, in the mid-1930s, was a C Type (225 feet long) Aircraft Shed, steel-framed, brick walled and featuring a wood and metal serrated-type roof.

On 1 April 1928 RAF Sutton's Farm re-opened with the arrival of Siskin IIIas of No 111 Squadron commanded by Sqn Ldr Keith Park MC DFC, who, during the Battle of Britain, was Air Officer Commanding No 11 (Fighter) Group, which included the Hornchurch Sector. That latter name, Hornchurch, superseded Sutton's Farm on 1 June 1928, to avoid confusion with RAF Sutton Bridge.

Hornchurch became a two-squadron station on 15 January 1930 when No 54 Squadron re-formed to fly Bulldog IIas. At the start of 1931 No 111 Squadron also acquired Bulldog IIas, taken to Northolt on 12 July 1934 to make space for No 65 Squadron, re-formed at Hornchurch on 1 August 1934 and equipped with Hawker Demons; a year later more Demons arrived. No 74 Squadron, reinforcing the RAF at Hal Far during the Italian-Abyssinian war, on 21 September 1936 commenced its lengthy, distinguished tenure of Hornchurch. No 65 Squadron re-equipped with Gauntlet IIs in July 1936, No 54 Squadron in September 1936, and No 74 in April 1937. All three squadrons now used Gauntlets.

Control of Hornchurch passed from the Fighting Area to No 11 (Fighter) Group, HQ Hillingdon House, Uxbridge, on 1 May 1936. The latter became part of Fighter Command, formed on 14 July 1936. Hornchurch, a Sector HQ, was a major element of the evolving fighter defence layout.

In April 1937 No 54 Squadron re-armed with Gladiator Is, No 65 Squadron following suit in June 1937. Advances more fundamental came in February 1939 when Spitfires reached Hornchurch for 74 Squadron; No 54 Squadron re-equipped with them in March and No 65 in April 1939. Hornchurch then held a highly formidable fighting force. On 11 August 1939, with the war clouds gathering, plans to safeguard that asset were practised when No 54 Squadron quickly dispersed to Rochford, pretending to evade German bombing of Hornchurch. By the end of August the station's buildings had been camouflaged.

*Sopwith Camel C8368 of No 189(N) Training Squadron at Sutton's Farm in October 1918. (Bruce Robertson collection)*

From 1 September 1939 the Station Operations Room was manned twenty-four hours a day. Ironically, almost traditionally, it was at night – 0250 on 4 September – that the station's first 'scramble' order was given and six Spitfires of 74 Squadron were sent to engage 'raiders' (actually straying Whitleys) reported off Essex. The second scramble came at 0640 on 6 September when 74 Squadron was ordered to respond to a He 111 fifty miles out in the Thames Estuary. On a weather reconnaissance, it so soon swung north and turned for home off Cromer, allowing the public all-clear to sound over a very wide area at 0900. Meanwhile North Weald's No 56 Squadron Hurricanes had also set out to engage. No 74 Squadron Spitfires, mistaking two stragglers as enemies, promptly shot them down, while a third force-landed near Wherstead. The so-called 'Battle of Barking Creek' was certainly nothing to be proud of, and 'friendly fire' was not a term in those times.

There were further scrambles, but not until 20 November was there combat. German bombers were at this period flying reconnaissances over Sussex, Kent and the Thames Estuary, and fighters were scrambled to engage. At 1245 three of 74 Squadron came across what they identified as a 'He 111' at 27,000 feet, heading easterly about fifteen miles south-east of Southend. They fired, scored hits, and watched the raider follow erratic tracks. Eventually a He 111 crashed 100 miles off Felixstowe. Hornchurch claimed its first kill, and the enemy airmen were rescued by HMS *Gipsy*, soon to be sunk off Landguard Point by a German magnetic mine.

*Spitfire 1s of No 74 Squadron shortly before the outbreak of war.*

Tough combat followed the enemy's massive onslaught of 10 May 1940 during operations from forward bases – mainly Rochford and Manston. On 13 May Sqn Ldr Leathart was the first from Hornchurch to engage a Bf 109, but such engagements soon became daily events, both over the English Channel and France. On 25 May 1940 No 19 Squadron, on detachment, undertook protection patrols from Hornchurch during operation *Dynamo*, before returning to Duxford on 6 June.

Throughout June the Hornchurch squadrons were busy; for example, on the 17th No 54 patrolled Abbeville and engaged three Ju 88s. Many sorties were reconnaissances over French airfields, and No 54 Squadron logged 330 operational flying hours in June. In July the battle area was closer, as German aircraft attacked English Channel shipping. On 12 July No 54 Squadron twice engaged Do 17s (some escorted by Bf 109s) trying to bomb ships off Dover. Ferocious fighting took place on 25 July, 'Black Thursday', first when Ju 87s and Bf 109s attacked shipping between Deal and Dover, then when RAF fighters were protecting two RN destroyers challenging German MTBs off Calais and the Luftwaffe responded. After an intensive period, No 54 Squadron retired on 31 July to rest at Catterick. No 74 Squadron carried out similar operations, both squadrons making plentiful use of Manston and Rochford.

HM King George VI visited Hornchurch on 27 June to decorate five officers. Sqn Ldr J A Leathart of 54 Squadron received the DSO, Flt Lt A C 'Al' Deere of 54 Squadron the DFC, Flt Lt A G 'Sailor' Malan of No 74 Squadron the DFC, Flt Lt R R Stanford Tuck of 65 Squadron the DFC, and Plt Off J R 'Dizzy' Allen of 54 Squadron the DFC. All destined to become well known, they had been much involved in recent battles. The King was visiting a rather small grass aerodrome encircled with an 18-foot-wide perimeter track. A few ground defence pillboxes were sited at strategic points around the perimeter, and four Bofors guns were ready to ward off the Luftwaffe.

There was much sharp, tough fighting before the main Battle of Britain attacks began in mid-August 1940. Hornchurch was attacked more than twenty times, the most memorable raids occurring on 24 and 31 August.

On 22 August 264 Squadron, flying Defiant turret fighters, was ordered south in case expected large formations of bombers made daylight raids on London. That would allow Defiants to be deployed in the intended bomber destroyer style. Instead, the squadron was ordered to Manston and immediately went into action in a style for which it was never intended. Before it could even adopt a battle formation three of the Defiants were shot down and Sqn Ldr P A Hunter, their leader, was last seen heading out across the Channel chasing a Ju 88. The saddened remnants of 264 were ordered to Hornchurch.

Throughout the morning of 24 August Luftwaffe fighters performed 'feints' over the Channel, trying to confuse British radar and cause fruitless scrambles, as large raids crossed Kent, including two forces bound for Hornchurch and North Weald. When Hornchurch came under attack by He 111s and Ju 88s, No 264 Squadron was in the throes of scrambling. Heinkel 111s of Raid H8 in formation at 15,000 feet aimed their bombs at the aerodrome, which in total was hit by only six. Predicted AA fire proved very accurate, the fourth salvo from battery N11 at 1541 scoring a direct hit on a He 111, knocking out its port engine before a fighter sent it to its doom at North Ockenden. AA Battery N20 seriously damaged the wing of another He 111. Most of the bombing involved areas around Dagenham, Upminster and Rainham, many single bombs falling widely. III/KG 53 retreated along the Thames Estuary minus five He 111s. But, Hornchurch had more to face.

*Spitfire 1s of 222 and 603 Squadrons on the field at Hornchurch in late August 1940.*

That well-known event of the period overtook Hornchurch on 31 August when a formation of II/KG 3's Dornier 17s arrived just as Spitfires of 54 Squadron were taking off to engage, so they bombed them. Flt Lt Deere (in R6895) and Sgt J Davis (X4235) had amazing escapes. Deere's aircraft had a wing and its propeller ripped off, then skidded for about 200 yards inverted. Plt Off E F Edsall's Spitfire (X4236) fared little better, although it did not overturn; he scrambled out and extricated Deere from his wreck. The third Spitfire, flown by Sgt Davis, was blasted into the air and crashed two fields away. AA gunners claimed one of the three Do 17s shot down – generally credited to 151 Squadron and 310 Czech Squadron – which at 1325 fell near Canewdon. Reconnaissance aircraft immediately sought evidence of the raid's effectiveness, one spying Do 17 being destroyed twenty miles off Bawdsey.

In the afternoon fighter-bombers of Erpro 210, attacking radar stations in Kent and Sussex, failed to stop them operating. The same unit and a few hand-picked Ju 88 crews made small-scale attacks on Hornchurch and Biggin Hill before in early evening another sharp blow was delivered. More than 300 enemy aircraft mounted six raids against airfields in Kent and near London, opposed this time by twenty squadrons. In ferocious fighting around Hornchurch, Spitfires of 54 and 603 Squadrons claimed two Bf 109s but lost three of their number. At Hornchurch most bombs fell wide, although two Spitfires on the ground were destroyed and an airman was killed.

Newcomer 222 Squadron first operated on 29 August when, with No 603 Squadron, it responded to 7 September's tea-time opening of the main assault on London and took part in the big fight on 15 September.

For its protection the Station Operations Room was, on 15 October, moved to more spacious accommodation at Lamborne Hall, Romford, where it functioned for the remainder of the war. That same day saw 603 Squadron operate with Spitfire Mk Is for the last time; on the 17th it began operating Mk IIs.

Squadrons using Hornchurch between 1 May 1940 and the end of 1940 were:

| Squadron No | Period | Aircraft |
|---|---|---|
| 54 | entire period, many detachments | Spitfire I |
| 74 | 31.9.36-27.5.40 | Spitfire I |
| 65 | 28.3.40-29.5.40, 5.6.40-28.8.40 | Spitfire I |
| 92 | 23.5.40-25.5.40, 9.6.40-18.6.40 | Spitfire I |
| 19 | 25.5.40-5.6.40 | Spitfire I |
| 222 | 28.5.40-4.6.40, 29.8.40-11.11.40 | Spitfire I |
| 266 | 14.8.40-21.8.40 | Spitfire I |
| 264 | 22.8.40-27.8.40 | Defiant I |
| 600 | 22.8.40-12.9.40 | Blenheim I(f) |
| 603 | 27.8.40-3.12.40 | Spitfire I (II 10.40) |
| 41 | 3.9.40-23.2.41 | Spitfire I |
| 64 | 10.11.40-27.1.41 | Spitfire I |

**NB** Squadrons made frequent use of Rochford satellite and Forward Airfields. No 54 Squadron was sited at Hornchurch 20.6.31-28.5.40, 4.6.40-25.6.40, 24.7.40-28.7.40, 5.8.40-3.9.40. An obvious odd-man-out was 600 Squadron flying Blenheim I(f)s. Hornchurch was its first war station, which it made use of between 2.10.39 and 16.10.39 and again from 20.10.39 to 29.12.39. Although it used Manston and Northolt, Hornchurch remained its main base to which it returned in August 1940 due to the heavy bombardment of Manston, and flew some night sorties before moving to Redhill.

Following the Battle of Britain, RAF fighter and day bomber squadrons engaged in operations over France and the Low Countries. The first *Circus* operation involved Hornchurch and took place on 7 January 1941, Spitfires of Nos 41 and 64 Squadrons providing cover to six Blenheim bombers of 114 Squadron attacking in France.

Hornchurch remained heavily guarded against possible invasion. Ground defenders numbering nearly 300 sometimes manned check points on adjacent public roads where identity cards, civil and military, needed to be shown. A 4.5-inch anti-aircraft battery positioned to the west of the airfield was backed with eight Bofors guns and RAF personnel using Vickers machine-guns.

By mid-1941 Sutton's Farm had become part of the aerodrome and was accommodating additional Spitfire dispersal standings. No 54 Squadron was here for the last time between 13 June and 4 August 1941. Then came Canadians, No 403 (RCAF) Squadron, which, after three weeks, moved to Debden. On 19 August Hornchurch Spitfires provided cover for the 18 Squadron Blenheim that, during a raid, dropped over St Omer an artificial leg for Wg Cdr Douglas Bader, shot down and captured – minus a leg – earlier that month.

Defensive operations and offensive escorts to *Circuses*, *Rhubarbs* and fighter sweeps (or *Rodeos*) were undertaken throughout 1941, including mid-summer escorts for heavy bombers making day raids and some other operations planned to reduce pressure on the USSR. Autumn saw the enemy introduce his Fw 190, providing a tough opponent for the Hornchurch Spitfire Vbs.

The squadrons rotated through Hornchurch in 1941, all flying Spitfires, were:

| Squadron No | Period | Type |
|---|---|---|
| 64 | 10.11.40-27.1.41, 31.3.41-8.5.41, 14-16.5.41 | Spitfire I (II 2.41) |
| 611 | 27.1.41-13.11.41 | Spitfire II (V 6.41) |
| 54 | 23.2.41-31.3.41, 20.5.41-11.6.41, 13.6.41-4.8.41 | Spitfire II |
| 603 | 16.5.41-12.11.41 | Spitfire V |
| 403 (Can) | 4.8.41-28.8.41 | Spitfire V |
| 64 | 17.11.41-31.3.42 | Spitfire V |
| 411 (Can) | | Spitfire V |
| 313 (Czech) | 15.12.41-7.2.42 | Spitfire V |

Throughout the year squadrons used Rochford forward base.

As soon as the winter weather faded, offensive operations – *Rodeos* and *Rhubarbs* – were resumed, with *Circuses* involving Boston bombers. German fighter-bomber activity against coastal targets increased, demanding rapid response often achieved too late.

A tragic event in June 1942 was the loss of the Hornchurch Wing Leader, Wg Cdr 'Paddy' Finucane, who died when his Spitfire V (BM256) was hit by ground fire, forcing it down in the English Channel.

Most of the squadrons at Hornchurch during 1942 flew Spitfire Vbs, but a great advance came when in July No 64 Squadron became the first to receive the outstanding Spitfire F IXb, powered by a two-speed-blower Merlin 61, which much enhanced its performance at higher altitudes. The squadron introduced the IX to operations on 28 July, and two days later, while providing top cover to Hurribombers of 174 Squadron attacking St Omer/Fort Rouge airfield, they claimed four Fw 190s during combat. The Hornchurch IXs were more than a match for them, and also provided essential support to USAAF B-17 raids, which were now commencing.

Autumn saw squadrons rotating through the station, a few exchanging Spitfire Vbs for Mk IXs. On average a squadron flew about ten operational hours a day. Defensive patrols were still needed, mainly to counter German fighter-bombers making hit-and-run raids. On a few occasions, when cloud was plentiful, a few German bombers ventured over Britain in daylight.

Squadrons based at Hornchurch during 1942, all flying Spitfires, were:

| Squadron No | Period | Type |
|---|---|---|
| 313 (Czech) | 6.3.42-30.4.42 | Spitfire V |
| 122 | 1.4.42-8.6.42 | Spitfire V |
| 64 | 1.5.42-20.7.42 | Spitfire V |
| 81 | 15.5.42-17.7.42 | Spitfire V |
| 154 | 7.6.42-27.7.42 | Spitfire V |
| 122 | 17.7.42-29.9.42 | Spitfire V |
| 64 | 28.7.42-8.9.42 | Spitfire IX |
| 340 (French) | 28.7.42-23.9.42 | Spitfire V |
| 453 (RAAF) | 23.9.42-7.12.42 | Spitfire V |
| 132 | 2.10.42-9.10.42 | Spitfire V |
| 122 | 3.10.42-16.11.42 | Spitfire IX |
| 122 | 9.12.42-18.5.43 | Spitfire IX |
| 350 (Belgian) | 8.12.42-1.3.43 | Spitfire V |

*Spitfire Vbs of 64 Squadron seeking protection in a revetment in May 1941.*

Offensive operations, *Rodeos*, sweeps, escorts and cover duties continued throughout 1943. Combat was less common, but on 8 April, when the Hornchurch Wing was near Abbeville, its ground controller warned Wg Cdr J R Ratten, Wing Leader, of enemy activity. Six Fw 190s fast dived into cloud before another eight appeared. Ratten ordered No 122 Squadron to hold up-sun at 27,000 feet, leaving 453 Squadron to attack. Brief was the encounter, but Ratten and Flt Lt Andrews each damaging an enemy aircraft. Only half the section was near enough to open fire before the enemy found safety in cloud. Even fleeting engagements were relatively rare due mainly to the Allied numerical superiority. The mock invasion of the Pas de Calais, operation *Starkey* of September 1943, failed to rouse the Luftwaffe into battle. An interesting participant, Hornchurch-based, was No 239 Squadron flying Mustang Is. The intention had been to place them at Detling, but Hornchurch was better able to hold the squadron, which carried out convoy protection during *Starkey* from its advanced base at Odiham.

The Hornchurch Wing became increasingly involved in pre-D-Day operations. On 15 November 1943 No 135 Airfield HQ formed and took control of Nos 66, 129 and 350 Squadrons before leaving in February 1944. No 412 R&SU arrived on 2 January 1944 to support 34 Wing, moving away into 84 GSU, also in February 1944.

During the latter half of 1943 squadrons here participated in escort and feint operations within large scale *Ramrods*, themselves sometimes distractions for USAAF heavy bomber raids. Often flying in broad sweeps around the main attack force, Spitfires protected light and fighter-bomber forces attacking airfields, bridges, rail and military targets, and by the end of 1943 flying bomb or *Noball* features.

Long-resident No 129 Squadron typically participated in such activities, occasionally engaging German fighters. Arriving in late June, it took over 453 Squadron's Mk IXs and on 1 July began operations by escorting P-47s over France. On 4 July Fw 190s were encountered and Flt Sgt Woodall was shot down. Many relatively uneventful *Ramrods* followed before dog-fights broke out on 27 September during *Ramrod 271,* a B-26 raid on Beauvais/Tille airfield, when twenty Fw 190s and some Bf 109s entered the fray. Further fighting took place on 3 October when B-26s attacking Schiphol were being given high cover. For such operations the Spitfires' limited duration, even carrying long-range fuel tanks, often meant dependence upon forward bases – as on 11 November, when the Wing provided 1st Fighter Cover over the Valognes area. In good weather two such operations were now being mounted in one day, for the tempo was ever increasing. So were tactics, for on 22 December the squadron flew at zero feet escorting a Mosquito strike on V-1 sites.

Weaving to escape flak, two Spitfires collided near St Saens. Not surprisingly, after intensive activity, the squadron retired to Peterhead on 17 January, there to rest.

Fighter squadrons based at Hornchurch in 1943 were:

| Squadron No | Period | Aircraft |
|---|---|---|
| 350 (Belgian) | 8.12.42-1.3.43 | Spitfire V |
| 350 (Belgian) | 13.3.43-15.3.43 | Spitfire V |
| 64 | 15.3.43-28.3.43 | Spitfire IX |
| 453 (RAAF) | 27.3.43-28.6.43 | Spitfire IX |
| 222 | 29.4.43-30.12.43 | Spitfire IX |
| 129 | 28.6.43-17.1.44 | Spitfire IX |
| 239 | 14.8.43-9.43 | Mustang I |
| 485 (NZ) | 18.10.43-21.11.43 | Spitfire IX |
| 350 (Belgian) | 30.12.43-10.3.44 | Spitfire IX |

January 1944 saw the arrival of 504 Squadron, and in March No 349 replaced Nos 66 and 350 Squadrons, but Hornchurch was nearing the end of its prime role, and fighter squadrons were taking up places nearer the invasion beaches. On 4 April, 222 Squadron bade farewell for the last time, and No 349 left a week later, then it was time for No 504 to go. The operational end came on 19 May 1944, when Nos 80 and 274 moved out.

In December 1943 No 20 (Fighter) Wing, 84 Group, formed to control Nos 135 and 136 Airfields, No 123 replacing the former on 10 March 1944. The Wing moved to Thorney Island on 9 April 1944, and was replaced by 25 Wing, superseded by 25 Sector, formed on 12 May to control 150 Wing, which left for France in August 1944.

Squadrons based at Hornchurch in 1944-45 were:

| Squadron No | Period | Aircraft |
|---|---|---|
| 504 | 19.1.44-30.4.44 | Spitfire IX |
| 485 (NZ) | 4.3.44-9.4.44 | Spitfire IX |
| 229 | 10.3.44-4.4.44 | Spitfire IX |
| 229 | 24.4.44-19.5.44 | Spitfire IX |
| 349 | 11.3.44-11.4.44 | Spitfire V |
| 274 | 24.4.44-19.5.44 | Spitfire V/IX |
| 80 | 6.5.44-19.5.44 | Spitfire IX |
| 278 ASR (det) | 13.11.44-15.2.45 | Spitfire V |
| 116 AAC | 2.5.45-26.5.45 (disbandment) | Oxford, Spitfire V |
| 287 AAC | 3.5.45-15.6.45 | Oxford, Spitfire V, Beaufighter |
| 567 AAC | 14.11.44-13.6.45 | Martinet |

Hornchurch operations room stood down soon after the last fighter squadron left. Perchance that made sense, because the V-1 attacks and much ground-based opposition would have made using the airfield hazardous. Many flying bombs came down in the Hornchurch area, the station being a base for a building repair unit attending to official needs.

In late 1944 Hornchurch became a major Personnel Despatch Centre, December 1944 alone seeing nearly 2,000 personnel passing through. After VE-Day many ex-prisoners of war passed through Hornchurch on their way to release.

From mid-November 1944 to mid-February 1945 a detachment from 278 Squadron carried out air-sea rescue duties, mainly assisting Allied bomber crews ditching off the East Coast. Also, from mid-November 1944 No 567 AAC Squadron used Martinets for local gunnery practice, then moved to Hawkinge on 16 June 1945 to become an APC. No 287 Squadron, which came in early May, left for Bradwell Bay to join an APC.

Its glorious days as a fighter station long over, Hornchurch transferred to Technical Training Command in June 1945. The PDC closed in 1947 and the aerodrome was placed on care and maintenance. A new lease of life began on 1 July 1948 when No 17 Reserve Flying School formed to fly Tiger Moths and Ansons; the school disbanded on 31 July 1953. On 7 December 1950 No 1 Civilian Anti-Aircraft Unit formed, taking over 34 Squadron's AA target provisioning for RN Chatham. Initially Short & Harland operated the unit, Airwork running it from 1 July 1954 until

*Tiger Moth N9215 of No 17 RFS*
*Hornchurch. (via George Burn)*

closure
on 31 December 1956. Still here was No 1959 Reserve AOP Flight, which moved in on 17 October 1955 and flew Auster 4s, 5s and 6s before disbanding on 10 March 1957. Also at Hornchurch was No 100 Wing, re-formed on 23 March 1956, which became the RAF Christmas Island Reinforcement Party and left for Lyneham in November 1956.

ATC gliding began with No 146 GS, opened on 17 August 1946. It became 614 GS on 1 September 1955 and moved to North Weald on 1 February 1962. No 142 GS, which arrived on 1 August 1953, disbanded on 1 September 1955. The Officers' Advanced Training School arrived on 25 July 1947 and closed on 25 October 1948. On 1 April 1952 the station became the Aircrew Selection Centre, a role it performed until the ASC moved to Biggin Hill on 9 April 1962. Hornchurch closed on 1 July 1962 when the holding party withdrew. Next year the site was auctioned and sold for a mere £517,000. Hoveringham Gravels bought the flying ground, a property developer the technical site. Once the gravel had been removed the quarry became a refuse tip, most surely a tragic end for such a distinguished and historically important RAF station.

Its buildings have been demolished, replaced by a housing estate whose roads carry names of the famous who flew from Sutton's Farm and RAF Hornchurch, while Mitchell Junior School, built where SHQ once stood, is named after the late R J Mitchell, whose fighter was such an important item here in the darkest days of 1940. West Havering School was built where once the Officers' Mess grandly stood, while Airport Way follows the route once taken by the perimeter track. We cannot preserve every tangible item from our great, unexcelled past, but we should most certainly tell our children to hold and maintain very firmly the heritage won at such great cost at such places as RAF Hornchurch.

**Main features:**
*Grass area:* N-S 4,800ft, NE-SW 4,800ft, E-W 4,800ft. *Hangars:* two Type A, one C (225ft), twelve Blister. *Hardstandings:* two Blenheim Type, ten Spitfire Type, seven frying-pan, seven 30ft square Sommerfeld. *Accommodation:* RAF officers 192, SNCOs 29, ORs 592; WAAF officers 24, SNCOs 38, ORs 728. Accommodation in 12.44 based upon the needs of Balloon Command.

## HORNE, Surrey

*51°10N/00°04W 190ft asl; TQ332435. 6½ miles SE of Redhill, to W of the A22*

Horne, one of the most northerly Advanced Landing Grounds, was laid out early in 1944 to provide a simple base for invasion support. Apart from two Sommerfeld 'runways' and dispersals, and the tented domestic accommodation, there was little else. Horne came alive on 28 April 1944 when 142 Airfield HQ arrived, accompanied (briefly) by Spitfire IXs of 56 Squadron. On 30 April Nos 130, 303 and 402 Spitfire Squadrons moved in. With the invasion near, the holding unit, under 85 Group 2TAF, was re-designated No 142 (Fighter) Wing on 12 May, which retained the three Spitfire Squadrons. On 18-19 June 1944 they left, No 604 Squadron and its Mosquitoes briefly joining the Wing prior to its departure for Hartford Bridge on 25 June 1944. Having played a brief useful part the airfield saw no further military use.

**Main features:**
*Runways:* NE/SW 4,800ft, NW/SE 4,800ft, both Sommerfeld Tracking, like the perimeter track. *Hangars:* four Blister. *Hardstandings:* thirty-two Sommerfeld aircraft parking pads. *Accommodation:* tented only.

## HUNSDON, Hertfordshire

*51°31N/02°08W 254ft asl; TL426138. Adjacent to the B180 about 3 miles NW of Harlow*

Construction of two-runway Hunsdon, an 11 Group station, began on 9 October 1940. SHQ opened on 22 February 1941, and on 3 May No 85 Squadron moved in from Debden. A detachment of a dozen 242 Squadron Hurricanes, commanded by Sqn Ldr Whitney Straight, joined them on 8 May for operational night-flying and training.

Shortly after No 85 Squadron arrived, conversion to Havoc night-fighters began. In July No 1451 Flight, equipped with Turbinlite Havocs, arrived. Next came Hurricanes of No 3 Squadron, which arrived on 10 August 1941 to operate as Turbinlite 'satellites'. The night Blitz over, trade was scarce.

On 1 July 1942 No 1530 Beam Approach Training Flight formed at Hunsdon, and moved to Wittering on 23 November 1942. In September 1942 No 1451 Flight was re-numbered No 530 Squadron, which received a quota of Hurricane night-fighters. With the Turbinlite outclassed by radar advances, No 530 Squadron disbanded on 25 January 1943. No 85 Squadron moved to West Malling on 13 May 1943, and the following day No 3 Squadron also left for West Malling. They were immediately replaced by No 157 Squadron's Mosquitoes from Bradwell Bay, joined on 1 June by No 515 Squadron, flying Beaufighter IIfs. No 157 Squadron flew intruder missions before leaving on 9 November, its place being taken by 410 (Canadian) Squadron, also flying Mosquitoes.

December brought more changes. No 515 left for Little Snoring and 100 Group on the 15th, and a fortnight later No 410 departed for Castle Camps, making way for three 2 Group Mosquito VI fighter-bomber squadrons, which landed on 31 December after attacking V-1 launch sites in France. Nos 21, 464 (RAAF) and 487 (RNZAF) came from Sculthorpe, Norfolk, to allow for a reduction in transit time to their operational scene. More *Noball* attacks followed, then, from Hunsdon on 18 February 1944 and led by Gp Capt P C Pickard, the three squadrons set out on operation *Jericho*, the breaching of the walls of Amiens prison. Mosquitoes of 464 and 487 carried out the bombing while No 21 held off in reserve. The prison walls were breached and 258 prisoners escaped – among them more than half of the patriots awaiting execution. Gp Capt Pickard circled to assess the success, and Fw 190s shot down his Mosquito. Also operating from Hunsdon was famous Mosquito IV DZ414 'O Orange', flown by Flt Lt 'Charlie' Patterson, responsible for the famous film of the show and many others.

To be even better placed for night interdictor operations connected with the invasion, mid-April 1944 saw the Mosquito FB VI squadrons leave for Gravesend, allowing No 410 Squadron back on 29 April for night patrols connected with Overlord.

One of the most unusual events of that period started at 2235 on 14 June 1944 when Flt Lt Walter Dinsdale and his radar-operator, Jack Dunn, set out in Mosquito XIII HK476 'O Orange' for their patrol zone, Fighter Pool No 1, at the beachhead. In clear weather they were vectored south towards reported bandits. Several contacts were obtained simultaneously and Dinsdale's controller called, "Bandits in your immediate area" and guided Dinsdale on to the slow-moving target. Closing in, Dinsdale lowered his undercarriage and flaps to avoid overshooting.

Closing to 1,000 feet, the target was identified as a Junkers 88, apparently carrying a V-1 above its fuselage, and flying slowly towards shipping off the Normandy beachhead. Dinsdale closed to 750 feet and opened fire on the starboard wing, causing a terrific explosion. Flames enveloped the cockpit and port wing before the enemy banked slowly to port, entering a steep diving turn before exploding on the ground at 2340 with a terrific explosion, some 25 miles south-east of Caen.

*A Mosquito NFII of 157
Squadron, Hunsdon, wearing
'night ranger' camouflage.*

Back at Hunsdon the crew maintained that they had shot down a Junkers 88 carrying a V-1. A few days later a *Mistel* was seen in daylight, revealing the true nature of the composite aircraft – a piloted Bf 109 'carrying' an unmanned, explosive-laden Ju 88, the first of which shot down had fallen to Dinsdale and Dunn.

On 17 June 1944 No 410 Squadron moved to Zeals, Wiltshire, and was replaced next day by No 409 (Canadian) Squadron, which remained until 23 August. A string of Mosquito night-fighter squadrons was subsequently Hunsdon-based, beginning with No 29 (June 1944 to February 1945) and followed by No 264 (July 1944 to August 1944), No 418 (August 1944 to November 1944), No 219 (August 1944 to October 1944), No 410 (September 1944), No 488 (RNZAF) (October 1944 to November 1944), and No 151 (November1944 to March 1945). All gradually moved forward, and in the first week of March along came Nos 154 and 611 Mustang Squadrons, and No 501 flying Tempest Vs.

No 154 disbanded on 31 March 1945, then Nos 441 and 442 Canadian squadrons, flying North American Mustang Mk IIIs, arrived to carry out long-range bomber escorts. Both Mustang squadrons moved out on 16 May 1945, and three days later the station was reduced to a care and maintenance basis. Hunsdon was finally abandoned by the Air Ministry on 21 July 1947.

**Main features:**
*Runways:* 086° 5,250ft x 150ft, 214° 4,200ft x 150ft, asphalt. *Hangars:* one Bellman, four Over Blisters, twelve Extra Over Blisters. *Hardstandings:* eighteen for twin-engined aircraft. *Accommodation:* RAF officers 100, SNCOs 140, ORs 2,000; WAAF officers 5, SNCOs 3, ORs 268.

## HUSBANDS BOSWORTH, Leicestershire

*52°20N/01°02W 505ft asl; SP645828. By A5199 10 miles NE of Rugby*

Ready for use by March 1943, this Class 'A' temporary wartime bomber airfield became active on 28 July 1943 as No 14 OTU Market Harborough's satellite airfield, when the parent, equipped with Wellington IIIs/Xs, moved out of Cottesmore. For just over a year it served in that role. On 15 June 1944 part of 14 OTU became the nucleus of a new late-war formation, No 85 OTU, administered by 92 Group. Having no satellite its three-quarters OTU establishment was set at thirty plus ten Wellingtons and four plus nil gunnery trainers, Master IIs replaced by Hurricane IIcs. The OTU disbanded on 14 June 1945.

The station's association with Market Harborough was renewed when between July 1946 and September 1947 it served as an aircraft sub storage site. Between May 1947 and 31 July 1950 it functioned as a sub storage site for 216 MU Sutton Coldfield, a variety of ground equipment items being kept here. Thereafter it saw no more military use. A grass strip 3,940 feet long and 295 feet wide is currently operated by The Soaring Centre for winch and aerotow gliding and microlight flying.

**Main features:**
*Runways:* 273° 6,000ft x 150ft, 223° 4,200ft x 150ft, 343° 4,200ft x 150ft, concrete with tar and wood chip surface. *Hangars:* four T2. *Hardstandings:* thirty-six spectacle type. *Accommodation:* RAF officers 213, SNCOs 469, ORs 854; WAAF officers 10, SNCOs 48, ORs 300.

The wartime control tower remains, with a helipad alongside.

## KELMSCOT, Oxfordshire

*51°42N/01°39W 230ft as; SU240980. 2¹/₂ miles ENE of Lechlade*

Kelmscot landing ground resulted from the requisitioning of land immediately north of Kelmscot village, and the result was an unusually L-shaped landing ground. Even in its prime only eleven buildings were erected here, grouped on the north-west side. Included was one Over Type Blister hangar (12512/41), a dining and recreation hut, and two Handcraft Type airmen's barrack huts (2886/42). A 36 feet by 16 feet Nissen hut served at the main dispersal area, and another (10024/41) as the control building in lieu of a conventional tower.

As Watchfield's RLG, Kelmscot was used for beam approach training. Two miles east of the Faringdon-Burford road was the outer marker, the inner marker being sited at the threshold to No 1 Flying Lane. The main beacon lay west of the landing strip. A 'flying lane' (vector 09/27) or grass landing strip 4,200 feet long and 150 feet wide was supported by two other very short flying lanes orientated roughly north/south and north-west/south-east. Airspeed Oxford pilots practising blind approach techniques used the long lane. For these purposes Kelmscot came into use on 17 October 1942, and remained available to No 1 Blind Approach School until the end of 1946. It was disposed of by 1948.

For a week in May 1944 Kelmscot was closed to flying and used as a drop zone for paratroops brought overhead in Dakotas of 46 Group. These last-minute practices for the Normandy assault commenced on 7 May 1944 with exercise *Noggin*, an early-morning drop by the 1st Polish Parachute Brigade jumping from eighteen Down Ampney Dakotas. Next day fifty Dakotas on exercise *Nark* – ten from each of five squadrons – brought troops of the 1st Polish Brigade in greater numbers. Release was lower and in one case from an aircraft flying too low, which resulted in casualties, four of them fatal.

Exercise *Noggin II* took place on 10 May, fifty Dakotas delivering troops of the 2nd Polish Brigade. Next day came exercise *Nark II*, forty-nine Dakotas providing the airlift in addition to five acting as pathfinders. Flying out of Down Ampney, the troops were again of the 2nd Polish Brigade. Exercise *Nark III*, held on 12 May, comprised twenty-seven Dakotas and two pathfinders, the aircraft being drawn from Nos 48, 233 and 271 Squadrons. Relatively small exercises, they made good use of Kelmscot.

**Main features:**
*Grass landing lanes:* E-W 4,200ft, NW-SE 3,000ft. *Hangars:* one EO Blister. *Hardstandings:* nil. *Accommodation:* nil

---

## KENLEY, Surrey

*51°18N/00°05W 557ft asl; TQ328580. 5 miles S of Croydon, off the A22*

"Kenley? No, never heard of it. Don't you mean Biggin Hill?"

The way to fame is usually through chance. Despite its action-packed history, well-known heroes, horrendous bombing, squadrons responding valiantly to the call, and a large share of offensive days, none was sufficient to provide Kenley with the fame that Biggin Hill enjoyed. The latter, though, managed public acclaim in wartime and knew Sir Winston well.

Constructed on the small area called Kenley Common, it lay a few miles from Croydon Aerodrome, which in the Second World War served as its satellite. Opened in summer 1917 as No 7 Aircraft Acceptance Park, it had fourteen paired hangars, each 170 feet long and 80 feet wide.

*A Bulldog IIa of No 3 Squadron. (R S Allam)*

*The Barrack Huts at Kenley Aircraft Acceptance Park in 1918.*

Prepared within those for service were DH 9s from Cubitt, Short and Whitehead; Dolphins from Darracq and Sopwith; Camels from Hooper; RE 8s from Napier; Salamanders from Sopwith; SE 5s from Vickers (Crayford) and Handley Page aircraft from the Croydon factory.

In summer 1918 Kenley also served as a mobilisation centre for squadrons intended for operations in France. First in was No 88 from Harling Road in April 1918, which stayed briefly until the 20th. No 108 arrived in mid-June and took its DH 9s to France on 22 July. No 110 moved in from Sedgeford on 15 June and, armed with DH 9as, left for France on 1 September 1918. No 91 Squadron re-formed at Kenley on 4 July 1918 and flew Dolphins, staying until 3 July 1919. No 95, which arrived on 1 October 1918, disbanded in November.

On 13 April 1919 No 1 Communications Squadron took up station to run, using F 2bs and DH 9s, a regular service between Kenley and Paris during the Peace Conference. It apparently became part of the Air Council Inspection Squadron, renamed No 24 Squadron on 1 February 1920. No 84 Squadron had just arrived, remained in cadre form and disbanded on 30 January 1920. No 39 Squadron, at half strength with DH 9as, arrived on 18 January 1922 and left on 8 February 1923.

There were other changes too. The Photographic Experimental Section had formed on 21 May 1918 from the Photographic Flight, Kenley, with a departure date uncertain. No 1 Group, which became Southern Area, moved to Kenley in December 1919, was renamed Inland Area in 1920, became HQ 6 Group on 19 May 1924, and disbanded into the Fighting Area on 20 May 1926. The Signals Co-operation Flight left Biggin Hill for Kenley on 15 December 1922, became the nucleus of No 13 Squadron formed on 1 April 1924, received F 2bs and departed for Andover on 30 June 1924.

Kenley had previously been chosen to be a Permanent RAF Station, and received a facelift while flying continued. On the southern approach to London, it was an obvious choice for a fighter station under the 1923 Steel-Bartholomew Plan. Evidence came when No 32 Squadron re-formed at Kenley on 1 April 1923, equipped with Snipes. In December 1924 it re-armed with Grebe IIs, and with Siskin IIIas in April 1928, then Bulldogs in September 1930. On 20 May 1926 the Fighting Area formed, absorbing HQ No 6 Group Kenley and taking control of fighter squadrons to be part of the Inland Area from 1 June 1926. ADGB controlled them from its Uxbridge HQ from 7 July 1926. Bearing no relationship to such activities, No 24 Squadron left for Northolt on 15 January 1927.

That made room for No 23 Squadron, which arrived from Henlow on 6 February 1927 using Gloster Gamecocks. In April 1931 it received Bulldogs, in one of which Douglas Bader, who had joined the squadron the previous August, lost his legs in a flying accident at Woodley Aerodrome. No 23 Squadron moved to Biggin Hill on 17 September 1932, No 32 joining them four days later, allowing Kenley to be closed for major reconstruction. Completion in May 1934 allowed SHQ Upavon with Nos 3 and 17 Squadrons and their Bulldogs to change stations.

The Italian attack on Abyssinia gave rise to an increasingly dangerous situation, and on 4 October 1935 No 3 Squadron was among those despatched to East Africa. In their absence No 2 Mechanical Transport Store opened in December and stayed almost to the outbreak of war in 1939. As for No 3 Squadron, it returned on 28 August 1936 to find No 17 Squadron flying Gauntlets; on 3 September 1936 it parted with its 'B' Flight, which became No 46 Squadron. On 8 March 1937 another new squadron, No 80, re-formed, then left for Henlow on 15 March. Expansion was coming with a vengeance, for on 1 June 1937 No 615 (County of Surrey) Squadron AAF formed as an Army Co-operation squadron using Audaxes and Hectors. No 3 Squadron in August 1937 re-equipped with Gladiators, and on 15 November 1937 moved to Digby. No 615's role changed when on 7 November 1938 it was reconstituted as a Gauntlet armed fighter squadron.

On 2 May 1939 No 3 Squadron, equipped with Hurricanes since October 1938, moved to Biggin Hill, and No 17 Squadron, still flying Gauntlets, moved to North Weald on 23 May 1939. By August the landing ground was all but out of use due to runway construction. Gauntlets of No 615 Squadron remained until 2 September 1939. No 56 Elementary & Reserve Flying Training School, surprisingly formed on 24 August 1939, hastily closed when war was declared, after receiving only six Tiger Moths and three Harts.

Building work on the enlarged aerodrome was being carried out by Constable, Hart & Co. Three pairs of hangars were demolished, leaving the GS Shed, permitting the two runways – north-west/south-east and north-east/south-west, measuring 3,000 feet and 3,600 feet respectively – to be laid. Leading off the perimeter track were twelve concrete revetment pens allowing for three single-engined aircraft per pen. Fuel storage totalled 35,000 gallons of aviation spirit – half the norm – 8,000 gallons of motor fuel, and 2,500 gallons of oil. Ammunition storage amounted to a million rounds of .303in.

LAA aerodrome defence comprised four 40mm Bofors guns manned by the 31st LAA Battery, two 3in guns manned by the 148th AA Battery, and a few Lewis guns. Along the north side in 1940 was the parachute and cable (PAC) installation, designed to fire a salvo of rockets that burst to release small wire-carrying parachutes that were intended to ensnare low-flying aircraft or dive-bombers.

With much reconstruction the station had been relatively under-used in the first months of the war. Then on 8 May 1940 253 Squadron arrived with Hurricanes, and operated over the Channel before moving to Kirton-in-Lindsey, Lincolnshire, on 24 May. Supplementing it came No 64 Squadron, which arrived on 16 May, followed by Nos 615 on 20 May and No 3 Squadron on 21 May, both flying in from Merville, France. Much battered, they retired to Wick on the 23rd. Next day 17 Squadron came for a stay lasting till 6 June 1940, when it took its Hurricanes to Hawkinge. From the start of the war Croydon was used as Kenley's satellite.

June found Nos 64 and 615 Squadrons based at Kenley, which was HQ 'B' Sector of No 11 Group with Gatwick and Redhill available for emergency use. Like so many other squadrons, those at Kenley moved almost daily to forward aerodromes from where they engaged in the fighting as the Battle of Britain unfolded, the first major battle – involving 615 Squadron – occurring on 14 July when Ju 87s and Bf 109s were engaged off Portland. Shipping patrols and operations off Kent predominated until the Luftwaffe began its heavy attacks on fighter airfields. Kenley's turn came shortly after 1300 on Sunday 18 August.

Slipping in very low over Newhaven, nine Do 17Zs of KG 76 attacked the aerodrome at 1322 from between 50 and 100 feet. The leading three bomber crews machine-gunned the station's anti-aircraft defences before dropping their bombs on the north-east part of the camp, leaving their colleagues to deal with the hangars and sick quarters. Five minutes later came the high-level force flying at 10,000 feet and arriving via Dungeness. Their bombs hit three hangars, the Station Armoury and Station Sick Quarters, and variously damaged eight aircraft (including six

*Hawker Demon K1954 traversing gun fighter of No23 Squadron.*

Hurricanes of 615 Squadron). Delayed-action HEs were also dropped. No 111 Squadron tackled the low-flying element, two Do 17Zs being brought down by parachute and cable defences, one crashing near the aerodrome boundary. About a hundred bombs fell, twelve personnel died and twenty were injured. No. 615 Squadron, responding as quickly as possible to the attack, was caught by rear-support Bf 109s, causing Flt Lt Gaunce to bale out near Sevenoaks. Plt Off Hugo was wounded and force-landed. Plt Off Looker's Hurricane, set on fire, landed at Croydon, Flt Lt Sanders was shot down near Kenley, and Sgt Walley was killed when he crashed at Morden, Kent. Kenley was now in a terrible condition and 615 Squadron's remaining aircraft diverted to Croydon. Conditions there were also extremely bad, more bombs having caused a serious fire. There was devastation in Purley Way and at the Rollason works. No 64 Squadron, which made many claims, was able later to land at Kenley, on a narrow flag-marked track. Fires still raged six hours after the raid, and phone lines were down, generally disrupting 11 Group activity at Kenley and at Biggin Hill, which had been similarly attacked. Both were vital Sector Stations.

Next day No 64 Squadron was replaced with Spitfires of No 616 Squadron, No 615 having to wait until the end of August for exchange with the Hurricanes of 253 Squadron. No 616 Squadron was moved to Coltishall on 3 September. Over the previous fifteen-day period four pilots had been killed, five wounded and one made a prisoner of war. Of the twenty pilots of 616 Squadron who had flown in, only eight flew out to Coltishall, from where 66 Squadron came as a replacement.

Kenley was repeatedly bombed through the remainder of the Battle of Britain, suffering damage and casualties. On 17 October nine aircraft on the ground were hit, and in November it received a night attack , two men being killed and further damage being sustained by a hangar, living accommodation and offices. As a result of the raids, Station HQ had been set up in High House, Whyteleafe Road, from where it moved to Petterswood in Torwood Lane in September 1941.

Kenley's own, No 615 Squadron, returned on 17 December 1940 and was joined early in 1941 by No 1 Squadron. Both arrived to take part in the day offensive begun in January over France. *Rhubarbs, Circuses, Rodeos* and a wide assortment of escort and patrol operations became part of daily life throughout the year.

Squadrons based at Kenley between January 1940 and 31 December 1941 were:

| Squadron No | Period | Aircraft |
|---|---|---|
| 615 | 4.40-France | Hurricane I |
| 3 | 20.5.40-23.5.40 | Hurricane I |
| 17 | 24.5.40-6.6.40 | Hurricane |
| 253 | 8.5.40-24.5.40 | Hurricane I |
| 64 | 16.5.40-19.8.40 | Spitfire I |
| 615 | 20.5.40-29.8.40 | Hurricane I |
| 616 | 19.8.40-3.9.40 | Spitfire I |
| 66 | 3.9.40-11.9.40 | Spitfire I |
| 501 | 10.9.40-17.12.40 | Hurricane I |
| 615 | 17.12.40-21.4.41 | Hurricane I |
| 1 | 5.1.41-7.4.41 | Hurricane I/II |
| 302 (Polish) | 7.4.41-29.5.41 | Hurricane II |
| 258 | 21.4.41-10.6.41 | Hurricane II |
| 312 (Polish) | 29.5.41-20.7.41 | Hurricane IIb |
| 602 | 10.7.41-14.1.42 | Spitfire V |
| 452 (NZ) | 21.7.41-21.10.41 | Spitfire II/V |
| 611 | 13.11.41-3.6.42 | Spitfire II/V |

**NB** Additional to the above, in 1940-41 the two Lysanders of 11 Group ASR Flight were sometimes held at Kenley. Squadrons made much use of Redhill.

At the beginning of 1942 Gp Capt Victor Beamish became Station Commander. A much-admired, popular leader, he frequently flew with the Kenley Wing, and it was he who discovered the German warships making the 'Channel Dash' in February 1942. Tragically, when flying with the Wing on 28 March and engaging enemy fighters, he and three other pilots were lost.

On 14 May 1942 the first Canadian squadron to be based here, No 402 (RCAF), arrived from Fairwood Common for a two-week stay, and on 8 July No 616 returned to Kenley where, in 1940, it had been so terribly mauled. In August No 402 Squadron returned, and No 308 (USA) Fighter

Squadron came for a taste of operations. It was soon replaced by the 4th FS, 52nd FG, which flew Spitfire Vbs on operations between 27 August and 11 September during its brief stay. No 401 (RCAF) Squadron arrived on 24 September, and on 14 October No 421 Squadron came for two days. No 412 (RCAF) Squadron arrived on 2 November, the all-Canadian Kenley Wing forming on 25 November.

Throughout 1943 Kenley was home to the Canadian UK-based Spitfire squadrons, which, from March 1943, had as Wing Leader the famous Wg Cdr 'Johnnie' Johnson, the RAF's top-scoring Second World War fighter pilot. The RCAF squadrons waged a highly intensive offensive campaign, including complex fighter support activity during *Ramrods*. Only one 'RAF' fighter squadron, No 165, was Kenley-based at this time, when re-organisation for the coming invasion of France was under way.

On 4 July 1943 the Kenley Wing was renamed 127 Airfield HQ, part of No 17 (RCAF) Wing, holding 403 and 421 Squadrons, which, on 6 August 1943, moved to Lashenden. No 419 R&SU formed on 24 January 1944 and, as 419 (RCAF) R&SU, was placed in 83 Group TAF, becoming the Group's GSU in February 1944 prior to moving to Hurn on 20 March. On 4 March 1944 Kenley Sector was amalgamated with Biggin Hill, the need for offence having closed much of the home defence structure. The last operation from Kenley was undertaken on 13 March 1944 when Nos 403, 416 and 421 Squadrons escorted bombers to Namur, Belgium. On 16 and 17 April those same last three squadrons at Kenley, Nos 403, 416 and 421, moved to Tangmere, leaving behind a small holding party. HQ No 17 Sector, controlling Nos 122, 126 and 127 Wings, formed on 12 May out of 17 (Fighter) Wing, and moved to Old Sarum on 6 June.

Since September 1939, the Kenley Sector had claimed 603 enemy aircraft and another 231 probables.

Squadrons based at Kenley between 1 January 1941 and April 1944, all flying Spitfires, were:

| Squadron No | Period | Type |
| --- | --- | --- |
| 485 (NZ) | 10.41-7.42 | Spitfire V |
| 452 (Aus) | 1.42-3.42 | Spitfire V |
| 602 | 4.3.42-17.7.42 | Spitfire V |
| 402 (Can) | 14.5.42-30.6.42 | Spitfire V |
| 611 | 3.6.42-13.7.42 | Spitfire II/V |
| 616 | 8.7.42-29.7.42 | Spitfire VI |
| 350 (Belgian) | 16.7.42-31.7.42 | Spitfire V |
| 111 | 28.7.42-21.9.42 | Spitfire V |
| 402 (Can) | 13.8.42-19.3.43 | Spitfire IX |
| 4 FS, 52 FG (US) | 25.8.42-13.9.42 | Spitfire V |
| 401 (Can) | 24.9.42-22.1.43 | Spitfire IX |
| 412 (Can) | 8.11.42-28.1.43 | Spitfire IX |
| 421 (Can) | 1.43-3.43 | Spitfire V |
| 416 (Can) | 1.2.43-29.5.43 | Spitfire IX |
| 403 (Can) | 23.1.43-6.8.43 | Spitfire IX |
| 411 (Can) | 21.3.43-7.4.43 | Spitfire IX |
| 421 (Can) | 5.43-8.43 | Spitfire IX |
| 165 | 8.8.43-17.9.43 | Spitfire V |
| 403 (Can) | 14.10.43-17.4.44 | Spitfire IX |
| 421 (Can) | -17.4.44 | Spitfire IX |
| 416 (Can) | 3.44-17.4.44 | Spitfire IX |

**NB** 1941 to 1944 saw the squadrons making plentiful use of Kenley's satellite at Redhill, with squadrons moving between the two bases and still operating as part of the Kenley Wing.

June 1944 saw Kenley close to flying, for the balloon barrage, flown to help engage flying bombs, was close. On 28 June a V-1 fell just south of the station, causing damage to houses and the station cinema.

Kenley was transferred to No 46 Group Transport Command on 1 July 1945, and on 1 August 1946 became HQ No 61 Group Reserve Command. Between March and April 1945 No 103 Air Disarmament Wing trained personnel for their task in Germany. Over the next eighteen months Kenley also served as a storage site for captured German and Japanese equipment, including parts of V-1s and V-2s. A small number of German POWs housed on the aerodrome helped to renovate buildings.

*Kenley and 64 Squadron under attack from a low-flying Do 17Z during the 15 August 1940 raid.*

The possibility of using Kenley for light commercial flying was explored, Westminster Airways operating a passenger service from the aerodrome in 1946-47. It shared the only available hangar with No 61 Group Communication Flight, formed at Kenley on 10 September 1946 and here until it moved to Biggin Hill. No 61 Group HQ was amalgamated with 65 Group on 1 February 1951 and emerged as 61 (Southern Reserve) Group on 1 January 1957.

Throughout the 1950s Tiger Moths and Austers of two Auxiliary AF Reserve AOP Flights, Nos 1957 and 1960 (parts of 661 Squadron), flew from the station. No 1957 formed on 1 February 1949, the other on 1 May 1949, and both disbanded on 10 March 1957. No 143 Gliding School and

*'Scramble' time for 64 Squadron at Kenley in the summer of 1940.*

*Anson C 12 PH774 RCE-H
of No 61 Group
Communications Flight
Kenley.*

London University Air Squadron made use of it, the latter between 12 January 1956 and 1 April 1957. In 1951 *Angels One Five* was filmed at Kenley, and in the late summer of 1955 Kenley was location for another film, *Reach for the Sky*, in which Kenneth More played the part of Douglas Bader.

Although RAF Kenley officially closed on 1 May 1959, Reserve Flights functioned here until 1964, when the sole remainder was No 605 Mobile Signals Unit, which had moved in on 26 September 1963. After it left on 21 February 1966 the station was placed on care and maintenance. Remains of the two General Service Sheds were completely destroyed by fire in October 1978.

Kenley's technical site passed to Army control, together with married quarters. Remembered as one of those stations where 'the Few' achieved immortality, Kenley has long been the home of Air Cadets No 615 (Volunteer) GS, formed out of 143 GS on 1 September 1955. Its gliders were destroyed in the major hangar fire of 23 October 1978, the School re-opening phoenix-like – and certainly in Kenley style – in 1981 and continuing to the end of the century.

**Main features (December 1944):**
*Runways:* 212° 3,600ft x 150ft, 312° 3,000ft x 150ft, asphalt. *Hangars:* one Belfast Truss GS Shed (two-bay), four O Blisters, four EO Blisters. *Hardstandings:* eighteen single-engine. *Accommodation:* RAF officers 142, SNCOs 2, ORs 478; WAAF SNCOs 3, ORs 122.

## KIDDINGTON (also known as GLYMPTON), Oxfordshire

*51°54N/01°22W 450ft asl; SP438230. 5 miles NW of Woodstock, off the A34, 1 mile NE of Glympton*

Kidlington's RLG opened near Glympton in the summer of 1940, and Harvards and Oxfords of 15 SFTS used the field in 1940-41. Further use was made by Kidlington's glider OTUs in 1942, and early in 1943 it came under 20 (P)AFU, which it spasmodically served until June 1945. This was a very primitive site, having neither hangars nor permanent accommodation.

**Main feature:**
*Landing ground:* NNE-SSW 3,078ft grass run.

## KIDLINGTON, Oxfordshire

*51°50N/01°19W 272ft asl; SP475I53. 6 miles NW by N of Oxford, by the A34(T)*

Kidlington has a varied history. Conceived as Oxford Airport, wartime expansion conferred upon it a rectangular array of huts and roads and metal hangars, bringing it into line with similar training establishments. It originated in 1938, No 26 E&RFTS opening here on 24 June. First in was Audax K7552, the School's strength mounting to three Ansons, a couple of Audaxes, seven Hinds and ten Magisters before the outbreak of war, when it closed. Alongside them, from 1 July 1939, there had been three Tipsy Trainers of the Oxford Flying Club. Running Kidlington was Airtraining (Oxford) Ltd, a subsidiary of General Aircraft Ltd.

On 9 September 1939 Battles of 52 Squadron dispersed here for a few days because Kidlington was now Abingdon's satellite. They left when their parent unit moved to Benson, and Kidlington came under 4 Group Pool, Abingdon.

Late 1939 saw its transfer to 6 SFTS Little Rissington, and when that station became waterlogged, 'E' and 'G' Flights of 6 SFTS, together with 'F' and 'H' servicing parties and the

*Kidlington tower in December 1988, with the wartime Watch Office marked by bay windows alongside to the right. (Geoff Phillips)*

Advanced Training Squadron HQ, moved to Kidlington on 8 January 1940. Kidlington also became unusable following heavy snow on 27 January, and was barely serviceable when in mid-March it needed to close again.

Kidlington was now operating as an RLG for 6 SFTS, which unit was suddenly ordered to leave in mid-August 1940. Bombing of Brize Norton raised an urgent need for the station to disperse its complement, so half of the ITS 15 SFTS and ground staff quickly moved into Kidlington on 19 August 1940. Kidlington was still a rudimentary site, although major expansions continued. Campsfield House was requisitioned for dormitory use. Airtraining (Oxford) had two hangars in which they had switched from pre-war flying school activity to aircraft overhaul under the CRO scheme, which led to work on Hurricanes and later Mustangs. The arrival of 15 SFTS increased Kidlington's importance within 23 Group, extended on 31 August 1940 when the remainder of ITS 15 SFTS moved in from South Cerney, where it had lodged after its Middle Wallop home had become a fighter station. On 31 August 1940 Kidlington held fifty-six Harvard Is and two Oxfords.

*The replacement tower at Kidlington, in May 1990. (Geoff Phillips)*

HQ 15 SFTS arrived on 1 October 1940, the remainder of 15 SFTS following on 17 October. More than a hundred Harvards were now on charge and building well advanced. On 1 November 1940 15 SFTS acquired Weston-on-the-Green as a second RLG.

The need for all the dispersal activity was audible when at 1515 on a rainy 3 November 1940 a Ju 88 raced low over the technical site from the north-east, dropping five bombs. One ricocheted its way through the station armoury, while another hit a hangar before bouncing back into the armoury and exploding. Two others burst on the landing ground, where the fifth rested unexploded. The Ju 88, machine-guns blazing, scurried into cloud, flying south-westerly. One person was killed, and two seriously injured. The armoury and Hangar 4, together with an Air Training Co hangar, were all seriously damaged, and two Harvards burnt.

Throughout the winter of 1940/41 Harvards and Oxfords used Kidlington, then most of the Harvards were taken to Southern Rhodesia and replaced with Oxfords. Another Ju 88 called on 27 February 1941. As it came in along the Woodstock road at about 300 feet a Kidlington gun post crew opened fire as, returning it, the raider retreated.

The state of the landing ground was hindering flying, and on 28 February 1941 a Flight from 15 SFTS moved to Watton. On 8 March the use of that operational station increased when two separate Flights, each of five aircraft, moved there for flying training. The need for detachments was alleviated when on 30 June 1941 the new RLG, at Barford St John, opened.

Kidlington was in an increasingly busy area, which added to the risk of accidents. At 1603 on 22 May 1941 an Oxford of 15 SFTS hit a balloon cable and fell in Beechwood Avenue, Coventry. The switch from Harvards to Oxfords had taken place over several weeks, from the start of 1941 and throughout the year. Concern that winter would bring a poor surface resulted in the start of runway-laying in autumn 1941. On 23 December, with the customary two Sommerfeld track runways available, Oxfords of 'J' and 'K' Flights 15 SFTS returned from Weston-on-the-Green, forced out by the formation of 2 GTS. Next day a letter to Kidlington confirmed that 15 SFTS was to close. A new 'No 15', called 15 (P)AFU, would to form at Leconfield in January 1942. Intake at 15 SFTS ceased, but courses in hand completed their training programmes, Oxfords continuing to fly from here until 11 April 1942.

On 1 January 1942 No 1 Glider OTU controlled by 70 Group formed at Kidlington, to provide trained glider pilots with operational skills. Before this scheme became effective, the Horsa had been selected as the assault glider, side-lining the Hotspur. A few OTUs were formed, and a glider pilot attending one found himself flying a Hotspur towed by an antique Hector as before. A second glider OTU formed at Kidlington in February 1942, and both were re-named as 101 and 102 OTUs soon after. They functioned until June 1942, when the HGCU opened at Shrewton.

A party left for Shobdon on 28 May to form 5 GTS, then, on 13 July, the remaining Hotspur organisation and SHQ Kidlington combined to form 4 GTS. Kidlington had lost its RLG at Barford St John on 10 April, and now switched to using Kingston Bagpuize. No 4 GTS amalgamated with Nos 1 and 2 GTSs to form No 20 (P)AFU on 10 March 1943. The new unit used Oxfords and made use of Croughton until November 1944. Flying also took place from Kidlington and Hinton before unit disbandment on 21 June 1945. A non-flying unit then formed at Kidlington, No 1 Aircrew Holding Unit, and stayed until September 1945. No 265 MU was also here and at Grove between October 1945 and July 1948.

On 1 July 1946 the Oxford Flying Club re-formed, and was re-named the Oxford Aeroplane Club in February 1947. The Oxford UAS, which moved in from Abingdon on 14 April 1949, departed on 12 January 1959. In 1958-59 Goodhew Aviation and Derby Aviation operated an Oxford-Jersey service using Marathons and Dakotas. Kidlington also became an outlet for Piper aircraft run by Vigors Aviation.

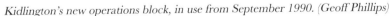

*Kidlington's new operations block, in use from September 1990. (Geoff Phillips)*

In 1961 British Executive Air Services, part of Pressed Steel's airport and aviation business, ran courses leading to Private Pilot Licence standard. In August 1961 the Oxford Aviation Co and the Pressed Steel business merged. January 1962 saw the establishment of CSE Aviation, and BEAS started its first helicopter training business at Kidlington in 1962. BEAS's Flying Training Division was renamed Oxford Air Training School in 1963. In May 1964 OATS became the first such to be CAA approved for the training of CPL students. In 1964 Pressed Steel sold its Oxford Airport BEAS business to CSE Aviation, except for the helicopter facility.

In September 1981 ownership of the airport passed from Oxford City Council to CSE Aviation for £1.4 million, and in September 1986 a financial investment holding company, Oxford Airport Holdings Ltd, acquired a substantial holding of CSE Aviation shares. This led to an ambitious programme to improve OATS facilities as well as the airfield. Runway 02/20 was extended at its northern end and DME was installed.

In January 1988 OAHL acquired the whole of the issued share capital of CSE Aviation. When in September 1988 Murray McLean, Chairman and Chief Executive of CSE Aviation, died, Alan Youdell took his place. There was then a large investment in modern buildings and equipment. In January many of the wartime buildings were demolished and soon the wartime Officers' Mess was no more. The dome trainer survived – to 4 November 1989. Kidlington's first control tower was built in 1957 and replaced in 1960. A new upper control room was added to its top in 1968. In 1989-90 the tower was rebuilt, and a new operations building replaced the wartime example. New flight simulators and Line Orientated Flight Simulators were installed.

More changes followed. In September 1990 a new company formed by amalgamating CSE Aviation with AB Nyge Aero (the Swedish General Aviation) resulted in Nyge CSE Aviation AB, probably the largest general aviation company in Europe.

During the 1990s several charter companies established offices at the Airport and in 1992 McAlpine Helicopters moved its main base here. By 1998 more than 10,000 commercial pilots from eighty countries had trained at OATS.

Changes to company structure continued. In August 1997 CSE Aviation was bought by Close Investment Management, and in August 1998 CSE Aviation became Oxford Aviation Services Ltd, which in 2000 was bought by BBA Group, a major aviation and engineering group.

Not surprisingly, Kidlington is a strictly 'prior permission only' airfield with a variety of civil aircraft coming and going in an extremely busy flying area. As long ago as 1968 Oxford Airport had 223,270 aircraft movements, second only in Britain to Heathrow, which had 247,417 movements that year. It remains a hyper-active airport.

**Main features:**
*Runways:* 024° 3,420ft Army Track, 351° 3,420ft grass, 286° 3,936ft grass. *Hangars:* seven Bellman, ten Blister (65ft), one Horace civilian. *Hardstandings:* four rectangular. *Accommodation:* RAF officers 140, SNCOs 310, ORs 980; WAAF officers 8, SNCOs 6, ORs 454.

The current basic layout comprises four *Runways:* 02/20 1,200m, asphalt; 30/12, the first hard runway, was built in 1970 by widening the northern taxiway; 02/20, the second hard runway, was built in summer 1974 and extended in 1988 to 1,500m with the licensed Landing Distance Available being 1,200m; 760m asphalt; 03/21 902m, grass; 09/27 884m grass.

---

# KIMBOLTON, Cambridgeshire

*52°19N/00°23W 241ft asl; TL105695. 1 mile N of Kimbolton by Spaldwick road*

Kimbolton, prepared in 1941 as Molesworth's satellite, is generally thought of as a USAAF B-17 base, but on 29 November 1941 it received Molesworth's first aircraft – not a Fortress but a Wellington IV destined for 460 Squadron. Kimbolton and Molesworth had been built as potential bases accommodating part of an RAF Bomber Command force of B-24 Liberators. That plan changed after America was dragged into the war, at which time they were sharing 460 Squadron's Wellingtons until those moved to Breighton in early January 1942.

Japan's attack on Pearl Harbor and American entry into the war had a dramatic effect upon the airfield situation. The planning had been for a new RAF bomber group, No 8. Suddenly all changed with the decision to place US bombers, and later fighters, on airfields in Britain. None having been envisaged for such use, an almost desperate search for suitable airfields ensued. Many

Midlands airfields were surveyed, Molesworth and Kimbolton being chosen during January 1942, both for US occupation by the summer.

Much work was needed to bring Kimbolton to the required state, an RAF opening-up party arriving on 31 July 1942. The first Americans – of the 91st Bomb Group – which moved in on 13 September, were soon joined by some of the first B-17Fs to reach Britain, their increased clear transparency areas and elongated transparent noses readily differentiating them from B-17Es. They wore single-tone bronze-green upper surfaces, and had a dark shade of grey on their under surfaces, which toned-down their appearance when compared with B-17Es of the 97th.BG.

Brief was their stay. Wellingtons of 11 OTU Bassingbourn were moving to the inland OTU area, which released an elaborate Permanent Station with newly built hard runways, facilities readily accepted by the comfort-loving visitors who, in October, eagerly forsook Kimbolton's spartan nature for the splendour of mock Georgian Bassingbourn. Personnel en route for operation *Torch* replaced them at Kimbolton. Claims that the 91st moved because the runways could not withstand B-17 operations are only partially true, the main reason being to allow for force expansion. To accommodate a four-squadron USAAF bomber group Kimbolton needing further increased facilities on a number of counts. It remained administered from Molesworth.

On 30 March 1943 it was again divorced, and on 20 May another group of Americans began arriving. The eleven officers and 1,646 men, who had disembarked from the *Aquitania* at Glasgow, manned four squadrons of the 379th Bombardment Group. With them were support personnel of the 82nd Service Group, 171st QM Company, 1094th and 1773rd Ordnance Companies and the 379th Servicing Squadron. On 21 May another 115 officers and 203 enlisted men moved in. Six days later more arrived from AAF Station 109, Podington, then came B-17Fs for the 379th BG. At noon on 1 June 1943, Kimbolton was formerly transferred to USAAF control, the property 'deeds' passing to Colonel M Preston.

The 379th BG, whose operational debut had taken place the previous day, was to fly 330 operations, more than any other Group in the 8th AF BC. They first operated against U-boat installations at St Nazaire, then other raids included attacks on strategic targets including factories, oil plants, storage depots, submarine pens, airfields, communications centres and industrial items, including some in distant Poland and Norway. Special targets raided included the IG Farben chemical plant in Ludwigshaven, an aircraft factory at Brunswick, the ball-bearing works at Schweinfurt, and synthetic oil plants at both Merseburg and Gelsenkirchen. The 379th also played its part in the 1st Air Division's operations leading to the Normandy landings, the Arnhem assault, the Battle of the Bulge and the Rhine crossing. Final bombing sorties were flown on 25 April 1945, and for its excellent operational record between May 1943 and July 1944 the 379th was awarded a Distinguished Unit Citation. A second such commendation followed a courageous operation without fighter escort, mounted against an aircraft factory on 11 January 1944.

*B-17F 230298 'Busy Baby' of the 525th Bomb Squadron, 379th Bomb Group, by a T2 hangar on 8 April 1944. USAF*

*B-17E 19100 FR-U formation assembly ship of the 379th Bomb Group photographed on 24 July 1944. 'Birmingham Blitzkreig' of the 97th BG in 1942, it wears white stripes on its olive drab coat. USAF*

The final tally of operational sorties showed 10,492, the bomb tonnage dropped being 26,459 and the number of operations a record 330. Of the 379th 'K in a triangle'-marked aircraft, none became better known than B-17G 42-40003 'WA-H', named 'Ol' Gappy', which was credited with 157 operational sorties. The 379th vacated Kimbolton on 16 June 1945, for Morocco and Casablanca.

The runways and perimeter track next echoed to the sound of marching by new RAF entrants posted to the recruit training centre here. Although Kimbolton's two T2 hangars saw little further use, the airfield hit the headlines in November 1971 when an abortive attempt was made by a Syrian flying a Piper Cherokee to smuggle illegal immigrants into Britain, an exercise brought to a dramatic end by a farmer. Little remains of Kimbolton's wartime days.

**Main features:**
*Runways:* 330° 6,000ft x 150ft, 210° 4,200ft x 150ft, 270° 4,200ft x 150ft, concrete, tarmac and asphalt. *Hangars:* two T2. *Hardstandings:* fifty loop type. *Accommodation:* USAAF officers 421, EM 2,473.

## KING'S CLIFFE, Northamptonshire

*52°34N/00°29W 251ft asl; TL025980. 6 miles S of Stamford, ENE of King's Cliffe village by the Wansford road*

Commonly called Wansford and officially 'K2', this site was acquired early in 1940 as a second satellite for Wittering and took its designation from Fighter Sector 'K'. Wittering housed a number of squadrons, making the acquisition necessary. In July 1940 work commenced on laying a perimeter track, the intention being that this and the runways would be completed within three months. Wimpey had the contract.

It was 1941 before King's Cliffe began to be used by Spitfire IIas of 266 Squadron. In August 1941 Mk Vbs replaced them, then on 24 October No 266 completely moved into WB2 King's Cliffe, a new title. No 266 had vacated WB3 Collyweston preparatory to Typhoon conversion at Duxford. Giving a foretaste, R7590 visited King's Cliffe on 25 January 1942 and returned to Duxford next day. On 29 January Spitfires of 266 Squadron joined it.

Spitfire Vbs of 616 (County of Yorkshire) Squadron replaced them, arriving in sleet and snow; King's Cliffe seemed a poor substitute for Kirton-in-Lindsey. February 1942 was cold and cheerless, and HRH The Duke of Kent called when the war news was grave. Even lower morale came on 12 February 1942 when German capital ships sailed unchallenged through the Straits of Dover. Ten 616 Spitfires raced to Matlask, six subsequently supporting Whirlwinds of 137 Squadron, which searched unsuccessfully for the German ships.

King's Cliffe was too far from France for Spitfires to operate directly over the Continent, so 616 Squadron would join a 12 Group Wing, fly early to West Malling, refuel, operate and return to King's Cliffe in the evening. The first such venture took place on 12 April, involving thirty-five Spitfire Vbs of 412, 609 and 616 Squadrons. The *Circus* operation took them to Hazebrouck, two of 616's Spitfires failing to return.

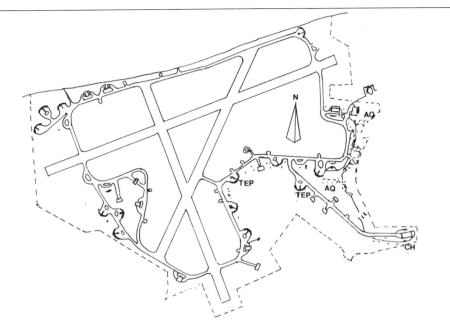

## KING'S CLIFFE

King's Cliffe began life in 1940 as a primitive Unbuilt Satellite for Wittering, its second, as the other, at Collyweston, was scheduled for development. An early addition was an encircling perimeter track to ease bad weather activity. Set alongside were thirteen curved Fighter Pens (7151/41 or 11070/41), each planned to contain two fighters and all placed well apart and facing in different directions to achieve maximum protection. Two of them were larger (TEP) than the others, and intended to hold two twin-engined aircraft, in effect Blenheims or Beaufighters. An unusual item in the area was Building 57, a steel Callendar Hamilton Hangar (6649/37) (CH).

Following the decision to upgrade the station, three runways were added, together with eventually thirteen small circular unprotected hardstandings linked with the perimeter track. A further dozen square pads each accommodated one Blister Hangar of the 65-foot-wide steel EO Type (13084-7/41). One Blister Hangar (13024/41) served in the MT yard. The flying control building (FCW/4514) was of temporary brick construction.

There were 141 mostly 1940-41 listed items (including hardstandings) on the main site, of which eighteen were Laing buildings, thirty-two of Temporary Brick type and a few with wooden construction. Two Laing buildings (196/41) served as squadron offices and another fourteen as Airmen's Quarters, unusually within the main site. The Operations Room and Crew Briefing Room were both brick-built. Surprisingly few prominent changes came during the USAAF tenure.

Next day No 616 Squadron participated in a *Rodeo*, and on 15 April operated twice. During the afternoon the 12 Group Wing (411, 609 and 616 Squadrons) covered eight Hurribombers attacking Desvres. Enemy fighters challenged and Flt Lt Johnson damaged a Fw 190 before Sergeant Millar, also of 616 Squadron, was rescued after ditching off Dungeness. Two days later, during the Lancaster dash to Augsburg, 616 Squadron's Spitfires diverted enemy attention. By the close of April, No 616 had flown seven offensive sweeps in a Wing generally led by Wg Cdr Jamieson. On 29/30 April six pilots tried their hand at night-fighting during the bombing of Norwich.

An excited 616 Squadron received its first high-fighting Spitfire VI, 'A-Apple', on 22 April 1942. Pressure cabin insulation made entry in full flying gear difficult, the cabin temperature was high at lower altitudes and on the climb, and although the engine had a higher altitude rating than others, it was far from the desirable Merlin 61 two-stage variant. The Mk VI was heavy, and propeller refinement much needed. The planned four-bladed propellers remained in short supply and some Mk VIs were at first adapted to have inferior three-bladers. But 616 at least had its first high flier with which to conduct combat at great heights.

May 1942 was a busy month, with some Mk VI training carried out at Boscombe Down. Five sweeps using Spitfire Vs were flown, two on May Day when Plt Off Brown claimed a probable Fw 190. Another took place on 4 May while 616's fourth Spitfire VI touched down at King's Cliffe. *Rodeo 19* was flown with 19 Squadron on 6 May, then on 9 May No 616 Squadron took two Mk VIs on its first sweep, together with ten Mk Vs and Spitfires of 411 Squadron. These joined forty-eight Spitfires of the North Weald Wing, all returning without combat. No 616 Squadron then concentrated on Mk VI handling, and by 24 May fourteen Mk VIs were on strength.

During the rainy afternoon of 25 May, coastal radar plotted a Dornier 217E east of Mablethorpe, heading southwards. After it flew over the Wash, then inland, two Spitfires of 411 Squadron and four of 616 Squadron were scrambled. The Dornier flew to about fifteen miles east of Bramcote at between 7,000 and 10,000 feet, 616 Squadron engaging and probably damaging it near Leicester. The event was sad for 616 Squadron because return fire from the Dornier damaged Perspex in a Spitfire's cockpit glazing, causing Plt Off Brown to lose an eye. The Do 217 dropped four bombs near Belton, Rutland, before its exit over the Wash. This was not the expected baptism of fire for the high-altitude fighter.

Conversion complete, and seventeen Mk VIs in hand, No 616 Squadron resumed operations over France, making a diversionary sweep with 610 Squadron in the Le Touquet-Boulogne area on 3 June, and another two days later with Nos 610 and 611 Squadrons. These were the only two such operations from King's Cliffe in June 1942, excessive heat in the tightly enclosed Spitfire cockpits halting operations until 15 June, after which training resumed.

On 3 July No 616 Squadron was detached to West Malling, reinforcing 11 Group during an intended commando assault on the French coast. On 7 July it returned to WB2 (still commonly called Wansford) for an overnight stay, the Squadron moving to Kenley next day, swapping places with Spitfire Vbs and 485 (NZ) Squadron. The New Zealanders came for a 'rest' and flew four operations during the Dieppe landings before busying themselves supporting US 8th AAF B-17s and RAF day raids from advanced bases.

On 8 September 1942 No 93 Squadron's Spitfire Vbs arrived from the Isle of Man to work up for operation *Torch*, and departed in mid-October. No 485 Squadron moved temporarily to Kirkeston, Northern Ireland, on 24 October. On 23 November it returned, leaving for West Hampnett on 3 January 1943.

The squadron's brief absence was supposed to make way for 12th AF Americans similarly preparing for operation *Torch*. Instead, it was 8 December 1942 before USAAF Bell P-39 and P-400 Airacobras of the 347th Squadron, 350th Fighter Group, arrived. For three weeks Airacobras in British colours and US national insignia were seen and heard for, on the climb, their Allisons very noisily hauled the fighters aloft with a sound peculiar to their breed. On 4 January 1943 they left on the long journey to Africa, there to join their ground echelon.

Almost immediately the US 56th Fighter Group arrived and soon received P-47C Thunderbolts. However, King's Cliffe's facilities remained insufficient for intensive operations. One squadron, No 63, lodged at Wittering, leaving the 61st and 63rd at King's Cliffe. With the airfield non-operational, this was a suitable time to build better runways, blast pens and additional

*'The camp' at King's Cliffe in
1944. via (Dave Benfield)*

*A P-51D of the 79th FS, 20th FG.*

accommodation. By May 1943 what had been little more than a large meadow with a few Blister hangars was now a full airfield.

Early in April 1943 the 56th Fighter Group moved to Horsham St Faith. The RAF re-possessed King's Cliffe and, in May, No 91 Squadron's Griffon-engined Spitfire XIIs arrived, leaving for Hawkinge on 21 May. Commencing on 14 June Miles Masters of No 7 (P)AFU were here for two weeks. No 349 Squadron returned from overseas, assembled at Wittering and, with one Spitfire V, moved to King's Cliffe on 29 June. After working up using Spitfire Vbs, it left for Wellingore early in August.

King's Cliffe's most active period commenced on 26 August 1943 when the 77th and 79th Squadrons, 20th Fighter Group, USAAF, brought along the latest Lockheed P-38H Lightning fighters. In early September the USAAF took over the base. Accommodation shortage caused the Group's 55th Squadron to lodge at Wittering until 27 May 1944, when the 55th found room at King's Cliffe.

P-38s suffered from engine and supercharger problems, to clear which the 20th's P-38Hs were passed to the more experienced 55th Fighter Group at Nuthampstead. The 20th – far from operationally ready – received replacement P-38Js in October. Recognisable by the deep air intakes accommodating radiators, shifted from the wing leading edges and fitted ahead of the engines, additional fuel tankage and a possible 150-gallon drop tank increased the still-air non-combat radius of action to more than 600 miles. Operationally, about 400 miles was a realistic figure.

The 20th Fighter Group cautiously commenced operations on 5 November 1943, eight P-38s of the 79th Fighter Squadron tagging along with P-38s of the 55th Fighter Group. Full-scale operations from King's Cliffe began on 28 December 1943. Aerodynamic problems were far from over, however, and to the end of its operational career with the 20th Fighter Group the complex single-seat P-38 was far from easy to cope with. Nevertheless its range made it useful, P-38s seeing seven months of active service at King's Cliffe.

For the 20th, 8 April 1944 was a day to recall with pride. Cheated of joining a main bomber force operation by misty conditions, the Group secured permission for a special, one-off strafing mission. Forty-eight P-38s left King's Cliffe, their targets being around Salzwedel, some eighty miles from Berlin. A highly successful venture, the 20th claimed twenty-one enemy aircraft destroyed on the ground and four in the air, and attacked rail traffic for the loss of two Lightnings. P-38s had hitherto been mainly used for bomber support, low-level strafing by a fighter fitted with turbo-superchargers for high-altitude work seeming strange. But that item had given trouble, forcing P-38s to be used for lower, medium-level operations.

What now transformed the P-38 was the fitting of a clear nose in which a bombardier could, just, be accommodated, and, as bombing leader, he could mark the target for attack by conventional P-38 fighter bombers. There were few 'droop snoot' P-38s, but the 20th had one by April 1944 and first used it during an attack on Gutersloh airfield. More such attacks followed.

*P-51D-5-NA KI-K 'Little Lady' of the 55th FS, 20th FG.*

The afternoon of 5 May 1944 saw King's Cliffe's P-38s commencing their important pre-Normandy invasion task, patrolling south of the Isle of Wight to cover Allied troop convoys advancing slowly towards France.

In July 1944 P-51 Mustangs began arriving at King's Cliffe. The 20th Fighter Group had claimed eighty enemy aircraft shot down for a loss of eighty-seven P-38s before, on 20 July, the 20th's P-51s began operations. Bomber escorts, fighter-bomber raids and low-level locomotive strikes followed in the months ahead. They were busy during the Ardennes battles and the Rhine crossing. One of their more unusual missions came on 11 September 1944 when they escorted B-17s and, after their bombing, proceeded to the USSR. They then protected the bombers returning via Hungary and Italy before landing back at King's Cliffe on 17 September 1944.

The last of 312 operations flown by the 20th Fighter Group from King's Cliffe took place on 25 April 1945, the 20th returning to the USA the following October. King's Cliffe became a Holding Unit for German POWs awaiting repatriation, under the control of the RAF's 28 Group. The Unit closed in July 1947. King's Cliffe was then held on care and maintenance, serving as an ammunition storage area for No 93 MU between August and December 1952. The RAF vacated the site in January 1959, and it was sold for private use later that year.

**Main features:**
*Runways:* 210° 5,100ft x 150ft, 210° 3,975ft x 150ft, 350° 3,300ft x 150ft, tarmac. *Hangars:* one T2, four Blisters, eight '55 Special'. *Hardstandings:* eleven cement pads, fourteen PSP, thirteen revetments (from Spitfire times). *Accommodation:* USAAF officers 151, EM 1,267.

## KINGSTON BAGPUIZE, Oxfordshire

*51°40N/01°24W 300ft asl; SU410965. 5 miles W of Abingdon, S of the A415*

Kingston Bagpuize, built on flat land south of the village, had excellent approaches. Between January and May 1942 No 3 EFTS used Kingston as an RLG, then from 9 March to 19 July 1942 it was a satellite for 1 GTS Thame, whose Hotspurs and tugs undertook circuit training.

When a glider pilot refresher school for those trained already was suggested, Kingston and Thame were considered. Nothing came of this and, between January and April 1943, Kingston was used by 4 GTS. Between 10 March and 28 July 1943 it served as a satellite for 20 (P)AFU. Plans to enlarge the airfield were then implemented.

When a 70 Group opening party arrived on 30 January 1944 to take over from the contractors, they found that the USAAF had already moved in. On 7 February 1944 an advance party of the IXth AF also arrived. American interest was not so much in operating from the station but in trying out a wire mesh PSP covering laid over the original runway surface. The Commander of IXth AF came to inspect it in March and observed rapid operational turn-round of fifty P-47s drawn from the 368th Fighter Group, Greenham Common. Next day the Group mounted three operations from here, testing the efficiency of the novel runway surface They again used Kingston on 13 April 1944.

Another day of intensive flying to test the runway further took place 6 May 1944 when P-47s repeatedly landed, showing that frequent repairs were necessary. A B-17, short of fuel, visited briefly on 25 May, and on 15 June circuits by C-47s trying out the runway showed little wear on its surface. In late June 1944 the experimental wire mesh was removed, trials being deemed complete by August. Kingston was dormant until 14 December 1944 when 3 MU took over the site. By then all PSP had been removed and the airfield closed. Most of the site was in the process of being de-requisitioned. The sub-site that 3 MU had established was eventually closed on 14 June 1954.

**Main features:**
*Runways:* 022° 6,000ft x 150ft, 080° 4,200ft x 150ft, both PSP; a third NW/SE 4,200ft PSP runway was removed in autumn 1944. *Hangars:* two Butler (US) design, one T2, two large Blisters, one small Blister. *Hardstandings:* fifty PSP. *Accommodation:* USAAF officers 136, EM 2,838.

---

## LANGLEY, Buckinghamshire

*51°30N/00°32W 100ft asl; TQ025795. E of Slough, alongside railway line*

That an aircraft manufacturer of the calibre of Hawker Aircraft Ltd did not have its main production centre adjacent to a flying ground is unexpected. Instead, completed airframes were conveyed from Canbury Park Road works, Kingston-upon-Thames, to Brooklands. There they were erected, then test-flown. The Hurricane prototype was thus treated in October 1935 two weeks before its first flight on 6 November 1935. Contracts involving large-scale Hurricane production led to the Hawker-Siddeley Group negotiating financial loans, which, by November 1936, had doubled the company's capital to £4 million. They also included £30,000 for the purchase of Parlaunt Park Farm at Langley, where a large new factory and adjacent aerodrome were built. The Langley factory was completed by the end of 1938, and Hurricane production began there. It soon reached one aircraft per day – five a day in 1942. At the outbreak of war the three Hawker factories – Brooklands, Langley and Kingston – were employing 4,000 people.

Hawker now had a suitable base for trials and development, the Tornado prototype making its first flight from Langley on 6 October 1939 and the prototype Typhoon on 24 February 1940. Amazingly, the Germans made very little attempt to interrupt any Hawker activity. One bomb at Canbury Park Road caused more confusion than damage, a raid on Brooklands did little damage, and Langley was barely touched. Hurricane production, so vital to winning the 1940-41 battles, was thus able to proceed little hindered.

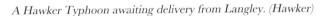

*A Hawker Typhoon awaiting delivery from Langley. (Hawker)*

*Hurricane II Z3777 about to be flight-tested from Langley.*

The second Typhoon prototype first flew, from Langley, on 3 May 1941, and Hawker, looking for an alternative engine, first flew the Bristol Centaurus Typhoon on 23 October 1941. A few production Typhoons were Langley-built in 1941-42, the first flying on 26 November 1941. However, production here until 1943 was concentrated on Hurricanes and their development.

By 1942 Langley had become involved with the Tempest, the Mk I prototype flying on 24 February 1943 and the first Mk II on 28 June, a week after Bill Humble had first flown production Mk V JN729 on the 21st. Tempest V production gathered pace in 1943, then in 1944 came the Fury, the prototype of which flew on 1 September. Fury development here was followed by Sea Fury production after Tempest II production faded.

Although suitable for large aircraft like Lancastrians, Yorks and Tudors, upon which some work was undertaken, Langley, being a grass airfield, was unsuitable for jet aircraft. Furthermore, by 1948 Heathrow activity made test-flying thereabouts impracticable. Aircraft building switched to Hawker's Richmond Road factory and other sources, and in 1950 Hawker Aircraft decided to acquire tenancy of Dunsfold airfield. In 1959 the Langley works was taken over by Ford Motors.

**Main features:**
The grass landing ground and grass runways were bordered on their southern side by assorted, extensive industrial buildings.

*Sabre-engined Hawker Fury Mk 1 LA610 at Langley in mid-1946.*

## LEAVESDEN, Hertfordshire

*51°41N/00°25W 65ft asl; TL 095002. NW of Watford, S of Abbots Langley*

On land called King George V Playing Fields (known locally as 'Mile Field' because of its dimensions, and part of Hunters Farm), a large aircraft production unit was built, together with an adjacent flying ground. The 300-acre site, owned by Watford Corporation, was purchased by the Government in 1940, and a 3,033-foot-long runway was laid, supplementing two large factory complexes and hangars used for final assembly.

The premises were leased to London Aircraft Productions (LAP) building Halifaxes and the Second Aircraft Group (SAG), the latter under the general administration of the de Havilland Company, which administered its factory area.

*Production of Mosquitoes by the Second Aircraft Group in 1943.*

During the Second World War both Halifax bombers and Mosquito fighter-bombers were built at Leavesden. To allow the heavies to take off safely from the relatively short runway, installation of much of their equipment was undertaken elsewhere. More than 4,000 Mosquitoes were assembled at Leavesden during the war years.

Such activities ceased in 1946 when Leavesden became the service department for civil repairs of de Havilland aircraft. Repair and servicing of DH piston engines was also undertaken, and later turbine engines, which led to a re-organised Leavesden being expanded into the de Havilland Engine Company base.

*Halifaxes formed a considerable proportion of Leavesden's wartime output.*

Transition to the manufacture of the jet engine was progressive and involved new techniques and new equipment. When the lease of the Stonegrove works expired in 1954, Leavesden was equipped and ready to take the full production load of both piston-engine and gas-turbine manufacture.

With changes to the aircraft industry, management of Leavesden changed from de Havilland to Hawker Siddeley, which in February 1961 sold the site to Bristol Siddeley Engines; this led finally to Rolls-Royce occupying the site. The basic work carried out here did not, however, change. Small jet engines were handled here.

The 300-acre site, where more than 3,000 people were at one time employed and on which was situated the Rolls-Royce Aero Division Leavesden and Leavesden Aerodrome, was owned by the Ministry of Defence and leased to Rolls-Royce through the Property Services Agency. Rolls-Royce Leavesden designed, developed, manufactured and overhauled a range of gas-turbine engines for civil and military helicopters.

Two main factory areas remained at the Leavesden site, an experimental and development area where engines were designed and developed, and the production build and machine shops. Parts for the giant RB211, destined for the wide-bodied airliner market, and the RB199, the powerplant of the multi-role Tornado, were also manufactured here.

Leavesden Airfield was not only used for Rolls-Royce Aero Division's comings and goings. It was a publicly licensed aerodrome run by Rolls-Royce and open to all aircraft operators. It served executive, commercial and private flyers of light and medium aircraft, and was fully equipped with navigational and landing aids airspace. The final aviation occupant was the Leavesden Flight Centre. Like Langley, Leavesden was sited in a very busy area – indeed, movements to and from in 1990 totalled 60,000. That problem and defence cuts brought an end to flying here in March 1994.

In 1994 the Millennium Group Ltd began using some factory buildings, which, on lease from Rolls-Royce, were converted by Eon Productions into film studios. Sets for top films have been built and the clear outside backdrop put to good use. Films produced at Leavesden Studios include Star Wars Episode 1: The Phantom Menace and Goldeneye.

**Main features:**
Two concrete runways were featured, together with a large industrial complex.

*Beech D 18S G-ATUM in March 1968, typical of the unusual aircraft seen at Leavesden. (John Strangward)*

## LEICESTER EAST, Leicestershire

*52°36N/01°02W 469ft asl; SK015660. 4 miles SE of Leicester*

A standard wartime airfield with the usual three concrete runways and encircling perimeter, Leicester East officially opened on 15 October 1943 and was placed in 38 Group. First in was No 196 Squadron, which arrived on 18 November 1943 from Witchford, bringing Stirling IIIs. After re-equipping with Stirling Mk IV glider-tugs, it moved on 7 January 1944 to Tarrant Rushton.

On 23 November 1943 another Stirling III squadron, No 620, moved in from Chedburgh to convert to Stirling Mk IVs received during February 1944. These flew supply drops to the French Resistance before moving to Fairford on 18 March 1944.

On 5 January 1944 No 190 Squadron re-formed here, also equipping with Stirling GT IVs, departing on 25 March 1944. Then came change with the formation, on 3 May, of No 107 (T) OTU, which trained crews to operate Dakotas for 46 Group. On 26 March 1945 the OTU was redesignated No 1333 Transport Support Conversion Unit, although the role changed little. The unit moved on 25 October 1945 to Syerston.

That was the last RAF flying unit based at Leicester East, and following its departure the station was placed on care and maintenance. That ceased on 31 December 1947 and the site was officially abandoned.

For many years it has been used as a

*The control tower photographed during the July 1986 PFA Rally.*

civilian airfield, the base of Leicestershire Aero Club, and in 1977 was named Leicester Airport. The renovated original control tower serves the club. Other Leicester occupants include Heli Air and Ultra Air.

**Main features:**
*Runways:* 107° 6,000ft x 150ft, 051° 4,200ft x 150ft, 165° 4,200ft x 150ft, concrete. *Hangars:* four T2. *Hardstandings:* forty-eight spectacle type. *Accommodation:* RAF officers 116, SNCOs 283, ORs 1,152; WAAF officers 10, SNCOs 16, ORs 340.

Currently runway 10/28 940m x 30m, asphalt, occupies a section of the wartime runway and there are two short asphalt runways, 04/22 490m x 18m and 15/33 495m x 18m. There are two 418m grass runways, 06/24 and 16/34, in the centre of the metalled runway complex.

## LITTLE HORWOOD, Buckinghamshire

*51°57N/00°52W 385ft asl; SP795315. 2½ miles NE of Winslow*

Due to Cheddington being transferred to the Americans, Little Horwood replaced it as 26 OTU's satellite with effect from 3 September 1942, and was used for Wellington conversion training. The OTU's Gunnery Section also moved here, together with No 92 Group Communication Flight, which arrived from Bicester on 16 September 1942 and stayed until disbandment on 15 July 1945.

Little remains of this 92 Group airfield. Apart from 26 OTU's Wellington IIIs and Xs few other aircraft used it. One exception came on 23 January 1943, when, with fuel short and the weather bad, B-17s operating from Chelveston landed on return from Lorient.

Tomahawks equipped No 1684 BDTF, formed here on 5 June 1943, and transferred to Wing, the parent station, on 17 July 1943. To ensure like standards, No 92 Group Screened Instructors' School also formed here, on 17 April 1944.

On 26 August 1944 the strength No 26 OTU was reduced to three-quarters OTU level and flying ceased at Little Horwood. This left 92 Group Communication Flight in occupation, using an

Oxfords, Ansons, Tutors and Proctors. On 16 October 1944 the OTU returned to full-strength level, which included fifty-four Wellingtons. Parts of the unit – including the Gunnery Section's Hurricanes – returned to Little Horwood.

On 24 July 1945 No 92 Group SIS closed, on the same day as No 91 Group Navigation Instructors' School moved in from Honeybourne. Although the latter closed on 31 October 1945, No 26 OTU Wing survived until March 1946, its home being earmarked for post-war civilian use. Not so Little Horwood, where flying had ceased on 30 November 1945, although the satellite was administered by 26 OTU until 15 January 1946.

It was immediately occupied by 71 MU, a salvage recovery and repair unit that remained until disbandment on 15 November 1947. Following the usual strip-down, the site was disposed of.

**Main features:**
*Runways:* 295° 6,000ft x 150ft, 170° 4,200ft x 150ft, 236° 4,200ft x 150ft, concrete. *Hangars:* one T2, one B1. *Hardstandings:* thirty for heavy bombers. *Accommodation:* RAF officers 124, SNCOs 304, ORs 802; WAAF officers 2, SNCOs 3, ORs 293.

## LITTLE RISSINGTON, Gloucestershire

*51°51N/01°41W 707ft asl; SP211189. 4 miles S of Stow-on-the-Wold*

'Business Park', the notice proclaims. Nothing new in that.

In its RAF days Little Rissington, partly constructed using native Cotswold stone, was always in business. While 8 MU on the southern side backed the fight, flying training was intensively conducted from the northern side.

RAF Little Rissington came to life between 20 and 25 August 1938 as 6 FTS moved in from Netheravon bringing Harts and Audaxes, received in October 1935, and a few Hawker Furies, soon joined by Ansons. During June 1939 the pernicious, unpopular sounds of Harvard engines and fast-tip-speed propellers began shattering the sky. With a motley collection, 6 FTS went to war.

Constructed as a Permanent RAF Station, Little Rissington was composed of the usual array of tasteful-looking buildings all designed to do as little damage to the rural scene as possible. Many of the pre-war Married Quarters are now privately occupied, the camp's streets retaining symbolic names. Little Rissington's four C Type hangars (6045/36) still flank a curving apron. When the station opened it had an Aircraft Repair Shed (6116/34) behind No 3 Hangar, to deal with damaged aircraft, and a so-called 'fort type' Watch Office erected by the apron in front of No 3 Hangar. Most buildings were to the rear of Nos 1 and 2 Hangars, sloping ground to the east limiting development. Main Stores (2056-61/34) and Workshops (2046/34) were to the rear of the No 1 Hangar. Barrack blocks were of three types: Type P (2363/37, for fifty-two men and three NCOs), Type Q (582/36 for sixty-four men and three NCOs) and Type R (2277/34, for eighty-four men and three NCOs). The Sergeants' Mess (102/55) could accommodate sixty-five SNCOs, with quarters for twelve. To the north of the parade ground was the Airmen's Dining Room, capacity 450 men, with the Institute (5062-66/36) on the upper floor. The Officers' Mess (566/37 1459/37), for 108 officers, was situated on the northern edge of the camp.

No 6 FTS shared the station, for on 11 October 1938 No 8 Aircraft Storage Unit (re-named 8 MU on 7 February 1939) opened under Sqn Ldr D W Dean. Its task was the preparation of aircraft for service within its bulky D Type hangars and grass-covered Lamella 'mounds' favoured for ASUs. On 3 September 1939 there were 268 aircraft in store. Additionally, Wellingtons of 215 Squadron scattered here for safety when war began and stayed for a fortnight.

On 3 September 1939 the FTS became No 6 Service FTS, whose Intermediate Squadron expecting Harvard Is had to make do with Audaxes and Harts to train pilots following their elementary training. A fleet of up to forty-four Ansons equipped the Advanced Squadron from which pilots were briefly detached, for operational and armament training, to Penrhos in October-November 1939, and Hullavington in December 1939-January 1940. Then the snow fell fast, drifting deeply over Little Rissington, sited on the roof of the cold Cotswolds. However, it did not stop 8 MU helping the courageous Finns to defeat the Russians, despatching Blenheims to the Bristol Aeroplane Co for preparation in that distant conflict. Flying from Rissington being almost impossible, 'E' and 'G' Flights, with two servicing parties, and the

Advanced Squadron HQ moved to Kidlington early in January 1940. A week later Kidlington was out of use due to the thaw, which extended into February. Only the southern and western sections of Rissington's landing ground were usable, for essential flying. Kidlington briefly closed again in March, but by late April all was well. Resumed armament training began at Warmwell in May 1940, by which time operational training schemes were in play. Establishment now called for forty-five Harvards and sixty-three Ansons.

On 24 June 1940 6 SFTS became a twin-engine training school only. Biplanes had been phased out in early 1940, and by May the establishment was for forty-five Harvards and sixty-three Ansons. Now the plan was to replace both types, although in September 1940 108 Ansons remained on establishment. In November Oxfords began to replace them, Ansons being required for overseas training schools.

Dispersal of the SFTS aircraft around the airfield perimeter called for anti-intruder/sabotage defences. Fencing off large areas and patrolling them being largely impossible, many aircraft just had to be vulnerably housed in hangars – particularly the remaining biplanes, which were also susceptible to inclement weather. In May 1940 No 8 MU held about 350 aircraft, many closely packed in Lamella hangars.

Deterioration in the international situation prompted the OC 8 MU on 24 June 1940 to keep a Spitfire ready for 6 SFTS Staff Pilots for use in local defence. With more than 400 aircraft at Little Rissington in mid-1940, it was certainly an inviting target. Some trainers remained at Kidlington until July, when use began of RLG Windrush. Mid-June found 8 MU holding, among others, fifty-eight Battles, thirty-nine Hampdens, twenty-one Magisters, thirty Spitfires and twenty-one Tiger Moths. Some were temporarily dispersed to Watchfield, Worcester, Stoke Orchard and Great Shefford. Stored, dismembered aircraft were held 'in purgatory' at Luton (from 1940 to 1942) and Portsmouth (1940 to 1941).

The arrival of around a hundred Blenheims in July 1940 brought fresh concerns, especially when, on 29 July, a raider dropped seventeen bombs, harmlessly, in fields $3^1/_2$ miles away. Windrush RLG was now used for night-flying, allowing Little Rissington to stay unlit.

A bold aircraft enthusiast would have discovered Little Rissington holding much to fascinate. In August 1940, for instance, fourteen Mohawks and three rare Curtiss Cleveland biplanes arrived, but to discourage strangers sixty civilians of the ASU and SFTS formed a Home Guard battalion on 28 August. Three days later an invasion alert caused the manning of fourteen brick blockhouses and fourteen concrete pillboxes around the aerodrome perimeter.

Autumn's increased accident rates at training schools were harming courses. On 29 September 1940, for instance, Anson N9821 collided with Oxford P9039 of 2 SFTS three miles south of Little Rissington, killing all the aircrew. On 29 October 1940 two Ansons, N9737 of 11 AONS Watchfield and N5285 of 6 SFTS, collided ten miles north of Stow-on-the-Wold. Such serious accidents were relatively rare, although on 23 May 1941 – by which time establishment was for 112 Oxfords – two of them collided over their home station.

At a second RLG, Chipping Norton, 6 SFTS had commenced circuit flying on 16 November 1940 to further lessen congestion. Integrating 8 MU's mixed aircraft often brought problems – like MU storage. Partial alleviation came in 1940 when dispersal commenced at Satellite Landing Grounds including Great Shefford, Pembridge, Watchfield, Worcester and Stoke Orchard, where the Gloster Aircraft Co established a sub-factory. Further changes to the SLGs under 8 MU control came in February 1941 when No 3 SLG Middle Farm came into use, with No 28 Barton Abbey acting as sub-station from February 1941 to August 1942. By October 1941 more than ninety aircraft were in store at Middle Farm. Control of 8 MU switched to 52 Wing on 21 April 1941, and on 30 June the stock included twenty-seven Hampdens, ten Mohawks, nine Proctors, thirty-seven Spitfires and 120 Oxfords.

The ever-increasing RAF night-bomber strength made instrument flying training ever more essential. Equally important was bad weather landing approach training. In October 1941 No 23 BAT Flight formed, was re-named No 1523 BAT Flight in January 1942, and usually held eight Oxford IIs. It functioned at Little Rissington until November 1945, and disbanded on 17 December 1945.

As a result of extensive flying training overseas, No 6 SFTS, within 23 Group, in April 1942 became No 6 (Pilots) Advanced Flying Unit. Using Oxford IIs, this and other (P)AFUs provided pilots trained overseas with experience of flying in European conditions. In June 1942 6 (P)AFU's establishment stood at 115 Oxfords and four Ansons. An additional thirty-four Oxfords, previously on 2 (P)AFU strength, were received on 14 July 1942 when Akeman Street RLG came into use. Additional Oxfords arrived conveniently, for during the previous month 6 (P)AFU had assessed the Blackburn Botha for use as an advanced trainer. Declared quite unsuitable, 6 (P)AFU's Oxfords were left to continue filling the circuits at Little Rissington and its RLGs.

Runway building was undertaken at Little Rissington during 1942. Night-flying was feasible there because of reduced enemy night activity. Little Rissington's triple runway pattern was useful to 8 MU allowing Horsa gliders erected here, as well as Hotspurs, to be towed away by Whitleys. During 1942 8 MU mainly handled Hampdens, Oxfords, Spitfires and, in particular, Wellingtons. Aged biplanes including Harts, Hinds, Hectors and Audaxes – useful for glider training schools – were overhauled. By early 1943 Spitfires were prominent among Hampdens, Wellingtons, Tomahawks, Halifaxes, Typhoons and a few Kittyhawks. March 1943 saw No 8 MU take over administration of No 34 SLG, Woburn Park.

No 6 (P)AFU's Oxfords seemed ever to proliferate. In May 1943 establishment rose to 163 Oxford I/IIs, four Ansons and a Tiger Moth to serve a pupil population of 350 being trained at three RLGs as well as at the parent station.

Rare aircraft were still assigned through 8 MU in April 1944, among them ten Hengist gliders taken into 'purgatory' storage at Rawcliffe Paper Mill. At that time the MU held, scattered over all sites, an amazing 520 aircraft, and had opened another 'purgatory' store at Northolt.

Increased BAT training became available to 6 (P)AFU in May 1944 when Nos 1516 and 1517 BAT Flights at Pershore and Chipping Warden respectively began assisting. Although the intensity of flying training in the Rissington area was already high, 8 MU's holding increased dramatically, particularly of Wellingtons. In November 1944 it was ordered to concentrate upon dispersed storage of at least 600, and more were to follow. At the end of the year 757 aircraft were on charge, including Wellington Mks III, X, XIII and XIV. A year later the holding had swollen to a staggering 1,388 aircraft, for which reason No 107 Sub-Storage Unit at Honeybourne and No 108 at Long Marston were opened.

Little Rissington's three RLGs remained in use to the end of European hostilities, and when training ceased at 6 (P)AFU on 26 November 1945, the unit had trained 5,444 pilots, and its pupils had been given 705 gallantry awards including four Victoria Crosses.

On 17 December 1945 No 6 (P)AFU reverted to being 6 SFTS, with a new establishment of fifty-four Harvard IIbs (twelve of which had arrived in October), two Ansons and a Magister. Control of Little Rissington remained with 23 Group. On 25 April 1946 No 6 SFTS moved to Ternhill, making way for part of the Central Flying School, the RAF's most prestigious training formation. Re-formed at Little Rissington on 7 May 1946, it was derived from an amalgamation of the ECFS and Nos 7 and 10 Flying Instructors' Schools. Its core task was the training of flying instructors, and basic instruction was handled at South Cerney, leaving advanced training instruction to be given by two Harvard squadrons at Little Rissington. Prentices began replacing those in July 1947, then in 1953 Provosts took their place. In 1960 Jet Provost T3s ousted their predecessors, T4s and T5s later being used. Post-war the RLGs used were Enstone (May 1946 to December 1950), Moreton Valence (1949 to 1951) and Wellesbourne Mountford (1951).

There were numerous syllabus adjustments, major re-organisation taking place on 1 January 1951. The basic element remained at South Cerney, while at Little Rissington were the Ground Training Squadron, the Examining Wing to check all flying instructors, two Harvard squadrons and a Meteor Flight. In May 1952 all were gathered under the title CFS (Advanced) Little Rissington. Multi-engine training courses had earlier been run using Mosquito TIIIs, then Varsities. The first jet flying involved Meteor T7s and later Vampire T 11s. Rissington's 'Vintage Pair', a T7 and a T11, which collided and crashed at a Mildenhall Air Fete, were a reminder of those days.

On 1 June 1957 CFS Basic and Advanced combined at Little Rissington, and next year CFS formed 'The Pelicans' using Jet Provost TIs, soon replaced. Much later came 'The Skylarks' flying Chipmunks. Although part of CFS, the 'Red Arrows' were never based at Little Rissington. RLGs – still needed – were Aston Down (June-November 1964 and August 1965-February 1976), Fairford (1964-66) and Kemble (October 1955-April 1976).

No 8 MU closed on 1 July 1957. In its place was much smaller 250 MU, re-formed on 1 March 1957 as an MT Servicing Unit, disbanding on 31 October 1959.

The 1970s saw steady contraction, CFS Little Rissington using mainly Jet Provost T3s, 4s, 5s and SAL Bulldogs. Group status was withdrawn on 9 February 1974 when the School passed under the control of 23 Group. For Little Rissington this marked the commencement of closure. On 12 April

1976 HQ CFS, the Examining Wing and Jet Provost Squadron moved to Cranwell, the Bulldogs to Leeming, and Little Rissington closed as a functional station within Training Command. On 31 August 1976 SHQ Little Rissington closed and the RAF vacated the station, which was handed to the Army Department on 1 September 1976 and named Imjin Barracks.

During 1982 the Americans established a medical centre around a hangar within a fenced-off compound, which had links with Upper Heyford. After having it on stand-by during the 1992 Gulf conflict, the USAF moved out.

Flying has not ceased here, for on 29 November 1977 No 637 (Volunteer) Gliding School arrived from Gaydon and currently flies Vigilant T1s for ATC use.

**Main features:**
*Runways:* 050° 4,695ft x 150ft, 100° 3,450ft x 150ft, 140° 3,105ft x 150ft, concrete and tarmac. *Hangars:* School site: two C Type, three Bellmans, one ARS, seven 69ft Blisters, ten 65ft Blisters; MU site: two D Type, six E Type, two C Type, eight Robins, three Super Robins. *Hardstanding:* nil. *Accommodation:* RAF officers 151, SNCOs 250, ORs 916; WAAF officers 9, SNCOs 2, ORs 362.

## LITTLE STAUGHTON, Bedfordshire

*54°14N/00°21 225ft asl; TL120615. 4 miles W of St Neots*

Pforzheim was rarely attacked, a raid by 250 aircraft of 1 Group and fifty of 6 Group being an unusual event. No 8 Group, the Pathfinders, fielded sixty-one aircraft, including eight Lancasters of 582 Squadron, Little Staughton. One was flown by the Master Bomber, Captain Edwin Swales DFC, South African Air Force, who in 'M for Mother', PB538, reached the target area as a fighter engaged it, putting an engine and the rear guns out of action. As Swales continued his role a German fighter repeatedly attacked, rendering a second engine useless.

His task completed, Swales set course for home in an almost defenceless aircraft. By the time friendly territory was reached it was clear that the aircraft could not safely land, and Swales decided that his crew must bale out. He flew the aircraft as steadily as possible and, moments after the last man baled out, PB538 crashed at Chapelle au Bois, near Monchaux, France. Swales was killed, and for his courageous action was posthumously awarded the Victoria Cross.

During the last year of the war Little Staughton's 582 Squadron led a number of raids. Even more importantly, it was from here that *Oboe* Mosquitoes of 109 Squadron marked targets, sometimes for all of Bomber Command.

On 1 December 1942 475 American airmen and twenty-eight officers arrived at Little Staughton to prepare the Advanced Air Depot, 1st Bombardment Wing, which placed B-17s at this airfield, alias AAF Station 127. Little Staughton had previously attracted a variety of aircraft, the first to land being an Anson from Finningley, which called on 7 December 1942. By February 1943 three T2s were in place, and on 1 May 1943 the station passed into American hands. Unusually, some Robin hangars had been added. Throughout 1943 the base was a maintenance depot. An

*Mosquito B16 RV295 'K' of 109 Squadron on dispersal at Little Staughton.*

agreement to place RAF Bomber Groups within geographical groups led on 1 March 1944 to Little Staughton passing to No 8 Group, PFF, Bomber Command. On 1 April a Flight from 7 Squadron and another from 156 Squadron arrived to amalgamate as No 582 Squadron, Lancaster equipped. Next day much of 109 Squadron, PFF, arrived from Marham, where runway building was to commence. Mosquitoes of 109 Squadron had been marking pre-invasion targets and undertaking extensive diversion and nuisance raids on Germany.

On the night of 4/5 April 1944 No 109 Squadron opened Staughton's impressive operational record with raids on Essen where 4,000lb 'cookies' were dropped, on Cologne, Krefeld, Aachen and Rheinhaussen. That first night proved to be one of the few when an *Oboe* Mosquito failed to return – 'S Sugar' crashed in the North Sea.

Lille marshalling yards on the night of 9/10 April 1944 were 582 Squadron's first target, with seven crews operating. Next night the squadron raided Laon and Aachen. By the end of April it had visited Cologne, Dusseldorf, Karlsruhe, Essen and distant Friedrichshafen, suffering its first loss (JA933) on 22/23 April, which was one of two aircraft marking Laon. By the end of April 1944 No 582 Squadron had flown 120 sorties, and No 109 190. May was busier, 320 sorties being flown by 109 Squadron and 173 by the Lancasters of No 582.

On 23 May 1944, at 0300 hours, Anson LT476 of 13 OTU, on a cross-country flight, was attacked by an intruder – probably an Me 410 of V/KG 2. The Anson, hit by cannon fire, force-landed at Little Staughton. One of the crew had baled out, the pilot had serious abdominal wounds and the navigator a thigh injury.

For both squadrons the opening of the Normandy invasion brought a busy night marking coastal batteries. During July 1944 628 sorties were flown from the station, and in August 620, which indicates the activity level.

Although losses were lower than at many bomber bases, operations were far from uneventful. On 22/23 May, for example, Sqn Ldr H W B Heley, flying at 18,000 feet in JB417-R, had an incendiary bomb hit his Lancaster's port rudder. Another lodged in the port outer engine before exploding. Heley completed his bombing run, then ordered the crew to prepare to bale out as flames were now trailing behind the wing. A searchlight picked out the bomber and it was seven dangerous minutes before the flames went out. Between Cologne and Gladbach predicted flak hit the Lancaster, yet it still made England.

Near Mepal, Heley switched on his navigation lights because there were many aircraft about. Moments later an Me 410 attacked the Lancaster from below and astern. With the rear turret out of action, JB417 was highly vulnerable. Although enemy fire raked the bomber none of the crew was injured. Despite the loss of hydraulics, JB417 made an emergency landing at Little Staughton, after which the crew discovered that a 500lb GP bomb had 'hung up'. An eventful sortie for sure.

The first daylight operation for No 582's Lancasters came during the evening of 30 June 1944 with Villars Bocage as target. No 109 Squadron also participated. Thereafter, daylight operations became quite common, with 582 Squadron concentrating upon them during the first half of August. Both squadrons took part in tactical bombing raids, including operation *Tractable* on 14 August, and Lancasters of 582 Squadron marked for a day raid on the Ghent-Terneuzen Canal on 18 August. In early September No 582 helped to reduce Le Havre's garrison to submission, before Calais and Boulogne received similar treatment. On 3 October the target was West Kapelle, with Gp Capt P H Cribb as Master Bomber in 582's ND750.

Rarely did enemy fighters successfully engage Bomber Command's heavies in daylight, but an exception came on 23 December 1944. To attack Cologne's Grimberg marshalling yards seventeen Lancasters of 582 Squadron and a 109 Squadron Mosquito set out in fine weather. Intense flak on the run-in damaged eleven Lancasters, a mixture of Bf 109s and Fw 190s then swept through the fighter screen, engaging the bombers over the target. Lancaster 'T Tommy', flown by Captain Swales, was attacked by eight Bf 109s and a Fw 190, which one of his gunners claimed. Wg Cdr Clough's crew fought it out with a Messerschmitt. Twelve of the Lancasters placed their bombs at the southern end of the railway yard, but it was costly for Little Staughton, five Lancasters and a Mosquito failing to return.

Barely had the returning Lancasters touched down when four Mosquitoes of 109 Squadron took off to join another thirty-six attacking Seighburg. Four more were among the fifty-eight sent to Limburg. During December, 582 Squadron lost seven Lancasters, and by the close of the year it had flown 1,588 sorties, including 147 in December, during which 109 Squadron lost five Mosquitoes in the course of 284 sorties.

Nine crews of 582 Squadron participated in the notorious Dresden raid, four as blind illuminators, one a blind marker, one a blind skymarker, one a primary visual marker, and two as visual centres, all of whom returned safely. The complexity of Pathfinder operations is well illustrated by even this small portion of the force. On the same night six other crews of No 582 marked the synthetic oil refinery at Bohlen for 200 bombers of 4 Group and fifteen of 6 Group. Chemnitz was twice No 582's target at this time. Operations by 109 Squadron included a daylight raid on 6 March when Wesel was bombed by six Mosquitoes leading other 8 Group Mosquitoes. The leader of the first formation collided with a Mosquito off Southwold, leaving Flt Lt Carnegie to force-land his Mosquito at Woodbridge.

Offensive operations by Little Staughton's three-Flight squadrons ended on 25 April 1945. Only one of 109 Squadron's aircraft was able to mark the Wachenfels SS Barracks at Berchtesgaden, the rest having technical problems, then came the final fling. Wangerooge's guns were targeted for twenty-five Lancasters of 582 Squadron, and eight crews of 109 Squadron were marked. Both squadrons participated in food drop operations for the starving Dutch in operation *Manna* in early May, and 582 Squadron retrieved POWs in operation *Exodus*, particularly from Juvincourt and Lubeck, and brought them back to Westcott.

'Cook's tours' of damaged Germany followed. Mosquito crews continued training, their squadron being earmarked for retention. Some of their practice raids were experimentally intercepted by Meteors. The end for 582 Squadron came on 10 September 1945, its Lancasters being flown away to Mepal and Wyton. On the afternoon of 28 September all of 109 Squadron's Mosquitoes left for Upwood, ending Staughton's operational days.

On 19 October 1945 Typhoon RB390 of the Station Flight crashed nearby, five days before Transport Command took control of the airfield, which, on 10 October 1945, was declared non-operational. Tempsford billeted 300 of its men here from late November. Flying had not entirely ceased, for on 28 November a Dakota landed and, on the 30th, an Anson. But during December 1945 Little Staughton was placed on care and maintenance.

There was considerable discussion as to whether this and Thurleigh could be linked by a long runway for the NAE, the reckoning being that high-speed aircraft needed very long runways. However, the idea was abandoned, although RAE Bedford had links with Little Staughton. Brooklands Aviation handled servicing, etc, of Valettas, Varsities and target-towing Mosquitoes here, and for many years it has been used by private light aircraft; in 2003 a 923m by 46m section of runway 07/25 remained in use, the airfield being run by Colton Aviation Ltd.

**Main features:**
*Runways:* 250° 1,920ft x 150ft, 310° 1,340ft x 150ft, 010° 1,000ft x 150ft, concrete and tarmac. *Hangars:* three T2, eight Robins. *Hardstandings:* fifty frying-pan and loop. *Accommodation:* RAF officers 213, SNCOs 600, ORs 1,415; WAAF officers 5, ORs 120.

## LOUGHBOROUGH, Leicestershire

*52°47N/00°13W 40ft asl; SK525215 (Second World War). 1¹/₂ miles NW of Loughborough*

Loughborough has had two airfields, both connected with Brush Coachworks Ltd. That existing in the First World War, from October 1915 to April 1919 and known as Loughborough Meadows, was owned by Brush Electrical Engineering Company, and was used to test-fly the company's aircraft. Brush produced here eighty-seven Farman Longhorns, 350 Avro 504As, Js and Ks, an experimental Henri Farman Astral, twenty Short 827 seaplanes, and 142 Short 184 seaplanes, all except the seaplanes being test-flown from Loughborough Meadows.

In the Second World War the Loughborough factory again built aircraft, although the airfield was re-sited north-west of the town, a grass field with a maximum run of 2,000 feet. Brush Coachworks Ltd test-flew the 335 DH 89 Dominies that it built between March 1943 and March 1946. The Dominies were towed tail-first to the flying ground where the mainplanes were fitted. Hampdens were also repaired by Brush. Closed in 1947, the airfield now rests under an industrial estate.

**Main feature:**
The grass field was alongside the Brush factory.

*An aerial view of Luton in the 1960s, the Percival factory in the central foreground.*

## LUTON, Bedfordshire

*51°52N/00°02E 526ft asl; TL120210. 2 miles E of the town*

Luton has long been far more than a hive for Monarchs, 737s, 'Brits' and easyJet. Here Percival aeroplanes, what some would regard as real aeroplanes, were once made. Prior to the present site, a landing ground existed $2^1/_2$ miles to the north-west until it was outflanked by Luton town's ribbon development. In its place came a new grass aerodrome officially opened on 16 July 1938. Luton Corporation's desire for a municipal airport differed from Birmingham's, for it had a firmer financial and economic base. It was Council eagerness to attract new industries to the town that led to Captain Edgar Percival vacating Gravesend and moving his production base to Luton. Percival was already achieving success with the Gull series and the Mew Gull racer.

The airfield, on high ground east of Luton, was constructed where conditions were usually clear, whereas the low-lying town was often mist-clad. This thoughtful original positioning makes the present airport well sighted, and has made it suitable as a diversion airfield. Percival's factory lay to the north of the adjacent industrial site and to the left of the approach road.

The company moved to Luton in 1936-37, building and levelling of the aerodrome taking place in 1936. Percival's Gull had first flown in December 1935, and during the move further Gull variants were being planned. Work was also being undertaken on the twin-engined six/seven-seat Percival Q.6, the last new pre-war design, first flown in 1937. Vega Gull and Q.6 production occupied the firm in 1938. Fifteen Vega Gulls were supplied to the RAF and a specialised military variant followed.

The Air Ministry desired to open an Elementary & Reserve Flying Training School in the area. Discussions in 1936 led to agreement in April 1937 for Marshall of Cambridge to operate the School. Ten days after the aerodrome officially opened, two Hawker Harts landed for use by 29 E&RFTS, which began functioning on 1 August 1938. While it was never a large School, the airfield attracted a wide variety of light aircraft in pre-war days, and many famous fliers sampled the delight of a Gull or the sight of that beautiful, turquoise Q.6, 'EYE'.

Percival's military Gull, the Proctor, first flew from Luton on 8 October 1939, by which time Captain Percival had left the company. Proctor I deliveries commenced in March 1940, and some also went to the Royal Navy. Proctor I production at Luton totalled 222 aircraft.

As work on the Proctor Mk II was under way, much else happened. Into the western area of the airfield, where some T2 hangars had been erected, moved a small, somewhat secretive organisation, the Napier Flight Development Unit. Napier's factory was in Acton and the firm had managed to establish the Napier Experimental Engine Installation Unit at Northolt in 1937, to carry out flight trials of its H-type Dagger engine, testing of which was under way in 1938. That year witnessed bench-running of the mammoth twenty-four-cylinder H-section in-line Sabre engine. An output of 2,000hp seemed amazing at that time, making it a favourite choice for a multitude of new aircraft types. However, problems with the engine were endless, and seemingly insurmountable, but with essential planned airframes relying on the Sabre, cancellation was impossible, and its development was forced to acceptable levels. Eventually, only two fully operational wartime aircraft were Sabre-powered, out of more than thirty designs for which it was intended.

To test the powerplant a Fairey Battle, L5286, went to Northolt on 18 August 1939 to have a Sabre installed. Another Battle, K9240, fitted with a Dagger, flew mostly from Farnborough. While the Battle was suitable for a variety of engines, it lacked space for comprehensive measurement equipment and was a makeshift test-bed. Napier's flight facility was edged out of Northolt to Luton during March 1940 to make more space available for Northolt's fighters. From Luton the fixed undercarriage Battle was busily flown, testing its Sabre until March 1941, when RAE Farnborough took charge in an attempt to sort out the engine's problems.

Others were also about to move. Short Brothers operated two E&RFTSs, one at Rochester (No 23), the other at Sydenham, Belfast (No 24). At the outbreak of war the two amalgamated at Sydenham as No 24 EFTS, and training of pilots for the Fleet Air Arm continued there. The 1940 collapse of France led to Battle bombers being placed at Sydenham to prevent a German attempt to land in Ireland, and 24 EFTS was forced to find space elsewhere. Leicestershire airfields were considered, but the choice finally fell upon under-used Luton, whither the EFTS moved on 17 July 1940. Two courses under way had to live under canvas, and servicing of the unit's Miles Magisters was undertaken in the open. Each course trained about thirty pupils.

By the end of August 1940 there had been limited enemy action near Luton, then a major assault came in the late afternoon of Friday the 30th when a score of Heinkels bombed the airfield's factory area. Although twenty-eight bombs fell within the airfield boundary, there was little damage and no serious casualty level. One night a parachute mine penetrated the roof of the Percival factory where it dangled some twenty-five yards from where RAF Luton's Orderly Officer was on night duty!

For No 264 Squadron, fame came as fast as it went. It was the first squadron to operate Boulton Paul Defiant turret fighters, but losses forced its withdrawal to safer skies, and the Battle of Britain further proved it outmoded. Then 264 Squadron was switched to night-fighting, to undertake which 'B' Flight moved to Northolt on 12 September 1940. Seven days later Sqn Ldr Garvin moved the Flight to Luton and used sick quarters as the operations room, with tents in the north-west corner of the airfield for the duty crews. On the night following arrival, the Defiants commenced patrols west of London under Northolt's control.

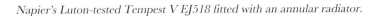

*Napier's Luton-tested Tempest V EJ518 fitted with an annular radiator.*

Nightly operations were punctuated by a spectacular accident. At around 0530 on 7 October 1940 veteran Defiant L7018 was commencing its take-off when, as it raced along the flare path, it hit the wing tip of a stationary aircraft, setting the latter ablaze. The Defiant momentarily became airborne, then fell upon a large tent, the combination bursting into flames. Amazingly, the three tent occupants escaped with only slight injuries.

Great excitement greeted Plt Off Hughes and Sgt Green, who, flying N1621, shot down a Heinkel 111 near Brentwood at around 0130 on 16 October. This was 264's first night success, and the only occasion when a Luton-based aircraft successfully engaged an enemy aircraft.

Throughout the Battle of Britain the Sabre Battle, L5286, was active. It logged more than 1,000 flying hours during four years of active service, which ended on 7 December 1943. Between 10 May 1940 and 17 August 1941, a Hereford was also at Luton, helping to solve oil problems plaguing the Dagger. The Napier Sabre engine proved to be as difficult to develop as any, so the arrival in late 1940 of P1774, the first of the bulky, inelegant Gloster-built Folland 43/37 designed from the outset as test-beds, was most welcome. P1774 was at once used for Sabre I flight development, and later for the equally important Sabre II engine-cooling trials. P1776 arrived at Luton on 29 March 1942 to help test the Sabre II and various radiators before it crashed on 28 August 1944. P1780 was Luton-based from January to August 1943. Napier's test facility also attracted Sabre-powered operational aircraft, the first in the summer of 1941 being a Typhoon Ia used for engine oil pressure and temperature trials, cylinder tests and engine-cooling investigations. Meanwhile 24 EFTS flew long hours using Magisters, some of which, from the summer of 1940, used Barton-in-the-Clay RLG for circuit flying. One of the highlights of the stay of 24 EFTS came on 23 May 1941 when Sir Winston Churchill and a famous retinue visited. Their opinions of the Sabre will probably always remain secret!

At Luton 24 EFTS still concentrated upon training pilots for the Fleet Air Arm. There were ninety-nine pilots undergoing instruction when the School left Luton and moved to Sealand on 7 February 1942.

In 1941 Percival's drawing office designed the Proctor III, but only its prototype was built here. Instead, the company constructed 775 Airspeed Oxford Is, 575 Mk IIs and six Oxford Vs in its by now much enlarged factory. Woodworking skills were even better utilised by building 195 Mosquito XVIs and fifty Mosquito PR 34s at Luton, leaving Messrs F Hills & Son ('Hillson') of Manchester to build the Proctors. A further Proctor re-design during 1942-43 led to the four-seater Proctor IV radio trainer, only eight of which were Luton-built.

The second production aircraft type to have a Sabre was the Blackburn Firebrand heavy naval fighter, the prototype of which, DD804, fitted with wing-root cold air intakes, was at Luton in 1942-43 for 200 hours of flying in an attempt to clear its 2,250hp Sabre III engine. The Sabre required a large radiator, and a novel manner of reducing its drag was tried on Typhoon R8694, which arrived at Luton in August 1942; it had the radiator wrapped around its Sabre IV in annular style. Such a radical change would have upset production lines far too much, although in August 1944 a Warwick III, HG248, arrived for similar fitting, and trials lasted into post-war years.

*'Hello, nice to see you at the Euravia check-in desk' in Luton's first post-war terminal.*

The development of a two-speed supercharged Sabre was an obvious progression, but Napier went further, designing the E 118 three-stage supercharger Sabre in connection with which Folland P1778 test-flew its ducted radiator. The main final wartime Sabre work revolved around making it suitable for the Tempest V, the first of which, EJ518, arrived at Luton on 29 May 1944. Napier, keen to push the annular radiator on the Sabre VI, fitted an example to this aircraft. When it force-landed in late 1944, Napier continued the task using a newly acquired Warwick.

In 1944 Napier held up to twenty aircraft for engine development. One tricky problem being investigated was the addition of a wing-root oil cooler to allow the Tempest VI to operate in hot climates. Another Tempest, NV768, had an annular radiator; this unusual-looking aircraft was later fitted with a drag-reducing ducted spinner, adding 15mph to its top speed. This was to have been a standard post-war fitting to the Napier turbo-prop engine, which was test-flown in the noses of two Lincoln bombers, RF402 and RF530. At Luton a Bristol Phoebus was installed in the belly of another Lincoln, RA643, and the Napier-patented electro-thermal Spraymat de-icer system was first tested on Viking VL229, which served for seven years, then on a Lincoln.

Another Lincoln, SX973, was fitted with a Napier Nomad, a large compound engine intended for the Saro R.2/48 seaplane, a very-long-range South Atlantic patrol aircraft. After much work on both, their rejection was a bitter blow for Napier and Saro, and when the Napier Eland-powered Rotodyne was also cancelled, the future became very bleak.

'Of course, we have the most modern of facilities here at Luton.'

Some success attended the Gazelle engine for the Bristol 192, and the Double Scorpion rocket motor in Canberra WK163 hurled the aircraft fast, high and into the world record class. Cloaked in general euphoria, behind the scenes it was viewed as a 'spy-plane' for operation at around 70,000 feet. Instead, lack of orders for Napier's engines saw the company's demise before the 1960s ended.

Soon after the 1939-45 war ended Percival pursued the Proctor's civil potential by putting the Proctor V – a civil version of the Mk IV – into production at Luton, selling it at home and abroad. Equally important was a three-seat trainer design to Specification T.23/43, the RAF's main post-war intermediate trainer, the Percival Prentice, Luton-built between August 1947 and August 1950.

*Luton's more spacious 1980s terminal, since replaced.*

*An external view of the 1980s terminal.*

Recalling its elegant Q.6 airliner, Percival also designed a new twin-engined, high-wing, five/eight-seater, the Merganser, which first flew on 9 May 1947. With DH Gipsy Queen engines it was clearly under-powered. Re-design and the fitting of Alvis Leonides engines resulted in the eight/ten-seater Prince and military Pembroke. Variations of both were built and others projected, but it was the Provost trainer line that brought most success when it became accepted as the replacement for the RAF's Prentice. All Provosts were Luton-built in the large hangar and works to the left of the approach road at the old entrance to the airport site.

Vaguely resembling the Provost and retaining side-by-side seating for instructor and pilot came the Jet Provost, a natural development. All the Mk I and III versions were Luton-built. During production of the Mk IV, Percival became Hunting-Percival, then Hunting Aircraft was overtaken by the British Aircraft Corporation.

At that time the company had, in a building on the opposite side of the road from the production line and strongly guarded, a mock-up of its very elegant P.107 airliner, development of which BAC undertook, enlarging it into the highly successful BAC 111, examples of which often operated into and out of Luton in later years.

Alongside Percival, Luton Flying Club, of pre-war origin, re-opened after the war. Much publicity surrounded news that the notorious Neville Hume, who cruelly murdered in Bournemouth for sexual satisfaction, flew with the club, even doing so during its first post-war air display on rainy 10 June 1946. Hunting, already associated with Luton, had two Proctor Vs on view that day. Others RAF Proctors were being overhauled, and keeping them company was Jean Batten's Vega Gull (*G-ADPR*, but still marked AX866. Luton-based Hunting Aerosurveys displayed its Dragon Rapide, *G-AEAL*. By Hangars 3 and 4, used by the Napier Installation Experimental Establishment, were two Typhoons, the aged R7712 keeping company with RB450. Warwick III HG248 still retained its wartime grey-green-blue transport finish, beside which Tempest NV768 looked immaculate. During the show a Tempest VI, EJ823, was demonstrated, making this a small yet memorable display. There was not the slightest portent of the airfield's coming transformation.

*Pembroke WV733 on the field outside the Percival works.*

Luton acquired an asphalt runway after the war, although not before Eagle Aviation obtained hangar space and, in the early 1950s, kept some of its Avro Yorks here. Expansion of charter business was slow, mainly ex-military low-load-factor aircraft being costly to operate. For a better view a new control tower opened in 1952.

In 1958 great change began when Luton Council decided, cautiously, to expand its aerodrome into Luton International Airport. At the time Napier was floundering and Percival's future was not assured. Before the decade was out Derby Aviation was running scheduled internal services from Luton, and in 1960 charter operations were commenced by Autair, using the 5,532-foot runway and departure buildings, which, as part of the briefing and operations area, remained for many years at the base of the old control tower.

An important event was the 1962 establishment of Euravia, which in late 1964 became Britannia Airways. In 1968 Monarch Airlines was formed, and indications of the rapid growth of Luton Airport can be appreciated from the fact that in 1961 there were 580 commercial movements, whereas in 1980 they totalled 26,358, with a 1972 peak of 31,257. Runway extension to 7,054 feet was made in 1966. Another £750,000 was spent on a new passenger terminal, the new combination eroding Southend's tourist traffic. In 1969 one-fifth of all inclusive tours involving flying departed from Luton.

Autair became Court Line in 1969 and entered the inclusive tour market, undercutting fares and introducing Lockheed TriStars. In 1972-73, 3,145,658 passengers passed through the airport, making its operation highly profitable. Then, quite suddenly, during the middle of the tour season in August 1974, came the catastrophic collapse of Clarkson/Court Line. Court had charged too little in an attempt to increase trade and fill seats in a highly competitive environment. It had, however, given an enormous boost to holiday inclusive tours, particularly to Spanish resorts. Luton's passenger total fell dramatically, to 1,920,275 in 1974-75, but after about five years business had recovered well and in 1979-80 some 2,230,568 passengers passed through Luton. A 1978 Government White Paper listed Luton as vital to the UK's transport system.

Although it had a flight path sensibly taking aircraft to the south of the town, Luton Airport long suffered a tedious misfortune. Taxiways to the runway led directly from the apron to its northern side, but not to the end, which meant backtracking along the runway prior to take-off, thus impairing operational efficiency. Approval for the necessary improvement was a long time in coming, possibly linked with Government obsession with Stansted, which it persists in promoting despite the terrible damage it brings to a most beautiful part of England's countryside.

Following the Court Line collapse, Luton saw Britannia Airways predominate, its 737s and 767s being a large part of the 1980s and early 1990s scene. Monarch Airlines – still using Luton – operated Bristol Britannias, which were replaced by 757s and Airbuses. In 1986 Monarch Crown Service was operating to Spain, and a new name appeared, Ryanair, which operated to Eire.

The 1980s saw holiday tour operators switch from first-generation jets to quieter, more economic Boeing 737s, and recently to the sophisticated Airbus family. A boost to Luton came from the decision of Royal Mail to use it as the overnight base for Datapost distribution.

By 1979 airlines were flying out of Luton to sixty-five countries, so Luton Council approved plans for a fine terminal building costing some £6 million, which was opened in 1985 by HRH The Prince of Wales. The airport was making a healthy profit, and the future looked encouraging. But aviation carries investment risks, and there were always those who asked what a local Council was doing running an international airport, however successfully. In 1986 the Luton Airport Act required the establishment of the airport as a company having a management board. The following year Luton International Airport became a Limited Company with Luton Borough Council the sole shareholder. In 1990 it was officially named London Luton Airport, from where Ryanair departed in 1991.

In the 1990s the airport was sold amid some acrimony. Eventually it came into the hands of the present operator, London Luton Airport Ltd, with the Council as an 'arm's length' shareholder. The new management developed new business links, including the start of Airtours flights, increased employment levels and built a new access road. It was now that taxiways from the main east apron, new cargo apron and centre, as well as from the General Aviation Parking Area, fed into a perimeter track that led to the eastern hold for the now 7,087 feet by 150 feet 08/26 asphalt Cat 3 ILS-equipped runway. Although three lead-offs remain available, to reach the south-western end of the runway still requires backtracking. A new control tower was also built, and superior passenger terminal facilities flanked by an improved bus terminus. There was also another major change to exploit, deregulation in Europe. No longer would fares be held at one price for each service and style – they could be decided upon by the operator.

Hitherto, large national carriers had offered a fair range of routes without strong competition and had little incentive to lower fares. Deregulation opened the door to a new style of operation, and easyJet was founded on the beliefs that passengers want safe, on-time, low-cost travel. As with Court Line, the new operator set out to fill seats by setting low fares and including various inexpensive promotions to attract awareness of regular deals on offer. After the catastrophic events of '9/11' the company moved quickly, cutting fares by 10% and attracting customers back faster than many airlines that increased fares to stem losses. Passengers would need to book easyJet flights direct with the operator through the internet or by telephone, removing the middleman, the travel agent. Perhaps most important, the company would run for easier maintenance a single-type fleet suitable for European sectors of up to four hours. Absence to a large extent of on-board catering would help to reduce turn-round time. For a major hub easyJet chose Luton.

By 2003, easyJet, Europe's largest low-cost airline, was into its seventh year, had shown a profit for the previous six years, and was operating on 105 routes serving thirty-eight airports. Between January 2002 and January 2003 easyJet carried 17.7 million passengers, nearly half on some routes being business passengers. At Gatwick and Schiphol easyJet is the second most frequent user.

Although Ryanair has returned to Luton one does not need to be at Luton long to realise the dominance there of easyJet. By summer 2003 the range of travel on offer included flights to Amsterdam, Athens, Faro, Malaga, Nice, Palma, Paris Charles de Gaulle, Nice, Scotland, Zurich and others. It is best to be a regular internet user to make a booking.

*An easyJet Boeing 737 taking off in hazy weather with Luton's latest tower behind.*

How long the popularity of low-cost airlines will be maintained is unpredictable. An economic turn-round, for instance, might lure business passengers back to personal-service national carriers. Unforeseeable events of many sorts could change the pattern of travel. Demands for more space, movement and special on-board facilities might quite quickly alter the scene – and so might very large aircraft like the Airbus A380. At present, though, and probably for some time to come, easyJet remains good news for London Luton Airport.

In marked contrast with earlier times, scheduled services now accounted for 70% of the volume of traffic. McAlpine handles a lucrative and mainly VIP charter business involving, by the 1990s, expensively fitted Falcons, Gulfstreams and, more recently, Global Express bizz-jets.

Remnants of wartime and even pre-war Luton remain. The large hangar by the west side of the apron takes in the two pre-war hangars, joined and modified. Napier's T2s are used for bizz jets. Percival's factory was overtaken by now largely vanquished Vauxhall Motors. What seems lost – not entirely due to high and essential security measures – is the friendly atmosphere so prevalent in the past and enjoyed by millions setting off for a place in the sun, or venturing to very distant places. For many years Luton provided a distinctly more intimate service than airports usually offer. Now one senses that the pressure is clearly directed to making money, and probably has to be for company survival. Sadly, Luton is no longer quite such a special place, just a part of a less satisfying market forces world.

**Main features:**
*Runway:* 08/26 7,087ft x 150ft, asphalt. *Hangars:* one modified T2, assorted large civilian-designed hangars. Large general aircraft parking to west, east apron from which Taxiway D leads north to cargo apron. New Taxiway A connects all parking areas with the runway.

## MARKET HARBOROUGH, Leicestershire

*52°29N/00°57W 360ft asl; SP710890. 2 miles NW of Market Harborough*

Market Harborough, a mid-war airfield built in 1942/43, was constructed due to the need to expand the number of UK airfields in order to accommodate large numbers of US units in Britain. A typical temporary three-runway wartime airfield for bomber-type aircraft, its prime use was as a home for No 14 OTU. Moved from Cottesmore to make way for a US Troop Carrier Group, that unit brought along Wellington IIIs and Xs at the end of July 1943. Simultaneously, a companion new airfield, Husbands Bosworth, became its designated satellite.

To cope with increasing needs for bomber crews, part of 14 OTU was hived off on 15 June 1944, and at Husbands Bosworth formed the nucleus of No 85 OTU. As a result No 14 OTU was reduced to a three-quarters strength, in which state it remained until disbandment on 24 June 1945.

The only unit change during 14 OTU's stay was the arrival on 3 February 1944 of No 1683 Bomber (Defence) Training Flight flying Tomahawks – but not for long, because in March Hurricane IIcs replaced them. The Flight disbanded on 1 August 1944.

After a period on care and maintenance, Market Harborough was occupied by 273 MU, which, in February 1946, established No 113 Sub-Storage Site here. Handling large numbers of aircraft, it needed much additional space. Martinet target-towers were stored then scrapped here, together with Horsas from 6 MU, the unit that took over the business on 28 April 1947. The sub-site closed on 3 October 1949 and activity here ceased.

**Main features:**
*Runways:* 140° 5,700ft x 150ft, 180° 4,200ft x 150ft, 290° 4,200ft x 150ft, concrete and tarmac. *Hangars:* four T2, one B1. *Accommodation:* RAF officers 171, SNCOs 628, ORs 892; WAAF officers 10, SNCOs 15, ORs 427.

## MELTON MOWBRAY, Leicestershire

*52°44N/00°53W 400ft asl; SK750155. 2 miles E of Melton Mowbray*

By mid-1943 RAF overseas operations required a steady flow of replacement aircraft. Far East operations were also soon likely to need much support, although a positive decision was taken whereby the USA would provide many aircraft needed in that theatre. Long-duration aircraft – like the Lincoln and Hornet – would be developed in Britain, also particularly for that theatre. For use in the Near East, Middle East and SEAC, fighter aircraft needed to be shipped, with some twin-engined machines being flown out via staging posts. Larger aircraft, after special preparation, could to be flown out if crews were given suitable training. That task was partly undertaken at Melton Mowbray.

A typical three-runway, temporary wartime bomber-style Class 'A' airfield, built in late 1942-43 and inland of the operational area, Melton Mowbray began its active life within 44 Group, Transport Command, when No 4 Overseas Aircraft Preparation Unit formed here on 1 September 1943, principally to handle types as diverse as Bostons, Beaufighters, Wellingtons and later Stirlings. To train crews to fly mainly 'twins' overseas, Nos 306 and 307 Ferry Training Units arrived on 14-17 October 1943. On 1 December 1943 No 304 FTU, which concentrated on ferrying larger aircraft, joined them. Then on 15 January 1944 the three units became 304 FTU to train crews for all overseas ferrying tasks.

Following training, crews joined No 1 Ferry Crew Pool, which moved into Melton Mowbray on 14 January 1944 and held for practice small numbers of Beaufighters, Beauforts, Mosquitoes, Wellingtons and Warwicks. Its stay was brief, for on 16 March 1944 No 1 Ferry Unit (FU), Pershore, absorbed it.

On 5 July 1944 the local OAPU dropped its 'overseas' prefix, becoming No 4 APU. Further rationalisation followed on 9 October when it merged with 304 FTU, becoming 12 Ferry Unit, now also handling Dakotas and Halifaxes and adding Liberators, Venturas and some smaller aircraft to its repertoire in 1945.

Sundry other units passed through Melton Mowbray, like the Mk X Airborne Interception Radar Conversion Flight, formed here on 29 August 1944 to provide conversion training for Mosquito crews in the Middle East, whence it departed, via St Mawgan, on 8 September 1944. Dakotas of No 107 OTU flew from here in September 1944, and later that year No 1341 (Special Duties) Flight made transit en route to the Far East. On 28 September 1945 a special Flight to operate Stirling Vs overseas began life here as 'J' Flight, moving to the Middle East on 5 October

1945 and becoming No 1588 Heavy Freight Flight on 10 October 1945. By then Melton's task was being undertaken elsewhere, and on 7 November 1945 12 FU closed, leaving Melton to fade away.

**Main features:**
*Runways:* 157° 6,000ft x 150ft, 296° 4,200ft x 150ft, 035° 3,900ft x 150ft, concrete. *Hangars:* four T2. *Hardstandings:* twelve spectacle type, eighteen aprons. *Accommodation:* RAF officers 115, SNCOs 414, ORs 1,472; WAAF officers 10, SNCOs 24, ORs 288.

## MOLESWORTH, Cambridgeshire

*52°23N/00°25W 240ft asl; TL008775. E of Thrapston*

Planned in 1939, hill-top Molesworth featured outstandingly excellent approaches. It was one of a clutch of bomber bases intended for RAF Bomber Command Liberators equipping 8 (Bomber) Group, but which was abandoned early in 1942. All the earmarked airfields were similar in formal and general layout featuring one J Type metal hangar and only essential additions.

Its interesting, unusual history began when the RAF opening party arrived on 15 May 1941. Vacillation over Liberator policy meant that it was 15 November 1941 before any squadron moved in. At Molesworth that involved a new Australian bomber squadron, No 460, formed from 'C' Flight 458 Squadron and armed with the American-engined Wellington IV, a version unusual in the area. Kimbolton, already Molesworth's satellite, actually attracted the first Wellington for 460 Squadron, which positioned itself there on 29 November. No operations were flown before 460 Squadron left for Breighton on 5 January 1942, Molesworth's first association with operational flying occurring three days later when a Wellington of IX Squadron landed here from operations.

The station's next occupants were crews of 159 Squadron, who had learned to operate Liberators at Polebrook. They had no aircraft of their own, stayed only briefly, and on 12 February 1942 departed by train from Thrapston. Next day thirteen Blenheims of 'A' and 'B' Flights, 17 OTU, moved in, for Upwood had become unserviceable. Some returned home on 17 February, the remainder in March.

On 27 February 1942 Molesworth was honoured with a visit by General Ira Eaker USAAC, who brought along four of his staff to view the station's potential as a B-17 base. Major improvements followed, including runway extensions and additional dispersal areas. More accommodation was built and two T2 hangars were added. Another unexpected interlude began on 13 March 1942 when thirteen Master IIIs and three Hurricanes of 5 SFTS Ternhill arrived for a month's stay.

Preparations gathered pace in May 1942 for the establishment of 'No 2 Depot'. On 10 May the station was placed on care and maintenance, then, during the evening of 12 May, trains arrived at Thrapston bringing the advance US guard under the command of Major M C Carpenter. Throughout May more Americans moved in, and early in June ground personnel of the 31st Fighter Group stayed briefly. In mid-June, personnel of the 5th Photographic Squadron also staged through, but the greatest excitement greeted the arrival on 9 June 1942 of the 15th Bomb Squadron, which was to operate from here. Later that day it took on charge a couple of RAF Boston IIIs and a doubtless nervous Tiger Moth.

Crews of the 15th were told to explore using the Douglas A-20 in a night-fighter/interdictor role. Switched by the British to day-bombing, the Americans wanted to find out for themselves which role most suited the A-20. Having no operational aircraft of its own, the 15th borrowed Boston IIIs from the RAF, and for operations was attached to No 226 Squadron RAF, Swanton Morley. Headed by Captain Kegelman, a USAAF crew aboard a 226 Squadron Boston on 29 June 1942 carried out the first USAAF bombing raid on a European target, Hazebrouck marshalling yards. The 15th BS acquired RAF Bostons in July and decorated them with the US star insignia.

More personnel arrived on 14 July, their crusade being the effective operation of their vaunted Flying Fortress. Regarding the precise date of arrival of the first B-17F Fortress there seems uncertainty, but I first noted one at Molesworth on 5 August.

The 5th Photographic Reconnaissance Squadron left on 10 September, the 15th Bomb Squadron three days later. All was then clear for the arrival of the 303rd Bomb Group, which left Biggs Field, Texas, and began moving into Molesworth on 12 September after a five-day Atlantic crossing on the RMS *Queen Mary*. By the end of the war in Europe the 303rd was to fly, in the course of 364 operations, more operational sorties (10,721) than any other 8th AF Bomb Group.

Not until 17 November 1942 did sixteen B-17Fs of the 303rd fly their first operation, U-boat pens at St Nazaire being the target. Bombs were brought back, however, for on arrival the target was thickly cloud-clad. Next day they tried for La Pallice, bombed – and discovered that they had hit the previous day's target! A few days later they redeemed themselves as the only Group to bomb Lorient during a difficult operation.

Committed to action, 'Hell's Angels' joined in most major attacks by the 8th AF, including the Wilhelmshaven raid of 27 January 1943, when the 8th AF introduced itself to the Fatherland. It visited Hamm on 2 February.

It was 18 March 1943 when the courage so suddenly demanded on operations was dramatically displayed by Lt Jack W Mathis, bombardier aboard *The Duchess,* a B-17F of the 358th Bomb Squadron. As the aircraft was running in to the target a shell burst close to the nose, hurling Mathis back into the fuselage. Horrifically wounded, he summoned the courage to drag himself back to the bombsight and released the bomb load before he died. He was posthumously awarded the Medal of Honor.

Raids on Germany took the group to well-known targets including Huls synthetic rubber factory, Bremen's shipyards, Hamburg, Frankfurt and Schweinfurt. Many targets in France were attacked both prior to, and following, D-Day, by which time another member of the 303rd, Technical Sergeant Forrest L Vosler, also of the 358th, had been awarded the Medal of Honor . He was aboard *Jersey Bounce Jr* during the Bremen mission of 20 December 1943, when heavy flak was encountered, after which German fighters pestered the damaged Fortress. Vosler, seriously wounded, continued with his task, aiding the defence of the B-17. Eventually the aircraft ditched in the Channel. Despite terrible wounds, Vosler held another member of the crew aboard until both were transferred to a dinghy. After ten months' treatment Vosler was invalided out of the Air Force.

As well as courageous men, Molesworth was the base of famous Fortresses. One was the B-17F *Hell's Angels,* 41-24577 of the 358th Bomb Squadron, the first B-17 to complete twenty-five operational sorties over Europe. Another was *Knockout Dropper,* the first B-17 to manage seventy-five sorties – the equivalent to three crew tours. As 41-24605 it had arrived in Britain in October 1942, joined the 359th Bomb Squadron, became 'BN-R' and brought its crew home each time without any being wounded.

During the Oschersleben raid of 11 January 1944, when the 303rd was leading the 1st Air Division, ten of its B-17s were shot down by intense fighter onslaught. The courage of all won the group a Distinguished Unit Citation.

The 303rd flew its final mission on 25 April 1945 and bombed Pilsen in Czechoslovakia. In early June the Group was transferred to North Africa for transport duty.

The RAF repossessed Molesworth on 1 July 1945, with affinity to things American continuing. Nos 441 and 442 Canadian squadrons had on 16 July brought along their Mustang IIIs and IVs. On 27 July 1945 a still rare sight and sound was the arrival of Meteor IIIs belonging to No 1335 Conversion Unit, moving in from Colerne. Their role was to convert piston-engined fighter squadron pilots to jet aircraft.

Both Mustang squadrons disbanded on 10 August, and were replaced by 234 Squadron from Hutton Cranswick. On 7 September 1945 Mustang IVs of 19 Squadron also moved in. While here they managed to acquire blue and white nose chequerboard markings, despite official frowning. March 1946 saw Spitfire XVIs replace the Mustangs, the squadron leaving on 28 June 1946. Spitfire IXs of 129 Squadron arrived from Brussels on 9 November 1945 and left for Hutton Cranswick on 3 December. No 124 Squadron, at Molesworth from August to 6 October 1945, flew Meteor IIIs. In late October 1945 No 222 Squadron came from Weston Zoyland for Meteor conversion. The first accident involving one of the jets happened on 15 October 1945; short of fuel, it came down two miles from Polebrook.

In November 1945 the first of several foreign delegations came to see the Meteor, but whether they knew of November's highlight is doubtful. At about 0100 on 20 November a guardroom Corporal heard an unexpected roar. A Meteor was making an unauthorised flight! A roll-call showed that Plt Off J E Adam was missing, together with EE316. The general hullabaloo brought the special investigation branch hurrying along and 12 Group held a court of enquiry.

On 11 December 1945 No 222 Squadron left for Exeter. Next in was 234 Squadron, in mid-February, leaving for Boxted in March following Meteor conversion. Between September and October 1946, Tempest IIs of 54 Squadron were based here, then the station was placed on care and maintenance.

Molesworth's clear approaches and good weather record led to it being funded for improvement by the USA in July 1951. A long, single runway was laid, superimposed upon the conventional three-runway site, the base re-opening for flying in February 1954. The new occupant was unusual, for it was the 582nd Air Re-supply Group, which arrived later that month bringing a dozen B-29As, four Grumman SA-16A amphibians, three C-119Cs able to use RATO gear, and a C-47. The B-29s' role, secretly guarded, was said to include 'supply dropping and giving assistance to crews who had come down in difficult terrain'. Also undertaken was leaflet dropping. A few B-45s of the 47th Bomb Wing were at Molesworth in mid-1956 while their home base had runway repairs.

On 25 October 1956 the 582nd ARG dissolved into a new 42nd Troop Carrier Squadron (Medium) directly controlled by USAFE through HQ 3rd AF. Gone were the B-29s, their place taken by C-119Cs and a few C-54s. C-47s and SA-16As merely switched owners. This unit's stay was brief for, on 31 May 1957, it came under Alconbury's control before being de-activated there on 8 December 1957. Transport aircraft continued to call for some time because Molesworth was a supply depot for the USAF as well as a reserve airfield. A few 'weather reconnaissance' Boeing WB-50s made use of Molesworth in the late 1950s.

The 1980s saw Molesworth hit the headlines as the second base for US cruise missiles stored within the 550th TAM GLCM Alert and Maintenance Area, which straddled what was once the long runway. Four Flights, each able to launch sixteen missiles, were based here once the unit was complete in 1988. Their stay was brief, removal coming when the Cold War had thawed. Molesworth retains US links.

**Main features:**
*Runways:* 191° 6,000ft x 150ft, 255° 4,200ft x 150ft, 309 4,200ft x 150ft, concrete and tarmac. *Hangars:* two T2, one Type J. *Hardstandings:* fifty frying-pan. *Accommodation:* USAAF officers 443, EM 2,529.

---

## MORETON-IN-MARSH, Gloucestershire

*51°59'N/01°40'W 420ft asl; SP230350. 2 miles E of Moreton-in-Marsh*

'Much Binding in the Marsh' of 1940s radio fame originated from the name of an airfield on the fringe of the market town of Moreton-in-Marsh. There the link ceases, for this Cotswold airfield played a largely unsung yet important part during wartime.

Why Moreton-in-Marsh, on the Fosse Way, was so named is uncertain. It could be due to marshland around, or its situation on a 'march' or county boundary where Gloucestershire and Oxfordshire meet. What is certain is that construction of the 1939 planned airfield started in 1940, with 3,000-foot runways well advanced by October 1940. Already judged too short, one was extended to 4,200 feet and the other two to 3,300 feet. None were finished when on 21 January 1941 the RAF moved on to sodden marshland, confirming one possible airfield title meaning. Roofing of the J Type hangar was still incomplete, the framework for two T2s was being erected, and only the foundations of the other pair had been laid.

Drainage was a common problem at new airfields due to them occupying flat areas, while in summer many became parched, dusty plains until grass took a strong hold. For safety, 75-yard-wide strips on each side of metalled runways were rolled hard in case aircraft swung off them, or needed to make 'soft ground' belly landings.

Although under the control of Edgehill, Moreton-in-Marsh opened as 21 OTU with three Wellington Ics and two Ansons, the latter for navigation training. The OTU's No 1 Course opened on 1 March 1941.

Aware of that activity, the enemy twice attacked the station. On 3 April 1941 two large HEs exploded on the landing ground, and on 8 May 1941 a shoal of incendiaries fell on the west side of the airfield. No 21 OTU was by now operating, and on 28 April 1941 its Wellingtons dropped leaflets on Paris. However, such activity was very limited, the OTU being too busy training crews for the many Wellington bomber squadrons.

On 24 November 1941 a directive sealed 21 OTU's activity for much of its future. It would train crews exclusively for Middle East Wellington squadrons, members of the first such course completing their training on 14 December 1941. On returning after a week's leave, each crew spent ten days in Despatch Flight, preparing to make a night flight across France to Malta – later via Gibraltar – then proceeding to Egypt or beyond. For a crew with limited experience, such an undertaking was not to be faced lightly. There was no other feasible way of delivering the aircraft apart from withdrawing crews from operational squadrons, and loss rates were surprisingly low. The first flight to Malta left on 1 January 1942, such activity being now concentrated at Harwell and Moreton.

A second batch of seven crews left Moreton on 15 January 1942, following which fifteen crews were despatched each month, rising to eighteen in April, then twenty monthly. Take-off accidents involving the very heavily laden aircraft were inevitably serious. On 6 May 1942 a Wellington Ic, swinging on take-off, suffered a burst tyre, swerved and rammed X9934 being armed at dispersal. Both aircraft burst into flames, personnel in X9934 being lucky to clear the aircraft before its bombs exploded. Three men were, however, injured.

No 21 OTU contributed to the 'Thousand Plan' operations, ten Wellingtons flying from Moreton to bomb Cologne on 30/31 May 1942, and seventeen for the Essen raid. In all three crews made early returns and Wellington W5618 was lost. Moreton-in-Marsh sent seven aircraft to Bremen, T2974 landing back at Honington after being engaged by a night-fighter.

Formed at Bassingbourn, No 1446 Ferry Training Flight moved here during May, its role being the handling of the despatch overseas of Wellingtons. It became operational during June 1942, first despatching Wellingtons for Nos 99 and 458 Squadrons. Then it took over half of the commitment of 1443 Ferry Training Flight, Harwell. From July 1942, for safety reasons, all Wellington flights to the Middle East were routed via Cornwall on a track taking them out over the Atlantic. Exceptions were Wellington GR VIIIs, whose range problems limited them to shorter flights. In July 1942 No 1446 Flight despatched thirty-six Wellingtons overseas.

Between July and September 1942 No 21 OTU reinforced bomber raids by participating in *Grand National* Main Force bombing of German targets, then reverted to normal training. During October 1942, in keeping with other 91 Group OTUs, and to explain Allied attacks on French colonial territory, *Nickelling* was resumed, five sorties being sent to the Paris area on 24/25 October. Another round came on 18/19 November, during which engine trouble forced down T2574 at Lysse, near Petersfield, Hampshire, killing the crew of four. That month twenty-two Wellingtons left Moreton-in-Marsh for the Middle East.

In December 1942 No 1446 Flight, holding twelve Wellingtons as well as Ansons and Oxfords for ferry crew training, despatched thirteen Wellington VIIIs, while 21 OTU supplied reading matter to the residents of Nantes. Similar activity took place in February 1943 after leaflet distribution to Parisians. The Ferry Flight, redesignated No 311 Ferry Training Unit on 1 May 1943, moved Wellingtons to the Middle East until disbandment on 1 May 1944.

Spring 1943 found 21 OTU's establishment set at fifty-four Wellingtons, seventeen Ansons and four target-towers. By then the Unit was participating in *Bullseyes*. The first two Martinets received on 27 April 1943 were placed at Enstone, designated 21 OTU's satellite on 12 April. At the end of August and in the first week of September 1943, 21 OTU briefly resumed bombing operations, targets in the Pas de Calais being attacked during the *Starkey* feint operation.

Change overtook Moreton-in-Marsh and other OTUs with the fitting of a second navigator's table in the aged Wellington Mk Ics still used here. Anson navigational trainers could now be dispensed with. Two *Nickelling* operations were flown in mid-September 1943, then bad weather prevented any in October, by which time 21 OTU was instructed to fly a dozen *Nickels* monthly. In November thirteen were despatched when the OTU was contributing to six *Bullseyes* a month.

What remains surprising is that 21 OTU was in 1944 *still* flying operational sorties using obsolete Wellington Ics. It appears that the last British-based Wellington Ic operational sorties were flown, from Moreton-in-Marsh, on 6 February 1944. Prior to that, three certainly delivered leaflets on 22 January. On 6 February, among six Wellingtons operating over France were R1523 (once with 311 (Czech) Squadron), X9818 (once of 101 Squadron), Z8840, with a lengthy front-line career, DV844 and DV896. Does any reader have memories of flying in these old stagers? Survival rates of Moreton's Wellingtons were remarkable. Participants in the leaflet-dropping operations on 14/15 January 1944, for instance, included L7890, which had entered OTU service at Pershore on 9 April 1941 and progressively served with Nos 22, 21, 15 and 21 OTUs between 2 December 1943 and 22 February 1944. Also operating that night were R1523, used by 3 PRU between 30 March and 27 July 1941, and N2736, delivered to Hendon in January 1941, passed to 221 Squadron in May 1941 and transferred to Moreton-in-Marsh on 8 January 1942. R1523 even survived the war, not being struck off charge until March 1946.

Changeover to Wellington IIIs and Xs at Moreton came during January 1944, Mk Xs first operating on 14/15 January; soon after they were flying from Enstone, and sorties were flown from there in March, in which month unit strength quickly rose, for thirty-five Wellingtons had reached 21 OTU upon the closure of 15 OTU Harwell. Moreton-in-Marsh was congested with Wellingtons – until the trusty old Ics were ferried away. Increased numbers of newer Wellingtons raised the number available for operations to twenty, two being the Type 423 variant so that 21 OTU could, if necessary, drop 4,000lb bombs; normally the OTU's aircraft carried 500lb bombs.

*Bullseyes* continued, and in March the first exercise Eric was flown. Sixteen *Nickels* were mounted in April 1944, including leaflets warning the French to expect heavy attacks on transport targets. Diversion feints were flown over the North Sea in May, to mislead German night-fighter controllers.

For a year Martinet target-towers had doubled up as fighters, giving gunners training, but from 26 April 1944 Hurricanes replaced them. All Wellingtons here were now Mk III/Xs, the nominal strength still being fifty-four.

Operational flying ceased after July 1944, but unlike many OTUs No 21 did not disband at the end of hostilities. Instead, it moved to Permanent RAF Station Finningley in November 1946. Moreton-in-Marsh was taken over in December 1946 by No 21 (P)AFU from Wheaton Aston, which resulted in a swarm of Oxfords descending. No 21 Group, Flying Training Command, controlled the station from 9 December 1946.

No 1 Refresher School arrived from Enstone on 17 December 1946, raising the Oxford population to sixty-two aircraft. Seven Magisters and fifteen Harvard IIbs were added in January 1947 before very heavy snowfalls halted flying, which was not resumed until 9 April 1947. A drastic reduction followed, half the Oxfords being declared surplus.

On 6 August 1947 No 21 (P)AFU and No 1 Refresher School amalgamated, becoming No 1 (Pilot) Refresher Flying Unit. 'A' Flight used eleven Oxfords, 'B' Flight ten Wellington Xs, and 'C' Flight nine Harvards and seven Spitfire XVIs. On 10 January 1948 this unit followed its predecessor to Finningley, leaving Moreton-in-Marsh under care and maintenance.

An RAF medical school then opened, a 'medical flying squad'. Following its closure in 1951 came Harvards of No 1 Flying Training School, training pilots and also acclimatising to European conditions those trained overseas. In December 1951 it became the last FTS to re-equip with Prentices.

Little Rissington and Valley aircraft made use of Moreton-in-Marsh, but its runways were too short for safe jet flying. No 1 FTS closed in 1955, the station again passing to care and maintenance. Later that year the Home Office commandeered it for training RAF 'H' Class reservists in fire-fighting techniques in a nuclear war, which continued until 1959.

Civilian and auxiliary fire service training for civilians then commenced, and Moreton-in-Marsh became an annexe of the Fire Service College at Dorking. On 14 June 1966 it was announced that the Fire Service Technical College was opening at Moreton-in-Marsh to train middle-rank fire service personnel. Training has been repeatedly re-orientated to take account of the complex latest problems and threats facing the fire services, particularly caused by toxic materials and chemicals, and when fighting industrial fires. Staff College Dorking closed on 30 June 1981, senior staff courses then being run at Moreton-in-Marsh from 1 July 1981, when the Fire Service College re-opened here, where it still operates behind high trees.

**Main features:**
*Runways:* 218° 4,800ft x 150ft, 157° 3,300ft x 150ft, 277° 3,300ft x 150ft. *Hangars:* one Type J, four T2. *Hardstandings:* thirty frying-pan type. *Accommodation:* RAF officers 150, SNCOs 477, ORs 1,460; WAAF officers 12, SNCOs 24, ORs 400.

---

## MOUNT FARM, Oxfordshire

*51°40N/01°09W, 139ft asl; SU578963. E of Berrisfield, 8 miles SE of Oxford*

Gravel workings mark the site of what was once Benson's satellite, named Mount Farm. Dispersing to this Unbuilt Satellite in July 1940 came Battles of 12 OTU, whose crews received initial conversion training by day and night, a gooseneck flare path being laid for the latter activity. Personnel and the troops guarding the site relied upon tented accommodation and facilities. Following the alarming attack on Stanton Harcourt, a few light machine-guns were placed to protect Mount Farm, which, by mid-August and because of its good situation, had been chosen for development. Concrete runways were fast constructed in the hope that they would be ready for use in mid-September 1940. That was over-optimistic – it was two months later before the runways came into use.

Policy changes relating to Unbuilt and Built Satellites had then come about. Initially for dispersing aircraft, they were, from September 1940, to be extensively used for night-flying training, thereby lessening the need for Permanent Stations to be lit at night. In the case of 12 OTU, Battles were to be phased out in favour of Wellingtons, which would become 1 Group's main type. High-intensity flying made runways necessary at OTUs, especially in winter. Benson, the Parent Station, still had a grass surface unsuitable for much Wellington flying, whereas Mount Farm's runways were available for day and night flying of Wellingtons. Extension of those runways by 900 feet was ordered to be undertaken when feasible.

On 1 December 1940 No 12 OTU was reduced from a Battle-armed full OTU to a half-strength Wellington OTU flying from Mount Farm and Benson. Half-strength resulted from the decision to move the PRU from Heston to Benson in December 1940. By January 1941 training of Wellington crews by 12 OTU was well under way. It was briefly interrupted in the early afternoon of 27 January by a low-flying raider, using low cloud cover, which penetrated to the Benson area. Two bombs fell about half a mile from Mount Farm, whose LAA guns fired unsuccessfully as the bomber hurried away to bomb Benson. During night-flying, a second attack resulted in thirteen 50kg bombs falling on Mount Farm. One cratered the north-east/south-west runway and two burst on the peritrack; an NCO was killed, three men were injured and two Wellingtons and a Magister were damaged. A third attack came on 12 May 1941 when a bomb produced a 50-foot-diameter crater, again on the main runway, which was further damaged by a smaller bomb. Another fell on the perimeter track and fifteen more on waste ground. Such attacks were an annoyance, as was the intention.

Benson's role as the PR centre caused 12 OTU's relocation to Chipping Warden, then No 15 OTU Harwell took control of Mount Farm on 23 July 1941, which became its Second Satellite. With runways, and following general upgrading, Mount Farm was now used for operational flying, including night diversions. On 10 July 1941 nine Hampdens of 61, 106, 144 and 408 Squadrons and two Wellingtons of 218 Squadron, returning from attacks on Aachen and Osnabruck, homed here.

Benson received No 1416 Flight on 5 September 1941, and on 17 September it became 140 Squadron. Mainly equipped with PR Spitfires, it held a handful of Blenheims for night reconnaissance. To relieve pressure on Benson, now packed with PR aircraft, the station re-possessed Mount Farm in January 1942, 140 Squadron placing four Spitfires here on 23 January. Operations, however, were despatched from Benson due to the need for special pre-flight briefing. In the event of a German invasion of Britain, 140 Squadron would have maintained a visual and photographic watch on developments, and the squadron had, for that reason and the likelihood of heavy losses, a higher establishment than most PR squadrons.

Mount Farm served as a dispersal airfield for increasing numbers of Benson's PR Spitfires until 4 May 1942, when both 'A' and 'B' Flights of 140 Squadron moved in while concrete runways were being laid at Benson. Mount Farm now accommodated up to ten PR Spitfires variously known as Mk V, Type F, G and Mk Ia, together with six Blenheim IVs and a Tiger Moth. From Mount Farm the Blenheims flew night photo reconnaissance flights using photo flashes. Spitfires flew daylight PR sorties over France, and with the Dieppe raid being prepared, that area received much attention from 140 Squadron. After the raid's postponement, a second busy period required new intelligence. Between 15 and 22 August 1942, sixty-three of the seventy-five Spitfire sorties flown from Mount Farm were successful, many being to the Dieppe area. On 17 August 1942, when the Squadron flew twenty-two Spitfire sorties, many covered Dieppe. Plt Off L G Smith, flying R7115, made six runs across the port, obtaining fine results from 30,000 feet.

Blenheim operations were becoming increasingly hazardous. Twice towards the end of June 1942 crews reported night-fighters, so Blenheim sorties ended with a night reconnaissance to the Cherbourg Peninsula on 15 August 1942. Spitfire operations continued until 15 March 1943, when 140 Squadron moved to Hartford Bridge. Mount Farm's future was then re-orientated.

Gearing up for a tactical PR role was the 13th PR Squadron, USAAF, which had reached Podington on 2 December 1942 and was awaiting space at a suitable base. Mount Farm being ideal, the 13th moved there on 16 February, bringing along some Piper L-4 Cubs, although it was to operate with P-38 and F-5 Lightnings. Before they arrived, reverse Lend-Lease Spitfires formed a major element of the squadron's equipment and were used to obtain target damage assessment photographs following 8th AAF attacks.

On 12 May 1943 the 14th PR Squadron (Light) arrived, also to operate P-38s, F-4s and F-5s, and later Spitfires. The 22nd Photographic Squadron (Light) reached Mount Farm on 8 June, also to use P-38s and Spitfires. From a humble start Mount Farm was now really important.

Photo-reconnaissance operations by the 13th Squadron commenced on 28 March 1943. On 7 July the three squadrons became part of the 7th Photographic Group, then the 14th started operating. Activated on 1 May 1943 as the 7th Photographic Group, it was renamed the 7th PR and Mapping Group, then the 7th Photograph Group (Reconnaissance) on 13 November 1943. Name changes indicated alterations in operational purpose. A fourth squadron, No 27, joined the Group on 4 November and commenced operations on 20 December 1943. It, too, operated P-38s, F-4s and F-5s over a wide area, and on 6 March 1944 a Spitfire made the first USAAF PR sortie from Mount Farm to Berlin.

An important contribution to the forthcoming invasion of France was photographic reconnaissance for the production of maps needed by ground and air forces. Enemy transport movements, installation features and weather information were recorded. L-5 Sentinels were used to maintain contact with those urgently needing information for planning. As D-Day approached, Continental airfields, towns, ports and targets, including those in the Low Countries, were all watched by the 7th.

During July 1944 attention was diverted to photographing V-1 activity, and in August 1944 to gathering information for further updating maps as the US Army quickly advanced. Photographs were also provided for September's airborne assault in the Netherlands, and in December 1944 for the Battle of the Bulge. In the last months of the war, P-51s assigned to the Group escorted its reconnaissance aircraft. On 9 November 1944 No 27 Squadron moved to France, returning later to Chalgrove. HQ 7th PR Group (Reconnaissance) moved to Chalgrove on 8 April 1945, followed by the three squadrons. The other three squadrons disbanded during December 1945 after flying post-war damage assessment flights.

Mount Farm returned to the RAF on 1 May 1945. Coming full circle, it became Benson's satellite once more, from 22 June 1945 to 19 October 1946. No 8 OTU was here until 4 July 1946, when that, too, took the path to Chalgrove. Mount Farm then became a depot for surplus military vehicles. By 1949 it had become a designated Agricultural Airfield, being finally sold for civilian use in 1957. Large gravel pits soon removed the one-time airfield.

**Main features:**
*Runways:* 240° 4,800ft x 150ft, 120° 3,300ft x 150ft, 170° 3,300ft x 150ft, asphalt. *Hangars:* four 69ft Blister, four 65ft Blister. *Hardstandings:* twenty-four loop type. *Accommodation:* USAAF Officers 206, EM 1,617.

## NORTHOLT, Middlesex

*51°33N/00°25W 126ft asl; TQ100850. 3 miles E of Uxbridge*

One of the first custom-built military aerodromes in the United Kingdom, Northolt's greatest claim to fame is providing a home for the RAF's first Hurricane eight-gun fighters. For much of the war it provided succour to many Free Poles, and in peacetime was used by BEA and European airlines until Heathrow could accommodate them. Northolt's story is long and complex, and following the closure of RAF Uxbridge the station will assume even more importance.

Desire to use land for an aerodrome near Northolt began in 1910, negotiations for acquisition took place in 1912, but not until the start of 1915 did construction begin, on the selected 283 acres. Six aircraft sheds each measuring 200 feet by 60 feet, as well as a twin-hangar comprising similar units, were erected together with workshops and wooden barrack huts.

One of seven night-landing grounds for the defence of London, its name was derived from nearby Northolt Junction railway station – now called South Ruislip. Its first occupant, following official opening on 1 March 1915, was No 4 Training (ex-Reserve) Aeroplane Squadron, which came from Farnborough. No 18 Squadron RFC, hived off at Northolt on 11 May 1915, left for Mousehold Heath on 16 August 1915.

By then a BE 2c always stood operationally ready – two examples later in the year – with primitive lighting allowing night operations. On 12 October 1915 No 11 Training (ex-Reserve) Squadron formed out of 4 RAS to undertake the essential night-flying training using BE 2cs, Martinsydes and Curtiss JNs. Northolt became part of the 78th Wing on 13 December 1915.

Landing ground drainage problems arose in the winter 1915-16, making flying difficult, for taxiing from the north side hangars down the slope to the flying ground was nigh impossible. Eight square acres – still just visible from above – were clinker-covered to assist, but not until 1925 were the drainage problems satisfactorily solved.

On 13 January 1916 Training (ex-Reserve) Aeroplane Squadrons became Reserve Squadrons (RS). One such, No 19 RS, which arrived from Hounslow on 1 February, was upgraded on 15 April 1916 to become well-known as No 39 home defence squadron, and left soon after. During 1916 other squadrons also formed at Northolt then moved elsewhere. No 40 RS, formed on 5 July in 18 Wing, left on 21 August for Port Meadow in the 21st Wing, and on 8 December No 43 Squadron, flying Avro 504Ks, BE 2cs and a few Bristol Scouts, came from Netheravon to re-arm with Sopwith 1½ Strutters before heading for France in mid-January 1917. Captain H H Balfour (later Lord Balfour of Inchrye) was one of the Flight Commanders, and later became Air Minister.

Squadron processions continued through 1917, with No 11 RS, flying BE 2cs, RE 7s, 1½ Strutters and a few Avros, arriving in January. After it left for Rochford, No 2 RS, an elementary training squadron using Maurice Farman Shorthorns, replaced it. On 16 February 1917 came No 35 RS from Filton, an advanced flying training squadron using BE 2cs, and by summer 1917 Bristol F-2Bs. On 31 May 1917 Reserve Squadrons were renamed Training Squadrons.

Two Brisfits of 35(T) Squadron made history on 13 June 1917 when at 1119 they left to 'patrol' with other fighters facing eighteen Gothas raiding London. Airborne within two minutes, Captain C W E Cole-Hamilton in A7135 spotted the Gothas over Hackney. They bombed, he chased, and beyond Ilford the pilot and his gunner, Capt C H Keevil, both scored hits on a bomber they chased. Near Southend return fire killed Keevil. The other F-2B flown by 2/Lt J Chapman had engine trouble. This was the only engagement during the 1914-18 war involving Northolt aircraft, although operational daylight sorties were flown on 4 July, 7 July and 22 August 1917.

Fairey Aviation, with a factory in Hayes from late 1916, was using Northolt for test-flying by 1917. To Northolt by road came the Fairey-built 142-foot wingspan Kennedy Giant (No 2337, designed by J C H MacKenzie Kennedy). It was erected in the open because no hangar could accommodate it. Lt F T Courtney, an instructor with No 35 TS, attempted to fly the machine in late 1917; he headed down the field's southerly slope as he opened to full throttle, and the Giant rose to about 100 feet, then touched down in soft ground. It flew no more, and was dumped in Northolt's north-western corner. Among types successfully flown here were the Fairey III series and Fox production aircraft.

Foreigners came to Northolt in considerable numbers for training after the United States was dragged into the war, Americans and a few Russians passing through from July 1917. No 74 Squadron, flying Avro 504s, formed here on 1 July 1917, and left for London Colney nine days later. No 35 TS provided a nucleus of No 2 Training Depot Station, opened on 7 August 1917, before moving to Oxford on 16 December. It was replaced the same day by No 86 Advanced Training Squadron using Sopwith Camels and Avro 504s.

February 1918 saw the organisation of training squadrons again reviewed, resulting in Northolt's squadrons, Nos 2, 4 and 86, amalgamating as 30 Training Depot Station on 15 July 1918. Each of its three Flights had an establishment of eighteen aircraft and forty pupils, later twenty-four aircraft and sixty pupils. After the war ended 30 TDS was rapidly wound down. In May 1919 No 30 TS re-formed, only to disband on 15 March 1920. Remaining was No 4 Squadron, which had brought along its RE 8s on 13 February 1919 and stayed until 30 April 1920.

June 1919 saw the arrival of the South-Eastern Area Communication Flight, at the aerodrome nearest to the RAF Depot (later HQ) Uxbridge. Light transports were now available, as well as flying refresher courses for officers. The Coastal Area Flight, which arrived on 1 April 1920, merged with the resident Flight to become the Inland Area Communication Flight, which in turn became the Home Command Communication Flight, on February 1927. Within it was the Parachute Training School, which, with its Vimy, departed for the Home Aircraft Depot Henlow in late 1926.

Northolt was, in July 1919, licensed as a joint RAF/civil flying field, allowing the Central Aircraft Company to operate a flying school and charter organisation, and to manufacture aircraft, among them the Centaur, a large-cabin biplane first flown in May 1920. Closure overtook the firm in January 1927.

Military activity increased when No 12 Squadron re-formed at Northolt on 1 April 1923 as a bomber squadron armed with DH 9As. No 41 Squadron re-formed with a Flight of Sopwith Snipes, replaced in 1924 with two Flights of Siskins. No 12 Squadron departed for Andover on 23 March 1924, leaving No 41 to re-equip with Bulldogs in October 1931.

Aircraft accommodation needed attention, and three original wooden flight sheds were replaced by a steel-framed 'A1' Aircraft Shed. New barrack blocks and 1920s-style Messes were built, while the landing ground was enlarged.

On 1 May 1923 HQ Superintendent RAF Reserve was established at Northolt, from which on 14 May 1925 stemmed HQ for the AOC Superintendent Reserve and Auxiliary Air Force, which moved to London. Part of the latter was established at Northolt, where No 600 (City of London) and No 601 (County of London) both formed on 14 October 1925 as light bomber squadrons flying DH 9As. No 601, commanded by Sqn Ldr Lord Edward Grosvenor, became popularly known as 'The Millionaires Squadron', said to have had six millionaire members at one time. The peacetime training programme followed a regular pattern – 'club' flying training at weekends, a summer camp and RAF Hendon Display participation. On 15 January 1927 No 601 departed for Hendon, No 600 following three days later.

On 15 January 1927 No 24 (Communication) Squadron replaced them, its role being the conveyance within the UK of high-ranking officials and military personnel. Within the squadron the Air Pilotage School formed on 26 October 1931. Flying practice for pilots on the Air Ministry staff was also given, drawing upon the assorted aircraft on strength including Avro 504s, Bristol Fighters, DH 9As, DH Moths and Fairey IIIFs. HRH the Prince of Wales (later the Duke of Windsor) and Prince George (then Duke of Kent) both received flying lessons from Sqn Ldr D S Don, CO of No 24 Squadron. The special section disbanded in April 1932.

Maintaining the civilian-military link, Fairey Aviation's famous Long-Range Monoplane K1991 first flew from here on 4 November 1928, but in 1929 such activity ceased, for the company moved to new premises at the Great West Aerodrome.

On 9 July 1933 No 24 Communication Squadron moved to Hendon. Northolt was to become a fighter station protecting London's western flank, and the policy change attracted 111 Squadron, which, on 12 July 1934, arrived with Bulldogs from Hornchurch. Soon after, an important organisation began formation, the Air Fighting Development Establishment, which opened on 20 October 1934. Its task was to discover capabilities and best tactics for the operation of fighters and bombers. In 1939 AFDE organised for Parliamentarians a display of the latest British military aircraft, during which the Westland Whirlwind fighter prototype appeared. Its unusual configuration and high-speed passes won it instant notoriety as 'The Crikey', a name taken from a then current Shell slogan, 'Crikey, that's Shell, that was!' The organisation gradually expanded, becoming the Air Fighting Development Unit in July 1940, which in mid-December 1940 moved to Duxford and, in 1943, to Wittering.

Northolt's proximity to the capital has always influenced it, and in 1935 the University of

*Hawker Demon K5685 of No 23 Squadron.*

London Air Squadron opened here equipped with Avro Tutors and Hawker Harts. No 41's tenancy ended in October 1935 with detachment to Aden in response to the Italian-Abyssinian War.

Re-armament raised Northolt's importance and on 1 May 1936 it became part of No 11 Group and Fighter Command, and on the same day Northolt's Station Flight became 11 Group Communication Flight. On 21 December No 23 Squadron and its Hawker Demon turret fighters enhanced station strength, remaining until 16 May 1938 when Wittering was ready for them.

A new fighter squadron, No 213, flying Gloster Gauntlet IIs, re-formed at Northolt on 8 March 1937 and left for Church Fenton on 1 July. More momentous was the arrival on 15 December 1937 of L1548, the first Hawker Hurricane to join an RAF squadron, giving 'Treble One' a starring role in the Expansion Scheme. The work-up was not without accidents, the first fatal crash involving L1556, flown by Fg Off Mervyn Bocquet, occurring on 1 February 1938, when the aircraft dived into the ground next to Western Avenue between Hillingdon and Ickenham. More spectacular, for better reasons, was an amazing dash by Sqn Ldr Gillan, flying a Hurricane from Edinburgh to Northolt and achieving an average IAS of 408mph – thanks to a very strong tail wind.

While 111 Squadron learned to master its fine Hurricanes, Northolt had a facelift. Two 225-foot C Type Hangars were added, and in the north-east corner five H Type Barrack Blocks. In 1939 two paved runways, each 2,400 feet long, were laid, making Northolt one of the few RAF airfields to have such when war was declared. At that time Northolt's resident squadrons were No 25, which took up its war station on 22 August; No 111, which moved out on 27 October 1939; and No 600, which arrived on 25 August re-armed with Blenheim I(f)s.

Between 15 September and 4 October No 600 Squadron dispersed to Filton. Two days previously No 65 Squadron brought along the first Spitfires to be based here. Northolt's Blenheim fighters, operating out of Bircham Newton on 26 November 1939, were involved in the afternoon strafing of He 115 minelayers at Borkum.

Gp Capt (later AVM) S F Vincent took command of the station in January 1940, occupying the post during the Battle of Britain. Early in the war Northolt began using Heston as its satellite aerodrome, and in February 1940 a dummy aerodrome with wooden Hurricanes and a dummy flare path was completed on a golf course at Barnet. Plans to paint Northolt's buildings in wavy stripes of green, black and brown were, Vincent pointed out, incongruous within a suburban area, and would compromise the disguise. Eventually, each hangar was painted to resemble two rows of houses with gardens between. Large black areas, representing trees and bushes, were applied to the perimeter track and runways, and a stream painted on each runway led to a pond at the intersection. Lines of tar applied to grass areas represented hedges outlining fields, as they had been prior to 1915. Northolt and its surroundings suffered relatively little from bombing, so maybe the unusual and thoughtful camouflaging of the airfield protected it.

Improvements continued through spring 1940, an additional perimeter track leading westwards to new dispersal areas. On the airfield now were thirteen twin dispersal Blenheim Pens, with adjacent wooden huts for air and ground crews. Around the field Bofors guns were positioned, and air-raid shelters dug for a Detachment of the 2nd Battalion, The London Scottish Regiment, which was defending the aerodrome.

*Hurricane L1559 of 111 Squadron refuelling from the 'Zwicky', 1938-style.*

*Pilots of No 111 Squadron, smart in their 'whites', discuss how to spend the day.*

As Northolt was some way from the opening skirmishes of the Battle of Britain, No 257 Squadron began moving to Hawkinge or Tangmere to participate with increasing intensity. No 43 Squadron withdrew partially to Northolt for a brief rest, but was soon also flying from Hawkinge before re-assembling at Tangmere on 8 August. From Tangmere on 12 and 15 August No 257 Squadron took part in tough fighting. The day after arriving at Northolt No 1 Squadron RCAF was thrice scrambled and began using Croydon and North Weald for operations. On 31 August Northolt's squadron twice scrambled from base, for the enemy was flying in daylight deeper into Britain. No 1 Squadron (RAF) was now very busy, using Hawkinge, Manston, North Weald and Rochford.

At the height of the Battle there was another newcomer. From elements of No 1 Warsaw Squadron, Polish Air Force, Major Zdzisiwkasnodebski and Sqn Ldr R G Kellett put together a Polish-manned squadron, No 303 (Kosciuszko), established at Northolt on 2 August 1940. It became operational on 24 August and at 1530 had a dozen Hurricanes on patrol and packed with enthusiasm for the fight. On the 30th they had a running battle with the foe over Kent, fought again next day from home base, and fought even harder on 2 September. Operating with Northolt's other squadrons the Poles threw themselves into battle with amazing ferocity during the first major London raid on 7 September, and operated three times on the 15th. For more than four years Polish squadrons were very active training and operating in Northolt's sky.

Squadrons based at Northolt between January and 31 December 1940 were:

| Squadron No | Period | Aircraft |
|---|---|---|
| 65 | 2.10.39-26.3.40 | Spitfire I |
| 601 | 16.1.40-15.5.40 | Blenheim I(f) |
| 253 | 14.2.40-8.5.40 | Hurricane |
| 92 (detachments) | 9.5.40-9.6.40 | Spitfire I |
| 600 | 14.5.40-20.6.40 | Blenheim I(f) |
| 609 | 19.5.40-5.7.40 | Spitfire I |
| 1* | 18.6.40-9.9.40, 13.12.40-5.1.41 | Hurricane I |
| 257* | 4.7.40-15.8 40 | Hurricane I |
| 43 (detachments) | 23.7.40-8.8.40 | Hurricane I |
| 303 (Polish)* | 2.8.40 (formation)-11.10.40 | Hurricane I |
| 1 RCAF | 17.8.40-10.10.40 | Hurricane I |
| 229* | 9.9.40-15.12.40 | Hurricane |
| 615 | 10.10.40-17.12.40 | Hurricane I |
| 302 (Polish) | 11.10.40-23.11.40 | Hurricane I |

* Northolt-based during the Battle of Britain

No 1 Squadron replaced No 229 on 15 December, and 601 replaced 615 on 17 December. No 303, which had rested at Leconfield since October, returned on 3 January 1941 to join Nos 1 and 601 to participate in the opening offensive operations. No 1 Squadron moved to Kenley mid-January, and as 1941 progressed Polish units arrived, fought, patrolled, rested, re-equipped and were involved in many *Circus*, *Ramrod* and *Rodeo* operations while maintaining a defensive posture, sometimes involving the use of Forward Airfields due to Northolt's inland position.

Heston's April 1942 rise to station status resulted in Northolt's reduction to a two-squadron station, and the two Polish squadrons at Heston now flew with Northolt's as a Polish Wing.

Long-expected Luftwaffe activity over inland Britain in daylight during August 1942 brought considerable concern. Involved were Ju 86R bombers based at Beauvais and operating almost in the 'stratosphere'. Engaging these lone raiders at more than 40,000 feet needed special skills and equipment, for which the High Altitude Flight formed at Northolt in late August 1942. Re-named the Sub Stratosphere Flight, it equipped with specially modified Spitfire IXs and Mosquito MP 469s, the six pilots selected for the unit including famous Russian-born Plt Off Prince Emmanuel Galitzine. On 10 September 1942 he intercepted a Ju 86R at 42,000 feet, north of Southampton, damaging its port wing in what may well have been the highest combat of the Second World War.

Another special unit, formed on 28 May 1942, was the Defiant Flight. Operating generally under the code-name *Moonshine*, they were predecessors of the *Mandrel* radar-jamming aircraft, whose role was to neutralise the effectiveness of enemy early warning radar ahead of a bomber force. On 1 October 1942 the Flight became No 515 Squadron, which, to allow more experimentation, moved to Heston on 29 October. In a formation of nine, in daylight and with little success, they had preceded the USAAF's first combined B-17/B-24 participation in *Circus 224* of 8 October, directed at Fives/Lille steel works.

Throughout 1942 and 1943 Northolt's Spitfire squadrons, relying usually on Forward Airfield Support within the Tangmere Sector, took a very active part in the daylight offensive acting as escort or strike fighters. On 4 November 1943 Northolt's current fighter squadrons, Nos 302, 308 and 317, were placed under HQ No 131 Airfield HQ (Polish), and with Heston were part of No 18 Fighter Wing, No 84 Group, 2TAF. On 1 April 1944 the Airfield left for Deanland in an historic move that ended Northolt's career as a fighter station.

Fighter squadrons that had been Northolt-based between January 1941 and April 1944 were:

| Squadron No | Period | Aircraft |
| --- | --- | --- |
| 303 (Polish) | 3.1.41-16.7.41 | Hurricane I/Ia, Spitfire I/II (from 1.41) |
| 306 (Polish) | 3.4.41-7.10.41 | Hurricane IIa, Spitfire II (from 7.41) |
| 308 (Polish) | 24.6.41-12.12.41 | Spitfire II/V |
| 315 (Polish) | 16.7.41-1.4.42 | Spitfire I/II/V |
| 303 (Polish) | 7.10.41-16.6.42 | Spitfire II/V |
| 316 (Polish) | 12.12.41-22.4.42 | Spitfire V |
| 317 (Polish) | 1.4.42-30.6.42, 7.7.42-5.9.42 | Spitfire V |
| 306 (Polish) | 16.6.42-13.3.43 | Spitfire V |
| 315 (Polish) | 6.9.42-1.6.43 | Spitfire V (IX 11.42-6.43) |
| 515 | 1.10.42-29.10.42 | Defiant II (*Moonshine*) |
| 308 (Polish) | 29.10.42-29.4.43 | Spitfire V |
| 303 (Polish) | 2.2.43-5.2.43, 1.6.43-12.11.43 | Spitfire V (IX from 6.11.43) |
| 316 (Polish) | 12.3.43-22.9.43 | Spitfire V |
| 124 | 26.7.43-20.9.43 | Spitfire HF VII |
| 302 (Polish) | 21.9.43-1.4.44 | Spitfire IX |
| 317 (Polish) | 21.9.43-2.12.43, 18.12.43-1.4.44 | Spitfire IX |
| 308 (Polish) | 29.10.43-8.3.44, 15.3.44-1.4.44 | Spitfire IX |

On 25 March 1943 RAF Transport Command was created with Air Chief Marshal Sir Frederick Bowhill in Command, and Northolt, the only airfield in the London area suitable for heavy transport aircraft, was useful as the Command's London terminal. With use increasing, the station's short north-south runway closed when the fighters departed in April 1944, allowing for additional parking spaces to be provided, and the main runway was extended. A Type B1 hangar had been erected to the west of the main hangars, supplementing fourteen Blister hangars erected around the aerodrome in 1941.

There was another service the station would perform before completely switching to transport use. Removal of the fighter squadrons made way for the arrival on 8 April 1944 of No 34 (Reconnaissance) Wing, 2TAF, and its three squadrons, whereby this unique day and night, high- and low-level tactical reconnaissance formation was positioned close to HQ SHAEF. No 34 Wing

*Battle of Britain Hurricane P3039 flown by 'Freddy' Rosie, commander of 229 Squadron, at Northolt.*

embraced No 16 Squadron, flying Spitfire PR XIs for daylight reconnaissance, No 140, flying Mosquito PR IXs and XVIs, and No 69, re-formed on 5 May 1944 using Wellington GR XIIIs specially adapted for night reconnaissance over battlefields, involving flare-dropping. No 34 Wing operated independently from an encampment at the west end of Northolt.

No 16 Squadron's Spitfires, active before D-Day, flew daylight sorties over the Normandy battlefield and adjacent areas once the invasion started. No 69 Squadron began operations on 5/6 June 1944, operating from Northolt intensively until 1 September's move to Balleroy on the Continent. No 140 Squadron concentrated on night photography of road and rail targets as well as front line and movement of reserve forces once the invasion of Normandy started.

Believing that close contact with the invaders ashore in France might be difficult, No 1697 Air Delivery Letter Service Flight formed at Hendon on 22 April 1944, and moved to Northolt on 9 May. Equipped with Hurricanes, the Flight began document delivery to France on 10 June, made sixty-eight landings there during June 1944, and continued the service into the autumn. Fearing that Hurricanes might be at a disadvantage in poor weather, No 1322 Flight formed using Ansons that 1697 Flight had used. The new unit began operating on 24 October 1944 and formed the main part of the ALDS Squadron formed at Northolt on 20 December 1944, which operated from there until moving to Germany on 12 June 1945. By then its remit had extended to carrying personnel as well as official mail.

By May 1944 VIP Avro Yorks were occasionally calling for passengers, Hendon's runways being too short for them. ADGB Communication Squadron, formed on 1 May 1944, became Fighter Command Communication Squadron on 10 November 1944, and stayed until a move to Bovingdon was made on 9 July 1947.

Considering its position, Northolt was fortunate to escape enemy attention, although on 30 July 1944 a V-1 exploded on the south side of the airfield, causing little damage.

RAF and USAAF transports were now coming and going daily. With heavy aircraft requiring ever longer and stronger runways, early 1945 saw construction of a new north-west/south-east PSP runway. The existing north-east/south-west runway was resurfaced and work started on an extensive concrete aircraft parking apron along the airfield's southern side, spreading before passenger and freight terminals.

*Lord Louis Mountbatten's York taxies before setting out from Northolt.*

*BEA Viking 1B G-AIVD*
*shortly before touch-down*
*at Northolt in August 1950.*

On 20 February 1945 five Dakotas arrived on detachment from No 271 Squadron Down Ampney to operate under 110 Wing (until 2 April 1945) scheduled military/Government passenger services to Brussels. No 246 Squadron absorbed the VIP York activities of the Metropolitan Communications Squadron.

On 1 February 1946 Dakotas of the European Division, BOAC, (alias BEA) started operating civilian passenger services from Northolt to Paris, Brussels and Amsterdam. Northolt was lent by the Air Ministry to the Ministry of Civil Aviation from 4 February 1946. By March 1946 a concrete north-west/south-east runway was ready for use, likewise a new control tower built in the airfield's north-west corner. Civilian flying fast increased as foreign airlines started services into Northolt. Among them were Alitalia, ABA Swedish Airlines, Aer Lingus, Czech Airlines, Danish Airlines, LOT, DNL, and Swissair, mostly using DC-3/Dakota/C-47s, later DC-4 Skymasters. Autumn 1946 saw the introduction of Vikings by BEA.

By 1952 most airlines were using Heathrow, and in October 1954 Northolt returned to RAF control. Almost five million passengers had passed through during the course of around 300,000 scheduled airline flights. As well as the civilian airliners, RAF Dakotas had operated services to Berlin, Buckeburg, Warsaw and Vienna, and sundry other British and foreign military aircraft called.

With traffic reduced, runway resurfacing and improvements to buildings were again put in hand and completed by mid-1957. Remaining First World War hangars had at last gone. Hendon's long resident, the Metropolitan Communications Squadron, arrived in November and Northolt became part of Transport Command.

There were a few alarming moments, as on 1 June 1960 when an Anson of Bomber Command Communication Squadron encountered an engine failure on take-off and was forced to set down on top of the Express Dairy, South Ruislip. Fortunately there was neither fire nor serious injuries. On 25 October 1960 Northolt unexpectedly hosted a Pan American Boeing 707, which in landing required every foot of the 5,500-foot runway. The pilot, heading for Heathrow, had mistaken Harrow's gasholder and Northolt's north-east/south-west runway for Southall's gasholder and Heathrow's 23L runway – today's approach aids and talk-down were not then available. The 707 was stripped of its seats before being flown out

April 1969 saw Northolt hit the headlines when Sqn Ldr Thompson took off in a Harrier to make a practice run to New York as part of the Daily Mail Transatlantic Air Race. Six hours and 37 minutes later he landed vertically at Floyd Bennet Naval Air Station, the first vertical take-off jet to make an Atlantic crossing.

On 3 February 1969 Nos 32 and 207 Squadrons re-formed at Northolt, No 32 from the Metropolitan Communications Squadron, and No 207 from the Southern Communications Squadron, recently arrived from Bovingdon. No 32 Squadron operated HS 125s, Whirlwinds,

*BEA Viking G-AIVI on the*
*north side at Northolt in*
*1947.*

*With just a 1951 slatted fence protecting the public enclosure, Dakota G-AMFV cruises by. How things have changed!*

Andovers and a Gazelle to transport Government officials and senior officers of the three Services. No 207 Squadron, using Bassets and Devons, transported senior RAF personnel within the UK before its disbandment.

Changes made to the Royal Flight resulted in No 32 Squadron becoming No 32 (The Royal) Squadron on 1 April 1995 and the arrival of the Royal aircraft at Northolt in 1995. It was to this station that Princess Diana was flown, in a BAe 146 following her tragic death.

In 2003 the squadron held two VVIP BAe 146 CC2s, six BAe 125 CC3s and three AS355F-1 Twin Squirrel HCC.1 helicopters. Station Flights held one Islander CC2. BAe 125s from Northolt were used to transport senior officers during operation *Telic*. The proximity of Maritime HQ Northwood increases communication flying, which, for a time, led to Coastal Command Communication Flight (and later 18 Group Flight) being based here.

*A view over Northolt's southern terminal in 1965. (Bruce Robertson collection)*

Northolt has long supported several 'lodger' units, among them No 1 Aeronautical Information Documents Unit, here since 1956 and responsible for the output of Flight Information Publications (FLIPs) for service use.

A long-arm pendulum has swung, for, as in the 1920s, there is once more a civilian-military mix at Northolt, well placed to handle private, executive and charter flights, as well as Government and military visitors. Thus, Gulfstreams park among foreign Beech Kingairs, RAF 125s and many other types. Single-engined aircraft are not allowed to visit, and civilian aircraft movements are limited to twenty-eight per day. That activity is controlled by Northolt Handling Ltd, which takes care of about 7,000 civilian movements a year. Further restrictions limit aircraft size to twenty-seater international and thirty-seater domestic aircraft. Northolt is strongly secured, for it is used by the Royal Family as well as HM Government and HM Armed Forces.

A poignant, prominent reminder of wartime years remains, the Polish War Memorial at the south-eastern corner of the airfield. Constructed of York stone, it is surmounted by a bronze eagle. On the rear face of the monument are the words 'I have fought a good fight, I have finished my course, I have kept the faith'. Who can fairly disagree that Northolt too – and so many in the RAF – have done just that?

**Main features:**
*Runways:* 260° 5,400ft x 150ft, 205° 2,940ft x 150ft, both asphalt, 308° 4,800ft x 150ft, Sommerfeld Tracking. *Hangars:* one A1, two C Type, 225ft. *Hardstandings:* two twin-engined type, thirty single-engined type. *Accommodation:* RAF officers 145, SNCOs 203, ORs 1,405; WAAF officers 14, SNCOs 13, ORs 496.

Northolt now has one asphalt runway, 07/25 5,525ft x 1650ft, with a taxi track to the north side and a disused runway. Direct taxiways link the apron only with the western end of the runway, the opposite end being reached via part of the shortest unused runway. Two helipads are marked on the south-side apron, one on the north side.

---

## NORTHLEACH, Gloucestershire

*50°N/01°50W, 682ft as; SP110155. 12 miles NE of Cirencester, by the A429*

Although an RLG near Northleach was planned in 1940, it did not come into use until 2 November 1942 when a Flight of Master GT IIs and Hotspur gliders from 3 GTS Stoke Orchard took up residence. Their stay was brief due to the airfield's poor surface, and they returned to Stoke Orchard awaiting an improved state.

Spasmodic use followed, Northleach being raised to Unbuilt Satellite status in May 1944, still administered by Stoke Orchard. Between 21 and 23 October 1944 No 3 GTS was forced to leave Stoke Orchard because the grass airfield there was also in poor state. The School moved to Zeals and activity at Northleach ceased. The site then returned to agricultural use.

**Main features:**
Available *Grass runs:* N-S 2,250ft, E-W 3,150ft. *Hangars:* two 65ft Blister. *Hardstandings:* nil. *Accommodation:* RAF Officers 14, SNCOs 23, ORs 66, using Nissen huts by the landing ground boundary.

---

## NORTH LUFFENHAM, Leicestershire (Rutland)

*52°37N/00°36W 350ft asl; SK940050. Approximately 6 miles W of Stamford, north of the A6121*

A strange, incongruous experience it was. Barely had I left sleepy little Luffenham village when I found myself in Canada, or so it seemed. French chatter and red maple-leaf motifs abounded, the latter readily visible on the brightly shining silver Sabres from which dangled, 1940s-style, their pilots' kit awaiting donning on the order to 'Go', and fast. Instead of the customary Meteor T-7s of RAF squadrons, RCAF pilots carried out their continuation training using Canadair-built T-33s, while supplies arrived from Europe in RCAF Bristol 170 Freighters. Both were in evidence on that July 1954 day at the height of one of those so memorable, large-scale home air defence exercises in an era that converted North Luffenham into little Canada, whose bright Canadair fighters plugged the gap until Swifts and then possibly Hunters armed Fighter Command.

---

*Lancaster PB437 of No 1653 HCU North Luffenham. (John Rawlings)*

This austere bomber base, surrounded by agricultural land and on a plateau 350 feet above sea level, was destined for a surprisingly long and varied life. It was designed in 1939, as is clear from the two J Type hangars backed by flat-roofed permanent technical and domestic buildings. Construction started early in 1940, and at the time of opening in December it had only a grass flying field. Perhaps because it was sited outside operational Bomber Group areas, its first use was, surprisingly, as a home for de Havilland-operated No 17 EFTS, formed here on 18 January 1941 to train pilots using Tiger Moths, Magisters and Ansons. The School moved to Peterborough in mid-July 1941.

North Luffenham began serving its intended purpose on 17 July 1941 when Hampdens of Nos 61 and 144 Squadrons, 5 Group, arrived. Although No 61 Squadron was flirting with the awkward Avro Manchester, they were never operated from here. Instead, the squadron participated in Main Force raids using Hampdens until October 1941, when Manchester activity intensified. Full conversion commenced at Woolfox Lodge, North Luffenham's satellite, in November. No 144 Squadron continued operating Hampdens from the parent station, having for company a detachment of Canadian No 408 (Goose) Squadron from Balderton, between 27 January and 17 March 1942. No 144 Squadron was busy during the start of the 1942 tough bomber offensive, but not for long, as the squadron and its Hampdens had been selected for transfer to Coastal Command and on 6 April carried out its last Hampden bomber raid from the station, target Essen. On 21 April 1942 No 144 transferred to Leuchars, Fife. As for No 61 Squadron, on 27 March it had formed at Woolfox Lodge a conversion flight equipped with two Manchesters and two far better Lancasters. It left for Syerston on 5 May 1942, and the station was transferred to No 91 Group.

No 29 OTU North Luffenham opened in 7 Group on 21 April 1942, and equipped with Wellington Ics and IIIs, Ansons, Lysanders and Defiants. No 7 Group became 91 Group on 11 May, its new OTU producing eight crews in time for the Bremen 'Thousand Plan' raid of 26 June 1942. To make maximum use of the airfield 12 (P)AFU used it at night as an RLG.

To permit upgrading of North Luffenham, No 29 OTU moved to Bruntingthorpe early in June 1943. Although closed to flying, North Luffenham was, from January 1944, the centre for Hamilcar glider assembly and modification under MAP auspices, in a B1 hangar and three T2 hangars erected on the northern edge of the airfield.

The reconstruction resulted in a customary three-runway Class A airfield re-opened in March 1944 within No 23 Group, Flying Training Command. On 2 March 1944 the Heavy Glider Conversion Unit started moving in from Brize Norton, allowing that station to become an operational base. Horsa troop-carrying gliders towed by Whitleys became a common sight until September, when Albemarles replaced the latter. On 16 October 1944 the HGCU returned to its previous home, better sited for its activities.

*Valetta VW849 NU-K of No 240 OCU North Luffenham.*

Reversion followed when on 1 November 1944 North Luffenham again became a bomber station. Units, once part of No 31 Base, were moved north, with North Luffenham as HQ 73 Base, Bomber Command. Incorporated in the Base were 1651 HCU Woolfox Lodge, 1658 HCU Bottesford, and 1669 HCU Langar (the last two between 1 April and 1 August 1945). On 27 November 1944 No 1653 HCU arrived at Luffenham from Stradishall, its established strength being thirty-two Lancasters, showing the change overtaking HCUs, now bidding farewell to Stirlings. More realistic fighter affiliation resulted from the addition of two Beaufighter night-fighters to HCUs, supplementing pairs of Spitfire Mk Vs and Hurricane Mk IIs.

Its task ended, 1653 HCU moved to Lindholme on 28 October 1945. North Luffenham then fell quiet until the arrival early in December 1946 of No 21 HGCU equipped with Dakota and Halifax tugs and Horsa and Hamilcar gliders. In effect, a slimmer HGCU was returning, which died on 5 December 1947, just before the arrival of two other airborne forces training units. No 1333 TSCU, flying Dakotas and Oxfords, and 1382 TSCU moved in during mid-December 1947, and on 5 January 1948 combined to form No 240 OCU. Its role was the operational training of crews for light and medium transport aircraft. Mainly Dakota-equipped, Valettas, Ansons and Devons were also on strength before the unit moved to Dishforth on 28 March 1951.

Ever ready to survive, North Luffenham joined 25 Group and received its first jets with the formation on 1 May 1951 of No 102 Flying Refresher School. This gave flying practice for fighter pilots who had held ground jobs, etc, enabling them to resume front-line flying in an expanding RAF facing new challenges. Between now and its closure on 15 November 1951, Meteors, Vampires, Spitfires and Harvards populated the station.

Far greater change followed, with the arrival on 1 November 1951 of No 1 Fighter Wing, Royal Canadian Air Force, whose squadrons were flying Vampire FB 5s. The decision to place operational Canadian fighters here brought about extensive modifications to the airfield. On the north side at both ends of the main runway were laid Operational Readiness Platforms, into which were fed telescramble lines allowing for fast response. Spread before the J hangars and the northern metal hangars were two Aircraft Servicing Platforms. Both subsidiary runways were abandoned, together with the long southern section of the perimeter track linking both ends of the main runway.

When the RCAF squadrons arrived, part of NATO being seconded to 12 Group, Fighter Command, for the air defence of the UK, they brought along Canadair F-86E Sabres. Totalling in theory seventy-five, the Sabres equipped Nos 410, 439 and 441 RCAF Squadrons.

*F-86 Sabres of No 439 Squadron RCAF on exercise standby 24 July 1954.*

The Canadians began moving out at the end of 1954, No 410 departing on 14 November for Baden Soellingen, Germany, and No 441 on 20 December for Zweibrucken, Germany. On 31 March 1955 No 439 moved to Merville, France.

On 1 April 1955 the station returned to the Royal Air Force, and yet again North Luffenham changed track by involving itself with All-Weather fighter training. On 17 April 1956 Meteor night-fighters of No 228 OCU Leeming began using North Luffenham for flying training while their base received a major facelift. In October 1956 Valetta T.4 AI operator trainers came into use. The unit, which ceased flying from here on 25 January 1957, then retired to Leeming.

Replacement came the same month when 238 OCU, Colerne's AI School, moved to North Luffenham, equipped with Valettas and Brigand T.4s and T.5s for basic AI training. Meteor NF 11s/14s served for operational practice until the unit disbanded on 13 March 1958.

There were six weeks of jet flying left for the station. In mid-February the Hunters of 111 Squadron came on detachment while their North Weald runway was resurfaced. When they left for home, North Luffenham's days as an airfield were all but ended, but not its thirst for active front-line activity. It was placed on care and maintenance, then by the end of the year work was under way to build the Thor Intermediate Range Ballistic Missile administrative HQ. Three Thor launch sites were constructed, with more at North Luffenham's four satellite stations – Folkingham, Harrington, Melton Mowbray and Polebrook.

The station re-opened on 1 October 1959, No 151 (Air Defence Missile) Wing HQ then being here. Thor missiles arrived in USAF C-133 Cargomasters during 1960, Americans from the Douglas Aircraft Company assisting in the overall operation. In 1960 two Bloodhound Mk I squadrons re-formed, No 62 at Woolfox Lodge and No 257 at Warboys, and on 1 June 1961 the HQ unit at North Luffenham became No 151 (Surface to Air Missile) Wing, 12 Group, to control them. On 30 December 1962 the Wing's operational status was removed and it became No 151 (SAM) Servicing Wing, which, on 31 March 1963, took on the support of two more Bloodhound squadrons, No 242 at Marham and No 266 at Rattlesden. With the run-down of the V-Force, which Bloodhounds protected, summer 1964 saw its role end, disbandment taking place on 30 September. Mid-August 1963 had seen the last Thor complex close here, the last fixed-wing aircraft leaving the station on 27 September 1963, carrying a Thor surface-to-surface missile.

*Brigand AI trainers of 238 OCU.*

North Luffenham's survival was now vested in a variety of ground units. November 1963 brought from Upwood the Radio Technical Publications Squadron, which produced documentation needed for servicing sophisticated electronic equipment. After missile activity ceased in 1964 the station passed to Signals Command and provided a home for the Midlands Radar Unit. In 1969 Signals Command became No 90 (Signals) Group within Strike Command, which in 1972 was transferred to Maintenance Command, soon re-titled Support Command.

In 1971 North Luffenham also housed No 63 Squadron, Royal Air Force Regiment, Rapier (Ground to Air) Missiles, which left for Germany in 1974. The early 1970s saw a limited return of fixed-wing aircraft, Chipmunks giving ATC and CCF air section cadets a summertime taste of flying. Rumours of closure were rife, but North Luffenham was not prepared to surrender. It now also housed the Aviation Medical Training Centre, undertaking medical checks and running courses for Medical Officers, Flight Sisters, Decompression Chamber Operators and Air Ambulance Attendants. The station also attracted the Ground Radio Servicing Centre (GRSC), the RAF Language School and the Midland Radar Unit, which still provides an air traffic service for all off-airways aircraft between the Thames Estuary and Tyneside, and also covers airfields in Lincolnshire, East Anglia and the Midlands. 'Shortage of resources' inevitably bore down, reducing the variety of activities at this RAF station with such a variety of memories. It is still an important surprisingly untidy military base.

**Main features:**
December 1944: *Runways:* 260° 6,000ft x 150ft, 190° 4,200ft x 150ft, 320° 4,200ft x 150ft, concrete. *Hangars:* two Type J, three T2, one B1. *Hardstandings:* thirty-two loop type, eighteen frying-pan. *Accommodation:* RAF officers 108, SNCOs 182, ORs 1,828; WAAF officers 11, SNCOs 10, ORs 290.

In the mid-1950s many of the dispersal pads were replaced by using two standard fighter ASPs and ORPs. Both shorter runways were disused.

## NORTH WEALD, Essex

*51°43N/00°09E, 283ft asl; TL488044. 2 miles NNE of Epping*

Chris Cole, the much-missed enthusiast and Air Ministry Press Officer, was sensibly handling the inquisitive brigade at a time when spinning was performed by aeroplanes and not peculiar, deceitful characters. Air Chief Marshal Sir Harry Broadhurst (who shot down a He 111 near Acklington as the squadron's first Second World War victory) was at North Weald on 30 April 1957 to present a Squadron Standard to 'Treble One'. Following that we were to be treated to the first PR display by a new aerobatic team, the 'Black Arrows'. Its eleven Hunters – Mk 6s, the latest to serve – were drawn up in a semi-circle, in front of which 'A' and 'B' Flights paraded while No 4 Regional Band of the RAF played sensible music.

Teacups chinked, buns disappeared, then the guests headed for 'The Tower' – except for Chris Cole and one keen accomplice, the only ones interested in touring the line, shooting the jets. Three Hunters retained camouflage, while eight had been painted gloss black, with four-inch red serials and red nosewheel door letters. We reckoned the once-tried 'Golden Arrows' scheme might have looked more exciting, and discussed the rejected 'Red Arrows' scheme for all-red Hunters bearing 'RAF' in giant white letters on the under surfaces.

*'Treble One' Squadron Hunter F6s and crews.*

The General Salute sounded as the Air Chief Marshal took his place. Wg Cdr Sutton, Station Commander, handed the Standard to a bearer, then the Chaplain-in-Chief, Canon A S Giles, blessed it. Lively Sqn Ldr Roger Topp spoke, hats popped on and off, then the squadron, in smart finery without a scruffy camouflage outfit in sight, marched off. Sir Harry headed for VP971, his very shiny Devon. Following went the AOC-in-C Fighter Command, being driven to his Devon, VP968. AOC 11 Group had to make do with an Anson. Someone else, who had arrived in 'his' Vampire, had it privately tucked away, out of sight behind a civilian Rapide.

The pilots were soon in their Hunters, white-coated 'chiefies' standing ahead of each. As their hands were lowered in unison, engines came alive, then nine Hunters taxied out, led by XG193, for a massed take-off.

Their performance was superb, so far unsurpassed for sure. Fast jets of exquisite form, they jostled into many formations, generated some smoke, then after the 'swan's neck' came the bomb burst, the most spectacular yet, followed by a loop and very low, fast crossovers. The team reassembled then broke for landing, touch-downs being at about 140mph. Mike Thurley would be last man home.

What we did not expect was a sudden, astonishing, awful finale. On landing each pilot wasted no time in clearing the short runway. Some, having no time, were hurrying to the runway edge, for they knew that the last man in was in trouble. Low on fuel, he knew his landing would be difficult for he had no means of braking. We watched with increasing alarm as he was clearly approaching very fast and almost shaved the top of the boundary hedge. To everyone's amazement the aircraft, power now off, touched and porpoised, touched again, bouncing upwards to about 30 feet, then hit the runway hard a third time before the pilot suddenly relit and applied full power, intending to go round again. His tailpipe could only have been an inch above the runway on that third attempt. Unknown to him he had torn off the nosewheel strut and, being about three-quarters of the way along the runway, he was immediately told to shut off all power. He slammed the nose down, slewed right onto the overshoot, crossed a nearby road and bumped against a ridge. That ripped off the nose, and as it did so we saw an ejector seat shoot out at a low angle as 'H' XG203 turned into a horrid black inferno. Thurley, who had been catapulted almost horizontally into bushes, was collected, taken for a quick medical and declared in amazingly good state. Miracles clearly do happen, engineered in this case by Martin Baker.

Some of us stood for some time in silent dazed amazement, while others, who had shown scant interest in the Hunters, were now gruesomely demanding to visit one. The more responsible guests were taken to the Mess for tea and a chance to overcome their concern, together with that of the pilots.

*Hurricanes of 56 Squadron against the backdrop of Epping Forest in the summer of 1940.*

We had not been there long when there was a flurry of excitement, enormous excitement. Incredibly, Mike Thurley was briefly joining us! There was great delight and astonishment that he was able to do this. Between sips of his tea he spoke of what he had endured. His was a great escape, truly the stuff of legend.

North Weald was an important military airfield for many decades until its unsuitability for extension, close proximity to public complaint and limited strategic value brought its demise. Built in 1916 west of North Weald Bassett village, its first occupant arrived in August 1916, a detachment from 39 Squadron based at Woodford. On Sunday 1 October 1916 2/Lt W J Tempest took off in a BE 2c from North Weald to engage night raiders approaching London. After an almost two-hour patrol, he spotted zeppelin L 31 entangled in searchlight beams, closed and shot it down over Potters Bar, for which feat he was at once awarded a DSO.

May 1917 brought the Gotha bomber threat, to thwart which the two detached flights of No 39 Squadron, operating from Sutton's Farm (later Hornchurch) and one at Hainault Farm (Fairlop), moved to North Weald, from where the squadron now busily operated as an entity.

On 22 May 1918 No 75 Squadron and its Bristol F-2Bs joined it. No 39 Squadron left for France a few days before hostilities ceased. No 75 Squadron disbanded on 13 June 1919, and No 44 Squadron with Camels replaced it on 1 July and disbanded on 31 December.

Bleak was North Weald's future until the 1922/23 Steel-Bartholomew air defence plan earmarked it for development as part of London's air defences. Reconstruction started in 1926, re-opening taking place on 27 September 1927 under Wg Cdr A G R Garrod. Prominent already were two A Type hangars – one still present – and permanent brick and slate barrack blocks built to 1922 plans and sited in the station's south-east area. As was customary at fighter aerodromes, space was left for a third hangar to be built between the two if needed.

No 56 (Fighter) Squadron vacated Biggin Hill on 11 October 1927, bringing Armstrong-Whitworth Siskin IIIas under Sqn Ldr C H Elliott-Smith AFC. No 56 will ever be linked with the great Captain Albert Ball and Captain J B McCudden, awarded between them two VCs, five DSOs, three Military Crosses, and a Military Medal. On 1 April 1928 No 29 moved in from Duxford, also flying Siskin IIIas, to make up the usual two-squadron twenty-aircraft-per-station strength. Both squadrons re-armed with Bristol Bulldog IIas in 1932, by which time North Weald was commanded by Wg Cdr Sholto Douglas MC DFC.

In March 1935 No 29 Squadron began re-arming with Hawker Demon two-seater fighters, and on 4 October 1935, with the Abyssinian crisis serious, left for Egypt. When the international situation calmed, the squadron headed for home, reaching North Weald on 12 September 1936. Shortly before, on 4 August 1936, as part of the RAF Expansion Scheme, 'B' Flight of No 56 became the nucleus of 151 Squadron.

Demons from Martlesham Heath, flown by 64 Squadron, were here for the summer air defence exercise between 30 July and 13 August 1937. On 22 November 1937 No 29 Squadron moved to Debden.

*A Hawker Demon of 604 Squadron, North Weald.*

No 56 Squadron received its first Hurricanes in May 1938, whereas No 151 Squadron, still operating Gauntlet IIs, faced the Munich Crisis accompanied by Demons of No 604 (County of Middlesex) AAF Squadron at this, its war station, between 29 September and 3 October 1938. High was the alert state, with live ammunition being belted. Re-armament and expansion then raced ahead, 151 Squadron getting Hurricanes in December 1938. Less fortunate, No 17 Squadron – which to allow much rebuilding vacated Kenley on 23 May 1939 – arrived still flying Gauntlets, replaced with Hurricanes during June.

On 2 September No 17 Squadron left for Debden, its war station. North Weald went to war with two Hurricane squadrons and the Blenheim I(f)s of No 604 Squadron, which returned on 2 September. Among their fliers were Plt Off John Cunningham and his gunner Jimmy Rawnsley, who later achieved fame as a top-scoring night-fighter team.

North Weald at this time extended over 400 acres between Weald Hall Lane, Church Lane and the Epping-Ongar road. Two paved runways had been laid, some of the first at a British fighter station. Quite narrow, that running north-south was 2,800 feet long, the east-west runway measuring 2,750 feet in length. North Weald, HQ Sector E, 11 Group, had also seen steady improvements made to its buildings.

During the first hours of war the station was at high alert, raids being expected. The first call came at 0300 on 5 September 1939, when 56 Squadron was brought to readiness. It never took off, the order to 'scramble' going instead to Nos 151 and 604 Squadrons, at 1215. No enemy was encountered.

At 0640 on 6 September 56 Squadron was 'scrambled'. 'A' flight was to patrol over Harwich-Colchester at 11,000 feet as a He 111 had been detected in the outer reaches of the Thames Estuary. 'B' Flight protected Ipswich, and at 0710 two more Hurricanes set out to join them. Spitfire pilots of 74 Squadron spotted the spares and, concluding that they were enemy aircraft, shot down both, killing Plt Off Hulton-Harrop and wounding Plt Off Tommy Rose, who baled out from his stricken aircraft. The Heinkel headed north well out to sea, leaving the 'friendly fire' incident to became the 'Battle of Barking Creek'.

North Weald was soon making use of Martlesham Heath as a forward airfield, which also served Debden. Squadrons were detached for short or long stays. On 22 October No 56 Squadron began flying shipping protection patrols from Martlesham.

The next serious alert came on 17 November when He 111s were located off the Dutch-Belgian coasts. Again, there were no engagements and within a few weeks severe winter weather saw snowploughs removing many tons of snow from the runways. In mid-January 604 Squadron left for Northolt, and Blenheim I(f)s of No 25 Squadron arrived from Martlesham Heath to replace them.

No 56 Squadron returned to North Weald on 28 February, then plied to and from Martlesham with only a skirmish to record – until May 1940. The German assault on the West changed everything, the station's fighters soon being in the thick of the fight over the Channel and France, sometimes trying to protect Blenheims attempting to halt the German advance. On 21 May 'B' Flight 56 Squadron joined 229 Squadron to form a composite unit that flew from Vitry-en-Artois to be more useful. Filling the space at North Weald was 111 Squadron, which moved out to Croydon on 4 June to allow the much-battered Hurricanes of 56 Squadron to return after a mauling.

*A camouflaged Gloster Gauntlet II of 151 Squadron by an 'A' Type hangar in the autumn of 1938.*

Using South Coast forward aerodromes, Nos 56 and 151 Squadrons covered the BEF's withdrawal from France, with close-by Stapleford Tawney available as the station's dispersal satellite.

In mid-June 25 Squadron took its turn at Martlesham, to be better placed for night-fighting. Otherwise the squadrons protected shipping often from South Coast aerodromes while awaiting an inevitable German onslaught on Britain. It began early in July and witnessed North Weald's fighters performing very courageously.

Through rain and cloud German aircraft reconnoitred the outer Thames estuary on 9 July, gathering details of a large FN convoy assembling. At 1245 a German strike force and a Bf 110 diversion mounted by III/ZG 26 were approaching the South Coast, and No 43 Squadron Hurricanes damaged two of them.

The main force was engaged by six 11 Group squadrons including 'A' Flight No 151 Squadron, which, soon after 1300, left North Weald with the Station Commander, Wg Cdr Victor Beamish, flying Hurricane P3807. Within a few minutes the six Hurricanes were facing about one hundred enemy aircraft, bombers operating at around 12-15,000 feet protected by top-cover Bf 109s stacked to 20,000 feet. Despite the daunting odds, a Hurricane section went for the bombers with No 151 fighting for its life. Midshipman O Wightman, shot down, was rescued by a trawler, but the bomber formation had been split, with all but one group making for home and leaving the ships undamaged. There were more such engagements when success would be far less.

In mid-August the Luftwaffe opened its offensive against fighter stations, those in Kent and Surrey receiving most attention. North Weald's Hurricane squadrons were called upon to reinforce 11 Group squadrons as required. Enemy bombers gradually thrust more deeply and during the afternoon of 18 August eight raids approaching via the Blackwater and Thames estuaries crossed the Essex coast. Nos 54 and 151 Squadrons responded, preventing the bombing of Hornchurch and North Weald. The bombers instead unloaded on Medway targets.

On 24 August the principal afternoon activity began at 1520, four large raids crossing Kent, two bound for Hornchurch and North Weald. As Hornchurch came under attack by He 111s, North Weald was bombed at the same time, about fifteen He 111s of III/KG 53 entering from the east at 12,500 feet and following the main road to the aerodrome, where about 200 bombs fell on or around the target. Both the Officers' and Airmen's Married Quarters were severely damaged. Nine members of the Essex Regiment who were in a shelter that received a direct hit were killed, and ten other personnel were injured. Wg Cdr Beamish seemed to be everywhere, encouraging all by the fine example he set.

Bf 109s covering the Heinkels, with fuel shortage looming and too high to intervene, left bomber protection to supporting Bf 110s, which, for once, guarded their charge well against some fifty RAF fighters by then active. Although there were many casualties at North Weald, damage was mainly caused to the radio station and huts, a fire in Epping Forest producing a deceiving huge pall of smoke after 300 incendiaries ignited. The extent of the afternoon raids was such that nearly all of 11 Group's serviceable aircraft had operated, for intelligence sources had suggested that London was about to be bombed. Warned of the potential development, at around 1600 Keith Park had asked 12 Group's Commander, Leigh Mallory, to provide cover for 11 Group stations north of London. No 12 Group responded by attempting to marshal a large group of fighters over Duxford to defend London, but it took too long to assemble. Without ample practice the scheme was impracticable, so instead six 19 Squadron cannon-armed Spitfires, ordered to North Weald, arrived in time to see the smoke rising from there and also around Hornchurch. Before gun stoppages occurred (caused by spent cartridges jamming in breeches because the cannon had to lie on their sides in the thin wings), the Spitfires claimed three Bf 110s. All told, five bombers were destroyed and four fighters. Fighter Command lost eight aircraft and three pilots.

On Saturday 31 August the Luftwaffe returned in force. Radar gave warning of 200-plus aircraft, and near the coast they split into groups, seeming to be heading for North Weald. No 56 Squadron put up twelve Hurricanes, but before they could attack the Dorniers they were 'bounced' by escorting Bf 109s and 110s, losing four of their number almost immediately. They had now lost eleven aircraft in five days of hard fighting and No 56 was being wiped out. So, on Sunday 1 September, the squadron's seven remaining Hurricanes, now without a Commanding Officer, moved to Boscombe Down to re-form and rest. They were replaced that same day by No 249 Squadron, led by Sqn Ldr John Grandy, a future Chief of the Air Staff. The same day No 151 left for Digby; it, too, was without a Commanding Officer and held only ten serviceable aircraft.

*All-black Hunter 6
in the trial 'Golden
Arrows' paint
scheme at North
Weald.
(Private source)*

The heaviest bombing of North Weald occurred on Tuesday 3 September. It was the first carried out by Do 17Zs, about fifty, preceded by a large force of forward-support fighters. Approaching along the Thames estuary, the raid again raised fears that London was the target, and caused Park to place sixteen squadrons (122 fighters) over Kent and Essex by 0940. Suddenly the formation turned north near Southend, swung westerly, then lined up to carpet-bomb North Weald. No 249 was being turned round when the warning sounded, and many of the Hurricanes, racing across the field to get airborne, had tanks only partially replenished. By the time the raiders appeared all the station's serviceable aircraft were airborne, but 249 Squadron had a serious height disadvantage. Bombs started falling before the Hurricanes could engage the raiders. Hangars were hit and gutted by fire, the operations block and many other buildings were damaged, and in the MT yard many vehicles were set alight. Lots of other buildings were damaged. More than 200 bombs fell on the station, many on the south-western corner of the landing ground. However, although heavily cratered, it remained available for daytime use. Casualties totalled four killed and thirty-seven injured.

Three Blenheim crews of 25 Squadron had scrambled to help fight the Dorniers, that unusual event proving disastrous when Hurricane pilots erroneously attacked them. Sergeant Powell, gunner in Plt Off Hogg's aircraft, crawled to the nose, only to find his pilot slumped dead over the controls. He baled out, leaving L1512 to crash near Greenstead Green, Essex. Sqn Ldr Loxton landed safely, but Plt Off Cassidy had to force-land his damaged Blenheim L1409 at Hatfield Heath. As the enemy was making for home, cannon Spitfires of 19 Squadron tried to dispose of the Bf 110s, only to encounter the usual gun stoppages. Hurricanes of Nos 1, 17, 46, 257 and 310 Squadrons were soon on hand to force the escorting Bf 110s into combat. Despite the sharp raid, North Weald remained operational. Fate was certainly unkind to 25 Squadron, for when Plt Off Rofe made a night patrol and engaged three raiders, heavy AA guns fired upon his Blenheim, twice putting it into dangerous spins. But all was not failure: Plt Off Herrick in another Blenheim shot down two night raiders. In recognition of his leadership and drive, Wg Cdr Victor Beamish, who frequently flew with his squadrons since his appointment as Station Commander in July, went to an investiture at Buckingham Palace on 4 September 1940 to receive his DSO from HM King George VI. Throughout the remainder of the month he flew operationally at every opportunity, for he was no 'chairborne warrior'.

On 2 October the station was visited by ACM Sir Hugh Dowding, and on the following day by Captain Balfour, Under Secretary of State for Air. On 8 October No 25 Squadron moved to Debden and No 257, led by Sqn Ldr Stanford Tuck, arrived from Martlesham.

Attacks on aerodromes in the south and east were continuing, although generally on a smaller scale. On 27 October dense cloud provided cover for a Do 17 that dipped from cloud, dropped eight bombs, then re-entered the cloud. Two days later the station, caught off guard, was bombed and machine-gunned by Bf 109s, which dropped more than forty 50kg bombs, causing considerable damage. No 249 Squadron was taking off when the enemy attacked, and the first three Hurricanes were airborne when a 50kg bomb exploded to their right. Sergeant A G Girdwood was killed when his Hurricane, taking much of the blast, was blown ahead of the others, hit the ground and burst into flames.

On 7 November No 249 was replaced by No 46 Squadron, which moved in from the Stapleford Tawney satellite. The intense fighting of summer and autumn was now replaced by monotonous patrols over coastal shipping, costly in manpower, fuel and aircraft maintenance.

Squadrons based at North Weald from September 1939 to 31 December 1940 were:

| Squadron No | Period | Aircraft |
|---|---|---|
| 56 | 12.10.27-22.10.39 | Hurricane I |
| 151 | 4.8.36-13.5.40 | Gauntlet, Hurricane (from 2.38) |
| 604 | 2.9.39-16.1.40 | Blenheim I(f) |
| 25 | 16.1.40-19.6.40, 1.9.40-8.10.40 | Blenheim I(f) |
| 56 | 28.2.40-10.5.40, 12.5.40-1.5.40, 4.6.40-1.9.40 | Hurricane I |
| 111 | 30.5.40-4.6.40 | Hurricane I |
| 151 | 30.5.40-29.8.40 | Hurricane I |
| 249 | 1.9.40-21.5.41 | Hurricane I (II 2.41) |
| 257 | 8.10.40-7.11.40 | Hurricane I |
| 46 | 8.11.40-14.12.40 | Hurricane I |
| 56 | 17.12.40-23.6.41 | Hurricane I/II |

Activity in the period 1941-44 fell into seven phases. With the Battle of Britain won, German daylight operations against the UK passed into cloud-cover nuisance raids by lone bombers and Bf 109 fighter-bomber attacks, mainly on coastal targets. Both were difficult to intercept, and in the case of North Weald were challenged by Hurricane squadrons, No 242 and No 56 Squadrons, the latter back at its ancestral home until June 1941, when it left for Martlesham. Through that period North Weald's Hurricanes contributed to the escort of RAF daylight bombers raiding fringe targets in France, or took part in 'sweeps' designed to challenge the foe to fight. In February 1941 Mk IIbs (which had Merlin XXs) were received, and continued protecting coastal shipping.

A second phase is represented by squadrons re-arming in summer 1941 with Spitfire Vbs after some flirtation with Spitfire Mk IIas. Again, the squadrons using them – including No 71, the first US 'Eagle' squadron – carried out bomber support duties and sweeps while being available for home defence. Flying a bomber escort sortie in a Hurricane, Plt Off Dunn scored the 'Eagle' squadron's first victory, a Bf 109f shot down over Lille.

In May 1942 North Weald's 'own very specials', the two Norwegian Spitfire Vb squadrons, began a residence that extended to March 1944 with barely a break. On 19 May 1942 No 331 first tangled with Fw 190s, and on the 31st had its first confirmed success, a Bf 109f. In October 1942 both re-armed with Spitfire F IXbs, with which they carried out bomber support operations in particular, ever more intensively. They protected 2TAF and US IXth AF bombers, and aided raids by US 8th AF B-17/24s by providing forward support and rear cover.

Clear preparations for D-Day were inaugurated on 1 November 1943 when No 132 (Norway) Airfield HQ opened in 84 Group to handle the two Norwegian squadrons. Overall control of Nos 132, 134 and later 145 Airfields was vested in No 19 (Fighter) Wing, which re-formed at North Weald in December 1943 and became titled No 19 (Fighter) Sector on 12 May 1944. After learning to dive-bomb during January 1944, the Norwegian Airfield moved to Bognor on 31 March 1944.

On 15 November 1943 No 130 Airfield HQ formed to handle Nos 2 and 4 Squadrons, which, flying Mustang Is, arrived the same day. At the end of the month Nos 63 and 168 Squadrons replaced them, the former two squadrons moving into 123 Airfield, which 168 joined on 21 January 1944. As well as tactical training, the squadrons carried out shipping searches off the Netherlands and Belgium, and flew photo-recce sorties along the French coast and hinterland, gathering pre-invasion material before moving to Gatwick or Sawbridgeworth.

In March-May 1944 five Spitfire IX squadrons made brief use of the station: No 1 came to re-equip after using Typhoons, No 66 for training. The other three – Nos 33, 74 and 127 – after serving in the Mediterranean Theatre, were re-forming for a rear-support role, Lympne-based, for when the invasion of France began. Their specialised task was to protect squadrons from attack as they landed at UK bases after tactical sorties.

Following their departure in May, the station was quieter. As well as No 1 Air Delivery Flight, here between 4 July and 27 August 1944 to deliver aircraft to replace losses, ready for operations, two AAC squadrons arrived to provide 'targets' for AA gun crews. Both left in August 1944, making way for Spitfire IX and Mustang III squadrons, to help protect Halifax and Lancaster daylight *Ramrod* operations until the end of the year, when they moved forward. During this period North

Weald was a Fighter Sector Station controlling ten other stations: Forward Airfields at Andrews Field, Castle Camps, Hornchurch, Manston and Stapleford Tawney; Forward Airfields/Night Fighter at Bradwell Bay and Hunsdon; and other airfields at Bentwaters, Bottisham and Fairlop.

Squadrons based at North Weald from January 1941 to 31 December 1944 were:

| Squadron No | Period | Aircraft |
|---|---|---|
| 56 | 17.12.40-23.6.41 | Hurricane I, IIB (2.41) |
| 242 | 16.12.40-9.4.41 (Stapleford) | Hurricane I, IIb (2.41) |
| 22 | 5.41-19.7.41 | |
| 71 ('Eagle') | 23.6.51-14.12.41 | Hurricane II, |
| | | Spitfire IIa (8.41) |
| 111 | 20.7.41-1.11.41, | Spitfire IIa (Vb from 9.41) |
| | 13.12.41-22.12.41 | |
| 222 | 18.8.41-30.5.42 | Spitfire Vb |
| 121 | 16.12.41-3.6.42 | Spitfire Vb |
| 403 | 22.12.41-3. 5.42 | Spitfire Vb |
| 331 (Norwegian) | 4.5.42-30.6.42, 7.7.42-14.8.42, | Spitfire V |
| | 14.9.42-3.1.44, 3.3.44-31.3.44 | (Mk IX from 10.42) |
| 332 (Norwegian) | 19.6.42-31.3.44 | Spitfire Vb |
| | (less training detachments) | (Mk IX from 11.42) |
| 412 (Can) | 6.42-6.42 | |
| 222 | 7.7.42-1.8.42 | Spitfire Vb |
| 242 | 11.8.42-1.9.42 | Spitfire Vb |
| 486 | 28. 9.42-13. 10.42 | Typhoon Ib |
| 124 | 7.11.42-7.12.42 | Spitfire HF VI |
| 124 | 12.3.43-28.4.43 (for Spartan) | Spitfire HF VII |
| 4 | 15.11.43-30.11.43 | Mustang I |
| | (to Sawbridgeworth) | |
| 63 | 30.11.43-16.1.44 | Mustang I/Ia |
| | (detached to Benson 12.43-1.44) | |
| 168 | 30.11.43-21.1.44 | Mustang I/Ia |
| | (Llanbedr armament training), | |
| | 3.2.44-6.3.44 | |
| 268 | 17.1.44-7.2.44 | Mustang I |
| | (Llanbedr armament training), | |
| | 20.2.44-1.3.44 | |
| 2 | 22.2.44-29.3.44 | Mustang I/Ia |
| | (to Sawbridgeworth) | |
| 66 | 1.3.44-3.3.44 | Spitfire IX |
| 1 | 3.4.44-29.3.44 | Spitfire IX |
| 33 | 23.4.44-17.5.44 | Spitfire IX |
| 127 | 23.4.44-17.5.44 | Spitfire IX |
| 74 | 24.4.44-17.5.44 | Spitfire IX |
| 116 | 2.7.44-27.8.44 | Hurricane, Oxford, |
| | | Tiger Moth |
| 287 | 4.7.44-27.8.44 | Martinet, Oxford |
| 234 | 28.8.44-17.12.44 | Mustang III |
| 312 (Czech) | 27.8.44-3.10.44 | Spitfire IX |
| 310 (Czech) | 28.8.44-29.12.44 | Spitfire IX |
| 313 (Czech) | 4.10.44-29.12.44 | Spitfire IX |

Between 4 January and 20 June 1945 the station again accommodated an AAC squadron, No 285, together with Mustang Is of 26 Squadron, here between 21 January and 3 April 1945. No 1494 Flight, using Martinets and Master IIs, also functioned from the station, between 5 March and 30 June 1945. No 128 (Reconnaissance) Wing re-formed here on 7 May to oversee the movement of Nos 331 and 332 Squadrons to Norway, and left for Dyce on 14 May. On 10 May No 130 Squadron had also arrived, flying Spitfire XIVs; its stay was brief, however, for on 24 May it also moved to Dyce en route for Norway, where it was to serve as part of the stabilising force.

*Vampire F3 VG700 of 604 Squadron outside an 'A' Type hangar.*

For the first time for many years North Weald fell silent, but not for long. Remaining in occupation was the Fighter Command Radar School, opened in April and closed on 7 September 1945. On 1 July 1945 North Weald temporarily came under the control of No 46 Group, Transport Command. Next day No 301 (Polish) Squadron moved, in followed on 10 July by No 304 (Polish), both of which had recently re-equipped with Warwick C IIIs, the latter squadron holding on to a few Wellington GR XIIIs. Their stay was brief, 301 leaving on 4 September and 304 on the 6th, to occupy awaited space at Chedburgh. Their role was the operation of scheduled passenger and freight services to Greece, Italy and Norway.

On 1 August 1945 Essex Sector HQ opened. Renamed Metropolitan Sector in June 1946, it remained at North Weald until November 1957. On 15 September 1945 North Weald once more became its old self, for at midday, flying an assortment of Spitfires, many of the most famous fighter pilots set forth on a memorable first Battle of Britain Day commemorative flight over London with Douglas Bader, the Station Commander, well to the fore.

ATC gliding was carried out by No 129 GS from October 1946 to May 1958, as well as No 142 GS; they shared the station, which from October 1945 to September 1948 was occupied by No 9 Personnel Despatch Centre and trade selection boards.

Disarmament kept North Weald empty of fighters until 27 March 1949, when No 601 Squadron AAF brought along Spitfire LF XVIes, followed next day by 604 Squadron similarly armed. These were Reserve Command squadrons, which at North Weald became again part of 11 Group Fighter Command. In November 1949 the Auxiliaries began re-equipping with de Havilland Vampire F-3s, and they were joined in March 1950 by Vampires of No 72 Squadron. In 1951 the main runway was extended for safer operation of jet fighters.

Replacement of Vampires started in August 1952 when No 72 gave up its Mk Vs for Meteor F8s, followed the same month by 604 Squadron and in September by No 601. On 11 May 1953 No 72 Squadron left North Weald, which in October 1953 became once more a Sector Operations Centre and HQ Metropolitan Sector.

On 2 December 1953 No 111 Squadron re-formed at North Weald and equipped with Meteor F8s to complete the North Weald Wing. In June 1955 it re-armed with Hawker Hunter F4s, and in November 1956 started getting F6s. In the early weeks of 1957 'Treble One' learned that under Sqn Ldr Roger Topp it was to become the Royal Air Force Aerobatic Team, the 'Black Arrows', flying aircraft appropriately painted. On 11 March 1957 12 Group Modification Centre moved in from Horsham St Faith to became No 2 Modification Centre.

Drastic contraction of Fighter Command was initiated in 1957, with all the RAuxAF squadrons disbanding on 10 March. The axe also started falling on associated units and RAF stations.

*Warwick C III HG304 QD-P of No 304 (Polish) Squadron.*

The Battle of Britain Flight was temporarily at North Weald from 28 February to 16 May 1958 when, with its two Spitfires and a Lancaster, it found a new home at Martlesham. On 18 June 1958 'Treble One' ceremonially vacated North Weald, which, on 15 November 1958, was placed on care and maintenance.

On 1 September 1964 it was reduced to Inactive status, although No 614 (Volunteer) Gliding School flew from here between 1 February 1962 and 1 February 1965. A new phase in North Weald's life started with its transfer to the Army Department on 4 January 1966. The flying ground had been available to light aircraft and gliders, which led to its use for air shows from the early 1960s. In May 1968 North Weald became really alive in a manner it surely never expected, when makers of the film *Battle of Britain* brought along Spitfires pouring forth the delectable sound that only an early Merlin Spitfire can produce.

In August 1979 the airfield was sold to Epping Forest District Council for the princely sum of £660,000. All manner of schemes were put forward for its use. London Transport and other drivers practiced on the runways while transport firms filled the hangars with metal boxes. The best events were the arrival of 'Aces High', which resulted in mainly more aged and unusual aeroplanes moving in, and the splendid Fighter Meets of the 1980s. In the north-west area 'The Squadron' established itself as a centre for light aviation and enthusiasts, while along the western fringe developers on the M11 motorway probably dream of an interchange with a trading estate, a dome or some such unwelcome feature. Meanwhile, civilianised Jet Provosts show a distinct liking for the airfield, which in 2002/03 hosted more film stars, two C-54s.

North Weald Airfield Museum displays the station's distinguished history in the one-time SHQ situated by the one-time Main Gate, and is open (admission £1.50 – £1 for children and OAPs) from Easter to 31 November. Access is from North Weald village.

**Main features:**
*Runways:* 314° 4,800ft x 150ft, 027° 4,200ft x 150ft, tarmac and wood chip. *Hangars:* two Type A (250ft x 120ft), twelve Blister. *Hardstandings:* eleven single-engine Spitfire type, two twin-engined Blenheim type, twenty-one frying-pan (65ft). *Accommodation:* RAF officers 156, SNCOs 284, ORs 2,795; WAAF officers 36, SNCOs 52, ORs 537.

## NUTHAMPSTEAD, Hertfordshire

*51°59N/00°04E 460ft as; TL435345. 5½ miles SE of Royston*

Steady the rain at the break of dawn on 23 October 1943, but insufficient to thwart Alan Wright and I from checking out rumours that P-38s were at the 'new' Nuthampstead airfield.

Numerous reconnaissance aircraft tried to monitor our progress as we cycled by Duxford's display of fifty-eight grounded Thunderbolts. It was a hard ride because of the undulating terrain, and not until 1345 had we ascended Royston Downs and were closing in on Nuthampstead. Suddenly, to our glee, a P-38 zoomed around, confirming the tales (or tails?). Many engines burst into song as the afternoon detail prepared for flying, while groundcrews tried hard to clear the problems, wrecking operational prospects. Indeed, throughout the afternoon one could hear run-ups of offending Allisons.

Thunderbolts in increasing numbers intruded upon the scene and commenced low-attack training. Soon the fighters were engaging in combat practice above our heads. P-47 QP-V was chased over very low by P-38 17245 of the 343rd Squadron, and, as it banked, white vapour streamed from the wing tips. Judging by the animations decorating my diary entry, this may have been the first time I had seen anything quite like that. Certainly, despite their size, the P-38s showed surprising manoeuvrability.

Seconds later P-38 CY-S, which I noted as 267066, slipped in overhead, revealing its vital long-range tank racks. When the time to leave came it was accompanied with a fine send-off as eight 'CY'-coded P-38s roared away spectacularly. Heading home most satisfied, and with a notebook of memories, we were serenaded by the 'pop stars' of our day, a Beaufighter I escorted by a Martlet and a P-47 ahead of a highly unusual Spitfire Va with clipped wings and yellow under surfaces. What do our late breed of markings experts make of that 'impossibility'? Among parading UC-78s crept a smart Barracuda followed by 'a Mustang I in USAAF colours and markings'. No doubt, for it circled twice. Presumably to confirm for myself that unusual sight, I noted in my diary that evening that 'it *sounded* like an Allison-engined Mk I, too'. If it was instead a P-51B, then it must have been one of the very first flying in the UK.

Meanwhile the P-38s were milling around and had attracted a Mosquito II of 157 Squadron, an all-black example in use long after that scheme had been superseded. As dusk closed in a low-flying Cierva C-30a whirred its way westwards to end a very memorable outing. Problem aeroplanes the Lightnings were, but they were fine to watch.

As for Nuthampstead, not everyone was enjoying it, for it was muddy beyond belief, a tract of chalk mud, the worst mud of all. Memories of that surely remain with the US Army engineers who produced Nuthampstead in 1942-43.

The RAF took over the airfield in May 1943, and American fighters arrived in September, the air and ground crews manning three squadrons of the 55th Fighter Group equipped with assorted camouflaged P-38s, whose twin booms gave them their rather spooky, racy and highly unconventional appearance. Work-up took a month, by which time the P-38Hs among them were declared operational, and flew their first sweep, off the Dutch coast, on 15 October 1943. The P-38 had a good range, American bomber losses were heavy, and only fighter protection could reduce them. Therefore the P-38 was committed to Europe here and at King's Cliffe, with priority being given to the Nuthampstead Group as regards delivery of P-38Hs.

Their action radius, with two drop tanks, was about 400 miles, allowing little spare fuel for combat. Participation in sweeps and B-26 escorts over France took place from Nuthampstead in October 1943, then, on 3 November, the 55th set off in support of heavy bomber operations. The target for the B-17s was Wilhelmshaven, over which the P-38s engaged enemy fighters operating in its defence. The 55th claimed six enemy aircraft and was credited with three.

Two days later came another performance during a raid on Munster, to where B-24s were shepherded. Operating in four-finger formations, the sixteen P-38s claimed five enemy aircraft without loss, but all was not well with the P-38. Its two engines, which should have conferred additional safety, remained troublesome, particularly at low temperatures. Cockpit heating was extremely poor and, despite the vaunted turbo-supercharger, engine performance fell off rapidly above 20,000 feet, making the aircraft highly vulnerable in combat at this frequently flown altitude.

Around 15,000 feet, however, the P-38 was a fine performer, so it came to be accepted as a medium-altitude fighter. Just how vulnerable P-38s were was apparent on 13 November 1943 when forty-eight Lightnings escorted B-17s to Bremen. Seven did not return, and eight were damaged in combat. By the end of November the two P-38 Groups had lost eighteen aircraft, some without doubt as a result of engine malfunctions.

Little improvement came with the longer-range P-38J, whose theoretical radius was 640 miles if two 150-gallon drop tanks were carried. In reality it remained a little over 400 miles. One special prize nevertheless fell to the 55th during its Nuthampstead days when, on 3 March 1944, it became the first USAAF Fighter Group to fly over Berlin. The bombers it was escorting had aborted near Hamburg!

*B-17G 297810 of the 602nd BS, 398th BG Nuthampstead. (IWM)*

The development of Merlin-engined P-51s meant that the P-38's escort days were numbered, except at lower altitudes. A bright idea was to fit a transparent nose carrying, in cramped conditions, a bombsight and a bombardier. Such 'droop snoot' P-38s would lead other Lightning fighter-bombers into the attack from around 20,000 feet, the other pilots releasing their bombs as the leader's fell. The first such operation at that altitude was mounted in April 1944, each aircraft carrying a 1,000lb HE bomb and a drop tank. After twenty-eight bombs had been aimed at Coulommiers airfield, the P-38s strafed the ensuing confusion, and the defenders skilfully fired, bringing down the 'droop snoot'. Six days later, the 55th Fighter Group moved to Wormingford.

During February and March 1944 personnel of the 50th Fighter Squadron were briefly here, after helping to defend Iceland. They joined the 802nd Group at Cheddington in mid-March and appear never to have had any aircraft here or at their next base, where they remained until August 1944 before returning to the USA.

On 22 April 1944 the 398th Bomb Group, embracing Nos 600-603 Squadrons inclusive, moved into Nuthampstead, bringing unpainted B-17Gs. They arrived as the invasion build-up was intense, and participated in sustained attacks on V-weapons targets – one of which, the site at Sottevast, was, on 6 May 1944, intended to be the group's first target, but too late in formation, the 398th had to abort. Subsequently, it was to participate busily in operations to places near and far, target manifests including Berlin, Kiel, Merseburg, Munich, Munster, Saarbrucken and, of course, Normandy. The 398th fully supported battlefield operations, and flew its last sorties on 25 April 1945 while raiding an airfield near Pilsen. Thereafter it transferred POWs from Germany to France before pulling out of Nuthampstead in late May 1945.The 398th's personnel made the homeward journey in the liner *Queen Elizabeth*. Behind them lay 195 operations and the loss in action of fifty-eight B-17Gs.

Nuthampstead returned to the RAF on 10 July 1945, then became a sub-site of 95 MU, which used it as a weapons store until January 1948, and again between October 1949 and 30 October 1954. Between January 1948 and October 1949 it was a sub-site of No 94 MU, which also handled explosives. On 30 October 1954 Nuthampstead was placed on care and maintenance. The site closed in March 1959, some of its concrete dissolving into the M1 motorway.

*Nuthampstead's present grass strip and centrally sited hangar. (Mike Rudkin)*

There was the prospect of far more flying arising from a curious notion to build here a third London airport. Much of the clamour seems to have been a mixture of camouflage and diversionary kite-flying to disguise an intent to build that at Stansted or Maplin Sands – not to be completely confused with Joe Maplin's Holiday Camp of *Hi-De-Hi!* notoriety.

Light aircraft still use a 700m by 35m grass 05/23 strip, beyond which are remnants of the wartime runway. A 6-metre-wide farm track runs alongside the runway, and other very narrow 'roads' connect with the outside world. This private airstrip is operated by Nuthampstead Airfield Associates Ltd, and there is also a small hangar. In August a local ATC squadron usually organises a fly-in.

At 0505 on 10 December 1944 a V-2 rocket air-burst over Nuthampstead airfield, its remains making two craters on the base. This was almost the furthest inland penetration, and the longest flight made by a long-range rocket launched towards Britain, the unwanted record probably being held by the Henlow rocket.

**Main features:**
*Runways:* 230° 6,000ft x 150ft, 290° 4,200ft x 150ft, 350° 4,200ft x 150ft, concrete and tarmac. *Hangars:* two T2. *Hardstandings:* fifty spectacle type. *Accommodation:* USAAF officers 421, EM 2,473.

## OAKLEY, Buckinghamshire

*51°47N/01°04W 233ft as; SP640110. 8 miles ENE of Oxford, near the B4011*

Oakley will be remembered by many a prisoner of war who, after release from the Continent, experienced anew the soil of freedom by stepping on to it at Oakley, positioned in a flat, damp, wooded area.

Although Oakley appeared to be a standard wartime airfield, it was unusual in having three runways of differing lengths and only one T2 hangar and one B1 hangar. Ready before its parent, Westcott, it opened on 27 May 1942 as Bicester's second satellite and remained such until August 1942, when it was adopted by its intended parent. After 11 OTU moved to Westcott in September 1942, Oakley received some of its Wellington Ics. In autumn 1943 they were replaced with Hercules-engined Wellingtons. The OTU's Air Gunnery training section was based at Oakley, and from March 1943 flew Martinets. A few Hurricane IIcs came into use a year later.

A fully fledged bomber station in size and layout, night operational diversions could be accepted, as on 5 April 1944 when eight Lancasters of 106 Squadron landed from Toulouse. At 0230 on 7 June 1944 a Halifax was on approach from the south when the crew baled out, the bomber crashing near Benson. A more distressing accident happened here in the early evening of 9 June 1944 when Wellington LP252, making a low approach to runway 025, clipped a hedge then hit a passing Army lorry. Although it successfully landed, a soldier in the lorry was killed and four men were injured.

Conversion training for bomber crews was Oakley's primary role, which continued to the end of the war, during the final year of which crews were trained mainly for overseas service. After hostilities in Europe ended, orders were received to clear the B1 hangar and prepare it to provide refreshment and succour to hundreds of repatriated POWs who were flown here during May 1945. Although Oakley closed to flying in August of that year and was soon sold for agricultural use, it remains very visibly a wartime airfield.

*Oakley in 2003, its runways very much intact. (Mike Rudkin)*

**Main features:**
*Runways:* 209° 6,000ft x 150ft, 298° 5,100ft x 150ft, 249° 4,200ft x 150ft, concrete. *Hangars:* one T2, one B1. *Hardstandings:* twenty-seven heavy bomber frying-pan type. *Accommodation:* RAF officers 82, SNCOs 300, ORs 840; WAAF officers 4, SNCOs 8, ORs 225.

## OLD WARDEN, Bedfordshire

*52°05N/00°01W 110ft asl; TL155445. 2 miles W of Biggleswade*

Warm and sunny with a few puffy clouds, good company in the old 'Roller', a hamper packed with goodies and a bottle of bubbly – where better to combine them than at verdant, soothing Old Warden? On a calm balmy day, aeroplanes from the dawn of flying will also do their best to charm you. In surroundings somewhat akin to their childhood, they will bring the delightful sounds – and scents – of days long gone, for Old Warden is one of the world's last bastions of biplane, wood, dope and petrol. It is a shrine populated by professionals tending proper aeroplanes.

*Old Warden is a haven for old aeroplanes seeking new life, such as the Desoutter Mk 1 (mod) G-AAPZ shown under restoration. (Audrey Bowyer)*

Grateful we must be to the Shuttleworth family for assembling their collection. Sad, for sure, that Richard Shuttleworth never survived to enjoy the outcome of his dreams. Born in July 1909, endowed with ample charm, handsome, and with considerable ability, he delighted in things mechanical. He knew considerable wealth, which allowed for his education at Eton, and afterwards in France. He passed through Sandhurst, an Army career promoting his interest in aged machines. Although he learned to fly, he never forsook the love of unusual vehicles, delighting in conquering their fastidiousness. While he enjoyed motor-racing, most of all he came to adore old aeroplanes.

His first acquisition was a DH Moth, to fly which in 1932 a small airfield was prepared on part of the family's beautiful estate at Old Warden. When there was no flying, sheep safely grazed against a woodland backdrop. Richard Shuttleworth soon had a tiny Comper Swift and a couple of Desoutters. He added a DH 84 Dragon, once the transport of HRH the Prince of Wales.

His father had died when Richard was only three years old, although it was not until July 1932 that he succeeded to his father's estate. Hearing of an air race to be run in India, and reckoning it to be a worthwhile challenge, he set off on 28 January 1933 to participate, travelling there in his diminutive Comper Swift, like *G-ACTF,* presently part of the Shuttleworth Collection. A friend flew another. In the extraordinary tiny machine he crossed France, flew the length of Italy, pressed on to North Africa and, flying via Iran, arrived in Delhi twelve days after setting out. It was an amazing achievement. In the air race he was unsuccessful, and he returned more conventionally.

Mr A E Grimmer, with whom Richard became acquainted, was an Ampthill garage proprietor who owned in store a 1909 Bleriot XI and a 1910 Deperdussin Monoplane. Both had flown from Hendon prior to the First World War and needed much attention. Richard Shuttleworth wanted to restore them to flying state, so Grimmer, knowing that they would have a good home, let Richard have them. The famous Shuttleworth Collection had commenced, and the two trophies still perform at Old Warden.

Bringing them to flying condition was demanding of time, skill and cash, but both often flew before the Second World War, by which time Shuttleworth had acquired a 1912 Blackburn Monoplane from a barn near Wittering. Not until 1949 did this, the oldest British aeroplane still airworthy, resume flying.

Memories of the First World War still strong, Shuttleworth added aeroplanes of those times to his stock, including a Sopwith Dove and a post-war two-seat version of the Pup, which he converted into the single-seat fighter, named N5180 and still frequently demonstrated. The skill and patience needed for conversion work were displayed by Mr A Jackson, Chief Engineer and Manager at Old Warden.

When the international situation deteriorated in the late 1930s, Richard Shuttleworth joined the RAFVR. The outbreak of war found him at Upavon, then Ternhill, before a posting to 12 OTU Benson. The expectation was for him to join the accident investigation branch. He still managed the Shuttleworth Estate, and became friendly with a fellow officer, that well-known figure of modern Old Warden, Air Commodore Alan Wheeler, to whom the care of Old Warden was entrusted following the war. This was necessary for, in the early hours of 2 August 1940, Richard Shuttleworth was killed when flying in a Battle, L4971, which crashed at Ewelme, Oxfordshire.

In wartime the small airfield became an overhaul depot for Harvards, Proctors and Miles Magisters, an example of the latter (P6382) still flying from here. In peacetime a Trust was established to run the estate, which later became an educational charity. By the end of the 1940s it

*More 1930s than 1970s, the*
*Redwing G-ABNX at Old Warden.*

*Shuttleworth's true 1910 Deperdussin monoplane still flying in 2002 and eagerly awaiting*
*becoming a centenarian.*

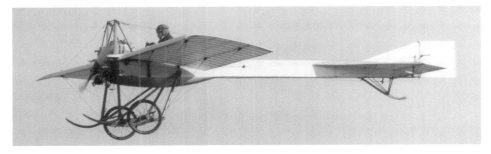

*An amazing sight in September 2002, the 1960s replica Bristol Boxkite, its struts and fabric*
*spectacularly back-lit.*

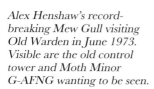

*Alex Henshaw's record-breaking Mew Gull visiting Old Warden in June 1973. Visible are the old control tower and Moth Minor G-AFNG wanting to be seen.*

was very active, most aircraft being tightly packed in the hangar near the main entrance, or in a small adjacent shed. Visiting on 11 April 1950 I noted, among others, the fuselage of Queen Bee LF858, Auster Vs, the 1912 Blackburn, Bleriot XI, 1911 Deperdussin and *G-EBKY,* the dismembered Dove-cum-Pup. Nearby were DH 60X Cirrus Moth *G-EBWD,* in a blue and silver scheme, a red and silver DH 60, *G-ABYA,* and Dessoutter Mk 1 Coupe *G-AAPZ,* all of which remain active.

Much later acquisitions have been superb replicas of the Boxkite and Avro Triplane used in the film Those Magnificent Men in their Flying Machines. Often flown are Shuttleworth's Avro 504K and SE 5a F904. The Collection held the only surviving LVG C VI, and Bristol F2B D8096, which once served the RAF in Turkey and was restored for the Collection in 1950/51 by the Bristol Aeroplane Company.

The inter-war years are represented by a fleet of de Havilland aircraft and the sole Parnall Elf. Avro Tutor K3215 has links with CFS, and 2 FIS Church Lawford. A splendid Shuttleworth treasure is the Gladiator, built using remains of two such machines. More recent additions have been a Sea Hurricane, Spitfire Vb AR501 in 310 Squadron colours, and what at Old Warden seems large – a Westland Lysander – well suited to the scene because of its STOL characteristics.

As the Collection enlarged so did the need for suitable accommodation for the rare machines. Visit now and a line of excellent hangars will be seen in which artefacts on show include photographs, power plants, model aircraft, a metal panel from the Brabazon I and a Concorde model from RAE Bedford. In a case a model of the R-101 dwarfs a model of a Boeing 747 to the same scale, and is a reminder that Cardington is very near.

*Fascinating 'visitors' are often seen, like the superb Belgian-operated Hawker Fury K1930, present in 2003.*

The Collection is open daily to visitors, apart from a few days at Christmas, from 1000 to 1700 hours; it closes a little earlier in winter. Worth visiting, too, is the Swiss Garden, part of the visually very satisfying estate vista. Close viewing of most aircraft, including those being restored, is possible in the hangars, a visit to which brings a chance for a close encounter with that highly enigmatic aeroplane, the DH 88 Comet Racer *G-ACSS*, which is in flying condition. Documentation relating to its spectacular performance in the 1934 MacRobertson Air Race is displayed in a hangar.

On selected Sundays between spring and autumn, the Collection flies its treasures, particularly during the summer Pageant when vehicles are paraded. Evening flying displays have in recent years become a popular feature, for calm conditions aid the flying of the old aeroplanes. Of all remaining active British aerodromes, none can equal the delightful atmosphere of unique Old Warden.

**Main feature:**
*Sole grass Runway:* 03/21 618m x 40m, restrictions apply. A recently extended crowd line affording excellent photographic opportunities extends from the control tower southerly to College Road.

## PANSHANGER (HOLYWELL HYDE), Hertfordshire

*51°48N/00°09W 250ft asl; TL266166. E of Welwyn Garden City to the south of the B1000*

On high ground between Welwyn Garden City and Hertford was Holywell Hyde, where, it is claimed, a landing ground was used pre-war by light aircraft. In 1940 it was the site of a quite elaborate de Havilland Hatfield factory decoy, built using scaffolding and canvas. Still called Holywell Hyde, it was cleared for use as an RLG, and came into use on 16 June 1941 for 1 EFTS Hatfield, which moved into it on 7 September 1942, thereby providing much-needed space for the de Havilland enterprise at Hatfield. The name change to Panshangar took place on 13 September 1943, by which time the School's main task was the grading of trainee pilots, a role that continued to the end of the war.

On 5 May 1947 the School became No 1 RFS. Tiger Moths were used, as they had been by No 1 EFTS, the change to Chipmunks starting in April 1950. Closure came on 31 March 1953.

Since the end of the war Panshangar has constantly been the haunt of privately owned and school-operated light aircraft, many, naturally, being de Havillands. In 2002 it was the home of Panshanger School of Flying, and was being run by East Herts Flying School, and Heli Air was also here.

*Anson T22 navigational trainer WB462 of 1 RFS. (John Rawlings)*

*A Bensen B7M Gyroplane at Panshanger 16 September 1962. (John Strangward)*

*Also visiting Panshanger on 16 September 1962 was Rallye G-ASAP. John Strangward*

**Main features:**
*Grass runs:* N/S 3,000ft, NE/SW 3,099ft, E/W 3,498ft, NW/SE 3,099ft. *Hangars:* two Double Extra
Over Blister, two Extra Over Blister, one Triple Standard Blister, one Double Standard Blister, one
Standard Blister. *Accommodation:* RAF SNCOs 3, ORs 40; the main accommodation was off-base.
  In 2003 grass runway 11/29 had a maximum length of 2,340ft and a width of 85ft.

## PENSHURST, Kent

*51°12N/00°10E 152ft asl; TQ522442. 4 miles NW of Tunbridge Wells*

Situated two miles north of attractive Penshurst and by the north side of the railway, a landing
ground covering 73 acres came into use in November 1917 as a base for No 2 Wireless School.
It trained wireless operators during a week-long course for activities related to home defence, for
which a fleet of DH 6s were also based here. Available for them were two 130ft by 60ft sheds.
Penshurst also served as the depot for wireless equipment, its repair and testing. The School closed
on 23 March 1919, then the airfield buildings were removed.
  Penshurst came alive again in the 1930s for private flying. A small hangar on the south side
supplemented a landing ground measuring 1,650ft by 960ft. During March 1940 No 15 EFTS
Redhill began to use Penshurst as its RLG, but the tenure was brief for on 2 June the School moved
to Kingstown, Carlisle. The site found further military use in 1942 when No 35 Wing, Army Co-
operation Command, began preparing it as a base for Auster AOPs. The first tenant, in September
1942, was No 653 Squadron.
  In mid-1943 spasmodically active Penshurst passed to No 83 Group. A detachment from
658 Squadron arrived in October and stayed until February 1944. In June 1944 the long stay of 653
Squadron ended, after which Penshurst remained on care and maintenance until 664 Squadron placed
its Auster AOP 4s and 5s here for a brief stay. Then the airfield was retained as an Inactive landing
ground within the Biggin Hill Sector of Fighter Command until military interest ceased.

**Main features:**
*Grass runs:* N/S 2,400ft, E/W 1,200ft. *Hangars:* nil. *Hardstandings:* nil. *Accommodation:* RAF
officers 26, SNCOs 10, ORs 156.

## PODINGTON, Bedfordshire

*52°13N/00°36W 330ft asl; SP955605. 3½ miles S of Rushden*

One of the first airfields in England fully occupied by the Americans, which hosted a larger
assortment of units than most, it is now known as 'Santa Pod'. Officially opened in August
1942 as Chelveston's satellite, it remained thus until Chelveston passed to the USAAF on 19 April
1943, when Podington became an independent station.

Construction was still under way when ground echelons of the 352nd Bomb Squadron, 301 Bomb Group, lodged here between 18 August and 2 September 1942 to prevent overcrowding at Chelveston They replaced the C-47 Dakotas of the 28th Troop Carrier Squadron, 60 TCG, the first USAAF unit to briefly use the base, here from 29 July to 7 August 1942.

Podington was much involved with the build-up of the 12th AF and operation *Torch*. Boston IIIs of the 15th Bomb Squadron (L), forced out of Molesworth by B-17s, were here between 13 September and 13 November 1942, when they left for North Africa. Personnel of the 5th Photographic Reconnaissance Squadron were at Podington from 10 September to 29 October 1942, when they, too, left for Algeria. Their place was taken by the 13th Photographic Reconnaissance Squadron, 3rd PR Group, here between 2 December 1942 and 16 February 1943.

The early months of 1943 found Podington out of operational use while fifty dispersal standings were laid and runways extended to permit B-17 operations. Nevertheless, between August 1942 and May 1943 the VIIIth BC CCRC used the station. With ten dispersals incomplete, three squadrons of the 100th Bomb Group arrived on 30 May 1943 for a brief stay, and, with thirty-two B-17s in hand, the 100th left for Thorpe Abbott on 8 June. Construction work continued into the summer, then the 92nd Bomb Group's B-17s arrived from Alconbury between 11 and 15 September 1943 and commenced operations, soon playing a major part in the 1st AD's bombing campaign.

During November 1943 PB4Ys of the 479th Anti-Submarine Group arrived from Dunkeswell and disbanded, its squadrons forming the nuclei of Special Operations Squadrons. The 92nd continued to participate in 1st AD operations to the end of the war. To increase the effectiveness of attacks against reinforced concrete fortifications, this was the Group that undertook trials of *Disney* rocket bombs, two of which could be carried beneath each B-17 mainplane. Only twice were operations flown using them, the close of hostilities rendering the weapons unnecessary.

In mid-June 1945 the 92nd left Podington for Istres, France. In the summer of 1945 RAF airfield construction units were based at Podington, which closed in 1946. The site, sold in 1961, is now the Santa Pod Raceway and Three Shires Riding Centre.

**Main features:**
*Runways:* 050° 6,000ft x 150ft, 290° 4,200ft x 150ft, 350° 4,200ft x 150ft, concrete and tarmac. *Hangars:* two T2. *Hardstandings:* thirty-two frying-pan/loop type. *Accommodation:* USAAF officers 421, EM 2,473.

## POLEBROOK, Northamptonshire

*52°27N/00°23W 230ft asl; TL095870. 5 miles ESE of Oundle*

Visit Polebrook and a bold memorial can be seen straddling the eastern end of what might have become the longest runway in Britain, nay in Europe, and probably far beyond. A possible extension from 5,850 feet to an amazing 14,000 feet was twice considered seriously, at first to make B-29 operations feasible. In the late 1940s the idea surfaced again, to make Polebrook V-bomber friendly after Upwood was pronounced unsuitable. Instead it was at Gaydon and Wittering where Valiants and atomic bombs settled. Polebrook instead became a Thor missile base and the runway was left to decay – with some assistance.

*A Fortress 1 of 90 Squadron running-up at Polebrook.*

Polebrook became the world's first operational Boeing B-17 Flying Fortress base. Their 1941 arrival was memorable for all whose lives were in any way touched by them. For sky-gazing folk the astonishing and hitherto unseen quartet of broad brilliant white contrails these high fliers etched over eastern England surely remains unforgettable. In reality the Fortress Is were all but useless, a truth that fast became a badly kept secret, and soon they became an unpleasant novelty item. After arriving at Watton during Easter 1941 they moved to West Raynham, Bodney and Great Massingham, all of which were 2 Group Blenheim day-bomber stations. None featured the necessary hard runways, so a search for something better was initiated; Polebrook, the building of which began in autumn 1940, was a chance choice. Pat Webster, leader of 90 Squadron, which was afflicted with the Fortress Is, taking an aerial look at Polebrook, reckoned it suitable, so to this new airfield 90 Squadron took its handful of 'Forts' between 27 and 29 June 1941.

Polebrook, land for which was acquired from the Rothschilds, was a 1939 design reduced to having only one Type J hangar (pattern 5836/39) for major servicing, but later supplemented by two T2s (8254/40). Three runways and a compact technical site, north of the main hangar, were featured. Parts of the technical site remain, as well as the main hangar, fire-damaged in 1979 then repaired and used to store agricultural items.

In the winter of 1940-41, before completion, Polebrook served as a dispersal airfield and later a satellite for the Blenheims of 17 OTU Upwood, a sleeping role retained until September 1941, when Warboys replaced it. Gp Capt A C Evans arrived to open the self-accounting station on 26 May 1941.

B-17s were based here long before the USAAF came to the UK; they were B-17Cs, whose operations were fraught with terrible problems. The fitting of effective turbo-superchargers to improve high-altitude flying was somewhat strange for the Americans cautioned the British about high-flying. They advised the RAF to employ them as trainers in advance of superior versions. Troubles likely during lonely, stratospheric flights were rightly forecast as enormous, but to an impatient Prime Minister they were challenges to be mastered. He was eager that the British should make the B-17C a success, to encourage more US backing in the war. Bombing Hitler, in Berlin, in daylight, from a mysterious and great height and in immunity, these were all notions to delight the Churchillian temperament. To accurately drop the small bomb load from above 30,000 feet needed a well-heated and sealed aircraft, ample oxygen and clear weather. Huge ports in the aircraft's sides needed to open in order to poke out the heavy .50in defending guns. When the huge windows opened, cold air flooded the fuselage, some as cold as -50°C. Absence of a pressure cabin demanded an elaborate oxygen system, portable bottles and the wearing of thick and heavy electrically heated clothing. Hand-traversed guns quickly froze to their mountings, further reducing the bomber's value. What was never in short supply was the courage and will to attempt to make the Fortress I a going concern.

On 8 July three Fortresses, starting the operational phase, set out for Wilhelmshaven in quite good weather, but only two reached the target area and only one attacked. Enemy fighters were spotted – and the Fortress's waist guns were frozen to their mountings. Survival came only because the fighters turned away. A 7-inch thick layer of ice on the tailplane of the third Fortress had forced its early return.

Bombing Berlin in daylight to deliver a puny load could neither harm the foe nor boost crew morale, so, due to the risks involved, Fortresses operated against fringe targets. On 24 July 1941 a trio from 90 Squadron led a daylight assault on German capital ships in Brest. Nuisance raids followed, limited by unserviceability, hazy conditions and other criteria. An attack, on 8 September 1941, on the *Admiral von Scheer* in Oslo docks virtually ended their operations, two of the four Fortresses being shot down. On 26 October No 90 Squadron sent a detachment to the Near East, where weather conditions favoured high-altitude operations. In December 1941 it was concluded that successful Fortress I daylight raids were almost impossible. Suggested night operations, too, were abandoned. High-altitude bombing, if resumed, would be by Wellington VIs – fitted with pressurised cabins. No 90 Squadron disbanded at Polebrook on 12 February 1942.

At the end of 1941 a new organisation, No 108 Conversion Flight, controlled by a new Bomber Command training Group, No 8 Group, came into being at Polebrook. It was the precursor of something larger, No 1653 Conversion Unit, which opened on 9 January 1942. The previous day Liberator IIs arrived from Snaith for the training of crews of Nos 159 and 160 Squadrons by the newly formed CU. It was to build to a strength of sixteen plus two Liberators, and use Grafton Underwood as its satellite station. After converting crews for two overseas bomber squadrons, it would provide crews for No 1 Group, whose Wellingtons were expected to be replaced by Liberators. Training of Liberator crews proceeded until, on 2 June 1942, the unit left for Burn. This period in Polebrook's history raises an interesting question – when did the first Liberators arrive at the station ? I ask because on 1 January 1942 I recorded seeing Liberator IIs (identity letters MX) flying in the area.

Whereas in June 1941 Americans went to Polebrook as businessmen, they were now about to engage in combat. On 11 June 1942 20 officers and 450 other ranks moved into Polebrook, followed by a further thirty-one officers and 465 men on the 12th. Yes, the Yanks had at last come, and to Polebrook, holy shrine of the B-17, to where they were to bring the first USAAF Fortresses in Britain. Men from these first postings were soon establishing themselves as the 340th and 341st Bombardment Squadrons of the 97th Bombardment Group, whose headquarters was set up at Polebrook. There, on 6 July, the first B-17E to come to Britain for operational purposes landed, and by 31 July thirty-eight were being shared by Polebrook and Grafton. To fly them there were forty-seven combat crews, who between them had flown more than 500 training hours since arrival.

For Americans accustomed to flying over wide, open spaces, crowded eastern England took some getting used to, and they did well to be operationally ready early in August. The 97th, at Polebrook and Grafton, was alerted for action on the 9th of that month and again on the 12th, but poor weather prevented operations. General Spaatz and Lieutenant General Eisenhower visited on the 15th, but it was 17 August that became the most auspicious day. Polebrook's part was limited, if important, for two small diversionary operations were mounted from the base. An hour ahead of Grafton's bombing effort, three B-17Es of the 340th Bomb Squadron, escorted by a swarm of RAF Spitfires drawn from Nos 121 ('Eagle'), 242 (RAF), 331 (Norwegian) and 403 (Canadian) Squadrons, under North Weald control, Nos 111, 308 (USA) and 350 (Belgian) Squadrons, under Kenley, and Nos 71 ('Eagle'), 124 and 232 Squadrons, controlled by Debden, flew some twenty-five miles out to sea towards Dunkirk. Further support came from nine *Moonshine* Defiants operating from Northolt. German fighters at St Omer and Courtrai were ordered to engage too late.

Another three B-17s, of the 341st Bomb Squadron, flew a feint towards Alderney to attract fighters from the Cherbourg Peninsula. Their crews were exposed to more risk than intended because they had taken off fifteen minutes too soon, and the six-Spitfire RAF escort was not available. The only problem the Americans encountered came from a flock of pigeons that intercepted a B-17 near Marlborough; some crashed into the bomber, injuring its navigator.

On 19 August a dozen B-17s of the 340th and 341st Squadrons, supporting the Dieppe operation, bombed the Abbeville/Drucat airfield. Later that day a Percival Q.6 touched down with General Eaker, here to find out first-hand about the latest operation. Another visitor was 12354, one of the first USAAF B-24s to be based in Britain.

Bombing raids from Polebrook soon included attacks on Amiens/Longeau on 20 August, Le Trait on the 24th, when Fw 190s damaged several B-17s, Wilton's shipyards at Scheidam on the 27th, and Meaulte on the 28th. On 5 September Polebrook's contingent and others raided Rouen/Sotteville. Return to the Potez Meaulte factory, on 6 September, brought the loss of B-17 124450, piloted by Lt Lipsky, 340th Bomb Squadron. This was a B-17F, examples of which the 97th received in late August.

An Ibsley-based P-38 called on 7 September, its suitability as a fighter bomber carrying a 1,100lb bomb being considered. That day the 97th returned to Wilton's shipyards. On 8 September came consolidation, with the 342nd and 414th Squadrons moving in from Grafton. On 2 October, using only B-17Fs, Meaulte and St Omer were attacked. A week later twenty-two B-17s participated in the largest US raid yet, on the Fives/Lille steel plant and Hellemmes railway works. On the 21st the Group suffered its heaviest loss yet, three B-17s missing from a Lorient raid.

On 18 November the 342nd and 414th Squadrons left for Hurn, and thence to North Africa, followed by the 340th and 341st on 25 November 1942. Polebrook was then extensively modified to accommodate a complete Group comprising four B-17 squadrons. One runway was extended to almost 6,000 feet, the others to 4,300 feet, and an unconventional taxi track was added.

Selected for Polebrook was the 351st Bomb Group, which came to Britain by sea during April-May 1943. The first of the B-17Fs to arrive was 229411, bringing the advance party on 15 April. Four squadrons (Nos 508, 509, 510 and 511) followed and commenced operations on 14 May. Thereafter the Fortresses raided Schweinfurt, Berlin, Hamburg's oil refinery, a locomotive factory at Hannover, communications targets in Koblenz and Mayen, factories and railway installations in Cologne, and harbours, V-weapon sites, submarine installations and tactical targets in France, Holland, Belgium and Norway. A famous personality at Polebrook 351st was film star Clark Gable, who flew operationally several times in 1943 while making a training film here.

A highly meritorious event during the 351st Group's stay came on 20 February 1944 when Leipzig held the target. One of the B-17s was badly crippled, its co-pilot killed and the pilot seriously wounded. The damage did not bring the aircraft down, so 2/Lt Walter E Truemper, the navigator, and Sgt Archibald Mathies, ball turret gunner and engineer, decided to nurse the B-17 home. After the aircraft was righted to allow some of the crew to bale out, it was heroically flown back to Polebrook. After circling, those aboard tried to land it. That proved very difficult, and after such a magnificent effort in bringing their wounded pilot home, the entire crew was killed during their third landing attempt. Mathies and Truemper were each posthumously awarded a Medal of Honor.

By the end of the first week of June 1945, the 351st, its last combat mission flown on 25 April against a Czech target, started returning to the USA. American tenure of Polebrook ceased on 10 July 1945, upon which date the RAF's 273 MU opened as a long-term aircraft storage centre with sub-sites at Market Harborough, Tempsford and Wratting Common, and satellites at Deenethorpe and Glatton. For the most part Stirling IV and V transports, together with Mosquito VIs and XVIs, were held prior to break-down. Ferry duty was carried out between 15 March 1946 and 30 April 1947 by Ansons and Proctors of No 3 Ferry Pool. No 273 MU closed on 15 September 1947, leaving the station to care and maintenance.

After ten years of dormancy, the unlikely happened when Polebrook became operational following the formation of No 130 Squadron on 1 December 1959, to operate three Thor missiles. They and the launch facility functioned in a high-security enclave on the airfield's southern side under North Luffenham control. The squadron disbanded on 28 August 1963, and the site was returned to the Rothschild estate in January 1967.

Polebrook's memorial is worth a visit, a private exhibition exists on site, and the village church contains interesting memorabilia. What does seem strange is that the first operational Flying Fortress base attracts less interest than many others.

**Main features:**
*Runways:* 250° 5,850ft x 150ft, 190° 4,200ft x 150ft, 310° 4,200ft x 150ft, tarmac on concrete. *Hangars:* one Type J, two T2. *Hardstandings:* fifty loop type. *Accommodation:* USAAF officers 443, EM 2,529.

## RADLETT, Hertfordshire

*51°43N/00°19W, 74ft asl; TQ155036. Just S of St Albans on E side of A5*

Magic, it was, sheer magic, when at the start of September 1946 during the first post-war SBAC Show, held at Radlett, one could examine closely many of Britain's late war and immediate post-war prototypes and their production derivatives. The Tudor 1, Concordia Meteor IV, Hamilcar X, Halifax transport, Seafang, Attacker – not to mention the Mosquito prototype W4050 proving that it could carry everything including a kitchen sink. All and many more were there, and lots of them flew, including the AW 52G, which was hauled off by the last active Whitley GT V. For two years 'Radlett' became a place of pilgrimage and joy before Farnborough snatched the honours.

Obscure in public mind, this portion of Hertfordshire long played a part in aviation. In 1916 on a 212-acre site close to nearby London Colney, a landing ground hosted Captain Ball's No 56 Squadron between 4 July and its departure for France with SE 5s on 7 April 1917. Reserve Squadrons used that site, as well as No 74 Squadron's Avro 504Ks and SE 5As between 10 July 1917 and 25 March 1918. London Colney also served as a Training Depot Station prior to its closure in December 1919.

Well to the south lay Hendon, close to which was the Handley Page Kingdom of Cricklewood. There, in September 1912, the company that was to become famous for its large aeroplanes moved into a collection of stables by Crown Lane, developed its purchase, began building BE 2As and

*The first Handley Page Heyford Mk 1, K3489, on Radlett's flying ground in 1934.*

*Handley Page Hampden L4032 at Radlett in 1938.*

soon its first 0/100 big bomber. Transporting such by road to test-fly from Hendon was impracticable, so the company acquired Clutter House Farm. Adjacent to its large factory, it converted it into a flying ground.

Keeping any aviation business going after the 1914-18 war was not easy, and from the aerodrome Handley Page ran an international air service, the first in the London area to be supported with its own Customs facilities. Cricklewood was not really suitable for such activities, which ceased on 21 May 1921, after a passenger aircraft crashed at Golder's Green on 14 December 1920. There had been the usual complaints about noise and 'low flying', mostly from houses only recently built around three sides of the aerodrome.

Handley Page, in any case needing a superior site for flying, found it by chance. Jim Cordes, assistant test pilot, collected an Avro Avian from Woodford, Manchester. As he returned towards Cricklewood he encountered bad weather and had no choice but to force-land. He chose a large field just north of Radlett village, lying between a railway line and Watling Street. It was also fairly close to the wartime London Colney landing ground. As a result, in June 1929, Handley Page bought the 154-acre Colney Street area used by Cordes. That allowed Cricklewood aerodrome to close to flying in February 1930. Although that land was sold, the Cricklewood factory remained Handley Page's main aircraft production centre almost to the company's demise.

By the end of 1929 a test flight hangar had been erected at Radlett, and on 7 July 1930 the aerodrome was officially opened by Prince George (later Duke of Kent). During the opening the HP 39 Gugnunc was demonstrated by Cordes. He began his take-off run from within the hangar and was airborne by the time he reached the open doors!

Radlett was a grass aerodrome with buildings alongside Watling Street, which marked the western boundary. Although small, it was suitable for the sedate aeroplanes of the time. To the early 1930s civil aircraft predominated, some prototypes being built here, and some at Cricklewood, where construction of Handley Page production aircraft generally took place. On 25 June 1930 the Heyford prototype's first flight was from Radlett, then on 11 November 1930 that beautiful HP 42 airliner *Hannibal* sailed aloft. On 21 June 1936 the Hampden prototype first became airborne from Radlett, and exactly two years later the first production example. To cope with increasing work, new flight sheds and a main production hall were erected at the Park Street area of Radlett. Extension of the landing ground followed in the Stone Wood direction, although the overall size was constrained by the main railway line and the main roads bounding the site. It was these confinements that resulted in the prototype Halifax being taken by road to Bicester for its first flight on 25 October 1939. That proved Radlett suitable after all, and the second prototype first flew, from Radlett, on 17 August 1940. Wartime flying by Hampdens and Halifaxes was plentiful, particularly for development of both types. The strange HP Manx was also test-flown from Radlett. Although runways were imposed by spring 1943, their length led to the Hastings being first flown from Wittering on 7 May 1946 and the Victor prototype being taken in imaginative disguise to Boscombe Down for its first flight of 17 minutes on 24 December 1952.

Hampden then Halifax components were in wartime transported by road from Cricklewood to Radlett for assembly and test-flying. The addition of more buildings meant demolition of an entire farm, after which even more land was necessary to meet wartime needs. Eventually the airfield boundary almost reached the River Ver. Eventually 1,590 and two prototype Halifaxes were Cricklewood/Radlett produced.

*A Halifax 1 passes low over Radlett and the 'old cars' used nightly in 1940 to block the landing ground.*

By the time hostilities ceased Handley Page's attention was already directed to the Hastings military transport and its civilian equivalent, the Hermes. During its maiden flight from Radlett on 2 December 1945, Hermes prototype *G-AGSS* encountered catastrophic aerodynamic problems resulting from elevator overbalance. After stalling, it entered an inverted dive and crashed on nearby Kendall's Farm, killing test pilots Talbot and Wright. The second Hermes, *G-AGUB,* first flew on 2 September 1947, just in time to appear at the second Radlett SBAC Show. Hopes were pinned on the Hermes IV, the nosewheel variant, first flown on 5 September 1948. Production of the Hermes was limited, making it a costly venture, and the turbo-prop Mk V was eclipsed by the Bristol Britannia.

In 1952 the company's Low-Speed Wind Tunnel was joined by a high-speed twin Nene-jet-engine-driven induced flow 4ft by 3ft closed working section wind tunnel capable of continuous running at around M = .92, which was built at the northern end of the site near the Centrifuge Test Rig. At Park Street were to be found structural test facilities needed for design work on the Victor V-bomber, the Experimental Hangar, drawing office and design centre, a water pressure test tank and other trials facilities. When the prototype returned from Boscombe Down on 25 February 1953 it landed on the newly paved 21/03 7,002-foot main runway with northern end overshoot. From this runway the first production Victor, XA917, made its maiden flight on 1 February 1956. Victors were assembled at

*The ill-fated Hermes G-AGSS at Radlett. (Eric Watts)*

*Hermes 2 G-AGUB at the 1947 SBAC Show.*

Blackburn Firecrest RT651 at the 1946 SBAC Display at Radlett.

Hastings TG499, carrying a trial freight pack, was test-flown from Radlett. (Eric Watts)

Victor B1s in Radlett's flight-test hangar. (HP)

Colney Street where a 675-foot-long, 150-foot-wide factory extension opened on 26 March 1956, leaving the experimental section at Park Street. That department was to be very busy with Victor development, including work on the B Mk 2 first flown on 20 February 1959. When production ended in 1963, a total of eighty-four Victors and two prototypes had appeared, and design work had begun to convert Victors into tanker and reconnaissance versions.

By then Handley Page – and indeed Radlett – had suffered a crippling blow with the death, on 21 April 1962, of Sir Frederick Handley Page. Very strong-willed and mightily proud of 'his' company, he refused to merge with any other, but as a result HP lacked the funds and 'power' to effectively compete in the tough new world. The company's success had come from its heavy bombers now being eclipsed by the ICBM, and its future now depended upon making its HP 137 Jetstream twin-engined feeder liner a success. Plans called for its manufacture in a new plant, The Jetstream Main and Sub-Assembly Buildings at Radlett, and with 200 aircraft on order the company looked likely to survive for a few more years. Unfortunately a major set-back arrived when Jetstream development costs tripled. So serious was the development that merely to break even orders for more than 1,000 Jetstreams were needed instead of the original 400.

*HP Herald G-APWI on Radlett's lengthy apron.*

In 1966 manufacture was entirely removed to Radlett, the Cricklewood factory being sold for other industrial uses. Available Treasury aid was of no use because sufficient Jetstream orders were unobtainable. The Receiver was called in and on 16 August 1969 Handley Page Aircraft Ltd was formed to continue only Jetstream production. American-owned Cravens Corporation, backing the new company, withdrew financial support after only six months, and on 27 February 1970 Handley Page went into liquidation. On 2 March the Handley Page Radlett workforce ended their employment. During April Victors for conversion into tankers were flown to one-time competitors at Woodford for completion. On 1 June 1970 Handley Page ceased to exist, and by September the Radlett shops had been reduced to shells. Nothing lasts for ever. Although the long runway and parts of the factory have survived, they are memorials to a passed phase of human endeavour.

**Main features**:
The lengthy main factory had an apron of the same length, to which were added three parking fingers for heavy aircraft. Alongside the main production hall and to the south was the large components shop and the Jetstream complex. The 7,002ft concrete runway – much of which remains – was laid prior to Victor flying. A secondary 15/33 3,891ft runway crossed it and was loop-joined to the main runway along the eastern side. A further, shorter runway linked Park Street with the main runway. Sporting and social areas were at the northern end of Park Street.

## READING (WOODLEY), Berkshire
See **WOODLEY**

## REARSBY, Leicestershire

*52°43N/01°02W 70ft asl; SK650140. NE of Leicester, SE of Rearsby village and the A607 road*

In the late 1930s a small grass aerodrome opened at Rearsby for use by Leicestershire County Flying Club. At nearby Rawcliff, Taylorcraft Aeroplanes (England) Ltd began in 1938, building under licence US-designed light aircraft, the first of which made its initial test-flight on 3 May 1939. By September 1939 twenty-three Taylorcraft light high-wing monoplanes had been built. To keep its team intact during the war, the company obtained sub-contract work from aircraft firms, while one of its own aircraft was acquired by the RAF for evaluation as an artillery air observation post. Success led to the other examples being re-engined with the Cirrus Minor, thereby changing them into Plus Model Ds. A further one hundred were ordered in 1941, these featuring larger Perspex windows and being named Taylorcraft Auster Is.

MAP had contracted Taylorcraft to repair Tiger Moths, and later in 1940 the company's part in the CRO organisation was extended to include Hurricanes. Needing a larger landing ground and increased factory space, the company acquired Rearsby, where four new hangars were constructed. Further contracts led the CRO repair work to involve Bostons, Havocs and later many Typhoons.

Regular upgrades of the Auster AOP led to the Mk III, which had increased engine power and additional cockpit glazing, the AOP IV and V, Lycoming-engined, and the Gipsy Major post-war Mk VI, which featured external slotted flaps for exceptionally slow flying. A complete re-design resulted in the Auster AOP 9, production of which took place at Rearsby between summer 1954 and early 1956.

On 8 March 1946 the company changed its name from Taylorcraft to Auster Aircraft Ltd. Interest was by now centred on civilian Auster variants, in particular the J/1 Autocrat, the J/4 and later the Aiglet trainer. By the late 1940s success was being dented by ever-increasing foreign competition from companies with large home markets.

*TJ707, the Auster AOP 6 prototype, at Rearsby.*

*Auster AOP Mk IV MT100 at Rearsby. (Auster)*

*The first post-war success was the Autocrat, like G-AGTV seen at Rearsby in January 1958.*

*Auster Aiglet Trainer G-ANWX at Rearsby in January 1957.*

In the late 1950s Auster tried unsuccessfully to enter the helicopter market, then in the early 1960s the company was taken over by British Executive & General Aircraft Ltd (Beagle), and the Rearsby branch became Beagle-Auster. A twin-engined light aircraft, the Basset, attracted a small contract placed by the RAF, which needed just such an aircraft for special communications flying.

Aircraft production continued until 1964, the last Rearsby-built aircraft being a Husky *(G-ASNC)* granted a CofA on 23 April 1964. In 1968 Beagle-Auster was sold to Hants & Sussex Aviation at Portsmouth, the business closing in 1969. As for the Rearsby works, they became a centre for light industry and the airfield was closed

**Main features:**
The small grass airfield adjacent to the Auster factory buildings lay to the south-east of Rearsby village. Grass runways were sufficient to permit wartime use by Typhonos and Bostons, which flew in for CRO attention.

## REDHILL, Surrey

*51°12N/00°08W 205ft asl; TQ300475. 2 miles SE of Redhill*

For an airfield that started life as a small grass field for light civilian aircraft, Redhill acquired considerable importance. Its first significant RAF association came on 1 July 1937 with the formation of No 15 Elementary & Reserve Flying Training School, operated by British Air Transport Ltd, which used Magisters and Hart variants. In September 1939 it became No 15 Elementary Flying Training School and continued using Magisters. Congestion at Redhill resulted in the acquisition during March 1940 of a relief landing ground at Penshurst. By late May 1940 southern England was obviously an unsuitable area for pilot training, so the EFTS moved on 2 June to Kingstown, Carlisle's pre-war airfield. With it went the Polish Grading & Testing Flight, formed on 15 February to assess Polish pilots, and using Magisters and Battles.

Redhill was now freed for operational activity. First in were Lysanders of No 16 (Army Co-operation) Squadron, returning from France, which lodged here between 2 and 29 June. Handling them was HQ 50 Wing, resident between 9 June and its disbandment on 6 August 1940. No 600 arrived from Hornchurch on 12 September 1940 and brought along Blenheim I(f)s; it remained until 12 October 1940, by which time it was starting conversion to Beaufighters. Immediate replacements were more Blenheims and Beaufighters, this time of 219 Squadron, which stayed until 10 December 1940.

By now a perimeter track encircled the grass airfield, from which taxi tracks led later to eight Blister hangars and a dozen double dispersal pens. The landing area was also extended, into an L shape, providing a main NE/SW runway and a shorter N/S runway, from which between May 1941 and January 1944 a succession of fighter squadrons operated. Nos 350, 611, 303, 310 and 312 Squadrons were particularly active on 19 August 1942, providing cover for the Dieppe combined forces raid. Fighter squadrons that used Redhill were:

| Squadron No | Period | Aircraft |
|---|---|---|
| 1 | 1.5.41-1.6.41, 19.6.41-1.7.41 | Hurricane I |
| 602 | 14.1.42-4.3.42, 13.5.42-17.7.42 | Spitfire V |
| 340 | 1.4.42-7.4.42 | Spitfire V |
| 308 | 1.7.42-7.7.42 | Spitfire V |
| 312 | 1.7.42-8.7.42, 16.8.42-20.8.42 | Spitfire V |
| 611 | 20.7.42-27.7.42, 1.8.42-23.9.42 | Spitfire V/IX |
| 350 | 31.7.42-7.9.42, 15.9.42-23.9.42 | Spitfire V |
| 303 | 15.8.42-20.8.42 | Spitfire V |
| 310 | 16.8.42-20.8.42 | Spitfire V |

For Redhill to be of much value it needed firm runways, so over the next few months Army Track was laid, 4,690 feet forming runway 087 and 3,170 feet producing runway 019. Some improvement to accommodation and general facilities was also made so that Redhill could play a very useful part in preparing for the invasion of France.

In February-March 1943 a pseudo '83 Group' was established, which was to control Nos 121 to 124 Airfields during the forthcoming mobility exercise *Spartan*. To support the true 83 Group, the 83 Group Communication Flight opened on 8 April 1943, became a squadron on 1 March 1944, and departed on 15 April 1944. By then there had been other developments, including the formation on 4 July 1943 of No 126 Airfield HQ, established to administer Nos 401, 411 and 412 Canadian squadrons. The unit left on 6 August. Already No 39 (Reconnaissance) Wing centre had arrived and stayed until 1 April 1944, running Nos 128 Airfield, which controlled Nos 168, 414 and 402 Squadrons, and No 129 Airfield, controlling Nos 140, 231 and 430 Squadrons.

In the summer of 1943 Redhill once again held operational squadrons as follows:

| Squadron No | Period | Aircraft |
|---|---|---|
| 66 | 10.8.43-13.8.43 | Spitfire V |
| 504 | 14.8.43-19.9.43 | Spitfire V |
| 131 | 16.8.43-17.9.43 | Spitfire V |
| 231 | 15.10.43-15.1.44 (disbandment) | Mustang I |

Now the run-up to the invasion began in earnest with the formation of No 83 Group Support Unit from the amalgamation of Nos 403, 405, 409, 410 and 419 ARFs. Its task would be to maintain a reserve of three aircraft and pilots for each 83 Group squadron. Redhill's commitment to the Normandy campaign was obviously very important, and the GSU moved forward to Bognor on 25 June 1944. Ansons had arrived on 18 May 1944 for No 1310 Flight, based here until 25 June to assist with the supply of aircraft and personnel to 2TAF squadrons in France. No 4 Overseas Air Delivery Unit formed under 46 Group Transport Command on 22 May 1944, also to assist in ferrying fighters to 83 Group in France. No 4 OADU advanced on 26 June 1944.

*Miles Whitney Straight G-AERV on Redhill's apron on a rainy day in April 1950.*

*Flamingo G-AFYH of British Air Transport Ltd sheltering at Redhill among RFS Tiger Moths.*

*Tiger Moth PG640 RCD-W of No 15 RFS Redhill.*

*Chipmunk T10 WB640 of 15 RFS.*

Redhill now resumed its place in the Biggin Hill Sector and, with the pre-invasion forces gone, No 116 Calibration Squadron came to fill the vacancy, arriving from Gatwick on 5 September 1944 and bringing a fleet of Tiger Moths, Oxfords and Hurricanes for AA radar calibration. On 20 January 1945 No 287 Squadron joined it, and brought along from Gatwick more Oxfords and Spitfires for anti-aircraft support tasks. Both squadrons departed during the first week of May 1945, leaving the station housing No 1 Aircraft Delivery Unit between 17 October 1944 and 14 February 1945. A small part of No 212 MU arrived in July 1945 for a brief stay, and had quit by the end of the year.

Civilian light aircraft flying was resumed in 1946, supplemented, from 1 April 1948, by No 15 Reserve Flying School using Tiger Moths, as well as a few Ansons for navigational training. The RFS later had several Oxfords, and before closure converted to Chipmunks. The reduced need for a large reserve force, mixed with the increasing complexity of modern combat aircraft, resulted in closure of the reserve schools programme in 1954, the end of No 15 RFS coming on 20 June. Redhill remained an active centre for light aircraft, private and club – and that included The Tiger Club, a popular entertainer at air shows in the 1950s and '60s. The airfield later became a helicopter centre, and remains as such as through the London Helicopter Centre, which sees plenty of movement by light aircraft of Cabair, Cloudbase Aviation and Redhill Aviation, among many others.

**Main features:**
December 1944: *Runways:* 087° 4,690ft, 019° 3,171ft, Army Track. *Hangars:* eight Blister type, nine pre-war civilian hangars. *Hardstandings:* twelve for twin-engined aircraft, twelve 50ft diameter frying-pan. *Accommodation:* RAF 30 officers, 333 ORs; WAAFs in requisitioned premises.

Redhill Aerodrome Ltd of 2004 lies within the Gatwick CTR. It has three grass runways, 01 850m x 25m, 08 897m x 30m, and 08 Left 678m x 50m. There are four helicopter training areas and two (08/26 and 01/19) heli-strips. Part of the wartime L-shaped extension has been closed.

## ROCHESTER, Kent

*51°21N/00°30E 436ft asl; TQ745645. SE of Rochester between the B2097 and the A229,with the M2 running close to the western side*

'Rochester' had, for many years, a double meaning.

Most famously, and for half a century, 'Rochester' meant 'Shorts', which also equated with 'seaplanes, Medway'. When the company decided to include floatplanes in its aircraft manufacturing programme, the aerodromes at Leysdown and Eastchurch, where its landplanes were flight-tested, were obviously unsuitable. It therefore bought a piece of land on the right bank of the Medway above the bridge at Rochester in 1913, and the following year built its Cuxton factory. Oswald Short supervised the works, which produced Short 184s and others.

After the Armistice there was a run-down of military contracts and Short's turned also to the manufacture of buses, cars and other products in order to keep solvent. Nevertheless, the company maintained its aircraft business, concentrating upon marine designs, in particular the 'Singapore' for the RAF and the 'Calcutta' passenger boat.

The most successful product of the Medway works was the Short 'C' Class or Empire flying boat, first flown in July 1936, of which twenty-eight were ordered. From the Empire boat came the superlative Sunderland, both products of the 1930s. The most spectacular was the Mayo Composite, which separated a number of times over the river. There was now a reversal of fortune; test-flying facilities for the boats were readily available, whereas there was no suitable aerodrome close by from which to fly any Short landplanes. Until 1933 civil types were being test-flown from Lympne or Gravesend.

Help was, perchance, about to unexpectedly emerge. In September 1933 Rochester Council purchased 105 acres of land situated between the Maidstone and Chatham roads for the purpose of developing not another housing enclave but a municipal airport. For Short's, good news came on 22 November 1933 when it was granted a lease on much of the land – with the proviso that the site would also be available for use as an airport, and retain private and public landing rights and facilities. With all that Short Bros agreed, and almost at once the local unemployed began levelling the ground and generally preparing the airport. Short Bros moved in even before any hangar was built, and during the 1933-34 winter the company famously erected its large Scylla four-engined biplane airliner in the open, where it faced gale and rain. Nevertheless, it first flew from Rochester on 26 March 1934.

*A Short Scion
Senior flying from
Rochester Airport.*

By the end of that year other firms were interested in Rochester, among them Pobjoys, which had a main works at Bedford and whose Rochester factory was erected in the north-western corner, directly across the field from Short Bros' large works. Proving its interest in the airport, Short's started air services on 9 June 1934, initiating a run to Southend. The cost of the 12-minute journey was 8 shillings single, 12 shillings return, the latter currently being around £30. There were also hangars for private owner and light aircraft use.

*The third production Short Seaford resting on the Medway.*

*Sunderland N9050 riding
the Medway beneath
Rochester Castle.*

A further boost came when, on 1 April 1938, No 23 Elementary & Reserve Flying School, operated by Short Bros, opened at Rochester, a hangar and other facilities being built for School use. A second hangar became available in summer 1938 when the E&RFTS expanded to allow training of Fleet Air Arm pilots. Such was the aircraft shortage that Avro 504Ns were briefly used, until Avro Tutors, Tiger Moths and Magisters became available. Intermediate and advanced training was given using Audaxes and Harts. Upon the outbreak of war No 23 E&RFTS merged with No 24 EFTS at Sydenham, Belfast, its place at once being taken by No 16 Group Communication Flight, formed on 3 September 1939 and remaining here until June 1941, using an interesting assortment of aircraft including an Airspeed Envoy and a Hornet Moth.

Short Bros' factory was extended in 1939, for the company now had two main lines, the Sunderland flying boat and the Stirling four-engined bomber, production of which started in 1939 at the Rochester works. Stirling delivery had barely started when, on the afternoon of 15 August 1940, the airfield was attacked by Do 17Zs of KG 3. Although many of their bombs fell among houses across the road from the main works, serious damage resulted and six Stirlings were made useless. Pobjoys' was also damaged. Stirling production was much disturbed, salvaged parts were being dispersed while the design department moved to Kidderminster. Rebuilding was soon under way at Rochester, although Stirling output was not fully resumed for almost two years. While the aircraft factory was repaired, Rochester Airport proved useful as an emergency landing ground for battle-damaged aircraft.

The second half of the war saw Stirlings again being built and test-flown at Rochester, while Sunderlands in all their clean-white splendour slipped into the Medway from their riverside birthplace. In the drawing office, well away from Rochester, plans evolved for the giant Shetland flying boat, launched on to the Medway on 24 October 1944, and the Seaford, the ultimate development of the Sunderland, first flown in 1944, its civilian cousin being the Solent. Ever a company to diversify, ideas were advanced for a fast shipboard strike and reconnaissance bomber, the Sturgeon.

When the war ended and the civil Silver Stirling was unwanted, production of that type ceased. Work continued, however, on the Short Sturgeon, prototypes being constructed. BOAC ordered Solents and used civilian Sunderlands, but the market for seaplanes like those and the Short Sealand

*A Short Bros advertisement for its magnificent C-Boat used in the 1937 Hendon Display programme.*

ONE OF THE EMPIRE FLYING BOATS
Constructed for
IMPERIAL AIRWAYS
by
SHORT BROS. (ROCHESTER) LTD.
ROCHESTER.     ENGLAND

*Bombing of Rochester Airport on 15 August 1940.*

was extremely limited. With the future looking none too bright, Shorts, as the company was now generally talked of, decided to rationalise. In 1946 it decided to move its business to Belfast, where since pre-war times it had been associated with Harland & Wolff, and where, in wartime, it had built on Queens Island many Stirlings in an Air Ministry-built factory. Thus Shorts of Rochester was no more once the last Solent, *G-AHIY,* left the river on 8 April 1948, the seaplane works closing in July. Other work was transferred to Belfast, and both Rochester factories and facilities closed.

There was, for a time, a Short presence still, as No 24 EFTS, run by the company, re-opened on 1 March 1946, and on 7 May 1947 became No 24 Reserve Flying School, flying Tiger Moths and Ansons, and later Chipmunks, Prentices and Ansons. It closed on 31 March 1953. No 16 Group CF had also returned to function here between January 1945 and March 1946. The Reserve element resulted in Shorts having an overhaul and repair contract between 1954 and 1959 involving target-towing Beaufighters, Mosquitoes and Sturgeons. Then the works handled Bailey bridges and other Army equipment until 1962. Alongside that activity Channel Airways operated out of Rochester, from 1960 to 1967, one of its Channel Islands services. Rochester Flying Club had begun using the airfield when civil flying restarted in 1946, and plentiful light aircraft and helicopters continue to use the airfield.

*Stirling N3641 during acceptance testing at Rochester Airport.*

*Prentice VS698 of No 24 RFS Rochester. (John Rawlings)*

The year 1962 saw the start of the present main activity at Rochester Airport when the old Shorts factory was acquired by Marconi Avionics, which eventually became part of BAe Systems, the current occupant. Outwardly the buildings look the same, the Board Room still topping the pillared main entrance. Inside there is a maze of cables and computers, carpets and cleanliness, for only in pristine conditions is it possible to manufacture anything so advanced as avionics such as a 'HUD' (head-up display) for an F-16 or the JSF. One building literally floats to ensure right construction conditions, and air-conditioning reigns supreme. People? Yes, they are there, but the numbers are few compared with yesteryear. It is so quiet, too, and much assembly is 'mechanically electrical'. "This is a night vision helmet for a helicopter pilot, that is an avionics component for Eurofighter. The history display cabinet shows our contribution to the US industry, to Airbus – and how far we have come from the early years of Jaguar," I was recently told.

"You haven't got a Stirling tucked away in another cabinet, have you?" I asked.

Sadly they hadn't kept one. In any case it would have long since withered at the sight of such amazing wizardry.

Light planes are quite active here, operators including Millen Air Services and Rochester School of Flying. On their side of the field there is the Medway Aircraft Preservation Society, which has the twin tail wheels of BF523, which I recall once poking through the mud in the Ijsselmeer and which is pictured in situ in *The Stirling Story* (Crécy). MPS restored Spitfire K9942 for the RAF Museum, so, with a few more pieces... No, I don't think we'll ever again see a Stirling at Rochester. If you want a good view of what's left, the Holiday Inn awaits you, built perhaps ominously on the one-time council airfield. As for the seaplanes, the M2 motorway passes over Cuxton Reach, which used to be their take-off area.

**Main features:**
*Runways:* Rochester Airport, run by Rochester Airport plc, remains a grass airfield of an unusual acute triangular shape. It has two main grass runways, 02/02 and 16/34, and there are three helipads at the runway ends. There are many peripheral industrial buildings.

## ROCHFORD (SOUTHEND), Essex
### See SOUTHEND

*An Avro 504J of No 198 (Night) Training Squadron at Rochford.*

## SALTBY, Leicestershire

*52°49N/00°42W 480ft asl; SK865265. 11 miles S of Grantham, W of the A1*

Upon opening in August 1941, Saltby was 14 OTU's satellite, a grass airfield within No 7 Group that attracted Hampdens, Ansons and, from 1942, Wellingtons. Lit at night, it was attacked three times by the Luftwaffe. In spring 1943 thirty-two Horsa gliders were flown in for storage.

Saltby was selected for upgrade to Class 'A' standard after No 14 OTU left Cottesmore for Husbands Bosworth in August 1943, freeing the satellite for development. Concrete runways were added, as well as four T2 hangars and one B1 hangar, and additional domestic areas.

On 18 December 1943 Saltby was transferred to the IXth AF TCC Substitution Unit. Runways completed in February 1944, Saltby was ready and the 314th TCG, US IXth Air Force, and four squadrons of C-47s/C-53s moved in and took over the stored Horsas. The 314th, which served within the XIIth Air Force in the Mediterranean Theatre, had acquired combat experience during the invasion of Sicily, and throughout April and May 1944 it flew day and night formations in preparation for D-Day.

On the evening of 5 June 1944 fifty-one C-47s and nine C-53s of the 314th TCG, carrying 1,007 men of the 508th Parachute Infantry Regiment, 2nd Battalion Regimental HQ and 42,838lb of ammunition and equipment, set off as part of the operation *Albany* force and dropped just after 0200 on 6 June. Of the force, eighteen aircraft were damaged and one was shot down near the DZ. Next day a re-supply mission was flown using fifty C-47s and two C-53s. Bad weather forced thirteen of them to abort, while thirty others suffered serious flak damage.

Between June and September supply drops continued, until 17 September 1944, when seventy-two aircraft of the 314th TCG took part in Market, carrying 1,015 paratroopers and 248 loads of equipment to DZ 'X' at Renkum, south of the Utrecht-Arnhem railway line.

Next day seventy-two aircraft took off from Saltby carrying 1,217 paratroopers, including part of the 4th Parachute Brigade, and 219 parapacks of equipment, for release at DZ 'Y', Ginkel Heath. Many aircraft were hit by AA fire and four fell near the drop zone. After the September airborne assault, the C-47s and C-53s flew freight and personnel-carrying missions to the Continent before moving to France early in March 1945.

The Royal Air Force retrieved Saltby in late March, No 1665 HCU arriving from Tilstock on 26 March bringing transport Stirling IVs and Halifax IIIs and a few Spitfires for fighter affiliation activities. Late May 1945 saw Saltby jointly used by the USAAF and the RAF. Curtiss C-46 Commandos of the 349th TCG transported from here men and supplies to Stavanger, Norway, including the British 1st Airborne Division. This busy time for Stirlings and Commandos produced one spectacular accident. At 2350 on 29 May Stirling IV PW386 swung on take-off and careered into a C-46, both aircraft erupting in flames. Flt Sgt Nettleton, the pilot, received cuts and burns while an American, asleep in the C-46, was killed. When on 30 May the thirty-three C-46s left Saltby, they had carried out seventy-three sorties and carried 1,163 personnel of the British 1st Airborne Division as well as more than 1,700,000lb of freight.

On 1 August the HCU departed for Marston Moor. Saltby then passed to care and maintenance, parented by Melton Mowbray, later by Wymeswold. Its active flying days were over. Later it was used by Nos 216 and 255 MUs, until 26 October 1948. After years as an Inactive site, Saltby was de-requisitioned in September 1955, then reverted mainly to agricultural use.

*C-47 2100894 of the 59th TCS, 314 TCG, Saltby.*

A 1,200m by 40m concrete/asphalt section of runway 07/25 remains, as well as 800m by 30m of the 02/20 concrete runway, and Saltby is used by the Buckminster Gliding Club. Its hangar and wooden clubhouse are on land leased from Buckminster Estates.

*Saltby remains, 2003. (Mike Rudkin)*

**Main features:**
*Runways:* 255° 6,000ft x 150ft, 196° 4,200ft x 150ft, 314° 4,200ft x 150ft, tarmac on concrete. *Hangars:* four T2, one B1. *Hardstandings:* fifty frying-pan type. *Accommodation:* RAF officers 61, SNCOs 325, ORs 608; WAAF officers 2, SNCOs 8, ORs 102.

## SAWBRIDGEWORTH, Hertfordshire

*51°50N/00°07E 320ft asl; 3 miles SW of Bishops Stortford*

The 1914-18 war saw many grass fields become emergency landing grounds, and one was near Sawbridgeworth. Some were developed into aerodromes, while others were superseded by more suitable sites nearby, sometimes used for private flying and aerial 'pageants' like the Spellbrook Flying Ground, also near Sawbridgeworth.

Different territory close by was in some instances chosen for large-scale development within the 1930s RAF expansion programme. Wartime Sawbridgeworth, several miles from the nearest First World War landing ground, was a development of a site by Mathas Wood used in the summer of 1937 by No 22 Group during major Army exercises.

Summer 1940 saw it enlarged, then re-opened on 15 June 1940. Lysanders of No 2 Squadron made early use of it before moving in on 24 October 1940. Tented accommodation was replaced by permanent buildings, supplemented with requisitioned premises, then further extension resulted in the adoption of the name Sawbridgeworth.

Initially the grass runway ran almost parallel to a nearby road, but in summer 1941 two Sommerfeld Tracking runways were laid to the west of the original site, giving the airfield an unusual layout. Metal tracking was laid primarily to enable Tomahawks to fly from here. Introduced in August 1941, when 34 Wing formed, they were found to be troublesome and prone to ground looping, and Lysanders remained – as an insurance.

Aircraft had dispersed at the woodland's edge until late-1941 'TE pens', often called 'Blenheim Pens', were built. They consisted of four earthen walls forming revetments, each holding a 'twin'. Barriers halved some pens, allowing dispersal of two fighters.

In March 1942 a third runway was laid, before No 2 Squadron re-armed with Mustang Is in April 1942. It was many months before the last Lysander and Tomahawk left, a common feature at Army Co-operation Command stations.

Late 1942 saw a typical wartime control tower opened and a T2 hangar added to supplement three Over and eight Extended Over Blister hangars. Fighter-bomber Typhoons of 182 Squadron were here from 7 December 1942 to 30 January 1943, returning to Martlesham Heath after flying one operation, against Bruges, on 3 January.

No 2 Squadron was detached to Bottisham between 3 February and 27 April 1943 in connection

*Sawbridgeworth-based Lysander T1532 of No 2 Squadron.*

with *Spartan*. During that time No 3226 Servicing & Commando Unit, trained to protect landing grounds, participated at Sawbridgeworth, whither came No 652 Squadron with its Auster AOP 1s on 21 February 1943. After re-arming with Mk IIIs, it left for Scotland on 30 March. Stapleford Tawney now became the station's satellite, until 1 June 1943, when that passed to 12 Group.

Formed on 8 August as 34 Wing's gunnery training unit, mid-May 1943 saw the arrival of the four aircraft of No 1495 (TT) Flight, which stayed until 10 July. On 30 June 2759 RAF Regiment Squadron came in from Stapleford Tawney, departing for Snailwell on 13 July.

No 2 Squadron left for Gravesend on 16 July 1943, Sawbridgeworth going to care and maintenance on 7 August. Two 83 Group R&SUs formed here, No 410 on 1 September and 409 on the 3rd, the former departing for Detling on 11 November and the latter to Kenley on the 10th. Both were to play major parts in *Overlord*. Other invasion support units that passed through in this phase included two field hospitals and two Casualty Air Evacuation Units, before flying was resumed in November.

On 12 November 1943 HQ No 123 Airfield from Thruxton brought along Mustang I/Ias of Nos 63, 168 and 170 Squadrons. Nos 63 and 168 Squadrons were exchanged for No 130 Airfield North Weald's No 4 Squadron on 30 November. It had come in January 1944 to convert to a PR role with a tactical bias, and flew Spitfire PR XIs and Mosquito PR XVIs. No 170 Squadron disbanded on 15 January 1944, making way for No 2 to return on the 29th, as part of No 130 Airfield, which departed for Gatwick and 35 Wing on 4 April, taking No 2 and No 4 with it and also No 268 Squadron and its Mustangs, which had arrived on 1 March. The first Spitfire PR XI sorties had been flown from here in that month, the first Mosquito PR sortie taking place on 20 March 1944.

No 126 Squadron, flying Spitfires, was re-established at Sawbridgeworth following service in MedMe, and was given an anti-intruder rear-support home defence role in *Overlord*. It arrived on 1 May and, after re-arming with Spitfire IXs, departed for Culmhead on the 22nd. That was the last flying unit based at Sawbridgeworth. The station was too far north for an active part in the Normandy campaign, to which it had nonetheless made very important contributions.

On 30 November 1944 the station passed to Maintenance Command. No 211 MU, at nearby Hyde Hall from 14 December 1942 until closure on 20 August 1945, had long been connected with the airfield. On 6 April 1945 No 247 MU formed here to handle fuel supplies, and remained until disbandment on 1 May 1946. On 31 January 1946 263 MU arrived from Stansted. Within a few weeks the landing ground was being prepared for agricultural use. On 16 March 1946 a sub-site of the very large 3 MU found space and stayed until June 1947. Thereafter the airfield was slowly replaced by rural encroachment, the Air Ministry releasing its hold in 1956.

**Main features:**
*Runways:* 306° 5,400ft x 150ft, 244° 4,200ft x 150ft, 188° 4,200ft x 150ft, Sommerfeld Tracking.
*Hangars:* one T2, eleven assorted Blister. *Hardstandings:* thirteen Blenheim type, fifteen 50ft
diameter frying-pan, fifteen Sommerfeld. *Accommodation:* RAF officers 69, SNCOs 87, ORs 840;
WAAF officers 4, SNCOs 10, ORs 120.

## SHELLINGFORD, Berkshire

*51°38N/01°31W 275ft asl; SU325940. 3 miles SE of Faringdon*

No 3 EFTS had an unusual origin, which lay in the Reserve Flying School that arrived at Hamble
on 1 April 1931. In June 1935 that became 3 E&RFTS, equipped mainly with Hart variants,
and when war began it became No 3 EFTS. The area around Southampton Water being very
hazardous in 1940, the unit's unusual, civilian-marked Avro Cadets moved to Watchfield in July.
There the EFTS ran into more problems, for mixing blind approach training with elementary pilot
training was hardly ideal, so it initiated a search for a practice landing ground to relieve Watchfield.
Kelmscot landing ground was a possibility, for Brize Norton made little use of it, but 50 Group
showed little inclination to settle for that. Despite the problems, 3 EFTS managed 1,935.40 flying
hours in August 1940 and had only two accidents. The search for a landing ground continued, and in
October the choice fell upon a small area near Shellingford, four miles east of Faringdon. Reckoned
to be a good site, although surface preparation was needed, its main attraction lay in the ease of
possible enlargement.

Nevertheless, December 1940 brought proposals from HQ FTC that 3 EFTS should instead
take over Wanborough RLG, dormant and awaiting use by Lyneham's SFTS. The EFTS replied
that Wanborough was unsuitable because its grass surface could not accept winter activity.

As flying increased at Watchfield, 3 EFTS decided, in May 1941, to accept Wanborough after all.
Command's response was that the site was now earmarked for Lyneham! No. 3 EFTS was therefore
authorised to use Kelmscot for practice forced landings. However, no Tiger Moths could be left there
overnight, for the site was unguarded. Also, at night it was obstructed by an odd collection of anti-
invasion landing vehicles placed there by a local farmer on behalf of the Air Ministry.

Closure of 11 AONS at Watchfield during July 1941 brought suggestions that 3 EFTS stay there,
but since early 1941 3 EFTS's choice remained the area near Shellingford. It had also already
interested higher echelons, and planning was going ahead to acquire it. On 6 September 1941 3 EFTS
was told that, because upgrading of Kelmscot was unlikely, and because a third Flight was to be
added, a move must come. The new 'C' Flight would be detached to the Shellingford landing ground
until that airfield won full station status and could accommodate the complete EFTS.

Shellingford was soon fit for use, a dispersal site for pupils now having dormitory accommodation,
from which they were conveyed to the airfield by motor coach. As yet there were no cooking facilities,
meals for the defence force permanently stationed there being brought from Watchfield. Tiger Moths
of 'C' Flight dispersed on the airfield, but inspections were carried out at Watchfield.

*Tiger Moth T5985 '13' of
No 3 EFTS Shellingford.
(via George Burn)*

September 1941 brought instructions from 50 Group that EFTS pupils should have night-flying experience to relieve pressure on SFTSs. This commenced at Watchfield on 25 September 1941, but only for instructors. Pupils began night-flying at Shellingford on 15 October 1941, where a Cranwell-type flare path proved satisfactory.

On 18 December 1941, with sufficient buildings erected, 3 EFTS moved its fifty-six Tiger Moths to Shellingford. The technical site had four hangars together with stores, lecture rooms, a Link Trainer, transport section, armoury, flight offices, crew room, parachute section, administration block, nine Nissen huts, three Laing huts for the defence force, and a collection of 'latrines – bucket seat type'. A communal site was established at Stanford in the Vale, where the Officers', Sergeants' and Airmen's Messes were, together with the NAAFI, and central ablutions. The Officers' and Sergeants' quarters were at dispersed Site 1, each with three sets of huts. Other sites were soon in use, and sick quarters were placed at No 5. In January the use of RLG Kingston Bagpuize was authorised. By mid-January 1942 enough accommodation was available for thirty cadets, and 3 EFTS started to use it as an RLG. Kingston Bagpuize was only briefly available to 3 EFTS so, on 16 May 1942, a detachment went to RLG Wanborough, no longer needed by Lyneham and which was making itself into a base for heavy transports. However, it was too far away from 3 EFTS to be of much value.

Army pilots first joined 3 EFTS in July 1942, for pre-glider flying training. They had to complete eighty hours' dual and solo flying before being posted to a GTS. Glider pilot courses became an important part of Shellingford's activity into 1943. Some measure of the activity at 3 EFTS may be judged from the 3,472.45 hours flown in March 1943, 209.05 of them at night. A steady flow of trainees passed through 3 EFTS in 1943 and Tiger Moths were about in profusion. Training of Army pilots continued spasmodically and, in September 1945, a period of glider pilot refresher training took place.

Shellingford resumed its association with Watchfield after the war, messing being switched to the latter station. In 1946 Royal Netherlands Air Force pilots trained at Shellingford. With the gradual wind-down of the RAF, 3 EFTS, like Shellingford, closed on 31 March 1948.

**Main features:**
*Grass Runways:* NE/SW 3,450ft, E/W 3,075ft, NW/SE 2,799ft. *Hangars:* four Bellman, eleven Standard Blister with taxiways to a field-encircling perimeter track. *Accommodation:* RAF officers 42, SNCOs 39, ORs 727.

## SIBSON, Cambridgeshire

*52°32N/00°23W 100ft asl; TL059960. 7 miles SW of Peterborough by the B671, S of Wansford*

Some airfields survive against all odds, and Sibson, in a sense, lies in this category. Close proximity to Wittering mitigated against it, but the ever-increasing size of Peterborough has helped Sibson. Visit it and one finds a grass airfield smaller than when the RAF used it, because the present Sibson lies adjacent to and north-west of the wartime airfield, and is thus not quite the same site. Wartime Sibson's grassland became an aerodrome by the addition of a few tents, and portable flares for night-flying. Use as Peterborough's RLG began in July 1940, and it was bombed the following month. At this time it was used for the training of naval pilots using Harts and Audaxes.

In January 1941 Sibson was transferred to Cranfield control, Oxfords flying from here until 14 SFTS left in June. On the 15th No 2 CFS Church Lawford acquired the use of Sibson for its Tutors and Oxfords, which flew from here until mid-January 1942. This unit shared Sibson with Peterborough until the latter regained control in July 1941. Use had been made of it by Tiger Moths of 25 EFTS, replaced by others of 17 EFTS, which carried out circuit training until the school disbanded on 1 June 1942. That date coincided with the formation of 7 (P)AFU at Peterborough, a unit that equipped itself with many Master IIs. Controlled by 21 Group, it placed its 'A' and 'B' Flights at Sibson on a permanent basis in August 1942. By mid-1943 there were two day-flying Flights and a night-flying Flight here. Increased flying brought about improvements and enlargements to a once spartan site, needed to cope with its increased use. A T1 (14) hangar (9659/42) was erected and existing buildings changed into SHQ (3825/43) and a Main Stores, which was sited in a Romney Hut (11279/42). A rest room was converted into a lecture block (745/41), while the control tower remained (13726/41). Two sub-sites existed, No 1 in the south-west corner dominated by a T1 (14) hangar. There was also a Blister hangar here, and High Leys Cottage accommodated flight offices and the rest room. Sub Site No 2 also had a

*Master II AZ705 '89' of 7(P)AFU.*

T1 (14) and flight offices. A typical 24,000-gallon fuel tank was placed nearby. Beside the main site was the instructional area. Four enlarged Over Type Blister hangars (12532/41) were added to the landing ground, which ultimately had three runways.

Throughout 1943 and into the summer of 1944, Master IIs of 7 (P)AFU were ever active in the area and, occasionally, one of that unit's Hurricanes. There was intense operational flying around Sibson, which with the amount of mixed flying from Wittering was hardly conducive to pilot training. Accordingly, 7 (P)AFU relinquished its hold on Sibson on 8 August 1944, and moved to long-established Sutton Bridge where the facilities, although antique, were far superior to those at Sibson.

Limited flying continued at Sibson to the end of 1944, then, early in 1945, it was placed on care and maintenance. Its proximity to Wittering rendered it a possible dispersal site, but Sibson closed on 21 May 1946 only to be again placed under care and maintenance in the hands of Flying Training Command. Fighter Command administered the station from 8 July 1946 to its closure on 1 October 1946.

Since the 1960s Sibson has been a popular centre for civilian flying, and became the Peterborough Parachute Centre for free-fall parachuting. It is the only airfield in Britain where the lanky Pilatus Turbo Porter was seen regularly. In 2004 the operator of Sibson is Walkbury Flying Club.

*Sibson's heaviest visitor? P-38 KI-D '051' of the 20th FG after ground looping. (via Dave Bradfield)*

**Main features:**
Wartime: *Runways:* NE/SW 3,300ft, N/S 2,700ft, grass. *Hangars:* one T1, three Standard 65ft Blister, one Double 65ft Blister. *Accommodation:* RAF officers 53, SNCOs 104, ORs 446; WAAF officers 2, ORs 35.

Current: *Runways:* 07/25 703m, 15/33 551m, grass.

## SILVERSTONE, Northamptonshire

*52°05N/01°00W 506ft asl; SP675420. 6 miles SW of Towcester*

Stirling Moss, Jack Brabham, Froilan Gonzales, Giuseppe Farina – names to thrill when Silverstone was a simple circuit around a converted airfield. From the start it was a Mecca for personalities whose none-too-powerful cars proudly displayed each driver's name. Then, all was for pure delight. Now the thrills emit from curious noisy contraptions screaming 'money'!

Silverstone's opening on 20 March 1943 was far more sedate. Upwood's 17 OTU had produced Blenheim bomber crews, but by 1943 that need had passed, so HQ 92 Group, on 10 April 1943, ordered 17 OTU to Silverstone to equip with Wellington IIIs on a three-quarter OTU establishment. Upwood's team moved in during mid-April.

On 6 May 1943 two Wellington Ics, arriving from Westcott, were the first bombers to land at Silverstone. They were making their final flights, for they had come for conversion into ground instructional airframes. Next day a Wellington III touched down, ten being here by mid-May. Training commenced on 1 June, No 62 Course changing role in mid-stream. OTU strength was set at 30 IE plus 10 IR Wellington III/Xs, raised on 26 June to fifty-four bombers. Additional were four Ansons, three Martinets, two Lysanders and briefly a Defiant.

The first *Bullseye* was attempted on 30 July 1943, all four participants being recalled. 'B' Flight moved into the satellite at Turweston on 2 August, then four crews flew the unit's first exercise Eric from Silverstone. The following night saw the unit's initial offensive sorties, four crews scattering leaflets over Arras, Lille, Roubaix and Tourcoing. Thereafter *Bullseyes*, *Erics* and *Nickelling* were undertaken on a 92 Group set rota.

On 28 August 1943 a Halifax of 434 Squadron landed back from Nuremburg, and two nights later Silverstone despatched its first bombing raid, two Wellingtons dropping twelve 500lb bombs on the Foret d'Eperlecque. Two similar night raids, eight sorties, preceded the climax to operation *Starkey*. *Bullseyes* played an increasingly important part in training, and on one such Sergeant Shearing, flying HE264, was intercepted by two enemy aircraft and luckily escaped. A Gunnery Flight formed on 24 November 1943 at Turweston, equipment now narrowed to Wellingtons and Martinets.

By the end of 1943 17 OTU had despatched thirty-three *Nickel* sorties, and No 71 Course passed out on 2 January 1944. Aircraft returning from operations were being diverted to Silverstone, as on 22 May 1944 when sixteen Halifaxes landed from Bourg Leopold. Another fourteen came on 26 July, together with some of the 100 diverted to 92 Group airfields on the 30th. Of seventeen Halifaxes arriving on 21 September, most had bombs aboard. The final *Nickel* was flown deeply into France on 14 August 1944, after which 17 OTU flew diversionary sorties confusing enemy radar. Life changed little before the war ended. During August 1945, when courses 110-115 were being trained, the OTU vacated Turweston, which ceased to be the satellite on 23 September 1945.

No 17 OTU remained intact during the initial post-war wind-down. In September 1946, attempts were made to find suitable replacements for the Hurricanes that had replaced the Martinets in 1944 for gunnery training. The Tempest V was too fast, the Harvard too slow, so Spitfires and Masters were to be used. Suddenly the news broke that 17 OTU was to move to North Luffenham in November 1946; that later changed to Swinderby, whence 17 OTU moved in November. Silverstone, placed on care and maintenance, was sold in 1947. In 1948 the first RAC Grand Prix was run here and, in May 1949, the British Grand Prix. There is still flying on race days, when helicopters bring in celebrities.

**Main features:**
*Runways:* 026° 6,000ft x 150ft, 068° 4,200ft x 150ft, 144° 3,900ft x 150ft, concrete with wood chips. *Hangars:* four T2, one B1. *Accommodation:* RAF officers 174, SNCOs 553, ORs 865; WAAF officers 10, SNCOs 13, ORs 392.

## SMITH'S LAWN, Berkshire

*51°25N/00°36W 50ft asl; SU971700. S of Windsor in Windsor Great Park*

Smith's Lawn originated before the war as a private landing strip, which in wartime looked likely to become an RLG. Late 1940 brought the unexpected when a Bellman hangar was erected and Vickers-Armstrong opened production at what was designated VAXI (Vickers-Armstrong Extension 1). Similar titles were not uncommon, unlike the erecting here of high-altitude Wellingtons. The sole production Mk V passed through, followed by sixty-four Mark VIs, of which eighteen were modified Mk V airframes. All were apparently flown out of Smith's Lawn, where, in 1944, Warwicks could be seen in storage.

Sited in the south-east corner of Windsor Great Park, between 14 July 1941 and February 1945 the landing ground also served as an RLG, for No 18 EFTS. Its other use was as a landing ground for USAAF L-4 Piper Cubs and L-5 Sentinels, bringing personnel for business and doubtless private purposes. After the war the site reverted entirely to its original state. Many sporting events now take place on Smith's Lawn.

## SOUTHAM, Warwickshire

*52°14N/01°22W 300ft asl; SP430615. 9 miles SE of Warwick*

In 1940, the grassy Southam Fields became an RLG for Tiger Moths of 9 EFTS Ansty until its disbandment in March 1944. Church Lawford's Tutors and Oxfords also used it in 1941. At this small airfield, Laing huts (1032/41) served as barracks and as an unusual combined Officers' and Sergeants' Mess. The medical section used a Nissen hut while flight office and crew room occupied wooden huts. On the east and west perimeters were four Blister hangars, including a couple of joined 69-foot EO Blister hangars bricked in at one end to act as a maintenance hangar – not unusual. Airfield closure came on 21 March 1944, after which Southam was used by Airfield Construction Units. On 18 December 1944 it was transferred to the Ministry of Works.

**Main features:**
*Grass field dimensions:* ENE/WSW 2,400ft, NW/SE 1,800ft. A few temporary buildings on the southern boundary. *Accommodation:* RAF ORs 69 only.

## SLOUGH (LANGLEY OR PARLAUNT PARK), Buckinghamshire
See **LANGLEY**

## SOUTHEND (ROCHFORD), Essex

*51°34N/00°42E, 25ft asl; TQ872895. 2 miles N of Southend-on-Sea, off the B1013*

To many, 'Southend' is synonymous with 'Pier' – still surviving. Others will think of Channel Airways or of the start of Continental 'hols' via a 'Freighter' or, more spectacular and a Colossus in its time, a Carvair. But military flying from Southend? In truth, and known as Rochford, it was as militant as any.

In 1914 a flat area near Rochford was identified as a suitable landing ground, which, in 1915, opened as RNAS Eastwood. From there, as early as the night of 31 May 1915, Flight Sub-Lieutenant A W Robertson reached 6,000 feet in his Bleriot Parasol while trying, without success, to intercept zeppelin L 38 far above him, heading in over Shoeburyness to carry out the first bombing of London. Subsequently two BE 2cs were positioned here, the station having been renamed RNAS Rochford by April 1916.

Its positioning on the approach to London made it of considerable value, and when on 15 September 1916 No 37 Squadron re-formed, one Flight, using BE 12s, was based at Rochford for air defence. Its value was evident in November, when the squadron responded to a day raid by an LVG CIV. By the start of 1917 the squadron, and its three bases, defended the area Rochford-Farmingham-Biggin Hill-All Hallows-Rochford, for which in March 'B' Flight placed 16 BE 12as at Rochford.

On 24 January 1917 No 11 Training (ex-Reserve) Squadron moved in from Northolt, becoming No 98 Depot Squadron on 8 February. Using Avro 504s, it trained pilots for home defence formations, changing its title (to avoid confusion with front-line squadrons) to 198 Depot Squadron on 27 June, and to 198 (Night) Training Squadron on 21 December 1917, which disbanded in May 1919. A similar squadron, No 199 Training (ex-Reserve) Squadron, had formed at Rochford on 1 June 1917 as 99 Depot Squadron, and was repositioned at East Retford on 23 June 1917.

To strengthen home defence, 37 Squadron's 'C' Flight (now here using BE 12s, soon to be replaced by 1½ Strutters) was supplemented with No 61 Squadron, formed at Rochford on 24 July 1917 and armed with Sopwith Pups. On 12 August eleven Gothas invaded the Southend sky to drop bombs that killed thirty-two people. Some bombs fell on Rochford.

Much attention had been devoted to night-fighting, but with limited success. When the Germans switched to using Gothas and the 'Giant' bomber at night at the end of 1917, patrols were carried out from Rochford usually by quartets of Pups flying at between 8,000 and 10,000 feet, and 250 feet apart. The squadron re-equipped with SE 5as in January 1918, and later with Sopwith Camels, easier to operate at night. On 5 December 1917 a Gotha crashed near the aerodrome; hit by gunfire near Canvey Island, the crew, seeing the aerodrome flares, attempted to land. A Very light that they fired being in the colour for the night, it was acknowledged, but on approach they hit a tree and crashed on a nearby golf course The crew became POWs, and when their aircraft was inspected a Very pistol accidentally fired, caused the wreckage to ignite.

On 1 January 1918 No 141 Squadron formed from a flight of 61 Squadron, but only held one Sopwith Dolphin dedicated night-fighter before moving to Biggin Hill on 2 February 1918. No 152 formed at Rochford on 1 June 1918 as a Camel night-fighter squadron, and during that month 37 Squadron left. No 152 Squadron moved to France on 18 October 1918, and No 61 Squadron disbanded in June 1919. Rochford thus had a hand in London's defences to the end of the war.

A brief exposure to civil aviation came on 10 May 1919, when a converted Handley Page 0/400 bomber delivered newspapers by parachute near Southend Pier. The last recorded RAF arrival of the period at Rochford was Bristol Fighter E2581, flown from Northolt by Lt Bromfield, which arrived on 4 December 1919. On 3 February 1920 he flew it to Eastchurch for its eventual display in the Imperial War Museum, Lambeth. Rochford, derequisitioned soon after the war, was briefly used for pleasure flying, wartime buildings were soon demolished, and the land reverted to farming.

In the early 1930s, after much campaigning, the decision was taken to open a municipal airport. In 1933 Southend Corporation purchased the land upon which the First World War aerodrome had existed, and the site was then prepared for Southend Flying Club and hangars were erected. On 18 September 1935 the airport was officially opened by Sir Phillip Sassoon, Under Secretary of State for Air, stylishly arriving in his Leopard Moth. Southend Flying Club, which also had a Leopard Moth and five Avro Cadets, ran the Airport, which was visited by many privately owned aircraft. Such was the local enthusiasm that prior to the opening of the airport, flying had taken place from a field just to the north of the airport site, referred to as Rochford and also as Holt Farm. From the airport Short Bros were soon using a Scion for an hourly five-shilling single service to Rochester. There were other runs, to Norwich and Portsmouth, which at that time would have seemed quite distant from Southend.

Military activity was resumed when Rochford became an Auxiliary AF summer camp venue. In summer 1937 602 and 607 Auxiliary Air Force Squadrons from Rochford made use of nearby weapons training facilities. No 34 Elementary & Reserve Flying Training School operated by Air Hire Ltd opened on 1 January 1939 to use Tiger Moths, Hart variants and Ansons, while the Flying Club here ran the Civil Air Guard scheme. The E&RFTS closed when the airport was requisitioned, in September 1939.

Renamed RAF Rochford, it immediately became a satellite of Hornchurch. With the war eight days old, Spitfires of No 54 (F) Squadron arrived from Hornchurch, and on 16 October Blenheims of No 600 (City of London) AAF Squadron joined them for four days. On 22 October No 74 ('Tiger') Squadron began the first of its five brief stays over the next nine months, departing by the end of the month, only to reappear on 3 November. On 13 February 1940 the 'Tiger' Squadron took part in the first engagement from Rochford, when a Heinkel 111 was damaged over the Thames estuary. A few days later a Dornier 17P was engaged.

No 616 (South Yorkshire) Squadron flew in on 27 May 1940 to help cover operation *Dynamo* before departing on 6 June. On 18 June Flt Lt 'Sailor' Malan, flying a Spitfire of 74 Squadron from Rochford, became one of the first two single-seat fighter pilots of the Second World War to destroy an enemy aircraft at night. On 25 June the Spitfires of No 54 Squadron replaced No 74 and stayed for a month, during which the action was hotting up.

Bombs first fell at Rochford at night on 2 August, although there was much activity over and around. The Rochford squadrons, and others briefly using the airfield, were by then in the thick of the fight. During the afternoon of 13 August Ju 87s escorted by Bf 109s set out to bomb Rochford, but thick cloud caused the raid to be abandoned. The most savage attacks fell on 28 August, when 264 Squadron was spending two days at Rochford.

Dawn reconnaissance flights along the south-east coast preceded an early build-up over France of He 111s and Do 17s escorted by Bf 109s of I and III/JG 51. They headed inland near Sandwich, preceded by fighter sweeps that were met by Hurricanes, including those of Nos 501 and 615 Squadrons, as well as a dozen 264 Squadron Defiants, which were unable to prevent He 111s of II and III/KG 53 from attacking Rochford. Bf 109s engaged the Defiants, trying to deal with the He 111s; No 264 Squadron destroyed a Heinkel and damaged another before the leader's Defiant (L7021) was shot down. Two more Defiants (L7026 and N1574) were destroyed, and N1569 force-landed. Of eight that returned to Hornchurch, five were damaged. Some fifteen Heinkels that reached Rochford faced ferocious AA defences – but still cratered its turf with 15 tons of bombs.

Rochford was attacked again, at 1240 by Raid 13H, which came in from the south-east and damaged buildings. Carried out by twenty-seven Do 17s of II and III/KG 3 attacking from 18,000 feet, the raid was delivered just too late to prevent 264 Squadron scrambling before bombs began bursting on the airfield. Spitfires of 54 Squadron positioned at 30,000 feet took on the bomber escort, Flt Lt Al Deere claiming a Bf 109, Flt Lt George Gribble another at the end of an eleven-aircraft line, and Sqn Ldr Leathart a Dornier. Chasing a Bf 109, Gribble (R6899) and Norwell (R6898) ended the fight so low that Gribble's shooting killed a cow. After landing, he discovered pieces of a tree lodged in his Spitfire. Deere (R6832) was less fortunate – he had to bale out. As the raiders were approaching Rochford, Hurricanes of No 1 Squadron downed a Do 17Z of 6./KG 3 on Rochford aerodrome, its crew becoming POWs. On 26 August another Dornier Do 17Z, of 2./KG 2, attacked by Flt Lt Saunders of 65 Squadron at 20,000 feet over the Channel, had coasted in to a belly-landing on Rochford, and a third battle-damaged Dornier 17Z-2 of 9./KG 3 crash-landed on the airfield on 2 September. Throughout the Battle of Britain, Rochford was repeatedly used by Nos 54 and 74 Squadrons as a forward airfield, sometimes as a bolt hole.

On 28 October 1940 Rochford became RAF Southend, with its own SHQ, but was still closely affiliated with Hornchurch. Defiants of 264 Squadron were here once more from 29 October to 27 November 1940. Two Spitfire squadrons here in December were No 603 (City of Edinburgh) from the 3rd to the 13th, and 611 (West Lancs) from 14 to 27 January.

Wg Cdr Basil Embry DSO (later Air Chief Marshal Sir Basil Embry GCB KBE DSO and 3 Bars DFC AFC), Station Commander since October 1940, was posted to the Middle East, and Wg Cdr J M Thompson assumed command as SHQ moved from 'Greenways', Hall Road, Rochford, to Earls Hall School. Southend was classified as a Forward Airfield for day fighters on 9 January 1941. Squadrons that rotated through the station, also to and from Hornchurch, from January 1941 to November 1943 were:

| Squadron No | Period | Aircraft | Notes |
|---|---|---|---|
| 64 | 27.1.41-31.5.41 | Spitfire II | Moved to Hornchurch |
| 54 | 31.3.41-20.5.41 | Spitfire II | Also Hornchurch 3.41-8.41 |
| 611 | 20.5.41-16.6.41 | Spitfire II, V from 6.41 | Hornchurch 27.1.41-13.11.41 |
| 222 | 19.7.41-18.8.41 | Spitfire II | |
| 402 (Can) | 8.41-5.11.41 | Hurricane IIb | |
| 603 | detachments | Spitfire V | Hornchurch 8.7.41-12.11.41 |
| 122 | detachments | Spitfire V | Hornchurch, period 1.4.42-18.5.43 |
| 313 (Polish) | 7.2.42-6.3.42 | Spitfire V | To Hornchurch |
| 411 (Can) | 7.3.42-31.3.42 | Spitfire V | |
| 64 | 31.3.42-1.5.42 | Spitfire V | Hornchurch 5.42-3.43 |
| 403 (Can) | 4.5.42-2.6.42 | Spitfire V | |
| 121 ('Eagle') | 3.6.42-23.9.42 | Spitfire V | Second US 'Eagle' Squadron |
| 19 | 16.8.42-20.8.42 | Spitfire V | For Dieppe raid |
| 350 (Belgian) | 23.9.42-12.42 | Spitfire V | To Hornchurch |
| 453 (RAAF) | 2.10.42-9.10.42, 6.12.42-27.3.43 | Spitfire V | |
| 222 | 27.3.43-1.4.43 | Spitfire V | |
| 137 | 12.6.43-8.8.43 | Hurricane IV | Converting from Whirlwind to new type |
| 611 | 6.9.43-13.9.43 | Spitfire V | |
| 234 | 16.9.43-9.10.43 | Spitfire V | |
| 350 (Belgian) | 13.10.43-31.10.43 | Spitfire V | |
| 349 | 26.10.43-10.11.43 | Spitfire V | |

During that long period Bf 109 fighter-bombers several times delivered low-level attacks. On 11 May 1941 the station received such an attack, ground defences destroying one and Southend's fighters another, which crashed near a hangar. Attacking Southend airfield on 26 October 1942, a Dornier 217E, hit by AA fire from No 2830 RAF Regiment, crashed into 350 Squadron's dispersal area and killed Belgian Warrant Officer Dyon. In bad weather on 9 February 1943 a lone Dornier 217 sneaked in below a flight of patrolling Spitfires, machine-gunned the airfield from a low level, then escaped. It was a reminder of the need for vigilance at all times in war.

A major influence on the station's future had been initiated with the arrival on 9 February 1942 of No 1488 (Fighter) Gunnery Flight and its Lysander target-towers. It split in April, No 2 Flight remaining. Southend moved from the Hornchurch Sector into North Weald Sector on 1 May 1942. On 17 August 1943 it re-formed No 2 Flight completely at Rochford, and on 18 October 1943 became No 17 Armament Practice Camp, operating eight Martinets. Its task was two-fold: towing fabric targets, it gave pilots a chance to improve their air-to-air firing skills, while it was also the centre where Spitfire IX pilots came to learn tactical strike and dive-bombing techniques. Acquiring the latter was a vital skill during the run-up to and beyond D-Day, for it made the unexcelled Spitfire IX into a fine fighter-bomber. The following listing shows the squadrons that attended 17 APC for intensive training against targets on the Essex marshland:

| Squadron No | Period | Aircraft |
|---|---|---|
| 66 | 16.11.43-30.11.43 | Spitfire IX |
| 317 (Polish) | 2.12.43-18.12.43 | Spitfire IX |
| 501 | 21.1.44-4.2.44 | Spitfire IX |
| 41 | 6.2.44-20.2.44 | Spitfire XII |
| 312 (Czech) | 22.2.44-3.3.44 | Spitfire IX |
| 331 (Norwegian) | 5.3.44-13.3.44 | Spitfire IX |
| 332 (Norwegian) | 21.3.44-27.3.44 | Spitfire IX |
| 313 (Czech) | 14.3.44-20.4.44 | Spitfire IX |
| 310 (Czech) | 28.3.44-3.4.44 | Spitfire IX |
| 222 | 4.4.44-11.4.44 | Spitfire IX |
| 302 (Polish) | 12.4.44-14.4.44 | Spitfire IX |
| 66 | 22.4.44-25.4.44 | Spitfire IX |
| 19 | 2.5.44-20.5.44 | Mustang III |
| 122 | 20.5.44-28.5.44 | Mustang III |

During the first few weeks of 1944 No 413 R&SU was at Southend before becoming part of No 84 GSU. The ATC also had a toehold after No 148 GS formed in November 1943 and commenced flying in July 1944 once D-Day had passed. Eventually it dissolved into No 141 GS, on 16 June 1949. Southend had reverted to Hornchurch Sector on 1 June 1943, and stayed within it until that Sector closed on 18 February 1944, when it returned to North Weald Sector, staying there until 1 September 1944, when Southend was reduced to care and maintenance and used for storage purposes by Balloon Command.

Southend was derequisitioned in 1946, and a civil flying licence was issued to Southend Corporation on 31 December of that year. Sqn Ldr Jack Jones formed East Anglian Flying Services, and the Municipal Flying School soon re-opened; by the time it closed in January 1964 it had trained 400 pilots.

Jack Jones was joined by Captain H A M Pascoe AFC and Captain Hugo Parsons DFC, their EAFS fleet in 1948 comprising five Rapides and a Miles Aerovan. Customs facilities allowed services to the Channel Islands and Ostend.

In January 1949 Bovingdon-based Aviation Traders Engineering Ltd (Atel) opened an overhaul facility at Southend to support Berlin Airlift aircraft. BKS formed in 1952 to operate a mixture of aircraft for cargo-carrying, eventually becoming part of BEA.

Air Charter Ltd, an Atel associate, was born in 1954, and in April the following year acquired two Mk 31 Bristol Freighters, building its fleet to six by December 1956 for its Channel Air Bridge. Each Freighter could carry three medium-sized cars and up to twenty-three passengers on the short transit to Calais – later to Ostend or Rotterdam.

*Southend Airport in August 1950, with Halifaxes awaiting Aviation Traders' attention. Taken from G-AJEO, flown by that so much missed truly great civil aircraft enthusiast 'A J Jackson'.*

Improving regularity, two tarmac runways were laid in 1955-56. The main 06/24 was 5,265 feet long and 120 feet wide, the secondary runway, 15/33, being 3,712 feet long and 90 feet wide.

Aviation Traders attempted, unsuccessfully, to enter the short-haul transport aircraft market with its own twin-turboprop, the ATL-90 Accountant. It was first flown on 9 July 1957, in the year that saw East Anglian Flying Services established with two Bristol 170s, supplemented in 1960 with Dakotas. In 1958 Air Charter combined with Airwork, Transair Ltd and Hunting Clan Airways to form British United Airways, led by the irrepressible (Sir) Freddie Laker. That same year Tradair Ltd introduced Vikings at Southend for modification and overhaul.

A big breakthrough – literally – came in 1958 when Atel began the design and conversion of DC-4s into Carvair car carriers. DC-4 G-ANYB, used in 1959 for 'no passport' day trips to Calais, became the prototype Carvair, first flown on 21 June 1961 and introduced in 1962.

Silver City and Channel Air Bridge joined on 1 October 1967 to become British United Air Ferries, whose Carvair services were extended to include Basle, Geneva and Strasbourg. Not until 1976 did Carvair services end, the last example being retired in April 1979.

In December 1962 BUA became a subsidiary of Channel Airways, which had been chosen on 29 October 1962 in preference to East Anglian Flying Services. Vikings, having operating passenger flights to Ostend in the late 1950s, were participants in some of the earliest package holiday deals. In 1963 Channel Airways took over Tradair Ltd, and the first Viscount 700 series entered service at Southend. In 1965 Channel Airways ordered HS 748s, and in 1966 acquired Viscount 812s from the USA. In 1967 British United Air Ferries left BUA, and on 1 October 1967 became British Air Ferries, whose headquarters moved to Southend, where a dozen Freighters were then based. From the 1950s Southend was busy with cross-Channel car ferry operations. However, keen competition from sea ferries brought an end to British Air Ferries' Bristol 170 services from Southend in 1967. More than half a million passengers and 600,000 cars had been carried on the cross-Channel services.

Overhaul and conversion, long a part of the Southend scene, saw Aviation Traders Engineering Ltd in 1968 converting BEA Vanguards into the Merchantman for freighter use. Channel Airways was now operating BAC 111s on a scheduled run to Rotterdam. Charter services were also flourishing, their operators including Braathens, Martinair and LTU, and on 8 April 1970 Boeing 737 G-AXNA of Britannia Airways made that type's first call. In 1971 came the first 707 arrival, N11RV, which came to Atel for maintenance

In a period of tough financial activity, February 1972 saw the liquidation of Channel Airways. British Midland Airways took over the company's Channel Islands services, but the end of Channel Airways meant a major drop in revenue for Southend, which Aviation Traders left in 1974. In 1975 passenger throughput fell below 250,000, in a year that saw British Air Ferries acquire fourteen HPR Heralds.

*Aviation Traders 98A Carvair G-ASHZ of British United Airways at Southend on 6 June 1964. (George Pennick)*

TAC/Heavylift moved into Atel's hangar in 1979 to undertake conversion of ex-RAF Belfasts to allow them to be used as civilian transports. In 1980 British Island Airways amalgamated with Air Anglia to form Air UK. The following year BAF acquired the British Airways Viscount fleet of eighteen aircraft, making it the world's largest operator of the type.

Harvest Air, here since 1974, won during 1983 the DoT contract for oil pollution control, using Islanders and DC-3s for aerial detergent spraying. Air UK left Southend in 1983, passenger figures falling to their lowest since 1958. In 1984 Heavylift Cargo Airlines set up Heavylift Engineering to carry out maintenance at Southend, from where Maersk Air started services to Denmark.

On 1 March 1985 operation of the airport passed from Southend Borough Council to British Airports International. Although passenger numbers were not high, there was plentiful assorted activity, which in 1988 made Southend Britain's fourth busiest airport. On 15 May a BAe 146 made its initial fare-paying flight, to Palma, then in 1989 Region Airways started a service to Paris using a BAe Jetstream. Freight figures were also the highest for fifteen years. Amalgamation of Baltic (UK) Airlines with BAF took place in 1989, leaving the company with seventeen Viscounts, the largest fleet in the UK.

A new ILS came into use in June 1992. The Council was now seeking another airport operator, and by 1994 was planning either to privatise the airport or close it. Luckily Regional Airports Ltd stepped in during March and agreed a 150-year lease, and London Southend Airport Co Ltd was established to run it. In 1995 the new owners refurbished the terminal, resurfaced the runway, redecorated some buildings, and demolished others. On 26 May 1995 the refurbished terminal officially re-opened. Government go-ahead was given in 1998 for the construction of a completely new passenger terminal to handle 300,000 passengers a year, and a railway station to provide a 48-minute link with London; the control tower will also be relocated. A longer runway would be beneficial, but that requires the moving and rebuilding of a church.

Around 1,300 people are employed at the airport, where more than seventy companies function. There are still a number of flying clubs here, among them the Southend Flying Club, School of Flying, Willow Air and Seawing Flying Club.

**Main features:**
Wartime: *Grass area:* NE-SW 3,900ft, E-W 3,300ft. Hangars (military): two Bellman, four Over Blister. *Hardstandings:* thirty-six twin-engined type. *Accommodation:* RAF officers 89, SNCOs 106, ORs 1,363; WAAF officers 4, SNCOs 6, ORs 163.
Current: *Runways:* 06/24 5,265ft (with ILS/DME and NDB), 15/33 3,710ft, asphalt. PAPI approach lights installed for 06/24 in 1985. The second runway has become a taxiway only. A large hardstanding area is spread before the main buildings.

---

## SOUTH MARSTON, Wiltshire

*51°34N/01°44W 280ft asl; SU185873. 4 miles NE of Swindon*

In 1939 construction commenced at South Marston (near Swindon) of a shadow factory for Phillips and Powis whose premises are, in MAP files, referred to as Flight Shed No 1. The labour force was recruited locally and particularly from among skilled wood workers at the GWR works. Their task was to construct wooden Miles Master advanced trainers.

Major change followed a bombing raid on Short Brothers premises at Rochester Airport early in September 1940 which wrecked repair work undertaken after the major attack of 15 August 1940. Shorts packed as much as they could on lorries and 60-foot Queen Marys for a move to a less exposed area. South Marston was chosen to become the main site of a new production centre. Temporary lodging for Short was found at Hucclecote near Gloucester where 28 Stirling Is were completed. The closed Rochester factory temporarily became derelict after Stirling N3636 was completed at the start of November 1940. Not until 1942 did Rochester Airport works re-open, delivery resuming on 28 March 1942 with Stirling N3719.

It was intended to extend the Miles shadow factory. Instead, materials earmarked for the purpose were diverted to nearby sites for Short at Blunsdon and Sevenhampton. Construction of a facility to build Stirlings came underway at South Marston. At Stratton St Margaret, they opened a drawing office used until late in the war. Short's set-up in the area was known as the Swindon Division, and in factory speak, the South Marston unit was known as Flight Shed No 2. Among the Stirlings generated were over 360 Mk IVs assembled and test flown at South Marston before production was completed during August 1944. The final Stirling delivery took place in October 1944.

As a result of the bombing of Rochester Airport followed by the seaplane works in 1941, Oswald Short suffering from ill health moved to Cornwall and Arthur Gouge became company Chairman. Following rejection of Short's scheme for the B.8/41 'Super Stirling' in Spring 1942 the company was pressed to build Avro Lancasters, something they strongly resisted. When Stafford Cripps became Minister of Aircraft Production he tried, without success, to persuade Short to build Lancasters. Unable under existing wartime regulations to force the company to change course, the government instead bought them out in 1943 thereby enabling MAP to by-pass the Board and resistant shareholders. In April 1943 – at which time the Swindon Division work force totalled 4,314 – came the decision to begin delivery in June 1944 of a batch of 100 Lancasters. Another 100 would be Lancaster IVs later named the Lincoln. Adding Avro bombers meant Short Brothers new management team would be wrestling with a variety of aircraft types - the Stirling, Shetland, Sunderland IV and now the Lancaster/Lincoln.

On 1 September 1943 Short's Swindon Division came under the management of Armstrong Whitworth Aircraft. Then, to avoid extensive effort required in starting a Lancaster line at South Marston, production was switched to other AWA factories. That allowed supervised output of vitally needed Stirling glider tug Mk IVs to be undertaken at South Marston, a task completed in August 1944 after which AWA moved out.

Master production at South Marston had ceased in 1942 by which time 549 Mk IIs and 602 Mk IIIs had been produced. Replacement of that activity began around February 1943 when Vickers-Supermarine established an assembly and flight test centre intended for a new range of Spitfires and Seafires powered by two-stage supercharged Rolls-Royce Griffon 61 series engines. These aircraft would be far removed from the original Spitfire, and a surfeit of mark numbers looked likely. Accordingly, a new name was chosen and Victor replaced Spitfire. Its existence was brief due to the unpopularity at the loss of such a prestigious name as Spitfire. The latter was reinstated and a new set of mark numbers in the 20s (40s in the case of the Seafires) was launched.

The new version entered production as the Spitfire Mk 21, the prototype of which first flew in December 1943 and in the hands of Alex Henshaw. On 27 January 1944 he made the first flight of a production F.21 LA187, and from South Marston. A variety of problems seriously beset the Mk 21 making it a year before the type was ready for squadron service. Its production was paced by that of the Seafire 45 components which, Castle Bromwich built, were assembled at South Marston before being test flown alongside Mk 21s throughout 1945. Seafire 46 and 47 output followed and was centred completely on South Marston where Spitfire 22s were built, also Mk 24 fighter-bombers which utilised parts produced for Mk 22s prior to the closure of Castle Bromwich. At South Marston refurbishment of Spitfire IXs for foreign air forces was also undertaken.

Production of Attacker jet fighter-bombers followed, for the Royal Navy and Pakistan. Then came the Swift, the first production Mk 1 being delivered in March 1953. All the Scimitars were manufactured at South Marston before the aviation works closed.

Cancellation of the Swift led Vickers to diversify at South Marston where a nuclear reactor for Winfrith nuclear power station was built, also equipment for the AERE Harwell. The Whitehead Torpedo works moved in (from Weymouth) and Vickers Hydraulics division arrived. Flying of a sort continued (and ended – apart from civilian flights using light aircraft) with the development and construction of the Vickers VA-1,2 and 3 hovercraft, the latter for British United Airways.

October 1977 saw a link with time past when Spitfire 21, LA226, arrived to guard the front gate. Now, with its aircraft industry days gone, South Marston is a motor car industrial complex.

Main features: Flying took place from two runways, 01/19 tarmac surfaced and 5,997ft long and another of concrete 3,839ft long. They were to the east of the large factory complex which comprised assorted shops, final assembly area and flight test shed.

**Main features**:
Flying took place from adjacent runways, 01/19 tarmac surfaced and 5,997ft long and the other of concrete, 3,839ft long. They were to the east of the large factory complex, which comprised assorted shops, final assembly area and flight test shed.

## SOUTHROP, Gloucestershire

*51°43N/01°44W 350ft asl; SP190035. 3 miles NW of Lechlade*

This hill-top RLG was more sophisticated than many. Sub Site 1, the servicing area in the south-west corner, had two 69-foot Blister hangars and a 4,000-gallon aviation fuel tank. Sub-Site 2, in the south-east portion, had seven 65-foot Over Type Blister hangars (12532/41). Technical and Instructional Sites were at the RLG's north end, the former comprising buildings of 1941-42 vintage, many of temporary brick construction or adapted Laing huts. The Technical Site held a 'T1 (14) 19' (9665/42) hangar. There was a two-bay MT shed, a fuel compound and a brick control tower (13726/41). The 1942-style Instructional Site contained the intelligence library, photographic block, armament training facilities and navigation training rooms. Four domestic sites were built in Macaroni Woods, as well as SSQ and the WAAF site.

Each of the four male domestic sites comprised Laing huts suitably laid out to accommodate six officers and two servants, or fourteen Sergeants, or a Sergeant and fourteen men. The Officers' Mess Type 68 (3440/41 and 10216/42), Sergeants' Mess Type 159 (3441/41, 10217/42) and Airmen's Mess Type 673 (3445/41, 10218/42) were at a Communal Site. The NAAFI block and games room, etc (3446/41), had facilities for 104 corporals and 625 men. The camp's high-level water tank (Type 20/41) held 50,000 gallons.

No 2 FTS was the first user in August 1940, continuing to do so after re-classification as No 2 (P)AFU on 14 March 1942. Upon its closure on 13 July 1942, Southrop passed to 3 (P)AFU South Cerney, whose satellite it remained until 22 January 1945.

**Main features:**
*Runways:* Army Track 230° 3,060ft, 330° 2,790ft, grass E/W 3,150ft. *Hangars:* one T1, nine 69ft Blister. *Accommodation:* RAF officers 70, SNCOs 180, ORs 570; WAAF officers 4, SNCOs 5, ORs 117.

---

## SPANHOE (HARRINGWORTH, WAKERLEY), Northamptonshire

*52°34N/00°37W 340ft asl; SP935970. Approximately 8 miles SW of Stamford, 4¹/₂ miles E of Uppingham*

Spanhoe was a typical well-dispersed 1943 Class 'A' bomber airfield with living accommodation, messing and SSQ on its southern side in and around Spanhoe Wood, after which it was named. An obvious title was Harringworth, but Spanhoe was chosen to avoid confusion with Harrington.

On 1 January 1944 the station was allocated to the 9th AFTCC Substitution Unit, and the 461st Signal Construction Battalion and the 309th Station Company Squadron moved in. Spanhoe officially opened on 7 January, and on 7 February the 315th TCG, comprising only the 34th and 43rd Squadrons, arrived from Welford Park bringing C-47s, C-53s, two Oxfords and Waco CG-4A gliders. By the start of April 1944 the strength had risen to sixty-one aircraft, thirty CG-4A Waco gliders and several Piper L-4As. As the Group trained, strength increased, and by May the 309th and 310th Squadrons had been added.

Large-scale night exercises were flown, forty-eight C-47s of the 315th beginning take-off from Spanhoe at 2230 on 11 May. By any reckoning this was a major event, comprising 432 aircraft of the 50th and 53rd Wings carrying more than 6,000 men of the 101st Airborne Division, and 369 aircraft of the 52nd Wing, each C-47/53 carrying a token two paratroopers of the 82nd Airborne. The latter had trained fully, so no risks were being taken with that element.

On 3 June 864 paratroopers of the 505th Paratroop Infantry Regiment of the 82nd Airborne Division overflowed into Spanhoe's facilities, many needing to sleep in a hangar. As the paratroopers were boarding for Normandy on 5 June a trooper near the 43rd Squadron aircraft accidentally dropped a hand grenade, which exploded, killing three paratroops and wounding fifteen, including the aircraft's radio-operator.

Soon after, forty-eight C-47/53s took off and, led by Col McLelland, headed for DZ 'O' near Ste-Mere-Eglise where a successful concentrated drop was achieved. By 0440 on 6 June 1944 all the aircraft were safely back in Britain, twelve of them bearing battle damage. After flying a re-supply mission, the 315th carried much freight to France and trained – not without drama, for at night on 8 July a C-47 of the 309th Squadron collided with another, both crashing near Tinwell, Rutland, killing eight aircrew and twenty-six paratroopers.

Between mid-August and mid-September three planned airborne operations – *Transfigure, Linnet* and *Comet* – were abandoned. Then came *Market*, planned for 14 September, for which 354 paratroopers of the 82nd Airborne arrived at Spanhoe from Braunstone Park camp. Then a three-day delay occurred before, at 1039 on 17 September 1944, an amazing force of ninety C-47/53s began take-off for their part in the Rhine bridges operation. Their DZ was just north of the River Maas, all except one aircraft making their drops and returning safely. Ground personnel then changed the US-type container racks to suit the British type, and next day fifty-four aircraft carried 462 paratroopers of the British 4th Parachute Brigade to DZ 'Y', Ginkel Heath. This time many aircraft were hit and some pilots complained at the poor level of fighter cover near the target. Bad weather then intervened, 700 Polish paratroopers brought to Spanhoe being unable to be dropped until 21 September. Bad weather also prevented operations on the 22nd, but on the 23rd forty-two aircraft carried 560 Polish paratroopers and 219 parapacks to Arnhem where, already, the battle had been lost.

After the operation, conveyance of freight continued against an expected move to Birch, which was cancelled. When on 24 March 1945 the 315th participated in operation *Varsity*, it lost nineteen aircraft, another thirty-six suffering damage. When the move came it was to Amiens/Glisy on 11 April.

Spanhoe returned to RAF use on 30 May 1945 and became part of the North Luffenham Base. No 253 MU, concerned with disposal and sale of surplus vehicles, moved in on 8 July 1945, its holding in March 1946 totalling an amazing 16,069 vehicles. When No 253 MU left, in spring 1947 the airfield closed. Subsequently some of its western fringe was the site of iron-ore mining.

**Main features:**
*Runways:* 078° 6,000ft x 150ft, 141° 4,200ft x 150ft, 205° 4,200ft x 150ft, tarmac on concrete. *Hangars:* two T2. *Hardstandings:* fifty spectacle type. *Accommodation:* RAF officers 126, SNCOs 37, ORs 1,579; WAAF officers 10, ORs 319.

## STANTON HARCOURT, Oxfordshire

*51°44N/01°24W 230ft asl; SP415050. 5¹/₂ miles W of Oxford*

In the late afternoon on 16 August 1940, with civilian workmen busy on a Stanton Harcourt hard runway, three enemy bombers suddenly strafed and bombed it. Five of Wimpey's workforce were killed, another four dying later. Anti-aircraft defences were subsequently installed, not only here but at all airfields being constructed. Stanton Harcourt, little damaged, had made a major contribution, even prior to opening.

On 3 September 1940 No 10 OTU – satellite Stanton Harcourt – commenced night-flying here, the satellite reflecting 10 OTU's activities until its closure on 15 January 1946. By August 1940 it was clear that night-bombing of Permanent Stations could result in considerable casualties, much damage to very-expensive-to-repair items, and the destruction of aircraft undergoing repair in hangars, which could result in a conflagration. Stanton Harcourt was almost certainly the first satellite to come into use for night-flying in order that the parent station could be unlit except for essential operations. Whitleys of 'C' Flight 10 OTU arrived from Abingdon on 10 September 1940, and thereafter concentrated on night-flying training. Shortage of aircraft caused the Flight to disband in February 1941, then 'A' Flight, converting crews to Whitley flying, replaced it.

Stanton Harcourt possessed an unusual layout, its three runways being far apart. The proximity of the River Windrush made flooding ever a possibility. Weapons were stored in the south-east of the airfield, main dispersals being on eastern and western sides. Personnel were accommodated in dispersal sites north of the village beyond the T2 and B1 hangars. Most buildings were of 1940 and 1941 vintage.

The runways were put to good use in July 1941 when Halifaxes of 35 and 76 Squadrons used Stanton as an advanced base for their daylight attack on the *Scharnhorst* in La Pallice.

Whitley V operational trainers provided most of the 1942 air activity, then on 12 January 1943 there occurred a most unusual event. In great secrecy Gp Capt van der Kloot landed famous Liberator AL504 *Commando* from Lyneham for operation *Static*. In darkness on 13 January *Commando* departed, carrying Sir Winston Churchill to the Casablanca Conference.

Re-organisation of 10 OTU came the following month. 'A' and 'B' Conversion Flights were now placed at Stanton Harcourt, as well as gunnery trainers. From 18 April until 31 December 1943, Oxfords of 1501 BAT Flight flew from here, the B1 hangar being added at this time. On 20 March 1944 10 OTU's flying was switched completely to Stanton Harcourt while two runways were laid at Abingdon. OTU strength was reduced to three-quarters in May, and soon after Hurricanes replaced the fighter-affiliation Martinets. Wellington Xs began taking over from the Whitley Vs in July, 10 OTU bidding farewell to its last examples in October 1944. On 16 November 1944 daylight flying was resumed at Abingdon, to where most of the unit had moved by early 1945. Stanton Harcourt retired from active use in the summer of 1945, and gravel workings now mark the spot from where Sir Winston left for that victory-planning conference in 1943.

**Main features:**
*Runways:* 056° 4,800ft x 150ft, 117° 3,300ft x 150ft, 177° 3,300ft x 150ft, tarmac. *Hangars:* one T2, one B1. *Hardstandings:* twenty-seven frying-pan type. *Accommodation:* RAF officers 40, SNCOs 164, ORs 509; WAAF officers 3, ORs 98.

## STAPLEFORD TAWNEY, Essex

*51°39N/00°08E 120ft asl; TQ493970. NE of London on the A113 between Chigwell and Ongar*

Visit Stapleford, now a popular private flying venue, and it is hard to believe that it holds such a varied, quite important niche in aviation history. It opened on 23 June 1934 as a base for 'no frills' Hillman Airways, which had outgrown the small field at Maylands from where it operated. Hillman had acquired 180 acres of land near Stapleford Tawney on a twenty-five-year lease for use as an aerodrome. Three small hangars each had a concrete apron, and there was an administration centre and a passenger terminal on the edge of a somewhat uneven grass flying field.

Edward Hillman, an Old Contemptible Sergeant Major and operator of Hillman Pullman Coaches of Southend, wanted to offer air travel to all without the trimmings. His flagship service would be to Paris. No meals, acceptable comfort and aircrew who needed to work quite long hours were part of the equation. He approached de Havilland for a seven-passenger, 120mph aircraft operating for threepence a mile and costing no more than £3,000. De Havilland provided him with the DH 84 Dragon, and on 1 April 1933 he began his Paris service with an aeroplane running on 9mpg at 105mph. Hillman's expansion very soon included a Stapleford-Liverpool-Isle-of-Man-Belfast service. With all going well, Edward Hillman suddenly died in December 1934 at the early age of 45. The company weathered the tragic blow and continued to expand, eight new DH 89 Rapides being introduced for daily services. At the end of June 1935, just after three DH 86s had been acquired, Hillman Airways moved to more prestigious Gatwick and was soon under some pressure, which resulted in its absorption by British Airways. 'EasyFly' had become 'EasyGo' – nothing much in creation is entirely new!

Denuded of a recent busy atmosphere, Stapleford was now empty except for a few private aircraft. It was the opening of No 21 Elementary & Reserve Flying Training School, run by Reid & Sigrist, that started its military career. Tiger Moths served for basic training, and Hawker Harts, Hinds and Audaxes for the more advanced. One who trained here was 'Johnnie' Johnson, the top-scoring RAF fighter pilot, who received five British decorations for gallantry and a similar number of foreign awards.

The outbreak of hostilities saw No 21 E&RFTS depart, and the requisitioned aerodrome was enlarged, a 2¼-mile concrete perimeter track 18 feet wide laid, and six double dispersal pens constructed, together with accommodation and administration buildings. The grass landing ground, measuring 3,000 feet north/south and 2,400 feet east/west, was camouflaged using soot to inscribe 'hedgerows', a common early war procedure. Stapleford, able to accommodate a fighter squadron, became North Weald's satellite in early 1940 and appears to have come into use in March 1940, when Hurricanes of Nos 56 and 151 Squadrons made overnight stays.

The first permanent resident was No 151 Squadron, dispersed from North Weald on 29 August 1940 and immediately operational. On 31 August No 151 was very busy when the Luftwaffe attacked North Weald and it shot down a Bf 109. During a second operation it destroyed a Do 17 near Hornchurch and another during a third patrol, but all at a price – two pilots and aircraft lost, their pilots injured. On 1 September No 151 Squadron swapped places with No 46 Squadron at Digby.

Next day No 46, in battle, destroyed a Bf 109, but Plt Off J C D L Bailey failed to return. The squadron was in action daily, and by 30 September had lost five more pilots.

*Bucker Bu 131 G-ASLI before the Thurston Aviation and Essex Aero Club hangar in April 1969.*

Bad weather restricted October's first two weeks, but on 15 October No 46 Squadron destroyed a Bf 109, losing two Hurricanes. On 25 October Plt Off W B Pattullo died after crashing into a house in Romford following combat with a Bf 109.

In September Stapleford accommodated briefly the small No 419 Flight, the nucleus of 138 Squadron, whose two Lysanders lodged here before proceeding to Stradishall and Bomber Command on 9 October. Two nights previously bombs had cratered Stapleford's landing ground, parts of which were soon converted into a quagmire by wet weather. On 8 November it was declared unserviceable, and No 46 Squadron was forced to find sanctuary at North Weald.

After five months Stapleford Tawney re-opened, and No 242 Squadron moved in from Martlesham Heath on 9 April 1941, bringing Hurricanes. Eleven days later, during the first operation, three Hurricanes collided in cloud over the Channel, killing their pilots, including the Commanding Officer, Sqn Ldr Treacy. Three days later Sqn Ldr Whitney-Straight took command of the squadron.

No 242 Squadron participated in sweeps over France and Belgium before moving to North Weald on 22 May. No 3 Squadron, flying Hurricanes, filled the vacancy, arriving from Martlesham Heath on 23 June to fly *Rodeos* and convoy escort patrols. In July and August detachments from 3 Squadron at Hunsdon co-operated at night with No 1451 Flight's Turbinlite Bostons and Havocs. No 3 moved to Hunsdon on 8 August, closing Stapleford's offensive career.

No 2 Camouflage Unit had arrived in June 1941, bringing Tiger Moths, Oxfords and Dominies with which to conduct aerial inspection and photography of camouflaged special sites such as factories, to check their levels of disguise.

When, on 22 December 1941, No 277 Squadron formed with an establishment of Lysanders and Walruses, Stapleford Tawney acquired a very important role, air-sea rescue in the Thames estuary and off Kent. Squadron HQ, major maintenance and pilot conversion were all established here, which, in early 1943, underwent upgrading. New domestic and messing buildings were erected near the main hangar, and eight Blister hangars were added. Machine-gun posts and pillboxes surrounded the airfield, which was further protected with small retractable Hamilton Forts.

April saw No 277 Squadron converting to Defiants, a dozen of which were in use by May; they could defend themselves while protecting downed aircrew awaiting launch rescue. Among second-line aircraft variously used here was a Koolhoven FK 43, a May 1940 Dutch escapee. On 7 December 1942 277 Squadron moved to Gravesend.

Another quiet winter ended in March 1943 when Stapleford, transferred to No 34 Wing Army Co-operation Command, became the satellite of Sawbridgeworth. No 656 Squadron, flying in from Westley, Bury St Edmunds, brought Auster AOPs and Tiger Moths. August saw the squadron depart for India, via Liverpool Docks. When TAF began forming in June 1943, the station – still Sawbridgeworth's satellite – transferred to No 12 Group. Official formation of 2TAF on 15 November 1943 resulted in a variety of non-flying units using Stapleford as a staging point in the run-up to *Overlord*. When No 2 Camouflage Unit left in September 1944, Stapleford's last wartime powered aircraft had departed. Stapleford Tawney remained a Forward Airfield in North Weald Sector until May 1945. Since summer 1944, No 142 Flight, for ATC training, had been flying from the airfield.

Stapleford Tawney was well within the area constantly being bombarded by V-2s from the Netherlands, and on 20 November 1944 one exploded in the centre of the landing ground, producing a 60-foot-diameter crater. Another, which rammed into the main camp site at mid-afternoon on 23 February 1945, killed seventeen personnel, injured fifty and caused extensive damage.

With remaining ground units gone, the station passed to care and maintenance on 11 May 1945. Thereafter, and during 1946, airborne forces at Wethersfield and Earls Colne used the landing ground as a paratroop DZ. Then the airfield slipped into a state of neglect, some sections being retrieved for agricultural use.

After the loss of Broxbourne, the Herts & Essex Aero Club acquired Stapleford Tawney in 1953. Hangars were renovated, together with other buildings. Private flying using Austers, M.38s, Geminis, Tiger Moths and others followed. In 1955 Edgar Percival formed a company under his name to produce at Stapleford his EP 9 crop-spraying aircraft, first flown on 21 December 1955. Nearly forty examples had been built when he sold his company. Production was switched to Blackpool in 1958.

As well as the Club and other private concerns and owners, Thurston Aviation used Stapleford as the base for an air taxi business before moving to Stansted in late 1978.

In 2003 the Herts & Essex Aero Club still operates the airfield, which is also used by the Stapleford Flying Club for pilot training.

**Main features:**
*Grass landing ground:* E/W 2,400ft, NE/SW 3,400ft. *Hangars:* one civil, four EO Blister. *Hardstandings:* six, built along the south-west boundary. *Accommodation:* RAF officers 33, SNCOs 68, ORs 731; WAAF officers 2, SNCOs 4, ORs 40.

In 2003 Stapleford Tawney occupies the same grass area with the imposition of a grass/asphalt 04R/22L 900m x 46m runway and a grass 715m x 46m 10/28 runway, with taxiways along the runway edges and a relief 04/22L-R runway.

## STRATFORD (ATHERSTONE), Warwickshire

*52°09N/01°41W185ft asl; SP215515. 3 miles SSE of Stratford-upon-Avon*

Authorisation for the preparation of a Built Satellite for 22 OTU's use was given on 18 June 1940, an advance party opening Stratford on 5 July 1941. Wellingtons were using it a week later. However, when Wellingtons from Wellesbourne were seen passing directly over the main runway at Stratford, its situation was clearly very dangerous. The station's original name was also unsuitable, for there was another airfield known as Atherstone.

Wellingtons of 22 OTU used Stratford until 15 November 1942, and when Wellesbourne's runways were re-surfaced, Wellingtons in plenty tarried here.

In November 1942 Stratford passed to 23 OTU Pershore, a three-quarter-strength OTU whose establishment amounted to forty-two Wellington Ics. When Gaydon opened as 22 OTU's satellite, pressure on the unit was also relieved when it was nudged out of Defford in April 1942 because that station joined 10 Group.

No 23 OTU's establishment was increased to full OTU level and maintained until 15 January 1944, when it again fell to three-quarters level due to needs for major work at Pershore. Stratford again became a 22 OTU satellite, from 7 March to 15 December 1944, permitting Wellesbourne to be increased to one-and-a-half OTU establishment from 15 March, giving it a strength of eighty-one Wellington III/Xs, thirty-three of them inherited from 23 OTU. Although the name and markings changed, many Stratford residents remained the same. When 22 OTU vacated the station it was transferred to the Signals Flying Unit at Honiley, which controlled it until flying ceased in late 1945.

**Main features:**
*Runways:* 192° 4,800ft x 150ft, 254° 4,050ft x 150ft, 320° 3,630ft x 150ft, tarmac. *Hangars:* one T2, one B1. *Hardstandings:* twenty-seven frying-pan type. *Accommodation:* RAF officers 47, SNCOs 126, ORs 1,308; WAAF officers 2, SNCOs 5, ORs 147.

## SYWELL, Northamptonshire

*52°18N/00°47W 365ft asl; SP825690. 6 miles NE of Northampton off the A43(T)*

All self-respecting towns and cities need an airport, and Northampton would do well to ensure that Sywell prospers. Closing such first-rate facilities in favour of modern ghettos is folly. It was in the 1920s that Northampton began to be served by an airport, built alongside Holcot Lane and wisely sited allowing plentiful flying in a non-built-up area, still the case when Lancaster IIs roared off in wartime.

The first landing at what became Sywell took place on 12 June 1927, the aerodrome opening taking place in September 1928, presided over by Air Vice-Marshal Sir Sefton Brancker, Director of Civil Aviation.

Subsequently, Northamptonshire Aero Club attracted DH Moths, air pageants and famous fliers. Financial problems in 1932 were resolved by improving an expanded airfield with a smart clubhouse complex, completed in 1934 and still used.

Military Sywell began when No 6 E&RFTS opened, run by Brooklands Aviation under Air Ministry contract and employing DH 60s and Tiger Moths. In April 1937 five Hart variants were added. In June 1939 its twenty Tiger Moths were supplemented by three Ansons, the syllabus being extended to include the training of air observers and air gunners. On 3 September 1939, when it became 6 EFTS, School strength included twenty-five Tiger Moths and sixteen flying instructors, and observer/navigator training passed to No 8 Civil Air Navigation School, formed at Sywell on 2 September 1939. Initial pilot training was undertaken by 6 EFTS using Tiger Moths throughout hostilities. Until the first War Course opened on 23 October 1939, the School provided short courses for flying instructors. Establishment by then had risen to fifty aircraft and twenty-four flying instructors.

*A Miles Gemini near Sywell's airport buildings in April 1957.*

Clearing the way for large-scale elementary pilot training, the navigation school, losing its civilian status, became No 8 AONS on 1 November 1939, then on 25 November was absorbed by 9 AONS Squires Gate. The civilian status of 6 EFTS also changed, for on 1 January 1940 all flying instructors were called up for RAF service, resulting in Sqn Ldr R W MacKenzie becoming Officer Commanding 6 EFTS; previously he had been CFI as well as Manager of Brooklands Aviation. Aircraft establishment now steadied at fifty-four Tiger Moths.

By the summer of 1940 No 6 EFTS was using the Denton RLG. The school held an enviable record, there being no serious injury to any pupil to the end of August 1940. However, billeting the increased numbers of pupils brought problems, and from the start of October 1940 they lived out, in Northampton. United Counties buses conveyed them to and from Sywell, where quarters could be occupied by airfield defence personnel guarding against 'fifth columnists' penetrating anti-sabotage defences. Sudden roadside checks were common around airfields, and anyone without an identity card – serviceman or civilian – could be faced with quite frightening moments. This facet of life continued well into 1942, making the pleasure of observing wartime activities a trifle hazardous.

November 1940 brought a sudden scare to the EFTSs. An instructor was diving Tiger Moth N6804 to restart its engine, which had stopped during a slow roll, and the leading edge of its upper starboard mainplane collapsed. The skilful instructor managed to land. There had been similar failings at the other EFTSs, and thirty-three Sywell Tiger Moths were immediately grounded for AID inspection. The conclusion was that the trouble was due to moisture permeating the structure when the aircraft stood at dispersals in all weathers – particularly in winter. Schools would have to watch for evidence of the problem.

With each course standing at sixty pupils, all from ITWs, high levels of aircraft utilisation were necessary. Flying accidents were surprisingly few, considering the combination of weather, congestion in the circuit, malfunction and inexperience. In September 1941, as Tiger Moth T6342 was gliding in to land, it was suddenly struck by Oxford V3980 from Kidlington. Both aircraft dived to the ground, killing their occupants.

Summer 1940 saw Brooklands Aviation open a repair unit within the CRO on the south-west side of the airfield. There it overhauled 1,841 Wellingtons, and in 1944 converted some into special interim transports.

An additional Flight for 6 EFTS in March 1942 added eighteen more Tiger Moths, allowing pupil establishment to rise by thirty, increasing the School's establishment to 210, for which 126 Tiger Moths were available. On 7 May 1942 a Grading Scheme was introduced, pupils – after twelve hours' flying – being awarded marks according to their flying ability. Arrangements were

*Attending Sywell's 'Flying For Fun' in 1983 is the Cassutt Racer IIIM G-BEUN.*

then made to remove from the School, by 13 May, all ab initio cadets, then re-organise 6 EFTS into six Flights of Graded Pupils. This pattern of instruction continued during 1943.

Opposite the airfield in a large factory Armstrong-Whitworth Aircraft was to have assembled Whitleys, then Manchesters, but plans changed before 1943, when assembly of Lancaster IIs commenced. They were flown out of Sywell for testing, the airfield grass area having been increased in July 1943.

Evidence of the intense local operational activity was apparent, with B-17 formations assembling overhead in the early morning before setting off for distant targets. Their return was often a sobering sight. Lost in cloud, the crew force-landed B-17 229860 at Sywell on 31 December 1943, clouting a Wellington's wing and knocking off its own tail. Forty minutes later 229888 also put down, short of fuel, and smashed its way through the boundary hedge.

To the end of the war Sywell was the base for 6 EFTS, with Wellingtons being overhauled. Post-war the work concerned Wellington T 10s, after which Brooklands overhauled Valettas and, between 1957 and 1971, Varsities, Mosquitoes and Vampires. Chipmunks and conversion of Mosquito 35s for target-towing were also attended to. Absence of a hard runway limited Sywell's value, but did not prevent Dakota overhauls during the Berlin Airlift. Most of Brooklands' *Varsity* and some Mosquito work was, however, undertaken at Little Staughton. A few Vampire T 11s made use of Sywell's grass.

Soon after the war the EFTS was reduced to four Flights, training of Frenchmen ceasing on 8 January 1947. Since 15 February 1941 Frenchmen had come to learn to fly RAF-style, both Army and Navy personnel, at what was often called the French EFTS, where a total of 1,932 Frenchmen – 1,707 from the Army – were trained. The final course was posted out from 6 EFTS on 21 April 1947, the School closing upon transfer to Reserve Command on 12 May 1947. Some exchange of Tiger Moths was effected and, as customary, a few Anson T 21s joined the School for navigation training. Chipmunks replaced the Tiger Moths, and Prentices briefly served at 6 RFS before its closure on 31 March 1953. For the training of National Service pilots, No 4 Basic Flying Training School, operating Chipmunks, opened at Sywell on 14 November 1951 and closed on 30 June 1953. To improve flight safety, a new control tower was built before the School closed.

Civil flying resumed at Sywell in 1947. The Northamptonshire Aero Club re-formed and Sywell became a prominent post-war light aviation centre. Such activity continued through the 1950s and 1960s. Between 1959 and 1965, Marathons, and later Dakotas, of Derby Aviation ran scheduled air services from Sywell, and in 1969 the first 'Flying for Fun' pageant took place. For the 1973 display the Popular Flying Association took over responsibility, making the airfield a yearly venue for light and home-built aeroplane enthusiasts. With around 400 visiting aircraft during a weekend, those occasions, in aesthetically satisfying surroundings, must now surely be viewed with much nostalgia. Although the PFA rally had outgrown Sywell, that event on a fine summer's day was a delightful experience.

Brooklands suffered a take-over in 1974, and in 1977 disposed of its Sywell interests. Sywell Aerodrome Ltd is now the operator and it remains a venue for private flying, retaining a shapely pre-war main civil flying centre. Users include the Northamptonshire School of Flying, the RB Flying Group and Sloane Helicopters. Large hangars also remain, but what Sywell really does need – and deserves – is a hard-surface runway.

**Main features:**
*Grass runs:* N/S 4,800ft, NE/SW 4,800ft, E/W 3,450ft, NW/SE 3,750ft. *Hangars:* one main civilian 200ft x 140ft, one MAP CRO repair 300ft x 115ft, one 110ft x 90ft, one AWA factory 300ft x 120ft, one 300ft x 100ft, one 200ft x 60ft, EFTS eight Standard Blister, three Double Standard Blister, four Double EO Blister. *Hardstandings:* nil. *Accommodation:* RAF officers 73, SNCOs 43, ORs 273.

In 2002 Sywell had three grass runways, 03/21 909m x 30m, 15/33 528m x 18m, and 07/25 700m x 18m.

## TEMPSFORD, Bedfordshire

*52°09N/00°15W 60ft asl; TL185140. 3 miles N of Sandy*

Proceed down the hill from Everton, follow the signposted bridlepath on the right, and enjoy a satisfying wander through the countryside. Soon you will join a concrete road – actually Tempsford's wartime peritrack – and moments later you will be at a runway threshold where you can imagine a Whitley or a Halifax setting off, not for a city but for a co-ordinated target, and departing cloaked in great secrecy. Tempsford was a very secret secret. In the distance rests a B1 hangar, best seen from the road; however, a brown object ahead is the main object of interest. Old, reasonably dilapidated, but luckily supported by interior brickwork and well-wishers, is the famous barn. On its north side is a notice board placed there by the East Anglian Aviation Society informing a passer-by that this was once part of the vanquished Gibraltar Farm. To the barn Special Operations Executive agents came to be equipped and kitted out before leaving on perilous adventures in Occupied Europe. Few barns in our entire history can have meant so much to both so few and yet so many.

Tempsford remains a place of pilgrimage whose past eclipses many a more picturesque and historic site. Imagine, on crossing that runway, a Halifax swinging on to final hold, allowing agents to quickly clamber aboard, faceless in the darkness, nameless to the crew and supremely brave. Surprising too that, at the time, quite a lot of what was taking place was publicly and quite widely known. When the 'NF' Whitleys and Halifaxes were at Tempsford, and easily observed climbing over the old A1, they were accepted as merely continuing their secret delivery activities in more seclusion than at Newmarket.

In 1936 there were plans for the conversion of Everton Heath into a 400-acre flying ground, but they were not proceeded with. Instead, Tempsford was built on rather marshy scrubland beneath the dominant greensand ridge and on part of the Astell Estate, of which Tempsford Hall remains a major feature. Airfield construction by Balfour Beatty commenced in late 1940 for the opening in late summer 1941, under 3 Group. The first to lodge upon the station were Wellington Ics of 11 OTU, here from 16 December 1941 to April 1942 while runway construction took place at Bassingbourn. Radio and radar navigation aids were being skilfully developed for Bomber Command at the time on a number of RAF stations in this region, and Tempsford became involved when, on 19 January 1942, the HQ and Wireless Development Flights of 109 Squadron brought along their Wellington Ics. Spring 1942 found 109 Squadron experiencing the unique misfortune of being the only squadron to attract Wellington VI high-flying pressure-cabin bombers. W5801 and W5802 spent a fortnight while their suitability as *Oboe* radio equipment carriers was explored, a task eventually given to Mosquitoes. Tempsford, with its approach roads sealed, was ideal for such secret goings-on. With 109 Squadron was No 1418 Flight, whose four Wellington IIIs arrived at the start of March 1942 for a five-week stay. They were used to develop radio navigation aids, before their removal to BDU Gransden.

Important as all that was, Tempsford's fame came from its association with 138 Squadron, which arrived on 14 March 1942 flying mainly Whitley Vs and having a handful of Westland Lysanders modified by Fairfields to have a fixed fuselage ladder and a long-range belly fuel tank. These Lysanders were used to land and retrieve agents in France and Belgium on moonlit nights – if discretion permitted. No 138 Squadron used dispersals around Gibraltar Farm.

No 161 Squadron, formed on 15 February 1942 under the command of Wg Cdr E H Fielden and barely existent, moved to Tempsford (via Graveley) in mid-April 1942 and used dispersals near the main railway line. Prior to arrival at Tempsford, 138 Squadron's Lysanders had been involved in nine pick-ups in France and one in Belgium, eight of them successful.

By the end of 1942 the Lysanders had set forth from Tempsford, usually via Tangmere, on a further thirty-eight such sorties. Until October 1942 No 138's main equipment was the Whitley V, but such was the importance of its task that in March 1942 it was awarded a few scarce Halifax IIs, which began replacing Whitleys in both squadrons the following October. Part of one Flight of 138 Squadron was manned by Polish airmen who, in September and October 1942, made particularly gallant attempts to penetrate deep into Poland. One crew managed, on 29 October, to deliver supplies to

*The Gibraltar Farm barn used for kitting out SOE operatives immediately prior to their operations. It is easily reached by following a public footpath.*

*Lysander V9367 MA-B of
161 Squadron photographed
on 4 August 1942. It joined
the squadron on 18
February 1942, and crashed
on 17 December.*

Warsaw, only to run out of fuel, which necessitated a ditching off Sheringham. This happened at a time when three Liberator IIs, attached to 138 Squadron, flew long-range sorties to Poland. They were soon placed in the special 301 Flight, which became 1586 Flight and which, in July 1943, proceeded to Brindisi, Italy, from where flights to the Polish Resistance movement were undertaken.

Of the brave associated with Tempsford, surely no one became better known than Wg Cdr P C Pickard. One of his moonlight exploits took place on 22/23 November 1942 when he and Flt Lt Bridges operated together to a field near Chateroux, flying in two agents and six packages and returning with three others and their luggage.

Most of the squadrons' work consisted of very accurate low-level supply drops to Resistance forces. A triangle of red lights was lit on the ground and a white code identity letter flashed downwind of the apex. Landings were later aided by a *Rebecca* homer and an 'S' telephone link, allowing the pilot to contact the reception committee. An extension of pick-up operations came with the delivery of Lockheed Hudsons to 161 Squadron. Whereas the one-man undefended Lysander could operate within a rectangle of 250 by 25 yards, the Hudson took a greater run. But it permitted much deeper penetration flights, as on 25/26 November 1942 when Gp Capt Fielden flew FH406 to Avignon, a 7½-hour flight, only to discover no reception committee awaiting his arrival.

November 1942 saw 'A' Flight, 161 Squadron, convert from Whitley Vs to Halifaxes. The squadron also had a special detachment at St Eval, flying two Albemarles for shipping co-operation sorties. Detachments from Tempsford were common, and at the end of 1942 some crews operated within the Mediterranean Theatre. Another departure from the usual SOE employment came when Lysanders and Whitleys of 161 Squadron made bombing raids, thus providing diversion activities while the usual operations were taking place.

Throughout 1943, when the moon was bright and conditions favourable, Lysanders of 'A' Flight, 161 Squadron, operated 111 successful pick-up sorties out of 157. Part of 138 Squadron was detached to operate in support of guerrilla forces in Libya, while four Halifaxes spent a short time in Russia. Wg Cdr Pickard left Tempsford in May 1943, by which time a number of pilots had become skilled at pick-up operations. One of the most successful months for operations was August 1943, during which sixty-six agents were dropped, as well as 194 packages and 1,452 containers in the course of 184 sorties. The first double Hudson pick-up, on 18 October 1943, witnessed both aircraft becoming temporarily and alarmingly bogged in damp ground. Wg Cdr R Hodges, Commanding Officer of 161 Squadron, landed first and picked up ten people. Fg Off J Afflick, who followed him in, airlifted out another ten. Years later Hodges was to discover that one of his then un-named passengers was a Mr Vincent Auriol, later President of France. Hodges became well-known in the post-war RAF, and at one time was station commander at Marham. John Afflick spent some time as a BEA Viscount pilot.

*Halifax II NF-W of 138
Squadron in December
1942.*

Double operations were fraught with great danger, only too apparent on 16/17 December 1943 when two Lysanders collided during a blind landing.

A very special operation took two Halifaxes to Norway, a ten-hour journey, to deliver paratroops whose task was to attack a heavy water plant. On 28 May 1943 a new unit, 1575 Flight, equipped with Halifaxes and Venturas, formed here before proceeding overseas a fortnight later.

During February 1944 the first mail pick-up was attempted. The Lysander used the antiquated pick-up hook with which it had been born and which had hitherto seemed so outdated in an era of radio contact.

Short Stirlings first came in numbers to Tempsford in February 1944 when a detachment from 149 Squadron took up residence to train in delivering containers to precise locations from very low levels.

For effective SOE operations it was essential that ample, regular radio communications be maintained with the Resistance. For that role Hudsons were used to fly 296 so-called Ascension Operations, mainly off the Dutch coast and at around 20,000 feet. Prior to the use of Hudsons, a few Havocs were employed for what became an evening ritual over East Anglia in the summer of 1942. Usually as a pair, they would climb to their operating altitude and parade to and fro gathering radio messages.

Immediately prior to D-Day, both 138 and 161 Squadrons supplied war material to Resistance forces throughout Europe. Poland, Austria and Yugoslavia were most easily reached from the south, and Tempsford's crews flew to the Mediterranean Theatre to undertake drops in those countries.

On 11/12 August 1944 No 138 Squadron flew its last Halifax sorties from Tempsford, thirteen aircraft supplying the *Maquis*. Lysander pick-up flights were now no longer needed. Between November 1942 and September 1944, Hudsons made thirty-six successful pick-ups out of forty-six attempted.

Rapidly 138 Squadron converted to Stirling IVs fitted with long-range tanks. No 161 Squadron flew its final Halifax sorties on the night of 1/2 September 1944 and began operating Stirlings on 8/9 September, No 138's having gone into action on 28/29 August.

By September 1944 drops were mainly to the Belgians, Danes, Norwegians and over a few areas of south-east France. By the end of 1944 they were also being undertaken over Germany, using Hudsons. The last agent-landing flight was despatched on 3 February 1945. Low flying made SOE operations hazardous, as on 20/21 March 1945 when three Hudsons, despatched to Germany, failed to return.

No 138 Squadron's association with Tempsford ended most abruptly when it moved to Tuddenham and re-equipped with Lancaster bombers. During its Tempsford operations it had delivered 995 agents, 29,000 containers and 10,000 packages in the course of 2,494 sorties, for the loss of seventy aircraft. No 161 Squadron operated from Tempsford to the end of European hostilities, completing its commitment when, on 3 June 1945, a Stirling flew to Brussels. Disbandment came on 14 June 1945. Tempsford crews had brought hope and succour throughout enslaved Europe.

As 161 Squadron disbanded, No 1 Transport Aircraft Modification Unit formed, a centre for the conversion of Coastal Command and bomber Liberators into transports. When this work finished, 1 TAMU moved, in February 1946, to Honington.

In mid-June 1945 Tempsford switched to 47 Group. No 426 (RCAF) Squadron arrived and rapidly converted to Liberator troopers for the Europe to India service, carrying out that task almost until disbandment on 31 December 1945. A Proctor and an Anson of 48 Group Communication Flight were also here until the unit disbanded on 15 May 1946. A detachment of 53 Squadron's Liberators arrived on 9 December 1945 and returned to Gransden Lodge in March 1946. No 102 Squadron also had a detachment of Liberators at Tempsford from early January to 28 February 1946, when it was dissolved into 53 Squadron.

Removal of the Liberators left Tempsford quiet. Maintenance Command took over the station on 7 August 1946, Polebrook's 273 MU establishing a sub-site here for the storage of Harvards and Mosquitoes in spring 1947. Tempsford passed to care and maintenance in June 1947, then transferred to Technical Training Command in October.

On 12 April 1961 many remaining buildings were sold and, in February 1963, 648 acres of the site were bought by the Astell family. It is surprising that with so much interest in SOE activities there is no large museum at Tempsford, with a Lysander sometimes demonstrating itself on the remaining length of runway.

**Main features:**
*Runways:* 251° 6,000ft x 150ft, 010° 4,800ft x 150ft, 309° 4,149ft x 150ft, concrete. *Hangars:* six T2, one B1. *Accommodation:* RAF officers 2,623, SNCOs 429, ORs 1,126; WAAF officers 10, SNCOs 8, ORs 250.

## THAME (HADDENHAM), Buckinghamshire

*51°47N/00°56W 84ft asl; SP755090. 6 miles SW of Aylesbury, NW of Haddenham village*

> "Welcome to Flying Legends 41! Look east and you will see the stars of our air show approaching, two Avro 504s retired in 1933 and, in this hour of need, rejoining the RAF front line."

On 27 April 1941 two of seven active, aged Avro 504Ns impressed for military service arrived at Haddenham. Sadly, nobody seems to have been brave enough even to click a Brownie!

Derivatives of the 1914-18 War, these venerable old souls had been lovingly adopted by civilians, making J8533 into *G-ADET,* while K2353 was renamed *G-ADBP,* both having recently 'volunteered' (impressed, actually) to again serve King and Country, as AX875 and AX874 respectively. A daring future had been planned for them: the towing of wooden sailplanes over the English Channel for release near the French coast. Thame-based, they would be then be testing German radar's ability to detect wooden 'gliders' in an escapade that could never for sure become one of life's most carefree ventures.

While British airborne forces did not originate at Thame, it nevertheless played a very important part in the development of military gliding, a task it shared with RAE Farnborough, CLE Ringway and General Aircraft at Hanworth. Thame (or Haddenham) was chosen because this 1938-built small, vacant, pre-war aerodrome developed by CTF Aviation was deemed suitably situated for the development of tactics involving the use of pre-war civilian light sailplanes, including the Falcon III, Kirby Kite and Rhonbussard, supplemented with engineless BA Swallows.

Following the fall of France, the decision was taken to form a British glider-borne paratroop force. A start was made using sailplanes hauled aloft by a collection of light aeroplanes based at Ringway, where a glider training school formed on 19 September 1940. This was a strange choice, for its future base was Side Hill, grassland on the eastern fringe of Newmarket, where horses cantered, Lysanders occasionally floated in and at least one Whitley had touched down intentionally. Glider pilot training in a busy operational area, where the enemy constantly nosed around, was hardly ideal. Nevertheless, the Glider Training Squadron arrived at Side Hill on 21 November 1940, left on 28 December and sensibly headed for a little aerodrome known as Haddenham, re-named RAF Detachment Thame.

Opening Thame provided plenty to occupy its new arrivals. No gliders were yet to hand, and the GTS found the landing ground strewn with obstructions to discourage the very activity it had come to promote. Quickly the rubbish was removed then burned in preparation for the impressive arrival of Britain's mighty airborne army.

It arrived almost complete – almost – and in formation. Composition? Five Tiger Moths, which managed an assault landing in an astonishing one minute, setting a target time for future airborne adventurers. Crew shelter was provided in a room of Yolsome House before more expansive accommodation became available at No 8, Church Road, Thame, a residence conveniently adjacent to the other ranks' quarters – in a tithe barn. All the troops were in their billets by 3 January 1941. Incredible it surely is that the mighty force that skilfully moved into Normandy in 1944, and fought with such colossal courage at Arnhem, should have been born in these pathetic circumstances. Such, though, is the manner by which the British have always gone about their fighting business, and probably always will, in order to win.

The glider forces' arrival at Thame was understandably not featured by the media of those days – particularly as the gliders arrived unspectacularly in over-sized suitcases. 'Gliders' is an incorrect description, all five being Kirby Kite sailplanes, which, by 5 January 1941, were ready for flight. Next day the General Officer Commanding-in-Chief watched an impressive parade of Tigers and Kites, which, in a wide formation, toured as far as Hartford Bridge. They turned, crossed White Waltham for the benefit of aviation enthusiasts (if any) and returned to Thame, where the 'gliders' cast off for a stream landing. Then the snow came, and ice needed to be swept from the wings of the aircraft.

Construction and improvement of Thame was under way, and by 11 January 1941 a dominant Bessoneau hangar was completed, together with three huts. Flying hours had so far amounted to 25 hours 33 minutes. Doubtless the administering 70 Group was pleased with the start, although the vulnerability of glider trains was disturbing. Surely fighters could easily pick them off? This needing investigation, so a ground party left Thame for Duxford on 17 January 1941 while another group acquired a Viking sailplane for trials. Five Kirby Kites, letters A to E, were towed to Duxford by 'The Tiger Club', and on 10 February a trial was flown, the five combinations being engaged over Royston Heath by AFDU fighters while Wing Commander Vasse observed from a Gladiator. During a repeat performance a GRU Defiant had, as its unlikely 'gunner', the famed Professor Melville Jones. All seeming fairly safe, and the gliders returned to Haddenham.

What was needed most were military transport gliders, not sailplanes, and between 15 and 18 February 1941 personnel from Haddenham inspected four real gliders, General Aircraft Limited Hotspurs in use at RAE Farnborough where another antique, a Handley Page Heyford bomber, towed them in train. Sqn Ldr H J Wilson, Aero Department, explained that the initial idea was to release troop-carrying gliders at 20,000 feet and 100 miles from their target, allowing them to approach stealthily. Tests revealed a very creditable 83-mile glide after release from 20,000 feet by a Hotspur, the prototype of which had been designed and built in three months. The towing method remained uncertain, the glider having hooks in the extreme nose, under the belly and in the tail to permit train tows, although wind tunnel tests showed that would be very difficult due to the dynamics involved.

Extremely elegant, the Hotspur 1's fuselage shape was derived from the profile of the R-100 airship. A moulded, transparent streamlined cockpit hood covered the two pilots seated in tandem, behind which six troops sat in line astern. They would jettisoned the fuselage roof then hopefully deplane in a few seconds after the glider slid to a halt on its lengthy skid. Shortly after take-off the wheeled undercarriage would have been jettisoned. Although twelve Mk 1s were completed, a policy change called for glider release close to the landing zone involving a steep descent. To achieve that, a braking parachute was experimentally fitted to a Hotspur. In order to meet the new requirement the aircraft's wing span was reduced from 61 to 46 feet, which removed the sailplane capability. Side bench seating and side doors for rapid exit for paratroops or ground troops were substituted. Soon the idea of gliders carrying paratroops was discarded. Gliders, simply equipped, were to be expendable after one operation. That effected tactics, life-span and durability.

BV134, the prototype intended eight-seater Mk 1, first flew in December 1940, but could safely carry only six armed troops. Its nose-towing quick-release hook had to be repositioned because of centre-of-gravity problems, the ultimate cure being a bifurcated tow-rope. BV137, the fourth Hotspur, and the first with the shortened span and enlarged ailerons, took a longer landing run, had a higher stalling speed and no brakes. In March 1941 came the decision to establish a huge glider force equipped with twenty-five-seater Airspeed Horsas. Hotspurs would now be used almost exclusively for training purposes, despite their lack of durability.

Twelve Army pilots reported at Haddenham on 3 March 1941 for the pilot training course. They would learn to fly Tiger Moths, then sailplanes, for it was 6 April before the first Hotspur for the GTS arrived by road. It was first flown on 9 April, towed aloft by Hawker Hector K8119. Finding suitable tugs had been a problem, then Malcolm Ltd quickly modified twenty-five unsuitable, unwanted Hector biplanes.

Haddenham's sailplanes and Tiger Moths had twice been demonstrated at CLE Ringway, and on 15 May 1941 were displayed for the local Home Guard, when the first long-distance Hotspur tow (of BV135 from Ringway to Haddenham) took place. That was useful preparation for a cross-country flight to White Waltham on 24 May. Next day the PTS and GTS mounted a display near Windsor for the King, and 5,000 Home Guard personnel. Following a paratroop drop from a Whitley and release of three Kirby Kites from Tiger Moths, a Hotspur was brought along by a Hector. Building GTS Thame was a protracted process with no room for complacency, and by September 1941 it seemed that for each three pilots trained, one Hotspur would be written off.

Haddenham's first Hotspur II, BT498, arrived on 14 October, and on the 22nd the GTS layout was as follows: Tug Towing Flight, with sixteen Hectors, two Tiger Moths and a Hind trainer for tug pilot conversion, and two Glider Flights, each established at eight IE and seven IR Hotspurs, the high reserves allowing for expected wastage. The actual holding totalled eleven Hectors, three Hinds, twelve Tiger Moths and those two Avro 504Ns (both sent to 71 MU on 12 December 1941 for disposal to ATC squadron, AX875 going to No 1458 at Deal, and AX874 to 1813 Squadron at

Merthyr Vale), but only eight Hotspurs. A further six Hotspurs had, on 13 October, been allocated to the Ground Training Unit. All needed erection and rigging at Haddenham, a tricky task complicated by control problems and tail heaviness for which no cures had been devised.

Formed on 4 November 1941, No 1 GTS Thame (whose title became effective on 1 December) had sixteen Army pilots on No 1 Hotspur Course, which also opened on 1 December under 23 Group, Training Command. An ideal Hotspur trainer was formulated based on Thame's experience. It would need a low-sited nose-hook to prevent the glider climbing too rapidly, and effective dual controls and instruments were deemed useful, together with wheel brakes and ballast. BV134 was modified accordingly. Even the limited experience so far showed the Hotspur insufficiently robust for training purposes. Wing and tail stresses had been underestimated, and there was excessive wear on the undercarriage because the glider was intended always to land upon its skid.

Loaded Hotspurs needed the pulling power of a Hector for take-off, but the run at Thame was insufficient in emergency conditions. Use of Kidlington was considered for gliders carrying ballast. Meanwhile, the first glider Operational Training Units formed and needed all the Hectors. The GTS would have to make do with Audaxes.

Nothing in the sphere of military gliding was simple. Fitting their activities into busy Midland air space was difficult, for Hotspurs and soon Horsas on tow were difficult to turn. Therefore, around Kidlington was established, in March 1943, the Central Gliding Area within the Barford-Thame-Kidlington triangle. Lengthy glider routes across the Midlands were also prescribed as, for example, Thame-Olney-Kettering-Barford and return, Kidlington to Tetbury or to Shrewton via Netheravon, as well as a long Barford-Pershore-Shrewsbury-Northwich-Ringway route, along which flights could be made at heights of up to 12,000 feet. Ample notice was needed by all Commands of such.

Glider activity rapidly increased in 1942, so No 1 GTS acquired the RLG at Kingston Bagpuize for use between 9 March 1942 and 25 July 1942. Thame's unsuitability, particularly for possible larger gliders, was obvious, and Training Command chose Croughton as a more suitable base for No 1 GTS, which began moving there on 22 July 1942 and completed the change on 3 August. A small portion of 1 GTS remained at Thame to become the Glider Instructors' School. Five months later the GIS closed, its task passing to a slimmed No 5 GTS Shobdon.

A new phase in Thame's career opened in April 1943 when the ATA (Training) Ferry Pool arrived from White Waltham and immediately sired the ATA Initial Flying Training School, which, Magister-equipped, quickly transferred its activity to Barton-in-the-Clay, where it remained until closure in 1945. On 5 August 1943 the Training Pool became No 5 (Training) Ferry Pool which, on 15 August, became No 5 Ferry Pilots Pool (or Ferry Pool), ATA. Using mainly Fairchild Argus I and II high-wing monoplanes together with Ansons, it was a major player in the delivery of aircraft between civilian aircraft production sources, repair units and military organisations. ATA light transports plied between airfields collecting ATA men and women and flying them back to the Pool HQ at the end of the day.

Thame was but briefly without towing activities, for in early 1943 the Royal Navy Air Experimental Department formed here to develop towed targets and target-towing gear. This attracted assorted aircraft types, including the Martinet, Defiant, Swordfish and Vengeance target towers.

Some trials concerned Lines Brothers' towed glider targets. Famous for their Frog Penguin plastic models, they were now producing full-scale target gliders, which were developed here for naval gunnery. The RNAED was replaced in May 1945 by the RAF's No 3 RC here until October 1945, when it moved to Ludham. Thame was left in the hands of RAF radio engineers and an overseas packing unit until station closure on 30 April 1946.

Civilian aircraft engineers then moved in to set up Chartair, and in 1947 Airtech Ltd opened an aircraft maintenance business, which led to Thame becoming the lair for civilian conversion of Stirling Vs, as well as Halifaxes and Dakotas. Airtech subsequently handled a variety of light aircraft, which the private grass strip at Thame continues to attract. Alongside is a light engineering and industrial estate using part of the wartime site.

**Main features:**
This grass airfield had a number of Blister hangars and two T2s, which post-war were used for large aircraft overhaul and modification programmes.

## THURLEIGH, Bedfordshire (see also Bedford)

*52°13N/00°28W 285ft asl; TL048602. 6¹/₂ miles N of Bedford*

Thurleigh opened on 24 July 1941 and by the end of that month the perimeter track, two runways of 4,800 feet and 3,300 feet, together with three groups of dispersal points were ready for use. On 9 October 1941 the station was switched from 2 Group to 8 Group, preceding the re-forming of No 160 Squadron here on 16 January 1942. Although several Liberator IIs joined it, they appear not to have been flown. Instead, on 12 February 1942 eight RAF officers shepherded no fewer than 524 obedient men of 160 Squadron from Thurleigh to their port of embarkation. This left ninety-six representing 160 Squadron, among them fifty-eight aircrew members with another five men 'AWOL'.

Four days later personnel of 18 OTU arrived, the remainder of 160 Squadron now leaving for Polebrook, and later to join 120 Squadron. Among the replacement Thurleigh residents were 127 Polish airmen, part of 18 OTU's detachment, which opened for business on 1 March 1942 using Wellington Ics. During the night of 18 May Wellington DV783 crashed on the aerodrome, five Poles aboard being killed. Almost simultaneously, but miles away, another Polish crew died when N2806 crashed. They were buried at Newark two days later. Five Wellingtons arrived from Bramcote on 3 June to retrieve some of the 18 OTU detachment, others left in lorries, and 2813 Airfield Defence Squadron remained to guard the airfield.

Work immediately began to improve the airfield for its main role, which commenced in the early hours of 7 September 1942 with the arrival of some 1,700 officers and men of the 306th Bomb Group, USAAF. After a brief rest they paraded to greet eighteen B-17Fs of the 367th and 423rd Squadrons. Alas, there was disappointment, for incomplete runways prevented landings and, after an impressive formation tour of the area, the Fortresses put down elsewhere. This was only a brief diversion, and in two formations the B-17s of the 423rd, 367th and 369th Squadrons made an even more impressive spectacle as they settled on 11 September. Two days later the Fortress crews were learning to fly in combat formation, and proving to the arriving 368th Squadron that the 306th was already active.

For the Group, 9 October 1942 was the big day, being the first occasion when a large number of American bombers literally drenched a clear sky with contrails as they roamed around getting into battle formation for the biggest USAAF raid so far. Take-off for Thurleigh's two-dozen B-17s began at 0732 for Target Z183, the Fives-Lille steelworks With the 11th CCRC, the 306th performed very creditably, nineteen crews claiming to bomb the target from around 22,000 feet between 0938 and 0946. Enemy fighters were very active, and the Group's crews had a clear and chilling view of 124510 of the 367th Bomb Squadron being shot down.

The 306th next operated on 21 October, twenty B-17s setting off for the Karoman shipyards at Lorient, an operation halted by poor weather resulting in the bomb load being jettisoned in The Wash. In November it attacked Brest on the 7th, Lille on the 8th, St Nazaire on the 9th and La Pallice on the 18th. On the latter occasion a dozen B-17Fs of the 306th joined twelve B-24Ds, eighteen B-17s of the 303rd BG and eighteen of the 91st BG. Flak was intense, one B-17 having an engine disabled and six of the crew injured. Bad weather in December reduced operations, Rouen marshalling yards being raided on the 12th and Romilly-sur-Seine on the 20th.

At the start of 1943 four Groups of B-17s were operating from Britain, the 91st, 303rd, 305th and Thurleigh's 306th, now the most experienced. Eighteen of its Fortresses set off for St Nazaire on 3 January, the 367th losing 124469, and the 369th 124470. Two more B-17s were lost when Lille marshalling yards were attacked on 13 January, and on the 23rd another attempt was made to bomb Karoman.

Field Order No 90 dated 26 January 1943 brought the news that all knew must come, the start of the US daylight onslaught on Germany. It informed the 91st, 303rd, 305th and 306th Bomb Groups that their next target would be the U-boat building yards at Vegesack, with Wilhelmshaven as reserve target. Fighter escort being impossible, the operation relied upon practised formation. The 101st CBW would lead with thirty-two B-17s of the 306th and 91st BGs, followed by the 102nd CBW with eighteen aircraft from the 305th and 303rd BGs. B-17s in the former formation would assemble in a line east of Peterborough-Bedford, make for St Ives and thence King's Lynn, arriving there at 1010, by which time the 102nd was to swing into line behind them. On a steady climb they would reach bombing altitude thirty-five miles from Baltrum Island, the 101st at 23,000 feet, the others at 25,000 feet. Orders stated that after bombing, they should turn left and retire between Wesermunde and Cuxhaven. Each B-17 would carry five 1,000lb bombs, and Colonel Frank

Armstrong, who led the first Rouen raid, would lead this operation in a B-17 of the 306th BG.

As planned, sixteen B-17s set off from Thurleigh. Two crews aborted before the others ran in towards Vegesack, which they found cloud-clad, making attack impossible. Therefore they pressed on to Wilhelmshaven, making that the first target in Germany to be bombed by the USAAF. Flak was encountered, as well as a few fighters. From the following Group, the 305th, a B-17 was seen shot down, and a Fw 190 was observed burning.

Now there was no holding back the B-17 Groups. On 4 February 1943 Thurleigh's Fortresses bombed Hamm, and tried for Bremen's Focke-Wulf factory on 26 February, when, due to cloud, they had to settle for Wilhelmshaven. On 5 April the 306th suffered its first major defeat when, although five enemy fighters were claimed, five B-17s were shot down when attacking Antwerp. That was a prelude to increasingly tortuous days ahead when Thurleigh's Fortresses struck deeply into Germany and beyond. The agonies and horrific hours their crews endured were vividly illustrated on 1 May when the 306th attacked St Nazaire.

Interception was ferocious and 1st Lt L P Johnson's B-17F, 229649 of the 423rd Bomb Squadron, was hit, causing a fire in the waist section and radio compartment. Sgt Maynard H Smith was in the ball turret occupying the position wherein one curled oneself in great discomfort while attempting to train two massive-looking guns. Only with the necessary physique could one even squeeze into place. Smith's turret was soon out of action and he crawled into the aircraft's fuselage to fight the fire aft. Three of the crew had abandoned the aircraft and the rear-gunner needed much assistance. Smith, realising someone was still controlling the bomber, decided to first set about tackling the fire, then he helped the rear-gunner before again tackling the forward blaze. Meanwhile Fw 190s were firing at the bomber. Smith hurled blazing ammunition boxes from the aircraft as escaping oxygen from bursting bottles fed the fires, which he fought for ninety minutes while also helping the tail-gunner. Despite the aircraft's plight, Johnson managed to land it at Predannack. Sgt Smith, on his first operational sortie, displayed such courage that he was awarded the Medal of Honor, the first to anyone in the 8th AF. Personnel of the 306th subsequently won many awards, the Group receiving a DUC when, in poor weather, they bombed an aircraft assembly plant at Bernberg on 22 February 1944. Losses were sometimes heavy, as during the October 1943 Schweinfurt raid, when ten B-17s were shot down before reaching the target.

Thurleigh's 306th BG was in continuous action over a longer period than any other in the 8th AF. Also, it stayed on one base longer than any other and, at the end of hostilities had completed 342 operations. Its final sorties were on 19 April 1945. Despite this it was not the best-known of the B-17 Groups, even though it held, within its 367th Bomb Squadron, the British Sovereign's daughter's namesake, Rose of York, a B-17 christened by Princess Elizabeth and which flew sixty-two successful missions. When returning from Berlin on 5 February 1945, it came down in the sea, taking with it a BBC war correspondent. By the end of the war the 306th BG had despatched 9,614 sorties and lost 171 aircraft in action. Unlike most, the 306th detached its squadrons to the Continent and overseas before moving to Giebelstadt, Germany, during December 1945.

In 1944 the Government decided that a new aeronautical research establishment would be built, embracing Thurleigh. Building commenced in 1946 and wartime Thurleigh became partly engulfed by a new airfield generally known as Bedford. A few buildings of wartime Thurleigh remain on wartime sub-sites, but Thurleigh aerodrome was absorbed within the new aerodrome, sometimes known by its predecessor's name.

**Main features:**
*Runways:* 054° 6,000ft x 150ft, 172° 4,200ft x 150ft, 288° 4, 200ft x 150ft concrete topped with asphalt. *Hangars:* four T2. *Hardstandings:* fifty-one mixed frying-pan and loop type. *Accommodation:* USAAF officers 443, EM 2,529.

## TURWESTON, Northamptonshire

*52°02N/01°06W 448ft asl; SP615384. 3 miles NE of Brackley*

Now known as Turweston Aerodrome operated by Turweston Flight Centre Ltd and utilising part of the wartime airfield, the site is to be found to the north of Turweston village, close to a picturesque wooded area; the name Turweston may commemorate a Danish soldier of long ago. It is best viewed after passing Whitfield, reached by turning off the A43(T) about 2¹/₂ miles north of Brackley. Climb the plateau and the remnants of brick huts seen to the right are part of a domestic site. Across farmland, firing butts in good condition may be glimpsed. The road passes close to the control tower (pattern Nos 13726/41 and 15683/41), near which parts of the perimeter track runway, huts and shelters remain.

Turweston has an involved history. In August 1941 No 12 OTU moved. taking Wellington Ics and Ansons from Benson to Chipping Warden, with Gaydon serving as satellite until Turweston temporarily replaced it. 'A' Flight of the OTU moved in on 23 November 1942, then in mid-April 1943 12 OTU moved to a permanent satellite, Edgehill. Turweston then became second satellite for 13 OTU, which, on 30 April 1943, brought its Mitchells here. No 307 FTU's Bostons also used the airfield between 1 and 18 May 1943. Turweston became Silverstone's satellite on 3 July, although Bostons and Mitchells remained until early August. They were replaced by Wellington IIIs of 17 OTU's conversion and general handling squadrons. On 24 November 17 OTU's Gunnery Flight formed at Turweston, equipped with Wellingtons and Martinets.

In late July 1945 17 OTU's Wellingtons were withdrawn, the bomber defence training flight leaving during August. Turweston closed on 23 September 1945, ceasing on 2 November 1945. On 21 January 1946 the station was transferred to the War Office, and Army vehicles soon littered the airfield awaiting public auction.

As well as being used for farming, part of wartime Turweston serves for a limited amount of flying. A section of asphalt runway 09/27, approximately 3,050 feet long and 60 feet wide, is used by the Turweston Aero Club and for PPR light aircraft activity. A parallel grass runway is available for tail-wheel aircraft. Part of the site is used for winch-launched gliding on Saturdays, and another area is used by a driving school.

### Main features:
*Runways:* 100° 6,000ft x 150ft, 040° 4,200ft x 150ft, 160° 3,300ft x 150ft concrete. *Hangars:* one T2. *Hardstandings:* twenty-seven heavy bomber type. *Accommodation:* RAF officers 93, SNCOs 312, ORs 622; WAAF officers 3, SNCOs 8, ORs 171.

---

## TWINWOOD FARM, Bedfordshire

52°10/00°29W 275ft asl; TL038549. 4 miles N of Bedford

"They should never have gone, they should never have let that plane take off," said the tall American in his 'pinks'. "What Goddam idea entered their heads we'll never know." True, true indeed.

T he weather at take-off time was too murky for Thurleigh to be used. Instead, on 15 December 1944 the USAAF UC-64 Norseman positioned itself at Twinwood ('Twinwoods' as it was colloquially known), and awaited a famed and popular passenger, Glenn Miller. He was about to be flown to Paris to arrange accommodation for the American band of the AEF.

What happened over the icy-cold Channel remains a matter of conjecture. His Norseman, a type ever noisily present in East Anglian skies at that time, sounded like a Harvard throwing a tantrum while resembling some ugly Soviet contraption. A most rugged beast, this giant single-engined aeroplane looked as if it could fly through a 5-foot-thick wall and emerge unmarked. Yet on Christmas Eve 1944 the news broke that Glenn Miller was missing, and that his transport had failed to make Paris. Furthermore, his Norseman had not even been tracked over the French coast. Somewhere off the Cherbourg Peninsula it seems to have came down in the sea, perhaps due to severe icing. Other theories suggest it was hit by a bomb jettisoned from a Lancaster. Whatever the truth, it just disappeared, bringing a tragic end for one who brightened the gloom of war.

Twinwood Farm has an interesting past. Named after the place upon which it was built, it was first used as an unbuilt landing ground long before it became a fully-fledged concern. Before the war the site interested Bedford Councillors as a possible area for a municipal airport. By mid-1941 14 SFTS Cranfield was using it for circuits by Oxfords prior to moving to Lyneham in August of that year. Twinwood then had a major facelift while remaining under Cranfield's control.

No 51 OTU formed at Cranfield in August 1941 to train night-fighter crews, and Twinwood re-opened too as its three-runway Built Satellite on 9 April 1942. It served the OTU until June 1945, and was populated first by very assorted Blenheims, including Mk Vs, then by mainly Beaufighter Is, all of which were used by pilots during type-conversion training.

In March 1943 Twinwood Farm briefly enjoyed intense fighter activity when a succession of Mustang I squadrons paraded through during exercise *Spartan*. Nos 164, 169, 239, 268 and 613 Squadrons were all briefly here.

The OTU, of which the station was a part, closed on 14 June 1945 and Twinwood Farm seemed finished. Instead, however, it remained a satellite of Cranfield until 1 February 1946. Already, behind the scenes, the decision had been taken to make it part of a grandiose scheme. To the north would be built a massive research establishment having an incredibly long runway reckoned necessary to flight-test the Brabazon I airliner and supersonic jets. Two Brabazons would be so large that, it was contended, a special maintenance area would be necessary. This, built on Twinwood Farm, would be linked with the research station by a mile or so of wide tracking. That entailed crossing the busy public road between Thurleigh village and Twinwood Tunnel Site. Travel that route today and one passes through a deep recess, and at one time there was a brief stretch of unexpected 'dual carriageway'. Over this point a bridge carrying a wide concrete taxiway would have passed. Like the Brabazon itself, the scheme never reached fruition. Twinwood, though, cemented its link with Thurleigh in another way, for its flying club used a Blister hangar and part of the runway, sharing it with crop-sprayers and other light aircraft.

There is now something very special at Twinwood Farm. The wartime control tower, where, in 2000, extensive, privately undertaken restoration work started, now contains on the ground floor the Glenn Miller Museum, a room devoted to RAF personnel who served here and a gallery of wartime art. Upstairs the tower has been laid out to look as it did in wartime. Adjacent is Twinwood Arena, able to hold as many as 10,000 people. A large grass area is surrounded on three sides by grassy banks with a woodland as backdrop. Here, special events can now be held. At long last a Glenn Miller shrine has been created for his many fans. A special private road to the events area leads off the A6 at Clapham Village just north of Bedford; for details phone 01234 350413. If you want to undertake the pilgrimage, you might like to start at Bedford Corn Exchange, the walls of which, 'tis said, still faintly vibrate to the Miller sound to get you in the mood!

**Main features:**
*Runways:* 330° 4,800ft x 150ft, 242° 4,200ft x 150ft, 278° 3,300ft x 150ft, concrete with wood and rubber chips. *Hangars:* six Blister type. *Hardstandings:* twenty-two special for twin-engined fighters. *Accommodation:* RAF Officers 70, SNCOs 118, ORs 740; WAAF officers 1, SNCOs 3, ORs 140.

## UPPER HEYFORD, Oxfordshire

*51°56N/01°15W 420ft asl; SP515270. 5 miles NW of Bicester*

"Come in Number One, your time is up," went the call – almost – to the Thunderbirds' leader over Upper Heyford on 19 June 1971.

Six bold flyers, after touch-down, each positioned his Phantom in front of the open-house crowd. At the simultaneous tweak of a switch each cockpit canopy rose and each aircraft's occupant stood to accept half-hearted rapture. While arms were at the salute, the Might of Uncle Sam was confronted by bulging, curvaceous lovelies courtesy of Uncle Hefner, who had kindly provided this feast of Bunny Girls for lunch.

To the twiddle of their tails the warriors almost fell down the cockpit ladders, eager to face the audacious fate in store, while not far away the Red Arrows were taxiing in. Power off, canopies up and to each Red Gnat also hurried a figure as well proportioned and aware of the ways of the world as any Bunny Girl. But there was one clear difference – the amply thick brown overalls of the RAF 'Chiefies' were in direct contrast to the lack of attire exhibited by the girls. Cocooned by RAF policemen and well-protected by groundcrews, the Arrows' pilots were quickly secured in a grey bus, faces long and thoughts obvious, for the Bunnies were whisking off their new playmates in taxis bound for the London playpens.

Placing America's F-111 swing-wing bombers at Upper Heyford seemed as incongruous as having Bunnies on the Flight Line. Sometimes the bombers squatted in hangars of the 1920s, built on this 1914-18 war training ground. Whether there were any real bunnies around in those distant days one can but muse. Certain it is that the surroundings could not have been further in style from 'smart' bombs, Blackbirds, popcorn, jeans and jammers.

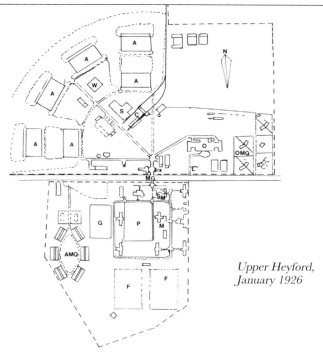

*Upper Heyford,
January 1926*

## UPPER HEYFORD
The re-developed Upper Heyford of the 1920s and 1930s exhibited basic features common to an RAF Home Station planned following the RAF re-organisation plans of 1922-23. Its Spartan layout was designed to accommodate and support three Single-Engined Day Bomber Squadrons intended for possible operations against France. By 1926 the need for such action was fast fading. The six Aircraft Sheds Type 'A', each intended for a Flight of small day-bombers, instead housed heavies after the policy change. Upper Heyford became a Two-Squadron Heavy Bomber Station, at which Hyderabads of 99 Squadron began to arrive on 12 December 1927.

Throughout its long, active life, Upper Heyford retained a wide and most impressive Main Gate (MG) entrance. Directly across the road bisecting the camp, another roadway led to the Domestic Site, more imposing than many.

Station Headquarters opposite the Guard House was just inside the aerodrome arena wherein buildings of basic need were sited. Included were the Operations Block, Main Stores (S), Main Workshops (W), Motor Transport Section and Sheds, Bombing Tower, Watch Office (for there was of course no control tower), power house, water tower, fire station and a contractor's yard fed by a railway link (C). Test butts for guns, the usual engine test house, lubricants store and bulk fuel installation were present, as well as the W/T R/T Station.

Within the Domestic Site were five Barrack Blocks Type 'C' built around the Parade Ground (P). Near the site entrance were the Sergeants' Mess and Institute. The Dining Room and Cook House (M), Station Sick Quarters, church, cinema and assembly hall were nearby. The strong accent on sporting activity within the service is evident from the two football fields (F) and a games area.

Provision of Married Quarters at RAF camps came after some lengthy consideration. Officers' Married Quarters were on the aerodrome side of the site close to the Officers' Mess (O). Quarters for Married Airmen (AMQ) were at the southern end of the Domestic Area.

Many RAF stations of the 1920s consisted of a square or oblong landing ground with buildings set within a rectangular area along one side. Upper Heyford was quite different, for the aircraft sheds were built in the south-east corner of the site and within an unusual convex-shaped technical site. The large bombers 'sailed' away then 'floated' into wind for landing, avoiding the limited built-up area of the station.

Upper Heyford was laid down in 1916. A year later Canadians arrived for the formation, on 20 January 1918, of No 123 Squadron, equipped with Sopwith Dolphins, which changed its name in 1919 to No 2 Squadron, Canadian Air Force, before leaving for Shoreham. A second such squadron, also Dolphin-equipped, was No 81, formed on 20 November 1918, which became No 1 Squadron, Canadian Air Force, then moved to Shoreham in March 1919. Upper Heyford closed in 1920.

The selection of the First World War airfield site for development followed the 1923 Defence Review. Although incomplete, it re-opened, as a bomber station, on 12 October 1927. Station Headquarters formed on 25 October, as well as the Oxford University Flight, which acquired three Avro 504Ns. That became Upper Heyford Station Flight on 4 November 1927. From Bircham Newton on 12 December came the advance party of 99 (Bomber) Squadron to prepare Upper Heyford to receive a dozen Hyderabads on 5 January 1928. As company they would have No 10 Squadron, re-formed two days previously. Upper Heyford was starting its long career as a bomber station, where, on 25 January 1928, 10 Squadron took on charge its first three Hyderabads.

Equipping was a long-drawn-out process, the usual plea of money shortage abounding. Not until 15 October 1928 did its second Flight form, also with Hyderabads, but on 26 April 1930 the squadron still had only six aircraft.

During 1929 the first Hinaidis reached 99 Squadron. Apart from their Bristol Jupiter engines they differed little from the Hyderabads. During 1930 the squadron began to receive later metal Hinaidis. Production remained pathetically slow into 1931, and Hyderabads were still with 99 Squadron. The first Hinaidi for 10 Squadron reached Upper Heyford on 9 December 1930, and by 1 April 1931 it held five. A change in emphasis came when, after its formation on 1 April, No 40 Squadron – the first to have Fairey Gordons – led to 10 Squadron moving to Boscombe Down.

No 18 Squadron was resurrected on 20 October 1931 and supplied with Hawker Harts. Its two other Flights – formed on 31 March 1932 – were joined by Harts of 57 Squadron on 5 September. Both squadrons became the core of the station's bomber force to the outbreak of war. Abingdon's availability brought space at Upper Heyford for 40 Squadron, repositioned there in October 1932.

Re-equipment long overdue, 99 Squadron soldiered on with its antiques until 14 November 1933, when it took on charge the RAF's first two Handley Page Heyfords. In sombre green, the Heyford had

*Hart day bombers of 18 Squadron over-flying 'A' Type sheds.*

*Hawker Hind light bombers of 57 Squadron heading for a fly-by at Hendon.*

a distinctive shape, making clambering aboard a memorable experience. Curious indeed seemed the attachment of the fuselage to the underside of the upper main-plane, causing fuselage entry to be made by means of a steep, narrow ladder leading from the lower mainplane on to which one had first to scramble. This peculiar arrangement allowed a dustbin turret to be fitted under the narrow-cross-section fuselage. Strange, too, were the very narrow tyres set within huge spats. After a crawl along the fuselage one emerged into an open cockpit high above the ground in this 'poor man's Stirling'. A few wriggles more and one was situated in splendid isolation in the nose-gunner's position, albeit being able to turn for company to the pilot close behind. A year to the day from receipt of its first Heyfords, 99 Squadron commenced moving to Mildenhall, which made space for Harts of 33 Squadron from nearby Bicester. A year later they hurried to Egypt, answering the Italian attack on Abyssinia.

Harts of 18 Squadron temporarily vacated Upper Heyford in January 1936 and were replaced by two lodger squadrons of Vickers Virginias, nudged out of Worthy Down, Nos 58 and 215, awaiting Driffield's opening in September 1936. No 18 Squadron then returned, Hind-equipped. Bomber Command had then formed, and Upper Heyford was in No 1 (Bomber) Group.

New squadrons came from Flights, 218 Squadron from 57 Squadron on 16 March 1936, the parent squadron re-equipping with Hinds in May. Then 57 Squadron surrendered its 'B' Flight on 4 January 1937 to become 108 Squadron, which left for Farnborough the following month. 'B' Flight of 57 Squadron became 226 Squadron and moved to Harwell in April 1937. Another Hind squadron, formed here on 18 May 1937, was No 113, which went to Grantham in August.

An event receiving wide publicity was the formation here in January 1938 of the Long Range Development Flight. Five much-modified Wellesleys, able to carry 1,290 gallons of fuel for their special Pegasus engines, joined the LRDF, commanded by Wg Cdr O R Gayford of Fairey Long-Range Monoplane fame. A 32-hour flight was made in July 1938 from Cranwell to the Persian Gulf. In November two aircraft made a spectacular record flight from Egypt to Australia non-stop in 48 hours, an achievement unbeaten for eight years.

Upper Heyford's bomber squadrons were ever-changing. Hinds of 218 Squadron left in April 1938, making way for the monoplane era. That began with Bristol Blenheim Is, and soon the station became one of their most prominent bases as 57 Squadron rapidly worked up with the wonder-bomber in March-April 1938, with 34 Squadron joining the sport in July, having vacated Lympne and left behind its Hinds.

In May 1938 No 18 Squadron received Blenheims, the three squadrons during the Munich Crisis waiting to become part of the 2nd Echelon, AASF, France, before the crisis passed. January 1939 found Upper Heyford placed in 2 Group, which, in February, shifted 34 Squadron to newly opened Watton. Upper Heyford faced the coming storm with some stability, as the base for two front-line Blenheim I squadrons, whose role within 70 Wing, Air Component, BEF, was to provide aerial reconnaissance for the British Army in France.

At the commencement of hostilities, Upper Heyford and its satellite field at Brackley (later known as Croughton) were immediately placed in No 6 Group and into a training role. Both Blenheim squadrons left for France as planned, 18 Squadron going to Amy and 57 to Roye, both on 24 September 1939.

On the day previous to that move, SHQ Finningley arrived, bringing two Hampden squadrons, Nos 7 and 76, to become the 5 Group Pool. No 76 was half Hampden-equipped, its other Flight using Anson navigation trainers. This training establishment ran until 22 April 1940, when SHQ closed and

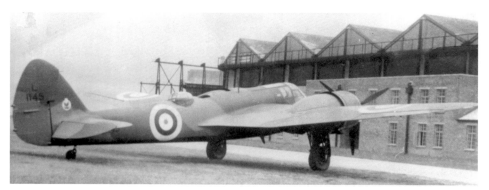

*Blenheim 1 L1145 of 57 Squadron in front of an 'A' Type hangar at Upper Heyford in the summer of 1938.*

5 Group Pool became 16 OTU within 6 Group. Steady expansion followed and, on 7 May 1940, the OTU received the first of nineteen troublesome Handley Page Herefords. A month later more Ansons arrived. On 13 August 1940 a spectacular crash occurred at midday. Two Hampdens, L4138 and P4339, barely airborne, collided in a gruesome smash when taking off from different grass runways.

On 25 and 27 July 1940, handfuls of Hampdens set off on leaflet-dropping sorties, carrying out the station's first offensive action. An operations order of 8 August called for up to eight such sorties weekly, in response to which Hampdens of 16 OTU delivered free reading matter to Caen, Rennes and Brest. Croughton landing ground began to be much used in July, accommodation being at Rastwick and Rectory Farms for groundcrews controlling the busy night procedures and equipment. More leaflet drops took place in October, then operations ceased.

Throughout 1941 Upper Heyford housed 16 OTU, training up to twenty-four one-pilot crews for Hampdens each month. The OTU was using widely spread accommodation, in Aynho Park, Fritwell Manor, Fucott House, Middleton, sundry stone cottages and in Nissen huts, which decorated the area around the station.

In April 1941, due to their poor serviceability record, the Herefords were posted away, to 5 B&GS. The established strength at that time was forty-nine Hampden/Herefords, thirteen Ansons, twelve Oxfords and sundry light aircraft.

Barford St John replaced Croughton as satellite in 1942, use also being made of Hinton-in-the-Hedges. Another advance came in April 1942, for by the end of that month 16 OTU had received twenty-three Wellington Ics; only the course under way flew Hampdens. The first Wellington joined

*Wellesley L2681 of the LRDF Upper Heyford.*

the OTU on 25 April, the first crew output being made on 5 June 1942. May had found 16 OTU half equipped with Wellingtons, sufficiently so for fourteen of them, and sixteen Hampdens, to take part in the Cologne 1,000-bomber raid from here.

For the Essen attack of 1/2 June, thirty crews operated, again in a mixed force. Hampden P2080 was attacked by a German fighter, in exchange for which the crew claimed to shoot down another. Twenty-three crews operated Wellington Ics in June's Bremen 1,000-bomber operation. More bombing raids were flown in July, August and September.

By March 1943 the OTU's strength had risen to fifty-seven Wellington Is, six Ansons, a Defiant and two Lysander target-towers. Alongside, enveloped in great secrecy, was 1473 Flight, whose origin lay within the RCM Flight of 109 Squadron. That formation had broken away on 10 July 1942 from the organisation that achieved fame as a result of its so-called 'beam-bending' activities in 1940. It was now an independent unit under Flt Lt C F Grant DFC, controlled by 80 Wing and administered by 92 Group. Using Ansons and Wellingtons, it monitored German radio beam activity while participating in *Window* trials for Bomber Command before moving to Finmere in 1943. No 1505 BAT Flight's Oxfords, also within 92 Group, provided beam approach practice from Upper Heyford between 17 December 1942 and its disbandment on 20 February 1943. Wellington IIIs came into use at 16 OTU in September 1942, their improved performance causing 92 Group to issue an order in November that four *Nickelling* sorties be flown per fortnight. From Upper Heyford leaflet-dropping was resumed on 27/28 November with drops in the Nantes area. In between *Bullseyes*, propaganda leaflets were dropped on Paris on 20/21 December 1942.

Such activities continued throughout 1943, in the autumn of which year Wellington Xs joined the OTU in increasing proportion. In 1944, too, the pattern of activity was all but the same. At the end of December, No 1655 Mosquito Training Unit arrived with an assortment of Mosquito bombers and trainers, together with a selection of Oxfords. The old 16 OTU disbanded, its title at once being conferred upon the new arrival, which also used Barford St John. For training bomber crews for 8 Group, 16 OTU's nominal strength in March 1945 stood at forty-five Mosquitoes of Mks 3, 4, 6, 20 and 25, supported, for navigation and light bombing training, by as many as thirty-two Oxfords, all under 92 Group control and shared in positioning with Barford.

The immediate post-war days witnessed a reduction in strength before 16 OTU moved to Cottesmore in March 1946. In its place came Dakotas of the Parachute Training School. Also brought here from Ringway was the famous parachute training tower, which moved to Abingdon in 1950.

The reason for that move was that the Americans were coming in June 1950. Ever since their 1948 return to Britain they had been asking to use four bomber bases in the East Midlands, that situation placing them behind fighter bases and the planned Eastern Missile Belt. After prolonged, heated discussions, mutual agreement was that four bases 'west of London' would be developed at minimum cost and with ample US financial input. Two would be Permanent RAF stations – which could only be Brize Norton and Upper Heyford. One of the temporary stations would be Fairford,

*F-100 0-53614 of the 20th TFW in a modified 'A' Type hangar.*

*B-47B 17057 during a 1956 TDY call at Upper Heyford.*

the fourth either Blakehill Farm or Mount Farm. Eventually a 'new' airfield was built on Greenham Common, much to the alarm of local residents. The minimum take-off run for a fully laden B-29 being 8,000 feet, the main runway at each new base was, for safety, to be 9,000 feet, with overruns allowing for jet bombers increasing it to 10,000 feet. A glide path of 1,100 feet was prescribed, and because of the size of US bombers the taxi tracks needed to be 100 feet wide. Runways, taxiways and dispersal pans would be made at least 2 feet thick.

Four Upper Heyford Barrack Blocks and the Airmen's Mess provided basic facilities for a US Engineer Aviation Battalion, a Maintenance Company, Ordnance Company, Engineer Depot Company and the Base Support Company. These units, soon to increase numerically, came to support the expanding SAC force moving into East Anglia and the Midlands. Barford St John remained Upper Heyford's satellite, like Middleton Stoney. Weston-on-the-Green, under Upper Heyford's control since 1946, became the home of the Air Position Plotting Unit on 9 August 1950. At the end of April 1951 it was transferred to No 62 (Signals) Group, RAF. On 15 May 1951, control of Upper Heyford passed completely to the USAF, formal handover from No 3 (Bomber) Group taking place on 1 June, when the 7509th Air Base Squadron took control.

With Upper Heyford's main runway only 6,000 feet long and 150 feet wide, the Americans' first task was to lengthen it to provide 9,592-foot runs for take-off and landing, and to lay an asphalt surface on the concrete. Improved operating facilities were added, including dispersal pans, and better personnel accommodation was built, those items seeing repeated upgrading almost to closure of the base.

The 7509th now being ready to support operational units, the Boeing KB-29Ps of the 93rd Air Refuelling Squadron began moving from Castle AFB on 1 December 1951. Like so many others they came for a ninety-day Temporary Duty (TDY) stay. Return home usually took place during the last few days of the third month, replacements arriving at the start of the following month. On 10 January 1952 the 3918th Air Base Group took over the running of the base, where the RAF's PTS retained lodger unit status.

American-built specialised facilities included a trio of nose docks for large aircraft and a new large maintenance building. Among various units at Upper Heyford in 1952 was the 98th Smoke Generating Company, able to provide a smoke screen in the event of air attack. Further airfield defence was soon provided by light anti-aircraft guns of the 4th AA Artillery Battalion.

In 1952 Upper Heyford hosted KB-29Ps of the 97th (February-May), 509th (June-August) and 2nd (September-November) Air Refuelling Squadrons, as well as KB-29Ms, whose role was in-flight hose and drogue refuelling of B-29s of the 301st ARS between December 1952 and February 1953. Sundry sections of KB-29s, B-50Ds and RB-50s made short stays before, in June 1953, the first B-47B Stratojets in Britain began using Heyford for flying training.

Soon, many B-47s and RB-47s would tarry or pass through before B-47Bs of the 22nd BW became the first to reside, from December 1953 to March 1954. On 5 February 1954 a B-47 was involved in a spectacular crash in Stoke Wood, 1½ miles from the end of the main runway, and not long afterwards the 303rd BW B-47Es were among the first based in Britain.

Mid-1954 witnessed the first landings at Upper Heyford by gigantic RB-36F and 'H reconnaissance aircraft of the 5th SRW main temporary base, Fairford. Although B-36s also visited, principally it was nuclear-armed Stratojets that made Upper Heyford their home. In September and October 1954 RB-47Es of the 26th SRW (3, 4 and 10 SR Squadrons) from Lockbourne AFB, Ohio,

*F-111E 68-073 of the 20th FW.*

were in residence, and between March and June 1955 three squadrons of B-47Es of the 310th BW from Barksdale AFB, La, were deployed here. B/RB-47s continued to come until 31 March 1965 when SAC occupancy ended, although Detachment 1, 98th SRW, arrived from Brize Norton in April 1965 to support RB-47H activity until 1967, moving to Mildenhall in December 1970.

On 8 February 1965 the running of Upper Heyford passed to the 7514th Combat Support Group (re-designated 7515th Tactical Group on 1 June 1965), which maintained it as a USAFE Dispersed Operating Base (DOB). That status terminated on 1 September 1966 with the arrival from Laon AB of RF-101 Voodoos flown by Nos 17 and 18 TRS, 66th Tactical Reconnaissance Wing, coming from France under Plan FRELOC. Upper Heyford now became a Main Operating Base. The 17th TRS started RF-4C conversion in February 1969 and was transferred on 12 January 1970 to the 26 TRW Zweibrucken because the 66th TRW was to be inactivated on 1 April 1970. Upper Heyford retained the other Voodoos until then, when they moved Stateside.

On 1 April 1970 the 20th Tactical Fighter Wing, flying F-100D/F Super Sabres, vacated Wethersfield, too small for its future equipment. The assignment brought a complete change of mission and very extensive modifications to its new base, making it the largest base of its kind in Europe.

On 12 September 1970 dramatic was the change when the first two F-111E swing-wing bombers touched down at Upper Heyford, the 20th reaching full complement on 29 July 1971. By September 1980 the F-111Es had flown more than 55,000 training sorties.

On 1 January 1984 a new squadron was activated under 20th TFW control, the 42nd Electronic Countermeasures Squadron. Its equipment was the EF-111A Raven ECM aircraft, the first of which arrived on 3 February 1984. On 1 July 1984 the 66th Electronic Countermeasures Wing was activated in the 17th AF at Sembach AB, and on 1 June 1985 the 42nd was placed under its control while remaining at Upper Heyford.

This was a time of great change and extensive building at Upper Heyford. To the long line of 'buzz-words' beloved by militants was added the magic word 'hardened'. Everything needed to be 'hardened', including, it seemed, the cookies that came with the coffee, sometimes with dunking resistance built in! Most prominent everywhere were concrete blocks, anti-terrorist spiked roller devices to deter the ramming of gates, increased or 'hardened' security devices and well-armed people. Most obvious were the 'HASs', the Hardened Aircraft Shelters. Upper Heyford eventually had more than 50, each intended to house one F-111. In its snug, warm home, the bomber – which curiously was called a fighter – could rest fully fuelled and armed awaiting an engine start to help its safer, quicker getaway. The steel-ringed shelters, concrete-cocooned, usually acquired a dirty brown external coat, while many buildings were given the 'farmhouse' look by being liberally dosed with cream and brown paint to give the appearance of a farm or civilian warehouse. In reality, when seen from above they looked quite nice, and very eye-catching. The serious thinking behind all this was that because a first strike nuclear intent by both sides was clearly impossible, fighting would be conventional. The shelters would have provided some protection to aircraft, but after wholesale destruction of Iraqi shelters in 1991 they came to be seen as giving limited dispersed protection, mainly providing cover from the elements.

*F-111E 003/UH at Upper Heyford in July 1975.*

On 14/15 April 1986 a few Upper Heyford aircraft played a part in operation *El Dorado Canyon*, the raid on Tripoli. Acting as airborne spares, 20th TFW F-111Es made a rapid take-off and flew around, but were not needed, unlike four of the five airborne EF-111As, which variously participated.

December 1987 saw USAFE's Project *Power Hunter* intelligence network come into play at Upper Heyford, then, during Exercise *Red Flag* in January-February 1988, the Wing was first to test *Durandel* 'runway buster' bombs.

Through 1988 the 20th TFW trained intensively. Between March and May 1989 its three squadrons used Incirlik AB, Turkey, for a Weapons Training Deployment using the Konya Range. Re-organisation of the many ground formations within the Wing was introduced by USAFE on 1 June 1989.

The early months of 1990 saw the Wing participating in major exercises, the 79th TFS taking part in *Cold Fire 90* (11-21 January), then the UK air defence exercise *Mallet Blow* held from 26 to 29 March. From 2 to 20 March the whole Wing had taken part in *Red Flag*, then in April was involved in a Weapons System Evaluation Programme, *Cold Hammer 90-7*, held at Mountain Home AFB, Idaho. The 77th TFS was at Aviano AB, Italy, for the NATO Southern Region exercise *Dragon Hammer 90* between 2 and 16 May, and the 79th took part in a Baltic maritime exercise, *Brazen Deed*, on 12 June. Wing strength was enhanced when on 1 July 1990 the 870th Contingency Hospital at RAF Little Rissington came under its control, the 2168th Communications Squadron, RAF Croughton, doing likewise on 25 September. By then Iraq had invaded Kuwait.

The 20th TFW had a detachment of F-111Es at Incirlik, Turkey, at the time that it became part of the 7440th Wing (Provisional), which embraced all USAF formations at the base. The F-111E force was increased to 23 and all were alerted for operation *Proven Force*, prevention of an Iraqi incursion into Turkey.

The build-up to *Desert Storm* saw EF-111As of the 42nd ECS move into Taif, Saudi Arabia, the squadron being re-assigned to the 20th on 25 January 1991. By then the 42nd had carved itself a special niche in history, for on 16 January, the first night of *Desert Storm*, an Iraqi Mirage, outmanoeuvred by a terrain-following EF-111, was caused to crash. By the end of the fighting the EF-111s had flown 252 sorties totalling 740 hours from Turkey, and another 219 sorties during 1,155 hours by day or night from Saudi Arabia.

Operations were also launched, early on 17 January 1991, from Incirlik. Initially the F-111Es operated in darkness at around 200 feet until suppression of ground defences allowed them to generally operate at around 20,000 feet. Among their targets were airfields, power stations, petroleum refineries and suspected nuclear development sites, all attacked mainly with 500lb and 2,000lb standard weapons supplemented by CBU-87/89 cluster bombs. The F-111E force managed 1,798 sorties delivering 4,714 tons of munitions without loss. Meanwhile, Upper Heyford had been preparing to receive troop casualties for onward movement to Croughton and Little Rissington, being made ready to cope with 2,000. In supporting the combat operations, 1,408 transient aircraft passed through Upper Heyford between January and June 1991.

Most of the F-111Es returned to Upper Heyford on 9 March 1991. On 6 April the 42nd ECS redeployed to Incirlik for operation *Provide Comfort*. Next month its Taif element returned to Upper Heyford.

Barely were the 20th crews home when they were needed for exercise NATO *Central Enterprise 91* held between 10 and 14 June. From 10 to 12 September the UK home defence exercise Elder Joust occupied them, and in October *Gunsmoke 91,* held at Nellis AFB. The 42nd ECS detachment had returned from Incirlik on 14 August, before the squadron rotated to Taif on 30 September. Next day the Wing was re-classified as the 20th Fighter Wing, the three squadrons (55, 77 and 79) being re-named Fighter Squadrons. Upgraded to Group status on 1 November, the 2130th at Croughton remained under the 20th's control.

Between 27 February and 13 April 1992 the 20th undertook training in the use of the GBU-12 LB laser-guided bomb during *Green Flag 92.* In May the 55th FS was detached to Aviano AB for *Dragon Hammer 92* before the Wing played a part in exercise *Excalibur.* By then its future was bleak.

Post-Cold War policy decreed that F-111s would all be withdrawn from Britain by the end of 1993 and that Upper Heyford would be closed in 1994. Accordingly, the last EF-111 return from Incirlik took place in June, and on 10 July the 42nd ECS was inactivated. The last EF-111 left Upper Heyford on 7 August 1992, although late that year several visited Lakenheath. On 23 April 1993 the 79 FS was inactivated, its last aircraft departing on 10 May. After taking part in *Excalibur 93* in June, the 77th FS was inactivated on 9 July, its last F-111 leaving in August. That left only the 55th, six of whose aircraft took part in *Incirlik Dynamic Guard* between 20 September and 8 October. The 55th was inactivated on 15 October. The last three F-111Es ceremoniously departed Upper Heyford on 7 December 1993, the runway 'officially closing' on 15 December 1993. Base closure was enacted on 15 September 1994, an official ceremony taking place on the 30th. A barely interrupted sight in Britain's skies since 1943, the 20th still maintains a presence here, for on 19 October 1993 F-111E 68-120 made its way to the Imperial War Museum, Duxford. As for the others, most were soon dispensed with, leaving 68-055 displayed at Robbins AFB, Georgia, and probably the best known of them, 68-020 *The Chief,* exhibited at Hill AFB, Utah.

With the Americans gone, there came the really big question: what should (and not what could) be done with Upper Heyford? For any land-cum-property developer the former base offered enormous potential income. Heyford Park, a settlement of 5,000 houses accommodating perhaps 18,000 inhabitants with questionable employment prospects, was mooted just as the last tyre left Heyford's runway. The local council wisely suggested that 1,000 houses were enough. From the other usual lobby came grandiose suggestions for a magnificent sports facility. Who would pay for development and upkeep seems to have been unclear, and the Government opted for such a construction at Sheffield. As with Bentwaters, the site began to waste away except for its runway, upon which thousands of unsold cars found a home, soon filling the hardstandings. The bulk of the technical site fell as usual to light industry, general trading and transport concerns. Like getting out of Aden, Afghanistan and certainly Iraq, nobody seems to have thought very intelligently how everyone can sensibly benefit when the military eventually waves 'goodbye'.

**Major features:**
*Runways:* 217 6,000ft x 150ft, 264 5,100ft x 150ft, 311 4,650ft x 150ft. *Hangars:* Six Type A. *Hardstandings:* 23 frying-pan type. *Accommodation:* RAF officers 202, SNCOs 62, ORs 1,184; WAAF officers 12, SNCOs 9, ORs 379.

*USAF period:* Runway 09/27, nominal length 9,592ft LCG II with dual overrun 120ft. Dual BAK-12 arrester gear. In addition to HASs, two Victor Alert large concrete areas were added in the mid-1980s' major buildings investment programme. Runways had adjacent warm-up pads.

## WARWICK, Warwickshire

*52°16N/01°36W 160ft asl; SP270635. 1¹/₂ miles SW of Warwick*

Just beyond the western edge of Warwick was a large, picturesque meadow which, in wartime, was requisitioned to become RAF Warwick, a Relief Landing Ground opened in December 1941 and placed in 23 Group during January 1942. Initially, Church Lawford's Oxfords and Tutors used it for instructor training.

On 1 October 1942 the training emphasis at Church Lawford changed. By the end of that month the unit there had become 18 (P)AFU, which at first retained the Tutors and Oxfords, but which soon equipped with only the latter, together with some Ansons. Warwick retained its status as an RLG for Church Lawford until the end of May 1945, when it was placed on care and maintenance.

Apart from the grass landing ground there was never much to be seen. Two Blister hangars (Over Type) were by the road, one remaining long after the war. Two more were in the south-west corner, together with six Laing huts (1032/41) for personnel. Two Nissen huts contained stores, and there was a fuel compound and water supply.

**Main features:**
*Runways:* NE/SW 3,150ft, N/S 3,150ft, both grass. *Hangars:* four 69ft Blister. *Accommodation:* RAF only – officers 2, SNCOs 4, ORs 88.

## WATCHFIELD, Berkshire

*51°37N/01°39E 331ft asl; SU240900. 7 miles NE of Swindon, by the A420*

Watchfield was the centre for beam and blind approach training, thereby making a major contribution to the safe return in darkness and bad weather of very many bomber crews.

Things were different at its birth in mid-1940, for the circuit was full of Tiger Moths brought in on 20 July by 3 EFTS, which hastened from Hamble – by Southampton Water – because of their vulnerability to enemy interference. By the end of July the EFTS was also using Kelmscot RLG because No 4 Air Observer and Navigator School had also moved in on 20 July, from Ansty, bringing its Ansons, which were supplemented by more. They belonged to 11 AONS, which was also quitting Hamble. Watchfield was certainly over-populated, and more occupants were to follow.

The intention had been for No 1 Blind Approach School to form at Watchfield on 2 August 1940, but lack of suitable equipment delayed that. Instead, the School commenced activity here on 28 October 1940 operated by AST, a subsidiary of Hawker Siddeley, which ran the other schools here. Four Ansons, together with two in reserve, joined the unit, as well as three wheel-type link trainers, by which time the station had become the most populated of its type in Europe. It was also destined to have a major role, training pilots in blind approach techniques.

Blind approach training had commenced at Mildenhall in March 1939 using Anson L9155 fitted with blind approach receivers (R1124/1125). Commanding the small training unit was Sqn Ldr R S Blucke, AFC. In July 1939 the Anson was allotted to 24 Squadron, Hendon, but VHF blind approach equipment was in full use at Boscombe Down, so the precious Anson moved there on 1 September 1939. A few days later it was positioned at CFS Upavon pending establishment of a Blind Approach Training Development Unit at Boscombe Down to where the Anson was transferred on 22 September 1939. More Ansons were then fitted with blind approach equipment for training. By May 1940. the twentieth short course was running.

On 6 June 1940 orders were received from 23 Group to immediately close the school. Wg Cdr Blucke was posted to HQ Bomber Command, and on 13 June 1940 the unit re-opened for totally different purposes. Establishment was increased to eight Ansons and three Whitleys for a new task, the investigation of very unusual enemy radio signals code-named 'Head-ache'. Operational control was vested in Fighter Command, the unit then holding only five Ansons with quickly installed special equipment. Pilots from the BATDU were posted to the new unit, including Flt Lt H E Bufton of 214 Squadron, who took command. He was subsequently to play a major part in

*Watchfield's specially modified control tower. (Geoff Phillips)*

developing and operating Bomber Command's radio bombing aids. But now, two days after arriving, he flew Anson N9945 to Wyton to commence intensive investigation of Germany's apparent extensive use of radio beams for navigation purposes and target marking.

By October 1940, after much success in discovering the German Gerat system, the unit's role had so much altered that, on the 14th, its name changed from Blind Approach Training and Development Unit to Wireless Intelligence Development Unit, a title in colloquial use since 30 September 1940. Meanwhile the need for specialised blind approach training was fast increasing as the hours of darkness increased and inclement weather arrived. Accordingly, two Ansons from the WIDU, R9828 and R9830, both carrying blind approach equipment, arrived at Watchfield on 20 October. Next day R9829 and R9837 joined them, completing the initial establishment for a new Blind Approach School. Secrecy was easy to achieve for the circuit was already full of navigation training Ansons. On the ground No 8 MU utilised some space for dispersed storage between September and November 1940.

Ground equipment for blind approach training was in short supply. The main beacon, as well as the inner and outer marker beacons, were of a no longer obtainable type made by Philips in Holland, and were more advanced than the British standard type. The main beacon had a system of phased aerials that reduced the twilight zone, and only at Amsterdam's Schiphol Airport had such advanced equipment been installed. Watchfield's quota had been shipped to Britain before the Netherlands fell. All the BAS Ansons at Watchfield had receivers working that system already used at Boscombe Down.

Six pupils arrived on 28 October 1940 to commence the first two-week course, involving twelve hours to a schedule prescribed by Wg Cdr Blucke. Training commenced with time on the Link Trainer, during which the trainees listened to blind approach notes on headphones and had the figure-of-eight procedures demonstrated.

From the start it was clear that there would be considerable training problems at this mixed-purpose busy station. Tiger Moths of the EFTS were ever active on circuit while Ansons set off on cross-country journeys. Flying control, from the tower, was vested in a Blind Approach School instructor, who saw to it that when an aircraft was on blind approach a red light on the tower was switched on, indicating to EFTS pilots that the incoming aircraft was at 100 feet in the direction of the main beam, irrespective of the wind direction. All aircraft on the ground had to remain stationary when the red light was on.

During the winter, training proceeded satisfactorily, despite a visit by the enemy on the evening of 27 February 1941. Incendiaries fell, together with a stick of five HEs along the south-east boundary of the airfield. Even less successful was a display of the blind approach equipment when the Inspector General, Air Marshal Sir W Mitchell, arrived in his Cygnet on 19 May 1941. He was about to watch the demonstration when a resistance burned out in the main beacon, putting everything out of use!

By mid-1941 installation of blind approach equipment had been extended to units in other parts of Britain. Equipment reliability and its accurate calibration needed to be regularly checked, so, in May 1941, the Blind Approach Calibration Flight formed at Watchfield, equipped with three Oxfords, the first aircraft of that type to be used for any blind approach duties. Over the next month, three more – V3888, V4026 and V4027 – arrived. Any slight increase at Watchfield brought problems, so it is hardly surprising that No 11 AONS closed on 19 July 1941 and No 4 on 30 August 1941.

Mid-August brought discussions as to the means of considerably increasing the output of trainees. Existing programmes called for eighteen hours each day, twenty-four hours seeming impossible to maintain because of enemy activity, unserviceability, etc. A scheme to train 1,100 pilots a year was to be put in hand, which meant an increase in aircraft establishment from six to fifteen, and of instructors from seven to sixteen. On 1 September 1941, as an interim measure, the establishment changed to twelve Ansons, an event soon overtaken. Blind approach training would now be part of the training syllabus at all SFTSs, where the standard aircraft type was the Airspeed Oxford. To achieve standardisation the decision was taken on 16 September 1941 to re-equip No 1 Blind Approach School with Oxfords. That also helped to dispel a generally held but erroneous notion that blind approach training could only be effectively carried out using Ansons because the Oxford was less well mannered. On the following day another three Oxfords (V4051, V4052 and V5054) arrived at Watchfield.

Another major change was instigated at Watchfield on 26 September 1941 when night-flying throughout the hours of darkness commenced, which depended upon a Cranwell-type flare path, power for which was supplied from a floodlight beacon. Flying took place every night in order to meet a new training programme, pupils now arriving at a rate of twelve every four days for the twelve-day course. In the twelve months ending 28 October 1941, 405 pupils were trained, 60 per cent for night-fighter duties. An enviable flight safety record had been achieved for there had been only one forced landing caused by a pupil knocking off some switches when changing to another seat – no other accident had marred the School's record. Additionally, pilots of the School had, since 13 March 1941, been training wireless mechanics. Introduction of the twenty-four-hour scheme, on 8 September 1941, improved the pupil output rate. In October 1941 the unit was re-designated No 1 Beam Approach School.

From Brasenose College, Oxford, the Regional Control School of Bomber Command moved into Watchfield on 15 December 1941, and became the School of Flying Control. Lecture rooms for the School became available after the departure of No 3 EFTS to Shellingford on 18 December 1941.

Trials of the Bell and Bobbitt trailing wire device, intended to inform the pilot accurately of his height, were conducted in January 1942. The first serious accident, involving Oxford AT775 flown by Sgt C M Rustron, occurred on 2 February. January had ended with snow and very cold weather, which extended into February. As the Oxford was approaching, ice accretion on the wings seriously increased, and snow obliterated the pupil's vision, forced him to make a very difficult blind landing. A stall developed, the port wing dropped and the aircraft side-slipped in from about 15 feet.

Four Dominies were allocated to BAS on 9 February 1942 to give SFC pupils air experience. On the following day came the first attempt to locate a suitable satellite airfield site for blind approach training. Initially a landing ground at Bushy Barn, Pusey, near Burford, was inspected, but it was quite unsuitable.

By mid-March 1942 another Flight was needed in order to train 1,450 pilots a year from April. Trials on 22 April 1942 proved that it was possible for an Oxford to be landed every five minutes if a revised holding pattern was introduced. By that time three SFC Dominies – X7491, X7492 and X7493 – had arrived, and in May Oxfords from Docking's BAT Flight were posted in to equip the new, additional Flight. To simulate night in daylight, synthetic night was tried using Oxford V4051, and on 16 May 1942 the aircraft was flying with blue window panels, its pilot wearing special goggles.

By July 1942 the association with the SFC had led to a new RAF trade, airfield controller. Things moved fast, and thirty-four trainees for the first two-week course arrived on 18 July. A few days previously, Oxfords of the Calibration Flight had moved to Bicester, easing pressure on Watchfield. By November use of existing beam approach equipment at Abingdon, Boscombe Down, Harwell and Little Rissington was being made, as well as equipment at Watchfield's new satellite, Kelmscot, which came into use on 17 October 1942. Because the other beams were available, each course now lasted a week. On 15 November 1942 the School of Flying Control moved and a detachment became the Airfield Controllers' School.

Sudden changes in weather posed major problems in the busy area, as on 6 January 1943 when general weather deterioration came quickly. One pupil landed safely at Kelmscot, which meant mounting an overnight guard on the aircraft. Officer Hutchison was over Otmoor on V4049 when ordered back to base. His homing equipment failed and over Watchfield he discovered that the undercarriage would not lock in the 'down' position. The aircraft had to be abandoned.

Activity was drastically reduced for six weeks early in 1943 while contact lighting was installed. A very wet airfield surface made laying a flare path impracticable, although some was possible at RLG Kelmscot.

Operational aircraft as well as others needed to be kept well away from busy Watchfield, except in emergencies. One such came on the night of 10 June 1943 when, at 0143, the Duty Flying Controller heard a large, low-flying aircraft. There was soon an explosion, then flames poured from wreckage a mile north-west of the airfield, marking where a Lancaster from Lindholme had crashed, killing the crew of seven.

*Anson NK273 of*
*No 1 BAS.*
*(Geoff Phillips)*

By July 1943 a second RLG, Wanborough, was in regular use, mainly for training airfield controllers. Up to 110 pupils at a time trained there, each course spending half its training period at this RLG. Kelmscot RLG was also busily used, and a few personnel manned Watchfield's Q-site at Kingston Warren.

It was Flt Lt James in Oxford 'H' who, at 1725 on 22 October 1943, gave the station warning of startling, impending disaster. Using his R/T he reported something akin to a whirlwind approaching the airfield from the south. Moments later it was possible to see from the tower a mass of nimbostratus cloud coming from the direction of Shrivenham, with a dark funnel hanging from it. Two Oxfords about to take off were ordered to taxi quickly back to the tower. The violent disturbance passed across the airfield towards the NNE, snatching a metal sheet off a hangar and depositing it in the middle of the landing ground. Oxford 'S' was lifted ten feet into the air, swung around, then dropped. Its undercarriage collapsed and the port wing crumpled. Two others were damaged before the intense storm died suddenly away.

At the end of 1943 the Beam Approach Technical Training School moved to No 1 RS Cranwell. The training of airfield controllers was transferred from Wanborough and Kelmscot to Watchfield and Kelmscot on 14 November 1943, allowing 3 GTS to place one Flight at Wanborough because Stoke Orchard was temporarily out of use. Wanborough was vacated by the School of Airfield Controllers on 2 December 1944 due to the poor state of personnel accommodation there, although the School still used the site.

March 1944 saw the area around Watchfield highly congested by an influx of transport aircraft and gliders taking part in increasingly extensive exercises. With control becoming ever more important, a master control for the whole area was established at South Cerney. Although Kelmscot remained the RLG for Watchfield into 1947, during 1944 it was used a number of times for parachute troop training exercises on a grand scale. Not until after D-Day was the BAS again able to use the RLG.

Watchfield briefly had an operational role that summer when a detachment of Ansons from the Air Navigation & Bombing School operated to assist 46 Group Dakota activities between the UK and France. It was here between 9 May and 11 July 1944 and joined the Sparrow (Ambulance) Flight of 271 Squadron, 46 Group, which was here between 2 June and 2 August 1944. Their role was to transport battle casualties from near the front line to reception hospitals in the UK. Assisting these activities was No 92 (Forward) Staging Post, Watchfield-based from 25 May to 13 July 1944.

A new BAT syllabus was introduced on 30 August 1944. Full cross-country in cloud would now to be practised at (P)AFUs by pilots undergoing BA training. During 1944 the course undertaken by a pilot at No 1 BAS consisted of three 'unhooded' introductory exercises: familiarisation and orientation, a figure-of-eight flown at constant height, and a normal approach procedure. During the 'hooded' training he again flew the 'eight' at constant height, the normal and back beam approach, visual and oral signal approaches, QDM homing procedures, homing without QDM, cross-country and, finally, engaged in night-flying. In addition to 1 BAS, several beam approach and radio aids training flights used Watchfield: No 1500 in 1943; No 1547, which formed on 1 June 1945 and was here into 1946; and No 1557, also formed on 1 June 1945 with double the normal eight Oxfords of these Flights, and transferred to 6 (P)AFU on 26 June 1945.

No 1 BAS disbanded on 1 January 1947, having latterly used a few Harvards as well as Oxfords. In its final months it trained pilots with the aid of two beams operated at Watchfield and Kelmscot, and used other beam systems within a radius of 100 miles. During six years of existence, 1 BAS aircraft had flown little short of 100,000 hours, some 8,500 pupils passed through the School, and only one accident involving injury had come about during QBI conditions – an amazing record, for sure, and a great contribution to victory.

Post-war Watchfield became the centre for training airfield and flying control personnel. The School of Air Traffic Control formed out of the School of Flying Control on 1 November 1946 and remained active, using Ansons, until January 1950, disbanding on 10 February 1950 when it became part of the Central Navigation and Control School. In the 1950s a new use was found for Watchfield – parachute training, and as a practice dropping zone for heavy loads from RAF transports – for which purpose it has long remained in use.

**Main features:**
*Runways:* NW/SE 4,200ft, NNW/SSE 5,100ft, grass. *Hangars:* five Bellman, five Over Blister. *Hardstandings:* eleven parking spaces on five roads leading to main hangars. *Accommodation:* RAF only – officers 130, SNCOs 168, ORs 391.

## WELLESBOURNE MOUNTFORD, Warwickshire

*52°11N/01°36 154ft as; SP265548. 5 miles E of Stratford-upon-Avon, off the B4086*

"Wellesbourne Mountford ? I've heard of it," I said. "It's near Stratford," I was told.
It was somewhere I came to know so well I would never forget it.

Manston had afforded what amounted to flexi-hours with ample lie-ins, late breakfasts and long lunch hours in which to enjoy the exotic visitors, which one day included a fly-past comprising a French AAC1 (Ju 52 in Gallic disguise), a French Air Force Baltimore and an Aeronavale Barracuda. Things passing have rarely bettered that.

Wellesbourne, by contrast, had little connection with aeroplanes. One needed to tread cautiously wearing ever-clean shoes – always. Even the 'station master' seemed uneasy when he passed the Main Gate where a particularly ferocious 'discip' couple resided. One forever displayed his over-large whitish teeth, and both had cultivated splendid moustaches that forever twitched. Even on the hottest summer's day, the senior one, the SWO, paraded his leather gloves. His suitably entitled swagger stick, which he clearly regarded as his magic wand, was eagerly supported by the rest of his personage as he watched and waited eagle-eyed for the unwary toppling from his brand of perfection. With fearsome delight he would swoop upon a hapless 'little man'. I once watched as he forced a sergeant to cross a COs parade 'at the double'. It was whispered that the camp barber's shop was his on account of the continuous trade with which he provided it. With an ugly grimace he bellowed the war cry, "Am I 'urtin' you, laddie? I'm treadin' on yer 'air!" If only I had been brave enough to retort, "No." Mind you, in an emergency one would have been very grateful for his brand of courage.

That is a personal memory of Wellesbourne shortly after the war, although it seems things were not much different at the start, for the station emerged from an outburst of British Government bullying in summer 1940. The Littler family, who owned the farm earmarked for RAF Wellesbourne, were ordered to remove their dairy herd in a matter of a few hours to make way for the Air Minister, losing much of their livelihood. They had no choice, and within hours the airfield construction team was following 1939 plans like those that resulted in austere Moreton-in-Marsh and Polebrook. All had a J Type metal hangar to allow for major servicing, a variety of pre-fabricated mainly concrete buildings and a goodly array of wooden huts across the road from the technical site. Plentiful concrete included three runways laid by John Laing & Co, a host of dispersal pans and a lot of static water tanks. The latter came to contain all manner of strange objects, including a fully made-up bed, and plans to immerse two unpopular souls were often mooted. But I digress. By March 1941 the station was ready for use.

*Wellesbourne photographed in 1948 from the SOP Anson.*

No 22 OTU Wellesbourne came into being on 14 April 1941 and soon equipped with 40 IE plus 14 IR Wellington Ics, supplemented by 14 plus 4 Anson navigation trainers. Before it was a going concern, during May 1941 the enemy delivered four attacks, during the first of which eleven bombs fell and slightly damaged the fire tender building. Three bombs fell near No 1 Dispersal in the second attack, and during the third a dozen bombs exploded on the north-east corner of the airfield, damaging two Wellingtons and an Anson. On 10 May a raider, believed to be a Heinkel 111, fired on a dispersed Wellington, then attacked the active runway and flare path. A stick of three bombs overshot on to a field by the village. By the end of May, in which 22 OTU managed a creditable 414 hours, the Unit was training three crews per fortnight, an output soon doubled. Further interruption came early on 5 June when a 500kg bomb smashed a dispersal hard standing.

Orders were received on 12 June 1941 for the OTU to carry out *Nickelling*, although it was the 23rd before practice bombing commenced using Prior's Hardwick Range. Flying hours in June reached 946. In August Lysanders were received for target towing and gunnery training, for Wellesbourne was expanding its scope. On 12 July its satellite at nearby Atherstone, later renamed Stratford, opened, to relieve pressure on its parent station. On 14 September 1941 'C' Flight moved there to carry out day and night type conversion flying.

With the satellite in use, and the parent active, an appraisal of the OTU was made by 6 Group, and serious dissatisfaction was expressed. Only one runway was completely satisfactory, one was too short for night-flying, and the other was downright dangerous, because it led directly towards high ground. Equally disturbing, the single runway at Atherstone – satisfactory by day and night – was in line, almost exactly, with one of Wellesbourne's. Only $3^{1}/_{2}$ miles separated the airfields, so that on take-off aircraft invariably overflew quite low one of the other fields. Little could be done to alter this, making a keen lookout and careful control essential.

In December 1941 the average serviceability at 22 OTU reached twenty-three Wellington Ics, three Ansons, a Lysander and a Magister. February 1942 saw hours total 1,796, showing that the OTU, while trailing behind others in 6 Group, was at least improving. It did little to improve matters when Wellington X9640 crashed and severed the station's main electricity supply.

Diversions and emergency arrivals from night raids increased in 1942 and reached higher numbers here than at most OTUs. As flying increased so did the accident rate, a serious crash occurring on 17 March 1942 when X9964 hit the 'A' Flight crew room in a corner of No 9 hangar. The Wellington's crew miraculously escaped unhurt.

Prior to the Cologne 1,000-bomber raid, some Wellingtons left for Elsham Wolds, and on 30 May 1942 No 22 OTU operated fourteen Wellingtons from Wellesbourne, eleven from Stratford and ten from Elsham. At the time of take-off from Wellesbourne there was torrential rain. From the operation four Wellingtons (three from Wellesbourne) were missing, two returned early (one of Wellesbourne's), and another from the parent station only reached Zeebrugge.

For the second 'Thousand Plan' raid No 22 OTU fielded thirty-four Wellingtons, twelve of them setting out from Wellesbourne, and all safely returned. Against Bremen, on 25/26 June, Wellesbourne despatched twelve aircraft, one of which did not return. Wellingtons from Wellesbourne also participated in *Grand Nationals*. Only two of the fifteen crews ordered to bomb Hamburg on 28 July took off, both failed to receive the recall message and were not heard of again. Next night the enemy replied, delivering incendiaries near Coldicote House, used as a WAAF billet.

On 1 September 1942 Wellesbourne's new satellite, Gaydon, came under its control, and until November – when Stratford passed to 23 OTU Pershore – 22 OTU had two satellites. Now one of the busiest OTUs in the country, morale was raised on 8 October with the arrival of the first Wellington III. Two months previously, Defiant target-towers had replaced the Lysanders. Most of the flying at that time had been undertaken from the satellites, retained now because the main runway at Wellesbourne was being resurfaced in preparation for increased use by the heavier Wellington IIIs.

Although alerted much earlier, 22 OTU had still not yet been *Nickelling*. When in November 1942 it was resumed by 91 Group – which had taken over the station – No 22 OTU was ordered to start leaflet-dropping operations in December 1942. Thereafter it provided the climax for crews about to complete operational training.

By this time 22 OTU was also participating in *Bullseyes* and taking part in 91 Group's exercise *Reduce*, a 10 Group daylight fighter affiliation activity flown over south-west England. ASR searches begun in August 1942, mounted to seek ditched bomber and Coastal Command crews.

In March 1943 *Nickelling* crews visited Clermont Ferrand. In April, the target for four more drops was Limoges, while another involved Le Mans. A crew on a Limoges operation had a very eventful journey, their aircraft being hit by flak that put its port engine out of use. At 13,500 feet the engine burst into flames, and it was hoped that when the fire died down the engine might re-start. Nevertheless the crew dropped their leaflets in the target area, by which time the rear turret was out of use. The pilot decided to fly home at around 5,000-6,000 feet to minimise chances of fighter interception, and he was soon flying as low as 300 feet, on one engine. Then the intercom failed, the directional gyro became unserviceable, and more flak was encountered when crossing an enemy airfield. With fuel low, the radio operator sent an SOS as he passed over the French coast. The main petrol supply and hydraulics had been severed over Le Mans and now the crew was guided by searchlights into Warmwell. The radio failed and the aircraft was belly-landed without injury to the crew, a splendid effort indeed.

Five more *Nickelling* sorties were flown in May, then in June the monthly commitment rose to seven *Nickel* sorties, which involved the dropping over Brest and St Nazaire of special leaflets intended to demoralise U-boat crews. Further sorties of this nature were undertaken on 9/10 July.

On 11 July 1943 No 312 Ferry Training Flight was established at Wellesbourne to train Wellington crews prior to the ferrying of their aircraft overseas. The surfeit of such Flights led to only limited activity, the unit disbanding on 17 December 1943.

For the August-September series of night raids on the Calais Peninsula during the run-up to operation *Starkey*, crews set off from Wellesbourne and Gaydon. Their first attack was directed against an ammunition dump in the Foret de Raismes. Half of 91 Group's effort of thirty-six sorties during *Starkey* was undertaken by 22 OTU. *Nickelling* was then resumed, usually to areas around Angers, Argentan, Granville, Le Mans and Rennes. By this time Wellington Xs were supplementing the Mk IIIs, Wellington Ics having been phased out at the close of 1942.

September 1943 saw trials at Wellesbourne using a Wellington fitted with a hood in place of a nose turret and a 1lb increase in boost pressure applied to its Hercules VI engines. Both features were successful, the go-ahead to remove nose turrets from Wellingtons being given, while permission to alter the boost was withheld. Some eighty-nine hoods were almost immediately obtained for Wellingtons, thirty being fitted to Wellesbourne's aircraft.

January 1944's returns showed that 22 OTU flew 2,221 hours that month, the third highest in the Group. *Nickelling* was at its peak and, in January, 22 OTU despatched eighteen sorties and delivered a record 2,788,000 leaflets. For those in Occupied France they warned of heavy raids to come on communications targets.

On 7 March 1944 No 22 OTU took control of Stratford, retaining it until 15 December 1944. Disbandment of 23 OTU Pershore resulted in many of its Wellingtons being transferred to Wellesbourne, as a result of which, from 15 March, the unit became a one-and-a-half OTU by strength. It was now the largest OTU, holding eighty-one Wellington III/Xs and six target-towers. Changes to courses resulted in two weeks ground school and eight weeks flying. The intake was twenty-four crews every fortnight, raising the crew population to 120 and the output to forty-six crews monthly.

Increased operational employment was ordered for all OTU Wellingtons, including those without front turrets. As a stand-by for the Normandy, a invasion reinforcement measure of up to twenty aircraft were to be regularly available. At Wellesbourne this included four Wellington Type 423s, each able to carry a 4,000lb bomb. Not surprisingly, March 1944 saw a further upsurge in 22 OTU's *Nickelling* effort, and, in the course of twenty sorties, 3,180,000 leaflets were delivered. The OTU also participated on 24/25 March in a special *Bullseye* routed over France to provide a diversion while the Main Force attacked Berlin.

Wellesbourne still attracted operational diversions. On 5 April 1944, for instance, twelve Lancasters of 61 Squadron, Coningsby, came after bombing Toulouse. Another busy night was 7 June, when eight Halifaxes of 420 Squadron landed after attacking Coutances, and L/429 Squadron arrived from Conde-sur-Noireau. On 14 June three Halifaxes came after mining operations off Lorient and St Nazaire. Ten East Moor Halifaxes landed on 25 August after bombing coastal batteries at Brest. These were but a few of the diversions at this time.

After four months, during which accidents averaged one per 1,000 hours, the OTU achieved an excellent rate of 3,600 hours accident-free in October 1944, but the following month showed far less favourable results. Wellington LN460 exploded over Broadway on 20 November 1944. An hour and a half later MF509, flying from Stratford, crashed in the Welsh mountains killing the entire crew. Two hours later again, MF505 was experiencing engine trouble at Wellesbourne. Winter weather brought many more diversions, one of the largest in February 1945 resulting in the arrival of twenty-four B-17s. To the end of the war this continued, fifteen Halifaxes of 415 Squadron, for instance, homing in on 14 April.

Hostilities in Europe ended, the wind-down at Wellesbourne was rapid. On 1 July No 91 Course completed training on the day that flying ceased at 22 OTU. But this was far from the end for the airfield. On 24 July 1945 both Wellesbourne and Gaydon were taken over by No 3 Glider Training School, equipped with Master IIs and Hotspurs and functioning until closure on

3 December 1947. Wellesbourne was then set aside for Technical Training Command.

First in was the School of Photography, which vacated Farnborough in the spring of 1948, although installing special equipment for the School delayed resumption of training until the following autumn. In May 1948 the School of Education arrived and remained until the end of 1950. Its coming aroused considerable ill feeling, SNCOs taking an understandably jaundiced view of school leavers with Higher School Certificates rising, literally overnight, to the often hard-won rank of Sergeant. Even greater ill-will was directed at those who, having somehow secured a university place prior to military service, were, upon joining the RAF, instantly elevated to the lofty realms of Pilot Officer.

Inside the J Hangar two war-weary aeroplanes made themselves available for camera fitment practice. One was Spitfire XI PL837, which had served with 400 Squadron, the other a Mosquito XVI, NS551, which had sacrificed itself in order to show the Americans what a real aeroplane was like. These shared the vast emptiness with Auster J/4 *G-AIJT* of the Spa and Warwick Timber Company, which had achieved the impossible, in those days, by basing its executive transport on a military aerodrome. Pale blue, and never looking very happy, was the unique Burgoyne Stirling Dycer, a light plane of the PFA type. The only military aircraft that flew was a solitary Anson 'TFAB', at one time NK312, and another, NK340, used by the SOP for aerial photography – rarely.

Whether the military preparedness, or lack of it, among Wellesbourne's martial men encouraged the Soviets or not we shall probably never know. But when the Cold War temperature fell it encouraged dramatic changes at a Wellesbourne that was still in excellent condition. An Advanced Training School was established in May 1950 which, in 1951, became No 9 Advanced Flying Training School, plentifully equipped with Oxfords and functioning until 1954. The School of Photography stayed until 1964, and with its removal came the departure of the Airfield Construction Branch based here since September 1958.

After thirty years I returned to see what had happened to the Wellesbourne I knew well. Set in a most attractive rural environment and backed by a wooded hillside, it was now but a shadow of its former self. Mrs Littler and her son spoke of hopes for a revival of flying, later realised. I motored on to see the …. my goodness, it had gone, the guardroom had collapsed into a heap of rubble!

Surveying the shattered remnants I thought long of the many characters I'd come to know there, for SOP and SOEd had, by their very callings, attracted the artistic and erudite, neither of which had much in common with Service life. Many of both often invested a 'bob' in Stratford, which secured standing room at the back of the theatre to enjoy Hamlet and a viewing of Claire Bloom.

There was also that magic moment when the SWO announced that his beloved Mess (gone, all gone, and overgrown by a housing estate) might win the Jolliffe Trophy until within moments I spoiled it with gigantic white footmarks across his wretched red floor! Years later I chuckled merrily when, in a rather more privileged stance, I patted the Trophy before its presentation to RAF Waterbeach, whose Mess in no way matched Wellesbourne's 'Palm Court'.

There was one last thing to do – collect a little piece of that guardroom. As I did so I smiled to myself at the pleasure some derived from an unregistered firm 'Passes Unlimited'. If that pair had known – but they've all been knocked down now.

As the Littlers said it would, Wellesbourne has come alive as an active light aircraft centre where you can join the Aero Troika Club and fly in a 'beautiful and unique aircraft from the golden age of aviation', alias an An-2 D-FKMA. I dread to think what the SWO would have said!

*Wellesbourne in 2003: five hangars remain, and a large industrial area now projects towards the landing ground. A housing estate occupies the previous Domestic Site.*

**Main features:**
*Runways:* 236° 4,200ft x 150ft, 187° 3,300ft x 150ft, 294° 3,300ft x 150ft, concrete with tarmac surface. *Hangars:* one J Type, four T2. *Hardstandings:* thirty frying-pan type. *Accommodation:* RAF officers 168, SNCOs 419, ORs 1,735; WAAF officers 8, SNCOs 20, ORs 281.

Operated by Radarmoor Ltd, Wellesbourne Mountford now has two asphalt runways, 18/36 912m x 23m and 05/23 596m x 18m. Aircraft park is by the Stratford main road, a perimeter track linking to the runway ends.

## WESTCOTT, Buckinghamshire

*51°50N/00°58W 262ft asl; SP711540. 10 miles ESE of Bicester by the A41*

Between 28 September 1942 and early October, Westcott became the new home of 11 OTU, removed from Bassingbourn to make way there for the USAAF. Using Wellington Ics, the unit trained bomber crews and, now part of 92 Group, participated in *Bullseyes*, the first of which took place on 26 January 1943. The average strength of 11 OTU at that time was fifty-two Wellingtons, backed by assorted gunnery training aircraft, the latter being based at the Oakley satellite. For communications purposes, an Avro Tutor was on strength until November 1943, Anson navigation trainers having been withdrawn early in that year. In spring 1943 Westcott provided a home for the four radio-trials Wellingtons of ECDU, 92 Group.

Hercules-powered Wellingtons, including Mk Xs, were introduced to 11 OTU in September 1943, thereby releasing Ics – in increasingly short supply – for 14 OTU. Leaflet drops to the French by Wellington IIIs and Xs were resumed in December 1943 after a long break.

Disposal of the remaining Wellington Ics took place in February 1944, and by the end of that month unit strength stood at three Mk IIIs and fifty Mk Xs. Conversion to type was now undertaken by 'A' and 'B' Flights at Oakley, where the Gunnery Flight was still based. *Bullseyes* and *Nickelling* were undertaken from Westcott where operational training took place.

At the end of March 1944 ground equipment began arriving from Harwell, whose OTU had closed. Westcott also took over much of its training commitment, and most crews at 11 OTU were training for service overseas. Since early 1943 bombers had been diverted here on returning from operations, eighteen Lancasters of the famous 617 Squadron landing early on 5 April 1944 after attacking distant Toulouse. At 0300hrs on 31 May 1944 a returning Lancaster overshot on landing with a 13,000lb bomb-load still aboard. After crossing the A41, the bomber halted near the D/F station and the occupants quickly got out. Flt Lt B C Bulmer, Flying Control Officer, was at the scene when, at 0330, the bombs exploded, killing him.

Westcott received diverted Halifaxes on D-Day. *Nickelling* continued, as on 19 July 1944 when four crews dropped leaflets on Le Mans, Angers, Nantes and Leval. From March 1944 Hurricanes supplemented Martinets for gunnery training. Following a fighter affiliation exercise on 30 July 1944 a Hurricane pilot returned to state that, five miles north of Westcott, he had witnessed the horrific sight of the wings being torn off a Wellington as it took evasive action.

To the end of hostilities, 11 OTU Westcott continued the training of bomber crews, its strength during March 1945 averaging fifty Wellington Xs, about half of them Oakley-based, together with four Hurricane IIcs and a Master II. Abrupt change came in May 1945 when Westcott became a reception airfield for receiving repatriated Allied prisoners of war. The first transports in were seven Dakotas that landed on 3 May, after which POW arrivals became a daily event, a very large number of men passing through to freedom. On 2 June 1945 fifteen true-to-name Liberators touched down bearing prisoners of war from Italy, more of whom arrived next day.

When 92 Group closed on 15 June 1945, the station passed to 91 Group, which was controlling 11 OTU when it disbanded on 3 August 1945. However, Westcott's useful days were far from over. German advances in rocket technology led to the Guided Projectile Establishment being set up here in April 1946. It was responsible for the development of ground-launched missiles until 1947, when its title changed to Rocket Propulsion Department, Royal Aircraft Establishment. Its role narrowed to development of rocket propellants, concentration being on liquid bi-propellant rocket engines after the German style. Engines for the RTV I and RTV II were developed between 1946 and 1951. Work on solid propellant motors commenced in 1949, the Solid Propellant Laboratory being created first, then an experimental filling factory completed in 1952, when plastic propellants were introduced. The 1950s saw diversification into other chemicals, various materials and combustion processes, for which further facilities were built.

Rolls-Royce was contracted in 1955 to build the liquid bi-propellant RZ1 liquid oxygen and the Kerosene engine for Blue Streak. Runs of the engine, far more powerful than any hitherto here, commenced in 1958. By 1960 more than 500 firings had taken place. After cancellation of Blue Streak in 1960, work continued on the engine for its use in the rocket Europa 1. Upper-atmosphere research followed the development, between 1955 and 1956, of the 17-foot-long Raven Motor, a component of the Skylark research vehicle.

The link with Farnborough ceased in August 1958 when Westcott became the Rocket Propulsion Establishment, where a variety of scientific programmes were initiated. Satellite propulsion interest remained until 1973, and since the late 1960s attention had been devoted to the problems of liquid propellant storage in Armed Services hands.

Not all Westcott's work had military overtones. After the wreck of the *Torrey Canyon* in March 1967, RPE was asked to carry out tests on the disposal of oil spillage by burning. Progress by November 1970 was such that in a major test 175 tonnes of crude oil were burned.

The Rocket Propulsion Establishment became the responsibility of the Procurement Executive of the Ministry of Defence in 1971, and in January 1973 merged with the Explosives Research and Development Establishment, Waltham Abbey. The Rocket Motor Executive moved to Westcott in 1975, further merging bringing the ERDE and RPE together as the Propellants, Explosives and Rocket Motor Establishment (PERME) in February 1977.

Work later undertaken involved boost motors for Sea Wolf and Sea Skua guided weapons, propellants for anti-tank weapons and air-launched cruise missiles, and static firing trials. Its purpose was to find possible points of failure during operations, or in manhandling. PERME had a site of 623 acres and a staff of about 700.

The steady run-down in operational requirements, and rationalisation of defence research and development, resulted in amalgamation of PERME with other MoD organisations. Some of the fixtures were then acquired by British Aerospace/BAe Systems, the present owners. Of wartime Westcott the control tower, somewhat modified, remains, runway and perimeter tracking can still be made out, and miscellaneous buildings survive, as well as a B1 hangar. An excellent view over Westcott can be obtained from high ground between Westcott and Ashendon, making the hazardous nature of flying from here only too obvious. The ground rises rapidly to the south, reaching its greatest height almost in line with the runway. The wonder must be that there were not more accidents.

**Major features:**
*Runways:* 250° 5,100ft x 150ft, 204° 4,200ft x 150ft, 004° 4,200ft x 150ft, concrete. *Hangars:* four T2, one B1. *Hardstandings:* twenty frying-pan. *Accommodation:* RAF officers 181, SNCOs 488, ORs 962; WAAF officers 10, SNCOs 9, ORs 339.

## WEST MALLING (KINGS HILL), Kent

*51°16N/00°24E 280ft asl; TQ680555. 5 miles W of Maidstone by the B228*

West Malling had an unlikely career for, starting as a First World War second-class landing ground covering a mere 47 acres, it became a major all-weather fighter station, one of Britain's most important.

On ground known as Kings Hill, the unpopulated, short-lifespan landing ground, measuring 650 by 380 yards, sat within a wooded area a mile and a half from West Malling railway station. Administered by No 53 Wing, it saw use by AW FK 8s of 143 Squadron and later in 1918 by their replacement SE 5as, which protected London and the South East from Gotha raids.

Resurrected in 1930 as a private aerodrome, the next year saw Kent Aeronautical Services using the field – now called West Malling – for modified SE 5as and a Sopwith Dove, the latter owned by Mr Lowe-Wylde. After his death the Dove was rebuilt in 1937-38 by R O Shuttleworth as a Sopwith Pup, still active as part of the Shuttleworth Collection.

More change, in 1932, saw the landing ground registered as Maidstone Airport. Two years later yet another company formed, Malling Aviation, which used an assortment of aircraft. Still unsettled, Malling Aero Club came into being in 1935 and took control. Air displays were held and visits made by famous visitors, including Alan Cobham and Amy Johnson.

From that varied start the little field achieved a much higher status when, at the start of the war, the Air Ministry requisitioned it. Extension, upgrading and building ensued, for RAF West Malling lay at the south-eastern corner of the fighter belt protecting London. The station received its first squadron on June 1940, No 26 (Army Co-operation) Squadron, forced to leave France and soon re-organised as part of the anti-invasion home defence force. One of its tasks was to reconnoitre the beaches of Kent, seeking any small parties of invaders. West Malling's main use, however, would be as a fighter station, and the first squadron was preparing to arrive. A designated satellite for Kenley, it would also be used as an advanced airfield for both Kenley and Biggin Hill.

In their first brush with the enemy Boulton Paul Defiant turret fighters had performed well, but the enemy soon discovered their serious limitations and blind spots. It was a second Defiant squadron, No 141, that flew into West Malling from Turnhouse on 12 July 1940. On 19 July they were ordered to the advance base at Hawkinge, where at midday they faced a Bf 109 onslaught launched from a position against which there was no chance of retaliation. Six Defiants were shot down, and 141 Squadron suffered a catastrophic blow. The remainder of the squadron immediately retired to Prestwick.

Their departure left Malling with only No 26 Army Co-operation Squadron and their 'Lyssies' to face the wrath of an enemy who began battering the station at around 0730 on 10 August 1940. The next raid, on the 15th, caused considerable damage and killed two airmen. Came the morrow and the Luftwaffe tried out a high-level attack. Although it caused no serious casualties, three Lysanders were badly damaged. Two days later Malling was dive-bombed, causing further damage and writing off another three Lysanders. Thrice more the Luftwaffe came before August ended, and on 3 September the onslaughts were resumed. There were now lots of wrecked aircraft, shattered buildings, plentiful craters to fill and UX bombs to avoid. No 26 Squadron must have concluded that West Malling was not a happy place, for later that day they moved to Gatwick.

By 12 September West Malling was starting to show signs of recovery when a lone raider suddenly peppered the station with anti-personnel bombs, one of which scored a direct hit on an Army post, killing six soldiers and wounding three others. Five times more bombs fell on the station before the month ended, so what had prompted so many air raids? As with Eastchurch and Detling, the Germans presumably perceived that this was another station from which the RAF would support Army attempts to prevent invasion forces landing on the Kent coast. As already stated it was classed already as a fighter station in the Biggin Hill Sector, although in the event of big trouble it might well have served a different purpose.

Although October brought no respite, repairs were sufficient to allow No 66 Squadron to arrive on the 30th, bringing its Spitfires. With them came 421 Flight, whose Hurricanes were replaced by Spitfires before the Flight moved to Biggin Hill on 6 November. Their role was to seek lone enemy aircraft and bomber formations (in case radar failed to detect them), and to observe enemy shipping activity in the English Channel.

No 66 Squadron moved to Exeter on 24 February 1941. The station still needed much repair, and at a time when the threat to London was very much by night. When a fighter squadron did arrive, on 14 April 1941, it was No 264 Squadron operating Defiants, more safely at night. It was joined on 27 April by 29 Squadron flying the more effective Beaufighter If night interceptor. Among its pilots was Guy Gibson, later of 'Dambusting' fame, who was gaining experience of night combat to translate to British bomber crews.

Extensive repairs had put the sole J Type back into use, and around the perimeter were sixteen Blister hangars. The landing ground remaining grass only, and two Sommerfeld track runways were later laid to permit all-weather operations. Later a SW/NE runway was substituted for one of them. The grass airfield measured 3,300 feet NE/SW, 3,900 feet SE/NW, 3,600 feet N/S, and 4,200 feet E/W. The N/S landing direction was later increased to 5,000 feet and the main E/W to 6,500 feet.

Throughout 1941 and to April 1942 No 264 Squadron flew night patrols and interceptions until moving on 1 May to Colerne to re-arm with Mosquito IIs. The Hurricane IIcs of No 32 Squadron that replaced them on 4 May used West Malling as their base, while being several times detached elsewhere for operational reasons; they eventually left on 9 September 1942. No 485 (NZ) Squadron supported the 19 August Dieppe raid from West Malling, more New Zealanders making use of the station during October.

No 1421 (Fighter) Flight formed at West Malling on 7 July 1941, and on 2 September 1942 No 1452 Flight was renumbered No 531 Squadron. Nominally it held the standard eight plus one Havoc (T) backed with Hurricanes. In the clipped noses of the Havocs were high-power Helmore searchlights, powered by batteries carried in the bomb bay. Early AI radar was carried to allow an enemy target to be roughly located, then it would be illuminated allowing the parasite wing-tip

Hurricane fighters to make the kill. However, improved airborne radar rendered the system obsolete, and the Squadron disbanded on 25 January 1943.

One of the more bizarre wartime events involved West Malling and took place on the night of 16 April 1943. A lone, single-engined aircraft was heard twice circling the airfield before it landed. It taxied to a halt and a groundcrew member climbed on to the wing to help the pilot out. As he did so he noticed the German Balkenkruz fuselage marking, so he quickly jumped clear. Already an officer had arrived from the control tower to arrest the pilot, with a fire tender and crash crew quickly on the scene to assist.

To their amazement, a second similar Fw 190 landed. The first pilot surrendered, whereas the second tried to take off. Shots from the fire tender hitting oxygen bottles in the pilot's cockpit led to an explosion. A third Fw 190 overshot West Malling's runway and careered into an orchard, while a fourth smashed into trees at Staplehurst. Some fifteen Focke-Wulf 190A fighter-bombers of I/SKG 10 had set out from the Poix area to make nuisance raids on south-east England. On several occasions such single-seat night raiders became disorientated and on this occasion apparently mistook West Malling airfield for their French base. Groundcrews were told that the Germans mistaking their position were enticed, in German, by a control tower officer, to sample British hospitality.

On 13 May 1943 No 29 Squadron, here since April 1941, moved to Bradwell Bay. During its stay it claimed forty-nine kills, and was replaced on its movement day by Mosquitoes of No 85 Squadron, commanded by famous Wg Cdr John Cunningham, here for a long stay. Next day fighter-bomber Typhoons of No 3 Squadron arrived for a brief stay, leaving for Manston on 11 June.

During August 1943 it was the turn of Nos 130 and 234 Spitfire Squadrons to use the station. Numerous Spitfire squadrons came for short stays and used West Malling as a forward station, well placed for operations over France. Replacing them on 20 October for a short stay ending on 7 November were Canadians of 410 Squadron and their Mosquitoes. They were replaced by 96 Squadron from distant *Drem* on 8 November.

West Malling was still accommodating day and night fighter squadrons. On 18 March 1944 Spitfire HF 7s of No 124 Squadron departed for rest at Church Fenton and were replaced by others operated by No 616 Squadron, which a month later left for armament training at Fairwood Common. Their replacement was 91 Squadron, which was flying the then new and powerful Griffon-engined Spitfire XIV. No 409 Squadron (RCAF) took its place here on 15 May, then a month later departed for Hunsdon.

When the V-1 flying-bomb offensive was launched in mid-June 1944, West Malling became an important base for squadrons pitted against the 'doodlebugs'. Although now classed as a Forward Airfield (Night Fighter), on 20 June No 96 Squadron made way for day fighter Spitfires of 322 Squadron. On 21 July No 85 returned, for it had the latest Mosquito, the fastest NF XIX, intended for 100 Group and Swannington-based. Soon supplemented by 157 Squadron, they chased V-1s until 29 August.

In the first two weeks of July three day fighter squadrons arrived, Nos 80 and 274 flying Spitfires IXs, and 316 using Mustang IIIs. They, too, chased flying-bombs, and were positioned here also to

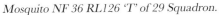

*Mosquito NF 36 RL126 'T' of 29 Squadron.*

*Meteor NF 12 WS612 'E' of 25 Squadron at West Malling.*

support daylight raids by Halifaxes and Lancasters. By the end of July Nos 91, 274, 316 and 322 Squadrons had left, leaving Nos 80, 85 and 157 remaining to intercept V-1 shoals. The Mosquitoes returned to Swannington in late August after the main offensive had stopped, and No 80 went to Manston. The station then closed for extensive reconstruction, and a 6,000-foot concrete runway was built to replace the longer of the two that had Sommerfeld Tracking.

Upgrading was completed in June 1945, at which time West Malling became a main rehabilitation centre for POWs returning to Britain. Its flying career was resumed on 10 September 1945 when No 287 Squadron and its Martinets, Oxfords and Spitfires arrived from Bradwell Bay. But West Malling's main post-war use started two weeks later with the arrival of an old friend, No 29 Squadron, and its Mosquitoes.

The proximity of naval gunners attracted target-towers, Vengeance TT IVs with Spitfire 16s of 567 AAC Squadron, which arrived on 26 April 1946 only to disband on 15 June, the same day as No 287 suffered the same fate.

By then the Auxiliaries were being resurrected. West Malling become the home of No 500 (County of Kent) Squadron, the first of whose Mosquitoes arrived on 10 May. Front-line fighters were represented by the Mosquitoes of No 25 Squadron, which joined them coming from Boxted in September 1946, and were joined on 16 April 1947 by Mosquitoes of No 85 Squadron. By then the squadrons were at half strength, and operating Mosquito NF 36s. Carrying heavy two-stage engines and well laden with radar, the Mk 36s were no match for bombers of the mid-1950s. As an interim measure, while the Javelin was being developed, the Malling night squadrons were re-armed with Meteor night-fighters.

Their numbers became greater as mini-re-armament took hold and on 28 February 1955, No 153 re-forming with an establishment of Meteors. The beginning of the reduction in Fighter Command's size began with the disbandment of the RAuxAF fighter squadrons on 10 March 1957, including No 500. The strategic situation was drastically changing, for ballistics missiles were starting to replace manned bombers. No longer was a costly huge fighter force needed.

In September 1957 No 25 moved to Tangmere, after having re-armed with Vampire NF 10s. No 85 moved to Church Fenton and No 153 to Waterbeach.

The airfield was then without a resident squadron, although it was a front-line station being maintained as a reserve station. Its value was apparent when on 5 August 1959 No 85 Squadron moved in from Stradishall bringing Javelins based here until 8 September 1960, when they left for West Raynham.

West Malling's days as an operational base had finished. In August 1964 it was placed on care and maintenance, but in 1965 re-opened when the United States Navy Facility Flight took up residence, bringing Douglas Super R4Ds and Convair C-131 communication and transport aircraft. The Americans were here until the Flight left for Blackbushe, which left flying to the ATC No 618 Volunteer Gliding School. Short Brothers moved its aircraft maintenance business at Rochester to West Malling, where it undertook work on Varsities and Chipmunks.

In 1970 Kent County Council bought the aerodrome, and some buildings were used as offices. In 1972 it served as a reception centre for Ugandan Asians arriving in Britain. Later it became the location of Tonbridge and Malling District Council's headquarters.

The airfield remained in quite a good state and attracted crowds when warbirds flying displays were held here. It was also used as a finishing centre for SAAB 340 commuter airliners, although the volume of production was too low for such activity to be sustained. Plans to turn it into a passenger and freight airport met the usual stiff local opposition, and instead it has become an industrial site.

## Summary of squadrons based at West Malling, 1940-60

| No | Dates | Aircraft |
|---|---|---|
| 26 | 8.6.40-3.9.40 | Lysander |
| 141 | 12.7.40-21.7.40 | Defiant |
| 264 | 14.4.41-1.5.42 | Defiant NF |
| 29 | 27.4.41-13.5.43 | Beaufighter, Mosquito |
| 32 | 4.5.42-14.6.42, 7.7.42-14.3.43 | Hurricane IIc |
| 616 | 3.7.42-8.7.42 | Spitfire V |
| 531 | 2.9.42-25.1.43 | Havoc NF, Boston III, Hurricane IIc |
| 85 | 13.5.43-1.5.44 | Mosquito |
| 3 | 14.5.43-11.6.43 | Typhoon Ib |
| 130 | 4.8.43-18.9.43 | Spitfire V |
| 234 | 5.8.43-16.9.43 | Spitfire V |
| 64 | 6.9.43-23.9.43 | Spitfire Vb |
| 350 | 7.9.43-18.9.43 | Spitfire V |
| 124 | 20.9.43-18.3.44 | Spitfire HF VII |
| 410 | 23.10.43-29.12.43 | Mosquito NF II |
| 96 | 8.11.43-20.6.44 | Mosquito NF XIII |
| 616 | 18.3.44-24.4.44 | Spitfire HF VII |
| 91 | 23.4.44-21.7.44 | Spitfire XIV |
| 409 | 16.5.44-19.6.44 | Mosquito NF XIII (detachment) |
| 322 | 20.6.44-21.7.44 | Spitfire XIV |
| 80 | 5.7.44-29.8.44 | Spitfire IX |
| 274 | 5.7.44-17.8.44 | Spitfire IX |
| 316 | 4.7.44-11.7.44 | Mustang III |
| 157 | 21.7.44-28.8.44 | Mosquito NF XIX |
| 85 | 21.7.44-29.8.44 | Mosquito NF XIX |
| 500 | 10.6.46-10.3.57 | Mosquito NF30 4.47-10.48, Meteor 3 7.48-10.51, Meteor 4 51-52, Meteor 8/51-52 |
| 25 | 9.46-30.9.57 | Mosquito NF 30/36, Vampire 5/NF10, Meteor NF12 |
| 85 | 16.4.47-23.9.57 | Meteor NF |
| 85 | 5.8.59-8.9.60 | Javelin F(AW) |
| 153 | 20.2.55-17.9.57 | Meteor NF 12/14 |

**Main features:**
*Runways:* 264° 6,000ft, Sommerfeld, replaced by concrete, 004° 4,980ft, Sommerfeld. *Hangars:* one J Type, sixteen Blister. *Hardstandings:* thirteen frying-pan, three for Spitfires, four for Blenheims, twelve temporary track. *Accommodation:* RAF officers 68, SNCOs 144, ORs 1,200; WAAFs billeted in requisitioned property.

## WESTON-ON-THE-GREEN, Oxfordshire

*51°52N/01°13W 260ft asl; SP535205. 3¹/₂ miles SW of Bicester by the A43(T)*

Weston-on-the-Green is another airfield whose survival is remarkable, particularly as it never has been much more than a large field. It has been quite important and must, in several respects, be unique. Additionally, it retains concrete evidence of its First World War days – albeit little more than foundations.

Apparently the site was acquired for military use in 1916. By whom it was first used is uncertain, but surviving records state that the amalgamation of Nos 61 and 70 Training Squadrons produced No 28 Training Depot Station, which opened here on 27 July 1918, and that Sopwith Camels and Avro 504Ks were used. Ground attack Sopwith Salamanders replaced the Camels before No 28 TDS closed in 1919. Establishment figures indicate that up to seventy-two aircraft may have resided here, where six aircraft sheds and a repair shed were provided. No 18 Squadron came from Germany on 2 September 1919 and disbanded on 31 December, and No 2 Squadron also arrived in September 1919 to disband on 20 January 1920. Activity ceased at the site in 1921. Under whose control it then was is uncertain, but even before the outbreak of war in 1939 RAF Brize Norton (whose satellite it had become) was administering the site. During the intervening years it had been used as grazing land.

On 2 September 1939, upon the order to scatter, No 90 Squadron (and probably 101 Squadron) hurriedly brought their Blenheims to Weston. Next day both squadrons repositioned at Brize Norton, although activity connected with them both continued at Weston-on-the-Green until mid-September. Bicester then used Weston for its Ansons and Blenheims, and when 13 OTU formed in April 1940 it came under that unit's control, remaining within 7 Group.

On 9 August 1940 Weston-on-the-Green was the first Oxfordshire airfield to be bombed. Late that night a stick of sixteen HEs fell in a two-mile-long line extending from Chesterton to the landing ground, upon which five bombs exploded without causing damage. A second attack came on 25/26 August when many incendiaries were scattered. The following night the Germans came again, and made seven more holes in Weston's field. The persistent Luftwaffe attacks were quite curious, and on 2/3 September another five HEs fell near Weston and one on Otmoor bombing range.

In summer 1940 No 13 OTU obtained more suitable satellites, allowing Weston-on-the-Green to become an RLG for 15 SFTS, Kidlington, from 1 November 1940. Harvards and mainly Oxfords were in the circuit daily and often at night. Early in 1941 part of the School moved to Weston, where a detachment of thirty men moved in on 20 February 1941 to service the aircraft.

Considerable local concern arose when, just after midnight on 12 August 1941, an intruder entered Weston's airspace and joined night Oxfords of No 24 Course. After engaging one, the Ju 88C intruder of I/NJG 2, flown by Ofw Busmann, came upon another and opened fire at 4,000 feet. W6629 promptly burst into flames and both Flt Sgt Julin-Olsene (Norwegian) and Leading Aircraftsman C P Blair were killed. Wreckage fell near Sturdy's Castle. Then the raider dropped six light bombs on the airfield. Seven Oxfords on the landing ground were damaged by strafing.

Protracted closure of 15 SFTS to clear way for glider training at Kidlington led to the contraction of the SFTS and the withdrawal of 'J' and 'K' Flights from Weston on 23 December 1941. By then No 2 Glider Training School was making use of Weston-on-the-Green. Orders for its formation out of No 1 GTS had been received at Thame on 4 December, and over the following few days Weston's state was examined. It had six domestic accommodation sites, in addition to a technical site where about 160 personnel resided. The communal site was 1½ miles away, and the dormitory site a further mile from it. For such dispersal a bicycle provided the ideal means of transport.

A party to open No 2 GTS here arrived on 8 December 1941. Airmen and NCOs would be accommodated in huts, while officers resided comfortably at Kidlington. On 22 December No 2 GTS was transferred from 70 Group Army Co-operation Command to 23 Group, Training Command.

*Hotspur training gliders at Weston.*

Although there was a serious shortage of Hotspurs, Hector tugs and tow ropes – not to mention flying instructors – training started early in January 1942 after conversion of pilots from Netheravon. Having had Hawker Hart experience, they were soon able to fly the Hawker Hectors. By the end of December 1941 No 2 GTS had eight of these, four of which were swapped for two dual-control examples at Thame. Another two, without towing hooks, were also suitable for pilot training, but maintenance was a problem with these ageing biplanes and their Napier Dagger III engines, further complicated by a shortage of suitable maintenance equipment. Having a few Hawker Hinds further complicated the situation.

Gliders were slow in coming, the first four arriving as a late Christmas present from 15 MU Wroughton, and assembled with the help of General Aircraft. This was none too easy, for tailplane warping was discovered and two gliders had to be borrowed from Thame to initiate flying. A general start had been accomplished, for on 28 December 1941 the first trainees reported to Weston-on-the-Green for flying training. Although 15 SFTS had left, one Over Type Blister hangar was set aside for the use of any of their night-flying Oxfords that might need emergency servicing.

Chronic was the shortage of tugs for training gliders, resulting in trials of a Fairey Battle at Weston in mid-December 1941, which quickly showed its unsuitability. In January 1942 the airfield became too wet for Hectors; they performed poorly in winter, and the Dagger's characteristics indicated that it would easily overheat in summer during towing activity. A more desperate search began for a replacement, which resulted in tests of a Kestrel XX-engined Hawker Audax, K5152. When towing a Hotspur, it needed a 2,460-foot run to clear 50 feet, and was far preferable to the Hector. Audaxes modified for glider towing were therefore acquired as fast as possible.

January 1942 also saw the completion of the twelve-bay Bessoneau hangar, to which another nine bays were added. Two more Over Type Blister hangars were being erected, together with another eight Hotspurs to occupy them.

Establishment called for thirty Hotspurs, 12 IE plus 4 IR, 2 Tiger Moths and a Hind (T). The first six-week glider pilots' course commenced on 2 January 1942, pass-out taking place on 17 February. Despite the poor surface, up to six tow lines were then in simultaneous operation, two of them being temporarily available for 1 GTS, for Thame was in an even worse state than Weston-on-the-Green. Five Audaxes arrived on 7 March, and others later that month; they did not entirely replace the Hectors, a few of which remained for full-load towing. Two more Blister hangars were erected in April 1942.

In March 1942 the projected Hotspur (T) became the Hotspur III and, in April 1942, all Hotspurs were ordered to be completed as training gliders. Some 370 had so far been built, and there were plans for ten to be modified to Mk III standard each week. Cost, and ever-changing requirements, led eventually to only fifty-two Mk IIIs being produced for glider schools.

With the Hotspur II in service, some modifications were clearly necessary. Tail skids gave trouble, so new designs were produced by various agencies, among them Weston's staff. The modification eventually adopted involved a backward extension of the foot of the skid, which was also made more flexible and able to withstand heavier shocks during landings.

There were three serious accidents in May 1942. One involved a glider that entered a very steep climb just after take-off and stalled as the tow rope was released. A high-point tow that developed as another Hotspur took off resulted in the glider being released quickly for a forced landing. Trouble with another glider's canopy, which opened in flight, brought another hasty touch-down. Throughout the month, night-flying was carried out here by Hotspurs of No 102 (Glider) OTU, Kidlington.

Search for more suitable landing grounds for glider training schools was under way. No 2 GTS conducted trials at Long Newton for its use by 1 GTS instead of unsuitable Thame. There was also a constant drive to improve the Hotspur. Gliders being built or in preparation depended upon a bifurcated tow rope, which required extra time spent fixing the hook-ups. Nose-point towing was developed and, by the end of May 1942, Hotspurs were being modified to have the nose-towing point featured by four gliders of 2 GTS by the end of the month.

Using outdated Hawker biplanes to tow gliders was increasingly unsatisfactory. Various replacement aircraft types were again considered, including an Airspeed Oxford tested here in May, before the choice fell upon the Miles Master II, the first of which arrived on 16 June for the addition of towing equipment. Three dual-control Master IIs were flown in on 28 June, conversion training being undertaken with the assistance of instructors from 9 (P)AFU. Two Hotspurs with nose-towing points were now in daily use. However, the Hotspurs were too tail-heavy for the Master tugs, so

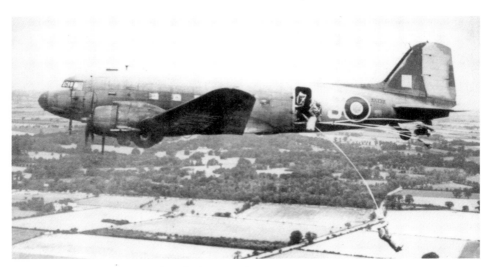

*Parachutists jumping from Dakota KK138 over Weston.*

ballast needed to be carried before research shared among the GTSs and RAE led to a cure through a change in the glider's tailplane incidence. By August 1942 the glider establishment had doubled and the tug strength was set at forty aircraft. On a fine day it was now possible to achieve as many as eighty tows out of Weston. Towing a Hotspur, the Master needed a 2,700-foot run to reach 50 feet. Standard manila tow ropes $2^{1}/_{2}$ inches thick were used for thirty-five launches.

On 2 September 1942 Master DL425 was towing HH518 from Weston and little height was being gained. Within moments the combination smashed into the steeple of Witney's church. Survival of the occupants was amazing, although their injuries were serious.

Intensive glider pilot training continued into 1943. Conditions at Weston at the start of February were so bad that 2 GTS was detached to Cheddington until 20 March 1943, when it returned to Weston. Drastic changes were by then under way, Air Ministry Works having decided in February that Sommerfeld Tracking runways and peritrack were essential at Weston prior to the next winter. Another decision was taken to close 4 GTS on 10 March 1943, because sufficient glider pilots had been trained. On that day the existing 4 GTS was re-titled 20 (P)AFU. Then it was the turn of 1 GTS to close, and to be dissolved into 20 (P)AFU on 24 March 1943, making Croughton a satellite of Kidlington. Finally, 2 GTS, Weston, ceased to function on 6 April 1943 and emerged the same day, and at Weston, as yet another part of 20 (P)AFU. Before that date different pupils arrived for training and soon three dozen Oxfords were based here. During March, 20 (P)AFU had received seventy-six Oxfords and three Ansons; its later strength was double that figure. Weston-on-the-Green was now a satellite of Kidlington.

AMWD, as good as its word, laid Sommerfeld Tracking in September 1943. Thereafter by day – and particularly by night – Oxford flying took place until 20 (P)AFU disbanded on 31 May 1945. Weston remained in 23 Group until 1 October 1945 when it came under 3 MU, which held it until 15 March 1946. Control then passed to Upper Heyford, a 38 Group station in Transport Command.

The Korean War brought weeks of high tension to many British airfields, and Upper Heyford was no exception. On 10 June 1950 Weston was placed at the disposal of Bomber Command, which held the station until 9 August 1950, when the Air Positioning Plotting Unit arrived. That was part of 62 Group under whose command Weston remained until 20 April 1951, when the site was placed on care and maintenance.

With so much air transport activity in the area, it was not long before Transport Command repossessed the airfield for use as a dropping area for exercises run by 1 PTS. Trainees were able to jump from a basket suspended below an LZ Kite Balloon that for many years drifted daily above the airfield. Over the years parachutists have also descended from Valettas, Beverleys, Argosys, Andovers and Hercules. During 1976 the parachutists' captive balloon was removed to Hullavington. Since then free-fall parachute jumping has very frequently taken place, both civil and military. Weston-on-the-Green is also home to the Oxford Gliding Club and the RAF Sport Parachute Association.

**Main features:**
*Runways:* 265° 4,500ft, 210° 3,600ft, Sommerfeld Tracking (removed post-war). *Hangars:* two Bessoneau nine-bay, two Bessoneau twelve-bay, one T2, four Double 69ft Blister, six Single 69ft Blister. *Accommodation:* RAF officers 47, SNCOs 216, ORs 434; WAAF officers 8, ORs 126.

Currently Weston-on-the-Green has three grass *Runways:* 10/28 2,985ft, 06/24 2,720ft, 01/19 2,265ft. The DZ has a 2nm radius based on the airfield's centre. PPR is needed before entering the circuit.

## WHITE WALTHAM (MAIDENHEAD), Berkshire

*51°30N 00°04W 130ft asl; SU850785. 2 miles SW of Maidenhead*

'Waltham', 'tis said, means 'Welcome'.

Never was that better fulfilled than in September 1945 when White Waltham's 'Air Pageant supporting the Air Transport Auxiliary Benevolent Fund' turned out to be one of the best of air shows. For a mere 23p, a GWR 4-6-0 loco towed us out of foggy, filthy Paddington, past the Kraft cheese works (and Tempest-packed Langley) to a Maidenhead displaying show proclaimers including Hurricane '8633' collecting money outside a cinema. A short bus trip took Alan Wright and me to White Waltham, where we arrived as an all-blue Miles M.38 was being chased by 'Maggie' R1901, followed by that great survivor, Miles Sparrowhawk *G-AGDL*. Throaty Firebrand TF IV EK637 banked steeply on approach while exclaiming a military message in an increasingly civilian world.

The half-crown entry allowed us close to Falcon IIIs, a Kirby Kite and a Kirby Cadet of the ATC GS, while overhead Harvard KF439 screamed at Mosquito VI SZ860. Both, like us, were clearly fascinated by passing all-silver RAF-marked Aerovan prototype U-O248 flying in Miles territory.

The static park was packed with 'goodies'. Argus II FK350 and Argus III HB658 reminded one that this was *the* home of those Fairchilds seen roaming Britain's balmy summer wartime eves when conveying home ATA ferry pilots after a hectic day. Local ATA trainers were also on show, including Harvard KF196 '4', and Coastal grey and white Hudson FK344 '5'. Not to be outdone, Anson NK957 appeared in an unusual overall dark green coat, pretending to be an early 'special forces' recruit.

Diverse visitors were a reminder of the multiplicity of types that ATA was delivering. Warwick GR V LM834, Typhoon JR263 marked HF-Z, Buckmaster T.1 RP176, into which we crawled, powered Hamilcar X LA704, RN Reliant FK878 alongside Sea Otter RD869, Hotspur III BT535, showing what Thame had suggested, and Wellington BJ712, displaying the hooded nose proposed by 26 OTU – all were for inspection. A slick Spitfire LF IX MK889 sheltered by Liberator C VI KH266 also among the endless assortment. BOAC York *G-AGNO* joined Dakota IV *G-AGKG* and Stirling IV EF323, while Barracuda RK461 and the Gloster E.28/39 rested in a hangar. Representatives of the ex-German Government – an Me 163, He 162 and Fw 190A-3 –

*White Waltham at the time of opening in 1936.*

*Fairchild Argus light transports were used by ATA as pilot ferries.*

shared space with Avenger FN766. Proving how clever it was, Cierva C-30a DR624 'KX-L' from Henley gyrated, joined by Hoverfly KK993 'KX-R', before 1415 brought along the latest Vickers, *G-AGOL,* the second Viking prototype. Then Lancaster PB388, marked 80-R, paraded within a stream of 'Lancs' trailed by a CB-17G. Three Boxted Meteor IIIs drowned out Lord Beaverbrook's speech, before Alex Henshaw, strapped to a Seafire 45, looped, upward rolled and steeply dived, giving a most stupendous aerobatic display. BOAC Lancastrian *G-AGMK* slipped in just before a trio of Benson Spitfire PR XIs (PM154, PM155, PM185) passed across. A superb showing of the 'new' Hawker Tempest II PR622 had it one moment high, the next incredibly low, all being interlaced with furious zooms skywards. That was in marked contrast with the stately passage of Sunderland V 'NS-C'. There was much, much more to thrill to before, for a tanner, a lovely old Thames Valley single-decker bus, RX 6247, hauled Alan Wright and me to meet GWR tank No 6990, which dragged us weary souls to Paddington. What a day it had been!

Memories of White Waltham would be incomplete without thinking of the five RAeS Garden Parties held there, in 1949 and then in the 1950s. A gorgeous girlfriend, nice little cucumber sandwiches, fine bone china chinking, cream piled high on strawberries, a chance to see and even 'bump into' massive Sir Frederick Handley Page, and all to the sound of the Fairey Works Band – that really was living. They surely presented the ultimate tea-tent experiences.

What, you may ask, do any such recollections have to do with White Waltham? In many ways they reflect what went on there for much of the war, for here was the HQ of the Air Transport Auxiliary, which exuded a refined, genteel side of flying brutish warplanes. Attractive ATA ladies, dark blue dressed, and smartly suited gentlemen pilots possessing high style and outstanding skill flew almost everything the British air forces ever used, to achieve which many were trained at White Waltham, whose grass was sampled by many exotic wartime aircraft.

White Waltham's 'B' Class aerodrome, built between the Shottesbrooke Estate and the main Bath road, had the Great Western Railway skirting its northern boundary. Asked to find a suitable base for a flying training school, de Havilland first chose Benson, but that had been earmarked to become an operational station. Instead, it purchased a 200-acre cornfield for development. As White Waltham aerodrome, measuring roughly 3,000 feet by 2,700 feet and 3 miles from Maidenhead, it opened on 16 November 1935 and served as home for a second flying school, born on 18 November 1935. Named No 13 E&RFTS, it provided ab initio training for pilots who flew mainly Tiger Moths together with Hart variants and Ansons. By 3 September 1939 some 600 pilots had been trained. Now renamed No 13 Elementary Flying Training School, it soon had an ELG at Waltham St Lawrence, and in April 1940 began making use of RLGs at Bray Court and Henley. Trainees included Flt Lt J. B. Nicolson, awarded the VC for his courage when flying a 249 Squadron

*The second Fairey Gyrodine G-AJJP, test-flown at White Waltham.*

Hurricane during the Battle of Britain.

White Waltham was subjected to a sharp attack on 3 July 1940 when at 1645 a Do 17 dropped a stick of bombs, killing one and injuring six personnel. Six Tiger Moths were destroyed and 25 damaged. On 20 December 1940 No 13 EFTS, after training some 650 pilots, moved to Westwood/Peterborough, making way for HQ main base and the training school of the Air Transport Auxiliary, founded by Gerard d'Erlanger, who, in the 1950s, became Chairman of BOAC.

ATA's very active association with White Waltham began on 15 February 1940 when No 3 Ferry Pilots Pool, using Tiger Moths and Magisters, formed with an establishment of nine aircraft and 40 pilots. On 1 May 1940 sections 'B' and 'C' (defined by the size and engine power of aircraft for which pilots trained) moved out. Section 'A' remained at White Waltham and on 5 November 1940 became No 1 Ferry Pilots Pool, alias Ferry Pool, ATA, flying Ansons and Arguses, before disbanding on 1 March 1946. The multi-role ATA Movements Flight formed in April 1942, relying upon Ansons, Arguses and Dominies.

Movement of large numbers of aircraft needed considerable planning and back-up, and in 1943 the aerodrome was extended, after which it became one of the busiest in Britain. From small beginnings ATA made 308,567 aircraft ferry flights during the Second World War. Of those, 78,500 were undertaken between February 1944 and January 1945, some involving deliveries to liberated Europe. The maximum number ferried in one day was 570, delivered on 21 February 1945.

Additional to ATA, along its southern boundary White Waltham hosted a variety of small RAF units. No 50 Group Communication Flight (CF) administering EFTSs was here between 2 September 1939 and December 1940, and 54 Group CF between April 1943 and 1 May 1944. Training Command CF arrived on 12 January 1940, and on 27 May 1940 split into Flying Training CF and Technical Training Command CF, the former leaving for Woodley on 15 February 1942, the latter staying until 6 November 1945. Army Co-operation Command CF formed on 1 January 1941 out of 22 Group CF, and was renamed 2nd TAF CF on 1 June 1943. It remained until late summer 1943.

On 14 October 1942 No 123 Gliding School opened, initially as No 3 Elementary GTS, and remained for many years, also making some use of Bray. Consolidated here again in February 1948, it became No 623 GS on 1 September 1955 and closed on 1 May 1963.

The RAF Staff College CF formed on 24 June 1946 and, larger than most, used Proctors, Oxfords, Dominies, a Hudson, Spitfire 16 and a Mosquito. On 14 November 1946 it passed to Technical Training Command, and in early 1948 moved to Andover.

Much associated with Reserve Command, White Waltham accommodated its CF from 10 September 1946 to 1 August 1950, when it became the Home Command CS, still flying Proctors, Ansons and Dominies. On 8 August 1950 the Home Command Examining Unit opened as a spin-off from Home Command Training Flight, using two Mosquito T3s, two Ansons, a Balliol T2 and a Chipmunk; it disbanded in 1951. On 31 December 1951 Home Command CS divided into Home Command Examining Unit and Flying Training Command CS, the former disbanding on 15 January 1959. Flying Training Command CS, flying Ansons, Chipmunks and a Pembroke, disbanded on 1 April 1964 on the formation of Southern CS at Bovingdon.

Final RAF representation was by the London University Air Squadron/ULAS based at White Waltham from 8 February 1959 until 10 August 1973, and No 6 Air Experience Flight formed here on 8 September 1959, which moved to Abingdon on 23 August 1973. It had been co-located with HQ Air Cadets, White Waltham-based from 1 May 1960 to 23 September 1968, when the

*The Rotodyne in Fairey's White Waltham flight-test hangar.*

*Fairey Junior OO-TIT at the
1950 RAeS Garden Party.*

HQ moved to Brampton. No 1 AEF was also here, between 7 February and 12 September 1959, and again from 10 September 1960 until 1 April 1963. Disbandment of RAF Home Command brought departure of the RAF, whose tenure – always on the airfield's southern area – ceased on 31 August 1973.

There had been other major players at White Waltham. During the first post-war year White Waltham was used by BOAC, then in November 1946 the Fairey Aviation Company, forced out of Heston and Heathrow, took over the main buildings and associated premises on the airfield's north side. A year later the company acquired the whole aerodrome, the West London Aero Club turning RAF Home Command and other commercial interests into lodgers. From here – until its demise – Fairey flight tested Fireflies and Gannets. The Duke of Edinburgh learned to fly at White Waltham in 1952, and for a while kept his DH Heron here.

Most of Fairey's helicopter and rotary wing development flying took place at White Waltham, Squadron Leader Arkell flying the Gyrodyne and setting up an international speed record for helicopters over a 3km course at the aerodrome. Later the Jet Gyrodyne was tested here, the Ultra-Light helicopter first flying on 14 August 1955. More spectacularly, it was at White Waltham on 6 November 1957 that Squadron Leader W R Gelatly took the Fairey Rotodyne, the world's first vertical take-off airliner, on its first flight.

Along the eastern fringe West London Aero Club re-established itself in 1946, utilising some Robin hangars. It now runs the airfield, where a goodly assortment of privately owned light aircraft remain, and Freestyle operates Pitts S-2As.

Since the days of the Domesday Book there has been a Waltham here, but where the 'White' came from uncertainty remains. Close-by Bray (where that changeable vicar hailed from) and quaintly named Tittle Row, Woolley Green and Touchenend do not provide clues. Maybe the answer lies with someone pure who dwelt in Maidenhead Thicket.

*Hawker Cygnet G-EBMB at the RAeS Garden Party on 6 May 1951. (John Strangward)*

**Main features**:
*Grass Runways:* 03 3,075ft, 07 3,330ft, 11 2,790ft. *Buildings:* When opened a large hangar was attached to offices together with a prominent flying control building in which were lecture rooms, the Link Trainer room and sundry offices. Hangar space developed into an industrial complex. There were Robin hangars on the eastern boundary and sundry blister hangars. RAF Home Command and contractors occupied assorted buildings on the southern boundary.

## WINDRUSH, Gloucestershire

*51°48N/01°43W 560ft asl; SP180120. 4 miles W of Burford*

It was near the end of a day when the fight to the south had been hard. Kenley was clouted, Biggin battered, Gosport bashed, Croydon and Manston too. Not long after twilight on that double summertime eve, around fifty German raiders headed inland where a number of rudimentary landing ground flare paths were lit to aid crews night-flying and distract German bombs away from Permanent Stations. At Windrush lines of lights edging the grass runway attracted the attention of a marauding Heinkel's crew, one of several raiders in the area that late Sunday evening of 18 August 1940.

Lining themselves with the RLG, a field calling itself RAF Windrush, they must have noticed ahead of them another aircraft. Their ten 50kg HE bombs fell close to the landing ground, one without exploding. As they burst, the Heinkel 111 closed on the aircraft ahead, Anson L9164 of 6 SFTS. Both aircraft were flying at about 1,000 feet, and as the Heinkel closed from 200 to 150 yards its front gunner opened fire. Sgt B Hancock in the Anson immediately switched off his navigation lights, banked to port and in a brilliant flash the German bomber rammed itself into the trainer. Eye-witnesses maintained that Hancock had deliberately turned into the bomber's path. Whatever the truth, a blazing inferno shattered within seconds to fall over fields about two miles south-west of the RLG.

The hours following were the most action-packed this little landing area would know, for, not long after, another enemy aircraft crashed near Northleach. Later on the 19th, Harvard P5788 of 6 SFTS crashed at Haselton, killing one and injuring the other member of the crew. At noon that same day Windrush passed from 15 SFTS to 6 SFTS, whose RLG it remained until its use ceased on 12 July 1945.

Windrush, which opened in early summer 1940, was serving by mid-June as an RLG for the aircraft of Little Rissington's 6 SFTS as much as for its parent unit, 15 SFTS. Both the ATS and ITS of the latter unit trained here, by day and night, in support of which they were allocated, at an early stage, three Nissen huts on the camp for their groundcrews on detachment. Between 27 July 1940 and 19 August 1940, care of the RLG was vested in 15 SFTS, then it returned to 6 SFTS, which had earlier looked after it.

The bright lights of Windrush seem to have been irresistible to the Luftwaffe, for on 2 September 1940 it returned, depositing a mile from the RLG some small HEs that failed to explode. Ten more were dropped a mile or so to the north-east of the site shortly after midnight on 11 September 1940, so Windrush was indeed diverting bombing away from major stations and not getting much hurt in the process.

During 1941 No 2 SFTS also used the landing ground, but Little Rissington's Oxfords mainly monopolised the circuit. On 22 April 1942 No 6 SFTS opened after re-organising as 6 (P)AFU, and Windrush was upgraded, becoming Little Rissington's satellite. Although the training programme was amended, the aircraft remained the same. Improvements to Windrush were made at this time. Nine Blister hangars were erected on the western side of the landing ground, now encircled by a perimeter track. Buildings grouped in the north-east corner served for instructional purposes, those in the north-west corner forming the communal site. In early summer 1942 two Sommerfeld Track runways were laid. Four collections of huts along the A40 road provided living accommodation.

On a fine, clear day the open plateau situation nearly 600 feet above sea level affords a vista of distant county after county. Somewhere in such a lovely setting with as beautiful a name as Windrush should never have known the tragedies that afflicted it.

**Main features:**
*Runways:* 011° 3,000ft, 071° 2,550ft, Sommerfeld Track. *Hangars:* one T1, five Double 69ft Blister, four Single 69ft Blister. *Accommodation:* RAF 132 officers, 142 SNCOs, 519 ORs; WAAF 4 officers, 2 SNCOs, 100 ORs.

## WING, Buckinghamshire

*51°40N/00°45W 450ft asl; SP860240. 7 miles N of Aylesbury, W of the village of Wing*

Clyffe, Foulness, Cublington – all have been suggested for transformation into international airports. All have – so far – been turned down, including the Roskill Commission's 1971 nomination of Cublington (alias Wing) as a site for London's third airport, which released the customary furore. No such opposition was voiced (or would have been tolerated) when in 1940 the same land was acquired for a temporary bomber airfield, which opened on 17 November 1941.

Although 26 OTU formed on 15 January 1942 under 7 Group control, it was March before all runways were clear of obstructions, and on the 18th a Tiger Moth was first to land. Wellington Ics fast joined it for No 1 training course, which opened on 25 April. Available were eight Ansons, and Wellingtons for conversion, with use being made of Cheddington. On 11 May 1942, control passed to 92 (Bomber) Group.

On 31 May twenty crews set out from Graveley, Huntingdonshire, for a part in the Cologne 'Thousand Plan' raid, which cost 26 OTU three crews. Of the remainder, fifteen took part in the following Essen raid and one more failed to return. Wellingtons of 26 OTU also participated in the June 'Thousand Plan' raid on Bremen. By August 1942, average strength of the OTU stood at thirty-four Wellingtons and eight Ansons. Two Lysander target-towers and a Wellington-equipped 'E' (Air Firing) Flight.

It was at this time that residents of Wing had a rare treat. Few interested in wartime 'new types', as they were colloquially called, failed to peer into a closely guarded copy of AP1480X, an official handbook containing silhouettes of experimental British aircraft. With no photocopier around, tracing paper knew its true place – against every page of this much-guarded loose-leaf treasure. Flick through those magic pages and a racy-looking six-cannon fighter named Experimental Aeroplane No 120, rumoured to be called the 'Whippet', attracted wonder. Seeing is surely believing, but nobody ever seemed to find anyone who had ever sighted the fighter, although many indulged in wishful thinking.

It was in reality one in a line of unusual aircraft from Martin Baker, best known for ejector seats and that other brilliant performer, the MB-5. Its forerunner, our 'Whippet', was really the MB-3, transported from Denham to Wing for long overdue flight trials. On 31 August 1942, in the hands of Capt H V Baker, it made its first flight. Sadly its existence was all too brief for, on 12 September 1942, its mighty Sabre engine failed the ensuing forced-landing and depriving Capt Baker of his life.

By then well-established, 26 OTU was participating in *Goodwood* bombing raids, including attacks on Dusseldorf, Bremen and Essen. All were flown from Wing, where, in October, the OTU's average total strength had increased to include two aged Wellington Is, two Wellington Ias, forty-nine Wellington Ics, six Ansons, three Lysander target-towers and a Defiant. Equipment changed little until February 1943, when the first ten Wellington IIIs were received to supplement fifty-two Mk Ics on strength. A further sixteen Mk IIIs came in March, re-equipment being completed in May, although Mk Ics lingered long after. It was August 1943 before a full switch to Hercules Wellingtons was made. During April three Martinets had replaced the other gunnery trainers.

More fascinating would have been the fruition of plans for operational Wellington VI high-altitude, pressure-cabin-equipped bombers to be stationed at Wing. They needed to be based well inland in order to reach their daylight operational height in good time. Flight trials encountered many problems, and a suitable pressurised rear turret was never developed. Various proposals were made for the use of the sixty or so Mk VIs completed, but the bombers were too specialised for anything other than their primary role, for which they were too slow.

Instead, 26 OTU started receiving Wellington Xs during July 1943, by which time only one Mk Ic remained at Wing. That month was auspicious for, during its course, 26 OTU despatched six effective *Nickel* sorties over France, the unit's first such employment. In mid-July a few Tomahawks of 1684 Bomber Defence Training Flight transferred from the satellite, Little Horwood. Although rated unsuitable for their task, they out-stayed their value; in mid-1944 three remained at Wing, although the Flight's main equipment was by then six Hurricane IIcs.

Operational bombing was briefly resumed when on 30/31 August, 2/3 and 8/9 September 1943 the Wellington Xs attacked ammunition dumps in the Foret d'Eperlecques during the build-up to operation *Starkey*, costing 26 OTU one crew. About 20 per cent of the OTU's strength consisted of Wellington Xs, the remainder being Mk IIIs, one of which, X3790, was involved in a spectacular

*Wing's most spectacular sight, the racy Martin Baker MB.3 R2492, first flown on 31 August 1942.*

incident on 7 August 1943. After hitting a tree, it crashed on to the roof of a house in Winslow High Street before careering across the street, where it clipped the top of the Chandos Arms before demolishing four cottages. Four of the crew and thirteen civilians died.

During the last three months of 1943 the OTU despatched twenty-six *Nickel* sorties from Wing. *Bullseyes* attracted far more effort, and during one of them Wellington BJ978, off course over the London IAZ, was hit by anti-aircraft fire. Enemy bombers were active that night.

A mixture of Wellington IIIs and Xs equipped 26 OTU almost to the end of the war, and half a dozen Hurricane IIcs had replaced the unit's Martinets at the satellite in April 1944. By June No 26 OTU's overall strength was twenty-six Wellington IIIs and thirteen Mk Xs, four Martinets, four Hurricanes, an Oxford I and two Oxford Mk IIs. June 1944 was a busy month, with Wing accepting operational bomber diversions. The highlight, though, was again a sombre accident. Wellington X HE854 was involved in a disastrous collision with a parked Wellington, two '60-footer' low-loaders and a hangar. A serious fire ensued, and three WAAFs with the lorries and the Wellington's co-pilot were killed. Take-off swings as a result of wrong power settings, engine problems and also undercarriage troubles plagued bomber OTUs.

Constant changes took place in crew requirements, resulting on 26 August 1944 in 26 OTU's strength being reduced by a quarter. Elements at the satellite were withdrawn and 1684 BDTF disbanded. The reduction was temporary, though, for in October No 26 OTU rose again to full strength. Two Warwick IIs were taken on strength, HG349 on 18 November and HG350 on 30 November, for assessment of that type's suitability for OTU employment, particularly as this and the Centaurus-engined Buckingham were considered likely to play an increasing part overseas and in the post-war Air Force. Wellington Xs formed three-quarters of the main equipment, and by February 1945 No 26 OTU held fifty-two Mk Xs and only seven Mk IIIs. Warwick trials were continuing, both examples remaining until autumn 1945.

The end of the war in Europe brought hectic activity because Wing was chosen to receive home-coming prisoners of war. The first contingent arrived on 9 April 1945 in thirty-three Dakotas, and totalled 819 men. By the end of April 1945 14,794 ex-POWs had passed through the station, chosen because its central position made it ideal for dispersal. On 8 May no fewer than 750 POWs arrived in sixty-one Lancasters and eight Dakotas, while an amazing 132 Lancaster landings were made at the station on the 15th. Of the 1,269 aircraft that brought POWs here in May, 518 were Lancasters. Tragedy struck once in what must have been momentous days for, on 10 May, a Lancaster carrying thirty-one POWs crashed on landing.

On 15 June 1945, with the disbandment of 92 Group, 26 OTU became part of 91 Group, and the following month the Gunnery Flight returned again from Little Horwood. Post-war training was on an ever-reduced scale and, on 4 March 1946, 26 OTU closed. Maintenance Command took control of Wing on 4 May, and the site was disposed of by April 1960.

**Main features:**
*Runways:* 258° 6,000ft x 150ft, 170° 4,200ft x 150ft, 302° 3,480ft x 150ft, concrete. *Hangars:* four T2, one B1. *Hardstandings:* thirty heavy bomber type. *Accommodation:* RAF officers 158, SNCOs 526, ORs 1,292; WAAF officers 10, ORs 501.

## WINKFIELD, Berkshire

*51°26N/00°41W 230ft asl; SU912726. 4 miles SW of Windsor*

A grass field near the village of Winkfield served as an RLG for Tiger Moths of No 18 EFTS Fairoaks between 28 May 1941 and 9 July 1945. Winkfield, with only a handful of buildings, closed soon after the war. The site was later used for radio and space communications research.

**Main features:**
*Grass runs:* N/S 1,995ft, NE/SW 2,940ft, E/W 1,890ft, NW/SE 2,310ft. *Hangars:* three standard Blisters, one Double Blister, one Extra Over Blister. Hardstanding: one. *Accommodation:* RAF officers 3, SNCOs 3, ORs 60; no WAAFs.

## WISLEY, Surrey

*51°19N/00°27W 44ft asl; TQ075575. E of Woking to the south of the A3 and east of the B2039*

Competition there may have been between Vickers and Handley Page, but they had one thing in common, the origins of their development and flight test centres. Just as Radlett was chosen after a forced-landing, so it was with Vickers. Captain Mutt Summers, Chief Test Pilot of Vickers-Armstrong, was flying a Wellesley when he encountered serious trouble and force-landed behind trees fringing the A3 London to Portsmouth road. His chosen field was about three miles from the Vickers-Armstrong Weybridge works.

*The first prototype Viking, G-AGOK, at Wisley in the summer of 1945. (Vickers)*

*Nene Viking G-AJPH at Wisley prior to flight-testing. (Vickers)*

*Valetta VL275, fitted with a multi-wheel undercarriage and tested at Wisley.*

Vickers built large aircraft and Brooklands/Weybridge was a small aerodrome. In 1942 the site where Summers had landed was surveyed, found worth developing, and purchased. It was then developed into an airfield for Vickers; a grass airfield known as Wisley, it came into use in 1943 and was used during the remainder of the war. From here the Windsor and later Warwick were tested, and on 22 June 1945 the VC-1 Viking *G-AGOK*, after erection here, was first flown. On 1 September 1946 Viking *G-AHOP* made the twenty-four-seater's first in-service BEA flight from Northolt to Kastrup. Elevator overbalance and icing problems caused grounding of the twelve in service in November 1946. Return to service came in April 1947 with the coming of the Wisley-tested stressed-skin Mk IB.

Wisley remained in use post-war and additional accommodation was built, making it a more elaborate main flight-testing centre. Production aircraft Weybridge-built usually ended their initial flight at Wisley and were delivered from there. A note of distinction came on 6 April 1948 when the Vickers Type 618, the twin-Nene Viking VX856 and the world's first pure jet transport, first flew from Wisley. It tested the Rolls-Royce Nene and was used for high-altitude trials. Components of the prototype Viscount were transported from Weybridge to Wisley from where the aircraft first flew on 16 July 1948. The prototype Valiant V-bomber made its first flight on 18 May 1951, from the grass at Wisley, although its next three flights were from Hurn's runway. With the considerable increase in size and weight the grass runway was obviously inadequate, and in 1952 a single paved runway, 7,500 feet in length, was laid. The prototype Vanguard first flew from the new runway, whereas the VC-10 prototype's maiden flight on 29 June 1962 was from Brooklands.

Neither Wisley nor its runway could solve an ever-increasing problem, the traffic density brought about by Heathrow and Gatwick, which made test-flying here difficult. As a result the British Aircraft Corporation, which took over Vickers-Armstrong, closed Wisley in 1973. Attempts to re-open it for civilian flying were abandoned after meeting much local opposition.

**Main features:**
Wisley consisted of a block of industrial hangars and flight shed along its western side. There was one, remaining, 7,500ft runway.

*The first Viscount prototype, VX211. (Vickers)*

## WITNEY, Oxfordshire

*51°47N/01°31W 355ft asl; SP335095. 1 mile W of Witney by Minster Lovell*

Not strictly a Second World War military airfield, assorted factory buildings still mark the position of the de Havilland Witney works where many military aircraft were overhauled or repaired before return to service. The factory overtook the Witney 1918-19 RFC/RAF training school west of Witney town, where training in fighter tactics was undertaken under the control of the 21st Wing.

Preparation started in 1917, but it was spring 1918 when three training squadrons moved to the aerodrome, where aircraft accommodation was to be in eight Bessoneau hangars supplemented by a General Service Shed and other wooden structures. First in on 30 March was No 24 Training (ex-Reserve) Squadron, quickly followed by No 8 Training (ex-Reserve) Squadron, both from Netheravon. On 30 April 1918 No 7 Training (ex-Reserve) Squadron joined them, the aircraft now here including Avro 504Ks, F-2Bs, DH 5s and RE 7s. All three squadrons disbanded on 15 August 1918, immediately being resurrected as No 33 Training Depot Station, which closed in September 1919. Its slim derivative, No 33 Training School, functioned until closure in April 1920.

Apart from limited civilian flying in the late 1920s, Witney saw little use until 1933, when Universal Aircraft Services Ltd formed, making use of the main hangar, followed the next year by Witney & Oxford Aero Club. DH 60s then became a daily sight. In 1936 the Witney Aeronautical College Ltd opened. By 1938 Witney was encountering financial problems, but the aerodrome remained functional. Updating had attracted some BA Swallows, and the Willoughby Delta Co, interested in developing a form of flying-wing. A variety of light aircraft used Witney, and Alan Cobham brought his 'flying *circus*' here, something one would not forget!

Soon after the outbreak of war the airfield was requisitioned and used as an RLG by 2 SFTS Brize Norton, one of whose Oxfords, P6796, crashed at the airfield on 2 February 1940. Also at the outbreak of war a dispersed site for contractor servicing of de Havilland aircraft was needed, and the company acquired Witney, where P E Gordon-Marshall became General Manager, ably assisted by Ken Brown. The first year of war saw work devoted principally to repair and overhaul, mainly of Tiger Moths supplemented by Dominies, Queen Bees and a variety of DH light aircraft used for communication purposes between units and factories. Two Bellman hangars were erected at the start of 1940 to cope with any increase in war work. For safety reasons the US Embassy Flight lodged here.

At 0530 on 22 November 1940 a raider released two HE bombs on Witney. They fell some way from the works, one exploding behind a brewery and the other in the church grounds. Some 200 houses were damaged, army vehicles on the Church Green were burned, and many shop windows in the High Street broken. The damage was far out of proportion to the bomb load. DH Witney was unaffected.

At Hatfield de Havilland had repaired the 150 Hurricanes called for in a contract completed in February 1941. Obtaining a second contract including specialised Sea Hurricanes, and needing additional space at Hatfield for Mosquito production, the work was switched to Witney, the new line opening in May 1941. Tiger Moth overhauls were transferred to Taylorcraft at Rearsby.

Under another contract Spitfire repair began in March 1942, extra hangar space being provided. All-metal Spitfires needed jigging, a challenge for those used to wood, fabric and metal frames. Witney was now a busy centre, with DH light aircraft still being handled. Gradually concentration fell upon Spitfires and DH 89s. According to the de Havilland Directors' Reports, Witney had by 15 August 1945 processed 1,450 aircraft, although the precise figure may be higher. In summer 1944 output had reached five fighters each week, the 373rd and last Hurricane being delivered in October out of a contract for 450, the others having been 'reduced to produce'. Some 205 Spitfires appear to have been completely overhauled, together with 802 de Havilland types. It is claimed that 450 aircraft in all were 'reduced to produce', with 6,000 removed components being repairable.

Witney works completed much of the final 150 Dominie contract. In September 1942 Brush Electrical secured a contract to build Dominies, Witney staff helping to initiate the task. When Brush production ended in March 1946, remaining components were transferred to Witney for completion. More than a hundred Loughborough-started Dominies were thus finished to civilian Rapide requirements, necessary expertise having been maintained in wartime because a limited number of DH 89 airframes were needed as Rapides for specialised civilian operators.

For a while de Havilland maintained the Witney facility, viewing it as a UK-based reception centre for de Havilland (Canada) products. In 1947 several of the earliest Chipmunks were assembled for sales promotion, then in 1949 Witney assembled the first DHC Beaver in the UK, but these were increasingly hard times and in August 1949 de Havilland moved out of Witney, transferring work to Leavesden. Land acquired for airfield extension in wartime needed to be returned to pre-war ownership, which much reduced the airfield's size and usefulness. Smiths Industries purchased the site in September 1949, opening a factory here in 1951. The General Service Shed survived to 1970, and a few First World War relics and wartime hangars remain.

**Main features:**
*Runways:* grass airfield with available runs of NE/SW 2,610ft, N/S 1,800ft, E/W 2,139ft and SE/NW 1,650ft. *Hangars:* six sheds, built in three pairs, and a major servicing shed were features of the First World War aerodrome. During the Second War a main pre-war hangar was supplemented with two Bellman hangars and at least two Robin hangars for CRO use. The factory producing DH 89s was alongside the Burford road and in the north-west corner of the site.

## WITTERING, Cambridgeshire

*52°36N/00°27W 273ft as; TF045025. 3 miles S of Stamford by the A1*

'Royal Air Force Wittering, Home of the Harrier'. Both are assured a special place in RAF history.

Wittering sits unusually at the summit of a grass bank rising from the A1 towards a bold plateau and retains a wide assortment of structures, some visible from the A1 being quite aged. Gone, though, are the pre-war and wartime 'twin box' Watch Office and Tower built in front of the three nine-bay C Type hipped hangars, one of which was reduced to an awful mess by the 1941 bombing. One remains, supplemented by a post-war 'Gaydon'-type large one and, more recently, a smaller custom-built hangar.

Throughout its long history Wittering has been an interesting station. It came into use during the First World War as Stamford, and between December 1916 and November 1917 housed FE-2bs of 'A' Flight, No 38 Home Defence Squadron. The 35th Wing Headquarters at Stamford opened on 22 September 1917 and closed on 9 April 1919, administered by No 1 Training Depot Station at Wittering between August 1917 and disbandment on 14 March 1919, and No 5 TDS at nearby Easton-on-the-Hill from 24 September 1917 until 14 March 1919, when it became No 5 Training School. As a companion 1 TDS had 'C' Flight 90 Squadron (formed from 38 Squadron) from September 1918 until its demise in June 1919. Stamford by then had been home mainly for 504s, Camels and Pups. At the end of 1919 it became a storage depot until placed on care and maintenance in January 1920.

Stamford's resurrection resulted from the air defence review of the early 1920s. Its name was changed to Wittering in May 1924, arrangements being finalised on 1 May for the removal of the RAF Central Flying School from Upavon to Wittering because the former station would be in an operational area. Wittering had been sufficiently rebuilt to allow the advance party of CFS to arrive from Upavon on 21 July 1926, and for the School to re-open on 17 October 1926. Many of Wittering's existing buildings date from that rebuilding period, a typical example being the guardroom, whose basic structure is typical of the 1920s. Wittering then had two hangars, an Aircraft Shed Double (322/17), reconditioned and half serving as a storage area, and a similar shed, half used as a workshop. Much of the old station had been remodelled, including Main Stores and SHQ (191/24). In a new Sergeants' Mess sixty-eight SNCOs could be accommodated, and in each of the four Barrack Blocks, New Type 'C' 242/23, three NCOs and sixty-four airmen. Station Offices (1799/25) and a Guardhouse (84/24) were later additions, likewise a 1924-style Officers' Mess. Airmen's Married Quarters were of 1922 design, whereas the Watch Office was to pattern 1926/27.

*Beaufighter 1f X7876 ZK-F of No 25 Squadron, Wittering.*

*The Officers' Mess at Wittering after bombing.*
*(M L Gibson)*

The main purpose of CFS was the training of instructors. Introduced by 'E' Flight in 1927 was a standard refresher course, and new training schemes were studied, some relating to blind flying. Instrument courses initiated in 1930 became a standard part of the CFS instructors' course. During its nine years here, CFS operated many aircraft types. Between 1926 and 1931 these included the Bristol F-2b, DH 9a, Lynx, Snipe, Grebe, Gamecock and Siskin. In 1931-32 Fairey IIIFs and Bulldogs were used, as well as a Vickers Victoria. Further changes in 1932-33 brought along Bulldog Trainers, Hawker Tomtits, Hart day bombers and Armstrong-Whitworth Atlases. CFS commenced its return to Upavon on 1 August 1935, completing the move on 2 September. Wittering had been selected as a fighter Sector Station, guarding northern East Anglia, with an extension towards Digby barring entry to the Midlands.

As an interim feature, No 11 FTS formed at Wittering on 1 October 1935 and equipped with Audaxes, Tutors, Harts, Gauntlets, a few Furies and later Ansons and Oxfords. A new Station Headquarters within Fighter Command formed on 11 April 1938 to control one single-seater fighter squadron and one multi-seat fighter squadron. No 11 FTS began moving to Shawbury on 13 May 1938, having recently been a lodger at this 12 Group station.

By then Wittering's appearance had again changed, a result of being selected as a Permanent Station. A 1935 contract required one 1917 hangar to be retained and three nine-bay C Type Aircraft Sheds to be constructed. Main Stores (2108/37) were erected in the centre of the Technical Site. AMQs to 1922, 1931, 1932 and 1933 specifications were upgraded and additional quarters built in 1934. There was a small southern extension to the camp, and on the field was laid a concrete taxi track, to which, in 1939, ten dispersal points were linked.

Wg Cdr D V Carnegi assumed command of Wittering on 16 May 1938 as 23 Squadron's Demons arrived. Two days later 213 Squadron's Gauntlets moved in from Church Fenton, and in August 64 Squadron's Demons came for the annual air defence exercise.

In October 1938 269 Squadron's Ansons were affiliated to 23 Squadron, whose Demons, now camouflaged, practised intercepting the newcomers. A winter conference held by Fighter Command at Wittering brought squadron Spitfires and Hurricanes together for the first time. News was given that 'as a temporary measure' 23 Squadron would arm with Blenheim I(f) ground attack fighters, each having a four-machine-gun belly tray. They joined the squadron with alacrity, for it was fully re-armed by the end of the year.

Companion squadron No 213 received its first Hurricanes on 16 January 1939, reaching establishment of sixteen on 3 March. A few days later the biplane era passed from Wittering. Numerous tactical exercises followed, including the involvement of French bombers, which 213 Squadron intercepted during a mock attack upon Birmingham on 17 August. A few days later mobilisation was ordered, and at 0800 on 3 September 1939, with German withdrawal from Poland unlikely, machine-gun posts around Wittering's perimeter were manned. Detachments from 213 Squadron proceeded daily to West Raynham and undertook convoy patrols off Norfolk. Blenheims of 23 Squadron commenced night stand-bys in October 1939, one Flight being at readiness while the other trained at Digby.

With Luftwaffe activity concentrated upon coastal shipping, No 610 Squadron arrived on 8 October to mount East Coast patrols. Ten days later there was a scramble for a possible 'bogey' off Wells-next-the-Sea, before winter weather turned very bad, limiting enemy activity. On 21 March 264 Squadron began detaching Flights of Defiants to Wittering for training, and on 4 April 1940 610 Squadron left for Prestwick. Detachments of 264 Squadron rotated, but April's main event was the arrival on the 7th of 266 Squadron, the groundcrews stylishly in an Ensign airliner. Three days later 266 Squadron joined the convoy patrol business.

Sudden German attack in the west resulted in the Defiants at once leaving for action. On 16 May 1940 'B' Flight, 213 Squadron, hurried to France via Manston, groundcrews following in a Bombay and Ensign, chased by the squadron's other Hurricanes. 'B' Flight joined Merville's 3 Squadron for an early morning patrol during which a group of Do 17s were attacked with uncertain results. Mid-morning 'A' Flight arrived and operated alongside 79 Squadron. Next day was busy too, and at midday on 19 May Merville was bombed, the Hurricanes being scrambled as much for survival as anything else. One Hurricane was brought down – by 'friendly' anti-aircraft fire – and Ju 88s were engaged. More patrols took place next day then, early on 21 May, 'A' Flight returned to Manston to operate over France from there and Biggin Hill, to where the entire squadron moved on 26 May to escort Blenheim raids and help cover the evacuation of the BEF, before returning to Wittering on 31 May. The station had, by then, opened its first satellite, Easton (alias K3), from where, starting on 26 May, No 266 Squadron nightly dispersed its Spitfires while 32 Squadron used the site each night.

With the Dunkirk evacuation under way, 266 Squadron's Spitfires moved to Martlesham and were earmarked for a possible move to France. Instead, they reinforced the Duxford Sector while that station's squadrons were away. It was 2 June before, operating from Martlesham, the Wittering Spitfires first patrolled over the retreating BEF, claiming a Bf 110 shot down and two Bf 109s damaged, for the loss of two Spitfires.

The Luftwaffe first directed its attention to Wittering on 6 June 1940. Lights were on at the Q-site when raiders arrived to deposit eleven bombs near Etton. On 9 June 213 Squadron went again to Biggin Hill, returned briefly to collect belongings on 18 June, then left Wittering for Exeter, moving not long before Wittering's Blenheims drew first blood.

Around midnight on 18/19 June 1940, a handful of KG4's Heinkel He 111s, operating ironically from Merville, crossed the Norfolk coast near Wells-next-the-Sea and were soon in the Wittering Sector and heading for airfield targets. Blenheims of 23 Squadron were ordered to intercept – easier said than done. Duxford's Spitfires were also despatched and, lacking AI radar, both stations' aircraft achieved surprising success in bringing down three Heinkels, two of which fell to 23 Squadron, one to Sqn Ldr J O'Brien and the other to Fg Officer H Duke-Woolley.

Wittering's Q-site was attacked again on 25 June, bombs falling half a mile away at North Borough. Air raid sirens wailed next night too, more bombs falling nearby, after 229 Squadron and its Hurricanes had arrived from Digby. On 29 June Plt Off Williams of 23 Squadron claimed an enemy bomber in the Norwich area.

Wittering was too far north for direct involvement in daylight raids during the Battle of Britain. Instead, its squadrons moved forward and reinforced 11 Group, 266 Squadron doing so on 12 August. 'Sailor' Malan's 74 Squadron replaced them at Wittering on the 14th. When, on 21 August, 266 Squadron returned from Hornchurch, among its Spitfires were some aged Mk Is with two-bladed

*A typical Wittering scene in 1944: the white Hampden AE373 sits behind a Spitfire F IX, and a Fw 190A noses into view. (Dave Benfield)*

wooden Watts propellers. No 74 Squadron was nudged north to Kirton, Nos 23 and 229 Squadrons making use of K3.

Each day during the summer of 1940, Wittering's squadrons were at readiness. On 31 August, for example, a day of hectic activity north of London, 64 Squadron defended the Wittering Sector, allowing 229 and 266 Squadrons to operate within the Debden and Duxford Sectors, before returning as usual to their base during the evening. Long overdue was replacement of 266 Squadron's aged Spitfires. It came in the form of Castle Bromwich-built Spitfire IIs, first taken into action on 7 September when two pilots over Yarmouth spotted a high-flying raider. They gave chase, and claimed to shoot it into the sea. A further change came on 9 September when 229 Squadron exchanged places with Northolt's No 1 Squadron. Then 23 Squadron moved to Ford and Middle Wallop on 12 September, night-readiness at K3 subsequently being provided by detachments of 29 Squadron, Digby.

Although enjoying some respite. No 1 Squadron was still available for action. On 15 September it provided rear support to 11 Group, by patrolling Duxford Sector during a day of intense fighting. Although there were warnings, September 1940 passed without Wittering being bombed. Two Hurricane pilots damaged a Ju 88 near South Cerney, and another pair chased a bomber out to sea, leaving it smoking. A trio of 1 Squadron's Hurricanes engaged a Do 17 near Banbury, and on 27 October others damaged a Do 17 near Feltwell. In late October 1940 No 266 Squadron exchanged its precious Spitfire IIs for Mk Is. Early on 28 October four small bombs fell in a field near a Bofors site by the A1. Next day was even more eventful, when eight pilots of 266 Squadron, operating with 12 Group from Duxford, engaged eleven Bf 109s. That day Blue Section shot down a Do 17 not far from Cambridge, but return fire pierced the coolant system of a Hurricane, forcing it to crash near Peterborough. A chase by 1 Squadron near Sutton Bridge on the following day resulted in the destruction of Ju 88A-4 L1+GS.

Sorties by lone raiders relying upon frontal weather became a disturbing item of life in the Eastern Counties, for one pass by a single bomber could bring destruction and alarm out of all proportion to the effort mounted. Combating nuisance raiders was difficult – sounding too many public alerts was playing the enemy game. Yet without the warning siren, morale could suffer. On 31 October, with cloud base too low for fighter interception, German bombers marauded over a wide area. At Wittering five air raid warnings sounded that day, and in the afternoon a delayed-action bomb fell in St Leonard's Street, Stamford, where there was machine-gunning, causing two casualties.

In November 1940, when the day battle in the south was declared 'won', the future could be viewed with a little more confidence. From Wittering, as from many fighter stations, much effort was now expended on shipping protection.

The appearance of a Wittering Wing comprising Nos 1 and 266 Squadrons was important, and they trained with 19 Squadron at Fowlmere, forming a 12 Group Wing for coming offensive operations as well as engaging German fighter-bombers over the South East. At night 29 Squadron still maintained stand-by forces at K3, where 151 Squadron placed part of its strength from 12 November.

Sixty bombs fell near Wittering on 20 November 1940, some at Barnack. Enemy night-bombers were often routed over or near Wittering when heading for the Midlands. Consequently, No 25 Squadron moved in from Debden on 27 November to engage them, being joined three weeks later by 151 Squadron, which brought its Hurricanes along from Bramcote. For the day-fighter role, 229 Squadron's Hurricanes replaced those of No 1 Squadron on 15 December 1940, and in the midst of these squadron moves command of the station passed from Gp Capt Harry Broadhurst to Gp Capt Basil Embry. No 229's stay was brief, for it moved to Speke shortly before Christmas, so that in the New Year Wittering and K3 housed Nos 25 (Beaufighter), 151 (Hurricane and Defiant) and 266 (Spitfire) Squadrons.

January 1941 was extremely cold. Heavy snow fell on four days, icy conditions making fire-fighting very difficult. A German bomber crew delivered a New Year's Day gift of four 50kg bombs to the rear of 25 Squadron's hangar, damaging the boiler house and coal compound. A clear, cold night with a full moon, 16 January was ideal for fighting – if one could withstand the cold. Contrails from enemy aircraft were that night clear to view over a wide area, and Plt Off Stevens of 151 Squadron scored his first success, Do 17Z 5K+DM Werke Nr 3456, of 4./KG 3, shot down near Brentford, Essex. After refuelling and re-arming, his Hurricane was off again and he brought down He 111H-5 AI+JK, Werke Nr 3638, of 2./KG 53 in the sea off Canvey Island.

*Havoc 1 'G' of No 532 Squadron at Wittering in the spring of 1942.*
*(J Cheney collection via Dave Benfield)*

Another clear night was 14 March, when at about 2300, with the moon bright and high, a Ju 88 raced low across Wittering, unloading six 250kg bombs and about a hundred incendiaries on to the camp. The first bomb penetrated the roof of 25 Squadron's hangar, smashing through the wing of a Beaufighter without exploding. A second bomb burst in the hangar roof, causing widespread damage. The third hit the airmen's cookhouse and the fourth exploded by the gas decontamination centre. A fifth went off by the Officers' Mess, shattering the Card Room and living accommodation above. The sixth burst on the squash court. Incendiaries set a hangar on fire, and burned out the station cinema and two barrack blocks. Surprisingly, although fires raged for an hour and a half and there was considerable enemy activity overhead, no more bombing took place. Three men were killed and seventeen injured, two of whom died later. It was one of the most effective night raids on British airfields, yet by noon next day Wittering was again fully operational.

On 23 March 1941 Wittering responded to the attack when, for the first time, Spitfires of 266 Squadron participated in an offensive strike using a forward base. At night both 25 and 151 Squadrons were very busy, and when Commander-in-Chief, Fighter Command, Air Chief Marshal Sholto Douglas visited the station on 10 April 1941, intensive operations were under way. While he was there Sgt Bennett of 25 Squadron destroyed a Ju 88, 151 Squadron scored a victory, and Flt Lt Armitage of 266 Squadron a possible.

*An aerial view in 1944. Note the twin GS Sheds bottom left, with naval aircraft beyond the 'C' Type Hangar. The A1 road crosses the top of the view. via (Dave Benfield)*

The end of the night Blitz was approaching, involvement in offensive operations increasing. On 15 April 1941 transition was apparent when 266 Squadron joined Nos 65 and 402 on a 12 Group Wing sweep over France. The emphasis at Wittering, though, remained on night fighting. Whereas night-fighter operations had so far been mounted from the satellite to keep the main base in darkness, the opposite policy was now in force. Sophistication of night-fighting and radar gear demanded even more elaborate facilities.

Although the night campaign against British cities was soon to cease, not so the bombing of Wittering. On 7 May nine medium-sized bombs were laid across the parade ground and on to a corner of a barrack block, five men being killed and ten injured. That night the enemy suffered more, 25 Squadron claiming three raiders.

Luftwaffe response was swift, for on 8 May Wittering was twice attacked. In fine, clear conditions, a diving intruder dropped ten HEs and incendiaries, killing Plt Off Carlin of 151 Squadron and damaging a number of aircraft, one of which was burned out. In the second attack of the night, five HEs and incendiaries fell by the Watch Office. Wittering's night-fighters claimed two bombers and engaged three more.

Undaunted, the Luftwaffe returned the following night, dropping four HEs. A burst water main was soon repaired, and one bomb hit a hangar girder but failed to explode. Plt Off Picknet of 25 Squadron landed soon after, having claimed to have shot down 'possibly a Fw 200'. And still the attacks were not over, for on 10 May, regarded as the last night of the major German night Blitz, four Hes aimed incendiaries at the camp overshot and burst close to Wittering village. The station's pilots claimed five enemy aircraft that night, although confirmation was not possible. German records list seven aircraft as 'unbekant'.

RAF activity over France was fast increasing, drawing 266 Squadron more into the fighting, mostly from the satellite. On 27 June, for instance, Sgt Lewis claimed a Bf 109 over France, but it cost two of the squadron's pilots. A fast fight developed on 3 July, two 109s being claimed and five damaged. In mid-July 1941 Lord Nuffield was entertained at the station, to which some of his earliest Spitfire IIs had been despatched. Next month 266 Squadron re-equipped with Spitfire Vbs. Autumn 1941 witnessed the opening of the second satellite, at King's Cliffe, to where 266 Squadron moved.

Defiants of 151 Squadron and Beaufighters of 25 Squadron were here at the start of January 1942. No 266 left the Sector and was replaced by 616 Squadron, but there was no successor to 25 Squadron, which moved early in January to Ballyhalbert. Room had been made for 1529 BAT Flight, which had formed on 1 November 1941 using Master IIs and moved to Collyweston (alias K3 and WB3) on 5 April 1942. Enemy night activity was now mainly devoted to anti-shipping operations. Defiants of 151 Squadron, patrolling over the sea on 19 February 1942, came across some Do 217s, one of which was shot down by Sqn Ldr Smith's gunner, Flt Lt Beale. That night three more Do 217s and a Ju 88 were engaged.

For *Circus* and offensive operations No 486 (NZ) Squadron came from Kirton on 9 April, permitting 616 Squadron to stand down for conversion to Spitfire HF VIs. It also had an unusual night defence role for a Spitfire squadron, since it was affiliated to No 532 Squadron, Wittering's Turbinlite organisation.

On 10 July 1941 No 1453 (Turbinlite) Flight, the third of ten, had formed at Wittering with a nominal strength of eight plus one aircraft. The mixture of Havocs and Bostons each carried a Helmore airborne searchlight in the nose, the first patrol being flown on 22 October 1941. At first the Flight operated with the aid of satellite Hurricanes of 151 Squadron, whose task was to shoot at any illuminated enemy aircraft. On 4 September 1942 the Flight achieved squadron status, becoming No 532, and was equipped with two Havoc Is (T) and six Boston IIIs (T) in mid-October, by which time it also had its own Hurricanes. Operations ceased after the squadron had participated in experimental night flights, during which attempts were made to illuminate enemy aircraft by dropping flares.

Disbandment came on 25 January 1943, by which time Wittering had achieved distinction for very different reasons. Basil Embry, never one to be left behind or out of the excitement, was greatly thrilled when, on 6 April 1942, the first Mosquito II for 151 Squadron touched down. Only 157 Squadron at Castle Camps had hitherto received Mosquito fighters, and Embry was determined that one from his station should draw first blood. Whether this was achieved will probably never be proven. No 151 Squadron began Mosquito operations on 30 April, the first claim to success being made on 29 May when, at dawn, Flt Lt Pennington engaged over the North Sea what he claimed to be a Heinkel 111. Eventually he was recorded as damaging a bomber.

Irrespective of total success or not, 151 Squadron achieved an enviable reputation as a night-fighter squadron. Re-equipment had come as the *Baedecker Raids* were under way, Wittering's fighters seeking trade off their Sector, bombers tracking along the coast. That the Luftwaffe had still not forsaken Wittering was clear when, on 25 June 1942, flares were lighting the area when bombs fell wide at Stamford. For much of the remainder of 1942, though, the night sky was largely free of enemy aircraft.

A new BAT Flight, No 1530, formed here on 23 November 1942, with six plus two Oxfords; it left for Collyweston in January 1943. That month witnessed the arrival of the 56th Fighter Group USAAF at King's Cliffe. Available accommodation was not to the American taste, and the 63rd Fighter Squadron, under Major Toky, lodged at Wittering with its P-47s until March 1943, when the Group left for Horsham St Faith. This move took place within a general re-arrangement of Allied squadrons in East Anglia following the departures to the Mediterranean Theatre and the arrival of many Americans. One of the decisions made was to pass Duxford to the USAAF, the aged station being of little operational value to the RAF.

This entailed the removal from Duxford of an assortment of organisations, each an enthusiast's joy to perceive. First to leave was 1426 Enemy Aircraft Flight, which, although Collyweston-based, made daily use of Wittering. On 25 March the Main Party, Air Fighting Development Unit, under Wg Cdr E S Smith, and the Naval Air Fighting Development Unit, commanded by Lt Cdr B H Kendall, between them saw to the movement of their exotic collection of aeroplanes. With armament, tactical and handling trials in plenty, there was little room for an operational night-fighter squadron and, on 30 April 1943, 151 Squadron fled to Colerne. Almost at once it was replaced by 141 Squadron's Beaufighters from Predannack, here for involvement in highly secret operations code-named *Serrate*. Using aged AI radar, they operated over enemy territory at night, trying to find and engage German night-fighters, thereby carrying out the first attempts to protect British night-bombers. Wittering, into the bomber world for the first time, served increasingly as a night-bomber diversion base. One of the first arrivals was Lancaster JA 691, which landed following an aerial collision with an enemy fighter.

Spectacular fighter operations were not a thing of the past, though, as was shown on 29 June 1943, when a very-long-range daylight trial penetration into France was carried out by two Mustangs of AFDU, flown by Sqn Ldr McLachlan DSO DFC and Ft Lt Paige, who between them claimed six enemy aircraft.

August 1943 found the Americans once more using Wittering. Accommodation problems remained acute at King's Cliffe when P-38s of the 20th Fighter Group arrived in late August, so the 55th Fighter Squadron positioned its aircraft at Wittering, where it remained until April 1944, participating in many operations, including an escort during the first attempted USAAF Berlin raid of 3 March 1944.

Wittering, wartime home for many famous RAF figures, came to be associated with Wg Cdr D R J Braham DSO DFC, a very successful night-fighter pilot involved with *Serrate* trials in 1943. Yet not all of Wittering's heroes were men. Late on 24 October 1943 Wellington DV839 of 14 OTU crashed and burst into flames. Cpl A Holden of the WAAF was quickly at the scene and, despite the danger, managed to drag the rear-gunner from the aircraft before the fire crew arrived. On 31 March 1944 she was awarded the British Empire Medal.

During October 1943 No 141 Squadron re-equipped with Mosquito IIs and moved to West Raynham and 100 Group in December. As the Americans left in April 1944, the Fighter Interception Unit was arriving from Ford, bringing Beaufighters and Mosquitoes for experiments with equipment and techniques. Included was some operational flying.

*Spitfire XII EN223 at AFDU Wittering for tactical assessment.*

By then Wittering was an aircraft enthusiast's paradise, as myself and Alan Wright discovered on 10 April 1944. Close to the road rested captured Focke-Wulf Fw 190A-3, PM173, camouflaged dark earth and green and with yellow under surfaces and a light blue spinner. Resting near were a Wildcat VI with a tiny fuselage serial (possibly JV684), Barracuda P9917 festooned with ASV aerials, Hellcat 1 JV124, an early clipped-wing Seafire, and Fulmar DR716. Although belonging to the Naval Air Fighting Development Unit based here, the fighters unusually wore dark green and a very dark grey upper surfaces with medium sea grey under surfaces. Either they were in the process of joining the Fighter Interception Unit based here, or wore an unusual naval night-fighter scheme.

Hoots of delight came as we enjoyed the rare sighting of a white Coastal Command Hampden, AE373. This, the last complete Hampden that we ever saw, wore on its grey-green upper surfaces an assortment of 'white' stripes, which I later discovered were night formation flying aids. By the Hampden was the friendly old Boston III, AF-Z, a useful photo-taking mount from AFDU's Duxford days.

Extending our scan we spied a Corsair Mk 1 curiously finished in dark earth and dark green with yellow under surfaces. Its four-bladed propeller was unusual, for the three-blader was normal. A second look at a Spitfire revealed it to be fitted with contra-rotating propellers. Surprised, I double-checked and certainly it had six blades. A closer look revealed it to be RB179, resting among a group of AFDU Spitfires, among them the unusual Mk Vc dive-bomber, BR372, later to be credited with five enemy aircraft. Mk IXb MH413-ZD-M was also there, and a couple of Mk IIbs, AF-I and AF-E – P8252. Beyond them towered Grumman Avenger FN785 with YO-P identity letters in bright yellow.

During the afternoon sixteen P-38s trundled around the peritrack from their south-west corner dispersals, revealing KI coding, yellow noses and spinners, and white fin triangles. Their take-offs in fours along the top of the plateau I still clearly remember.

Repeatedly enjoyed, overhead trudged C-47s, while to the north-west Whitleys could be seen depositing Horsas on to North Luffenham as BAT Flight Oxfords commenced circuit training at Wittering, interrupted by an arriving RAF Hornet Moth. A C-47 tugged a Waco CG-4A across before a bevy of Mosquitoes of FIU, joined by some Beaufighters, began local flying. Auster IV MT214, Lancaster CF-P and a Barracuda, unusually sporting a sky band around its rear fuselage, arrived. As the latter crossed the A1, it dangled its arrester hook. Then the contra-prop Spitfire took off amid, for those days, no mean din. Only Farnborough and Boscombe Down could compete with Wittering as far as assortment was concerned. Crashes were, however, commonplace, for the station's grass runways attracted flapless, brakeless, seriously damaged battle-damaged aeroplanes, some with engines out of use and with seriously wounded crew aboard – the station faced all such in 1944.

Shortly before the invasion's immediate build-up, Wittering hosted Auster IVs of 658 Squadron, the first of which touched down on 1 April 1944, the squadron leaving after a three-week stay here and at Collyweston. From Exeter on 14 April came an unusual organisation, the Gunnery Research Unit, bringing along one of the last Fairey Battles, which, with the GRU, accommodated itself at Collyweston.

*A Spitfire Vb by Wittering's 'C' Type hangar in 1943. (R D Frey via Dave Benfield)*

By May 1944 the Wittering area was packed with American transports, often involved in impressive night exercises, and bringing the bizarre wartime sight of large formations ablaze with navigation and station-keeping lights. That was still insufficient to prevent accidents and, late on 28 July, two C-47s collided north-west of the airfield, crashing at Ketton with heavy casualties.

Wittering was used as a night dropping ground for paratroops, while between the many activities here, 1530 BAT Flight continued flying until disbandment on 1 August 1944. Beaufighters and Mosquitoes, together with Fireflies and Fulmars, served with the FIU and, at the height of the flying-bomb assault, tested interception techniques. To be more ideally positioned the Unit moved to Ford on 23 August 1944.

On 5 August 1944, the day that NAFDU lost its Avenger in the Wash, another unusual event took place. An attempt was being made to establish a long-distance record free flight for a military glider, the trip from the south to terminate at Saltby. Luck ran out, however, and the glider came down at Wittering.

Removal of the FIU meant that, for the first time since 1938, Wittering did not house multi-seat fighters, although into 1945 it was classified as a night-fighter station in the Digby Sector. Instead, it became the centre for all advanced fighter training. On 3 August 1944 Air Marshal Sir Roderick Hill, AOC ADGB, proposed to the Air Ministry the formation of the Central Fighter Establishment embracing day-fighter and night-fighter wings. Liaison with day-fighter units would be undertaken by the Day Fighter Wing, ensuring that the latest technical developments and tactics were appreciated. It would include a Fighter Training Unit, arising from the existing Fighter Leaders' School, and would use Spitfires and Martinets.

Also within DFW would be the Typhoon-equipped Fighter-Bomber Wing of FLS. An Air Support Development Unit would be formed, and the existing AFDU re-established to comprise six twin-engined and twenty single-engined aircraft. In the Night Fighter Wing would be a training unit, as well as the FIU, established at twenty twin and five single-engined aircraft. Authority for CFE to form was granted on 4 September 1944, and FLS began moving into Wittering on 6 October. Command was vested in an Air Commodore when HQ CFE opened at Wittering on 26 October, and AFDU became the Air Fighting Development Squadron, the layout of the Establishment being somewhat different to that originally envisaged. In February 1945 the elements of CFE gathered at Tangmere.

Although the flying-bomb campaign was largely over when CFE formed, nuisance launches from He 111s flying low over the sea continued, and caused great concern when, on Christmas Eve 1944, the V-1s were directed towards Manchester. To guard against extension of such manoeuvres, 68 Squadron moved into Wittering on 2 February 1945, and flew its last Mosquito XVII and XIX sorties from here before moving to Coltishall on 27 February, re-equipped with the troublesome Mosquito NF 30s. With the squadron's departure, the operational wartime career of Wittering ended. Claims by the station's squadrons stood at 151$\frac{1}{2}$ enemy aircraft destroyed, 50 probables and 61$\frac{1}{2}$ damaged. The FIU laid claim to 82 V-1s. Before Training Command took control of the station, on 31 March 1945, NAFDU moved to Ford and the Enemy Aircraft Flight to Tangmere. Wittering then passed to 21 Group.

*Harrier GR 1s of No 1 Squadron by Wittering's fighter Type 'C' hangar.*

The European war had ended when Wittering received a talented visitor, Mr James Martin of Martin-Baker Aircraft. He had sought permission to use Wittering's runway for trials of his ejector seat idea using a Defiant, the best aircraft he could prise from the authorities, who, suspicious of the firm, offered him a particularly poor example – as he expected they would! In any case, he needed a speed of at least 400mph to test his device, and therefore abandoned the Wittering trials.

Summer 1945 found Wittering quieter than at any time since the early 1920s. On the station were some Americans of a fighter control unit, shortly to leave for New York. POWs were temporarily here pending rehabilitation. Wittering's first hard runways had been built in 1941, fighter operations being less affected by major works programmes than bombers. With two satellites to hand, it was easier than at most stations. With the war ended and jets thought certain to need long runways, the decision was taken to marry wartime Wittering with close-by Collyweston, and a long runway was built in 1945-46.

On 17 December 1945 the Flying Training Command Instructors' School arrived from Brize Norton, staying until 24 May 1946, by which time Fighter Command had repossessed the station, forcing the FTCIS to South Cerney.

Fighter Command regained Wittering on 1 May 1946 and placed it in the Eastern Sector. On 15 April No 41 Squadron's snarling Spitfire 21s arrived, and on 1 May No 219 Squadron's Mosquito NF 30s. They were preceded by a large road consignment of an important new shape, the Handley Page Hastings prototype, which flew for the first time from Wittering on 7 May, using the station's long runway for safety.

Spitfire XVIs of 19 Squadron moved in on 22 June 1946 after 141 Squadron re-formed here on 17 June, and received Mosquito NF 36s. A third night-fighter squadron, No 23, re-formed on 11 September and, equipped with the older Mosquito NF 30, replaced No 219, which left early in September. On 23 September drastic strength reductions came into force, each squadron's establishment being cut to 8 UE, and from the effective dates '(Cadre)' became a suffix to each squadron's identity.

On 23 January 1947 both 23 and 141 Squadrons vacated Wittering for Coltishall. The other two day-fighter squadrons moved to Church Fenton, also in 12 Group, on 23 April 1947. No 19 Squadron had commenced re-arming with Hornet Is on 10 October 1946.

On 20 April 1947 No 264 Squadron arrived to be Wittering's sole occupant, freeing Linton-on-Ouse to become home of a second Hornet Wing. Its Mosquito NF 36s were at Wittering until 13 January 1948, when they moved to Coltishall.

Training Command resumed control of Wittering on 20 February 1948, the second post-war phase opening when No 1 Initial Training School occupied the station, staying until 6 April 1950, after which activity fell to a low ebb, but with good reason. Wittering had been earmarked for improvement and use as a bomber station. The 0/26 9,052-foot asphalt runway was strengthened and a new 'Gaydon'-type hangar erected. In April 1950 – during rebuilding – the Air Ministry Servicing Development Unit moved in. Renamed Central Servicing Development Establishment on 1 June 1950, it remained until March 1953.

Wittering's transfer to Bomber Command and 3 Group in 1953 brought many changes, the most important of which was the establishment on 1 August of the Bomber Command Armament School. This was the organisation that, in secrecy and darkness on 7 November 1953, received the RAF's first Blue Danube atomic bomb. Called Strike Command Armament School from 30 April 1968, it remained in Wittering's environs until autumn 1971.

On 6 August 1953 Lincolns of 61 Squadron arrived, followed by others of 49 Squadron. Little was seen of either, for in November 1953 a 49 Squadron detachment moved to Africa and returned to Upwood. From March to June 1954 No 61 Squadron's Lincolns were in Kenya.

The jet age began for Wittering when, on 9 December 1953, No 76 Squadron re-formed here, equipping with Canberra B2s. On 25 February 1954 No 40 Squadron's Canberra B2s arrived from Coningsby and, on 3 April, No 100 Squadron moved in. August 1954 saw No 61 Squadron re-armed with Canberra 2s, completing the Wittering Wing.

The third post-war phase was brief, because Wittering was to become a V-Force base, for which specialised building took place. No 61 Squadron left for Upwood on 3 July 1955, and on 15 November No 76 went to Weston Zoyland to undertake air sampling following nuclear trials, like 100 Squadron, held at Wittering until disbanded on 1 September 1959. The movement of 40 Squadron to Upwood came about on 1 November 1956.

Although a fully operational station, new techniques and trials seem to become traditional at Wittering, the Bomber Command Development Unit (a sort of latter-day AFDU) moving in during July 1954. It was then that No 1321 Flight re-formed to carry out dropping, from a Valiant, of the case chosen for the *Blue Danube* atomic bomb. The Flight disbanded on 15 March 1956.

At the start of July 1955 Valiants of 138 Squadron, arrived to make Wittering the prime operational V-bomber station. No 49 Squadron followed on 1 May 1956. In the autumn of that year No 138 Squadron (detached to Malta) carried out attacks on Egyptian airfields during operation *Musketeer*. The task of participating in the Christmas Island nuclear weapons trials during 1956-57 had meanwhile fallen to 49 Squadron. BCDU wound down in March 1960, and 7 Squadron brought its Valiants here from overcrowded Honington on 1 September. The disastrous discovery that Valiants were suffering from metal fatigue ended this phase in Wittering's career. As a consequence, No 49 Squadron disbanded on 25 June 1961, followed on 1 April 1962 by No 138 and, at the end of September 1962, by 7 Squadron, ending the Valiant's days at Wittering.

Replacement would soon come about, for in March 1964 the Victor 2 Training Flight arrived. The Navigational Bomb Sight Development Unit and the Bombing & Navigation Systems Development Squadron formed here on 1 August 1966, while also here was the Victor 2 Trials Unit, from which 139 Squadron formed on 1 February 1962. On 1 May No 100 Squadron re-formed, also flying Victor 2s, for which the *Blue Steel* stand-off cruise missile was the prime weapon. Soon came the decision to operate Victors at low level, despite concern about the effect of strong turbulence on their structures. *Blue Steel* was phased out because of its limited low-level strike range. Consequently, No 100 Squadron disbanded on 30 September 1968, followed by 139 Squadron on 31 December; Victor 2s were then modified for Marham's in-flight refuelling squadrons.

Wittering was transferred to Air Support Command on 1 February 1969, the resident Strike Command Armament Support Unit becoming the RAF Armament Support Unit on 1 October 1971. By then the whole tenor of Wittering's activity had dramatically altered, with the first signs of a vertical-take-off era accompanying the arrival, in March 1969, of Whirlwind HC 10s of 230 Squadron. Control of the station was now in the hands of 38 Group.

*Victor B2 XL512 of 139 Squadron carrying Blue Steel relies upon a braking parachute on landing at Wittering in 1968.*

*Harrier GR7 ZD438 '50' of No 1 Squadron.*

*An oblique view of Wittering in 2002. (MOD)*

On 18 July 1969 No 1 Squadron arrived accompanied by a handful of Hunters. The squadron's main task was to explore the Harrier's potential by extending the work of the Harrier Conversion Team, formed on 1 January 1969, which became the Harrier Conversion Unit on 1 April 1970. It was further renamed No 233 OCU on 1 October 1970, its role being the training of Harrier pilots for squadrons. Harriers with little need for Wittering's long runway soon acquired world fame as first operational V/STOL combat aircraft.

November 1971 saw No 230 Squadron commence re-arming with Puma helicopters before moving to Odiham on 1 January 1972. To make full use of the extensive station, Hunter 9s of No 45 Squadron arrived from West Raynham on 29 September 1972. No 58 Squadron re-formed as an offshoot on 1 August 1973. On 2 September 1974 these squadrons formed a Hunter Wing, which had both training and operational commitments prior to disbandment on 26 July 1976.

Harriers of 1 Squadron and Sea Harriers will always be associated with the regaining of the Falkland Islands in 1982, when both types operated from the HMS *Ark Royal.* From No 1 Squadron fourteen Harrier GR3s were drawn for operations over the South Atlantic, three more being positioned on Ascension. During the conflict No 1 Squadron flew some 130 sorties and lost three Harriers, from which in each case the pilots ejected.

Wittering initially accommodated Harrier GR1/T2, then the GR3. Both versions were used by No 20 (Reserve) Squadron, born on 1 September 1992 by renaming No 233 OCU. The early 1990s saw the switch to the GR5, and the mid-1990s to the GR7/T10. In 2003 the squadron's listed strength was nine GR7s and six T10s.

Between August 1993 and April 1995 No 1 Squadron was deployed to Incirlik, Turkey, to participate in operation *Warden,* policing Iraq's northern exclusion zone. In August 1995 the squadron began, from Gioia Del Colle, Italy, to take part in operation *Deny Flight* over Bosnia.

Operational training aboard an 'aircraft carrier' was followed in November 1997 by No 1 Squadron's deployment aboard HMS *Invincible* to support operation *Bolton,* ensuring that Iraq complied with the United Nations' chemical weapons monitoring programme.

Early 1999 saw sixteen Harriers of No 1 Squadron and part of No 20 (R) Squadron back at Gioia del Colle, this time for a part in operation *Allied Force,* the air assault on Serbia in connection with the Kosovo campaign, during which they flew an average of twenty bombing sorties each day against power stations and bridges. On the first night No 1 squadron despatched four Paveway II LGB-armed Harriers with two escort aircraft. During the operation they attacked ammunition depots and similar military and police targets.

With the decision to form Strike Force Harrier on 1 April 2000, concentrated at Cottesmore, No 1 Squadron bade farewell to Wittering on 28 July 2000, leaving behind No 20 (R) Squadron, the RAF ASUPU Bomb Disposal Team, and No 37 Squadron, RAF Regiment Rapier FSC Squadron.

Wittering, now in 3 Group, is positioned alongside the busy A1, which brings traffic problems. Disposal of such a site would mean honouring an agreement calling for land acquired by the Crown to be returned to its previous owner in the state in which it was acquired. That would be very expensive in the case of Wittering.

**Main features:**
*Grass runs:* E/W 13,500ft, NE/SW 4,350ft. *Hangars:* Two C Type (225ft long), one GS Shed, one EO Blister. *Hardstandings:* sixteen. *Accommodation:* RAF officers 186, SNCOs 185, ORs 2,524; WAAF officers 20, SNCOs 28, ORs 470.

In the 1960s asphalt runway 08/26 (LCG III) was, as now, 9,052ft. Four H Type dispersal pads were laid for V-bombers at the western end of the airfield, each accommodating four aircraft. Hardstandings for Harriers were built among and by the hangars. Wittering's most striking item is its curious, onion-shaped water tower.

## WOBURN, Bedfordshire

*51°59N/00°36W 380ft asl; SP340970. Within Woburn Abbey parkland*

Every year in August Woburn Abbey hosts one of aviation's most soothing treats, the de Havilland Moth Club's Weekend Rally. On the great lawn spread before the gracious Woburn Abbey, home of Lord and Lady Tavistock, a swarm of de Havilland aeroplanes from wide and far settle in, periodically spreading their wings to the joy of their keepers and friends, for this is a Moth shrine.

It was from Woburn that aviation's great lady, the Duchess of Bedford, made her tragic flight in her DH 60GIII Moth Major, *G-ACUR,* kept at Woburn. She learned to fly in 1934, and on 23 March 1937, then aged 72, she took off alone from Woburn and was not seen again. On 2 April some interplane struts washed ashore at Great Yarmouth were thought to have come from a Moth.

What, though, of the military side of Woburn? Its wartime service started in 1940, when a large area east of the Abbey was requisitioned. Small Robin hangars were erected and areas between trees – affording excellent camouflage – were chosen for aircraft storage. When the first machine arrived is uncertain. The site, called No 34 Satellite Landing Ground, was assigned to No 6 MU Brize Norton in November 1941, and to quote a local person 'small aircraft were flown in for storage'.

Woburn's transfer to No 8 MU Little Rissington on 8 February 1943 was followed by spectacular activity. Amazing as it seems, it was not long before fully intact Stirlings were squatting between the many trees – presumably they were flown in – and photographs were taken for either *Picture Post* or *Illustrated* magazines. The Stirlings were there in 1945-46 and probably broken down in situ. Did you bring a Stirling into Woburn? If so, how and when?

*DH60 Moth taxys in among a sea of Moths in 1998 at Woburn.*

*DH90 Dragonfly G-AEDU getting airborne.*

*Remember me? My picture appears at Croydon. P.S. I'm almost an OAP!*

**Main feature:**
For the August rally grass run 01/19 550m (1,800ft ) x 30m (100ft) NW of the Abbey is used, at one end of which are lakes, with a public road at the other. There are plentiful trees, and to the E the ground rapidly rises to 460ft, so that the current landing area (only available for the Moth Club event) is quite small.

## WOODLEY (READING), Berkshire

*51°27N/00°53W 150ft; SU780732. 3 miles E of Reading*

In the south-west corner of Woodley there must have been a magic cauldron because of the amazing ideas that originated here and flowed forth within astonishing projects and highly attractive, fascinating, often very novel aeroplanes. Around it Fred and George Miles (whose company called itself Phillips & Powis Ltd) worked their spells and carried on their business. In the 1930s they first gave flight to Falcons, Hawks and Sparrowhawks, while for the RAF they produced the Magister and Master trainers. They also devised the RAF's only dedicated, mass-produced wartime target-tower, the Martinet and the astonishing M.52.

In their inner sanctum they devised spectacular designs like a canard tailless bomber ideal for jet engines, and the Miles M35 model naval fighter, whose flight-tested ideas were more akin to those of the forthcoming Joint Strike Fighter and have been applied to other supersonic designs. Yes, they had one of those too – they designed Britain's first supersonic research jet, which in mock-up looked like a rocket fitted with scimitar-shaped wings. The later American Bell XS-1 and others akin looked remarkably similar to the Miles M.52. Naturally, the British Government withdrew support from it. Various reasons have been advanced for the cancellation, but recently released documents reveal – after a deep search into their contents – that some at RAE Farnborough did not believe that the M.52 would attain Mach 1.0, and that if it did so it would be but briefly and in a somewhat hazardous dive. Since the project was cancelled there can be no certainty.

Apart from Miles, Woodley's association with RAF training matters was strong. On 25 November 1935 No 8 E&RFTS opened and, run by Phillips & Powis, used Hawk Trainers, Tiger Moths, Hart variants and Fairey Battles. Before the war the E&RFTS trained some 680 pilots and 100 navigators, and became No 8 EFTS at the commencement of hostilities.

Elementary flying training continued until 1942, then on 22 July No 10 Instructors' School (Elementary) opened to train instructors for EFTS service, and gradually replaced No 8 EFTS, which disbanded on 15 October 1942. During the change-over Tiger Moths replaced all but ten of the Miles Magisters.

*Miles M 18 'Magister II' U-0224 at Woodley.*

By the end of the war Miles Aircraft had delivered more than 5,000 aircraft, and repaired many others, including Spitfires. In 1945 the company was working on radio-controlled Queen Martinets, and the twin-engined Monitor target tug was entering production – soon cancelled – for the Royal Navy. In the civil field it had the Miles M.38 Messenger and the Aerovan.

No 10 FIS survived until 7 May 1946, although on 1 June 1945 its Miles Master Flight was disbanded, but four days later Tiger Moths arrived from Theale. With the disbandment of No 10 FIS, on 7 May thirty Tiger Moths/Magisters were gathered to equip a new No 8 EFTS, which became No 8 Reserve School on 3 March 1947. Its establishment was only twelve Tiger Moths and two Anson T1s (later Anson T21s) to provided facilities for VR navigators and signallers.

From 15 February 1942 until 31 March 1953 Flying Training Command CF/CS operated from Woodley and was used by Technical Training Command and 50 Group for communications purposes. The unit operated a variety of aircraft including an Anson C19, Harvard T2 and a Dakota C4, KK209, the C-in-C's aircraft.

Chipmunks began replacing the Tigers in 8 RFS during autumn 1951, although it was 1952 before the last Tiger Moth left. In January 1953 it was announced that seven of the twenty reserve schools were to close down – Woodley was one, and No 8 RFS disbanded on 31 March 1953.

*Avro 504K of the RAF College outside Phillips & Powis hangar in 1932.*

The Miles M 35 U-0235 naval fighter flying testbed. Its foreplane and layout were somewhat akin to the JSF, and were very advanced concepts in April 1942. (Miles)

The Miles M39b ⁵⁄₈ scale testbed of a canard bomber, at Woodley in May 1944, was another extremely advanced design. (Miles)

As for Miles Aircraft, the Maggies, Hawks, Messengers, Aerovans, Merchantmen and the Marathon four-engined feeder liner, upon which such high hopes had been pinned, had all fallen into liquidation during 1947. In an almost desperate last throw, Handley Page bought Miles Aircraft in 1948 and established Handley Page Reading to develop the Marathon and its larger derivative, which became the four-engined Herald, and later a production twin turbo-prop version.

The Miles Aerovan, such as G-AILC, incorporated rear loading – quite portentous.

Miles Monarch G-AFCR airborne from Woodley. (Phillips & Powis)

Where once the Libellula taxied you can now freely wander – for that talent, skill, magic has been 'developed', but not to the greatness of Miles. It has largely gone the way of so many airfields, being just a housing estate which embraces a small museum. How many living there know that it was at Woodley where Douglas Bader had the crash that deprived him of his legs?

**Main features:**
Grass area: SW/NE 3,000ft to 2,400ft. Hangars: one civil 420ft x 200ft, one Standard Robin, one Bellman, four Double EO Blister, one EO Blister. Accommodation: RAF officers 79, SNCOs 208, ORs 214.

**WYCOMBE AIR PARK (BOOKER),** Buckinghamshire
        See **BOOKER**

# Index

## Aircraft types and missiles

416 ACTION STATIONS REVISITED NO 2

## USAF/USAAF Groups/Wings

66 ECW ....355
66 TRW ....355
67 TRG ....86
68 BW ....67
68 SRW ....140
91 BG ....239
92 BG/BW ....61, 62, 67, 301
93 BW ....67
96 BG ....162
97 BG ....61, 161, 162, 239, 303
98 BW ....67, 140
98 SRW ....355
100 BW ....67, 78, 301
301 BW ....67, 91, 301
303 BG/BW ....264, 265, 354
305 BG ....89, 91
306 BW ....140, 345
305 BW ....67, 140, 162
307 BW ....67
308 BW ....67, 140
310 BW ....355
313 TCG ....100
314 TCG ....100, 318
315 TCG ....332
316 TCG ....100
320 BW ....67
349 ....318
350 FG ....242
351 BG ....304
368 FG ....244
379 BG ....239, 240
380 ....67
384 BW ....67, 140, 162
387 ....BG 93
398 ....294
401 BG ....120
436 TCG ....59
440 TCG ....59
492 BG ....87
582 ARG ....266
801(P) BW ....174
806(P) ....140

## USAF/USAAF Miscellany
2 CCRC ....87
11 CRCC ....61, 62
Barksdale AFB ....355
Carswell AFB ....140
Castle AFB ....67, 354
HsX ....91
Lake Charles AFB ....140
Limestone AFB ....140
Lockbourne AFB ....355
MacDill AFB ....67
Nellis AFB ....69, 357
Pathfinder School Ixth AF TCC ....100
Portsmouth AFB ....78
Red RichardI ....91
Westover AFB ....67

## USAF/USAAF Squadrons
2 Pursuit ....54
5 PR ....264
13 PR ....86, 269
14 PR ....86, 270
15 Photo Mapping Sqn ....61
15 BS ....160, 264
15 TRS ....86
19 TRS ....78
22 PR ....86
27 PR ....86
30 PR ....85
31 PR ....86
34 PR ....86
40 ARS ....67
42 ECS ....355-357
42 TCS ....266
42 TRS ....91
55 FS ....391
90 ARS ....67
93 ARS ....354
97 ARS ....354
99 ARS ....67
301 ARS ....354
307 Pursuit ....54, 161
309 (USA) ....161
314 Pursuit ....54
325 BS ....61
326 BS ....61, 62
327 BS ....61
321 ARS ....67
342 BS ....161, 162
364-366 ....BS 89
376 ARS ....67
414 BS ....161, 162
422 BS ....89
509 ARS ....354
551/552 FS ....87
653 BS ....86
858 BS ....87
859 BS ....174